Anonymous

The Manuscripts of Charles Haliday, Esq., of Dublin

Acts of the Privy council in Ireland, 1556-1571

Anonymous

The Manuscripts of Charles Haliday, Esq., of Dublin
Acts of the Privy council in Ireland, 1556-1571

ISBN/EAN: 9783337323967

Printed in Europe, USA, Canada, Australia, Japan

Cover: Foto ©Suzi / pixelio.de

More available books at **www.hansebooks.com**

HISTORICAL MANUSCRIPTS COMMISSION.

FIFTEENTH REPORT, APPENDIX, PART III.

THE MANUSCRIPTS OF CHARLES HALIDAY, Esq., OF DUBLIN.

ACTS OF THE PRIVY COUNCIL IN IRELAND, 1556–1571.

Presented to both Houses of Parliament by Command of Her Majesty.

LONDON:
PRINTED FOR HER MAJESTY'S STATIONERY OFFICE,
BY EYRE AND SPOTTISWOODE,
PRINTERS TO THE QUEEN'S MOST EXCELLENT MAJESTY.

And to be purchased, either directly or through any Bookseller, from
EYRE AND SPOTTISWOODE, EAST HARDING STREET, FLEET STREET, E.C., and
32, ABINGDON STREET, WESTMINSTER, S.W.; or
JOHN MENZIES & Co., 12, HANOVER STREET, EDINBURGH, and
90, WEST NILE STREET, GLASGOW; or
HODGES, FIGGIS, & Co., LIMITED, 104, GRAFTON STREET, DUBLIN.

1897.

[C.—8364.] *Price 1s. 4d.*

CONTENTS.

APPENDIX.

INTRODUCTION.

THE Book of the Privy Council in Ireland, here printed for the first time, commences on the twenty-sixth day of May 1556, and ends on the twenty-second of March 1570–71.

The manuscript is on paper of foolscap size; most of its leaves are written on both sides with wide margins. Some leaves are blank, but all are marked in front at head in Arabic figures, and the final leaf is numbered 343.

The penmanship throughout the book is in styles known in England at the time as "text," "secretary," and "Italic" hands. Throughout the manuscript the orthography in English and Latin is irregular, with many abbreviations; Irish local and personal names in it are written in semi-Anglicised and phonetic forms, which contrast strangely with the originals in Gaelic.

The writing of the first portion of the body of the book may be assumed to have been executed by or under the supervision of John Goldsmyth, who had been appointed Clerk of the Council in Ireland in 1543. Goldsmyth's name appears on two pages of the manuscript before us in connexion with transcripts of documents. After Goldsmyth's decease Ralph Coccrell was in August 1558 appointed Clerk of the Council, and became official custodian of this register.

In relation to the English Government in Ireland, and the methods of its administrators in part of the second half of the sixteenth century, this Council book furnishes new and original information. It also affords valuable aid towards supplementing the contents of State Papers and contemporary writings hitherto incomplete.

The limits of this Introduction, however, will only admit of brief observations on some of the contents of the Council book, and on circumstances connected with its preservation.

In the first years of the period included in this volume the office of Chief Governor in Ireland for England was filled by Thomas Radcliffe, Lord FitzWalter, Earl of Sussex. During his occasional visits to England, his brothers-in-law, Sir Henry Sydney, vice-treasurer, and Sir William Fitzwilliams, treasurer at wars, were appointed to act as Deputies or Lords Justices for the government in Ireland.

After the retirement of Sussex from office in Ireland the post of deputy governor there was, from 1564 to 1571, entrusted at intervals to Sir Nicholas Arnold, Marshal of the Queen's Army, Sir Henry Sydney, Dean Robert Weston, Lord Chancellor, and Sir William Fitzwilliams.

In the sixteenth century the Council in Ireland of the King of England was also known as the Privy Council. It consisted of the chief governor for the time being, with the Peers, Archbishops, Bishops, Lord Chancellor, Judges, principal State officials, and Deans of Cathedrals. The proceedings of the Council in Ireland were on important matters regulated mainly by instructions from the administrators of the Government in England, with whom constant communication was maintained.

The meetings of the Council in Ireland were held at Dublin, in the castle, Christ's Church, St. Patrick's Cathedral, St. Sepulchre's, the Archbishop's residence, or at Kilmainham in the priory which had belonged to the knights of St. John of Jerusalem. According to exigencies in local matters the Council met at Belfast, Drogheda, Dundalk, Leighlin, Limerick, Navan, Newry, Philipstown, Ross, Waterford, and other places.

In the period under notice the chief governor and members of the Council who took part in any of its meetings and concurred in its acts signed the record when written in this book. The autograph of the chief governor generally stands at the head of the entry for the day and the signatures of the other members who were present appear at the end. Many of the autographs of the English as well as of the Anglo-Irish councillors are partly abbreviated and indicate little skill in penmanship or orthography.[1]

Records are extant in the Council book of the delivery of the great seals and curial seals for Ireland of Philip and Mary in 1558 and of Elizabeth in 1559. In presence of the Council at

---

[1] *See* "Facsimiles of National Manuscripts of Ireland," Part IV., London, 1882,

Dublin the great seal was delivered by the Earl of Sussex to the Chancellor and those for the law courts to the judges. At the same time the seals previously in use were broken and defaced.

From an unique manuscript leaf formerly in the collection of Sir Robert Cotton it appears that the Earl of Sussex, Lord Lieutenant of Ireland, was authorised in 1561–2 to bring to Queen Elizabeth the Council book here printed as well as the official volume which immediately preceded it in point of date.[1]

The subjects which came under the consideration of the Council and on which entries appear in the Council book were diverse in character. Among them the following may be mentioned: Measures for expulsion of armed Scots from Ireland; transactions with and outlawry of Shane O'Neill; reduction of Ulster to shire ground; subjection of Leinster septs and conversion of their lands into counties; arrangements between the Earl of Clanricarde and his kinsmen with the town of Galway; contentions between the Earl of Ormonde, Earl of Desmond and Baron of Upper Ossory; revolt of the brothers of the Earl of Ormonde; imprisonment of Thomas Stucley; applications from Spain for Irish hawks and hounds; claims from foreign merchants on ships and cargoes; projects for a university at Dublin, and a free-school at Galway.

In the Council book are entered copies of Governmental "indentures" with native Irish lords, who under these instruments covenanted to become faithful subjects to England.

Among compacts of this class which appear here between 1557 and 1566, written in Latin, are those in connexion with

---

[1] The entry is as follows:—

"T. Sussex.—Memorandum: That where it is thought necessarie that the Quens majestie shulde see and consider certen thinges conteyned within the olde and newe councell bookes as well towching Shane Onele and others for causes of this realme: it is agreed by us the Lorde Levtenant and Councell whoes names be hereunto subscribed that the said twoe books shalbe caryed over to her Highnes by the Erle of Sussex, her Majesties Levtenant, and to [be] by him retorned hether at her Majesties pleasure.

Yeven at Kilmannin, the xiiii of January, 1561[2].

H. Dublin, canc.—Thomas Ormonde, Ossory.—W. Fytzwylliams.—Jaques Wingfeld.—Henry Radeclyffe.—Thomas Cusake.—Francis Agarde.—John Chaloner."

Endorsed: "A concordatum for carying over of the councell books."

MS. Titus B. XIII. f. 80, British Museum.

the following: O'Carroll, O'Connor Sligo, O'Donnell, O'Farrell Bane, O'Molaghlin, O'Molloy, and O'Reilly.

Latin, it will be seen from the present volume, was in those times often used in communications and transactions between the chief governor and Council and native Irish lords. A proclamation issued in 1557 by the chief governor and Council contained a notification that it has been written in Latin with a view to having it fully understood by the leaders in the Irish districts to whom it was addressed. The writer of a letter to the Privy Council at Dublin mentioned that the Bishop of Clonfert, uncle of the Earl of Clanricarde, as well as the brothers of that nobleman and other lords and gentlemen of Connacht of the best houses, could neither speak nor understand the English language. John Lie, gentleman, is mentioned in 1567 as interpreter to the State.

An agreement concluded between the Queen's commissioners and Torlogh Luineach O'Neill, chief of Tyrone in 1570–1, was written in Latin. It was entitled "Ordo concordie seu "pacis," and O'Neill was styled in it "principalis sue gentis "et cognominis." The style of diplomacy deemed effective for this Ulster chief is partly exhibited in the following passages in the instructions to Her Majesty's Commissioners accredited to O'Neill:

"You shall procure Tirriloghe Leonaghe to come to the Newry or Dundalk or as near the borders as you can, but if you cannot we refer to your discretions to make choice of the place of meeting as you shall think meetest; and even so of the time and the allowance of such persons as shall be sent to talk with you.

"You may put him in despair of all foreign help, the Queen of Scots being prisoner in England, the King there maintained by the Queen our mistresses power. France so wasted and weary of war at home they rather seek friendship with our Queen than any way to annoy her. Spain vehemently afflicted with Moors and otherwise in great towardness of amity with us."

The Council book contains hitherto unpublished documents of interest in connexion with Conor O'Brien, Earl of Thomond, the oath taken by him to renounce for ever the name of

O'Brien; two letters from Queen Elizabeth in relation to his flight to France, and his sojourn under surveillance in England. There are also papers here on his return to Ireland and unconditional submission in person before the Lord Deputy and Council.

Complaints were addressed to the Council by gentlemen and freeholders of parts of the county of Waterford against the Lord Power, "Captain of the Powers' country." They averred that Lord Power, over and above the number of kerns and horsemen allowed him by order of the council, frequently surcharged and burthened the county of Waterford with superfluous and extraordinary numbers of the companies of theEarl of Desmond, the Earl of Ormonde, and the Earl of Kildare.

The complainants added that the Lord Power, "according " to the custom of mere Irishmen," did at such times as he went to Dublin tax and cess the gentlemen and inhabitants at such sums of money for his expenses "as he thought good."

On settlements of controversies between persons of importance before the chief governor it would appear that the parties usually indicated their intended adherence to the compacts by placing their hands in his.

Notwithstanding Governmental condemnation of native Irish law we find that in 1558 the English administrators in Ireland issued a decree enjoining observance of orders made by Brehons in controversies between parties in a district of Tipperary.

In connexion with corn in Ireland, towards the middle of the sixteenth century it will be seen that the peck was the common measure. The rate for wheat by the peck was usually about four shillings, and twenty pence for the same measure of oats. For a bullock the price was twelve shillings, and for a hog two shillings and eight pence.

The Queen's monies current in Ireland and arrangements in connexion with coins formed the subjects of several proclamations issued at Dublin by the Lord Deputy and Council. Testons, "red harps," "rose half-pence," and particulars in connexion with them are mentioned in these ordinances.

Much of the Council's attention was necessarily directed to measures for defence of the English territories in Ireland, maintenance of forts and garrisons, and repression of hostile movements.

Many entries appear in the Council book in connexion with proclamations for "hostings," or military expeditions, as well as for "cesses" to supply provisions for Governmental purposes.[1]

At "hostings" the armed men between the ages of 16 and 60 from various districts, with their captains, were mustered under standards and ensigns bearing the red cross of St. George. The forces consisted of horse and foot, archers, gunners, galloglasses [2] and kerns. Compulsory service was also exacted from drivers with horses and carts, and from labourers, in large numbers, to open passes and roads, and to repair or build fortifications.

To provide against enemies from the sea, beacons were ordered to be set up along the coast of the English districts. Upon warning given by fire or smoke the captains of the localities, with the men under their command, were to take up their positions at the places assigned to them.

The ultimate courses adopted by the Lord Deputy and Council in relation to persons whom they had denounced as "traitors and rebels" are exhibited in two proclamations entered in the Council book. By the first of these, in 1556, one hundred pounds was offered to anyone who would bring in the "traitor and rebel," Donogh O'Connor, or his head. At the foot of this ordinance is a statement that two members of the council, the Archbishop of Dublin and the Bishop of Meath, "did forbear to assent to that portion of the order "which touched the life of man, lest they should incur the "danger of irregularity."

The second of the proclamations referred to was against Shane O'Neill of Tyrone, who, it was stated, had brought the "whole North of Ireland in subjection to him and under his "rule, wherein he had a scope of a hundred and twenty miles

---

[1] Brief excerpts from the Council book in relation to "cesses" are extant among the manuscripts collected by Sir George Carew in the early part of the seventeenth century.

[2] Heavy armed foot soldiers. The term "spar of galloglasses" was used to designate a galloglass soldier, with the bearer of his arms, and a boy to carry his provisions.

" long and a hundred odd miles broad." The Lord Deputy and Council denounced O'Neill as a rebel and traitor, and offered one thousand pounds for his body, a thousand marks for his head, and five hundred pounds to any person who by direct or indirect means killed him, " though he brought neither " the head nor the body." A notification in Latin concerning the proclamation against O'Neill was at the same time addressed by the Lord Deputy and Council to the Irish lords in Ulster. Portions of the English proclamation of the Council was embodied in the statute for the attainder of Shane O'Neill in 1569.

Commissions were, from time to time, issued by the Council for pursuing rebels with fire and sword in their own territories and elsewhere. Penalty of hanging was incurred by persons travelling by night unless they were accompanied by " some " honest men in English apparel."

The entries in the Council book are not in chronological sequence. From the 10th of December 1564, when Sir Nicholas Arnold was Lord Justice of Ireland, no acts of the Council are entered in this book till February 1565–6, at which time the office of chief governor was filled by Sir Henry Sydney.

The absence of entries in that interval may perhaps be accounted for by the dissensions which existed between Arnold and members of the Privy Council in Ireland.

Sir Henry Sydney in a letter to Cecil in 1567 wrote: " There " is no servant in Christendom that indureth greater toil of " mind and body than I do, nor that with so little assistance " wieldeth so weighty matters."

The contents of the Council book are printed without abbreviation in the present volume in the order in which they stand in the manuscript. To facilitate reference, head numbers have been prefixed to the entries and marginal notes indicating the pages of the original are given throughout.

In the Council book are entered forms of the oaths for Privy Councillors in Ireland. There is also here a copy of the oath administered to William Uscher or Ussher, who was admitted clerk of the Privy Council in Ireland in 1594.

At head of the initial page of the manuscript is a memorandum in which Sir William Ussher stated that on the 19th of September 1609, he " ended the table of all the particular "matters contained in this book."[1] Subsequently, for more than two centuries, the existence of this Council book appears to have been unknown to historical investigators.

Towards the year 1850 the Council book was purchased by Mr. Charles Haliday, Governor of the Bank of Ireland, Dublin, an assiduous collector of books and documents relating to Irish affairs. After the decease of Mr. Haliday in 1866 the manuscript was presented to the Royal Irish Academy, Dublin.

The table which Ussher compiled in 1609 to the Council book, and which is here printed, remained long in obscurity and apart from the manuscript to which it referred.

I have found that this table, bound with other papers, was for a time in possession of Sir James Ware, and that the volume in which it was included passed successively to Henry Earl of Clarendon, Archbishop Tenison, James Duke of Chandos, Dean Milles of Exeter, and finally to the British Museum.[2]

The book of the Privy Council in Ireland, which in order of date preceded that of 1556–1570–1, here printed, was styled the "Red Council Book." It was stated to have been commenced in 1542–3, but it appears to have contained copies of earlier documents, and, according to Sir Henry Sydney, was the oldest Council book of Ireland known in his time. The "Red Council Book" has long been regarded as lost, but a succinct table of its contents, apparently compiled by Sir William Ussher, has been preserved.[3] This table is printed for the first time in the present publication, together with lists[4] hitherto unpublished of contents of two council books of Ireland which are also missing, and which commenced respectively in 1571 and 1589.

It is to be hoped that through the labours of the Historical Manuscripts Commission these important volumes may yet be brought to light.

JOHN T. GILBERT.

Villa Nova, Blackrock, Dublin,
26th October 1896.

---

[1] James Howell, author of Epistolæ Ho-Elianæ, visited Dublin in 1639, with a view to obtaining a reversionary grant of Ussher's office as clerk of the Council. Ussher was then, according to Howell, "very aged and bedrid." He, however, survived till 1659.

[2], [3], [4] Add. MS. 4792.

ACTS OF THE PRIVY COUNCIL IN IRELAND,

1556–1571.

CORRIGENDA.

Page 32, l. 32, for *strange* read *stronge*.

„ 73, ll. 40, 41, for *sterling. The pecke*, read *sterling, the pecke ;*

„ 74, l. 46, for XCI. read XC.

„ 75, l. 5, for XCIA. read XCI.

„ 126, l. 40, for *handreth* read *hundrethe*.

„ 133, margin, for 178*b* read 187*b*.

„ 185, l. 11, for *subsequmtum* read *subsequentium*.

ACTS OF PRIVY COUNCIL IN IRELAND.

ACTS OF THE PRIVY COUNCIL IN IRELAND, 1556–1571.—MS. OF CHARLES HALIDAY, ESQ., M.R.I.A.—BY JOHN T. GILBERT, LL.D., F.S.A.

"The Lieger or counsell booke, made and sett fourthe by the right honorable sir Thomas Radcliffe, knight, lorde Fitzwalter, lord deputie of the realme of Ireland, who toke his othe in Christes churche,[1] and enterid into the governmente of this the king and quens majesties sayde realme, the xxvi[th] day of May in the seconde and thirde yeres of ther majesties moste prosperous raignes." fol. i.* 1556.

A proclamacyon : fol. 1.

T. Fytzwauters.—Forasmoche as the king and quenes majesties pleasure ys that all suche sommes of money as are due to be payed by their majesties to any maner of person within this their graces realme of Irelande shulde be aunswered and payed with all expedicyon, as well for anything payable by their majesties to the contry or otherwyse as for victailles and other necessaryes impressed to the souldyour :

We woll, and in their highness name charge and commande that all and every suche personne shall betwixte this and thende of xx[tie] dayes nexte comyng bryng in their bookes, taylles and severall bylles, mentyonyng ther perticular debtes, whiche bookes and skrolles we woll also shalbe brought and delyvered to the handes of us, the lorde deputie.

And for that we thinke yt not expedyente to burdeyne every perticuler personne[2] of the countrey to travayll hither with his sayde rekonyng, our pleasure ys that two of every paryshe or more (yf they thinke yt so good, beyng suffycientely auctorysed for the reste) shall make their repayre by the daye above lymyted, bryngíng with them their sayde severall wrytinges and taylles, or at any tyme betwixte this and the saide twentieth daye, wheare, God wylling, order shalbe taken for their indelayed satysfactyon and payemente as shall appertayne.

Yeoven at Dublin the xxvii[th] of Maye, 1556.—God save the kyng and the quene.

[II.] A lettre dyrected to the mayor and constable of the king and quenes majesties towne and castell of Knockefergus :[3] fol. 2.

We grete you well: And understonding that certeyn vyctailles and other like provysion lately pertaynyng to Hughe Mac Nele Oge remayneth at this preasente in your custody, we have thought good, for the saufekeping of the same provision, to give you in chardge that no parte therof be purloyned or dismynyshed but reserved entier till furder

[1] Dublin. [2] *Personne*] Parsonne, MS. [3] Carrickfergus, co. Antrim.

1556. order shalbe taken, and that in case any in those parties shall clayme or challenge to have any parcell thereof, we eftesones commande you to make no delyvery to any parson till our furder pleasure be signyfied in that behalfe.

And for that Phelym Baccaghes[1] sonnes have byn here with us, humbly submytting themselves to serve the kings and queenes majesties, lyke as by reporte they have of long tyme don, we shall requyre you in their honeste procedinges to use them accordingly :

And lykewyse yf the Skottes shall at any tyme attempte to annoye the same Phelyms sonnes, or any their servauntes and followers, and that they for refuge flye unto that ther majesties towne of Knockefergus, we shall requyre you in that case to be ayding and assisting unto them from tyme to tyme, and to succour them bothe within your sayde towne and lyberties of the same.

We also requyre you that for suche horses and men as they say they have with your good will so used to have amonge you, that they may still contynue the same til our furder pleasure be signyfied unto you, and so long as ye shall consider them to be good and faithefull subjects. Fare ye well. From Dublin this xxix[th] of Maye, 1556.

fol. 2*b*. Post scripta : Ye shall understond that the saide Phelym Baccaghes sonnes for any contencyon or varyance betwixte Phelym Duffe and them have promysed to kepe ther majesties peace and in no wyse the one to breake upon the other till we may take order ; and therefore we woll ye so signyfie to the same Phelym Duffe, to thintente he maye for his parte doo the semblable, and not to revenge their severall injuries till our repaire amonge them ; and so we woll ye chardge the saide Phelym Duffe in our name.

fol. 3. [III.]—Apud Dubliniam, tertio Junii, anno regnorum regis et regine Philippi et Marie secundo et tertio [1556] :

T. Fytswauters.—It ys concluded by us, the lord deputie, the lordes spirituall and temporall of the realme, and the reste of their majesties' counsaill of the same whose names be hereunto subscribed, that, for soondry consyderations towching the service of their majesties, the quyete of this their realme and subjectes and thexpulsing of the Skottes out of the northe partyes of the same, there shalbe a generall hostyng for six wekes, to be proclamed after the olde custome by wrytt, at the rate of thre plowe lande to a carte, and to begynne at such tyme as we, the sayde lorde deputie, for that purpose shall thinke moste requysite, who have nowe concludid upon the seconde daye of July nexte commyng, and to assemble the saide daye at Ratheskeaghe, besydes Dundalke.

H. Dublin, canc.[2]—G. Armachanus.[3]—G. Kyldare.[4]—Will. Midensis.[5]—Roland Baltynglas.[6]—J. of Slane.[7]—Richard Delvin.[8]—Christofor of Kyllene.[9]—P. Barnewall, lord of T[rymleteston].—Thomas Louithe.[10]—

---

[1] In Irish : baccach, lame ; Latinized—" claudus," *see* p. 9.
[2] Hugh Curwen, archbishop of Dublin, lord chancellor, Ireland.
[3] George Dowdall, archbishop of Armagh, primate.
[4] Gerald Fitz Gerald, earl of Kildare.
[5] William Walsh, bishop of Meath.
[6] Roland Fitz Eustace, viscount Baltinglas.
[7] James Fleming, baron of Slane.
[8] Richard Nugent, baron of Delvin.
[9] Christopher Plunket, baron of Killeen.
[10] Thomas Plunket, baron of Louth.

Wyll: Fytzwylliams. — Gerald Aylmer.[1] — John Bathe.[2] — Thomas Lokwood.[3] — H. Sydney.[4] — Francis Harbard.[5] — John Parker.[6] — John Plunket.[7] 1556.

[IV.]—By the lorde deputie and counsell : fol. 3b.

T. Fytswauters.—To all and every the king and quenes majesties officers, mynysters and subjectes, and to every of them to whome yt shall appertayne, gretyng :

Lattyng you wytt that forasmoche as yt ys consydered that their majesties forte and garryson in Lexe[8] ys at this present disfurnyshed of necessary provysion, (chieffely wheate and malte,) we have therefore, for the spedy revytailling of the same holde, by theas presents auctorysed capitayne Lyppiet and capitayne Portesse, bearers hereof, to take up in all places within the counties of Dublyn and Kildare suche proportion of grayne as they, or either of them, shall for the purpose aforesaide thinke requysite and expedyente, aunswering the partyes forthwith in ready money for every pecke of wheate and bere malte v.*s.*, sterling, the pecke, and for every pecke woote malte iii.*s.* iiii.*d.*, sterling, the pecke.

And furder we doo by warrante hereof auctorise theas saide bearers to take up for conveyance of the said corne from tyme to tyme garrans and horses, in all places within the saide counties, as their necessite in this case for the servyce of their majesties and supplie of the presente wante shall requyre, payeng likewyse at reasonable pryses redy mony for the same; willing and commanding all and every their majesties said officers at all tymes and in all places to be ayding and assisting the sayde Lyppiett and Portesse, or either of them, for the better execution hereof as shall appertayne and as they woll answer to the contrary at their perilles.

Yeoven at their majesties manour of Kylmaynan,[9] the vii[th] of June, 1556.

Post scripta: Provided alwaies that by vertue of this commission they shall not take above the nombre of thre hundred peckes, that is to saye, one hundreth peckes wheate, and two hundreth peckes malte, two partes wote malte and thother bere malte.

H. Dublin, canc.—Wyll: Fytswylliams.—John Travers.—H. Sydney.

[V.] Instrucyons given the xiith of June, anno 1556, by the lorde deputie and counsell to John Basyng, William Turnour, Thomas Smyth, Henry Cowley, William Piers, Thomas Browne, John Muns, Robarte Cowley, and Hughe Robarte, and to every of them, appoynted to goo with the quenes majesties shippes northwarde, and by them and every of them to be putt in execution as shall appertayne : fol. 4.

T. Fytswauters.—[1.] Furste: Smyth shall, with fyfty souldyours, enter the Mary Wylloby; Cowley, with fyfty others, shall enter the Gerfawcon; Thomas Browne, with Smythes pety capitayne, shall enter the Dooble Rose, with xxv.; and Muns, with thothers namyd in theas

---

[1] Chief justice, queen's bench, Ireland.
[2] Sergeant-at-law.
[3] Dean of Christ Church, Dublin.
[4] Vice-treasurer and receiver-general, Ireland.
[5] Appointed member of the privy council, Ireland, in 1547.
[6] Master of the Rolls, Ireland.
[7] Of Donoghly, co. Dublin.
[8] Now portion of the Queen's county.
[9] Kilmainham, near Dublin.

instructyons, shall enter the Flower-de-luce, with xxv; and they shall doo as hereafter followeth:

[2.] Item: The Mary Wylloby, Pierses two shippes, and his thre pynnaces shall take their course towardes the Scottyshe shore, and, repayring to the Banne[1] with as moche spede as they possibely maye, they shall by the waye on the Skottyshe coste destroye all the galleys they maye convenyentely come by.

[3.] Item: The Gerfawkon, the Dooble Rose, and the Flower-de-luce shall take their course the nexte waye to the Ragheryns with all possible spede; and, destroying all the gallies they shall fynde on the Irish coste by the waye, they shall staye at the Ragheryns,[2] about the landing place there, and not only destroye the gallies there, and kepe suche as be already within the ylande from ypsuyng oute, but also kepe all others, as well from Scottelande as from Irelande, from enteryng into the sayde ylande.

fol. 4b. [4.] Item: They shall not lande in any place excepte they may be assured to annoye the ennemye and retorne agayne withoute daunger of hurte or losse.

[5.] Item: They shall doo that in them lyeth to take all shippes, gallyes, or other vesselles that shalbe either at the sayde Banne or in eny other place apon the coste of Irelande, or that shall passe betwene Irelande and Scottelande, and generally to kepe the seas, that no shippe, galley or other bote passe betweene Scottelande and Irelande, or Ireland and Scotteland, with eny Skottes.

[6.] Item: They shall, as occasion shall serve, geve such warnyng one to another as they maye alwaies be in a readynes to succour the one other for their suertye.

[7.] Item: They shall with all convenyente spede as well advertise us of their dooinges as also of all other thinges that they can have any intelligence of towching the dooing of the Skottes and for thadvancemente of the quenes majesties service.

[8.] Item: They shall from tyme to tyme sende to Knockefergus to knowe whether there have come any advertysemente from us hither to be sente to them.

All whiche articles they shall observe as moche as in them lyeth as they woll aunswer to the contrary at their perilles.

H. Dublin, canc.—Wyll. Fytswylliams.—John Travers.—H. Sydney.

fol. 5. [VI.]—At Kylmaynan, the xviith daye of June, anno 1556:

T. Fytswauters.—Wheare the barone of Upper Ossory[3] appearing before us, the lorde deputie and counsaill, whoose names ar hereunto subscribed, for certeyn varyances moved and depending betwixte therle of Ormonde[4] and hym, hathe not onely for the fynall determynacyon of the same refused to stonde to order, but also apon demande of certeyne pledges to be by hym delyvered, for that he hathe no auctorytie or grounde for any order passed betwixte the same erle and hym to detayne them (as his owne lerned counsell affirmed) hathe very arrogantely and disobedientely used himselfe before us, bothe contrary his duetie to the king and quenes majesties and in contempte of our auctorytie: it ys condescendid and agreid that the same baron for suche

[1] Bann, river, Ulster. [2] Raghlin. [3] Barnaby Fitz Patrick. [4] Thomas Butler.

arrogancy and disobedyence shalbe commytted to ther highnes castell of Dublyn, there to remayne during our furder pleasure. 1556.

H. Dublin, canc.—Wyll: Fytzwylliams.—John Travers.—H. Sydney.—D. Hay of Sleade.

[VII.]—At Kilmaynan, the xixth of June, anno 1556: fol. 5*b*.

T. Fytswauters.—Wheare we, the lorde deputie and counsaill, have receyved the quenes majesties letters commanding us that after we shall have perused and considered the prestes and disbursementes and other the rekenynges of sir Anthony Sentleger duryng the tyme of his being deputie[1] here, and taken their accompte of the same, whether he shalbe founde indebted to her majestie or in surplusage, we shall take suche order as the debtes whiche the sayde sir Anthony oweth within this the realme of Irelande be paied and discharged of suche her majesties treasure as was of late sente over.

Forasmoche as thauditour can not, as he sayeth, for wante of certen bookes procede to the taking of the true accompte of the said sir Anthony, and yet yt appeareth unto us that her majesties pleasure and meanyng of her lettre ys his debtes shulde be payde:

We, therefore, the saide lord deputie and councell, have agreid and ordered that the saide debtes of the saide sir Anthony, being thre thowsande two hundreth threscore fourtene poundes, xiiii*d*., sterling, as appeareth by a booke delyvered by the sayde sir Anthony and subscribed with his hande, shalbe paied in forme following, videlicet:

That the saide sir Anthony shall enter in bonde of recognysance of five thousande pounde currante mony of Inglande to be forfayted to the quenes majestie, her heires and successors, yf, apon her highnes knowledge of the paymente of the saide iij^{mti}. ij^{c}. xiiij^{ti}, sterling, for the debtes of the said sir Anthony, her majestie shall not be contented therewith, but will that the saide somme paied for the saide debtes be demanded agayn of the saide sir Anthony. Then yf the same sir Anthony his heires executors or assignes doo not presentely repaye to her majesties use in her exchequer of Inglande the somme of thre thowsande, two hundreth fourteen poundes xiiii*d*. sterling, then the sayde recognysance to stande in full force and effecte in the lawe, etc. fol. 6.

H. Dublin, canc.—Wyll: Fytzwylliams.—John Travers.—H. Sydney.

[VIII.]—At Kilmaynan, the xxiiith. of June, anno 1556: fol. 6*b*.

T. Fytswauters.—Wheare the erle of Kildare[2] hathe presentely the garde and custody of the king and quenes majesties forte of the Dyngan in Offalley,[3] by order from the late lorde deputie and counsell, we, upon good consyderacyons and for that also we thought yt not mete at this presente to dismynyshe any parte of tharmye, considering our hosting and journey northewarde, have resolved that the same erle shall still contynue his chardge and have the custody of their majesties sayde holde till Mychelmas nexte. For whose chardge, as well in the saufe keping thereof to their highnes use, as in victailling and entertaynyng the garryson there, yt is condescendid and agreid that the saide erle shall have the somme of one hundreth poundes, sterling, to be receyved at the handes of their majesties thesaurour at warres here, and at Michelmas nexte the saide

[1] Under Henry VIII., Edward VI., and Mary.

[2] Gerald Fitz Gerald.

[3] Now part of the King's county.

1556. erle shall render and give uppe the saide forte sauffe and sownde, to be then disposid and commytted of truste to suche as yt shall please their majesties, or as we by their highnes appointemente shall thinke good.

H. Dublin, canc.—Wyll: Fitzwyllliams.—H. Sydney.

fol. 7. [IX.]—At Kylmaynan, the xxvith daye of June, anno 1556:

T. Fytswauters.—We grete you[1] well, and having consydered the contentes of your lettres, togither with the reporte of Thomas Browne[2] of your dooynges syns your departyng hens, we perceyve that you cannot according to our expectatyon lett the Skottes from entering and yssuying oute of the ylande of the Ragheryns, whiche yet kepyng therabontes defende the passing betweene lande and lande.

Wherefore, accordyng your requeste made to us by the saide Browne, wee shall lycense you to doo what to your discreacyons shalbe thought beste, so that you endeavour yourselves to thuttermoste of your powers to kepe the passage betweene lande and lande, and that you yourselves do take lande in no place excepte you maye sauffely retorne and advoyde the traynes of the Skottes whiche be very subtyll and doubtfull. And yf you shall have occasion to occupy any botes, as Browne saieth you dayly have, we have wrytten to the mayour of Knockefergus to ayde you in that you shall demaunde, willing you not to putt the queene to farther chardge then for your dooinges shalbe requysite, and in all thinges that may be for the better service of the quenes majestie to follow our former instructione as nere as ye maye.

H. Dublin, canc.—Wyll: Fytzwyllliams.—H. Sydney.

fol. 7*b*. [X.]—A proclamatyon sett fourthe the xxviith of June, anno supradicto:

T. Fitzwauters.—To advoyde contentyon that moght aryse betwixte tho souldyour and thinhabytante of the countrey, as well for their owne dyettes and their horseboyes, as also for the dayly chardge of their horses, it ys agreid and orderid by us, the lorde deputie and counsaill, that every horseman shall paye for every weke for hymselfe two shillinges sterling, for every weke for his horseboye viii*d*., and for every horse having but six sheaves of dooble bande, with haye and glaye accustomed, day and night, a penny sterling, and that every footeman shall paye for every weke for himselffe two shillinges sterling, and that no man shall demaunde of the souldyour more then the pryses above appoynted; nor the souldyour shall paye les then after that rate, as they will annswer to the contrary at ther perilles.

H. Dublin, canc.—H. Sydney.—John Travers.—D. Hay of Sleade.

fol. 8. [XI.]—Ordres taken by the right honourable the lord Fitzwalters, lord deputie and councell at Knockefergus, the xth of Auguste, anno 1556:

T. Fytzwauters.—[1.] Furste: We constitute and appoynte our trusty and welbeloved sir George Stanley, knight, marshall of tharmye in Irelande, to be generall of Ulster, requyring hym to use thadvyse of the reverende father in God, the bushop of Dune,[3] capitayne Warren, capteyn

---

[1], [2] This paper is not addressed, *see* p. 10.

[3] Eugene Magennis, bishop of Down.

Williamson and capteyne Gyrton, whome we appoynte commyssioners with hym to assiste hym in suche sorte as hereafter ys specyfied. 1556.

[2.] That the saide sir George shall as farre as in hym shall lye, mayntеyne the right of holy churche, and kepe and defende the mynystres therof from all outerages or wronges that by eny man shall be to them offerid, and cause suche churches as to hym shall be thought good to be reedyfied at the chardge of the countrey in all the parties of Ulster for as long tyme as he shall contynue generall there.

[3.] Item: We geve to hym auctorytie to parle with all men at his will duryng the tyme aforesaide.

[4.] Item. We give to hym auctoryte to geve protection to all suche men as he shall thinke good and to take and delyver pledges as he will duryng the sayde tyme.

[5.] Item: We give to hym power and auctorytie to heare and determyne all manner of controversies betwene partye and partie, the same not beyng matter of enherytance within Ulster for the saide tyme. fol. 8*b*.

[6.] Item: That he shall execute the marshall lawe in all cases to hym thought convenyente.

[7.] Item: That he shall cawse the men of the countrey there to manure suche parte of every plowelande as to hym shalbe thought suffi-ciente for the mayntenance of the countrey and furnyture of the king and quenes majesties garrysons lefte there duryng the saide tyme.

[8.] Item: He shall cawse to be pounyshed all those that shall commytt treasons, murders, felony, rape or any other crymynall offence, as to the offences commytted in those cases shall appertayne for the saide tyme.

[9.] Item: That he shall cawse to be levied, to the king and quenes majesties use, all of forfaytes that of right during his abode there shall to ther majesties appertayne.

[10.] Item: That he shall take, to the quenes majesties use, suche fortes as to hym shalbe thought good and cawse the same to be repayred at the charge of the countrey during the said tyme.

Item: He shall cawse the countrey to cutt pases wheare he shall thinke mete at ther own chardge for the said tyme.

[11.] Item: That he shall cawse every one of the dwellers of Clandeboye to be followers of hym that possesseth the grounde wheere the same were wonte to dwell and be followers. fol. 9.

[12.] Fynally: We requyre hym to use thadvyse of the sayde com-myssioners in all the premysses, as they or enny of them shall presente.

Wyll: Fytswylliams.—H. Sydney.

[XII.]—T. Fitzwauters.—Hec indentura, facta undecimo die Augusti, anno Domini 1556, testatur quod cum concordatum est per nos, dominum deputatum et consilium, una cum majori parte nobilium et generosorum in Ultonia, quod generalis taxatio fiet supra omnes domine regine subditos infra universam Ultoniam predictam pro meliori gubernamento et defen-sione ejusdem adversus Scotos: fol. 9*b*.

Ulterius concordatum est per nos, prefatum dominum deputatum et consilium, ex una parte, et comitem Tironie,[1] baronem de Dungennan et Macdonellum, galloglassum, ex altera parte, quod prefati comes, baro et

[1] Con O'Neill.

1556. Macdonell, regine nomine, levari facient in comitatu Tyronie quadringentas martas; de domino Ochane[1] quadringentas martas;[2] et de Magenyssa[3] quadringentas martas, easque omnes martas ad sustentationem quadringentorum galloglassorum et centum harcabusariorum pro uno anni quarterio contra Scotos implicare promittunt, et se ipsos obligant.

Et prefati comes, baro et Macdonellus obligant se per presentes non solum quod predicti 400 galloglassi et centum harcabusarii[4] presto et parati erunt ad mandatum generalis Ultonie, per dominum deputatum pro tempore existentem nominandum, pro uno anni quarterio, incipientis xxiiii^{to} die instantis mensis Augusti et desinentis xxiiii^{to} die Novembris proxime insequentis.

Sed etiam quod regine nomine levabunt martas predictas modo ut premittitur absque omni excusatione posthac pro se in premissis facienda. Et hoc modo eos pro servitio dictorum galloglassorum et harcabusariorum satisfieri confitentur.

fol. 10. Et ulterius concordatum est quod prefati comes, baro et Macdonellus non implicabunt aliquam partem quadringentorum galloglassorum et centum harcabusariorum predictorum adversus aliquos preter solos Scotos et illorum fautores absque speciali licentia inde in scriptis concessa per dominum deputatum seu generalem Ultonie pro tempore existentem.

Et ulterius concordatum est quod si dictus Ocane et dictus Magenissa aut aliquis eorum antedictas martas sponte dabit ad dictum comitem, baronem, Macdonellum, sive alicui eorum, aut eorum assignatis, regine nomine petentibus, quod tunc non licebit dictis comiti, baroni, Macdonello, neque alicui eorum, sive assignatis eorum, facere levari dictas martas in eos super aliquem illorum qui dictas martas sponte dedit.

Et si dictus Ocane et dictus Magenissa, aut aliquis eorum sponte non dabit dictas martas, quod tunc licebit dictis comiti, baroni et Macdonello facere levari dictas martas in eos seu aliquem eorum qui eas martas sponte non dabit ad vicesimum diem hujus instantis mensis Augusti absque dilatione.

Et si prefati comes, baro et Macdonellus aut aliquis eorum aliquid contra tenorem et formam hujus indenture commiserit, quod tunc dicti comes, baro et Macdonellus et quilibet illorum ad arbitrium deputati pro tempore existentis punirentur.

In cujus rei testimonium dominus deputatus et consilium ex parte una, et dicti comes, baro et Macdonellus ex parte altera hiis indenturis sua signa et sigilla alternatim apposuerunt. Data die et anno supradictis.—Wyll. Fytzwylliams.—John Travers.—H. Sydney.

fol. 10*b*. [XIII.]—A note for cesse of bieves concluded the xiiith of August, anno supradicto:

T. Fytswauters.—Memorandum: It ys condescendid and agreid by us, the lord deputie and counsell, with the consente and agreement of the lordes, capteynes and gentilmen of the contrey that theas bieffes following shalbe cessid in the parties of Ulster and levied to the quenes majesties use, aswell for the relieffe of ther highnes army and garrysons ther as for the provision of others towardes thexpulsion of the Scottes videlicet:

Phelym Duffe, in kyne, 800; Moriertaghe Oneyle, 100; Cormocke Oneyle, 100; Savage, 100; Macgwyer, 400; Mac Mahon, 400; Tyrone, 400; Magennesse, 400; Ochane, 400:

---

[1] O'Cahan, O'Kane. [2] Marts, beeves. [3] Magennis. [4] Arquebusiers.

Whereof the cesse of the saide countreys of Tyrone, Magennesse and Ochane to serve for the fynding of five hundred galloglasse for one [w]hole quarter towardes thexpulsion of the said Skottes, as may furder appeare by thindenture of covenanntes beforewrytten. 1556.

Wyll: Fytzwylliams.—John Travers.—H. Sydney.

[XIV.]—A protection grauntid to Shane Oneyle by the lorde deputie and counsell, at Kylmaynan, the xiiith of September, anno 1556: fol. 11.

T. Fytswauters.—Omnibus ad quos presentes littere nostre per venerint salutem: Sciatis nos, certas ob causas et considerationes ad id specialiter moventes, recepisse sub tutela et protectione regie et regine majestatum dilectum nobis in Christo Johannem Oneyle, filium domini comitis de Tyrone, dantes et concedentes eidem Johanni et suis sequacibus tenore presentium salvum conductum nostrum de tempore in tempus tam veniendi quam redeundi modo et form sequenti, videlicet:

Quod dictus Johannes Oneyle et sui predicti sequaces quoties et quando ad nos seu ad alios infra partes Anglicanas accesserint non erunt aliquo modo impediti seu arrestati per nos vel aliquem alium de illorum majestatum subditis nec preterea persequti vel molestati in sua patria vel confinibus ejusdem propter aliquam querelam adversus illos proponendam donec hujusmodi querele coram nobis vel nostris in ea parte commisionariis destinandis merito responderint, in quo casu si idem Johannes aut sui sequaces recusaverint nostris aut eorum stare ordinacioni et judicio, tunc bene licebit omnibus illorum celsitudinis subditis illum et suos antedictos sequaces de tempore in tempus prosequi et ad extremum juxta eorum demerita punire, hac nostra protectione in aliquo non obstante.

Data die et anno supradictis.

Proviso tamen quod si prefatus Johannes Oneyle aut aliquis sequacium suorum invaserit patriam alicujus subditorum regis et regine majestatum, seu eandem depredaverit aut aliquod aliud facinus commiserit, tunc licebit inhabitantibus terre illius tam dictum Johannem quam suos antedictos sequaces resistere, ac etiam illos ad eorum bona recuperanda juxta leges persequi, hac dicta nostra protectione non obstante. Quam protectionem volumus continuare donec per litteras nostras prefato Johanni in contrarium significaverimus. fol. 11b.

H. Dublin, canc.—Wyll. Fytswylliams.—John Travers.—H. Sydney.

[XV.]—Ordo domini deputati et consilii capta apud manerium de Kylmaynan, decimoquinto die Septembris, annis regnorum regis et regine Philippi et Marie, Dei gratia, tertio et quarto, inter Phelomeum Duffe Oneyle et filios Phelomei Claudi, concernens pertitionem seu divisionem patrie de Clandeboye nuper sub regimine Hugonis filii Nelani Juvenis, defuncti, ad remanendum et continuandum prout sequitur, durante beneplacito domini deputati pro tempore existente: fol. 12.

T. Fytzwauters.—[1.] In primis: Dictus Phelomeus Duffe, in recognitionem debite obedientie sue regie majestati, tradet et deliberabit immediate principali capitaneo seu generali exercitus regine majestatis in Ultonia pro tempore existenti castrum sive regium fortilagium de Bellfarste,[1] custodiendum et retinendum ad usum et proprietatem sue majestatis.

[1] Belfast. See "Facsimiles of National Manuscripts of Ireland," Part IV. 1, p. xxix. London: 1882.

1556. [2.] Item: Similiter ordinatum et consensum est quod dicti filii Phelomei Claudi habebunt et possidebunt pro parte sua in dicta patria de Clandeboye omnia terra, tenementa, castra, fortilagia et edificia, unacum ceteris proficuis, commoditatibus et advantagiis quibuscunque eisdem pertinentibus, jacentia et existentia ultra flumen ibidem juxta Bellfarste predictum (dicto castro de Bellfarste tantummodo excepto).

fol. 12b. [3.] Item: Ulterius ordinatum et consensum est quod prefatus Phelomeus Duffe similem habebit possessionem in omnibus terris, tenementis, castris, edificiis et ceteris proficuis ac commoditatibus quibuscunque dicte patrie de Clandeboye spectantibus ex hac parte dicti fluminis juxta prefatum castrum de Bellfarste currentis.

[4.] Finaliter: Conclusum et ordinatum est quod legitimum erit alteruter illorum mutuum habere accessum ad alterius patriam de tempore in tempus sine obstaculo aut restrictione, cum jumentis, catallis, et singulis eorum sequacibus tam pro sustentatione capienda cum opus fuerit quam pro meliori eorum defensione et tutela erga Scotos seu alios illorum inimicos, donec per dictum generalem et regiam potestatem ibidem auxiliari et defendi possint.

H. Dublin, canc. — Wyll. Fytzwylliams. — John Travers.— H. Sydney.

fol. 13. [XVI.]—Instructions for Androwe Brereton and others joyned in commyssion with hym in Ulster, geven by the right honorable the lord Fitzwalter, lord deputie of the realme of Irelande and counsell of the same, at Kylmaynan, the xvith of September, anno 1556:

T. Fytzwauters.—[1.] Furste: We constytute and appoynte our trustie and welbelouved Androwe Brereton to be Generall of Ulster, requyring hym to use thadvise of the reverende father in God, the busshope of Downe, Capteyn Roger Broke, Edwarde Brereton, Richarde Bethell and William Pierce, whome we appoynte commyssioners to hym for thexecution of all mattiers hereafter following or any others that shalbe for the service of the quenes majestie during their abode there.

Furste: We woll that the sayde Androwe and commyssoners as farre as in them shall lye shall maynteyne the right of holy churche and kepe and defende the mynysteres thereof from all outerage or wronges that by enny man shalbe to them offerid, and cause suche churches within Ulster as to them shalbe thought good to be reedified at the chardges of the contry during their abode there.

fol. 13b. [2.] Item: We give to them auctorytie to parle with all men, duryng ther abode there, at ther will as well by lande as by sea.

[3.] Item: We give to them auctorytie, during their abode there, to give protectyon to all suche men as they shall thinke good, and to take and delyver pledges at their woll.

[4.] Item: We give to them power and auctorytie to heare and determyne all maner controversies betweene partie and partye within Ulster, during their abode there, so as the same be no mattiers of inheritance.

[5.] Item: That they, during their abode there, shall execute the marshall lawe, in all cases to them thought convenyente.

[6.] Item: That they, during their abode there, shall cause the men of the countrey there to mannure such parte of every plowe lande as to them shalbe thought sufficiente for the mayntenance of the countrey and furnytur of the queenes majesties garrysons left there. 1556.

[7.] Item: That they, during their abode there, shall cawse to be pounyshed all those that shall commytt treason, murder, felony, rape, or any other crymynall offence, as to thoffences commytted in those cases shall appertayne.

[8.] Item: That they, during their abode there, shall cawse to be fol. 14. leveyed to the queenes majesties use all forfaytes that of right during that tyme shall to her majestie appertayne.

[9.] Item: That they, during their abode there, shall take to the queenes majesties use suche forts as to them shalbe thought good, and cause the same to be repayred at the chardges of the countrey.

[10.] Item: That they during their abode there, shall cause the counterey to cutt pases at the chardges of the countrey where the saide commyssioners shall thinke mete.

[11.] Item: We will that they shall not delyver eny pledge already taken but upon speciall lycence from us in wryting.

[12.] Item: We will that the saide generall and commyssioners shall from tyme to tyme call thayde of the countrey to joyne with them and so doo their beste for the clere expulsyon of the Skottes and takyng of their cattell.

[13.] Item: We will that the saide generall and commyssioners shall leavy of Phelym Duffe eight hundreth bieves, one hundreth of Savage, one hundreth of the capteyne of Kilultaghe, and one hundreth of Moriertaghe Oneile according to our appoyntemente with the saide Phelym, Savage, capitayne of Kylultaghe and Moriertaghe at our being at Knockefergus, and cawse the same bieffes to be sauffely brought to fol. 14b. Carlingforde or Dundalke wheare we shall upon knowledge from the said generall appoynte men for the receyving of them. Provided that the generall may detayne for the necessary victualling of tharmye suche nomber of the saide bieffes as to him shalbe thought good, aunswering to the queenes majestie six shillings viii*d.* sterling, for every bieffe.

[14.] Item: We will that the saide generall and commyssioners shall call the towne of Knockefergus to accompte for suche money and other thinges as they have receyved for the fortyfieng of their saide towne, and shall thereupon cause them to fortyfie the same with all convenyent spede.

[15.] Item: We will that the saide generall and commyssioners shall delyver Hughe McMoriertaghe yf Neyle his brother doo become pledge for hym.

[16.] Item: We will that the generall shall have full power and auctoryte, during the tyme of his abode there, texecute the premysses with thadvyse and consente of one of the said commyssioners, yf it happen the reste of eny occasion to be absente in suche place as he can not have their advyse at the tyme when yt shalbe expedyente to putt in execution the premisses or eny of them; otherwyse not withoute thadvyse and consente of the saide Broke.

[17.] Item: We requyre the same generall and commyssioners to use good advyse and deliberation in thexecution of the premysses.

H. Dublin, canc. — Wyll: Fytzwylliams.—John Travers. — H. Sydney.

1556. [XVII.]—At Dublyn, the xvii[th] of September, anno 1556.

fol. 16.[1] T. Fytswauters.—Memorandum: That wheare sir William Fitz-williams, knight, receyved in Inglande fyve and twenty thousande poundes to be transported hither and disbursed by the handes of sir Edmonde Rows,[2] knight, late vicethesaurour, for the defraye of ther majesties debtes here, the same sir Edmonde having a daye prefixed by the councell of England for the declaracyon of his accompte there, departid hens with that his declaracyon before the [w]hole somme aforesaide payed and employed according to their majesties pleasure in that behalffe: it is therefore accorded, condescended and agreid by us, the lord deputie and counsell, for the better servyce of their highness that the saide sir William Fitzwilliams shall paye and delyver unto sir Henry Sydney, knight, nowe vicethesauror (by wryting indented to be made betwene them two) all suche money, parcell of the saide 25,000 li., as yet remayneth in his custodye, and therupon that the saide sir Henry shall from tyme to tyme make furder paymente thereof to their majeste's use as by warrante from us, the lorde deputie, he shalbe dyrected and ordayned.

H. Dublin, canc.—H. Sydney.—John Travers.—D. Hay.

fol. 16b. [XVIII.]—At Kylmaynan the xix[th] of September, anno 1556.

T. Fytswauters.—Memorandum: Wheare, apon our late retoune from Knockefergus and other the northe parties, yt was thought good by us, the lord deputie and counsaill, that for specyall consideracyons us movyng there shulde certeyn souldyours to the nomber of threscore be retayned to serve there under capteyne Williamson, whiche bande enteryng into wages of the fifte of August laste were agayne discharged the xv[th] of September following.

H. Sydney.—John Travers.

fol. 17. [XIX.]—The generall hostyng northewarde againste the Skottes, sett fourthe by the right honourable the lord Fitzwalter, lord deputie of the realme of Irelande, the seconde of July and contynuyng for xlii. daies:

A note wherby the shrieffe of the countie of Dublyn shall knowe and warne such personnes as shall sett fourthe to this hosting, and howe:

The Barony of Balrothery:

John Parkar of Holme Patrike, master of the rolles, shall set forth in personne, with six archers on horseback - -	vi archers	on	horseback.
The justyce Cardyffe, of Turvy - -	ii	"	"
James Barnewell, of Brynmore - -	ii	"	"
Christofor Barnewell, of Gracedieu, in person - - - -	iiii	"	"
Richarde Fynglas, of Wespleston - -	i archer		"
Patricke Fynglas, of Westpleston, to sett fourthe in person - -	ii archers		"

[1] In margin: "This is wrong nombered, as may apere by the leef of folio 8, which is of same sheets and hath folio 9 ensueing it, which is of the same sheet with folio 14, that goeth nexte before this lefe."

[2] Sir Edmond Rouse, Vice-treasurer, Treasurer at wars, and Receiver of revenues of Ireland, appointed by patent 12 December, 1553, was succeeded by sir Henry Sydney in 1555.

		1556.
Roberte Preston, of Balmadon, to set fourthe	ii archers on horseback.	
Walter Cruce, of the Nall	ii " "	
Robarte Butteler, of Curduffe	i archer "	
John Travers, of Ballykey, in person	ii archers "	
Thomas Fizsymondes, of Curduffe	ii " "	
Richarde Fizsymonde, of Balmadroght, in in person	ii " "	
Bartholome Bathe, of Laundeston, in person	i archer "	
Matheu Begge, of Boranston	i " "	
William Cowran, of the Corraghe, in person	i " "	
Tallon, of the Weston, by the Nall	i " "	

The somme of this baronye amounteth to ten cartes, whiche cartes were converted into garrans after the rate of five garrans[1] to every carte and to every five garrans thre hable men to dryve them.

The Baronye of Cullocke[2]: fol. 17b.

The lorde of Howthe, in person	iiii archers on horseback.
William Talbot, of Malahide, in person	ii " "
The baron Bathe, of Dromconraghe	ii " "
The baron White, of Clontarffe	ii " "
John Plunkett, of Donshoghelye	iii " "
Nycholas Holywodde, of Tartayne	ii " "
Robarte Taylor, of Swerdes, in person	i archer "
Nycholas Stokes, of the same, in person	i " "
Patrike Russell, of the Scaton	ii archers "
Bartholome Russell, of Feltrym, and Thomas Russell, his brother, in person	i archer "
Thomas Wycombe, of Drynann, in person	i " "
William Blackney, of Sawcerston, in person	i " "
Patrike Caddell, of Caldelston	i " "
Christopher Foster, of Killeghe	i " "
Emery Howthe, of Killester	i " "
Markes Barnwell, of Donbro	i " "
Walter Golding, of the Grange, in person	i " "

The somme of this barony amounteth to six cartes dimid. (fredoms excepte) whiche was convertid into garrans as is aforesaid.

The Baronye of Newcastell:

Tharshebusshope of Dublyn	viii archers on horseback.
Edwarde Barnewell, of Dromnaghe, in person	i archer "
Robart Talbott, of Belgar, in person	i " "
Richarde Talbott, of Templeoge	i " "

The somme of this baronye amounteth to ten cartes, convertid as aforesaide into garrans.

---

[1] Horses. [2] Coolock.

1556. The Baronye of Castellknocke:

fol. 18. James Luttrell, now shrieffe of the countie of Dublin, in person	iiii	archers	on horseback.
Bartholome Dyllon, of Kappoke	iii	„	„
Thomas Bealyng, of Stradbally	ii	„	„
Roger Finglas, of Porterston, in person	ii	„	„

The somme of the cartes of this baronye amounte to seven, the same convertid as aforesaide into garrans.

The Barony of Rathedowne:

Sir John Travers, knight, in person	iiii	archers	on horseback.
Thomas Fitzwilliams, of Meryon, in person	ii	„	„

This barony amounteth to [*blank*] cartes, levyed alwaies in money, and to this hosting was not cessed, but did aunswer the marche caryadge.

The marches of the countye of Dublyn:

All the Walshemans countrey, Haroldes countrey, and the Archeboldes	xii horsemen,	xvi kern.
The Byrnes	xii „	xxiiii „
The Thooles,—waste.		

A note whereby the shrieffe of the countie of Methe shall knowe and warne suche persons as shall sett fourthe to this hostyng, and howe:

The Barony of Dulyke:

The lord viscounte of Gormanston	viii	archers	on horseback.
The justice Aylmer	iii	„	„
The justice Bathe	iii	„	„
Talbott, of Dardeston	ii	„	„
fol. 18b. Darcie of Platten, in person	iii	„	„
Caddell, of the Nall, in person	ii	„	„
Byrte, of Tullocke, in person	ii	„	„
Hamlyng,[1] of Smytheston	i	archer	„
Sarsfielde, of Sarsfieldeston	i	„	„
Bathe, of Colpe	i	„	„

The somme of this baronye amounte to ten[2] cartes, and the same convertid as aforesaide into garrans after the rate above lymited.

The Baronye of Skryne:

The lord of Kyllene; the lord of Donsany, in person, with the reste of the Plunketts	xxiiii horsemen.		
The barone of Skryne, in person	iiii	archers	on horseback.
Sir Thomas Cusake, of Lesmollen, in consideracyon of his absence, but	ii	„	„
Sir Christofer Chever, of Maston	iiii	„	„
Bathe, of Raphecke, in person	ii	„	„

[1] In margin: "Darsy of Platten must be heer."
[2] In margin: "Nota: xi. cartes, by the olde booke."

Keute, of Daneston - - - ii archers on horseback. 1556.
Cusake, of Gerardeston, in person - ii " "
Thomas Dillon, of Ryverston - - iii " "
Tankarde, of Castelton, in person - i archer "
Pentney, of the Cabraghe - - i " "
The kernes of the Polles,—cl.

The somme of this baronye amounte to nine cartes, to be convertid into garrans as afore.

The Baronye of Ratowthe:

Barnewell, of Kylbree - - - i archer on horseback.
Berforde, of Kyllrowe - - i " "
Talbott, of Robarteston - - - i " "
Delahide of Donshaghelyn, in person - i " " fol. 19.
Weaseley, of the Blackehall, in person - i " "

The somme of this baronye amounte to five cartes, convertid as aforesaide into garrans.

The Barony of Dunboyne:

Phepo, of the Rowan - - .. - i archer on horseback.

This barony ys in the [w]hole but thre cartes, whiche convertid into garrans after the rate above saide make fifteen garrans.

The Baronyes of Dece and Moyfenraghe:

The barone of Galtrym, in person - iiii archers on horseback.
James Dowdall, in person - i archer "
Flemyng, of Derpatrike, in person - i " "
William Brymyngham, of Castellrycarde, in person - - - i " "

The somme of theas two baronyes amounte in the [w]hole to twelve cartes, etc., as before.

The Baronye of Lune:

Sir Francis Harberte - - - ii archers on horseback.
Lynche, of Dunore - - - i " "
Rocheforde of Keranston, in person - i " "
The portereeffe of Atheboye - - viii " "

The somme of this baronye amounte to six cartes convertid as aforesaid.

The Baronye of the Novan:

The bushope of Methe - - - viii archers on horseback.
The lord of Trymletston - - viii " "
The barone of Novan - - - iii " "
The Justice Dyllon - .. - ii " "
Rocheforde, of Kylbryde - - iiii " " fol. 19b.
Barnaby Skurlocke, in person - - ii " "
Michell Cusake, in person - - - ii " "
Ivers, of Ratayne - - - i archer "
The portereffe, of Trym - - - iii archers "
The portereffe, of the Novan - - iiii " "
Myssett of Laskartan - - - - i " "

The somme of this baronye amounteth to ten cartes, convertid into garrans as before.

1556. The Baronye of Kenlys:

Sir Thomas Barnewell, of Robertston, in person - iii horsemen.
James Everarde, of Randelston, in person - - ii „
Mape, of Maperathe, in person - - - i horseman.
Drake, of Rahode, in person - - - i „
Betaghe, of Moynaltye, in person - - - iiii horsemen.
Ledwyche, of Cookeston - - - - i horseman.
Fitz John, of Fyanston, in person - - - i „
The sofferayne of Kenlys - - - - ii archers on horseback.

Somme of this baronye amounteth to nine cartes, convertid as before.

The Halfe Barony of Fower:

Balfe of Galmoweston, in person - - - - ii horsemen.
Barnewell of Moylaghe, in person - - - i horseman.
Tuyte of Baltrastyn - - - - i „

Somme of this baronye amounteth in the [w]hole but to two cartes, convertid as above, etc.

fol. 20. The Baronye of Mergallen:

Thomas Flemying, of Stephenston, in person - - ii horsemen.
White, of Clongell, - - - - - i „
Velden, of the Raffen, in person - - - - i „

Somme of this baronye amounteth to five cartes and converted as before, etc.

The Baronye of Slane:

The baron of Slane, in person - - viii horsemen.
Netherfielde, of Dowthe - - - ii archers on horseback.
Barnewell, of Stacallen, nowe - - iii „ „
Shrieffe, in person - - - iii „ „
Barnewell, of Rowston - - - ii „ „
Flemyng, of Syddan, in person - - i „ „
Ivers of Byngerston - - - i „ „

Somme of this baronye amounteth to five cartes, and putt to the use as afore.

A note wherby the shrieffe of Westmethe shall knowe and warne suche gentilmen as shall sett fourthe to this hosting, and howe:

The barone of Delven and his kynsmen - - - - - - xviii horsemen, xxiiii kerne.
Tuyte of Sonnaghe and Tuyte of Molenlee, in person - - v „ viii „
Petyte, in person - - - - iii „ iiii „
Tyrrell of Fertullaghe, in person - vi „ xii „
John Darcy, in person - - - vi „ xii „
The Daltons, in person - - - x „ xv „
The Dyllons, in person - - viii „ xvi „
Dallamare, in person - - - xii „ xvi „

A note wherby the shrieffe of the countye of Lowthe shall knowe and warne suche personnes as shall sett fourthe to this hosting, and howe : 1556.

The lorde prymate - - -	vi archers on horseback	
The lorde of Lowthe, in person, with the Plunkettes -	vi	horsemen.
Taffe, of Cockeston, in person - - - - -	ii	,,
The Dowdalles, in person - - - - -	iiii	,,
The Garnons, in person - - - - - - -	vi	,,
The Bedlowes, in person - - - - -	v	,,
The Taffes, in person - - - - - - -	vi	,,
Whyte, of Balregan - - - - - -	i	,,
Moore, of Barnemethe, in person - - - - -	i	,,
Clynton, of the Water, in person - - - -	i	,,
Clynton of Dromcashell - - - - - - - -	i	,,

This shire hathe no cartes, but the plowelandes are alwaies accustomed to be leavyed in money, saving only foure cartes oute of the barony of Ferrarde.

The countie of Kildare did not aunswer the accustomed cartes to this hosting, for that the erle of Kyldare, with the viscounte of Baltynglasse, and the reste of the gentilmen of the same shiere were appoynted to attende upon the lord deputie, who nevertheles wente not but remayned at home for deffence of the borders.

The cytie of Dublyn sett fourthe to this hosting with thre score archers and gonners well appoynted, having the cariadge of the countrey assigned unto them.

The towne of Drougheda dyd lykewyse sett oute to this hosting with forty tall feallowes well appointed. fol. 21.

The rysing oute of Yrishe lordes and capitaynes to this hosting :

The Byrnes, viz., Tege oge Obyrne, Edmonde Obyrne and Dowlyn -	xii	horsemen,	xxiiii	kerne.
The Cavennaghes : Morroghe Cavenagh with the reste - - -	xii	,,	xxx	,,
O'Karwell, with - - - - -	xii	,,	xxiiii	,,
Magoghegan, with - - - -	iiii	,,	xxiiii	,,
Omolmoye - - - - -	vi	,,	xi	,,
Omollaghlyn - - - -	iiii	,,	xxiiii	,,
Omadden - - - - - -	iiii	,,	xii	,,
Hugh Omadden - -	iiii	,,	xii	,,
Magennesse - - -	xii	,,	xxiiii	,,
Mac Mahon - - - - -	viii	,,	xv	,,
Capitayne of Ferney - - - - -	x	,,	xxx	,,
Savage - - - - -	iiii	,,	xiiii	,,
Orayly - - - - -	xl	,,	c	,,

Phelym Roo, with his accustomed rysing oute.

Ohanlon, with his lyke rysing oute.

Magwyer, in the same sorte.

The erle of Tyrone and the barone of Dongennan, with their accustomed rysing oute.

Bryan Omaghery, with his rysing oute.[1]

---

[1] In margin, at foot : "Totall of this hosting, videlicet : horsemen, 642 ; kerne, 662."

1556. fol. 21*b*. Therle of Ormonde, in person, with his rysing oute of horsemen and kerne.

The barone of Donboyne, in person, with his horsemen and kerne.

The barone of the Cahir, to sende his sonne or his brother to the hosting, with his accustomyd rysing oute of horsemen and kern.

The barone of Upper Ossoryes sonne, wyth his horsemen and kerne.

fol. 22. [XX.]—At the Dynghain, the fourth of October, 1556:

T. Fytswauters.—Whereas, before our going northwarde in the generall hosting against the Scottes, the right honorable therle of Kildare made request to us, the lord deputie and others of thier majesties counsell then present, to be discharged of the forte of the Dinghain, whereupon it was ordered by the said lord deputie and counsell that for diverse causes theym moving, the said erle shuld contynue his charge at their requeste, till the feast of Saint Michaell next folowing, as by the same order written in the counsell booke[2] more at leynght dothe appeare: consideryng nowe the said tyme prefixed to be cumme and paste, we have thought good to receive the said forte of the said erle, and to discharge him of any further burden in the keping therof; and therefore by this our warraunt doo will and require you, the said erle, to deliver the saide forte to captayne Henry Cowley, whom we have appoynted to receive the same, with all thinges therein by bill indented of your lordship and this our warraunt shalbe your discharge therein.

Memorandum: That the same day William Derby was admytted and placed in the rowme of gentleman porter at the said forte at the wages of twelve pence sterling per diem, and appoynted to have oon man in wages at viii*d*. sterling, per diem, in the first rowme that fallithe voide in any of the Englishe bandes.

fol. 22*b*. [XXI.]—At Dublyn, the seventh of November, anno 1556:

T. Fitzwauters.—Right trusty and welbeloved we grete you hartily well: And wheare by us and others of the king and quenes majesties counsell yt is thought very necessary and expedyente that contynuall watche shulde be kepte every wheare within this realme, according thauntyente custome of the same, aswell for preservacyón of you and others their majesties loving subjects as for thapprehension of theffes, outelawes and other like malefactors whiche in defaulte of suche watche and keping are sondry tymes encooraged to commytt by night dyverse stelthes, murders, burnyngs and other semblable attemptes, to the greate losse, ympoveryshing and utter displeasure of their majesties saide subjectes:

Wee, therefore, consydering as well the same as thextremyte of this wynter season, in which time suche evill dooers have moste scope and liberty to execute their malyce, woll and commande you in their highness names that devyding yourselfes into cyrcuytes you sende for and call before you the constable and other offycers within every your cyrcuytes, charging and commaunding them and every of them by vertue hereof diligentely to forsee and cawse contynuall watche to be kepte nightely, according the custome, in every towne, village and boroughe within their precyncte betwixte this and Saynote Patrikes tyde, nexte commyng.

---

[2] See page 5.

And in case any of the sayde wacchemen so appointed (wherunto 1556.
we eftesones charge you to have speciall regarde and conсyderacyon) make defaulte and kepe not the same accordingly, he to forfayte for every tyme so founde or knowen two shillinges, the one halffe to the king and quenes majesties, and thother moytie to the constable of the same towne, village or boroughe wheare suche defaulte shalbe founde.

And, furder, yf huyte or crye be made in any the places aforesaide, fol. 23.
and yf the nexte towne or village adjoyning to the same doo not aunswer the sayde crye, then to forfayte for every tyme six shillinges viii*d*., thone halfe to the quenes majestie, the other halfe to the partye that shall make declaracyon of the defaulte to any justice of peace within the cyrcuyte wheare the default shalbe made.

And, furder, the constable beyng in the towne when suche defaulte shalbe made, to suffer imprysonmente for xxiiii howres.

And to thintente this our order might be better knowen to the people, we woll that you shall cawse the constables within your severall lymytes to cawse the prieste in every paryshe churche to make declaracyon hereof ones every monneth during the tyme of the wacche.

Fayle ye not therefore to see the premysses duely putt in execucyon, as ye tender your owne commodyties, the quyete of this their majesties countrey and subjectes, and will furder aunswer to the contrary at your extreme perilles.

H. Dublin, canc.—Roland Baltynglas.—Willelmus Midensis.—Richard Delvin.—John Travers.—H. Sydney.—D. Hay.

[XXII.]—Apud Dubliniam, die [vii Novembris] et anno [1556] fol. 23*b*.
predictis :

Ryght trustie and right welbeloved and trustye and welbeloved we grete you hartily well : And wheare we be putt in understondyng that Henry Oneyle and other his servauntes and followers have of late not onely ryffelid and spoyled soondry marchantes and others repayring to Carlingforde and those parties, but also taken them prysoners, whom he still detayneth, alleaging, as we be enformed, that he hathe donne the same for suche injuries and wronges as Henry Dowdall and others upon the borders of Uryell have withoute any redres commytted againste hym and hys.

And forasmoche as for other more waightye affaires we can not convenyentely ourselves attende to call the partyes before us, having good affyance in your wysdomes and discreacyon for the upright and indyfferente orderyng hereof, we have thought good by theas our lettres to auctoryse you or any two of you as well as to call the saide partyes before you (grauntyng rather then fayle saufe condyte to the sayde Oneile for his accesse) and to here and examyn at large their severall grieffes and varyannces, as also to order and determyne the same betwixte them as to justice shall appertayne.

And in case ye shall fynde the sayde Henry Oneyle wilfull or disobedyente, and that he will neyther conforme himselfe to good order, nor yet enlarge those captives whiche he detayneth, with the restytution of their goodes, we woll then that with delyberate advyse and discreacyon ye shall procede to the plaging of hym in such sorte as, with the helpe of the quenes majesties power there he may be compelled to aunswer to reason ; lyke
as, on the contrary, we wolde he shulde be reasonably aunswerid yf fol. 24.
the said Henry Dowdall or others in those confynes have usid hym otherwise then appertayneth, having no mystruste but ye wyll use the

1556. thing with such discreation as nothing shalbe attemptid that of right and equyte ought not. And even so fare ye well. From Dublin, etc.

fol. 24b. [XXII.]—Apud Dubliniam, die [vii Novembris] et anno [1556] supradictis:

T. Fytswauters.—Forasmoche as yt ys consydered by us the lorde deputie counsaill, that the king and quenes majesties fortes and other their highnes holdes and garrysons are dysfurnyshed of necessary provysion (chieffely wheate and other grayne) for their presente relieffe, the tyme being nowe moste propice to putt the same in order:

And considering agayne what corne heretofore hathe gone out of the English Pale into Irishemen's countreyes, and ys dayly by dyverse as well grey merchantes and others commonly laden and conveyid withoute lett or restraynte, whereby grete darthe and skarsyte ys lyke unyversally to growe:

It ys therfore condescendid and decreed that from hensfourthe no suche grayne shalbe conveyid, laden or solde oute of the sayde Inglishe Pale into any Irishemans countrey, nor yet any foreyn suffered or permytted to comme apon the markett daies or other tymes into any the townes, villages or boroughes, to bye any corne, but that yt shall be taken as a forfayte and lawful for every man to seyse apon the same, the one halfe to the king and quenes majesties use, and the other moytie to the seyser himselfe:

Wylling and requyring and nevertheles in their majesties names straightely chardging and commandyng all and every their highness offycers mynystres and subjectes of what estate, degree or condycion fol. 25. soever they be not onely to have specyall eye and consideracion to the premyses, but also to be from tyme to tyme ayding and assisting all those that shall putt this our proclamacyon in due execution; not fayling hereof, as ye and every of yow tender your duetyes, the servyce of their majesties and the furtherance of the publique weale, and will furder aunswer to the contrary at their uttermoste perilles. Yeoven at Dublyn, etc.

Postscripta: This order to be executid and followed till suche tyme as the fortes beyng furnyshed we shall give lyberty to the contrary.

H. Dublin, canc.—Rowland Baltynglas.—Willelmus Midensis.—Richard Delvin.—John Travers.—H. Sidney.—John Plunket.—D. Hay.

fol. 25b. [XXIV.]—Articles of commyssion mynstred to A., B., and C., condescendid upon by us, the lorde deputie and Counsaill, the viiith of November, anno [1556] supradicto:

T. Fitswauters.—[1.] Furste: That proclamation[1] be made thorougheoute the [w]hole shiere that no ydle person or vaccabonde shall repayre or hawnte within the same shiere after eight dayes nexte after the same proclamacyon made, upon payne of hanging, onles he have a juste cawse. And lykewyse that no person travayle by nyght onles he be accompanyed with some honeste man in Inglish apparell upon lyke payne.

[2.] Item: After the same viii dayes, yt shalbe lawfull for the saide A. B. C. to apprehende and take all suche ydle personnes as thei shall comme by, and yf thei shall fynde any reasonable or juste cawse they

[1] In margin: "Theis be the articles annexed to the commission for mershall lawe."

shall have lyberty to pounyshe them at their discreacyon as well by 1556.
deathe or otherwise in cawses of death.

[3.] Item: The said A. B. C. shall likewyse have full auctoryte to apprehende and take all such person or persons as doo willingly ayde, supporte, or maynteyne any outelawe or open theffe, murderer, or rebell and to sende them to the lorde deputie and councell with certificate of their demeanour, and shall also seyse ther goodes and cattailles, and putt the same upon suretye, taking an inventary thereof; and upon proufe that the partye ys suche a malefactor as by the lawe he ought to forfayte his goodes, the two partes thereof to be to the king and quenes majesties use, and the thurde parte to the use of the saide A. B. C. towardes ther paynes and chardges.

[4.] Item: In case the saide A. B. C. shall in the nyght fynde any
suspecte person or personnes not having in his or ther company some fol. 26.
one honeste man in Englishe apparell, it shalbe lawfull to the saide A. B. C. to use them at their discreatyon; and if any suche personnes so travailling by night be by the same A. B. C. taken with the manuvre[1] of any stelthe, robbery, or murder, yt shalbe lawfull for them to hange them up at suche place as they shall think mete.

[5.] Item: In case the same A. B. C. shall, in the prosequutyng of any suche malefactor, call for ayde and assistence of any the king and quenes majesties subjectes, and he or they so callid and requyred to ayde refuse so to doo, onles he have a lawfull cawse, or in any case resysteth the sayde A. B. C., they shall certyfie the same to the lorde deputie and councell who will see hym or them so refusing or resysting to be grevously pounyshed and some recompence to the saide A. B. C. of his or their goodes so refusing or resisting.

[6.] Item: Whensoever the saide A. B. C. shall so travaill for the pounyshemente of suche malefactors, yt shalbe lawfull for them to take meate and drinke for horse and man in reasonable sorte, so as they excede not one night or two in every baronye within the shiere; the same to be taken in suche indifferente sorte as the countrey be not oppressid therewith.

[7.] Item: The sayde A. B. C. so taking any suspecte personne or fol. 26 b.
personnes shall examyne hym or them before the nexte gentilman of worshipe or the sofferayn or porterieffe or other nexte hedde officer of any towne or borough nexte adjoynyng, and fynding suffyciente mattier of deathe shall and maye putt suche malefactor to deathe, or otherwyse pounyshe hym or them at ther discreacyon.

[8.] Fynally: Yt ys ordered by the saide lorde deputie and counsaill that this auctorytie shall not extende to any gentilman or freholder that may dispende xx. *s.* lande by the yeare; and that, furder, the constable of every paryshe shall give warnyng to the preste or curate of the same to publyshe and declare the punyshment openly in the churche, to thintent that the people may not be ignorante of the same.

[9.] It ys also ordered and agreid that yf any suche suspectid personne so taken shall fayle of his soreyne[2] and the same so justyfied before the sayde A. B. and C., then yt shalbe lawfull for to pounyshe the same person by deathe or otherwise as to ther discreations shall seme good.

H. Dublin, canc.—Roland Baltynglas.—Willelmus Midensis.—Richard Delvin.—John Travers.—H. Sydney.

---

[1] Goods taken in the hands of an apprehended thief.

[2] "Sorohen," "sorrihin," a cess levied quarterly.

1556. [XXV.]—Apud Dubliniam, 8 Novembris, anno [1556] supradicto:

fol. 27. T. Fytswauters.—For the reformacyon of Lexe and other the king and quenes majesties countryes apon those borders, yt ys condescendid and agreid by us the lorde deputie and counsell, with thadvyse of the nobylite of the realme, that the sayde lorde deputie by lettres under his hande shall from tyme to tyme, when occasion of warre serveth, retayne suche nomber of kerne for that purpose as his lordship shall thinke good. The same holding to be cessid at his discreacyon within the counties of Methe, Westmethe, Dublyn, Uryell, Kildare, Caterlagh, Wexforde, Waterforde, Kylkenny and Tipperary; and so many of the saide counties to be cessid in money as his honor for the hyer and entertaynemente of the saide kerne shall thinke expedyente.

Memorandum: That, upon the debatying hereof, yt was fynally concludid that there shulde be cessid in the counties of Dublyn and Methe two hundreth poundes for the same purpose. The meanyng ys two hundreth poundes, sterling, ratabely upon the plowlandes.

H. Dublin, canc.—Roland Baltynglas.—Willelmus Midensis.—H. Sydney.—Richard Delvin.—John Travers.—D. Hay.

[XXVI.]—Apud Dubliniam, ix° die Novembris, anno [1556] predicto:

fol. 27*b*. T. Fytswauters.—It ys condescendid, concluded and agreid by us, the lorde deputie, the lordes and nobles of this realme, with the reste of the king and quenes majesties counsaill whose names are hereunto subscribed, that for the furnyture and vytailling aswell of their majesties fortes in Lexe and Offalley, as other their highness holdes and garrysons both in the northe and elsewhere, that there shalbe a unyversell cesse of corne and bieves; that ys to saye:

Foure thousande peckes whete, and foure thowsande peckes of malte, whereof the thurde parte beare malte, and the other two partes woote[1] malte; the pecke of whete and bere malte at thre shillinges iv. *d.*, sterling, and the pecke of woote malte at two shillinges iv. *d.*, sterling.

The [w]hole to be cessid and levied within the counties of Methe, Westemethe, Kyldare, Dublyn and Uryell, and to be devided in sorte as followeth, that ys to saye, in Methe and Westemethe foure thowsande peckes wherof thre thowsande in Methe and one thowsande in Westmethe, the one halfe wheate the other malte; in Kildare, xv hundreth peckes wheate and malte; in Dublin, other xv hundreth peckes whete and malte; and in the countye of Uriell one thowsande after like rate.

The counties of Wexforde, Waterforde, Kilkenny and Typperary to be lykewise cessid at the discreacion of the saide lorde deputie and as his lordship by his lettres shall appoynte, to serve for the furnyture of the
fol. 28. manor of Leighlyn and other the quenes majesties garrysons that shall upon occasion resyde on those bordres. And, furder, yt ys concludid that for the furnyture aforesaide ther shalbe cessid within the saide five shieres of Methe, Westemethe, Kildare, Dublin, and Uriell, one thowsande bieves; whereof, in Methe and Westmethe, six hundreth; in Kildare seven score, in Uriell seven score, and in the countie of Dublin six score; the rate of the saide byeffe at xii. *s.*, sterling.

All whiche proportyon of corne to be brought in as followeth, that is to saye, one parte by Christemas nexte, the seconde parte by Candelmas and the thirde parte by Saincte Patrikes tyde next following, with suffycyente

[1] Oaten.

cariadge appointid by the countrey for conveying of the same, after the rate of iv. *d.* the garran and vi. *d.* the man by the daye, to be delyverid at suche places as in the meane tyme by the saide lorde deputie shalbe appointed unto you, wheare they shall receyve ready money after the rates aforesaide aswell for the saide grayne as also for the bieves, which bieves we woll shalbe brought all in betwixte this and Christmas nexte, to thintent they may for store be putt in salte, considering that after tyme they will fall and abate their fleshe. 1556.

H. Dublin, canc.—Roland Baltynglas.—Willelmus Midensis.—H. Sydney.—Richard Delvin.—John Travers.—John Plunket.

[XXVII.]—Apud Dubliniam, ix° die Novembris, anno [1556] supradicto: fol. 28*b*.

T. Fytswauters.—Memorandum: Wheare soondry varyaunces and controversies have heretofore byn moved and are yet depending betwene the right honnorable the erle of Ormonde, on the one partye, and the baron of Upper Ossory on the other, for dyverse stelthes, boddlerages,[1] and other enormyties done by them and their tenantes, servantes and followers, upon ther severall contries, to the greate unquyetenes of themselves and moche to the losse and hinderance of ther majesties subjectes abyding under their severall rules:

It is ordered, condescendid and agreid by us that Robert Dillon, esquier, seconde justice of their majesties benche here, and John Plunkett, of Donshaghly, esquier, as commyssioners, indyfferentely electid and chosen, shall with as moche spede as thei may make ther repayre into the saide erle and barons countries, and there travailling from place to place as occasyon shall serve, learne and understonde, by all the lawfull wayes and meanes they maye, eyther by deposition of wittenesses or otherwyse, what hurtes and damages have byn donne by the saide erle and baron one againste another, or by any their tenantes, servauntes and followers or any thinhabitantes within their severall countreys; and the same so knowen shall ymediately putt in wryting under their handes and seales and sende yt unto us, the lorde deputie, with convenyente spede, to thende that we therupon may take suche order betwixte the saide erle and barone for a friendly concorde and quyetenes to be had betwene them, and for the better staye and fol. 29.
quyetenes of the countries from hensfourthe as upon due consyderacyon of the mattier shalbe thought consonante and agreable to justice.

And hereupon yt ys furder orderid and agreid that not onely the costes and chardges of the sayde commyssioners to be sustayned in this behalffe shalbe indyfferentely borne by the sayde erle and baron, but also that they shall give unto the saide commyssioners by waye of rewarde for their paynes taking in the premysses twenty markes, sterling, apece, to be paied in hande before their departure oute of the countries aforesaide.

H. Dublin, canc.—John Travers.—H. Sydney.[2]

[XXVIII.]—Apud Laughlen, ———[3] die Decembris, anno [1556] supradicto: fol. 30*b*.

Memorandum: That the xxixth day of November, in the third and fourthe yere of the most prosperus reignes of our most dred soveraigne lord and lady, the king and quenes majesties, etc.:

---

[1] Depredations.

[2] Ff. 29*b*. and 30 are blank.

[3] Blank in Ms.

1556. Conell Oge Omore, with the rest of the septes of the Omores in Lease, having before submittyed themselves to their majesties mercies, came before the right honorable the lord Fitzwaters, one of the kinges majesties prevy chamber, capitaine of theire majesties gentlemen pencioners and men at armes in England, and their majesties deputie of the realme of Irelond, and sir Henry Sidnie, knight, vicetresurer of Irelond, and John Plunket, esquier, two of their majesties previe counsell in Irelond, and eftsones humebly submitting themselves, acknowlegeing there offences, and demanding pardone therefore, referred themselves with all they had to the order of the sayd lord deputi.

Whereuppon the sayd Conell, and the rest of the Omores were appointed to repaire to the sayd lord deputy to Laughlen, the second of December next following, which they dyd, and then and there in opin presence, did swere uppon the holy evangelyst to be true for ever after to the king and quenes majesties and the crowne of Inglond, and to be obedient in all thinges to the lord deputy or governor of this relme for the time being; and that they sholde kepe secrete all suche counsell as for the better service of the queenes majesties the lord deputie or governor of this realme for the time being shold dysclose to them; and that theye shold not keep secrete but open to the deputy or governor of this realme all conspiraces against ther majesties, the good government of this realme, or the persone of the deputy for the time being.

fol. 31. And that they shold not mainteigne any rebell or outlaw but prosecute them to the uttermost of their powres, togethers with all suche of their owne nacions as shall start from any order taken with them by the sayd lorde deputy.

And, finally, openly confessing theire usurpacion of the countrie of Leax, and renounceing clerely all claimes they or any of them might make to any parte thereof, and to stand to any order the lorde deputy sholde take with them, they dyd receve of their majesties gyft, by thandes of the sayd lord deputy, suche porcions of the countrie of Leax as the sayd lord uppon their humeble submyssion, thought feete in their majesties names to geve unto them; they to pay therfore suche rent as by the sayd lorde deputie uppon a new survei shold be appointed, and to hold the same uppon such condicions as by the sayd lorde deputy shold be thought mete, and be expressed in a further state to be after made to them therin.

Untill which time the sayde lorde deputie dyd for their better assueraunce deliver to every of them a bill signyd with his hand, specifying the places appointed to them and comaunding all their majesties subjectes to suffer them to enjoy the sayd places in quiet; which they willingly recevid, and requieryd uppon their further service to be further consideryd.[1]

1556[-7]. [XXIX.]—At Dublyn, the xxix of January, anno 1556[-7]:

fol. 32. T. Fytswauters.—It ys ordered, agreid and concludid by the right honnorable the lorde Fitzwalter, one of the gentilmen of the kinges majesties prevy chamber, capitayne of all their majesties gentilmen pensioners and gentilmen at armes in Inglande, and lorde deputie of their majesties realme of Irelande, the nobilyte of this realme nowe assembled and the reste of their majesties counsell now preasente, that there shalbe commyssions sente fourthe for the taking up for their majesties of every ther majesties farmor of porte corne, the fifth pecke of all suche corne as

[1] Fol. 31b. is blank.

any of them doo farme of ther majesties. Their majesties to pay for every 1556[-7]. pecke the dooble pryce that every suche furste farmor payeth to ther majesties, and yf any such farmor have alyenatid his lease so as he onely receyve yerely proffyte thereby, and yf the second and thurde farmer receyve also gayne therby, then the burdeyne to be layed indyfferentely apon them all by the price that corne beareth in the nexte markett to the ferme where the corne ys demaundid, and the corne by them so provydid to be for ther majesties. Otherwyse, the farmor nowe holding the said lease to be answerable onely thereto.

And yf any suche farmor shall resiste any commyssioner for the gathering of the sayde corne, or the delyvery thereof at any place appoynted within ten myles of the place where the corne ys to be gathered, then commyssion to be sente to the shrieffe for assistence in he execucyon of the premysses, and the partie to be pounysshed for his contempte at the discreacion of the lorde deputie and counsell.

And yf yt happen the furste farmor to be deceasid and have fol. 32b. alienatid his lease for a yerely gayne, and the same gayn commeth now to any other person, then he that receyveth the gayne to aunswer the commyssion as aforesaide.

And yf yt happen ther majesties to alyenate any parcell wherunto any person ys farmor, as abovesaide, this order nevertheles to contynue during the terme of the lease, whosoever possesses the landes or the leases, for that som farmors paye their rente by a proporcyon ratid for every pecke or busshell, and som for every coople.

Our meanyng ys that where ther majesties receyve rente for the pecke this our order shulde be aunswerid by the fifth pecke; and wheare there ys receyvid for the coople, it should be aunswerid by the coople, rating two peckes for every coople.

H. Dublin, canc.—G. Armachanus.—Rolande off Cass[hell].—G. Kyldare.—Roland Baltynglas.—Willelmus Midensis.—S[ir] P[atrick] Barnewall, lord of T[rimleston].—Jenico, vic[ecomes] of G[ormanston].—Richard Delvin.—Thomas Louithe.—Thomas Leglinensis.—Chrystofor Donsany.—John Travers.—H. Sydney.—James Bathe, baron.—D. Hay.—John Plunket.

[XXX.]—Ordres taken at Dublyn, the 30th of January, anno 1556[-7]: fol. 33.

T. Fytswauters.—[1.] Furste, for the better avoyding of stollen goodes:

It ys orderyd, agreid and concludid by the right honnorable the lorde Fitzwalter, one of the gentilmen of the kinges majesties prevy chamber, capteyne of all their majesties gentilmen pensyoners and gentilmen at armes in Inglande, and lorde deputie of their majesties realme of Irelande, the nobylite of this realme nowe assemblid and the reste of ther majesties counsell nowe preasente, that no man from hensforthe shall bye in any markett towne eny horse, cowe, garran or other beste, but apon the markett daye betwene nine of the clocke in the mornyng and thre of the clocke at afternoone, and in the market place, and that every byer shall see at his perill that he know the seller to be a suffyciente warrante for the sale of the goodes.

And yf eny man bye any of the foresaide goodes otherwise then ys above written, and the same goodes be after chalenged and provyd to be another mannes, the byer not onely to be aunswerable for the goodes so bought, but also yf the same goodes were stollen to suffer twenty dayes ymprysonmente for his contempte.

1556[-7]. And yf any man have any stolne goodes, not byeing them as aforesayde, and can not declare he had them of a suffyciente warrante, then he not onely to aunswer the same goodes but also the other goodes provid to be stollen with them; and so from one to another for the better advoyding of the cooloryng of stollen goodes, tyll the same be tryed oute.

[2.] Item[2]: Yt ys by the consente aforesaide orderid, agreid and concludid that yf eny horse, cowe or other cattayll be stollen and the
fol. 33b. tracte followydd to a certeyn place and the owner or owners inhabitor or inhabitors thereof be before recorde requyred to putt the tracte oute of the grounde to them belonging and they shall refuse so to doo, they to aunswer the goodes. And yf huyte and crye be made and the inhabitors theraboutes doo not aunswer the same, and that yt be provid that the parties that followe the goodes susteyne losse therby, then they that did not aunswer the crye to satysfie the partye or partyes for his or ther losses so sustayned.

[3.] Item: For the more spedy execucyon of justice yt ys ordered, agreid and concludid by assente aforesayde that when the lorde deputie or counsaill in his absence shall remytt any mattier in controversye betwene partye and partye to the hearing and determynyng of suche as to hym or them shalbe thought good to graunte a commyssion therfore, and that the sayde commyssioners shall have h[e]arde and determyned the sayde mattier or mattiers, the saide comyssioners shall dyrecte commaundementes to the shrieffe of the countye to see execution done according to their order; and there shalbe generall commyssiones sente fourthe to all shrieves to give them auctorite for the doing of the premysses, and to retorne every six wekes his dooinges therin to the lorde deputie and in his absence to the lorde chauncelor.

[4.] For thadvoyding of contentyons that dayly doo aryse, it is furder orderid, agreid and concludid that no man shall in his owne cawse from hensforth take any stresse of his owne auctorytie any man aunswerable to the lawes for any mattier that he shall not by the lawe be admytted
fol. 34. to strayne in. And yf any man doo contrary to this order, he to suffer ymprysonmente for twenty dayes, and make fyne to ther majesties as to the lorde deputie and counsell shalbe thought mete.

[5.] Item: For thadvoyding of the greate maynteynyng of malefactors, yt ys by assente aforesaid orderid and concludid that yf any man appoynted by commyssion from the lorde deputie, or in his absence from the lorde chancelor, for thapprehending of any malefactor or malefactors, and that in the seking or pursuyng of suche malefactor or malefactors, he whiche hathe the commyssion and auctorytie shalbe by any man resisted, or that eny man shall refuse to ayde every suche commyssioner in thapprehending of every such malefactour, wherby it shalbe provid there hathe ensuyd any hinderance to the taking of suche malefactor or malefactors, that then the partie so resisting or refusing shall suffer ymprysonmente for one monneth and fyne to ther majesties at the will of the lorde deputie and counsell.

[6.] Item: For the better execution of all orders taken, yt ys likewyse orderid and concludid by assente aforesaide that every shrieffe, bayly, constable or eny other offycer or offycers who shalbe appointed to see any order putt in execution, shall every six wekes presente to the lorde deputie, or in his absence to the lorde chauncelour, all breaches of ordres
fol. 34b. that hathe byn done within their rule during the same six wekes and

[2] In margin: "For tractinges of stolne goodes."

that they shall, before the twentieth daye of next monneth, presente in sorte before appoyntid all such breaches of ordres as hathe byn made within their rules syns the sending fourthe of the saide ordres; after whiche presentemente they to followe the order above wrytten every six wekes. 1556[-7].

[7.] Item: For that ther ensuyth moche inconvenyence by the disorder of ydle people, yt is furder orderid by assente aforesaide that every man dwelling within the counties of Dublin, Methe, Westmethe, Uriell, Kildare, Caterlaghe, Kylkenny, Wexforde and Waterforde shall putt in writing the names of suche ydle men as they kepe and will annswer for the dooinges and delyver the same to such commyssioner as shalbe appointid for the recepte thereof, who shall delyver the same to the lorde deputie. And yf any man doo contrary to this order, he to be ponnysshed by ymprysonmente and paye fyne at the lorde deputie[s] and counsailles pleasure.

H. Dublin, canc.—G. Armachanus.—Roland off Casshel.—G. Kyldare.—Roland Baltynglas.—Willelmus Midensis.—Janico, vic. of G[ormanston].—D. Hay.—Richard Delvin.—Christofor Donsany.—P. Barnewall, lord of T[rimletiston].—Thomas Leglinensis.—Thomas Louithe.—H. Sydney.—John Travers.—James Bathe, baron.—John Plunket.

[XXXI.]—At Kyllmaynam, the xivth of February, 1556 [-7]: fol. 35.

Whereare Wylliam Saunders, of Learpoole[1], maryner, and one Wylliam Raubynson weere apprehended of late uppon suspicion to have brought into this realme thre shillinges of counterfete monny, and theruppon being commytted to the castell of Dublyn to ward, have remeyned there certayne dayes, for so moche as, upon examynacion of the matter, there apperythe no sufficient cause why the sayd Saunders and Raubynson shold longer be deteigned, it is condescended and agreed by us, the lorde deputy and counsell, that they shall furthewith be enlerged and set at liberti, and no further trobled for the same matter.

[XXXII.]—At Dublyn, the xxvth of February 1556[-7]: fol. 35b.

T. Fytswauters.—Wheare Rowry and Donough Oconner, with the rest of the gentlemen and usurpid inhabitantes of Offaly, apperyed at the Dinghan, the fourth of October last past before us, the lorde Fitzwaters, one of the gentlemen of the kinges majesties privy chamber, captaine of all their majesties gentlemen pencioners and men at armes in Ingland, and lorde deputie of ther majesties realme of Ireland, and there, in presence of the erle of Kylldare and others of the counsell, humebly submytting themselves, desieryed that they might be recevyed to their majesties mersy, and that being taken as true subjectes from thenceforthe they wold clerely deliver the country of Offallye which they wrongfully kept, and receve at their majesties hands suche porcions of the sayd country and uppon suche sort and condicion as we, the lorde deputye, shold in their majesties names appoint, with offer to stand to all other orders that by us, the lorde deputy, shold be taken. For performaunce whereof the sayd Donoughe willingly yelded himself to remeyne in hand with us, the lorde deputy, tyll suche time as all orders shold be by us in the premyses fully taken; and so continued untill the xvth of December after.

[1] Liverpool.

1556[-7]. On which day at the sayd fort the sayd Rowry, with the rest of the gentlemen and usurpid inhabytantes, eftsones apperyed before us and divers of the counsell, and together with the said Donough, being there with us in band, cravid eftsones at her majesties handes mercy with some
fol. 36. porcion of the country in sort above writon.

At which time, uppon their humeblenes and othe made uppon the holly evangelest to be true to their majesties and to the crowne of Ingland for ever, and to be obedient to the deputy for the time being in all thinges, to maintaine no rebell or outlaw, but to prosecute them to the uttermost within their rule, to put away all strangers from them, and to prosecute all suche to the country as shold refuse to stand to any order taken by the lorde deputy, we toke order that the sayd Donough shold, delivering sufficient pledges for himself and the rest, be inlarged, and that the sayd Rowry and Donough with the rest shold remeyne in the parties of Dowgesshell tyll every of them shold have their porcions severally appointed.

For the better dyspatch whereof the sayd Rowry and Donough, authoryssyed for the rest, weare appointed to repayer to us, the lorde deputy, to Laughlen on the Thursday in Crystmas next after, there to receve for them and the rest whose names they shold bring with them writen in a bill suche porcions of the sayd country as for every of them shold by us the lorde deputie in their majesties names be appointed.

At which day the sayd Donough appeeryd not, and for the better assueraunce on the parties of the sayd Rowry and Donough and the rest above writen to performe the orders that shold be taken by us, the lorde deputy, in their majesties behalves, and to do their dueties of allegeaunce and obedience as good subjectes, we not onely the sayd xvth day recevid theire pledges, videlicet, Rosse Mc Morghe for Donough
fol. 36b. Oconner, Bryan McPhelem for Rowry Oconner, and Murghe Oge for the rest of the country, uppon condicion that Rosse Mc Owyn shold come pledge in the place of Rosse Mc Murgh for Donough, Lenoghe Boy in the place of Bryan Mc Pheleme for Rowry, and in the place of Murgh Oge for the country, the severall pledges and suche as we shold appoint of every man of the country that shold receve of their majesties anny parte thereof.

Which done, the sayd Rosse Mc Murgh, Bryan Mc Phelime and Murgh Oge with all other pledges that remeined in the castell of Dublyn before our furst entering into Offally shold not only be deliveryd, but allso by consent of bothe sydes appointed therle of Kildare, then absent with the barron of Delvin, Omolloy and Magoghhagan, then present, to be slanties[1] uppon them to follow them to the uttermost uppon breche of any the premysses, which slanty the sayde erle being absent dyd after by his letters to us take uppon him, and the sayd barron, Omolloy and Magoghhagan, being present, dyd then and there take uppon them.

Syns which time the sayd Donogh and others have not onely broken divers dayes of theire apparaunce before us but also have most falsely and traytorusly conspieryed with divers other rebelles and traitoures and uppon somons resolvid not to come unto us, the lorde Deputy and counsell, then being in the sayd country of Offally, but combyned themselves togethers to kepe out and make warr against
fol. 37. their majesties and ther good subjectes have utterly refused to come in to us, wheareby it apperythe they dyd and do meane but to delay the tyme to utter the better their traytorus intent:

---

[1] Sureties.

It is therefore, in respect of the premysses and other speciall causses to us the lorde deputy and counsell knowen, thought good that there shold be with all spede posseble sharp warre made uppon the sayd Donogh with all others that take his part, and that the sayd Donogh and all that take his part shold be proclemyd traytoures thorowout their majesties realme of Irelond, and the erle of Kylldare, the barron of Delvin, Omolloy and Magoghhagan shall follow the slanty to the uttermost. The premysses to be put in execution with all spede. 1556[-7].

H. Dublin, canc.—G. Kyldare.—Willelmus Midensis.—J. of Slane.—P. of Trymbeleston.—H. Sydney.—Henry Radeclyff.—James Bathe.—John Travers.—John Plunket.[1]

[XXXIII.]—At Dublin, the xxvth of February, 1556[-7]: fol. 38.

Whereas the Oconors, with other their complices and folowers in Offally, acknowleaging of late before the lorde deputie and summe other of the counsaill their disloyall bihaviour and disobedience to the king and quenes majesties, made their humble submyssion theryn and, for declaracion of their goode conformitie, not only toke a corporall othe upon the holy evangelistes to be from thensfurthe trewe, faithfull and obedient subjectes, but also for the better performance therof did put yn such pledges as by the saide lorde deputie and counsaill were then required. Syns whiche tyme at the saide lorde deputies and dyverse of the counsaills late being in Offally, Donoghe Oconor, with certain other of the Oconnors and men of Offally, nothing regarding their duties, nether their submyssion, othe and putting yn of pledges aforesaide, traiterously combyneng themselfes with other rebelles and malefactors to kepe owte and make warre upon their majesties and their goode subjectes, have refused to cume yn to the saide lorde deputie and counsaill, and do provyde to prosecute their myschevous attempte to their uttermost power, shewyng theymselfes manyfestly to be traitours and rebelles against their majesties:

It is therefore thought goode to the saide lorde deputie, the nobles of this realme and the rest of the counsaill nowe assembled together, as well by this present proclamation to signifie the premysses to all their majesties loving subjectes, to thende they shulde advoyde suche daunger as therof might ensue, as also to denounce and publishe the saide Donnoghe Oconnor and his complices, with all his folowers, ayders and maynteyners, open traitours and rebelles against our soveraigne lorde and lady the king and quenes majesties, straitly fol. 38b. charging and commaunding that noo person, of what degree or condicion soever he or they be, shall in any wise ayde, maynteyne or succour the saide Donnoghe or any of his adherentes or folowers aforesaide with meate, drinke, or other relief upon payne to incurre the pennaltie that by the lawes of this realme is ordered for the punnyshement of suche as shall maynteyne traitours.

And it is further condescended and agreed by the saide lorde deputie, the nobles and counsaill aforesaide, that whosoever shall bring yn the saide Donoghe or his heade to the lord deputie shall have by way of rewarde oon hundred poundes, sterling; and, if he be an offendor himself he shall have a pardon for his offences past.

Memorandum: That we, tharchebusshop of Dublin, lord chauncelor, and the busshop of Methe, do consent to all thinges above writtin,

[1] Fol. 37b. is blank.

1556[-7]. saving what touchith the lief of man, whiche we forbeare to do lest we shulde incurre the daunger of irregularitie.

H. Dublin, canc.—G. Kyldare.—Willelmus Midensis.—J. of Slane.—P. of Trimletoston.—Henry Radeclyff.—H. Sydney.—John Travers.—James Bathe.—John Plunket.

fol. 39 [XXXIV.]—At Dublyn, the xxvth of February, 1556[-7]:

T. Fytswauters.—Where Donnoghe Oconor and diverse other of the Oconors and men of Offally, after they had submytted theymselves to the lorde deputie and counsell, sworne their obedience to the kinge and quenes majesties, and put in pledges for performaunce of the same, traiterously combyneing theymselves with other rebelles and malefactors conspired to make warre agaynst their majesties and their good subjectes, and refused at the said lorde deputies late being yn Offally to comme yn, and shewe their due obedience to their majesties, and then did and do provide to prosecute their traiterous intent, contrary to their duties of obedience; for whiche theire great disobedience contempt and treasons the said Donnoghe and his complices, their aiders and mayntayners, are denounced and proclaymed as open traitors agaynst our soveraigne lorde and lady the kinge and quenes majesties: it is thought good to the lorde deputie, the nobles of the realme, and the reste of the counsell nowe assembled, for avoideng of inconveniences that might ensue, and the better folowing of the said traitors, to geve warning to all their majesties loving subjectes by this present proclamacion that whosoever hathe any goodes or catailes of any person dwelling in Offally commytted to his or their custody ether upon cummericke[1] or otherwise, shall ether furthwith bringe in the same goodes and catailes to
fol. 39b. the lorde deputie, or elles deliver unto him a bille declaring the certayntie therof and undertake to answere it when it shall be called for; and whosoever shall doo the same justly, without frawde or covyne, shall receive by way of rewarde the thirde parte of the saide goodes and catailes so committed to his or their custodies and declared to the lorde deputie, onles the whole be restored agayne to the owner by the said lorde deputies order.

And whosoever shall concele any parte of suche goodes or catailes so committed to keping as is aforesaid, and not deliver the same to the lorde deputie, or elles a bille thereof as is above mencioned, (the same being duly proved against him) shall not only be reputed and taken as mayntaynor and aider of traitors, but also shall incurre daunger of all penalties and other forfaites that by the lawes of this realme is provided against the maynteynors of rebelles and traitors.

H. Dublin, canc.—G. Kyldare.—Willelmus Midensis.—J. of Slane.—P. of Trymletestou.—Heury Radeclyff.—H. Sydney.

fol. 40. [XXXV.]—At Dublyn the xxvth of February, 1556[-7]:

T. Fytswauters.—Forasmuche as Donoghe Oconor and other his complices and adherentes have of late, contrary to their othe and faithfull promise, shewed theymselves disloiall subjectes, and traiterously combyned with rebelles and malefactors to make warre against the kinge and quenes majesties and their good and quiet subjectes:

[1] Surety.

It is therfore thought expedient to us, the lorde deputie, the nobles of this realme and the reste of the counsell nowe assembled, that generall musters be made with all expedicion for levieng of labourers to be sent into Offally and the confynes therof for cutting of paces[1] and mending of towghors,[2] wherby their majesties army may the better passe, and the traitors more easily be pursued. The said labourers to mete at suche day and place as the lorde deputie shall appoynte, furnished with billes, axes, spades, mattockes, or other tooles mete for the purposes aforesaid, and to be emploid where his lordship shall appoynt, by the space of eight daies together, vitailed and provided in all pointes at the charges of the countrey whens they rise, as heretofore in like cases hathe been accustomed. And that letters furthwith shalbe sent into severall counties for the spedy doing of the premisses with all good endevor and diligence. 1556[-7].

H. Dublin, canc.—G. Kyldare.—Willelmus Midensis.—J. of Slane.—P. of Trymleteston.—H. Sydney.—Henry Radeclyff.[3]

[XXXVI.]—At Dublyn, the xxvth of February, 1556[-7]: fol. 41.

T. Fytswauters.—Upon consideracion of the controversies that of late have been moved, and are yet depending, betwene the baron of Dungannon and Shane Onele, related presently unto us, the lorde deputie, by the credible letters of the right reverende father in God, the lorde primate: it is ordered, condescended and agreed by us, the lorde deputie and counsell, for thappeasing of the said variaunces and for a good quietnes to be had betwixt theym, that as well the said baron as the said Shane, shall have, possesse and enjoy all suche landes, goodes, catelles, and folowers as ether of theym had and enjoyed before the tyme of Shanes late siknes; and that eche of theym shall furthwith redeliver to the other as well all suche landes or cuntreys as any of theym hathe taken from the other syns Shanes late siknes aforesaid, as also make restitucion on bothe sides of all suche goodes, catailes and folowers as any of theym hathe taken from the other within that time. The same to be doon indifferently by the oversight of the said lorde primate and the lorde of Lowthe, who shall by their discrecions appoynt the said baron and Shane to cume before theym at Dundalke at a day convenient, and there declare to theym this our order and see it put in execucion accordingly; doing theym bothe to understande that whosoever shall refuse to conforme himself to this our order (as we thinke they will not) the same thereby shall geve us cause to aide the other against him that so maketh default.

The like whereof we will doo against him that shall for his own mayntenance intertaigne any Scotto borne out of this realme to annoy the adverse parte.

This order to endure during the lorde deputie[s] and counsels pleasures.

H. Dublin, canc.—G. Kyldare.—Willelmus Midensis.—J. of Slane.—P. of Trymleteston.—Henry Radeclyff.—H. Sydney.—John Travers.—D. Hay.

---

[1] Passes.
[2] Causeways.
[3] Fol. 40*b*. is blank.

1557.
fol. 42.

[XXXVII.]—At Dublyn, the xxvii of Marche, 1557:

T. Fytswauters.—For the better defence of thinhabitantes of Leys,[1] Offally,[2] Irry,[3] Glanmeliry[4], and Slemarge,[5] and for the spedier repressing of suche as in those quarters might hereafter rebell, it is ordered, agreed and concluded by us, the lorde deputie and counsell, that there shalbe generall musters of labourers taken for the fortifieng of certayne places, cutting of certayn paces and mending of sundry towghors, within the said cuntreys, and that there shalbe cessed in the countie of Kildare, 400 labourers, in the countie of Kilkenny 400 labourers, in the countie of Dublyn 200 labourers, in the countie of Methe 500 labourers, and in the countie of Westmethe 400 labourers, for the doing of the premisses.

The said labourers to be furnished withe vitailes and toles at the charges of the cuntrey for eight daies and to repaire to suche places as by the lorde deputie shalbe appoynted at suche tyme as by his letters he shall signifie to the shiref of every countie his pleasure in that behalf.

H. Dubliu, canc.—H. Sydney.—Henry Radeclyff.—George Stanley.

fol. 42*b*.

[XXXVIII.]—The copie of the letteres [to sheriffs], sent furthe upon thordre afore writtin, for mustring of labourers:

We grete you hartely well: And wheras upon consultacion had of late for the better defence of the cuntreys of Leys, Offally, and others therunto adjoyneng, and to abate the courage of suche rebelles and malefactours as happily hereafter might seke to bring the same into disordre, it was thought expedient, concluded and agreid by us, the lorde deputie and counsaill then assembled, as well that certain fortificacions shoulde be made bothe alongest the borders and within the saide cuntreys, as also that paces shulde be cutte and toughers mended for the more easy passage of tharmy, and saulftie of the people travailing to and fro, and for that purpose that generall musters shulde be made of all the husbandmen and labourers within the counties adjoynante wherby a sufficient numbre of strange and hable workemen may be appointed to assemble together at tyme and place certain, furnyshed of vitailes and tooles necessary, and be employed in labor as we, the lorde deputie, shall take ordre:

These be therfor to will and requyre and nevertheles to charge and commaunde you in their majesties names to cause suche generall musters of labourers as is aforesaide to be made within that the countie of ——[6] with all expedicion, and chosing ——[7] of the best and moost hable men oute of the whole numbre, to appointe them to be in perfite redynes to assemble and mete all together the morowe after Lowe Sunday[8] next, in the mornyng, at suche place as by our the lorde

fol. 43.

deputies letters shalbe to the sherif of the saide countie signified, with sufficient furniture of tooles and vitailes for eight dayes.

At whiche tyme they shalbe further directed by us, the lorde deputie, for employment of their travaill aboute the purposes afore mencioned as best shall appertayne. We require also and straitly charge you, the sherif and sergeant of the saide countie, upon ordre herein taken, to

---

[1], [2], [3], [4], [5] Leix, Offally, Irry, Glanmeliry, and Slemarge were, by act of parliament at Dublin in 1556–7, constituted shires under the names of the King's County and the Queen's County.

[6], [7] Blanks in MS.

[8] The first Sunday after Easter-day, 18 April, 1557.

see the premyses put in due execucion without delay, as ye, and either of you, will answere for the contrary doing at your extreme perilles. 1557.

[XXXIX.]—Letters for generall musters of men of warre : fol. 43b.

We grete you hartely well. And where it is upon consultacion thought goode to us that there shulde be for dyverse respectes generall musters taken thoroughe oute their majesties realme in suche sorte as heretofore hath been accustomed, and by thordre of their majesties lawes in suche caces is appointed, and the same so taken to be to us with spede retourned, we shall therfor requyre you that dividing yourselfs into circuites ye do aswell take musters with all expedicion of all their majesties subjectes of thage betwene 16 and 60 within their majesties Countie of ——[1] and to geve warnyng to every man to be furnished with weapon and armoure according to the tenure of the statutes therein provided, and also to make a perfite booke of your doinges therin, and of every mannes name and furniture in every towne within the said countie, and to advertyse the same in due ordre to us before the last of Aprill next cumyng, and not to faile of any parte hereof as ye tendre your duties to their majesties.

Yeven at Kilmaynan, the xxviith of Marche, 1557.

[XL.]—A proclamacion for goode ordre betwene the souldiours and the countrey, xxvii° die Marcii, 1557 : fol. 44.

Where, by reason of the warres at this present in Offally for the chastiseng of the rebellis there, the souldiours as well horsemen as fotemen have occasion to passe and repasse daily throughe the borders and other places of thenglishe pale, and that we be enformed by the souldiours that they can not have meate and drinke for their money as they were wonte to have, but that the people in many places rather flee the townes when they see them cumyng, and raise the crye then mynister any reasonable ayde to them for their money, and on the other parte oftentymes complaynt is made to us that the souldiours passing in sorte above saide take meate and drinke and pay nothing therfore.

To the intente that the souldiours shulde be releved with vitailes for their money, as reason is they shulde, and that the people according to right shulde receyve money for the same, it is therefore ordered by us, the lorde deputie and counsaill, that whensoever any souldiour or souldiours shall passe throughe the countrey in any place within the Englishe Pale, and demaunde meate and drinke or horsmete, he or they who so demaunde shall call for the sergeant, constable, or other officer yf there be any, or otherwyse for two of the best men in the towne, and shall require them to see them for their money provided of that they require within the saide towne, and the saide sergeaunt, constable, other officer, or the two best of the towne thereupon shall see them furnished of all thinges fitte for them and to receyve money therefore and see the people paied.

And if ether the souldiour shall take any thinge otherwise then by this proclamacion is appointed, exceipte demaunding it as is above written, it shalbe denyed to him, or that any suche sergeaunt, constable, other officer or two of the best of the towne shall deny to see the souldiours so demaunding to be furnished of their demaundes and to receyive money therfor for the people, the souldiour so offending or the sergeant, constable, officer or two of the best of the towne so denyeng to see the fol. 44b.

[1] Blank in MS.

1557. souldiours sufficiently furnished for their money of suche thinges as shalbe within the saide towne, and every man advoiding the towne or raising the crye when the souldiours shall cumme, to be punished by imprisonmente and fyne at the lorde deputie and counsailles pleassur. And, therefore, for the better execution thereof, and to advoide the disordre that hereby daily doth arise, we will you, the lordes and gentilmen of the cuntrey, to take suche ordre with your tennauntes, in every of your townes, as by your goode diligence this our proclamacion may for the benefite of the cuntrey and the well ordering of the souldiours the soner take good effecte.

fol. 45. [XLI.]—Hec indentura, facta secundo die Aprilis, anno Domini millesimo quingentesimo quinquagesimo septimo [1557], inter honorabilem ac illustrem principem, dominum Thomam Radeclif, militem, Sussexie comitem, vice-comitem Fitzwauters, dominum de Egremounde et Burnell, unum generosorum private camere invictissimi domini regis, necnon omnium generosorum serenissime domine regine pencionariorum et generosorum ad arma in regno suo Anglie capitaneum, ac regni Hibernie predictis domino regi et regine deputatum, ceterosque de consilio regali in eodem regno, quorum nomina hic inferius scribuntur, ex una parte, et Gulielmum Ower Okarwell, de principali Okarwellorum familia in patria de Ely Ocarwell oriundum, parte ex altera, testatur quod predictus Gulielmus concessit, promisit et per presentes se obligavit tenere et firmiter perimplere dictis dominis regi et regine, heredibus et successoribus prefate regine, Anglie regibus, tenorem et formam articulorum sequentium :

[1.] In primis: Quod non solum Catholicam fidem et religionem, quantum in se est, promovebit et defendet, sed omnes etiam contradicentes aut renitentes pro suo posse corrigi in judicium vocari et debito modo per omnia puniri faciet.

[2.] Item : Acceptabit et recognoscet predictos dominum regem et reginam legitimos esse sibi principes, illisque heredibus et successoribus predicte domine regine adherebit contra omnes homines sicut fidelis subditus, et sicut ceteri ligei predicti regni Hibernie serviunt et obediunt servire et obedire debent.

[3.] Item : Predictus Gulielmus non adherebit nec confederabit cum inimicis aut rebellibus dictorum regis et regine aut successorum suorum sed illos pro viribus suis de tempore in tempus castigabit et prosequetur.

[4.] Item : Ulterius, dictus Gulielmus per presentes obligatur quod
fol. 45b regia majestas habebit omnes terras et possessiones suas proprias ac cetera omnia et singula debita ad suam celsitudinem spectantia tam ea que modo jacent et existunt sub tutela et gubernacione predicti Gulielmi quam que quovismodo posthac crescere et legitime provenire poterint ad illorum majestatum usus infra limites et jurisdictionem patrie de Ely predicte.

[5.] Item : Similiter prefatus Gulielmus promptus et paratus erit in propria persona sua ad serviendum dominis regi et regine heredibus et successoribus dicte domine regine ad mandatum domini deputati pro tempore existentis, cum duodecim equestribus et viginti quatuor turbariis bene armatis in omni suo magno progressu bellico vulgariter nuncupato hostinges[1], cum victualibus pro se et suis ad expensas patrie sue quandocunque et quociescunque hujusmodi domino deputato placebit

[1] In margin : "Note : rent : servyce of horsemen, kearne, and galloglas."

ad hoc assignare et demandare. Et in quolibet alio viagio et progressu subito contingenti serviet cum toto numero et potestate sua cum victualibus similter pro duobus vel tribus diebus. Et pro quolibet equestre faciente defectum (ut predicitur) forisfaciet et solvet pro quolibet die tres solidos et octo denarios et pro quolibet turbario pro simili defectu denarios vigihti. 1557.

[6.] Item: Predictus Gulielmus concessit et promisit pro recognicione obediencie sue et quia tenet dictam patriam de domino rege et domina Regina reddere et solvere singulis annis dictis dominis regi et regine, heredibus et successoribus prefate regine, duodecim libras legalis monete Hibernice, solvendas et tradendas officiariis suis annuatim in hoc regno ad festum Sancti Michaelis tantum.

[7.] Item: Prefatus Gulielmus ulterius concessit et promisit daturum se quolibet anno bonagium octoginta Scoticis, vulgariter nuncupatis galloglasses, pro uno quarterio anni. Et quod indilate dabit et solvet fol. 46. prefato domino deputato aut ejus assignatis centum viginti martos pingues (ut moris est) pro nominacione et admissione sua ad locum capitanei sue nacionis et patrie de Ely predicte.

[8.] Item: Prefatus Gulielmus non solum juramentum corporale prestitit super sacrosancta Dei evangelia pro bono complemento premissorum, sed finaliter concessit etiam et promisit, pro majori securitate fidelitatis sue erga regis et regine majestates, ponere obsides suos penes prefatum dominum deputatum vel alibi prout melius eidem domino deputato videbitur.

In cujus rei et omnium premissorum fidem et testimonium, tam predictus dominus deputatus et consilium quam prefatus Gulielmus hiis scriptis manus suas alternatim apposuerunt.

Data die et mense supradictis, annis regnorum Philippi et Marie, Dei gratia Anglie, Francie, Hispaniarum, utriuusque Sicilie, Neapolis, Hierusalem et Hibernie regis et regine, fidei defensorum, archiducum Austrie, ducum Mediolani, Burgundie et Brabancie, comitum Haspurgie, Flandrie et Tirollis tertio et quarto [1557].

[XLII.]—At Dublyn, the ixth of June, 1557: fol. 46b.

T. Sussex.—Where variaunce is depending betwene Brian Offerrall and Fiaugheney Mc Tege concerning the captainship of the cuntrey of Offerrall Bane, and betwene the bretherne and sonnes of Donell Bane and Fiaughe Mc Tege aswell for the deathe of the said Donell, lately slaine by Fiaughe, as also for the breache of the slanty taken by the lorde deputie and therle of Kildare upon the said Donell and Fiaughe for the keping of their majesties peas:

It is ordered, concluded and agreed by us, the lorde deputie and counsell, with the consent of the said parties, that they shall stande to performe and abide in the premisses all suche orders and determynacion for all the said matters as we, the lorde deputie and counsell, shall hereafter take therin:

And, for the better performaunce thereof and the surer keping of their majesties peas, that every of theym shall put their severall pledges into the handes of the lord deputie and counsell.

Videlicet, the said Brian, for him and his septe, Tirlaughe m^c Brian; the bretherne and sonnes of Donell Bane, for theym and their septe, Brian mac Moroughe; and Fiaughney m^c Tege, for him and his septe, Donell mac Fiaughney, Brian mac Fiaughney and Dermot m^c Huberte.

1557. fol. 47. And, further, whosoever brekithe this order to be chastised by the lorde deputie and counsell as to their discrecions shalbe thought good.

H. Dublin, canc.—James Desmond.—G. Armachanus.—G. Kyldare.—Cristopherus Tuamensis.—Jenico, Vicecomes of G[ormanston].—Thomas Darensis.—J. of Slane.—P. of Trymleteston.—Henry Radeclyff.—D. Hay.

fol. 47b. [XLIII.]—Apud Dublinam, tercio Julii annis regnorum regis et regine Philippi et Marie tercio et quarto:

T. Sussex.—It ys concludid by us, the lorde deputie, the lordes spirituall and temporall of the realme, and the reste of their majesties counsaill of the same whose names be hereunto subscribed, that, for sondry consyderacyons towching as well the repressing of rebelles as also the resysting of foreyne invasion, ther shalbe a generall hosting for fourty dayes to be proclamed, after the olde custome by wrytt at the rate of thre plowe lande to a carte, to sett fourthe the seconde daye of Auguste nexte, and to mete at suche place as upon the nexte consultacion had by us in the meane shall by proclamacyon be sett fourthe.

H. Dublin, canc.—G. Armachanus.—G. Kyldare.—Jenico, vicecomes of G[ormanston].—W. Midensis.—Roland Baltynglas.—P. of Trymleteston.—Christofer Donsany.—Thomas Louithe.—Allexsandyr[1] off Fernys.—Christoffor of Kyllen.—Thomas Darensis.—D. Hay.—Henry Radeclyff.—George Stanley.—Gerald Aylmer, justice.—Robert Dyllon.—James Bathe.—John Plunket.—Francis Agarde.

fol. 48. [XLIV.]—At Dublyn, the xxiith of July, 1557:

Memorandum: That where upon the consultacion and agreement of this last generall hosting next before written aswell as at the other the laste yere, the cuntreys of the Englishe Pale alledge that they have of their owne benevolence been further charged then they heretofore have been accustomed to be.

It is therfore condescended and agreed by us the lorde deputie and counsell that this increase of charge growen and growing at these two laste hostinges and afore mencioned, shalbe no president to burden the cuntreys hereafter with the like, but that the same shall stande chargeable from hensforthe with as muche as of auncient custome they have been wonte to beare and no further.

fol. 48b. [XLV.]—This indenture, made at Dublin, the xxiiiith day of July, anno 1557, betwixte the right honorable the lorde deputie and counsaill of the one partie and John Bremengham and his son Waltier Bremengham of the other partie, witnesseth:

That wheras question was moved betwene the saide parties towching the castell of Kannafad the saide lorde deputie and counsaill alledging the same to pertayne to the quenes majestie by reason that a certayne somme of money was defrayed for the buylding therof out of the kinges Majesties treasure and a comon cesse was levied of the countrey by ordre directed from the lorde deputie and counsaill then being for the same, whiche was doon for the speciall service that the same castell may doo, it lyeng on the frontier betwixte the Englishe Pale and Offallyly upon thentringe of the long foorde called Aghefadda.

[1] Alexander Devereux, bishop of Ferns.

And the saide John and Waltier alledging that the saide castell appertaynethe to them selfes, for, as they sayed, it is buylded upon their propre enheritaunce and that they have employed, as they alledged, more chardges upon the buylding therof then the saide lorde deputie and counsaill have doon either in money or cesse, of whiche allegacions controversie is like to rise towching the right of the saide castell: 1557.

Notwithstandinge for that the same coulde not presently be herde and determyned for lacke of the proufes and that there is present nede of service to be doon by the castell, it is thought goode that the saide John and Waltier shude dimise and to ferme lett, like as by these presentes they do demise and to farme lett to the saide lorde deputie and counsaill their whole interest in the saide castell and the bawne annexed to the fol. 49. same for terme of thre yeres nexte ensuynge the date hereof, yelding and payeng for the same castell and bawne onely to the saide John or Waltier their heyres or assigne the somme of six shillinges and eight pence sterling yerely at the feaste of Sainct James thappostell.

Provided that the premises shall in no wise be impediment or hinderaunce to the right or title that the quenes majestie pretendethe to the saide castell, and also the saide John and Waltier have convenannted and agreid that in case it shall seme requisit to the lorde deputie and counsaill for service to be doon at thende of the saide terme to take the saide castell and bawne for more yeres that they shalbe contented to lett the same after the foresaide rate.

In witnes wherof the saide lorde deputie and counsaill and the saide John and Waltier have unto the partis of this indenture interchangeably subscribed their handes, the day and yere above specified.

[XLVI.]—Hec indentura, facta xxiii° die Julii, anno Domini millesimo quingentesimo quinquagesimo septimo [1557], inter honorabilem et prepotentem dominum, Thomam Radclif, prenobilis ordinis garterii militem, Sussexie comitem, vicecomitem Fitzwauteres, dominum de Egremounde et Burnell, unum generosorum private camere invictissimi domini regis, necnon omnium generosorum serenissime domine regine pencionariorum et generosorum ad arma in regno suo Anglie capitaneum, ac regni Hibernie predicte domino regi et regie deputatum, ceterosque de consilio regali in eodem regno quorum nomina hic inferius scribuntur ex una parte, et Bernardum, filium Mauri Offarrall,[1] in patria de Offarrall Bane, percella de Annaly,[2] parte ex altera, testatur quod predictus Bernardus concessit, promisit et per presentes se obligavit tenere et firmiter perimplere dictis dominis regi et regine heredibus et successoribus prefate regine, Anglie regibus, tenorem et formam articulorum sequentium: fol. 49b.

[1.] In primis: Quod non solum Catholicam fidem et religionem, quantum in se est, promovebit et defendet, sed omnes etiam contradicentes aut renitentes pro suo posse corrigi in judicium vocari et debito modo per omnia puniri faciet.

[2.] Item: Acceptabit et recognoscet predictos dominos regem et reginam legitimos esse sibi principes, illisque heredibus et successoribus predicte domine regine adherebit contra omnes homines sicut fidelis subditus et sicut ceteri ligei predicti regni Hibernie serviunt et obediunt aut servire et obedire debent.

---

[1] In margin: "Note: Rent of beves of alle hers sarvyce of horsmen and kearne."
[2] Now part of county of Longford.

1557. fol. 50. [3.] Item: Predictus Bernardus non adherebit nec confederabit cum inimicis aut rebellibus dictorum regis et regine aut successorum suorum sed illos pro viribus suis de tempore in tempus castigabit et prosequetur.

[4.] Item: Ulterius, dictus Bernardus per presentes obligatur quod regia majestas habebit omnes terras et possessiones suas proprias ac cetera omnia et singula debita ad suam celsitudinem spectantia, tam ea que modo jacent et existunt sub tutela et gubernatione predicti Bernardi quam que quovismodo posthac crescere et legittime provenire poterint ad illorum majestatum usus infra limites et jurisdictionem patrie de Offarrall Bane predicto.

[5.] Item: Similiter prefatus Bernardus promptus et paratus erit in propria persona sua ad serviendum dominis regi et regine, heredibus et successoribus dicte domine regine ad mandatum domini deputati pro tempore existentis, cum sex equestribus et triginta turbariis[1] bene armatis in omni suo magno progressu bellico, vulgariter nuncupato hostinges, cum victualibus pro se et suis ad expensas patrie sue quandocunque et quociescunque hujusmodi domino deputato placebit ad hoc assignare et demandare, et in quolibet alio viagio et progressu subito contingente serviet cum toto numero et protestate sua cum victualibus similiter pro duobus vel tribus diebus et pro quolibet equestre faciente defectum (ut predicitur) forisfaciet et solvet pro quolibet die tres solidos et octo denarios, et pro quolibet turbario pro simili defectu denarios viginti.

[6.] Item: Predictus Bernardus concessit et promisit, pro recognicione obediencie sue et quia tenet dictam patriam de domino regi et domina regina reddere et solvere singulis annis dictis dominis regi et regine, heredibus et successoribus prefate regine, quinquaginta martos pingues[2] annuatim, ad festum Sancti Michaelis tantum tradendos

fol. 50b. officiariis suis vel in defectu martorum solvet pro eis tantundem pecunie quantum ex veteri consuetudine solitum est solvi.

[7.] Item: Prefatus Bernardus ulterius concessit et promisit daturum se quolibet anno bonagium centum Scoticis vulgariter nuncupatis galloglasses pro uno quarterio anni. Et quod indilate dabit et solvet prefato domino deputato aut ejus assignato centum martos pinguas (ut moris est) pro nominacione et admissione sua ad locum capitanei nacionis et patrie de Offarrall Bane predicto. Et quod respondebit et exsolvet de tempore in tempus ad illorum majestatum usus omnia Offarrall Bane ante hac ex consuetudine solvit aut solvere debuit, et que ad illorum majestates quovismodo pertinet aut pertinere debent.

[8.] Item: Prefatus Bernardus non solum juramentum corporale prestitit super sacrosancta Dei evangelia pro bono complemento premissorum, sed finaliter concessit etiam et promisit pro majori securitate fidelitatis sue erga regis et regine majestates ponere obsides suos penes prefatum dominum deputatum vel alibi prout melius eidem domino deputato videbitur.

In cuius rei et omnium premissorum fidem et testimonium tam predictus dominus deputatus et consilium quam prefatus Bernardus hiis scriptis manus suas alternatim apposuerunt.

Data die et mense supradictis annis regnorum Philippi et Marie, Dei gratia, Anglie, Francie, Hispaniarum, utriusque Sicilie, Neapolis, Hierusalem et Hibernie regis et regine, fidei defensorum, archiducum Austrie, ducum Mediolani, Burgundie et Brabancie, comitum Haspurgi, Flandrie et Tirollis, quarto et quinto [1557].

---

[1] In margin: "His risinge out: six horsemen, thirty kearne".
[2] In margin: "His rent: fifty fatt beoves."

[XLVII.]—By the lorde deputie and counsaill, at Dublin, Julii xxvii°, 1557: 1557. fol. 51.

Where variaunce hathe been moved betwixte Lucas Otoole, in the behalfe of himself and the rest of his septe whether of them ought of right to have the spending of Glancapp in the Tooles countrey, for the deciding wherof and for a quietnes hensforthe to be had, bothe parties were agreed to abide the sayeng of the freholders of Glancappe, forasmuche as the saide freholders appearing this day before us, the lord deputie and counsaill, have made a corporall othe upon the holy Evangelistes that Glancappe is not nor ought of right to be charged with any expences to any of the saide septs of the Tooles but hathe been accustomed to be at the comaundement of the lorde deputie for the tyme being and used to pay yerely unto him certain wood.' cariages[1] and other duties to be defended against all other that by violente and wronge wolde exacte any thing upon them, which ordre was taken in the tyme that sir Edward Ponynges, knight, supplied the place of deputacion[2]:

It is therefore nowe ordered concluded and agreed by the saide lorde deputie and counsaill that nether the said Lucas Otoole nor Phelym Otoole nor any other of the Tooles hensforth shall have any spending uppon the tennauntes of Glancapp but that they shalbe free from all exaccions that any of the Tooles aforesaide should burden them withall and stande only chargeable to suche impositions as the lorde deputie for the tyme beinge shall taxe and set pon them. fol. 51*b*.

[XLVIII.]—At Dublin, xxix° Julii, 1557: fol. 52.

T. Sussex.—Forasmuche as it is thought expediente to the lorde deputie and counsaill that the more parte of their majesties waged kerne shall remayne in Leyes and Offally for the defence of those quarters and not goo forthe to this next generall hostinge: fol. 52.

It is therefore resolved by the saide lorde deputie and counsaill that there shalbe fifty kerne intertayned into wages for sixe weekes to goo forthe to the nexte hosting and then to be discharged onles for further respectes of service it shalbe thought goode to intertayne them for a longer tyme.

H. Dublin, canc.—H. Sydney.—Henry Radeclyff.—George Stanley.—Frances Agarde.—D. Hay.[3]

[XLIX.]—Proclamatio facta per dominum deputatum et consilium, apud campum prope Mulighe,[4] xvi° Julii, 1557: fol. 53.

Cum illustris ac prepotens dominus Thomas, Sussexie comes, prenobilis ordinis garterii miles, vicecomes Fitzwauteres, dominus de Egremounde et Burnell unus generosorum private camere invictissimi domini regis omnium regis et regine in regno Anglie generosorum pensionariorum et generosorum ad arma capitaneus, ac regni Hibernie deputatus, pro certo habens tam Donaldum Oconor, cujus manifeste prodiciones et conspiraciones adversus illorum majestates non solum vulgo sunt cognite, sed complures etiam traditores, rebelles et exleges, qui justam illorum majestatum punicionem et legis contempto vindictam devitantes, ac eo pacto expulsi tam extra limites de Leys et Offally quam de aliis locis ubi tunc habitabant nuper accessum suum fecerunt ad partes rivo de Shanon adjacentes, et in fol. 53*b*.

[1] In margin: "Note: Wood to be carryed to the deputy."
[2] 1494–5.
[3] Fol. 52*b*. is blank.
[4] Meelick, co. Galway.

1557. diversis Hibernicis patriis ex utraque rivi parte constitutis, facile inveniebant qui illos foverent ac in omnibus opem et auxilium subministrarent, inter quos quidam Omaddinorum qui castellum de Mulighe et ejus confines in sua possessione habebant pre ceteris manifestius indicium benevolencie sue erga prefatos traditores rebelles, et exleges fecerunt,
fol. 53b. tametsi non ignorabant prefatum Donaldum et omnes qui illius sequuntur partes aut quovismodo opem et auxilium suppeditant per proclamacionem publice factam pro traditoribus reputari, et ideo in extremum illorum majestatum legum discrimen incurrere.

Resolvebat igitur per maturam deliberacionem et advisamentum reliquorum illorum majestatis consiliariorum, regis et regine exercitum secum ad predictum castellum de Mulighe traducere, pro debita castigacione tam predictorum Omaddinorum si in sua traditoria obstinacia persisterent quam aliorum in illis partibus habitancium qui simile quicquid auderent ad animacionem traditorum et illorum majestatis regalisque dignitatis contemptum.

Ac itaque veniens coram predicto castello ac offerens majorem favorem et misericordiam, rebellibus qui tum antedictum castellum tenebant quam pro illorum meritis par erat, justissime provocatus fuit per illorum manifestam pervicaciam obstinatam et traditoriam disobedienciam, ac recusacionem illorum majestatis authoritati cedere, vi et potentia adversus illos uti, quibus coacti sunt pro salva vite custodia secreto se subducere et sic duriter evadendo castellum[1] vacuum relinquere, unde factum est quod idem castellum nunc (sicut de jure debet) in illorum majestatis legitima et reali possessione existit.

Prefatus ergo dominus deputatus et consilium volentes ac optantes omnes illorum majestatum subditos de via aberrantes per clemenciam et mansuetudinem potius quam per rigorem et extremitatem in ordinem ac debite sue obediencie cognicione reduci, quanquam non est illis ignotum prefatum
fol. 54. Donaldum Oconor et reliquos traditores, rebelles et exleges predictos victualia ac reliqua necessaria tam secreto quam publice nuper sibi subministrata habuisse in diversis patriis ex utraque parte rivi de Shanon existentibus, tamen quandoquidem capitanei patriarum predictarum prefata domino deputato modo venient ad Mulighe accessum suum ad illum fecerunt, offerentes imposterum bonum et fidele servicium illorum majestati prestare secundum illius ordinacionem commodissimum duxerunt per hanc proclamacionem publice denunciare ac significare, quod sicut contenti sunt abstinere a justa punicione delinquencium nec illis debitat penas juxta illorum merita infligere sub spe bona melioris frugis posthac proventure sic per presentes in regis ac regine nomine firmiter injungunt ac dant in mandatis omnibus et singulis (tam patriarum predictarum capitaneis quam reliquis illorum majestatum subditis ibidem habitantibus sub pena lese majestatis quod omnes imposterum sedulo caveant quomodo, sic denuo peccent diligenterque prevideant ne predicto Donaldo Oconor vel cuicunque alteri traditori rebelli aut exlegi de Offaly, Leys vel de quacunque preterea patria ad illos quo auxilio fugienti opem, auxilium seu adjumentum quovis modo ferant ac ministrent nec alicui Omadinorum qui castellum de Mulighe nuper possederunt neque illis qui idem
fol. 54b. castellum nuper tenebant, presertim Johanni More Ogleshane, Conoghyr Ogleshane, Johanni Boy McFlyne, Brianno McDonell, Willelmo Moile, Dermicio McAndro, Donaldo Odouilishe, Donello McFynell et Hugoni

[1] The capture of the castle of Meelick was referred to in a letter from the king and queen, dated Richmond, 31 July, 1557, to the lord deputy Sussex.—State Papers Ireland, Public Record Office, London. It was also noticed in a paper entitled "A journey by the earl of Sussex," from 10 July to July 18, 1557, by Athlone pursuivant of arms.

Oboran, nec eorum alicui secreto vel in propatulo intra sue authoritatis limites, sed quod predicti capitanei publice generalem monicionem dabunt omnibus sub se habitantibus pro apprehensione omnium et singulorum traditorum rebellium exlegum et malefactorum antedictorum ubicunque fuerunt inventi. 1557.

Et si imposterum probatum ac manifestum fuerit predictum Donaldum Oconor nuper possessores castelli de Mulighe, qui illud nuper illorum jure et nomine tenebant, seu quemvis alium traditorem, rebellem, exlegem, aut malefactorem superius specificatum, post hanc proclamacionem publice factam accepisse cibum, potum aut reliqua ad suos usus necessaria, sive permissos esse secreto vel publice existere aut manere in aliquo patriarum predictorum quod tunc capitaneus ejusdem patrie unde victualia vel alia necessaria sunt subministrata seu quevis alia persona antedicta ubi forte secreto vel in aperto existent aut manebunt respondebit pro eo facto ut superius est declaratum, et prosequetur ac punietur tanquam rebellis eo quod traditoribus et insigniter delinquentibus auxilium et adjumentum subministravit.

Atque hec proclamacio pro ultima mencione accipiatur quia fol. 55.
hujusmodi gravia ac notabilia crimina posthac committenda, non tam facile imposterum impunita evadent sicut modo sunt pretermissa, sed si occasio dabitur cum extremo rigore et severitate punientur.

Ac insuper prefatus dominus deputatus et consilium dant in mandatis ac firmiter injungendo precipiunt omnibus regis et regine subditis tam capitaneis et officiariis quam privatis personis quod auxiliantes et assistentes erunt hiis qui relicti erunt in castello de Mulighe pro defensione et salva custodia ejusdem in omnibus que racionabiliter ab illis requirent. Significavit ulterius quod si contingat aliquem illorum seu quemvis alium eo venientem sive inde abeuntem injuriam, detrimentum seu corporis lesionem de via capere quod tunc capitaneus illius patrie ubi nocumentum est illatum respondebit pro facto, quo in casu neque ignorancia neque aliqua alia excusacio locum habebit aut admittetur.

Postremo, prefatus dominus deputatus et consilium volunt quod omnes et singuli capitanei patriarum in hiis partibus mittent ad castellum de Mulighe pro hujus proclamacionis exemplari Latine scripti, in eum finem ut idem melius intelligere queant, et se ad illius debitam execucionem sicut par est accomodare possint.

Deus salvos faciat regem et reginam.[1]

[L.]—A proclamacyon sett fourthe by the lorde deputie, the nobles fol. 56.
of this realme and the reste of the king and quenes majesties counsaill assembled at Dublyn, the xx^th^ of October, the fourthe and fifte yeares of ther majesties raignes:

Wheare ther be many of the horsemen and kerne of Lex, Offalley, Irry, Slemarge, and Glanmoulyry,[2] retayned in dyverse partes of this realme, and that the sayde horsemen and kerne so retayned lyving openly in quyete and good order doo not onely secretely ayde the outelawes and rebelles with suche things as they maye, but also as yt dothe moste manyfestly appeare, goo personally also with them in the nyght to burnynges, spoylinges, stelthes and murdres, wherby ther majesties good subjectes receyve moche hurte and the rebelles the better hable to achieve ther myschevous and trayterous ententes when they be so secretely aydid and guyded by suche as to open shewe doo no hurte and after the facte commytted doo the nexte daye shewe themselves in open company as thoughe they were gilteles thereof.

[1] Fol. 55b. is blank. [2] *See* page 32.

1557. It ys therefore orderid and decreid by us, the lorde deputie, the nobles of this realme and the reste of ther majesties counsaill then present, that whosoever shall apon lycence or otherwyse detayne or kepe any horseman or kernaghe of the countreys above wrytten, and shall not within viii dayes after the proclaymyng of this our order within the contrey or
fol. 56b. countreys wheare he shall dwell presente in wryting the name or names of so many horsemen or kerne as he shall so detayne of the sayde countreys to us, the lorde deputie, or to sir Henry Ratclyffe, knight, livetenante of the said countryes, that then every man so fayling shall forfeyte for every horseman or kerne so detayned contrary to this our order one hundreth poundes sterling, the same to be levyed to ther majesties use ymediately upon the proving of the premysses and the moytie thereof to be geven to hym that shall give thinformacyon of the person so detayned contrary to this our order.

fol. 57. [LI.]—By the lord deputy:

Wheare we dyd heretofore, uppon divers and good respectes, restraine sir Henry Radclyf, knight, leivtenant of Leyse, Offally, etc. from the prosecuting or anoying of any of the borderers of the sayd countries duering the time of our late jorney in the northe, allthough the sayd borderers shold in any thing ayd or assist the rebelles, by reason whereof there hath succeeded divers hurtes commytted by the rebelles with the ayd of the sayd borderers, and more are lyke to ensue yf spedy remedy be not had therin forasmuche as divers and often warninge have bene gevin by us to the sayd borderers that they shold forbeare to ayd the rebelles with men, victuells or any other succors and that notwithstanding they do from tyme to tyme contemne our sayd warninge and comaundementes. We do therfore, for the avoyding of further hurt that myght ensue, geve by thes presentes licence and auctoryty to the sayd sir Henry aswell to take pledges of all men and in all places wheare it shalbe provyed that any goods under his rule taken by the rebelles hathe ben recevyd, and the same pledges to deteine till restitucion be fully made; as allso to plage, ponyshe and prosecute with sword and fier and other warlyke maners, all Iryshmen and their contries wheare he shall justly prove that the sayd rebelles shalbe by any meanes ayded, succored or relevyd from henceforthe:

And further that the sayd sir Henry shall and may geve to any of
fol. 57b. his deputyes in ether of the countries licens under his hand wryting to do any parte of the premyses when himself for any respect shall not think fytt to go in persone, which licence shalbe a discharge for his deputy or deputies:

And further that the sayd sir Henry or his deputy, licenced under his hand wryting, shall and may execute the mershall law uppon all manner of persones that shall be found gylty of the premyssis.

Yevin at Dublyn, the xxi[th] of October, 1557.

fol. 58. [LII.]—At Dublyn, the xx[th] of October anno 1557.

It ys condescendid concludid and agreid by the lorde deputie, the nobles of this realme and others of the quenes majesties counsaill, that for the presente furnyture of the fortes in Leix and Offalley and other ther majesties garrysons ther shalbe a ceasse of corne and bieves leavyed oute of hande in forme following, that ys to saye:

In Methe six hundreth peckes corne, the two partes malte and the other wheate and six score bieves; in Westmethe thre hundreth peckes, the two partes wheate the other malte, and threscore bieves, and in the countie of Kildare thre hundreth peckes and threscore bieves, divided in sorte as ys aforesaide. 1557.

[LIII.]—Apud Dublyn, 21 Octobris, 1557: fol. 58b.

T. Sussex.—It ys agreed, resolvyd and concluded by us, the lorde deputy, the lorde channseler, therle of Kylldare, sir George Stanlye, sir John Alen, Fraunces Agard and John Plunket, that their shold be for divers grete and urgent respectes us moving, and for the more suerty of the good state of this realme, sharpe warre made with all posseble spede uppon Shane Onele, the same to be orderyd from tyme to tyme as to the lorde deputy shalbe thought best.

H. Dublin, canc.—G. Kyldare.—George Stanley.—John Alen.—Jo. Plunket.—Francis Agarde.—D. Hay.

[LIV.]—Apud Armagh, xxv[th] Octobris, 1557: fol. 59.

Memorandum:—Yn the furst jorny that was made uppon Shane Onele we whose names be under wryten came after the taking of the pray to Armagh and finding there a grete masse of butter, corne and other victuells, wherewith Shane myght have meynteigned a gret nomber of Scotts for a whole yere to have the better done his determyned hurtes uppon their majesties good and Inglyshe sobjectes, dyd resolve for meny grete respects us moving that their shold be inquiery made of all victuells and other goodes whatsoever belonging to the churches or mynysters.

And uppon sequestring the same into suer places which was done the spoyle of the rest shold be gevin to the army and whatsoever cold not be carryed away shold be getheryd together and burnt; and finding after that the masse was so grete as the same cold not by any meanes be carryed away or duering our abode there getheryd and put into one or severall places, for that allmost every house was fylled with one or other kind of victuell, it was resolved that the victuelles shold be burned in the places wheare they lay, the lorde prymates and deanes houses only reservyed, and those onely to be taken out and getheryd together that were bestowed in any holy place.

All which the premysses were done with as muche reverence to the holy places and preservacion of images and other ornamentes of the churche and favor to the mynysters as by any meanes in suche a case we cold devyse.

Concordat cum originali: Ex. per me, Johannem Goldsmyth.

[LV.]—At Dublyn, the xxix[th] of November, anno 1557: fol. 59b.

T. Sussex.—It ys agreid resolved and concludid by us, the lorde deputie,[1] the nobles of the realme and the reste of the king and quenes majesties counsayll assembled at Dublyn, the daye and yere above wrytten, that for the preasente furnyture of the fortes in Lexe and Offally and other ther majesties garrysons in those parties ther shalbe a cesse of twelve hundreth peckes corne to be indyfferently cessid within the shieres of Methe, Westmethe, and Kildare, that ys to saye: in Methe, six hundreth peckes, whereof two partes malte and the thurde parte wheate, the pecke of wheate and beare malte at foure shillinge sterling, and woote malte at eight

[1] In margin: "Mem. That the countye of Dublyng was not cessed in this cesse, for that the sayed countye was cessed for the furniture of the lord deputies howse."

1557. grotes sterling the pecke; in Westmethe thre hundreth peckes divided in like sorte and at like rate and pryce; and in the countye of Kildare other thre hundreth in semblable sorte. The same to be levied betwixte this and the xth of January nexte, and to be sente: forsomoche as shall come oute of Methe to the town of Trym, and that oute of the countye of Kyldare to Athie, and that out of Westmethe to be delivered at the forte in Offalley.

H. Dublin, canc.—G. Kyldare.—Thomas Ormonde, Ossory.—Roland Baltynglas.—Christofor Donsany.—H. Sydney.—Henry Radeclyff.—Gerald Aylmer.—Thomas Louith.—Patryk of T[rimletiston.]—James Bathe—Robert Dyllon.—J. Travers.—G. Stanley.—John Alen.—Thomas Lokwod.—Thomas Harbart.—John Parker.—Francis Agarde.—Jo. Plunket.

fol. 60. [LVI.]—At Kilmaynan, the last of November, anno 1557:

T. Sussex.—Forasmoche as it is considered by us, the lorde deputy and counsell, that the quenes majestiesfortes and other their highness holdes and garizons are disfurnished of necessary provision, chiefly wheate and other grayne for their present relief the tyme beinge nowe most propice to put the same in order and consideringe agayne what corne heretofore hath gone out of the Englishe Pale into Yrishe mennes countreyes and is dayly by diverse as well grey merchantes and other commonly laden and convoyed without lett or restraynt wherby great derth and skarcitie is lyke universally to growe:

It is therefore condiscended and decreed that from hensforth no soche grayne shalbe conveyed laden or soulde out of the saide Englishe Pale into enny Yrishmans countreye nor yet enny forayne suffred or permitted to come upon mercate dayes or other tymes into anny the townes, villadges or b[o]rough townes to buy anny corne but that it shalbe taken as a forfeyte and lawfull for every man to seyse uppon the same, the one halfe to the king and quenes majesties use and the other moytie to the seysor himself.

Willinge and requyringe and neverthelese in their majesties names straytly chardginge and commandinge all and every their highnes officers, ministers and subjects of what estate degree or condicion soever they be
fol. 60b. not onely to have especiall eye and consideracion to the premisses but also to be from tyme to tyme aydinge and asstinge to all those that shall put this our proclamacion in due execucion; not faylinge herof as your and every of you tender your dueties, the service of their majesties and the furtheraunce of the publyque weale and will further aunswere for the contrary doing at your uttermost perill.

II. Dublin, canc.—G. Kyldare.—Roland Baltynglas.—D. Hay.—Henry Radeclyff.

fol. 61. [LVII.]—By the lorde deputy and counsell:

T. Sussex.—Where for the reformacion of Leys and other their majesties countreys on those borders order was taken by us, the lorde deputie and counsell, at Dubleyn, the viii[th] of November anno 1556, that the lorde deputie shulde from tyme to tyme when occasion of warre servithe retayne suche number of kerne for that purpose as his lordshipe shall thinke good, the same to be cessed by his discrecion within Methe, Westmethe, Dublyn, and other counties. At which tyme it was concluded that there shulde be cessed for the intent aforsaid within the counties of Methe and Dublyn cc.*li.* sterling, to be taken ratably upon the ploughe landes:

It is therefore nowe thought expedient that the said cc.*li.* be levied forthwith and delivered to the treasurer at warres to be employed upon the waging of kerne to pursue the outlawes, and where also the Polles have made defaulte to sende such number of kern to the laste generall hostyng as they ought to have done. 1557.

It is further or ordered that the accustomed fynes which were wonte to be taxed upon theym, making suche defaultes, shall also be levied forthwith and delivered to the treasaurer at warres for the intent aforsaide the said two hundred poundes and forfaites of the Polles to be employed for the waging of kerne as the lordes justices in thabsence of the lords deputie shall thinke good.

Yeven at Kylmaynan, the second of December, 1557.

H. Dublin, canc.—H. Sydney.—Henry Radeclyffe.—George Stanley.—John Alen.—John Parker.—John Travers.—Fraunces Harbart.—Frances Agarde.

(1556.)

[LVIII.]—At Laughlyn, the xxvi of Decembre, 1556:

Whereas in the matter depending in variaunce betwene Francisco Dies, Spaniarde, factor and attorney for certaine merchantes of Spayne, playntif, and Henry Corneilson, late of Myddelbroughe in Zelande, defendant, upon the demaunde of certain wares and merchandises laden in Flaunders in the saide Henryes barke called the Sprite Volant of Middelbroughe and discharged of late in the havon of Waterford and there solde, imbeseled or otherwise bestowed by the saide Henry, it presently appearethe unto us, the lord deputie, by a booke or certificate sent unto us from the maior and bailife, of Waterforde subscribed with their hands, wherunto the seale of office of the mairaltie there also is affixed, that parte of the saide goods afore mencioned were by the saide Henry solde to sundry personnes, parte also were by him geven awaye, and parte comytted to the secrete custodye of dyverse men, or conveyed to Rochell and other places to be solde. fol. 61*b*.

Forsomuche as upon deliberate examynacion of the matter, and hearing thallegacions on bothe sydes, the saide Henry hathe not produced nor shewed before us, the saide lorde deputie, any sufficiente authoritie or matter to beare him in the sale, gifte, bargayneing awaye or imbeseling of the saide merchauntes goods without ther consent or knowleage:

It is nowe therfore ordered, decreid and concluded by us, by the mutuall consent and agreement of the saide Francisco and Henry, in maner and forme as hereafter particulerly is declared:

First that all suche goodes, parcell of the premisses, as remayne unsolde, and are mencioned in the said maiors and bailiffes certificate, in whose custody soever they be, shall presently be brought in and delyvered into the handes of the maior, bailiffes and aldermen of Waterforde, and that the money, billes of dette and other specialties receyved for such other percelles therof as heretofore were soulde by the saide Henrye or any other factors or doers for him, shall also in like sorte and in the same kynde of coyne that it was receyved be delyvered to the same maior, bailiffes and aldermen without fraude coveyne or delaye. fol. 62.

Item: Where certain parcelles of the saide goodes were geven awaye by the saide Henrye to sundry personnes, the saide Henry shall cause the same to be restored and delyvered to the saide maior, bailiffes and aldermen or answere unto them the just value and price thereof. So shall he doo for all suche other things as by enquiry, deposicion of witnesses or otherwise are knowen, founde and tryed to be purloigned or embeselid by the saide Henry, and are mencioned in the saide certificate made by the maior and bailiffes of Waterforde aforesaide.

And where it appeareth by the saide certificate that parte of the saide goodes were sent to Rochell and there solde and some dowte and

(1556.) difficultie arisethe howe muche the saide Henry ought to aunswere, for that the certificate sent from Rochell under the handes of the poyzmaster and the publique notary there, makith declaracion that so muche wares were there uttered and solde by James Donytt, the said Henryes factor and by oon John Salynger as that there was receyved for the same two thowsand sixe hundrethe forty nyne frankes and a half, whereof the saide James, upon his othe solempnely made before the maior of Waterford, fol. 62b. hathe denyed to be by him receyved at Rochell any more then nynetene hundrethe tenne frankes and thirtene sowse, so that there remaynethe in suspence seven hundreth thirty and eight frankes and seventene sowse, to be tried whether the same ought to be aunswered by the saide Henry or noo :

It is therfore ordered by us that the saide Henry shall make undelayed payment to the saide maior, bailiffes, and aldermen of as muche money as is acknowleaged to be by his saide factor, James Donyll, receyved at Rochell for the same, and to stande chargeable also for the rest mencioned in the saide certificate from Rochell, onles he within the compasse of oon yere bring newe certificate from Rochell, under the towne seale, to lessen or utterlye advoide his present charge in that behaulf:

And hereupon it is further ordered that if the saide Francisco immediatly upon payment, restitucion and satisfaction made as is aforesaide, shall delyver to the saide Henry a good, sufficient and lawfull acquittaunce and discharge for his indempnitie against all personnes touching the premisses as by counsaill learned shalbe devised, then the said maior, bailiffes and aldermen shall furthwith delyver to the saide Francisco all the saide money, goodes and speciallties so by them receyved as is aforesaide.

And if the said Francisco shall not be hable to geve suche sufficient discharge therin to the saide Henry as may acquite him of all claymes hereafter to be made by any the principall owners of the saide goods, fol. 63. then all the money, goods and specialties aforesaide to be and remayne wholy sequestred in the saide maiors, bailiffs and aldermens hands, to be by them saulfly kepte untill the saide Henry shalbe sufficiently discharged thereof and ordre taken by us for delyvery of the same to the right owners as to justice appertaynethe.

And it is also further ordered by us by consent of bothe parties that the saide Francisco shall presently allowe and defalke upon the saide Henryes accompte as well the fraught of his saide barke, according to the bargain made in Flaunders at the firste lading of the goodes, as also all suche other reasonable and necessary costs and charges as he hath susteyned syns that tyme aboute the same goodes, so farre forthe as the saide maior, bailiffes and aldermen shall thinke and saye that the saide Francisco in conscience is bound to paye and allowe.

And that the saide Henry shall imediatly retorne to Waterforde and there yelde his body to prison till he for his parte shall have performed this our ordre, or elles put yn sufficiente surties for the due performaunce and accomplishement of the same. And that doon shall also enter into newe baudes with sufficient suerties in fyve hundrethe poundes to be answereable and furthcomying at Waterforde at all tymes by the space of oon yere next after the date of this our ordre tanswere for all suche other goodes parcelles of the saide Spanyardes clayme and lading within his barke aforemencioned as within that tyme shall happen to be founde oute as solde or imbesiled by him, and are not yet knowen nor come to light.[1]

[1] Fol. 63b. is blank.

[LIX.]—Pledges taken by the lorde deputie and lefte at his departinge: fol. 64.

Of Ocarroll: his sonne, at Catherlaughe. The castell of Lemyvanan with therle of Ormonde.

Of Omulloy: Tybot Omulloy; Fargnanym Omulloye, at the forte in Leyse. Tybot Omulloyes son with Fraunces Cosbye.

Of Megohegan: his son:—with therle of Kildare.

Of the Donnes: severall pledges:—with therle of Kildare.

Of Mecowghlan—his son:—with Fraunces Cosbye.

Of Brasill Omadden:—his brother:—with Fraunces Crosbye.

Of Melaughlyn Omadden: a pledge: with Fraunces Cosbye.

Of Phelym Duffe: his brother, Con Mc Nele oge, in the castell of Dublin.

Pledges promysed to be delyvered and their othes taken therfore:

Of Henry Oneyle: one.—Of McMahon: one.—Of M^cgenyse: one.

[LX.]—By the lord justice and counsaill at Dublin, vi^o Marcii, 1557[-8]: 1557-8. fol. 65.

H. Sydney.—Memorandum: That wheare Art Omolloye, late capten of Ferkeall, neither according his ductie ded attende on the lorde justice in a journey against the rebelles of the Occonnors: neither yeat being sent unto, uppon resonnable securitie to him offred to come to the same lorde justice did, repaier, but utterlie refused the same, and that further after the said lorde justices entrie made in to the said countrey of Ferkeall and going to the house of the said Omolloye, ded than and during the said lorde justices aboade there, contynuallie absent himself, persisting in his said wilfull refusall without any just cause or occasion to him mynistred so to do.

And albeit that the said lorde justice ded than also sende unto the said Omolloye, offring not onlie securitie as aforesaide, but also pardone for him, his wief, children and followers, yeat uppon his wicked and trayterous pretence appearing than partaking with the said rebelles, both contemned the same, and further as a perverse enemye and rebell in the departng of the said lorde justice out of the said countrey, in trayterous manner with a great power of men in warrlike arraye ded set uppon the said lorde justice and army in the strenght of a pase within the said countreye, whear in the conflict theldest sonne of the said Omolloye with others of his faction was than and there slayn and vaynquished.

Forasmochie as the said Omolloye, by suchie his trayterous behavior and open rebellion, hath deserved not only to forfait and lose his dignitie, name and roume of captein of the said countreye, but also to be further persecuted and ponished as a traitor.

And therewith considering the fidelitie and good service of Tibot Omolloye, brother to the said Art, besides other good respectes and considerations we the said lorde justice and others, whose names are herunto subscribed, have thought mete and expedient to appoint, ordeigne and constitute the said Tibot Omolloye to be chief captein of the said countrey fol. 65b.
of Ferkeall and to passe a graunt thereof unto the same Tibot by the king and queenes majesties lettres patentes accordingly.

The same Tibot to be bounde to certein articles conteigned and expressed in a payer of indentures in that behaulf devised, the tennor wherof followeth in the next lefe:

[LXI.]—Hec indentura, facta septimo die mensis Marcii, anno Domini fol. 66.
millesimo quingentesimo quinquagesimo septimo [1557-8] inter honorabilem virum Henricum Sydney, militem, thesaurarium domini regis et

1557-8. domine regine ad guerras, ac justiciarius regni sui Hibernie, ceterosque de consilio regali quorum nomina inferius scribuntur ex una parte et Theobaldum Omulloye in patria de Ferkeall[1] alias vocata Omulloyes countrey, gent (*sic*) ex altera parte, testatur quod predictus Theobaldus concessit, promisit et per presentes se firmiter obligavit tenere et firmiter perimplere domino regi et domino regine, heredibus et successoribus prefate regine, Anglie regibus, tenorem et formam articulorum sequentium :

In primis : Quod non solum Catholicam fidem et religionem, quantum in se est, promovebit et defendet, sed omnes etiam contradicentes aut renitentes pro suo posse corrigi in judicium vocari et debito modo per omnia puniri faciet.

Item : Acceptabit et recognoscet predictos dominos regem et reginam, legitimos esse sibi principes, illisque heredibus et successoribus domine regine predicte adherebit contra omnes homines sicut fidelis subditus et sicut ceteri ligei predicti regni Hibernie serviunt et obediunt aut servire et obedire debent.

Item : Predictus Theobaldus non adherebit nec confederabit cum inimicis et rebellibus dictorum regis et regine, aut successorum regine predicte sed illos pro viribus suis de tempore in tempus castigabit et prosequetur.

Item : Ulterius, dictus Theobaldus per presentes obligatur quod regia majestas habebit omnes terras et possessiones suas proprias, ac cetera omnia et singula debita ad suam celsitudinem spectantia, tam ea que modo
fol. 66*b*. jacent et existunt sub tutela et gubernacione predicti Theobaldi quam que quovismodo posthac crescere et legitime provenire poterint ad illorum majestatum usus infra limites et jurisdictionem patrie de Ferkeall predicte.

Item : Similiter, prefatus Theobaldus promptus et paratus erit in propria persona sua ad serviendum dominis regi et regine, et successoribus regine predicte ad mandatum locumtenentis deputati seu justiciarii Hibernie pro tempore existentis, cum quatuor[2] equestribus et duodecim turbariis, bene armatis, in omni suo magno progressu bellico vulgariter nuncupato hostinge, cum victualibus pro se et suis ad expensas patrie sue quandocunque et quocienscunque hujusmodi locumtenenti deputato vel justiciario placebit ad hoc assignare et demandare. Et in quolibet alio viagio et progressu subito contingente serviet cum toto numero et potestate patrie sue, cum victualibus similiter pro duobus vel tribus diebus. Et pro quolibet equestre faciente defectum ut predicitur forisfaciet et solvet pro quolibet die tres solidos et quatuor denarios et pro quolibet turbario pro simili defectu denarios viginti.

Et predictus Theobaldus concessit et promisit daturum se quolibet anno bonnagium[3] pro uno exercitu Scoticorum, vulgariter nuncupato a battayll of galloglasses, pro dimidio unius quarterii anni.

Ac eciam quod indilate dabit domino justiciario aut assignatis suis centum martos pingues (ut moris est) pro nominacione et admissione sua ad locum capitanei[4] nationis et patrie de Ferkeall predicte.

Et quod respondebit et exsolvet de tempore in tempus ad illorum
fol. 67. majestatum usus omnia que Omolloye antehac ex consuetudine solvit aut solvere debuit et que ad illorum majestatum usus quovismodo pertinent aut pertinere debent, seu imposterum concedi aut de jure pertinere dignoscetur.

---

[1] Now portion of the King's county.

[2] In margin : "His risinge out."

[3] In margin : "Bonaugh for half a quarter of a yeare to a battayle of galliglasses."

[4] In margin : "100 beoves for his name of captaine."

Item: Prefatus Theobaldus concedit per presentes quod locumtenens, deputatus, vel justiciarius pro tempore existens scindet et scindi mandabit aliquam arctum viam, Anglice vocatam a pase, in dicta patria de Ferkeall ad voluntatem ipsorum locumtenentis deputati et justiciarii seu eorum alicujus pro tempore existentis. 1557-8.

Et quod ipse Theobaldus de tempore in tempus escurabit et manutenebit eas vias vocatas pases, que per mandatum dicti domini justiciarii nuper scisse fuerunt aut que imposterum ad mandata locumtenentis deputati et justiciarii seu eorum alicujus scindi precipientur sumptibus et laboribus patrie sue predicte.

Item: Prefatus Theobaldus non solum juramentum corporale prestitit super sacrosancta Dei evangelia pro bono complemento premissorum, sed eciam finaliter concessit et promisit pro majore securitate fidelitatis sue erga regis et regine majestates ponere obsides suos penes prefatum dominum justiciarium vel alibi prout melius eidem justiciario videbitur expedire.

In cujus rei testimonium et fidem omnium et singulorum premissorum tam predictus dominus justiciarius et consilium quam prefatus Theobaldus hiis scriptis manus suas alternatim apposuerunt. Data die et mense supradictis, annis regnorum Philippi et Marie, Dei gratia, etc.[1]

[LXII.]—At Dublin, the xviiith of March, anno 1557[-8]:

H. Sydney.—Forasmochie as the fort in Leix stondeth presentlie in case to be fournished with corne and that the doing therof may be with lesse bourden and trouble of the countrye in the carieing and conveighing of the same corne to the said fort: it is considered, condescended and agreed by us, the lorde justice, and others whos names ar hereunto subscribed, that a cesse of corne shalbe hadd within the fyve sheres,[2] wherof some to pay money or corne, and some corne only, besides the carriage therof: fol. 68.

That is to saye, oon cesse in the countie of Lowth of four hundred peckes of whete or in steade of the same liii*li.* vi*s.* viii*d.*, sterling.

In Est Methe four hundred peckes of wheate or in lieu therof liii*li.* vi*s.*, sterling.

In Westmeth two hundred peckes of whete or therfor xxvi*li.* xiii*s.* iiii*d.*, sterling.

In the county of Dublin[3] four hundred peckes wherof half in wheate and half in malt, the thirde parte of the same malte [to be] berre malt.

And in the countie of Kyldare oon hundreth peckes, wherof fifty in wheat and fifty in malt, the thirde part of the same malte berre.

All which severall corne to be delyvered as folloeth: for Lowth, at the Novan, to thands of John Wakeley; for EstMethe, at Tryme, to the handes of sir George Stanley, knight, marshall of tharmy here; for Westmethe, at Molingarre, to thande of the same sir George; for Dublin, at the Nasse, to the portrief there; and for Kyldare, to be delyvered at Athy to the portrief likewise there. fol. 68*b*.

---

[1] Fol. 67*b*. is blank.

[2] In Leinster: Dublin, Louth, Kildare, East Meath, Westmeath.

[3] In margin: "The consideracion whyther the countie of Dublin in this cesse is cessed as moche as Meth, which is not equall after the rate of circuyte ground nor plow landes, is because a great parte of the countie of Kildare and other borders be so wasted, that they cannot be chardged with a ratable cesse, so as in that respect the fort sholde be in lack of fornyture if this cesse wer not passed as it is, otherwise the countie of Dublin was never compared to Meth in eny cesse or chardge.—Henry Sydney."

1557-8. And for suche money as is afore appointed to be paid for the said corne so severallie to be cessed as aforesaid the same money to be paid for the said corne to thandes of the vice thesauror of Irlande for the tyme being.

And it is further concluded by us as aforesaid that as well suche money as is afore lymyted to be paid for corne, having election thereof, as also the said corne to be cessed and caried in manner before expressed, shalbe cessed, levied and collected and also delyvered and paid, as said is, before the first of Maye next, without further tract or delaye in eny wise.

And also that for all the said corne so to be cessed and delyvered in manner afore declared payment to be made at the delyvery therof in the severall places before expressed by thandes of thaffornamed persones appointed to receyve the said corne after the rate of iiii*s*., sterling, the pecke both for wheate and berre malte, and for ote malte after the rate of ii*s*. viii*d*. the pecke.

H. Dublin, canc.—G. Kyldare.—W. Midensis.—Roland Baltynglas. —Christofor Kyllen.—J. Slane.—Thomas Louth.—P. Barnewall of T[rymleteston].—George Stanley.—Henry Radeclyff.—John Travers. —John Alen.—F. Harbart.—Francis Agarde.

1558. [LXIII.]—Apud Dublyn, secundo Maii, anno 1558:

fol. 69. T. Sussex.—It ys condescendid, concludid and agreid by the right honourable therle of Sussex, lorde deputie of the realme of Irelande, with the advyse and consente of the nobilite and the rest of the king and quenes majesties counsaill, that the watches before devysid for the good staye of the countrey and defence of the borders shalbe of newe sett fourthe and proclameyd, and that beakons shalbe fourthwith erectid in such places upon the see costes for the warnyng of the countrey as by the saide lorde deputie shalbe thought mete and expedyente.

And wheare dyverse bodderagges, hurtes and stelthes have byn commytted and donne, as well by Orayly and his followers apon the Englishe Pale as by the same Pale apon the sayde Orayly and the countrey under his rule. Wherein, notwithstanding severall ordres and commyssions dyrectid oute for the pacyfication and determynyng of the same, ther ys as yet no dyrecte ende taken:

fol. 69*b*. Yt ys therfore ordered and agreid that new commysioners shall by the saide lorde deputie be chosen and appoyntid for that purpose, and the same ymediately apon suche letters as his lordeshipe shall dyrecte to the sayde Orayly with his aunswer agayne to the same, to be putt in execution accordingly.

Furder: Yt ys condescendid and agreid that where order for musters to be taken in the severall baronyes within thenglishe shires was lately by speciall commyssion sett fourthe and comaundid by the late lorde justice and counsell, that certificate shalbe made ymediately what ys by the same commyssioners don therin, and in case they have not as yet putt in execution to procede fourtwith to the taking thereof according the said order.

G. Kyldare.—Jenico of G[ormanston].—Oswaldo Massingberd, prior.[1]—J. Slane.—P. Barnewall of T[rymleteston].—Richard Delvin. —Christofor Donsene.[2]

[1] Of Kilmainham, co. Dublin.
[2] Christopher Plunket, baron of Dunsany.

[LXIV.]—Apud Dubliniam, xiiii° Maii, anno 1558 : 1558.

It ys orderid by the lorde deputie and counsaill that after a corporall othe by us mynystred to the lorde Power he shall have lycence to departe for thapprehension of suche men as shall by us be delyvered to hym in a lybell, wherein he shall doo his utter endeavour to bryng them in betwixte this and Trynyte Sonday nexte ; and ymmediately after the sayde feste he hymselfe to make his repayre unto us or suche commyssioners as by us shalbe appointed ; and then, in all mattiers of controversy depending as well betwixte the sayde lord Power and the mayour and cytezens of Waterforde as also betwene hym and the gentilmen and freholders of the countrey, order shalbe taken accordingly. fol. 70.

LXV.]—Apud Dubliniam, xvi^to die Maii, anno 1558 : fol. 70b.

Wheare the manors of Rosegarlande and Kilcohan, in the countie of Wexforde, were, under their majesties lettres patentes, by sir Anthony Sentleger, then lorde deputie here, leassid to Fraunceis Agarde, esquire, whose intereste in the same farmes Anthony Colcloghe had and enjoyed. And after, apon thoffice of seneschalship of the saide countie given to Phillip Isam and suggestion by hym made to the quenes majestie he obtayned her graces lettres dyrected to the right honnorable the lorde Fitzwalter, lorde deputie of Irelande, and to the lorde chauncellor of the same, commaundyng them by vertue of the sayde lettres to call in the sayde Anthony Colcloghes lease, and ymediately apon the cancellyng thereof to make oute a newe lease of those parcells to the sayde seneschall as in the saide lettres ys furder expressid. Wherupon the saide Anthony, fynding himself moche wronged, made his humble suete to the quenes majestie beseching her in pitying his case to gyve order for his remedy, whoose highness, by her instructions delyverid to us, her saide deputie, under her graces hande and here enrollid, dyd in the behalf of the sayde Anthony inserte this clawse following :

And where humble requeste hathe byn made unto ther majesties on the behalfe of Anthony Colcloghe, who by their highenes order was put fol. 71.
out of possessyon of the manors of Rosegarlande and Kylcohân and his lease thereof cancellid, ther majesties will and pleasure ys, apon due consideracion of the case, that ther saide deputie cawse ther chauncelor ther to give unto said Colcloghe a constat of that his lease in suche forme as in like cases ys accustomed to be grauntid, and therby restore hym to the tryall of his right and intereste ; with suche furder order as to the upright execution of justice in that case appertayneth.

Whiche clawse, by waye of questyon we sente unto the judge and other ther majesties lernyd counsaill to knowe their resolution upon the same, who concludid as followeth :

We thinke and take the lawe : yf Anthony Colcloghe had the possession of the above namyd manors by force of the saide lettres patentes above specyfied, at tyme of cancelling of the same, and nowe having a constat of the same oute of the chauncery, then he to be restored to his former estate and possession, like as he had at tyme of the saide cancelling.

Wherupon, wayeng ther resolucyon, and having the same confirmed with ther hands, we did call bothe the parties before us and gave order that the saide Anthony shulde be restored agayne to the possession of the saide farmes and that the said seneschall shulde advoide the same, lyke as the said Anthony and Patrike Browne, by our order and dyrection were apon their majesties former lettres secluded from the same. Whiche order taken by the lorde chauncellor apon our resolucyon we fol. 71b.

1558. have, for the like observation thereof, on the saide Anthony Colcloghes behalf, cawsid the same to be insertid in the fyne hereof as followeth:

Thorder taken bytwene Phillip Isam and Patrike Browne ys that the said Patricke shall have and enjoye all the lande and profites till Mychelmas nexte ensuyng the saide order, paying all suche rentes as was due unto ther saide majesties at Mychelmas aforsaid, and that the said Patrike shulde sowe all his fallowe at his pleasure, payeing to Phillipe Isam for every acre of the same fallowe a bushell of suche corne as shalbe sowen upon the premysses after the measure usid in the said countie of Wexforde, and that the said Phillipe shall have fourthwith a chamber within the house of Rossegarlande for to buylde apon the premisses at his pleasure, and at Mychelmas to have the possession of the [w]hole housses, moving no tenantes oute of their tenanteryes till Maye.

Whiche order we woll that the saide Phillip Isam, Anthony Colcloghe and Patricke Browne shall nowe also observe and kepe in advoyding of the possession of the saide Phillipe so as yt may appeare either partie to have advoydid the possession by like order and therby indyfferente justice mynystred.

T. Sussex.—H., cancellarius.—Henry Sydney.—Geo. Stanley.—Henry Radeclyffe.—John Parker.—Gerald Aylmer.—John Travers.

Concordat cum originali:—John Goldsmyth.

fol. 72. [LXVI.]—At Dublyn, xvi to Maii anno 1558:

Wheare complaynte was made to us by James Dillon, farmor of the castell of Ardenegraghe in Dillons countrey,[2] Thomas Dillon and his kynsmen enherytors of the same againste Geralde McOlyver FitzGeralde for the deceytefull entery and forcible detayndure thereof contrary the statutes in that behalffe provided:

The erle of Kildare, beyng then presente at the tyme of the complaynte, did vouche the saide Geralde to have don the same by commandemente, and that he wolde make answer thereunto, requyring for his title to the said castell to have a daye to bring in suche evidence as he had to shewe.

Whereupon we gave respite to this daye, at whiche tyme the said erle appearing by his lernyd counsell shewid no materiall or suffyciente wryting to maynteyne the saide Geraldes crafty entery and forcible detayndure.

We, therfore, the lorde deputie and counsell whose names are subscribed, doo order and decree that the saide erle of Kildare shall ymediately cawse the possession of the said castell with thappurtenances to be advoyded and to suffer and permytt the saide complaynantes quyetly and peasibely to enjoye the same according their former estate.

And for the tryall of the title the same to be orderid as the parties hereafter, apon shewing furder mattier, shalbe agreable to justice.

fol. 72b. [LXVII.[1]]—Apud Dubliniam, xxivto Maii, anno 1558:

Wheare Abraham Kerste, factor and attorney, for Hubarte Van de Saude and John Hone, of Andewarpe, merchantes, againste Henry Walshe,[3] late of that your towne mayor, and other thinhabitantes of the

---

[1] Not addressed, but apparently intended for Peter Dobben, mayor of Waterford, 1557–8.

[2] In West Meath.

[3] Mayor of Waterford, 1556–7. *See* account of municipal archives of Waterford in Tenth Report of Royal Commission on Historical MSS. Appendix V., 1885.

same, before this came before us to the poynte of judgmente, saving that ther was objectid by the saide Henry and his counsaill that the sauffe condyte shewid fourthe was not vaylchable, alleaging that the date therof was extincted a yeare before the taking of the shippe and goodes now in clayme and bought in your saide towne: 1558.

Forasmoche as the saide Abraham hathe presentid unto us an auctentique instrumente from the state of Andewarpe, as well declaring the saide shippe and goodes to be their owne, as also that the sauffe condyte was vaylable and good, and the date thereof according the computation and prescription of all Brabant wherof the said citie of Andwarpe ys a member; wherby it appeareth to us that the saide sauffe condyte was in strenght and vaylable and that the said Abraham and thother merchantes have sustayned greate wronge and domage:

We, therfore, the saide lorde deputie and counsaill, whose names be hereunto subscribed, adwarde, order and decree that you shall fourthwith and ymediately see the saide Abraham restored to all suche goodes or the like goodes as he ys factor for and came to your handes or the handes of any thinhabitantes of your saide citie in every state or condition:

Or elles to agree with hym for the value of them according as the markett then was, so that he have no furder cawse in this behalfe to complayne, and hereof not to faile upon the payne of a thowsande poundes.

T. Sussex.—Hughe, cancellarius.—Oswalde Massingberde.—Henry Sydney.—Henry Radecliffe.—Gerald Aylmer.—George Stanley.—John Travers.—John Parkar.—Francis Agarde.—Thomas Cusake.

Concordat cum originali:—John Goldsmith.

[LXVIII.]—Ordo domini deputati et consilii capta cum domino Orayly[1], apud Kylmaynan, xxv^to^ Maii, anno 1558: fol. 73.

[1.] Primo: Quod ipse arbitramento et ordinationi commissionariorum per nos jam assignatorum stabit circa restitutionem et debitam satisfactionem per quoscumque sub ejus gubernatione fiendam in iis que contra confines Anglicanas commiserunt ac pro complemento et observatione hujus rei corporali se juramento astringet quod illos obsides in manus baronis de Slane aut magistri marescalli deliberabit infra octavum diem Junii proxime futurum, qui juxta nostram conclusionem fuerint assignati.

Similiter et idem dominus de Slane aut mareschallus in manus suas suscipiet eos ex confinibus Anglicanis versus quos dictus Orayly aliquam hujusmodi querelam seu occasionem habet.

Et sic penes se detinebit quousque debita per illos fiat restitutio secundum quod adjudicabitur diesque restitutionis hujusmodi hinc inde certus prefigetur ac limitabitur.

Et quemcunque constitutum terminum pretergredi seu violare contigerit penam dupli incursurum seu forisfacturum, quod si pars delinquens eandem penam sic forisfactam unacum adjudicata restitutione non persolverit infra decem dies proxime tunc sequentes tunc dictus dominus de Slane aut mareschallus pignus sufficiens capiet pro solutione ejusdem tam restitutionis quam pene, quo satisfacto, pignus hujusmodi iterum dimittet.

[2.] Item: Quod omnia hujusmodi bona que per filium suum Eugenium capta fuerant post ultimam ordinationem habitam apud Kenlys plene in integrum restituentur.

[1] O'Reilly.

1558. fol. 73b. Et dictus Eugenius propterea quod more guerrino seu bellico invasit partes Anglicanas ipse infra decem dies post datam presentium ad dominum deputatum accedet ad pardonacionem suam pro tali crimine humiliter postulandum.

Et insuper pro redemptione seu fine transgressionis sue dabit centum vaccas domine regine.

[3.] Item: Quod dictus Orayly obligabitur ad respondendum pro omnibus suis filiis et aliis quibuscumque personis sub ejus jurisdictione existentibus quatenus ipsi et quilibet ipsorum se erga suas majestates bene et fideliter gesserint, et pro pace observanda versus omnes suarum majestatum subditos Anglicanos. Et si aliquis ex patria sua in hoc articulo deliquerit; quod ipse delinquentem in manus domini deputati tradet aut pignus sufficiens pro restitutione dampni commissi.

[4.] Item: Quod ipse sine speciali licencia domini deputati non conducet nec in sua patria remanere quovismodo permittet aliquos Scotos aut alios extranee nationis quoscunque.

[5.] Item: In sua patria remanere non permittet absque licencia domini deputati aliquos ex stirpe Omore sive Occhonor aut ullum ex eorum sequacibus nec aliquos alios cujuscunque generis qui rebelles exstiterint contra suas majestates, quin eos omnes pro virili et posse suo quantum in illo fuerit apprehendere conabitur et apprehensos ad manus domini deputati perducet.

fol. 74. Et si contingat aliquos hujusmodi malefactores seu rebelles ad patriam dicti Orayly, illo ignorante, subterfugere et habita inde noticia dictus dominus deputatus ad illum scripserit pro apprehensione hujusmodi malefactorum, quod tunc prefatus Orayly summam diligentiam et operam suam prestabit ut illos capere posset, captosque ad dominum deputatum perducet aut cuicumque ipse assignaverit.

Ac etiam quod omnes latrones et hujusmodi predones qui furtum aliquod seu rapinam commiserint in partibus Anglicanis et illud infra patriam illius subduxerint, apprehendi faciet et apprehensos ad vicecomitem illius comitatus propinquioris transmittet et rei sublate quoad melius poterit restitutionem faciet.

Eadem et similis ordinatio erga illum observetur, si in partes Anglicanas quicunque fuerit ab illius jurisdictione ita surreptum.

Et quod neque ille ullos exules in patriam Anglicanam in patria sua demorare permittet neque ullus ex patria Anglicana aliquem exulem in patriam suam in partibus Anglicanis demorare permittet.

[6.] Item: Quod dictus Orayly portabit omnia onera et servicia regi majestati debita tam in promovendo exercitu equitum et turbariorum, quociens opus fuerit quam in solvendo solito numero Scoticorum quemadmodum debet aut temporibus elapsis solvere consuevit.

fol. 74b. [6.] Item: Quod ipse per totam suam jurisdictionem monetam regiam debito suo valore recipi faciat sicuti per partes Anglicanas passim et ubique currit.

Et pro omni premissorum perfecta observatione suscepit corporale juramentum; ac si deliquerit in aliquo premissorum, solvet domine regine mille martas.

Ac etiam concordationem istam proclamari faciet in patria sua et sigillum suum et sigilla filiorum suorum et omnium liberorum tenentium patrie sue hiis scriptis apponi faciet et nobis illam mittet ad perpetuam rei memoriam.

fol. 75. [LXIX.]—At Rathetothe, the xxvii[th] of Maye, anno 1558:

T. Sussex.—It ys condescendid, concludid and agreid by us, the lorde deputie, the lordes spirituall and temporall of the realme, and the reste of the king and quenes majesties counsaill of the same, whoose names be hereunto subscribed, assemblid at Rathetothe the daye and yere above wrytten, that for soondry erneste respectes and consideracyons tending as well to the furtherance of ther majesties servyce, as for the resisting of foreyn invasion yf any shulde chaunce, that ther shalbe a generall hosting proclamed by wrytt, according thauncyente custome, for fourty dayes, after the rate of thre plowe lande to a carte. 1558.

The same to sett fourthe within ten dayes nexte after proclamacyon made for that purpose, and to be orderid and devydid in suche sorte as within the saide proclamacyon shall be prescribed unto the cessors of the severall baronyes within every the shieres leviable.

H. Dublin, canc.—G. Kyldare.—W. Midensis.—Oswald Massingberd, prior.—Thomas Darensis.[1]—J. Slane.—P. of Trymleteston.—Christofor Kyllen.—H. Sydney.—Henry Radeclyff.—Gerald Aylmer.—John Parker.—Thomas Cusake.

[LXX.]—At the Navan, this xxiii^th^ of September, 1558: fol. 75b.

H. Sydney.—Memorandum: That lyke as yt was concluded and agreid by the right honorable the lorde deputie and others the lordes of the counsell at Dublin, nowe at the said lorde deputies late departure[2] to the seas, that one hundrethe good and hable kerne shoulde be cessed for defence and saluegarde of the borders of the countie of Methe next unto Offally, even so we, the lorde justice and counsell, with others of the nobylyte whose names are hereunto subscribed, do confyrme the same, willing and commanding that their chardge shalbe indifferently leavyed upon the [w]hole countie of Mythe, during the space of six wyckes, and that they be at thappointement of suche as are nominated in the commyssion which is under the brode seale.

Jenico, vic. of G[ormanston].—W. Midensis.—P. of Trymleteston.
—Christofer Donsene.—Gerald Aylmer.—Robert Dyllon.—
Thomas Cusake.

[LXXI.]—At the Navan, this foresaid xxiiith of September, 1558: fol. 76.

Memorandum: Where yt was concluded by the right honorable the lorde deputie and counsell, at his lordeshipes departure to the seas, that Thomas Flemyng shulde have the leading of one hundrethe kerne of the Polles, to serve in suche places of the northe as the saide lorde deputie did appoint, with thurtie one dayes victaill, and that the said Thomas shulde have the intertaynement of twenty of the same nomber towardes his paynes for leading of the rest:

---

[1] Thomas Leverous, bishop of Kildare.

[2] "December the fourth [1557] the lord lieutenant was recalled from Ireland, who, together with his lady, went to Houth, seven miles from Dublin, and from thence into England. Upon this transportation of my lord lieutenant, and his delay in England, after the first day of the ensuing March, the parliament, that was adjourned at Droghedagh, was dissolved. The second day after my lord lieutenants departure, [Hugh] Curwine, [archbishop of Dublin,] chancellor, and [sir Henry] Sidney, treasurer of the army, were made justices, after they had taken the oath in Dublin, at Christchurch, before the great altar. Having first heard mass, they received the royal sword from [sir George] Stanley, the marshal (with whom Sussex had left the sword to be delivered to them). They enjoyed the place till the sixth of February [1557-8] on which day Sidney, by the queen's command, alone was constituted justice, and received the sword in the same church, after the accustomed manner."—Annals of Ireland, by sir James Ware.

1558. And notwithstanding that the intertaynement of every kerne of the same Polles going to hostinges was used to be butt foure pence sterling by the day, yett nevertheless for that their travell in the said jorney is paynefull and trowblesome, and victaill more dearer nowe then before yt hathe bene, yt is condescended and agreid that for their wages, victaill and cariadge during the tyme of this jorney every kerne to have sex pence sterling per diem, not meaning that this shalbe a president whereby to chardge the countrey at any tyme hereafter with any more then as they have bene accustomed to pay heretofore.

fol. 76*b*. [LXXII.]—An othe taken by the erle of Thomonde and the gentilmen of Thomonde, the xth of Julii, anno 1558:

To be true and faithfull to the quenes majestie, her heires and successors, and her graces deputies for the tyme being.

To conceale no mattier that shalbe prejudiciall to her majestie, her heires and successors, the crowne of eny her realmes, or the person of her deputie for the tyme being.

To serve her majestie, her heires and successors, with all your force againste all foreyn ennemyes, civile rebelles and traytórs, whensoever you shall by her majestie, her heires and successors or the deputie be commaundid.

To maynteyn no foreyn ennemy or civell rebell and traytor within your countrey, but upon commandement from her majestie, etc. or the deputie, ye shall endeavor to apprehende all suche foreyne ennemyes traytours and rebelles and them to delyver as ye shalbe commandid.

To see all the freholders of the countrey to be maynteyned in ther right and kepte from unlawfull exactiones or extortions by others, and not to putt eny other impositions upon them then the capten of the countrey heretofore hathe by custome rightfully usid to doo or suche as by appoyntemente from ther majesties and the lorde deputie ye shalbe lycensid to doo.

fol. 77. To renounce for ever the name of Obryne and not to suffer eny suche name to be given to your selfe or eny other within your contrey, nor to levy any duetie as by the name of Obryne but by the name of erle of Tomonde and so to be callid in all places.

To be from hensfourthe a true and faithfull friende to the mayor and citezens of Lymerike and to mynyster justice upon all suche as shalbe within your rule that shalbe offenders againste the saide citie.

And according ordres taken heretofore ye shall not make clayme to anything on this side the Shennan.

For the gentilmen:

To be true and faithefull to ther majesties and ther deputie for the tyme being, and under them to serve truely therle of Tomonde and to yelde to hym as by the name of erle of Tomonde all suche dueties as of right did heretofore belonge to the capitayne of the countrey of Tomonde by what name so ever he were callid.

To renounce the name of Obryne to be at eny tyme hereafter usid amongst them nor ther capitayn and ruler to be callid by eny other name then erle of Tomonde, and to hym and his heyres to adhere and serve according to the tenor of ther majesties lettres patentes grauntid to the saide erle and to followe and prosecute to the uttermoste the traytor Donell Obryne and all others that shall take his parte and all others that shall goo aboute to usurpe the name of Obryne.

For performance hereof to putt in ther severall pledges.

[LXXIII.]—The indenture betwixte therle of Ormonde and therle of Desmonde and his son, the lorde Geralde,—[1]Julii, anno 1558: 1558. fol. 77b.

Memorandum: Wheare greate matier of contencion long tyme hathe dependid betwene the right honorable the erles of Desmonde and Ormonde, concernyng as well the title of the pryse wynes of Youghall and Kynsale as also the boundyng of the countie of Typperary, how farre the liberties doo extende and whether the manors of Clomell, Kilfeakill and Kilshelan, being within the said countie, ought to aunswer to the saide lybertie. The saide erle of Ormonde claymyng by his patente of graunte of the saide libertie that the same extende in all places within the same countie withoute anye exception of any parte thereof other then in the saide letteres patentes by speciall wordes ys exceptid and the saide erle of Desmonde, claymyng title to the said pryse wynes of Youghall and Kynsale, thorough long contynuance of possession in hymselfe and his ancestors; and also supposing that the boundes of the saide countie extende not so farre as the saide erle of Ormonde pretendeth to have liberty; and that the said abbay lands whiche he hathe in farm within the saide countie together with the saide manors ought not to aunswer to the sayde liberty by the saide graunte:

Thoroughe whiche contencions ther hathe happenyd dyverse harmes and injuryes in praying and wasting of contries as well by the saide erle of Desmonde and the lorde Garrett, his sonne, upon therle of Ormonde, fol. 78.
as by therle of Ormondes brethren upon the saide erle of Desmonde and lorde Garralde, and in eschewyng of more contencion and such inconvenyence as by the same might ensue dyverse wayes. The said erles of Desmonde and Ormonde and the said lorde Gerald appearing before us submytting themselves to our order in all ther contencions.[2]

[LXXIV.]—Recognisances apon the erles of Desmonde and Ormonde, etc.: fol. 79.

Coram domino deputato et consilio regie majestatis, apud Lymericum, xii°, die Julii, anno 1558:

Ego, Jacobus, comes Desmonie, et Geraldus, filius, fatemur nos debere regie majestati duo milia librarum sterling':

The condicion of this recognysance ys suche that if the saide erle and Geralde performe observe and fulfill all and singuler the contents of payre of indetures made betwixte them and the erle of Ormonde, bering date the xi[th] of July, anno 1558, then this recognysance to be voyde, otherwise, etc.

Coram deputato et consilio regie majestatis, apud Lymericum, xii° die Julii anno 1558.

Ego, Thomas, comes Ormonie, fateor me debere regie majestati duo milia librarum sterling':

The condicion of this recognysance ys suche that if the saide Thomas doo performe all and singuler the contentes of a payre of indentures made betwixte the said erle and James, erle of Desmonde and Gerott, his son, for his parte to be performyd bering date the xi[th] of July, anno 1558, then this recognysance etc., otherwise, etc.

---

[1] Blank in MS.

[2] Fol. 78b. is blank.

1558. fol. 79b. [LXXV.]—An indenture betwixte the erle of Desmonde and the lorde Roche,—[1] Julii, anno 1558:

Memorandum: That for the matier in varyance of long tyme depending betwene the right honorable the erle of Desmonde and the lord Roche and Davy Roche, sonne and heire to the saide lord Roche, yt is by bothe ther consentes agreid and orderid by us, the lorde deputie and counsaill, whose names be hereunto subscribed, that the same erle shall ymediately delyver —[2] son and heire to the saide David Roche, nowe in his hande as pledge with the sayde erle, the saide David, payeng for his chardge the somme of—[3] currant money of Irelande, and the same somme to remayne in the handes of the mayor of Lymerike saufely to be kepte till the said somme of —[4] be paid to the said erle or to suche as he shall appoynte and that the saide lorde Roche and David shall from hensforthe enjoye ther countrey callid the Roches countrey, with all other ther rightfull enherytance, withoute imposition or exaction to be layed upon them or ther contrey by the saide erle or any of his by extorte power, and that the freholders nor thinheritors of the same dwelling in the said contry shall not hensforthe (in eschuying inconvenyence and trooble to the countrey) be retayned by the saide erle, but shall remayne to serve the saide lorde Roche and David (and that the said erle shall delyver presentely to the said lorde Roche and David all suche castelles as he detayneth from thinheritors of the same countrey wrongfullye withoute pretence
fol. 80. of any former order or arbytremente given for the same to the saide erle. And suche castelles and landes as the saide erle pretende title unto by purchase, arbytremente, morgage or other enheritance, the same title to be examyned before tharchebushop of Cashell, the bushope of Lymerike and sir Thomas Cusake, who be chosen and appointid by us as arbytrors indifferente with the consentes of the said erle, the lorde Roche and David Roche, to end and determyne as well the same as all other ther contencions and after the saide arbitrors to order the possession of the saide castelles accordingly:

And for the better performance of the ordre whiche the sayde arbitrors shall take betweene the saide erle, lorde Geralde, his sonne, and the lord Roche and David, his sonne, the lorde Geralde to delyver unto the saide arbitrors handes suche pledge as the said David Roche for himselfe and his father shall name, the same pledge to remayne in ther hands for performance as well of all suche debte, restitution or amendes to the parties grevid as shalbe adwardid againste the saide erle and lorde Geralde. If the saide pledge by the sayde lorde Geralde be not sufficient to aunswer the same, then the saide erle to delyver the saide arbytrors suche other sufficient pledge for aunswering the said lorde Roche and Davides demaunde as the saide David shall name, and the saide David to remayne as pledge in the handes of the saide arbitrors for performance of ther
fol. 80b. lordshipes arbytremente to the saide erle and lorde Geralde.

Providid alwaies and also we doo order that all former arbytremente, decreeis, ordres or judgements that hathe passid betwene the said erle the lorde Geralde, the lorde Roche and David, or any of them that shalbe provid before the saide arbytrors that hathe byn orderid with ther mutuall consentes the same to stonde in force according to theffecte thereof and the saide arbitrors to ratyfie and confyrme the same in all thinges and to proceed to thordering of the reste.

And for keping of ther majesties peace the saide erle and lorde Geralde and the saide David Roche hathe aswell taken ther corporall othes before us, as also bounde in severall recognysance to the king and

[1], [2], [3], [4] Blank in MS.

queenes majesties every of them in m.*li.* to be rerid of ther goodes and cattelles, etc. 1558.

[LXXVI.]—An indenture betwixte the erle of Desmonde and Tege McCormoke, xvii° Julii anno supradicto [1558]: fol. 81.

Memorandum: Wheare Tege McCormocke complayned before us, the lorde deputie and counsaill, at Lymeryke, the xviiith of June, 1558, againste the right honorable the erle of Desmond and the lorde Gerott, his son, of dyverse praies, killing, burnyng, spoyling, keping of castelles and expulsing hym oute of his landes and countrey, besides the retaynyng of —[1], son to the saide Tege, in pryson—[2] yeares and more, withoute juste cause, as he affyrmeth: To the whiche complaynte the saide erle and lorde Gerott, appearing before us, denyeng parte of the saide complayntes to be true, and justyfieng his dooinge in the reste againste the said Tege, as well in claymyng title to his contrey of Muscry, affirmyng the saide Tege to be bastarde and that the saide erle, as in right of the ladye his wiffe, being right enheritrix to the same, as she affirmeth, ought to have the same, as for other dyverse causes:

But for that the saide contentyons being great, presentely coulde not be orderid for lacke of tyme to trye and examyne the same and to thentente to have the same indyfferently endyd and determyned, the saide erle and lorde Gerott, his son, for ther parte, and the saide Tege, in the behalfe of hym and his countrey, for his parte, with thadvyyse and consente of us the lorde deputie and counsaill, whose names are fol. 81*b*. under written, at Lymerike, the day and yeare aforesayde, did submytt themselfs to stonde, observe and obaye the order, decre, arbytremente and fynall judgemente of the moste reverende father in God, Rowlande, archebusshop of Casshell, and the reverende father in God, Hughe, busshop of Lymeryke, and sir Thomas Cusake, arbytrors indifferently chosen betwene them to ende ther saide contentions (the title of lande and tryall of bastardy only exceptid):

The same order to be indentid and signed with the handes of the saide arbytrors and delyvered to the saide parties on this syde the fest of Petri ad vincula nexte ensuying, and for the better performance of the sayde order given by the saide arbitrors betweene the said parties as well as the saide erle and lorde Gerott, as the said Tege McCormoke stonde bounde to other in two thousande pounde besides that that eche of the partyes shall delyver such pledge into the hands of the sayde arbitrors saufely to be kepte as every of them shall chuse upon other.

And furder, we, the lorde deputie and counsaill, whoose names are subscribed doo order and decree that the said erle of Desmonde shall delyver to the handes of the saide arbitrors —[1] son to the saide Tege, remaynyng in his custody and keping as pledge ther to remayne till the said Tege delyver thother suffycient pledge into ther saide handes fol. 82. as shalbe named being in his possibilitie to doo, and after the saide pledge delyvered, as afore, then the saide arbytrors to enlarge the saide son to his said father.

And furder we order that eche of them shall kepe the king and quenes majesties peace to other their men, followers and countreys, withoute taking of exactyons, cesse of galloglas horsemen or kerne or imposing of any other chardges or entery upon others countreys and in especyall on Muscry, but onely to stonde to the order of tharbytrors, and this upon payne of thre thowsande poundes to be forfayte to our soverayne lorde and lady the king and quenes majesties, etc.

---

[1], [2] Blank in MS.

1558. fol. 82b. [LXXVII.]—In hac indentura tripartita facta die mensis Julii anno Domini 1558, apud villam regiam Galvic[1] inter honorabilem et prepotentem virum Thomam Radeclyffe, Sussexie comitem, prenobilis ordinis gartherii militem, dominum de Egremonte, etc., et ceteros de consilio regali quorum nomina subscribuntur, ex una parte, honorabilem virum, dominum comitem de Clanrycarde[2], pro se et omnibus singulisque generosis et aliis quibuscunque inhabitantibus patrie de Clanrycarde, ex secunda parte, et maiorem, ballivos et communitatem dicte ville regie de Galvia, ex tertia, continentur quedam ordinationes facte per dictum dominum deputatum et consilium pro meliori gubernacione dicte ville et patrie, ut testificantur quedam convenciones et compositiones reciproce inter se invicem pacte sicut hic sequitur :—

[1.] In primis : Dictus comes, generosi et ceteri de Clanrycarde et maior et communitas dicte regie ville non solum Catholicam fidem et religionem quantum in ipsis est promovebunt et defendent, sed omnes etiam renitentes et contradicentes pro eorum posse corrigi, in judicium vocari et debito modo puniri facient :

Juramentumque corporale susceperunt quod observabunt pacem regiam erga se invicem, quodque stabunt omnibus ordinacionibus que pro presenti constituentur per dictum dominum et consilium in omnibus materiis in controversia dependentibus inter se aut eorum aliquos.

Et pro finicione omnium contentionum que imposterum inter eos aut eorum aliquos contingere possint et que antehac contigerunt et non sunt determinate, proque quiete meliori inhabitantium dictarum patrie et ville, fol. 83. dictus dominus deputatus et consilium constituerunt et per presentes constituerunt dictum dominum comitem de Clanrycarde, archiepiscopum Tuamensem,[3] episcopum Clonfertensem,[4] maiorem[5] ville regie de Galvia pro tempore existenti, Thomam Martyn et Nicholaum Filium Stephani Lynche aut aliquis eorum sex, quinque, quatuor, tres vel duos, quorum dictus comes, dictus archiepiscopus aut episcopus predicti semper fore unum et dictus maior, dictus Thomas vel dictus Nicholaus semper fore alium, commissionarios regios tam ad audiendum et examinandum quam ad terminandum atque finaliter finiendum omnes causas atque materias in controversia jam existentes aut que imposterum existent inter dictam villam et dictam patriam aut aliquam personam aut personas in eisdem aut earum aliqua habitantes, quorum ordinationes erunt bone et valentes.

Et ut dicte ordinationes eo melius perimpleri atque perfici possint dictus comes in dicta patria et maior pro tempore existens in dicta villa distringent et sufficientia districta sive pignora capient pro solutione et satisfactione omnium earum rerum que per dictos commissionarios erunt decreta sive ordinata et eadem districta sive pignora tradent ad manus partium quorum intererit donec fuerit solutio facta juxta dicta decreta sive ordinaciones.

Et etiam per dictum dominum deputatum et consilium ordinatum et constitutum est quod omnes dicti commissionarii convenient ad villam predictam xxvj^to die hujus mensis, ac postea ad finem stipulatorum lx. dierum et sedebunt quamdiu eis libuerit pro executione premissorum, et si aliquis eorum se absentem tenuerit, nisi specialiter ad negotia regie majestatis assignatus tunc fuerit, et tunc in eisdem occupatus fuerit

---

1 Galway.
2 Richard de Burgo, earl of Clanricarde.
3 Christoper Bodkin, Archbishop of Tuam.
4 Roland de Burgo, Bishop of Clonfert and Elphin.
5 Ambrose Lynch Fitz Martin.—*See* account of archives of Galway in Tenth Report of Royal Commission on Historical MSS. 1885, App. v. 417.

presens taliter delinquens forisfaciet domine regine pro quolibet die quinque markas. 1558. fol. 83*b*.

Et ulterius constitutum est per dictum dominum deputatum et consilium quod ipse dictus comes in patria et maior pro tempore existens in villa pro posse eorum perimplebunt, perficient et execucionem facient omnium decretorum et ordinationum que per ipsos dictos commissionarios erunt facta sive edita.

Et si aliquis eorum non fuerit habilis ad exequendum predicta decreta, alter eorum auxilium ad posse suum ei dabit tociens quociens dictis commissionariis visum fuerit conveniens, ita ut pro meliori executione premissorum auctoritatem suam junctim et divisim exercere possint et valeant, ut predicitur.

Et predictus comes promisit et concessit pro se et omnibus dictis inhabitantibus patrie de Clanrycarde, et pariter ordinatum est per dictum dominum deputatum et consilium quod ipsi nullum omnino impedimentum dabunt alicui persone sive aliquibus personis quominus possint libere et ad placitum eorummet ire ad mercatum dicte ville de Galvia diebus ad mercandum constitutis, videlicet, quolibet Mercurio et Sabbato et ibidem libere vendere suas res quas vendere voluerint.

Et quod si aliquis aperte sive secrete prohibitionem fecerit contra hanc nostram ordinacionem forisfaciet regie majestati pro qualibet prohibitione sic directe vel indirecte facta in contrarium ejusdem xl. *li*. leviandas per dictum comitem de Clanrycarde infra viginti dies postquam talis prohibitio probata fuerit fuisse facta coram dictis commissionariis, dimidium ejusdem fore ad usum regie majestatis et aliud dimidium ad usum ejusdem comitis ejus labore in leviando penam predictam.

Et ulterius ordinatum est per dictum dominum deputatum et consilium regium quod singuli inhabitantes in dicta patria permittent inhabitantes ville regie predicte quiete et absque ullo impedimento, gravamine aut exactione secum transferre de tempore in tempus omnes tales decimas quales eorum aliquis emerit aut aliquo alio justo modo acquiret pro uno aut pluribus annis. fol. 84.

Et quicumque aliquo modo prohibebit aut impedimentum dabit contra premissa alicui persone in contrarium dicte nostre ordinacionis et sic coram dictis commissionariis probatum fuerit forisfaciet duplicem valorem rei detente ei cui injuria commissa est, et simplicem valorem regie majestati pro contempte leviandum et dividendum ut supra.

Et quod inhabitantes dicte patrie permittent inhabitantes dicte ville regie negotiare et transire per omnes partes dicte patrie de Clanrycarde libere cum bonis et mercibus suis et eadem venditioni exponere et ea vendere sicut melius volunt et queant absque aliqua custumia aut exactione inde solvenda alicui persone.

Et pari modo quod omnia que vel pro pecuniis suis ement vel pro mercibus commutabunt vel aliquo alio justo modo acquirent secum adducere atque transferre possint et queant absque ullo impedimento sive molestatione aliquorum.

Et si aliqua parcella dictorum mercium aut bonorum contigerit esse capta ab aliquo manu forti in contrarium hujus nostre ordinationis quod dominus soli in quo eadem bona, merces, pecunia aut commoditates fuerint capta non solum solvat parti injuriate justum valorem captorum infra decem dies postquam idem fuerit juste probatum coram dictis commissionariis verum etiam pro contemptu forisfaciet domine regine dimidium valoris bonorum sic captorum leviandum et dividendum ut supra.

1558. fol. 84b. Proviso tamen quod si dominus soli probabit coram dictis commissionariis infra decem dies postquam talis violencia facta fuerit quod per alienos servos vel sequelas facta fuerit, et nomina eorum dicet, quod tunc (si non erit dolus in illo) ipse liberabitur a tali solutione et dominus dictorum servorum sive sequelarum persolvet omnia premissa.

Ac etiam quod pariformiter maior, ballivi et inhabitantes ville predicte permittent dictos inhabitantes patrie de Clanrycarde venire et negociare in dicta villa libere cum bonis et mercibus suis et eadem venditioni exponere et vendere prout melius volunt et queant absque aliqua illicita custumia inde solvenda.

Et quod omnes commoditates que vel pro pecuniis ement vel pro mercibus commutabunt vel aliquo alio justo modo acquirent secum auferre possint et queant absque ullo impedimento sive molestatione aliquorum.

Et si aliqua parcella dictorum bonorum mercium aut commoditatum contigerit esse capta per aliquem infra dictam villam et quod dictus maior restitutionem non faciet indilate postquam iniuriatus querelam suam maiori dabit quod dictus maior forisfaci et, etc. ut supra.

Et insuper dictus dominus deputatus ordinavit quod nemo in dicta villa districtum sive pignus capiet pro aliquo offenso sive crimine commisso extra libertatem ville predicti ab aliquo de inhabitantibus patrie predicte de Clanrycarde, et pariter quod nemo de inhabitantibus patrie de Clanrycarde districtum sive pignus capiet de aliquo inhabitanti dicte ville pro aliquo offenso sive crimine per ipsum commisso infra libertatem dicte ville nisi ut per ordinationem dictorum commissionariorum assignatum fuerit sub pena pro tali districto sive
fol. 85. pignore sic capto primum reddere pignus statim parti aggravate et perdere debitum pro quo pignus captum erit.

Et etiam forisfaciet regie majestati valorem debiti pro quo pignus est captum fore leviandum et dividendum ut supra.

Proviso tamen quod pro certo et approbato debito arrestari possit quevis persona donec dederit fidejussores ad respondendum coram dictis commissionariis in proxima eorum cessione sive congressu.

Et quod nemo dicte patrie de Clanrycarde petet aut requiret salvum conductum veniendo ad dictam villam regiam pro aliquo debito alicui inhabitati ville pertinenti neque aliquis de dicta villa petet aut requiret aliquem salvum conductum a dicto comite aut aliquo alio de patria eundo ad patriam pro aliquo debito alicui de patria pertinenti.

Et quod si fortassis talis salvus conductus fuerit petitus et ex aliqua parte concessus quod erit nullius momenti aut valoris sed totaliter frustratus.

Et quod omnes ordinaciones predicte erunt boni valoris et effectus inter dictam villam et McWillelmum Burke et omnes de ejus regimine, Okelly, Omadden, Offlarty, Omayly et omnes sub eorum et cujuslibet eorum regimine omnia forisfactura levianda ut supra.

Et pro perfectione omnium et singulorum premissorum non solum dictus comes pro se et patria predicta verum etiam dictus maior, ballivi et consilium ville predicte susceperunt coram nobis corporale juramentum ac etiam fecerunt fidele promissum super eorum cujuslibet ligea fidelitate erga regiam majestatem quod premissa omnia et singula perficient et perimplebunt.

fol. 85b. Finaliter: Dicti commissionarii fideliter promiserunt et corporaliter juraverunt ut supra premissa diligenter inquirent ac directam celerem et justam ordinacionem ac sententiam in omnibus causis coram eis venientibus pronuntiabunt, et quod easdem cum omni expeditione in executionem ponent et poni curabunt ad optimum eorum posse et quantum in eorum potentia fuerit possibile. 1558.

Et ulterius ordinatum est quod unusquisque generosus dicte patrie de Clanrycarde dabit nomina omnium de ejus sequela et tenentium et servitorum in scriptis infra quadraginta dies post datum presentium ad manus dicti comitis et dicti maioris, pro quibus omnibus respondebunt de tempore in tempus pro eisdem tam pro perfectione dictorum ordinacionum quam omnium aliorum factorum per eos.

Et quod nemo de patria predicta retinebit aliquos respondend' alienigenas imposterum et si jam aliquos habent eos exspedient.

Ac etiam nos, dictus deputatus et consilium, requirimus, regioque nomine stricte mandamus dictos commissionarios quod non permittent aliquam personam temporalem gaudere illegitime aliquibus possessionibus ecclesiasticis, neque aliquam personam spiritualem gaudere aliquibus possessionibus ecclesiasticis contra formam statutorum in tali casu provisorum.

Proviso semper quod nichil in hiis indenturis expressis prejudiciale erit libertatibus et privilegiis dicto ville neque in aliquo extendetur citra ut inhabitantes dicte ville privilegiis et libertatibus suis libere uti non possint.

[LXXVIII.]—An order towching Okarwell,[1]—[2]Augusti, anno 1558:

Memorandum: Where William Ower Okarwell, beyng of late by us made chieffe capitayne of his nation, and appoyntid to have the name of Okarwell, hathe behavid himselfe so traytorously towardes ther majesties as it ys by us thoughte expedyente to deprive hym of the same title and name and to proclayme hym traytor, we wyshing the good order of that countrey have by the consente of the reste of the Okarwelles and others the freeholders of Ely appoynted Tege Okarwell, called ——[3] Tege, and claymyng as eldeste of that name to be capitayn of his nacyon, and to have the name of Okarwell, so as the same Tege shall aunswer to ther majesties oute of the countrey of Ely all such dueties as heretofore others beryng the name of Okarwell were bounde to doo and shalbe expressed in his lettres patentes that shalbe grauntid to hym of the same, and that all thinhabitantes of Ely shall aunswer to the same Tege all suche dueties as of right belong to the name of Okarwell and to the capitayne of that nacyon and countrey: fol. 86.

And where Molrone Okarwell, sonne to Calloghe Okarwell, was of late falsely betrayed in parlementes by the said traytor William Ower, we order that all things taken the same day from the saide Molrony shalbe presently redelyvered to him by Tege ——[4], apon his retorne, and for all other controversies betwene party and party in the contrey every man to stonde to suche order as shalbe by the breyhouns taken betwene them in the pretence of Tege or by his assignmente, and further that the same Tege, now Okarwell, and all others within the countrey shall to the uttermoste of ther powers pursue and followe to the dethe the same William Ower, Shane atlerane, Shane McPiers and every of them and that all the gentilmen and freholders of the saide countrey shall putt in ther pledges into the handes of the saide Tege, now Okarwell, for performance of the premisses. And for the full performance of all and singular the premysses as well the same Tege, nowe Okarwell, Molrone mac Colloghe, Shane ——[4] McGylshill, with the reste of the freholders fol. 86b.

[1] O'Cearbhaill, O'Carroll. *See* p. 34.

[2], [3], [4] Blanks in MS.

1558. of the countrey, have taken a corporall othe upon the holy Evangelists and the blessid sacramente of the aulter, as also we, the lord deputie, and the erle of Ormonde are become slanty to pursue the breakers of this order to the uttermoste.

fol. 87. [LXXIX.]—Certen notes enterid the xxvii[th] of Auguste, anno Domini 1558:

That John Grace, of Fowlkes courte, ys become suertye for Kedaghe Fitzpiers Omore to be fourthcomyng at all tymes at the lorde deputies calling.

[LXXIXA.]—Quarto Septembris, anno supradicto [1558]:

That the erle of Kildare hathe bownde himselffe to the lorde deputie and counsaill that he shall have ready to aunswer at all callinges Arte Omolloye, Phelym Omolloy and Margarete Occhonor, pardoned at his requeste.

fol. 87b. [LXXX.]—Apud Dubliniam, xxi° die Octobris, anno 1558:

H. Sydney.—For the matter in controversy betwixte the cessors of the barony of Kenlys in the countie of Methe, on the behalffe of our soverayne lorde the king and quenes majesties, and one John Hammon of the New haggarde in the right and title of William Nugiente gentilman, who claymeth to have the same Newe haggarde and the landes thereof free from all manner of cessis and other impositions putt upon the said barony for the servyce of ther majesties:

Forasmoche as upon the mattier harde and debatid before us and severall depositions and wyttenes also produced on either syde, ther appered no sufficient grounde or mattier wherby the saide New haggarde shulde be free and exempte (saving onely that the saide Hammon alleagid to have a dede approving the saide fredom, whiche nevertheles he did not exhibite, nor yet coulde shewe before us any suche wryting:

Yt is orderid and decreid by us, the lorde justice and others of the counsell whose names be hereunto subscribed, that the sayde New haggarde shalbe contrybutary and aunswerable to all cessis, hostings and journeys as the reste of the said barony was, ys and shalbe from tyme to tyme till the saide dede or other more sufficient mattier then hathe yet appearid be exhibited.

H. Dublin, canc.—P. Barnewall of T[rymleteston].—John Travers.—James Bathe.—Patryk Whit, barone.—Robert Dyllon.—John Plunket.

fol. 88. [LXXXI. 1.]—Inter recorda scaccarii de termino Sancti Hillarii anno regni domini Henrici, nuper regis Anglie octavi xxxvi:[1] rotulo xiii°.

Certeyn warrantes for hawkes and houndes grauntid to the marques of Saria as followeth:

Right trusty and welbeloved and trusty and right welbeloved, we grete you well: Letting you wytt that upon instante suete made unto us by our right trusty and right entierly beloved coosen and counsaillour, the duke of Abberkirke[2] of Spayn, on the behalffe of the marques of Saria and his sonne, that yt moght like us to graunte unto the saide marques and to his saide son, and to the longer liver of them, yerely

[1] A.D. 1534. [2] Albuquerque.

oute of that our realme of Irelande two goshawkes and foure greyhoundes; forasmoche as the saide duke hathe don unto us in attendance upon our person in thies our warres very acceptable pleasure and servyce, and for that we be enformyd that the sayde marques beareth unto us speciall good wyll and affection, tendering as well the contynuance of the same, as the erneste requeste of the sayde duke, whose doughter the said marques sonne hathe in marriage, we have byn movyd to graunte his suete in that behalffe. And therfore our pleasure ys that by vertue hereof not onely you, our deputie for the tyme beyng, shall take order for the delyvery of the saide hawkes and greyhoundes unto such person as the said marques and his son, or the longer lyver of them, shall yerely with their lettres addresse unto you for that purpose, but also that you fol. 88b.
our thesaurour, shall, of suche our treasure as from tyme to tyme shall come to your handes, contente and paye the chardges of byeng of the saide hawkes and greyhoundes. Whereof our further pleasure ys that all our audytors and others having chardge of our accomptes there shall make unto you juste allowance from yere to yere during the saide terme, and thies our lettres shalbe a sufficiente warrante and discharge unto you, our saide deputie, treasauror, and to all other to whome in case yt shall appertayne as yf we did yerely addresse severall lettres for execucion of our pleasure in the premysses accordingly.

Yeoven under our signet at our pallayce of Westminster, the ix daye of December, the xxxvi[th] yere of our raigne.[1]

To our right trusty and welbeloved counsaillour, sir Anthony Sentleger, knight of our order, deputie of our realme of Irelande, and one of the gentilmen of our prevy chamber, and to our trusty and right welbeloved counsaillour, William Brabazone, esquier, vicethesauror of our said realme, and to our deputie and vicethesaurour for the tyme being, and to all others to whome in case yt shall appertayne.

[2.]—Inter recorda scaccarii de termino Sancte Trinitatis, anno fol. 89.
regni domini Edwardi, nuper regis Anglie, sexti secundo:[2] rotulo xliii[tio]:

Edwardus sextus etc. Universis et singulis ad quos presentes littere nostre pervenerint, salutem et sinceram dilectionem: Studium et affectum quem nobilis atque illustris vir, don Fernandus de Castro, marchio de Saria, erga clarissime recordationis serenissimum parentem nostrum semper antea gessit ut in nos postmodum veluti hereditario quod benevolencie nomine transtulit ita ipsius bene affecte voluntatis memores vehementer eum amamus charumque habemus, intelligentesque vario aucupii et venacionis genere animi recreandi gratia ipsum plurimum oblectari, volumus ea quoque in parte nostram in eum affectionem vicissim declarare, annuatim itaque illi dedimus et concessimus in nostro Hibernie regno duos accipitres seu falcones, quos goshawkes dicimus, et quatuor leporarios canes que eorum volatu, cursu et opera in suis aucupiis et venationibus quando ita volet uti possit.

Proinde nostro in dicto Hibernie regno deputato harum litterarum nostrarum virtute et vigore injungimus et mandamus ut predictum accipitrum et canum numerum ex prestantiori quidem genere eidem marchioni vel cuicunque ille commiserit nomine nostro prospitiat atque consignet. Et quemadmodum hoc utcumque exiguo signo nostri animi gratitudinem testari cupimus, ita ab eodem deputato nostro quod hiis litteris mandamus prompte factum iri non dubitamus.

---

[1] A.D. 1534. [2] A.D. 1548.

fol. 89b. In cujus rei testimonium has litteras nostras fieri fecimus patentes, manu nostra subscripsimus ac sigilli nostri appensione jussimus communiri.

Date in regia nostra Westmonasterii, die 24 mensis Junii, anno Domini millesimo quingentesimo quadragesimo octavo, regni vero nostri secundo.[1]

fol. 90. [3.]—Philippus et Maria Dei gratia, rex et regina Anglie, Hispaniarum, Francie utriusque Sicilie, Jherusalem et Hibernie, fidei defensores, archiduces Austrie, duces Burgundie, Mediolani et Brabantie, comites Haspurgi, Flandrie et Tirolis: omnibus ad quos presentes nostre littere pervenerint salutem:

Intelligentes sincerum et singularem animi affectum quem illustris et nobilis vir, don Fernandus de Castro, marchio de Sarria, erga serenissimos pie memorie principes patrem et fratres nostros semper gesserit et erga nos in presenti gerit, et quod dictus marchio aucupii et venacionis lusu magnopere oblectatur, sciatis quod nos de gratia nostra et ad mitiorem in illum affectus declarationem, dedimus et concessimus et per presentes damus et concedimus predicto marchioni duos accipitres sive falcones, quos gossehawkes dicimus, et quatuor canes leporarios annuatim habendos et percipiendos dicto marchioni vel deputatis suis in regno nostro Hibernie per manus deputati nostri ejusdem regni nostri, proinde dicto deputato nostro per presentes mandamus quatenus predictum accipitrum et canum numerum
fol. 90b. ex prestantiori genere in eodem regno nostro provenientium prefato marchioni aut suis in hac parte deputatis tradat, tradi vel faciat. Volumus insuper quod si duo vel tres anni aut plures antequam dictus marchio per seipsum aut deputatos suos dictos accipitres et canes in forma precedenti recipiet fuerunt elapsi, nichilominus tot dicti numeri eidem marchioni tradentur quot a retro fuerunt quandocunque illi placuerit.

Et ad uberiorem voluntatis et gratie nostre erga dictum marchionem significationem, damus et concedimus posteris dicti marchionis, hoc est heredibus masculis ex corpore ejus procreati ut ipsi quoque duos accipitres sive falcones, quos gossehawkes dicimus, et quatuor canes leporarios annuatim per manus deputati pro tempore existentis percipiant.

In cujus rei testimonium has litteras nostras fieri fecimus patente. Testibus nobisipsis apud Westmonasterium, quintodecimo die Septembris,
fol. 91. annis regnorum nostrorum quinto et sexto [1558].

Per ipsos regem et reginam.

Hec vera est copia originalis confecta et sigillata et examinata verbatim per Ricardum Ravener.—Queque originalis est sub magno sigillo Anglie forma prescripta.—Ric. Ravener.[2]

1558. [LXXII.]—Apud Dubliniam, xij° die Novembris, anno 1558:

fol. 92. T. Sussex.—Memorandum: We, the lorde deputie, the lordes and nobilitie of the realme, with the reste of the king and quenes majesties counsaill assembled at Dublyn and considering as well the disfurnyture of their highnes fortes in Lexe and Offalley and other their majesties holdes and garrysons, as also the tyme of the yeare to be moste propyce for the vyctualling of the same, concludid upon a generall cesse, as well of wheate and malte, as bieffes, swyne and other provision for the [w]hole yere, the same to be levyed in maner and forme following that ys to saye:

[1] A.D. 1548.

[2] Fol. 91b. is blank.

In the countie of Methe, one thousande forty six peckes wheate and one thousande eight hundred seventy six peckes malte, whereof the thurde parte to be beare malte: the wheate and bere malte at foure shillinges sterling the pecke and the woote malte at two shillinges eightpence the pecke. 1558.

In the countye of Dublin: six hundred and four peckes wheate and one thowsande eight peckes malte, after like rate, pryce and division as before.

In the county of Kildare: six hundred and four score peckes wheate and seven hundred four score peckes malte, after the like rate and division.

In the countie of Uriell: six hundred ten peckes wheate and eight hundred and sixty peckes malte after like rate or division.

In the countie of Westmethe: three hundred thirty nine peckes wheate and five hundred and ten peckes malte after the same.

The [w]hole proporcyon to be brought in to the places appoyntid by Whitsontide nexte at the furtheste, that ys to saye: fol. 92*b*.

The corne of Methe[1] to the towne of Trym.

The corne of Kildare and also of Caterlaghe to Athye.

The corne of Uryell to Drogheda.

The corne of the countye of Dublyn to the towne of the Nasse:

And the corne of Westmethe to suche places as by commyssion hereafter shalbe appointed.

And for the cesse of bieffes and swyne to be levied in Irishemens contries and apon parte of the shieres westewarde ther[e] ar[e] lettres to be written:

To Oraply for bieffes two hundreth and one hundreth swyne;

To the Annaly, one hundred bieffes, swyne fifty;

To Magoghegan, fifty bieffes; swyne twenty five;

To Macoghlan, bieffes, thirty and fifteen swyne;

To Okelley sixty bieffes, and porkes thirty;

The Byrnes, kyne one hundreth and fifty swyne;

The Tooles of Omayle, twenty bieffes and ten porkes;

The countie of Caterlaghe, one hundreth forty beffes and twenty swyne;

Upper Ossory, one hundreth bieffes and fifty swyne;

The county of Typperary one hundred bieves and fifty porkes;

The county of Waterforde, one hundred bieves and fifty porkes;

Farny, fifty kyne and twenty five swyne;

Hughe Oge of Dartry, thirty kyne and fifteen swyne;

The Rayllies beyonde Sucke,[2] sixty bieffes and thirty porkes;

Macmahon, one hundred kyne and fifty swyne;

The bieffe at twelve shillings sterling and the porke at two shillings eightpence sterling.

Yt ys furder concludid that in the county of Wexforde ther shalbe cessid five hundreth peckes wotes at sixteen pence sterling the pecke;

In the countye of Kylkenny two hundreth peckes wootes at twenty fol. 93. pence sterling le pecke;

And in upper Ossory thre hundreth peckes wootes, at like rate.

The saide wootes to be delyverid as followeth, that is to saye:

They of Wexforde at the towne of Wexforde; those of Kilkenny at Leighlyn and they of Ossory at the forte in Lexe.

---

[1] In margin: "Memorandum: It is ordered that the corne of the baronyes of Donbyn and Ratothe shall be caryed to the Nas" [Naas.]

[2] The river Suca.

1558. And furder it ys orderid that the said corne shalbe delyverid at three severall tymes in Trym, Dublin and Kildare, according to the pecke of Dublin; and Lowthe after the measure of Drougheda; and for the wootes of Kilkenny and Ossory according to the measure of Kilkenny; and those of Wexforde after the pecke of Wexforde.

H. Dublin, canc.—Roland Baltynglas.—W Midensis.—Oswald Massingberd, prior.—J. Slane.—Christoffor Kyllen.—P. Barnewall of T[rymleteston.]—Christofor Donsany.—H. Sydney.—Richard Delvin.—Henry Radeclyff.—Robert Dyllon.—John Travers.—Thomas Cusak.—James Bathe.—J. Harbart.—John Plunket.[1]

fol. 94. [LXXXIII.]—Apud Dubliniam, 12 die Novembris, anno 1558:

T. Sussex.—Memorandum: That the twelfth of November, anno 1558, and in the fifth and sixth yeres of the raignes of our moste gracious soverayn lorde and lady Phillip and Mary, by the grace of God, king and quene, etc., the right hounorable therle of Sussex lorde deputie of the realme of Ireland delyvered in the counsaill chamber at Christes Churche to the moste reverende father in God, Hughe,[2] archebusshop of Dublyn, lorde chauncelor of the said realme, ther majesties greate seale of the same, newly sente over, and tooke of hym the olde seale whiche was ther presently defacid and broken in preasence of us whose names are hereunto subscribed:

And lykewyse the same tyme delyverid thother seales of the three ordynary courtes, videlicet, the chieffe place, thexchequer and common place, taking from thens the olde seales of the same, whiche were there in lyke sorte broken and defaced, videlicet, the seale of the chieffe place to justice Dillon; the seale of the common place to justice Talbott; and the seale of thexchequer to sir John Alen, to be deliverid to the barons of the same.

H. Dublin, canc.—W. Midensis.—J. Slane.—Christofor Kyllen.—H. Sydney.—Thomas Cusake.—George Stanley.—Henry Radeclyff.—John Plunket.—F. Harbart.[3]

fol. 95. [LXXXIV.]—Hec indentura, facta vicesimo secundo die mensis Januarii, anno Domini millesimo quingentesimo quinquagesimo octavo
1558–9. [1558–9] inter honorabilem virum Henricum Sydney, militem, dominum justiciarium regni Hibernie, et alios consiliarios domine regine ejusdem regni, quorum nomina inferius subscribuntur, ex una parte, et Willelmum Ower Occarwell[4] de principali Occarwellorum familia in patria de Ely Occarwell oriundum, ex altera parte, testatur quod cum dicta domina regina nunc per litteras suas patentes, gerentes datum xxi° die Januarii anno suprascripto, perdonaverit, remisserit et relaxaverit prefato Willelmo Ower Occarwell omnes et omnimodas prodiciones tam majores quam minores (personam suam regiam, nec fabricacionem false monete non tangentes) rebelliones, murdra, homicidia ac alia enormia et malefacta quecunque. Ac jam dictus Willelmus Ower Occarwell seipsum humillime submiserit et ad locum, statum et dignitatem capitaneatus totius patrie de Ely Occarwell predicte restitutus, reerectus et stabilitus existat, modo ordinatum et conventum est inter partes predictas sub forma sequenti:

[1.] In primis: Quod dictus Willelmus Ower Occarwell non solum Catholicam fidem et religionem quantum in se est promovebit et defendet,

[1] Fol. 93b. is blank. [2] Curwen. [3] Fol. 94b. is blank.
[4] See page 63.

sed eciam omnes contradicentes, et renitentes pro suo posse corrigi, in judicium vocari, et debito modo per omnia puniri faciet. 1558-9.

[2.] Item: Acceptabit et recognoscet predictam nunc dominam reginam legitimam sibi esse principem, illeque heredibus et successoribus suis adherebit contra omnes homines sicut fidelis subditus et sicut ceteri legei predicti regni Hibernie serviunt et obediunt aut servire et obedire debent. fol. 95b.

[3.] Item: Quod predictus Willelmus non adherebit nec confederabit cum inimicis aut rebellibus dicte domine regine aut successorum suorum sed illos pro viribus suis de tempore in tempus castigabit et prosequetur.

[4.] Item: Dictus Willelmus obligatur per presentes quod dicta domina regina habebit omnes terras et possessiones suas proprias, ac cetera omnia et singula debita ad suam celsitudinem spectancia, tam ea que modo jacent et existunt sub tutela et gubernacione predicti Willelmi quam que quovismodo posthac crescere et legitime provenire poterint ad usum ejusdem domine regine infra limites et jurisdictionem patrie de Ely Occarwell predicte.

[5.] Item: Similiter, prefatus Willelmus Ower Occarwell promptus et paratus erit in propria persona sua ad serviendum dicte domine regine et successoribus suis, ad mandatum domini deputati seu justiciarii Hibernie pro tempore existenti, cum duodecim equestribus[1] et viginti quatuor turbariis, bene armatis, in omni suo magno progressu bellico vulgariter nuncupato hostinges, cum victualibus pro se et suis ad expensas patrie sue quandocunque et quotiescumque hujusmodi deputato seu justiciario placebit ad hoc assignare et demandare.

[6.] Et in quolibet alio viagio et progressu subito contingenti serviet cum toto numero et potestate sua cum victualibus similiter pro duobus vel tribus diebus. fol. 96.

[7.] Et pro quolibet equestre faciente defectum (ut predicitur) forisfaciet et solvet pro quolibet die tres solidos et quatuor denarios; et pro quolibet turbario pro simili defectu denarios viginti.

[8.] Et predictus Willelmus concessit et promisit pro recognicione obediencie sue et quia tenet dictam patriam de domina regina, reddere et solvere singulis annis eidem domine regine, heredibus et successoribus suis duodecim libras legalis monete Hibernie, solvendas et tradendas officiariis suis annuatim in hoc regno ad festum Sancti Michaelis Archangeli tantum.[2]

[9.] Et prefatus Willelmus ulterius concessit et promisit daturum se quolibet anno bonnagium octoginta Scoticis, vulgariter nuncupatis galloglasses, pro uno quarterio anni.

[10.] Et quod indilate dabit et solvet prefato domino justiciario aut assignatis suis centum viginti martos pingues (ut moris est) pro nominacione et admissione sua ad locum capitanei sue nacionis et patrie de Ely predicta.

[11.] Item: Prefatus Willelmus non solum juramentum corporale prestitit super sancta Dei evangelia pro bono complemento premissorum, sed finaliter concessit eciam et promisit pro majori securitate fidelitatis sue erga dictam dominam reginam, heredes et succesores suas ponere obsides suos penes prefatum dominum justiciarium vel alibi prout melius eidem domino justiciario videbitur. fol. 96b.

In cujus rei et omnium premissorum fidem et testimonium tam predictus dominus justiciarius et alii de consilio regali subscripti quam prefatus Willelmus hiis scriptis manus suas et sigilla alternatim apposuerunt.

---

[1] In margin: "Note: horsemen." [2] In margin: "Note: rent."

1558-9. Data die et anno Domini suprascriptis, anno vero metuendissime domine Elizabethe, Dei gratia, Anglie, Francie et Hibernie regine, fidei defensoris, etc. primo [1558-9].

fol. 97. [LXXXV.]—By the lord justice and counsell [1558-9]:

H. Sydney.—Memorandum: That the viith of January, the furst yere of our most dere soverayne lady quene Elyzabethes raigne, we, the lord justice and other of her majesties counsell whose name be herennto, for redresse of sondry prayes and other grete ennormyties attempted betwene Ofarroll bane and Faughney[1] McTeig for the moytie of tanestshippe of the Offarolles countrey called Clantane, Offarroll bane pretending to have by his letteres patentes as well the captenshippe allotted to Offarroll bane, as also the said half tanistshippe of Clantane, as lardgely as any other like capten have sithens the dyvision of that countrey into twoo captenshipps had and enjoyed the same:

And Faughney, on the contrary parte, pretendid for that he had by election the tanestshippe of the said countrey he ought to have the commodyties and prouffyttes of the [w]hole tanestshipe of the said Clantane:

Which contencion and cause of sondry myschiefes being by us throughly examyned as well on the one parte as the other, is founde that the half tanestshippe of the said Clantane of anctientie sithens the dyvision of the captenshippe have bene pertenente to Offarrall bane and so to that use ever leavied, and that Faughney without right thereunto by force and usurpacion hathe detayned the same:

We have ordred that the said Farrall bane from the date of his letteres patentes enjoye the half tanestshippe from hym kepte by the said Faughney:

And that for all manner controversies and other challendges betwixt them and any other the quenes majesties subjectes they shall ether of them putt into the erle of Kildares handes suffytient pledges as well for the preservacion of her highness pease, as restytucion to suche as right
fol. 97b. shall have adjudged unto them by indifferent persons chosen by ether of them, and in case they cannot agree, the umpershippe to be to the said erles adwarde and determynacion, and that Faughney shall remayne in thandes of the said erle untill we, the lorde justice, shall signifie our furder pleassure in that behalf.

G. Kyldare.—Jenico, vicecom: of G[ormanston].—Roland Baltynglas.—Richard Delvin.—George Stanley.—John Parker.—Francis Agarde.

fol. 98. [LXXXVI.]—Apud Dubliniam, ultimo die Julii, anno regni regine Elizabethe primo [1559]:

1559. H. Sydney.—Memorandum: That upon summons gyven to the lordes spirituall and temporall and other her majesties counsell, it is concluded by us, the lord justice, the lordes spirituall and temporall and the rest of her majesties counsell of this realme, whose names be hereunto subscribed, appering upon the saide summons, the rest being absent by excuse, that for sondry and urgent consideracions towching the service of her majestie, the quiete of this realme and her highness subjectes thereof, there shalbe a generall hosting for fortyone dayes proclamed, after the old custome by wrytt, after the rate of three plowe landes to a carte, to be in full readynes to sett forthe the last day of August next,

[1] Faghtna.

and to appere at suche place as the lorde deputie or the lorde justice shall by ther letteres appoint. 1559.

H. Dublin, custos magni sigilli. — G. Kyldare. — W. Midensis. — Oswald Massingberd, prior.—Christoffor Kyllen.—Crystofor Howthe. —John Travers.—John Parker.—James Bathe.—Robert Dyllon.— John Alen.—Thomas Lokwod, deane.—Francis Agarde—Thomas Cusake. —John Plunket.[1]

[LXXXVII.]—Orders taken at Dublin, xvii Augusti, 1559, betweene the baron of Upper Ossory and Edward Butler, esquier: fol. 99.

By the Lord justice.—Whearas the baron of Upper Ossery exhibited complaint before us in wryting particularly against Edmonde Butler, esquire, captaine of the countie of Kilkenny, in thabsence of the erle of Ormonde, declaring as well of the killing of sondry his men and followers as also for dyvers preyes and bodragges committed and done uppon him and his country by the said Edmonde his servants and others within his rule:

Wherof the said baron preyed amendes and restitucion according to right, and that the said Edmond appearing likewise before us and being chardged with the premisses ded likewise alledge sondry and many the like killinge preyes and bodragges to be done by the said baron and his countrey against thinhabitantes of the said countrey, which the same Edmonde, for want of due instruccions and being called before us uppon the sodeyn, coulde not presently shewe and declare in particularities:

Forasmoche as due prouf and tryall is to be made in place or places, whear the same ought and that we, for other occasions and impedimentes, cannot in person repeyer to these borders to call before us all suchie proufs as shall or may be produced for tryall of the trueth and certeintie on either side, and nevertheles desireous that due examynacion sholde be had in the premisses, and also order taken therin according to right and justice, have condescended that Luke Netervile, Nicholas White, captain fol. 99b. Heron, Frauncys Cosby, Patrike Sherlock, Olyver Grace, John Fitz Patrike and William Oge Ophelan or the moar parte of them, commissioners by us chosen indifferently for the hearing and report of the proufes of the said demaundes, shall have full power and authoritie to heare and examen the same and to proceade in manner and fourme following:

Fyrst: That they or the moar part of them shall resort and goo to Rathkwyle,[2] being on the borders of either of the said countreys, to be there the fyrst of September next, for the taking of the said examynacions and for certificat to be made unto us or the lorde deputie in that behaulf and uppon thapparaunce of both parties before the said commissioners or the moar parte of them to take as well on the part of the said baron as of the said Edmond Butler sufficient pledge to stonde to suchie order and decree as shalbe taken betwen them and the same pledge to be put in to thandes of captaine Heronn, saulfly to be keapt untill our or the lorde deputies determynat order and definicion shalbe geaven in the variaunces and demaundes on either side and that either of them accomplishe and performe the same accordingly:

We will also that all and every the prisoners within the compase of the demaundes taken by either partie and nowe deteigned with any of

[1] Fol. 98b. is blank. [2] Rathkeale.

1559. them shalbe furthwith put at libertie, and saulfly restored to their dwelling place without any maner of impedyment hurt or hinderaunce:

fol. 100. And the said commissioners shall proceade to take and receyve in wryting suchie bokes as either partie shall exhibit touching his severall demaundes against the other, and theruppon to heare and examen by all due weyes and meanes all suchie witnesses and proufes as either of the said parties shall produce for triall of the same demaundes or any part therof and the same to note accordingly as it may appeare wherof and for howe mochie the restitucion and amendes is to be made on either side to other:

And to thende our meaning may be accomplished herein for the playn full and due amendes and restitucion to be made either to other we will that the said commissioners hereby authorised allonly go to the prouf of the nombre and quantitie of the hurtes losse and domages and the full prouf of somoche to be entered in a boke as well on the one side as on thother, and so to make upp the totall some thereof, without prising or valuyng any part thereof, wherby the wholl so certified appearing unto us or the lorde deputie in particularities we or the lorde deputie may rate and taxe every thing for the partie whose hurte do excede the others according the due and veray value as to us or the lorde deputie in reason and equitie shall sieame to apperteigne:

Furthermore whearas One McLyse is challendged by the said baron to have done mochie hurt uppon him and his countrey, the particulers wherof to be delyvered unto the said commissioners in wryting:

And that the said Edmonde Butler disclaymeth in the said One to be within his rule or power whereby to geve him or amendes and

fol. 100b. restitucion for him according as shall or may be proved against him, the said commissioners authorised shall not allonly receyve and examen the said demaundes against him but also enquire whether he be within the reche and power of the said Edmonde or no, and if he be, than the said Edmonde to aunswer for him or produce his body to be aunswerable therunto:

Otherwise not being within his said rule and power to knowe, enquere and certify where and under whom the said One is, whereby order may be taken against him accordingly:

And to the entent that as well thinhabitantes of the county of Kilkenny may frely passe into all and every part of the barons countrey without hurt, let or hinderaunce and likewise thinhabituntes of Upper Ossery have free resort and recourse both to the market of Kilkenny and all other places within that countie for any their nedefull and convenient causes, we will that from hensforth either of thinhabituntes of the countye of Kilkenny and Upper Ossery shall permitt eche other so to do:

And that the said baron, for his part, shall see and cause the same to be observed and the said Edmond for him during his rule shall do the like, as they and either of them will aunswer and satisfy for the contrary:

Lastly: For that Luke Netervile and Nicholas White, being men lerned in the lawes and appointed commissioners to this busynes, must travaill farre from their dwelling places to their greate costes and chardges than other, it is ordered that either of them for and towardes their travaill, costes and chardges from the first day of his or their setting forthe in going to the place appointed untill their retorne to their own houses, allowing somoch tyme as hereunto is expedient, shall have for every daye xx*s*. sterling, to be borne indifferently by the said baron of Upper Ossery and Edmonde Butler, and to be paid unto thesaide Luke and Nicholas before their departure after thending of the said examynacions without tract, dymynucion or delays. 1559.

[LXXXVIII.]—Apud Dubliniam, xxii° Augusti, 1559: fol. 101.

H. Sydney.—Touching thadvauncing to the generall hostinge, latelie proclaymed by writt, for xii daies, to begynne the last of this moneth: In consideracion as well that the lordes of the quenes majesties most honorable counsaill in Englande have addressed to us, the lorde justice, their letteres bearing date Eltham, the iii. of August last, wherby the quenes highnes resolucion and theirs is further declared, as also that therle of Sussex, nowe appointed the quenes majesties deputie of this realme, is presently at the waterside, readie to come over, to whom the ordering of theis things are specially referred:

It is ordered by us, the said lorde justice and counsaill whose names are hereunto subscribed, that the said generall hosting shalbe deferred for and until the first day of September next:

And that nevertheles generall letteres shalbe writen and sent forth to all the sherifes and others, to whom it apperteigneth to geve warning and to make proclamacion in all places requisit within their offices and rules that all men chardgeable to the saide hosting faill not uppon fol. 101b. tenne dayes warning to be in areadynes, fournished to serve as they ought and to be at suchie place or places as shall uppon knowledge therof geaven be signified unto them, uppon suchie peynes and penalties as by the lawes statutes and customes of this realme is in suchie case provided.

H. Dublin, canc.—George Stanley.—John Travers.—John Parker.—John Alen.—James Bathe.—Thomas Lokwood, dean.—Francis Agarde.—Valentyne Browne.—John Plunket.

[LXXXIX.]—Apud Dublin, ultimo die Augusti, 1559: fol. 102.

T. Sussex.—Memorandum: We, the lorde deputie, the lordes and nobylyte of the realme, with the rest of the quenes majesties counsell, assembled at Dublin, and considering as well the disfurnyture of her highnes fortes in Lex and Offaly and other her majesties holdes, as also the tyme of the yeare to be most propice for the victaylling of the same, concluded upon a generall cesse as well of wheate and malte, as bieves, swyne and other provision for the [w]hole year:

The same to be leavied in manner and forme following, that is to say:

In the countie of Methe, one thowsande xlvi peckes wheate, and one thousand viij^q lxvvi. peckes malte, whereof the thurde parte to be beare malte:

The wheate and beare malt at iiii shillinges, sterling.

The pecke and the wote malte at ij^s viij^d sterling the pecke;

In the countie of Dublin: vj^c xiiii peckes wheate, and one thowsande viij peckes malte, after lyke rate, price and dyvision as before.

In the countie of Kildare: vj^c iij^xx peckes wheate and vij^c iij^xx peckes malte, after the lyke rate and dyvision.

In the countie of Uriell: vj^c x peckes wheate and viij^c lx peckes malte after lyke rate and dyvision.

In the countie of Westmethe: iij^c xxxix peckes wheate and v^c x peckes malte, after the same:

The [w]hole proporcion to be brought into the places by Ester next at the furthest, that is to say:

The corne of Methe, to the towne of Trym.

The corne of Kyldare and also of Catherlaugh to Athie.

1559. The corne of Uryell to Drougheda.

The corne of the countie of Dublyn to the towne of the Nasse.

And the corne of Westmythe to suche place as by commyssion hereafter shalbe appointed.

And for the cesse of byves and swyne to be leavied in Irishemens countreys and upon parte of the shyres westwarde, there are letteres to be wrytten :

To O Rayly : for bieffes ij^c and one c swyne.

To the Annally : c byeffess and fiftie swyne.

To Magoughegan : fiftie bieves xxxv swyne.

To Macoughlan : xxx bieffes and xv swyne.

To Okelly : lx byeves and xxx swyne.

The Byrnes : c byeves and fiftie swyne.

fol. 102b. The Toles of Omaile : xx bieffes and x swyne.

The countie of Catherlaugh : cxl byeves, xxx swyne.

Upper Ossery : c bieffes, fiftie swyne.

The countie of Typperary : c bieffes, fiftie swyne.

The countie of Waterforde : c bieves, fiftie swyne.

Ferney : fiftie bieves, xxv swyne.

Hugh oge of Dartry : xxx bieffes, xv swyne.

The Raylies, beyonde the Sucke : lx bieves xxx swyne.

McMahon : c kyne l swyne, the beef at xij^s, sterling and the porke at ij^s viij^d sterling.

It is furder concluded that in the countie of Wexforde there shalbe cessed v^c peckes wootes at xvi^d the pecke.

In the countie of Kylkenny : ij^c peckes wootes at xx^d sterling the pecke.

The said wootes to be delyvered as followethe, that is to say :

They of Wexforde at the towne of Wexforde, those of Kilkenny at Kilkenny :

And furdre yt is ordered that the said corne shalbe delyvered at iij severall tymes in equall porcions, that is to say :

The furst parte on this side Christenmas next, the secounde parte before Shroftide and the thurde and last parte before Whytsontide.

And that the corne of the counties of Methe and West Methe shalbe after the measure and pecke of Trym; Dublin, and Kildare according to the pecke of Dublin ; and Louthe after the measure of Drougheda ; and for the wootes of Kilkenny, according the measure of Kilkenny, and those of Wexfored after the pecke of Wexforde.

H. Dublin, canc.—G. Kyldare.—Roland Baltynglas.—Thomas Darensis.—W. Midensis.—Christofor Kyllen.—P. Barnewall, lord [of Trymleteston].—George Stanley.—Christofor Donsene.—H. Sydney.—Henry Radeclyff.—James Bathe.—John Allen.—James Wingfeld.—Thomas Lokwood, dean.—Francis Agarde.—Valentyne Browne.—Humffre Warne.—Francis Harbart.

fol. 103. [XCI.]—Apud Dublyn, octavo die Septembris, anno 1559 :

Memorandum : Thatt the eighth daye of September, anno 1559, and the first yere of the reigne of our most gracious soverayn lady quene Elizabeth, by the grace of god, quene of England France and Irland, etc., the right honorable therle of Sussex, lorde deputie of the realme of Ireland, delyvered att Saynct Sepulcres to the moost reverent father in God, Hughe, archebyshop of Dublyn, lord chauncelor of the said realme, her majesties greatt seale of the same, newly sent over, and tooke of hym the greatt seale which was there presently defaced and broken in presence of us whose names are hereunto subscribed : 1559.

H. Dublin, canc.—H. Sydney.—W. Fitzwylliams.—Henry Radeclyff.—James Bathe.—Jaques Wingfeld.

[XCIA.]—Item : the 27th day of October, 1559, a newe seale for the quenes benche wase delyvered to justice Plunket ; a new seale for the common place wase delyvered to justice Dillon ; and a new seale for thexchequer wase delyvered to baron Bathe ; and the old seales were then broken in the presence of us, the lorde deputie, justices and baron :

T. Sussex.—John Plunket.—Robert Dyllon.—James Bathe.

[XCII.]—By the lord deputie and counsell :

Where yt was agreid by us, the lorde deputie, the nobles of this realme fol. 103b.
and the rest of the counsell then assembled at Dublin, the last of August that ther shulde be a generall cesse of wheate and malte made for the furnyture of all her majesties fortes within this realme, at which tyme yt was ordered that the countie of Dublin shulde be contributory thereunto in the nombre of ——[1] peckes wheate and ——[2] peckes malte, whereof the thurde parte to be beare malte, the same to be delyvered at ——[3] by equall porcions at thre severall tymes, viz. the furst porcion before Hallontide next, the secounde before Candlemas and the thurde before Ester, according the measure of Dublin, we shall therefore requyre you and in the quenes majestyes name chardge and commande you, that waying discretely the ymportance of the cause, ye do ymedyately se the forsaide nomber of peckes of wheate and malte to be indifferently cessed within the said countie, and that ye take straight order with the cessors to see the same brought in at the dayes and places appointed: Wherein they shall for the better leaviing of the cesse and more sure answering of the pay to the pore people that shall beare the cesse followe suche order hereafter by us, the lorde deputie and counsell, shalbe to them under our hande wryting appointed and prescribed, ymedyately
upon which cesse so by you made ye shall advertise us the lorde deputie fol. 104.
under your hand wryting the just porcion of wheate and malte cessed upon every barony within the said countie according to your just dyvision thereof made, and the parties delyvering the corne at the day and place appointed shall receyve ther payment out of hande[4], that is to say, for every peck of wheate and beare malte, and for every pecke of wootemalte, ——[5].

So praing you to be dyligent in the premisses, we bid you hartely well to fare.

From Dublin, this xviiith of September, 1559, and in the furst yere of the most prosperous raigne of our soverayne lady quene Elizabethe.[6]

[XCIIA.—Form of order to cessors.]

Cessors, seriantes, collectors and all others the quenes majesties officers fol. 105.
in the barony of A. in the countie of M., to whom in this case yt shall apperteigne :

Where, in the dyvisione of the cesse of W., yt is ordred by the lordes and gentilmen of that countie, that ther shulde be alloted to the porcion of the baronie of Delvene A. ——[7] peckes wheate, and ——[8] peckes of malte, the same to be delyvered at three severall tymes by equall porcions : we will and commande you that ye cause the first porcione to be broghte

[1], [2], [3], [4], [5], [7], [8] Blank in MS. [6] Fol. 104b. is blank.

1559. wholy and fully to the Forte in Ophalie, so as it fayle not to be there the vth of Novembre next. At which day we have appointed Henrie Cowley to mete with you at Terells Castell for the more saulfe conductinge of you thethear.

And that the seconde porcione be also at the said Forte the xii^{th} of Januarie; and that the third porcione be also at the said Forte the first day of Marche, at which dayes we have also apointed the said Henrie to mete you at Terells Castell for your saulfe conductione.

Wherfore we chardge you as ye will answere to the contrarie at youre extreme perilles that ye faile not to see the saide porcions broghte into the said Forte at the said dayes.

And if eny mane shalbe negligente or willfull in the bringinge of his porcione, beinge warned therto by you, we then do aucthorise you and everie of you not onely to take ther stresse but also to complaine on them to the next justice of peace, whom we do by thes presentes aucthorise to commyt everye suche persone so by ye complained on to warde till ye shall declare to him that the persone or persons so committed shall have fully paied ther porcions.

fol. 105b. And commande all justices of peace within the said countie of Westmethe to see this oure ordre put in execucione as they will answer to the contrarie at their perilles.

And for the more juste and true paymente to be made by and to the contrey we will and commande you, the aforesaid officers, to make two perfite bokes, wherin shall be conteyned the names of everie manne within youre rule that oghte to bringe eny corne and the porcions which they oghte to bringe, wherof thone shall remaine with youre selves and the other with Henrie Cowley.

And at the daies before apointed ye shall youreselves in persone repayre with the cariers of the corne to the Forte and shall make entrie into everie of the bokes of the corne that everie manne bringethe, apon which entrie, so made by you, the said Cowley shall make paymente to the parties bringinge the corne, accordinge to the prices by us, the lordes of the realme and the reste of the councell in the cesse agreed.

Wherfore fayle ye not to see all the premisses put in execucione as every of you will answer to the contrarie at youre uttermost perilles.[1]

fol. 107. [XCIIb.]—Coppie of indentures betwene the viscount Montgaret and Thomas Fitz Henrie:

Wheras contencione hath longe depended before sundrie governors and counsailors of this realme, betwene the visconte Montgaret, and Thomas Fitz Henrie and Mathew Fitz Henrie, sonne and heire to the same Thomas, on thother partie, touchinge certein landes, tenementes and hereditamentes of fowre townes or villages in the Fausaughe Bentrie in the hundreth of Shilemalire in the countie of Wexforde, that is to say, Prycehagarde, Ballewarkely, Kilgibbone and Kylherie, which fowre townes or villages the said visconte Montgaret dothe alledge to be thenheritance of Fowke Dene, named late barone of Cahire, and so to have descended to Patricke Dene, sone and heire to the same Fowke, whose estate the visconte enjoyethe by purchase of the said Patricke Dene, which townes or villages also the said Thomas Fitz Henrie and Mathew dothe demande as the auncient inheritance of ther auncestors in the righte of ther maner of Maghmaine, in the said countie of Wexforde. The true title wherof, notwithstandinge longe travaile, to ther greate chardges hathe not ne coulde not hitherto bene determined

[1] Ff. 106 and 106b are blank.

nor ended but yet dependethe in controversie, and if order were not takene therein it were lyke to be cause of forther trouble and disquietnes betwene them. 1559.

Forasmoche as bothe parties, as well the said viscounte Montgaret and Patricke Dene as the said Thomas Fitz Henrie and his sonne, Mathew, have remitted thorderinge and finall determininge therof to us, the said lord deputie and consaile, whose names are herunto subscribed, and are contente to stande to owre order therin: We, the said fol. 107b. lorde deputie and consaile, by consent and agremente of the said visconte and Patrike Dene and Thomas Fitz Henrie and Mathew, his sonne, do order and by vertue herof awarde that the said visconte Montgaret, his heires and executors shall from henceforthe have, holde and enjoy forever for his parte towe of the said townes or villages, thone called Prishagard thother Ballewarkely, with ther apurtenances and all profites comodities and emolumentes growinge and risinge therof, and the said Thomas Fitz Henrie, his heires and executors to have holde and enjoy for ever for his parte thother two townes or villages, thone called Kilherie and thother Kilgibbone with ther appurtenances and all profites commodities and emoluments, growinge and risinge therof.

The which two townes or villages of Prishagard and Ballewarkely the said Thomas and Mathew by thes presentes dothe renonce unto the said visconte Montgaret, his heires and executors for ever all ther right title and interest that they or eny of them ther heires and executors hathe, shuld or oght to have in the said two townes of Prishagard and Ballewarkely or of and in eny of them.

And lykewise the viscont Montgaret and Patricke Dene, by thes presentes dothe renonce unto the saide Thomas and Mathew Fitz Henrie, ther heires and executors for ever all the right title and interest that they hathe, shulde or oght to have in the said Kilherie and Killgibbone or of and in eny of them.

And further, whereas there apereth to be controversie for and aboute fol. 108. the lymites meres and bandes of the said townes or villages we, the lorde deputy and consaile aforsaid, by the consente and agrement of the said visconte Montgaret and Patricke Dene and Thomas and Mathew Fitz Henrie have ordred that sir Henrie Radecliffe, knight, and captene Herne, sherif of the countie of Catherlaghe, shall call the contrey before them or suche and as manie as they shall thincke cane best enforme them of the true confines, meres and bandes of the said townes or villages, and therapon to appointe suche markes and meres betwene them as to ther discretione shalbe thoght fittest and most indifferent; which markes and meres they shall cause to be marked in suche sorte as they may endure and be knowene forever.

And further we order, by consent of the parties aforsaid, that the said sir Henry Radcliff and captene Herne shall cause an order indented to be made betwene the said visconte Montgaret and Patricke Dene, on thone partie and Thomas and Mathew Fitz Henrie on thother partie, wherunto everie of them severallie and jointlie shall putte ther signes and seales, wherein shalbe specified the lymites, confines and meres of the said townes and villages, with all markes and signes as they cane well name for the better declaracione and knowledge therof, and so to remaine as a perpetuall recorde of the said lymites, confines, markes and meares so apointed and made by the said sir Henrie Radecliffe and captene Herne, by the consent and assent of the said visconte Montgaret, Patrick Dene, Thomas and Mathew FitzHenrie and everie of fol. 108b. them.

In wittnes wherof as well the said lorde deputie and counsaile as the said viscont Montgaret, Patricke Dene, and Thomas and Mathew Fitz

1559. Henrie, in testimonie of ther whole, whole (*sic*) and free consents in and to the premisses, have to ether parte of thes present indentures severallie and jointly putt ther signes and seales, the xvth of November [1559], in the first year of the raigne of oure soveraigne lady Elizabethe, by the grace of God quene of Englande, France and Irelande, defendor of the faithe, etc.—Concordat cum originali.

fol. 109. [XCIII.]—The order takene betwene Francisco Dias, Hispaniarde, and Jhon Neyle and others of the marchantes of Waterforde, the 25th of November, 1559:

Thomas, earle of Sussex, viscont Fitzwalter, lord Egremonde and Burnell, knighte of the most noble order of the garter, captene of the gentlemene pencioners and gentlemen at armes, chefe justice and justice in oyer of all her majesties forestes, parkes and chases on this side Trente, and lorde deputie of Irelande: To all mene to whom thes presentes shall come gretinge:

Where in the matter dependinge in controversie betwene Francisco Dyas, Hispaniard, factor and atturney for certen marchantes Hispaniardes, plaintife, and Henrie Cornelisone, late of Middelborroughe, defendant, upon the demande of certene wares and marchandises ladene in Flaundres in the said Henries barke called the Sprite Volante of Middelborroughe, and dischardged of late in the havene of Waterforde and there sold, ymbeaseled or otherwise bestowed by the said Henrie, thorder whearof was committed by the quenes majesties especiall letteres.

There was order takene by us the lorde deputie that ther shuld be delyvered to thandes of Francisco Dias as well all such goodes as upon inquerie made by the maior and bayliffes of Waterforde was certified unto us in a boke signed with ther handes and sealed with the towne seale, and if eny of them were solde, then the money that was paied fol. 109*b*. for them to be redelyvered, as also all suche other goodes as within one yeare after mighte be proved to be solde, ymbeaseled or otherwise bestowed by the said Henrie or the value of them:

Wherein yt was also ordered by consente of both parties that the said Francisco shulde allowe to the said Henrie his freighte accordinge the bargaine made in Flaudres, with all suche other necessarie chardges susteined by the said Henrie aboute the saving of the goodes as the maior, bayliffes and aldermene of Waterforde shoulde thincke the said Francisco bounde in conscience to allowe, as in the said order,[1] beringe date at Laghlene, the xvi[th] of Decembre, 1556, more at length is declared.

Since which tyme thordre, not beinge fullie takene betwene them for Henries demandes, the matter was broght before sir Henrie Sidney, then lorde justice, duringe oure absence in Englande, who, for the better endinge of thes matters directed a commissione to certene mene in the citie of Waterforde to hire, examine and determine all matters in controversie betwene the said Francisco and Henrie, conteyned in twentie articles therunto annexed, and by his letters gave them his advice apone everie of the twentie articles, and so bothe in the commissione and letteres comanded them to make suche a finall ende as mighte in nothinge digresse from eny order takene by us before:

By vertue of which commissione and letteres, bering date the seconde fol. 110. of Februarie, 1557, the said commissioners did, without callinge the said Francisco to it, make a corrupte and unjuste ordre, wherein apon an untrue surmise that the said Francisco wolde not shewe his procuracione

---

[1] *See* page 45, fol. 61*b* of the MS., where the date is xxvi December, 1556.

nor fall to eny accompte, they did awarde the said Francisco to allow to the said Henrie two hundred and fourtie poundes for the chardges of his ymprisonment, wheras in dede he had one yeare and more before shewed his procuracione to us and gevene to [us] an accompte so fer as mighte be proved, and for that the said Henrie did not justlie and speedelie procede therein, he was by oure order committed to warde till he shulde fully accomplishe oure order, as in oure forsaid order and divers other orders therein takene doth more plainely appere. 1559.

And the said commissioners did also in the same order awarde divers other thinges unjustlie apon unjuste surmises and so dismissed the said Cornelisone, as in the said order, beringe date the xv[th] of May, 1558, doth more plainely appere.

Which order being made by vertue of the lorde justices commissione, dated the ii of Februarie 1557, was not made till the xv[th] day of May, after oure retorne into this realme, wherby ther order, besides yt was unjust and contrarie to ther commissione and our former ordres, was also in lawe voide, for that they did not execute ther commissione duringe the tyme that the lorde justice who gave them the commissione was in fol. 110b. aucthoritie.

Wherapon we, perceavinge the decepte whereby the said Francisco had bene defrauded of his goodes, contrarie to all righte and justice, for the space of two yeares and that the said commissioners did go about to cause the said Francisco to bere all chardges that the said Henrie had bene at by falslie delainge the said Francisco from the recoverie of his owne goodes, to the great hindrance of the marchantes Hispaniardes, who never for eny thinge coulde be done coulde attaine to the thirde parte of ther goodes ladene in the said shippe, and if they shuld also have beane judged to have unjustlie paied thos sumes of monie expressed in that ordre mighte not onely have throghe all realmes of justice complained of the injustice of this realme, but also have manifestlie proved that the Fleminge, as a thefe runninge away with ther goodes and spoylinge them of more then thone halfe therof, had also by order and color of justice a rewarde gyvene to him for his laboure:

Which indede procedinge onely of the corrupcion of the commissioners mighte nevertheles have gyvene goode grounde to all mene that shulde have herde the case to have accused the governors of this realme of corrupcione, who were nothinge giltie therin, [and] did ymediatlie take order that the said Henrie shulde be returned to the jayle of Waterforde till fol. 111. the said Francisco shulde be satisfied accordinge to oure former order takene, by vertue of which oure order the maior did committe the said Henrie to the jayle of Waterforde and there did detaine the said Henrie untill suche tyme as Jhon Neyle, one of the bayliffes, without knowledge of the maior or thother bayliffe or eny of the aldermene of the citie, did apon oure cominge to Dublin to take oure jorney by sea into Scottland, lett him out apon the suertie of James Dobene, Andrew Lyncolne, Nicholas Walche and Richarde Keny, who were bounde bodie for bodie to bringe the said Henrie to prison within twentie dayes excepte he did bring a dischardge for the indempnitie of the maior and bailiffes of Waterforde, as in the said bande, bering date the xxiii of Auguste, 1558, dothe further appere.

And where also at oure beinge at Waterforde the ——[1] of November, 1558, there was order takene by us and the councell then present, wherof sir Henrie Sidney was one, that the maior and aldermene of Waterforde shulde take a finall ende betwene the said Francisco and Henrie in all the

[1] Blank in MS.

1559. contencions and subscribinge the same and settinge ther towne seale therto they shulde sende it to us to thentent we mighte take order for the spedie execucione therof:

fol. 111b. Wherapon the said maior, bayliffes and aldermene did, according oure commissione, take a finall ordre therein, as aperethe by the same, beringe date the first of Februarie, 1558, signed with the handes of the maior, bayliffes and xi of thaldermene and sealed with the seale of the citie used in suche cases.

Forasmoche as the saide Francisco now aperinge before us hathe declared that he canne not be satisfied accordinge to thordre takene by the maior, bayliffes and aldermen of Waterforde, neither yet cane have the bodie of the said Henrie, accordinge the former ordres, for that he is now fledd out of this realme, and therfore besechethe to have some meane devised for his finall satisfaccione and depeache from hence:

Whereapon, callinge before us the said Jhon Neyle, James Dobenk Andrew Lyncolne, Nicholas Walche and Richard Keny, and findinge the premisses to be true, as well towchinge thordre of the maior, bayliffes and aldermene of Waterforde, as also for the fleinge of the said Henrie oute of this realme, falslie and untrulie leavinge them in dandger for him, we have in fine ordred, by thassente of the said Francisco and the said Jhon, James, Andrew Nicholas and Richard, that the said Jhon, James, Andrew Nicholas and Richarde shall, for ther full agrement, pay to the said Francisco two hundred markes, sterlinge, fol. 112. currant mony of Ireland, in consideracione wherof the said Francisco dothe by thes presentes gyve unto them and every of them a fulle dischardge for all matters he can objecte against them or eny of them for eny thinge towchinge the matter dependinge in controversie betwene him and the said Henrie; and that the said Francisco shall and may nevertheles recover against the said Henrie, whersoever he shall finde his bodie, all suche summes of monie as are due to him by the awarde of the maior, bayliffes and aldermene of the citie of Waterforde, signed with ther handes, sealed with the seale of the citie, used in suche cases, and beringe date the first of Februarie, 1558, deductinge allwayes the summe of two hundred markes, payed to the said Francisco by the forsaid Jhon, James, Andrew, Nicholas, and Richard, which summe of two hundred markes, so by them paied to the said Francisco the said Jhon, James, Andrew, Nicholas and Richard, junctly or eny of them severally, in the name of the rest, shall and may recover against the said Henrie, whersoever they shall finde his bodie or his goodes, together with suche losses as they have susteyned by his decepte and falshode.

In wittnes wherof as well we, the lorde deputie, as also we the said Francisco, Jhon, James, Andrew, Nicholas and Richarde have sett oure handes and seales to ether parte of these indentures.

Dated at Laughlen, the xxvth of Novembre, 1559, in the first yeare of the raigne of oure soveraigne lady quene Elizabeth, etc.[1]

fol. 116. [XCIV.]—[2]Ordered by the lorde liewtennant and counsaill, at Kylmaynan and Dublin, the last of June and firste of July
1560. 1560, as folowethe:

[1.] Firste that beakens be sett and good watche kepte upon all the accustomed places for all the sea coaste of the Englishe Pale wheare any

[1] Ff 112b., 113, 113b., 114 and 114b. are blank in the MS. The leaf which follows 114b. is numbered 116.

[2] In the MS. lines are drawn through the matter here printed under No. [xciv.]; and at head in margin is written: "vacat."

arryvall and landing of foreign enemyes may be doubted: the same to be diligently attended and contynued untill like ordre be agayne taken to the contrarye. 1560.

[2.] Item: That betwene this and the ——[1] daye of this instant moneth of July particuler muster shal be made in every baronye within the Englishe Pale of as many the quenes majesties subjectes dwelling or resident within every of the saide baronyes hable to welde weappon for defence of this her majesties realme (if suche neede were) as are above the age of xv. yeres and under the age of lx. yeres.

The same musteres to be taken by suche persons as the lorde lieutennaunt shall thereunto name and appoint particulerly for every of the said baronyes.

The whiche persons in the viewe of the saide musters shall discretely marke and note whiche men of all that multitude are goode and hable archers and whiche of them are furnished thereunto and whiche of them are unfurnished, and of them that are furnished, what their furniture is, and of them that are not furnished what furniture they lacke.

And in lyke maner of goode and hable bill men, and in lyke sorte of fol. 116b. meete and experte harquebuttieres. And in like maner distinctly for horsemen, kerne, gallowglasse, and all other sortes of the warr, noting in their bookes of the saide musters by convenient letteres or markes ensuying the name of every person mustered (if he be archer, billman or of other sorte), what furniture he hathe, by setting a prykke upon that kynde of furniture whiche he hathe and by leaving unpricked that kynde of furniture whiche he wantethe for that sorte of service, and marking acrosse in the mergent againste the name of every of the saide hablest men, to thende that suche order may thereupon be taken for the further furnishing of them with weapon and necessaries in that behaulf at reasonable price of the quenes majesties provision, as shalbe then thought expedient.

The same to be delyvered and commytted unto thandes and distribucion of some suche sufficient men within every of the saide baronyes as shall have charge and undertake that the saide weapon and municions so delyvered shalbe allways furthecomynge at the musters within that barony from tyme to tyme and not solde ne made awaye.

[3.] Item: That all those whiche shalbe comprised within those muster fol. 117. bookes of every baronye particulerly shalbe under the charge and leading of suche capitaynes as the saide lorde lieutennant will thereunto name and appointe, for every baronye two at the leaste, the whiche upon every occasion shall be attente, the one to receyve them at the generall place of assembley for that purpose appointed, the other with the ayde of the officeres of every towne to see them sett spedely furthe that none withdrawe ne remayne behynde.

[4.] Item: That at suche day and place as shalbe appointed by the saide lorde lieutenant and counsaill a generall mustre shalbe made of all the persons mustered and certified by the bookes of those particuler musters, with their furniture noted and appointed in those particuler bookes of musteres.

[5.] Item: That there be appointed and comaunded unto all the persons so mustered a place mooste apte and convenient to make their immediate and indelayed repaire unto, with their weapon and furniture appointed, upon every warnying geven by fyre or smoke from the afore mencioned beakons:

[1] Blank in MS.

1560. That is to witt at Ratowthe, for the counties of Methe and Westmethe, and Castell Knocke for the countie of Dublin.

The hill of Lyons for the counties of Kildare, Kilkenny and Catherlaughe.

fol. 117b. The hill of Monster Bois[1] for the countie of Lowthe; and for the countie of Weixforde suche place as by the seneschal and gentilmen of the countie shalbe thought mooste expedient bothe for the aunswering of the same countie and of the counties adjoyning:

There to gather and assemble under suche capitaynes as shalbe appointed to have the leading and chardge of them, and so to attende, redye to speede them further under the leading of their saide capitaynes unto such place as they shall be then commaunded unto:

And for every countie one capitayn to be appointed to have the charge and leading of all the horsmen of that countie, and also one generall capitain for all the fotemen of every countie, also for every barony one ensigne, to be provided upon the charge of the whole baronye, and for the horsmen of every countie one standert to be provided at the charge of the capitayne of the same.

For the countie of Kildare: the erle of Kildare and his substitutes to have the chief charge bothe of the horsemen and footmen and the sherif to attende on them in that behaulf.

For the footmen of the countie of Methe: the lorde of Gormanstown to have the chief charge, and the sheriff under him; and for the horsmen of the same countie: the lorde of Slane.

And for the horsemen and footmen of the countie of Westmethe: the sherife.

fol. 118. And for the horsemen and footmen of the countie of Kilkenny:——[2]

And for the horsemen and footmen of the countie of Catherlaughe: capitain Herne.

And for the horsemen and footmen of the countie of Lowthe: the lorde of Lowthe, and under him the sherife.

And for the horsemen and footmen of the countie of Dublin: the lorde of Howthe and under him the sherife.

And for all the countie of Wexforde: the seneschall.[3]

fol. 119. [XCV.]—The copie of the commyssions made oute for the musters, ——[2] die mensis Julii, 1560:

Com. Dublin.—Regina, etc. Dilectis nobis Hugoni, Dublin archiepiscopo, Hibernie primati ac cancellario nostro regni nostri Hibernie, Christophero, domino de Howethe, Johanni Pluncket, capitali justiciaro nostro banci nostri regni nostri predicti, Jacobo Bathe, capitali baroni scaccarii nostri regni nostri predicti, Ricardo Talbot, secundario justiciario nostro placei nostri regni nostri predicti, Patricio White, militi, secundario baroni scaccarii nostri regni nostri predicti, Johanni Travers, militi, Thome Lockwod, decano ecclesie cathedralis Sancte Trinitatis, Dublin, Patricio Barnewall, vicecomiti Dublin, Ricardo Finglas, servienti ad leges, Jacobo Barnewall, Thome Fitzwilliams de Holmepatricke, Christophero Barnewall de Gracedewe, Roberto Talbot de Bellegarde, Patricio Finglas de Wespelleston, Edwardo Barnewall de Drumnaghe, Rogero Finglas de Porterston, Willelmo Welshe de Carrickmayne, Johanni Burnell de Castell Knocke, et Thome Beling de Kilcoscane, salutem:

Sciatis quod nos de vestris fidelitate, circumspectione et industria ad plenum confidentes, ex assensu charissimi consanguinei et consiliarii

[1] Monasterboice. [2] Blank in MS. [3] Fol. 118b. is blank.

nostri Thome, comitis Sussex, ordinis nostri garterii militis, capitanei 1560.
generosorum pencionariorum nostrorum ad arma, capitalis justiciarius omnium forestarum, parcorum et chacearum nostrarum citra Trentam, ac generalis locumtenentis nostri regni nostri Hibernie predicti, simul fol. 119b.
et de consensu consilii nostri ejusdem :

Assignavimus et constituimus vos et quoscunque vestrum comissionarios nostros in comitatu nostro Dublin ac in crochiis et marchiis ejusdem, tam infra libertates quam extra, ad omnes et singulos subditos et ligeos nostros tam spirituales quam temporales, cujuscunque status, gradus, dignitatis aut condicionis existunt, coram vobis aut aliquibus duobus vestrum in unaquaque baronia dicti comitatus nostri, prout quisque vestrum nominatim ad unamquamque earundem baroniarum assignatur et delegatur per scedulam instructionum huic commissioni annexatam, indilate convocandi et venire faciendi ac cetus, conventus, monstraciones, ostentaciones et delectus bellicos habendi, procurandi, faciendi, conscribendi et exequendi seperatim in unaquaque baronia infra ac per totum comitatum nostrum predictum de et super omnibus et singulis hominibus ligeis et subditis nostris predictis in qualibet earundem baroniarum ac infra ac per totum comitatum nostrum predictum inhabitantibus, commorantibus seu degentibus :

Ac ipsos et eorum quemlibet ad bellicum apparatum et furnituram telorum, armorum, equorum hobellariorum, equitumque et peditum, secundum modum et quantitatem terrarum, tenementorum bonorum
et cattallorum suorum assesandi, censendi, conscribendi et arraiari et fol. 120.
preparari, inveniendi, procurandi et faciendi seperatim in unaquaque earundem baroniarum infra ac per totum comitatum predictum immediate, modo et forma prout in scedula instructionum huic commissioni annexata continetur, et magis plene liquet, omnibusque aliis melioribus viis modo et forma quibus uti seu perficere sciveritis et poteritis, juxta antiquas consuetudines, leges et statuta regni nostri Hibernie predicti ac instructiones predictas locumtenentis nostri generalis regni nostri Hibernie predicti vobis in hac parte directas, procurandas, faciendas, supervidendas et exequendas.

Et quum examinacionem hujusmodi ceperitis predictum dominum locumtenentem nostrum generalem sub manibus vestris particulatim, in primo die Augusti proximi, reddatis certiorem, hanc commissionem ei remittentes.

Et ideo vobis et cuilibet vestrum mandamus, etc.

Damus autem, etc. In cujus rei, etc. Teste, etc.

[XCVI.]—The instructions to the saide commyssion annexed: fol. 120b.

Firste: You shall according to your comyssion assemble yourselfes with all diligence at suche convenient place within the shire as you shall thinke moost mete, the xiii[th] day of this moneth of Julye, at whiche tyme[1] you shall divide yourselfes into severall companyes according as you be named, sorted and appointed by the instructions for every suche barony of the aforesaide countie, as unto every of your said severall companyes is by theise instructions severally allotted and assigned, so as you may make the musters with the more spede according to your comyssion and the statutes in that cace provided, and for the better guiding of the people at all eventes ye shall appointe to every barony one or two capitaynes,[2] such as you shall thinke fittest, the names whereof ye shall gyve unto the commyssioners for the musters of those baronyes to thintent they may at the taking of the musters declare the same to the people.

[1] In margin: "The tyme of the assemblie for the commissioners to muster against the tyme appoynted."

[2] In margin: "Capitaynes to be appoynted in everie baronye."

1560. Item: That doon you shall directe owte preceptes[1] to the constables of every barony within your allotmentes, comaunding them not only to appeare personally themselfes before you the xxii[th] day of this monethe of Julye, at suche place as ye shall appointe in every barony, and to bring in writing to be certified and delyvered unto you upon their othes the names and surnames of all persones inhabiting or resiaunt within
fol. 121. their severall rules being of thage betwene sixtene yeres and threschore yeres, but also to commaunde[2] all persones inhabiting or resiaunt within their saide rules of the saide ages to appeare personally before you at the saide day and place and to bring[3] with them all suche horsse, harneys, armour, bowes, arrowes, gonnes, weapon and all maner of warlike apparraill as they by any meanes can put in aredynes against that tyme for the service of the quenes majestie and defence of the realme. And every suche person as shall not upon suche warnyng appeare before you at the day and place appointed, being within the saide lymyttes of age and hable to welde weapon for defence of the realme, shall forfaite to her majesties use twenty shillings or suffer tenne daies imprisonment.

Item: You shall gyve order and speciall chardge that no horse or hackney be solde out of the English Pale to any whatsoever unles onely yt be to suche as are resyaunt in the Englishe Pale of the relme.

Item: You shall at the saide day appointed take the perfite musters of every suche person before you appearing, and, putting his name in writing, you shall view and take muster[4] of the person and his furniture, considere his hablenes and what sorte of weapon he hathe, and not only note the same briefly by one or two letteres in the mergent before his name:

That is to say, upon every hable archer h. a., upon every hable harquebus, h. ha., upon every hable billman, h. b., upon every hable horseman h. h., upon every hable kernaghe, h. k., and, upon him that you fynde not so hable, to leave out the firste h.

fol. 121b. But also note in like sorte by writing what horsse, armour and weapon every of them shall then have by thiese lettres: For a horsse, ho.; for a jacke, j.; for a speare, sp.; for a bowe, bo.; for a sheafe of arrowes, sh.; for a bill, b.; for a gonne, g.; for a sworde, s; for a habergen of mayle, h.m.

Item: Wheare ye shall finde defaultes[5] of weapon ye shall examyn the person what weapon he thinketh himself metest to use, and note the same weapon by letteres as aforesaide, and adde therto this worde 'want.'

Item: You shall then gyve commandemente unto them to kepe the weapon and furniture noted upon them, the whiche your booke[6] so perfitly made, togedther with the booke of every constable delyvered to you, ye shall sende unto us, the lorde liewtennaunt, by the firste day of Auguste next comynge, every booke by yourselfe so made to be subscribed with thandes of the commysioners that shall be presente at the taking of those musters.

And every booke of the constables delyvered unto you to be subscribed with the handes of the same constables whiche have delyvered it, and upon the heade of every person whiche shall make defaulte to be written thiese lettres: 'De.'

[1] In margin: "Preceptes to be directed to everie constable in eche barony to appeare themselves at the daie of the muster and to somon, etc."
[2] In margin: "To somon all between the age of xvi. and lx."
[3] In margin: "To bringe to the moosters horses, harness and weapon."
[4] In margin: "To mooster the person and to consider of his habilitie of bodie, and his weapon."
[5] In margin: "Defalte of weapon."
[6] In margin: "Mooster bookes to be made and to be certefied to the governor."

Item: When you shall have taken the saide musters, you shall gyve 1560.
generall commaundement that they be all in aredynes to muster togedther before the lorde liewtennaunt at suche place and day as he, upon proclamacion made in every barony within sixe daies warnyng[1] before the day of the musters to be before him made, shall appointe.

And if you finde any man unfurnished of suche horsse, armour or fol. 122.
weapon as by the lawes of this realme he ought to have, that then ye give streight commaundement to him that he be furnished thereof againste the day he shalbe appointed to muster before the lorde liewtenaunt, upon payne in the statutes expressed. And yf any man, being by the lawes of this realme bound to finde horsse, armor or any other kynde of weapon, do muster as servaunt or in liewe of any other, that then ye shall also note the same that noo excuse be made whereby the quenes majesties service might be hindered, and that you, the commissioners of eche barony, do cause your owne servantes and suche hable persons as remayne within your houses or under your rule to be at the said musters, well furnished with armor and weapon, as her majesties lawes and statutes doth allowe.

Item: You shall at the saide musters geve notice and commaundement, unto all those whiche shalbe comprised and writtin within the said musters of every barony within the saide countie severally that upon every warnyng geven by fyre or smoke from the beacons[2] and watche to be set and kepte in thaccustomed places, or opon every eskrie and alarme of them, indelayedly with their saide warlike and defencible aray and furniture appointed, immediately spede them and faile not to repaire unto suche place or places as you have by vertue of owre lettres and enstructions addressed to [you] for watche and warde appoynted, there to assemble and joyne with the rest of the power of the saide countie under the conducte and leading of such capitaynes as by you shalbe named as aforesaide:

And that as well all and singuler those capitaynes whiche according to this commyssion and instruction shall have been by you appointed, as also all and every of the saide persones mustered and appointed
under those capitaynes,[3] together with the whole power of the saide fol. 122b.
countie, shall be then attendant, redy and obedient to repayre and serve under the conduct, appoyntement leading and commaundement of the lorde of Howcthe[4] and of the sherife of the countie of Dublin, under him chief and generall capitayne, named and appointed by the lorde liewtennaunt and counsaill for the said countie in that bihaulfe.

Item: You shall geve commaundement that every barony in the saide countie do at the chardge and contribucion of the same barony provide them of a convenient and warlyke ensigne[5] with a redde crosse of Saint George therin, against the saide daye of musters.

All whiche the premysses you shall truly and uprightly do and execute, and of your doinges make true certificate to the lorde lieutenaunt, as aforsaide, by the firste day of Auguste,[6] aforsaide, as ye tendre the quenes majesties favor and thadvauncement of her service with the goode defence of this her majesties realme, your natyfe countrey.

---

[1] In margin: "Generall warning to be in readines to mooster before the governor and to be furnished with horsse, armour and weapon."

[2] In margin: "The men moostred to be readie to answere the beacons and to joyne with the residue of the forces of the countrey."

[3] In margin: "Shall repaire with the rest of the powre of the said countie."

[4] In margin: "Lord of Hoathe, capitayne of the countie of Dublin."

[5] In margin: "Everie baronie to have an ensign at theire own charges."

[6] In margin: "To make certificat to the governor."

1560. fol. 123. [XCVII.]—Capitain generall for the leading of the whole shire of Dublin :

The lorde of Howthe and under him the sherife of the same countie.

Thiese commyssioners under written appointed and allotted by thiese instructions for the severall musters of the baronye under written as ensuethe, that is to witt:

For the barony of Balrothery: James Barnewall.—Christopher Barnewall.—Thomas Fitzwilliams.—Patricke Finglas.

For the barony of Cowloke: My lord of Howeth.—Justice Ploncket. —Baron Bathe.—Baron White.

For the barony of Newecastell: My lord chauncelor.—Justice Talbot.—Robert Talbot of Bellegar.—Edwarde Barnewall of Dromnaghe.

For the barony of Castellknocke: Sergeant Finglas.—Roger Finglas, of Porterstowne.—John Burnell, of Castell knocke.—Thomas Beling, of Kilcoskane.

For the barony of Rathedowne: Sir John Travers.—The deane of Christes Churche.—Patricke Barnewall.—William Welshe of Carricke mayne.

fol. 123b. The like commyssion and instructions for the countie of Methe directed to the commyssioneres under written, videlicet, to the viscount of Gormanston, generall capitain appointed to have the leading of all the footmen of that shire, and the sherife of the shire under him :

The lorde of Slane, generall capitain appointed for the leading of all the horsemen of that shire :

For the musters of the barony of Dulyke: The said viscount of Gormanston.—Henry Dracott.—Thomas Darcy of Platten.—Mathewe Talbott, of Dardeston.

For the barony of Skryne: The lorde of Kyllyne.—The lorde of Donsanye.—Sir Christopher Chevers.

For Ratothe barony: Symon Barnewall.—Burforde of Killrowe.—Wesley of Blackhall.—Barnaby Everes.

For the barony of Donboyn: Christopher Ruchefort.—Phepo of Rowthan.—Michell Delahide.—John Scurloke.

For the barony of Deice: The baron of Galtrym.—Melior Hussey.—Lenam, of Adamston.—Delahide, of Assye.

fol. 124. For the baronyes of Moyfenragh withe Moygarr: Wellisly of the Dyngan.—James Dowdall.—Mathewe King.—Laurence Hamound.

For the busbops lands and Lenowes landes, Ballybogan and Casteljordan; The master of the rolles.—Richarde Croftes.

For the barony of Lune: Sir Olyver Ploncket.—Barnaby Scurloke.—William Bremyngeam.—Walter Lynche of Donnow.

For the barony of the Navan: The lorde of Tremleston.—The baron of the Navan.—Justice Dillone.—Rocheforde of Kilbrye.

For the barony of Kelles: Sir Thomas Barnewall.—James Evererde. —Patricke Ploncket of Gibbiston.—John Fitz Jones of Fyanston.

For the barony of Foure: Barnewall of Moillaghe.—John Ploncket, of Loghekrewe.—Balf of Galmoreston.—Tute of Baltraeston.

For the barony of Mergallen: Thomas Flemyng, of Stephenston.—White, of Clongell.—George Drake.—Velden of Raffyn.

For the barony of Slane: The baron of Slane.—Barnewall of Stockullyn.—Barnewall of Rowestowne.—Thomas Flemyng, of Syden.

For the towne of Athboy: The portrief of the same.

fol. 124b. The like commission and instructions for the countie of Westmethe, directed to the commysioners under written, videlicet: to sir Thomas

Nugent, knight, capitain generall appointed to have the leading of all the horsemen and footmen of that shire: 1560.

For the musters of all the territories of the Nugentes and their folowers: the saide sir Thomas Nugent.—James Nugent.

For the territories of the Tutes and all their folowers: Sir Ricarde Tute.—Mr. Ricarde Tute.

For the territories of all the Pettites and their folowers: Sir Garret Pettit and his son.

For all the Terrilles and their folowers: Sir Thomas Tirrell.—John Tirrell his son.

For the barony of Ferbill: George Fitz Garrett.—Garret Dareye.

For the territories of all the Daltones and their folowers: Mr. Marshall.—Richarde Dalton.—Henry McEdmonde Dalton.

For the territories of McGallis countrey and the Bryne: Thomas Straunge.—Garret Dillowne.

For Delamares countrey: Delamare.

The like commission and instructions for the countie of Lowthe directed to the commyssioners under written: fol. 125.

My lorde of Loweth, generall capitain appointed to have the leading of the horsemen of the same shire, and the sherife of the said shire for the footmen of the same.

For the musters of the barony of Ferrarde: George Plonket, sherife. —Richard Plonket of Newes.—Nicholas Dromgowle.—Christopher Dowdall of the Newton.

For the barony of Ardee: White, of Richardstowne.—Nicholas Tathe of Rahaster.—Peter White.—Robert Tathe of Mullagharrye.

For the barony of Lowthe: sir James Garlande.—Edwarde Garlande of Garlandston.—Nicholas Tathe of Balbragan.—Patricke Clynton of Dromcashell.

For the baronyes of Dundalke and Cowley: sir John Bedlowe, knight.—James Brandon, of Dundalke.—John Cashell of Dundalke.—Richard Bedlowe of Kilsaran.

The like commyssion and instruction for the countie of Kyldare directed to the commyssioners under writtin, videlicet; fol. 125b.

Therle of Kyldare, capitayn generall, appointed to have the leading of all the horssemen and footmen of that shire and his substitutes under him.

For the musters of the barony of Sawte: sir John Allen.—Thomas Lang.—Thomas Allen.—Patricke Sarsfelde.

For the barony of the Nasse.—Ewstace, of Castellmarten.—Sutton, of Tippar.—James Flatisburye.—Morice Fitzgarret, of Osberston.

For the barony of the Carbry: Henry Cowley.—Walter Bremyngham, of Donfert.—Walter Bremyngham of Carricke.—Bremyngham of Russelleswod.

For the baronyes of Oulterincy[1] and Okeythy: Aylmer, of Lyons.—Owgan of Racothie.—Olyver Sutton.—James Ewstace.

For the barony of Conalde.[2]—Garret FitzPhilip.—Garret Sutton.—Davy Ogan of Ladiston.—Edmonnde Mysett.

For the half barony of Kilcullyn: The lorde of Baltinglas and his substitutes.

For the barony of Kilka: Walter Pepparde.—Richard Wall.—James FitzGarrett of Grange Mollen.—Morice Ohikye. fol. 126.

For the baronye of Norraghe and Rabane: The baron of Rabane.—Garret Wesley, of Blackhall.—Richarde Ewstace of Tullaghgarry.—William Keyn.

[1] Oughterany. [2] Connell.

1560. For the barony of Offally: Sir Morice Fitz Thomas.—Raymonde Oge.—Thomas Moyle.—Thomas Fitz Edmonnde.

For the barony of Clean:[1] Edwarde Fitz James.—Garet Baron.—James Fitz Garret, of Donnowre.—Olyver Ogan.[2]

[XCVIII.]—By the lorde liewtenaunt:

fol. 127. Trustie and welbeloved we grete you well: And wheare for the service of the quenes highness we have thought good at this present to entertayne three hundreth sparres of her majesties galloglasses under your conducte for one quarter of a yere: we lett you witt that we have directed our severall mandates unto Obyrne and unto Omoloy and unto the capitaynes of the Analy to furnyshe you of your bonaght for the same accordingly, the which mandates you shall receyve herewith to be delyvered unto them, and therefore will and chardge you and every of you to assemble and prepare your saide numbre of sparres of galloglasses and with all expedicion receyve your saide bonaght appointed and furthewith be with them in redynes to her majesties service as you shall from us have comandement. Herof se you faill not in any wise.

Yeven at Rossegarlande, the xxii[th] of July, 1560.

To Alexandre M[c]Tirrelaughe, Tirrelaughe M[c]Donyll, Callonghe M[c]Tirrelaughe, and the rest of the capitaynes of the quenes majesties galloglasses, and to every of them.[3]

fol. 128. [XCIX.]—Per dominum locumtenentem regni Hiberniæ:

Dilecti, salutem: Quandoquidem expedire censuimus turmas aliquot ex galloglassiis cum suis capitaneis sub stipendiis et militia reginæ dominæ nostræ in presens tempus habendas, quodque vestri muneris est bonagium exhibere centum ac viginti sparris galloglassiorum ad servitium suæ majestatis in unum anni quarterium quottannis: vobis ergo ex parte suæ majestatis serio injungendo mandamus, ut expedite bonagium parari et exhiberi curetis capitaneis eorundem galloglassiorum suæ majestatis seu istarum litterarum latori pro centum ac viginti sparris galloglassiorum sub eorum ductu pro anni quarterio, dimidium vero ejusdem bonagii in victualibus, prout de more assuetum est.

Atque istuc facere nullatenus omittatis seu differatis vel excusetis, sicuti officii vestri erga majestatem suam memores estis; ac de alias respondendo cavetis.

Data sub signeto suæ majestatis e Rosgarlande, xxii[o] die Julii, anno regni majestatis suæ secundo [1560].

Dilectis nostris Ofarrall Bane et Ofarrall Boye, ac ceteris capitaneis de Aneley.

fol. 128b. [C.]—The generall hosting northwarde againste Shane Oneill, set furth by the most honorable erle of Sussex, lord liewtenant generall of the realme of Irelande, the xii[th] day of September, 1560, and contynue[yng] for xxx daies:

A note of the mandates or scedules directed to the sessoures of the baronyes particulerly:

Countie of Dublin:

Out of the barony of Balrothery: for the lord liewtenante, 5 cartes; Mr. Tresorer, 3 cartes; Richarde Fingles, of Kilsalhan, Patricke Fingles, of Waspelton, Barthillmew Bathe, of Lanndeston, 1 cart; Robert

[1] Clane. [2] Fol. 126b. is blank. [3] Fol. 127b. is blank.

Preston of Balmaden, Crewse of the Nall, Patricke Tallon, of Weston, 1 cart,=10 cartes. 1560.

Dublin:

Out of the barony of Cowlloke: for the lord liewtenant, 6 cartes; the lorde of Howthe, 1 carte; William Talbott, of Malahide, Taillour of Feltrym; Nicholas Stokes of Swordes, 1 carte,=8 cartes.

Out of the barony of Castellknocke: for the lorde liewtenant, 5 cartes; Barthilmewe Dillon, of Kepoke, Thomas Belyn, of Stradbalye, 1 carte. The barony of Rathdowne: Thomas Fitzwilliams of Merrion, Roger Fingles of Portreston, 1 carte,=7 cartes.

Out of the barony of Newcastell: for Mr. Treasourer, 3 cartes; the master of thordenance, 3 cartes; Marcus Barnewell, Walter Golding of the Graung, Justice Talbot, one carte; tharchebushope of Dublin, Talbot, of Belgarde,[1] Barnewell of Dromnaghe, 2 cartes,=9 cartes.

Out of the Barony of Rathdowne: for the quenes majesties secretary, in money, 1 carte.

Marche caringe: fol. 129.

Out of the crosse of countie of Dublin: for the lord liewtenant, 4 cartes; the master of thordenance, 6 cartes,=10 cartes.

Parte of the marches of the countie of Dublin: For the Welchmens countree and the Archebolds, 12 horsemen, 16 kerne; for the Birnes, 12 horsemen, 24 kerne; for the Towles,—waste.

Countie Methe:

Owte of the barony of Duleke: for Mr. Tresurer, 3 cartes; capitain Warren, 3 cartes; the viscount Gormanston, sir Geralde Aylmer, Talbot of Dardeston, 2 cartes; Caddell of the Nall, Birt of Tullock, Hamlyn of Smytheston, 1 carte; the baron of Skryne, Tancred of Castelltowne, 1 carte,=10 cartes.

Owte of the barony of Slane: for capten Warren, 3 cartes; Sarswell of Sarswelleston, Bathe, of Colpe, Netterfilde of Douthe, 1 carte; Barnewell of Stacallan, Barnewell of Roweston, 1 carte,=5 cartes.

Owte of the barony of Skryne: for Mr. Marshall, 3 cartes; James Barnewell of Bremor, Christoper Barnewell of Gracediew, John Travers, of Ballyky, 1 carte; Thomas Fitz Symons, of Curduff, Matthew Beg, of Boranston, William Coran of the Corraghe, one carte; The lorde of Kyllyne, with the rising out of the Plonkettes, besides their marche carriage, 2 cartes; sir Christofer Chevers, Pentney of Carbraughe, 1 carte; Bathe of Raffecke, Kent of Danyston, Golding of Pierston, 1 cart,=9 cartes.

Owt of the barony of the Navan; for Mr. Marshall, 4 cartes; Cusake of Gerradistowne, Thomas Dillon, of Riverston, 1 carte; the lorde of Trymbleston, the justice Dillon, Barnabe Skurloke, 2 cartes; the baron of the Novan; Michell Cusake, 1 carte; Richarde Kilbride, Evers of Retayne, Mysset of Laskartan, 1 carte; the portref of the Navan, the portref of Tryme, 1 carte,=10 cartes. fol. 129*b*.

Out of the barony of Ratothe and countie of Dublin: for Mr. Agarde 2 cartes; Caddell of Caddelston, Aymery Howth of Kellester, Thomas Wycombe of Drynan, Foster of Killieghe, 1 carte; sir John Travers, knight, Birforde of Kilrowe, 1 carte; Symon Barnewell, of Kilbrew, Talbot, of Robartestowne, Barnaby Evers, for Delahides lands, Wesley, of the Blackhall, 1 carte=5 cartes.

---

[1] [Belgarde] Belgrade, MS.

1560. Out of the barony of Dece: for captein Maners, 3 cartes; captein Audley, 4 cartes; the baron of Galtrym, James Dowdall, 1 carte,=8 cartes.

Out of the barony of Moyfenraghe: captein Girton and 20 of sir Henry Radcliffes men, 4 cartes,

Out of the barony of Lune: for Mr. Marshall, 2 cartes; capten Cuffe, 2 cartes; sir Francis Harbart, Lenche [of] Donnowre,[1] Rocheforde of Kerranston, the portreffe of Athboye, 2 cartes,=7 cartes.

Out of the barony of Kenles: for the quenes secretary, 1 carte; capitain Warren, 1 carte; capitain Maners, 1 carte; capitain Cuffe, 1 carte; sir Thomas Barnewall, James Arverde, 1 carte,=5 cartes.

Out of the barony of Mergallen: for the quenes secretarye, 1 carte; capitain Audley, 1 carte; Mathew King, 1 carte; Thomas Fleming, of Stephenston; White of Clongell, 1 carte; Veldon of Raffyn, the soveraigne of Kenles, Hill, of Alenston, 1 carte,=5 cartes.

fol. 130. Out of the barony of Dunboyne, and countie of Dublin: for Mr. Agarde, 1 carte; baron Bathe, baron White, Blakeney, of Saucerstowne, 1 carte; Hollywodde, of Tartayne, Patrike Russell, of Seton, Barthilmew Russell, 1 carte,=3 cartes.

Out of the half barony of Fowre: Mr. Agarde, in money, 1 carte; the quenes secretary, in money, 1 carte,=2 cartes.

Marche cariage: Flemyng, of Sydden, with the kerne of the Polles; Mape, of Maperathe; Drake, of Rathodd; James Betaught, of Moynaltie; Ledwiche, of Kokeston.

Cartes to sarve this journey in Methe: fredomes allowed:

Out of the barony of the Novan, cartes 10; out of the barony of Dece, cartes 8; out of Moyfenraghe, cartes 4; out of Dulyke, cartes 10; out of the barony of Donboyn, cartes 3; out of the barony of Ratothe, cartes 5; out of the barony of Skryne, cartes 9; out of the barony of Mergallen, cartes 5; out of the barony of Slane, cartes 5; out of the barony of Kenles, cartes 5; out of the barony of Lune, cartes 6; out of the half barony of Fowre, cartes 2,—summa, cartes 72.

In Dublin:

Out of the barony of Balrothry, cartes 10; out of the barony of Cowlloke, cartes 8; out of the barony of Castellknocke, cartes 7; out of the barony of Newcastell, cartes 10; out of the crosse of the countie of Dublin, cartes 10; out of the barony of Rathdowne, marche cariage and 1 in money,—summa: cartes 46.

In Louthe:

Out of the barony of Ferrarde, cartes 4; the barony of Ardye, the barony of Louthe, the barony of Dundalke and Cowley,—cessed for cartes in one hundreth poundes.[2]

In Kildare:

fol. 130*b*. Out of the barony of Sawte, cartes 6½; out of the barony of the Naas, cartes 7½; out of the barony of Carbrye, cartes 4; out of the barony of Outer Inne, cartes 3½; out of the barony of Okethye, cartes 2; out of the barony of Connall, cartes 3; out of the barony of Kilcullen, cartes 1½; out of the baronyes of Kilca and Mone, cartes 3; out of the barony of the Norraghe, cartes 2; out of the barony of Reban, cartes 2; out of

[1] MS. indistinct. *See* pp. 15, 92.

[2] In margin: "Videlicet, the hire of 25 cartes for 30 dayes, but they sholde answer for 39 cartes and a thirde parte of a carte, after the rate of 118 plowlandes in those baronyes conteyned." MS. damaged.

the barony of Offalley, cartes 3¼; out of the barony of Clane, cartes 3; summa: cartes 42½. 1560.

In Westmethe are nine baronyes and are not chardged with cartes but pay money when there is no rising out of the countrey:

Summa of all the cartes are 167½.

The rising out of the countie of Dublin and cariage appointed for the same:

Out of the barony of Balrothery:

James Barnewell, of Brymore, 2 men; Christofer Barnewell, of Gracediew, 4 men, = 6 men; out of the barony of Skryne, 1 carte ex com. Methe; Richarde Fingles, of Kilsalhan, 1 man; in person, Patricke Finglas, of Waspelston, and 1 man; Bartilemew Bathe, of Lawndeston, 1 man; out of the barony of Balrothery, 1 carte, = 4 men; Robert Preston, of Balmadin, 2 men; in person, Crewse of the Nall, and 2 men; Patricke Tallon, of the Weston, 1 man; out of the barony of Balrothery, 1 carte, = 5 men; John Travers, of Ballykee, 2 men; Thomas Fitz Symonde of Curduf, 2 men; Mathew Begg, of Borranston, 1 man; William Coran, of the Corraghe, 1 man, = 6 men; out of the barony of Skryne, 1 carte ex com. Methe.

Out of the barony of Cowloke:

In person, the lorde of Howthe, 3 men; out of the barony of Cowloke, 1 carte, = 4 men; in person, Talbot of Malahide and 2 men; Tailor, of Swerdes, 1 man; Nycholas Stokes, of Swordes, 1 man; out of the barony of Cowloke, 1 carte, = 5 men; baron Bathe, 3 men; baron White, 2 men; Blackeney of Sawcerston, 1 man, = 6 men. fol. 131.

Out of the barony of Donboyne:

1 carte ex com. Methe; Holywood, of Terteyn, 2 men; Patricke Russell, of Seton, 2 men; in person, Barthilmewe Russell, = 5 men; Caddell, of Cadelstown, 1 man; Amory Hoth, of Killester, 1 man; in person, Thomas Wycombe, of Drynan; Foster, of Killieghe, 1 man, = 4 men; out of the barony of Ratothe, one carte ex com. Methe; in person, Marcus Barnewall; in person, Walter Golding of the Graunge:

Out of the barony of Newcastle:

The justice Talbot, 1 man, = 3 men; out of the barony of Newcastle, one carte; tharchebisshop of Dublin, 8 men; in person, Talbot of Belgarde and 1 man; Barnewall of Dromnaghe, 1 man, = 11 men; out of the barony of Newcastle, 2 cartes.

Out of the barony of Castleknocke:

Barthilmew Dillon, of Kepocke, 3 men; in person, Thomas Beling, of Stradbally and 1 man, = 5 men; out of the barony of Castle Knocke, 1 carte; in person, Roger Finglas, of Portreston and 1 man; out of the barony of Rathedowne, in person, Thomas FitzWilliams, of Merion, and 1 man, = 4 men; out of the barony of Castleknocke, 1 carte; sir John Travers, 4 men; out of the barony of Ratothe, in person, Birforde, of Kilcrewe, = 5 men; out of the barony of Ratothe, 1 carte, ex com. Methe.—

The rising owte of the countie of Methe and cariage appointed for the same:

1560. Out of the barony of Duleke, [etc.]:

The viscount of Gormanston, 8 men; sir Geralde Aylmer, 2 men;
fol. 131*b*. Talbot, of Dardiston, 2 men, = 12 men; out of the barony of Duleke, 2 cartes; in person, Caddell of the Nall and 1 man; in person, Birte of Tullocke and 1 man; Hamlin, of Smithston, 1 man, = 5 men; out of the barony of Duleke, 1 carte; Sarswell, of Sarswelston, 1 man; in person, Bathe of Colpe; out of the barony of Slane, in person, Neterville of Douth and 1 man, = 5 men; out of the barony of Slane, 1 carte; in person, Barnwall, of Stacallan, and 2 men; Barnewall, of Roweston, 2 men, = 5 men; out of the barony of Slane, 1 carte; Flemyng, of Siddan, with the kerne of the Polles marche cariage out of the barony of Skryne; in person, the lorde of Killen with the rising out of the Plunkettes beside the marche cariage; out of the barony of Skryne, 2 cartes; in person, the baron of Skryne and 3 men; in person, Tankarde, of Castletown, = 5 men; out of the barony of Duleke, 1 carte; in person, sir Christofer Chevers and 3 men; Pentney, of Cabfaghe, 1 man, = 5 men; out of the barony of Skryne, 1 carte; in person, Bathe of Raffecke and 1 man; Kent, of Davyston, 2 men; Golding, of Pierston, 1 man, = 5 men; out of the barony of Skryne, 1 carte; in person, Cusake of Gerrardston and 1 man; Thomas Dillon, of Ryverston, 3 men, = 5 men; out of the barony of the Novan, 1 carte.

Out of the barony of the Novan:

The lord of Trymleston, 8 men; the justice Dillon, 2 men; Barnaby Scurloke, 2 men, = 12 men; out of the barony of the Novan, 2 cartes; in person, the baron of the Novan and 2 men; in person, Michaell
fol. 132. Cusake and 1 man, = 5 men; out of the barony of the Novan, 1 carte; Richarde, of Kilbryde, 4 men; Evers of Retayne, 1 man; Myssett, of Lascartan, 1 man, = 6 men; out of the barony of the Novan, 1 carte; the portref of the Novan, 3 men; the portref of Trym, 3 men, = 6 men; out of the barony of the Novan, 1 carte.

Out of the barony of Ratothe:

Symonnde Barnewell, of Kilbrew, 1 man; Talbot of Robertston, 1 man; Barnabe Evers, for Delahides landes, 1 man; in person, Wesley of the Blackehall and one man, = 6 men; out of the barony of Ratothe, 1 carte.

Out of the baronyes of Dece and Moyfenraghe:

In person, the baron of Galtrym and 3 men; James Dowdall, 1 man, = 5 men; out of the barony of Dece, 1 carte.

Out of the barony of Lune:

Sir Frauncis Herbert, 2 men; Lence of Donnowre, 1 man; in person, Rocheforde of Kerranston, the portref of Athboye, out of the barony of Lune, 2 cartes.

Out of the barony of Kenles:

Sir Thomas Barnewell, 3 horsmen; James Arverde, 2 horsmen, = 5 horsmen; out of the barony of Kenles, 1 carte; Mape, of Maperathe, 1 horsman; in person, Drake, of Rathhodde, and 1 horsman; in person, James Betaghe, of Moynalte, and 3 horsmen; Ledwiche, of Cokeston, 1 horsman = 8 horsmen. Out of the marche carriage to have their carriage.

Out of the barony of Mergallen : 1560.

Thomas Fleming, of Stephinston, 3 horsmen ; White, of Clongell, 2 horsmen, = 5 horsmen; out of the barony of Mergallen, 1 carte; Veldon, of Raffin, 2 horsmen; the suffreyn of Kenles, 2 men ; Hill, of Allenston, 1 man, = 2 horsmen, 3 fotemen. Out of the barony of Mergallen, 1 carte. fol. 132b.

Here is no mention of the baron of Slane and all the rest of the Plunkettes that are appointed to tary at home but are referred to use at your lordeshippes pleasures.

The citie of Dublin, for 60 men :

Out of the barony of Sawte, 6½ cartes ; out of the barony of Carbrye, 4 cartes. Item : 10½ cartes.

The towne of Drogheda, for 40 men :

Out of the barony of Ferrarde, 4 cartes.

The lorde lieutenante, 20 cartes :

Out of the barony of Balrotherye, 5 cartes; out of the barony of Cowloke, 6 cartes ; out of Castleknocke, 5 cartes; out of the crosse of Dublin, 4 cartes.

Mr. Thesaurer, 9 cartes :

Out of the barony of Balrothery, 3 cartes; out of the barony of Newcastell, 3 cartes ; out of the barony of Duleke, 3 cartes.

Mr. Marshall, 9 cartes :

Out of the barony of Skryne, 3 cartes ; out of the barony of the Novan, 4 cartes; out of the barony of Lune, 2 cartes.

Master of thordynaunce, 9 cartes :

Out of the crosse of Dublin, 6 cartes; out of the barony of Newcastle, 3 cartes.

Mr. Agarde, 4 cartes : fol. 133.

Out of the barony of Ratothe, 2 cartes ; out of Dunboyne, 1 carte ; out of the half barony of Fower in money for 1 carte.

Captein Waren, 7 cartes :

Out of Slane, 3 cartes ; out of Dulcke, 3 cartes; out of Kenles, 1 carte.

Captain Girton, the quenes secretary, and 20 of sir Henry Radcliffes men :

Out of the barony of Moyefenraghe, 4 cartes; out of the barony of Sawte, in money for ½ carte.

Captain Maners :

Out of Dece, 3 cartes ; out of Kenles, 1 carte.

Captain Cuffe :

Out of Kenles, 2 cartes ; out of Lune, 2 cartes.

1560. Captain Audley:

Out of the barony of Dece, 4 cartes; out of Mergalien, 1 carte.

Mr. Secretary and his men:

Out of the barony of Mergallen, 1 carte; oute of the baronye of Rathedowne, 1 carte in money; out of Kenles baronye, 1 carte; oute of the barony of Fowre, 1 carte.

Mathew King:

Out of Mergallen, 1 carte.

The cesse of Uriell remaynethe at your lordshippes pleasur and the cesse of Westmethe and the marche cariage among the Birnes, Tooles, etc.

Note that there remayneth one carte in the Newecastell unlymytted.

fol. 134. [CI.]—At Waterforde, the firste of Auguste, 1560:

T. Sussex.—Wheare it appeareth to us, the lorde liewtennaunt and counsaill, that a greate number of billes, causes and complaints exhibited unto us and remytted by us to the ordre and determynacion of dyvers persons rest by the negligence of them to whom the bills causes and complaintes be remytted utterly undetermyned so as the parties complaying without obteynyng of justice remayne still greved:

It is by us, the lorde lieutennaunt the nobiltie and counsaill, now assembled, agreed, ordered and concluded, that whensoever any bill, cause or complaynte shall be by us remytted to the hearing and determynacion of any person or persons, that the saide person or persons to whom suche bill cause or complaynte shalbe remytted shall, with suche convenient expedition at he or they maye, call before him or them the parties in the saide bill or complainte expressed and upon just examynacion of the matter shall take an upright and directe ordre, according to justice, whereupon he or they so by us authorised shall directe his or their letteres to the sherife of the countie or other the queenes majesties officer or officeres to whom in that case it shall appertayne to see justice mynistered and executed, according to the ordre by him or them so taken the copie whereof signed with his or their handes he or they shall sende to

fol. 134b. the saide sherife or other the quenes officer for his better instructing of that he shall have to doe.

And if any person or persons to whom any suche cause or complaynte shall be by us remytted, shall negligently or willfully deferre or delaye the juste ordering of the matter therin conteyned and to sende his or their letteres with the coppie of his or theirs ordre to the sherife or other officer for thexecution of the same, that then he or they who shall negligently or wilfully deferre or delaye the parties of justice in sorte above saide, shall upon due profe thereof before the lorde liewtennaunt and counsaill forfeite to the quenes majestie the juste value of somuche as the partie greved shall by due ordre recover against the partie upon whom he shall complayne of all suche thinges as in the bill of complaynte so remytted were declared.

Provided that if he or they to whom any suche bill cause or complaynte shalbe remytted shall with convenient expedicion advertise us of a juste cause why he or they cannot well ende that matter whereby he may appoint the determynacion thereof to some other that then he shall not be within the compasse of this oure ordre.

fol. 135. And if any sherife or other officer who shall receyve any suche lettere and coppie of ordre from any suche person or persons to whom any

suche bill cause or complaint shalbe by us remytted shall negligently 1560.
or wilfully deferre or delaye the juste execution of justice according to the ordre prescribed to him that then he shall forfaite to the quenes majestie upon juste profe thereof the juste value of the thing expressed in thordre.

Provided that if the sherifes or other officer be not of habilitie to put the same in execution that then he shall demaunde ayde of the chief person dwelling in that countie, and if the saide chiefe person shall refuse to ayde him, then the sherife to be discharged of all forfeiting and the chief person so refusing to gyve ayde to incurre the penaltie appointed to the sherife.

And for the better encouragemente of such as shall travaill therein it is ordered that the lorde liewtenunt and counsaill shall in all remyttalles wheare they think the partie or parties to whom the bill, cause or complaynt shalbe remytted worthie to have any recompence for their travaill, appoint what recompence the partie greved shall geve to them for their travaill.

H. Dublin, canc.—G. Kyldare.—Thomas Ormonde, Ossory.—Roland Baltynglas.—John Caroghmore.—Edmonde Dunboyn—Gerot Desmound.—G. Stanley.—W. Fitzwylliams.—Conor Thomonde.—Henry Radeclyff.—John Parker.—Jaques Wingfeld.—Thomas Cusake.—John Chaloner.—Francis Agarde.[1]

[CII.]—Orders[2] taken by the lorde liewtennant and counsaill fol. 136.
betwene the lorde Power and the gentilmen and freholders of the Powerne countrey, at Waterforde, the firste of Auguste, 1560:

T. Sussex.—Upon complaynt and mocions on either partie exhibited and brought before us by the lorde Power, capitain of the Powerne countrey, in the countie of Waterforde, and the gentilmen and freholders of that parte of the saide countie adjoyning to the citie of Waterforde, we, the lord liewtennaunt and the rest of the nobilitie and counsaill of this realme whose names are herunto subscribed, do ordeyne and adwarde articularly as ensuying:

[1.] Imprimis: Whereas there was heretofore certain orders by us made decreed and adwarded betwene the saide lorde Power and the saide gentilmen and freholders at Waterforde, the xxviii[th] day of Novembre, 1558, we do eftsones by thiese presentes ratifie and confirme all and singuler the saide orders to stande in full force and effecte.

[2.] Item: Whereas it hathe been complayned that the saide lorde Power over and above thexpences of theight horsemen and twelve kerne by our aforsaide ordre allowed unto him upon the saide countrey hathe dyverse tymes synce surchardged and burthened the same with superfluouse and extraordinary numbres of the companyes of the erle of Desmonde, the erle of Ormondes, the erle of Kildares and others cessed at his owne pleasure without thassentes or witting of the saide freholders and gentilmen, we do ordeyn that the saide lorde Power hensfurthe upon all suche occasions and upon all the chardges to be put upon the countrey for any causes shall geve warnyng to all the freholders of the countrey in the parishe churches where they dwell upon the Sonday before at what place and howre they shall assemble for that purpose.

And if the necessitie of the cace require more speede, then he shall geve warnyng thereof by the seriauntes at the mansion or chiefe howse of every suche freholder or gentilman within the saide countrey, and so fol. 136b.

[1] Fol. 135b. is blank.

[2] In margin: "Copia."

1560. order to be taken by the consent of the countrey for the indifferent bearing of those chardges when the same is occasioned by especiall lettere or commyssion for any cause touching the quenes service and when the comyng of any of them shalbe for their owne causes or pleasure then noon of the countrey to be chardged ne cessed with them but suche as be contented and geve their assent therunto.

[3.] Item: Whereas it hath been further complayned that the saide lord Power, over and above thexpences of the saide eight horsmen and twelve kerne, taketh capitaynes meate on them, whiche was not spoken of in the saide orders, it is by us nowe further for a more playne interpretacion of that article declared and ordeyned that the bushop of Waterforde and the sherife of the countie of Waterforde shall with thassent of the freholders cause the saide eight horsmen and twelve kearne to be indifferently cessed upon the whole countrey the seventhe of Auguste, and that the saide lorde Power shall be accompted for one of those eight horsmen, and at all suche tymes as he shalbe occasioned to goo abrode or travaill for thapprehending of malefactoures or for any other especiall or urgent service of the quenes majestie he may and shall take capitaynes meate and otherwise not:

And neverthelesse we do will his lordeshippe so to use and moderate the same as under collour of fayned service when there is noo cause he seeke not to oppresse the quenes majesties subjects there with capitaynes meate, being to his chardge comytted to be rather maynteyned and depended then impoverished and oppressed; and that at suche tymes as he shalbe occasioned to take capitaynes meate he do not bring any other trayne with him then is hereby to him allowed and this to contynue till further ordre be taken.

fol. 137. [4.]—Item: Whereas it hath been complayned that for all beoffes and corne cessed and taken uppon the saide countie for the furniture of the quenes majesties garrisons and fortes no payment hath been made to the countrey for the same, notwithstanding the saide lorde Power hathe receyved full payment of the quenes majestie for the same, we do ordeyne that touching all suche mattieres past as to come the money paied or hereafter to be paied for the same from the quenes majestie to thands of the lorde Power shalbe paied unto the countrey in the presence of the bushoppe of Waterforde and the sherife of the saide countie for the tyme being, whom we will and aucthorise by theise presentes to call upon the same and to see it doon.

[5.] Item: Wheare it is complayned that galloglasses have been cessed and charged upon the countrey by the lorde Power and some of the gentilmen of the same countrey at their will and discreation unnecessarily and not for any respecte of service to be doon to the queenes majestie, we do ordeyn and appointe that hencefourthe the saide countrey be not chardged with any galloglasses nor with any other imposicions other then is or shalbe appointed under thandewriting of the lorde liewtenant or governour of this realme for the tyme being:

And whereas also it hathe been particularly complayned by Peter Aylwarde, one of the freholders of the said shire, that wheare his chief howse in the said countie called Feathelyke, was wonte to have been cessed of auncient tyme but only after the rate of one plowelande and a haulf for the bearing of whatsoever cesses, claymyng the same in that sorte by an auncient fredome, and that sence the same by the lorde Power and his seriauntes hath been cessed and chardged after the rate
fol. 137b. of two plowelande: we do referre the same to be ordered by the lorde busshop of Waterforde, the sherife and gentilmen of the countrey, the

seventhe of Auguste, and all suche lyke caces that hereafter happen to be examyned adjudged and ordered by the freholders of the countrey in open assembly. 1560.

[6.] Item: Wheare it is further complayned that the said lorde Power, according to the custome of mere Irishe menne, dothe at suche tymes as he goeth to Dublin taxe and cesse the saide gentilmen and inhabitantes at suche soummes of money for his expences as he thinketh good, we do ordeyne that he shall not taxe ne cesse any imposicions upon the saide countie other then he shalbe appointed by the lorde liewtennaunt or governour of this realme for the tyme beinge.

H. Dublin, canc.— G. Kyldare. — Rolande Baltinglas. — George Stanley.—Jacques Wingfelde.—Henry Radecliffe.—W. FitzWilliams.—John Plunket.—John Parker.—Francis Agard.—Robert Dillon.—Thomas Cusake.—John Chaloner.

Examyned and conferred with thoriginall therof, written in parchement and signed by the counsaillors afore named, the duplicacion whereof is entered in the regester booke of the courte of Waterforde.

[CIII.]—Orders[1] for the cessing of the countie of Waterforde, taken by the lorde liewtennaunt and counsaill, at Waterforde, the firste of Auguste, 1560: fol. 138.

T. Sussex.—Wheare it is complayned by the lorde Power and the rest of the gentilmen of that countrey that all cesses imposed upon the countie of Waterforde be for the most parte [w]holye levied upon the Powerne countrey, and that all distresses taken for the nonpayment of the cesses have been taken upon the saide countrey, whearby they be muche impoverished:

We do ordeyn therfore that as well all cesses imposed upon the saide countie of Waterforde this last yeare passed as also that hereafter shalbe at any tyme by us imposed shalbe eqally cessed and divided upon the whole countrey by the consent of the bushop of Waterforde, the lorde Power, sir Morishe Fitz Garrett and the sherife of the countie, for the tyme being, and others the gentilmen and freholders of the saide countie so as every quarter may beare his juste porcion thereof: and for that it appearethe unto us that sir Morishe Fitz Garrett, contrary to his othe and our ordre taken herin the xxxviij[th] day of November, 1558, hath not aunswered the porcion allotted to be borne upon the diocess for the saide laste yere, we ordre that the saide sir Morishe shall remayne in the maiors custody till he have seen restitution made to the lorde Power of so muche thereof as was allotted to his porcion and for his defaulte was paied by the saide lorde Power and gentlemen of the Powern country or elles untill he hath put in sufficient suretie therfore unto the saide maior: fol. 138b.

And for the like imposicions cessed upon the saide whole countie for thother yere before this last yere passed, forsomuche as the saide sir Morishe Fitz Garrettes countrey lay that yere waste, we do ordre his countrey to be freed therof for that yere, and all the saide sesse and imposicion for that yere levied or imposed on the saide countie of Waterforde shalbe equally borne upon the rest of all the same countrey to be differently sessed and divided upon the same by the saide lord bushop of Waterforde, the lord Power, the sherife of the saide countie, and others the gentilmen and freholders of the saide residue of that countie.

---

[1] In margin: "Copia."

1560. And if there be any other in the countrey that have not paied his parte, we auethorise the lorde Power and the sherife for the tyme being to take a sufficient distresse for the payment thereof and the same to deteyne till they have receyved payment for so muche as shall come to his parte, whiche they shall see repaied to suche as hathe alredy made payment to the quenes majestie of the premysses, of their doing wherin they shall advertise us with expedicion.

Item: For the more indifferent cessing of every quarter, we do ordre that the bushop of Waterforde, the lorde Power, sir Morish FitzGarrett, and the sherife of the countie, the seventhe day of this moneth, at a place to them thought fitt, shall assemble the freholders of the whole countie, at whiche tyme they shall appoint for every quarter two sufficient cessours who shall from tyme to tyme sesse equall upon the quarteres to
fol. 139. them appointed suche porcion of the sesse as shalbe allotted to the quarter under their sessing by thappointment of the saide bushop, lorde Power, sir Morishe and the sherife, at whiche tyme the porcions shalbe also allotted to every quarter for paymente of the sesses imposed upon the whole countrie thiese two yeres passed, as aforesaid.[1]

[CIV.]—Orders[2] taken by the lorde liewtennaunt and counsaill,
fol. 140. betwene the erles of Ormonde and Desmounde, at Waterforde, the firste day of Auguste, 1560:

T. Sussex.—Firste althoughe for thunlawfull assembles made of late by eche of the saide erles it were convenient that either of them shulde be at the least grevously punnyshed by long imprisonement and great fynes, yet considering their humble submyssion with repentaunce of their mysorders and promyse never tattempte the lyke hereafter:

It is ordered by us, the lorde liewtennante and counsaill, that thoffences of the saide erles therin comytted shalbe to every of them for this tyme remytted and forgeven, chardging neverthelesse either of them to take hede how they attempte the like hereafter, as they will advoide thextremitie of the daungiers that by the lawes of the realme doth thereunto bilonge.

Item: In correction and punnyshment of their breaches of the former ordres, it is ordered and adwarded that eche of the saide erles shall paye and delyver two hundreth kyen at Laughlyn before the xx[th] of Seiptembre nexte, to come towardes her majesties buylding in Leyse, as a knowleage for their breaches of orders, which we advise them tattempte no more hereafter least we be therupon forced to cause them pay the whole forfaitures.

Item: For thobserving of her majesties peace from hensfurthe by eche of the saide erles, their men, folowers and servauntes, it is ordered that eche of the saide erles shall delyver unto the undernamed commyssioners, to be by them brought and delyvered unto the lorde liewtennaunt, for to remayne pledges at his pleasure and appointmente, during suche tyme as to him and the rest of the counsaill shalbe thought expedient, the persons here mentioned, that is to witt, John Butler, Piers Butler, and Edmunde
fol. 140b. Comyn of Toloncane for the erle of Ormonde; and John Fitz James of Desmounde, the white knight and John Browne for the erle of Desmounde.

Item: It is ordered that for a further assuraunce and bande for the saide observing of her majesties peace, eche of the saide erles shall acknowledge to stande bounde unto her majestie in two thowsannde

[1] Fol. 139b. is blank.

[2] In margin: "Copia."

poundes, and for the payment of the same the mannor of Kylmanyn in the countie of Waterforde with Glanowbirie and all therto bilonging to be lyable of therle of Desmoundes syde, and the mannor of Blacke Castell in the countie of Methe, with all therto bilonging of the erle of Ormondes syde, and the same recognisaunce and bande uppon eche bihaulf to be in force till it be revocqued. 1560.

Item: It is ordered that eche of the said erles shall bring in and delyver unto thandes and ordre of the said commyssioneres all such persones as be named in the severall billes subscribed with thandes of the saide erles, and that the saide erles shall from tyme to tyme delyver unto her majesties commyssioners for the tyme being all suche their men as shalbe demaunded by any of her majesties commyssioners and that for the observing and fullfilling of this article, eche of the saide erles dothe acknowleage to be bounde unto her majestie in a thowsaunde pounde.

Item: It is ordered that sir George Stanley, knight, marshall of her majesties armye, sir Thomas Cusake, knight, and John Parker, master fol. 141.
of the rolles, shalbe her majesties commyssioners, auethorised to heare and determyne all causes presently in controversie betwene the saide erles for them, their men, folowers and servauntes; and the commyssoners, to be at Clonmell for that purpose the fyftenthe day of this instant Auguste.

Item: It is ordered that eche of the saide erles shall acknowledge to be bounde unto her majestie in one thowsande poundes tabyde, fullfyll and perfourme both presently and from tyme to tyme all suche orders and adwarde as they the saide commyssioners or any other commyssioners hereafter shall adwarde upon the saide causes nowe in controversie or hereafter to be in controversie.

And further that the saide commyssioners and all other commyssioners hereafter shall at their discreation take pledges of the saide erles for the perfourmaunce of their saide orders and adwarde.

Item: The order taken betweene the saide erles at Waterforde, the xxi[th] day of Novembre, 1558, is ratified and confirmed in all pointes, saving in suche as specifie any arbitrement or umpiershippe and those clauses to be voyde for that tharbitratoures and umpieres did not conclude.

For the full perfourmaunce of all whiche the premysses eche of the saide erles have not only subscribed thiese presentes but also are sworne upon the holy Evangelistes, by them corporally towched in the presence of us, the saide lorde liewtennaunt and counsaill, well and truly fol. 141b.
to observe and performe the same and every parte and percell thereof.

H. Dublin, canc.—Thomas Ormonde and Ossorie.—G. Kyldare.—Rowlande Baltinglas.—Gerot Desmound.—Conor Thomonde.—Roland of Cass[el].—William Fitz Williams.—Edmunde Dunboyne.—Henry Radeclyff.—George Stanley.—John Plunket.—Jaques Wingfeld.—Fraunceis Agarde.—Robert Dillon.—John Parker.—John Chaloner.

Examyned and conferred with the copie of thoriginall writtin in parchemente and signed by the counsaillours aforenamed and delyvered to the marshall at Waterforde.

30 Julii, 1560. Post meridiem.—Geven in at Waterforde: fol. 142.

The names of such persones of the erle of Desmoundes men whom the erle of Ormonde requireth to be furthcomyng to aunswere to hurtes commytted by them sethens the last submyssione and orders taken betwixte bothe the saide erles, the xxv[th] of Maye, 1560, hereafter ensueth:

Firste: John O Carwell alias Shane Etlea, proclamed traitor.

Piers Grace, with dyverse malefactours of his company.

1560. Lysaghe McMoroughe Oconnor.
John Fitz Geralde, the erles brother.
Thomas Fitz Geralde, son to Morice Etotane.
McBrene Ogownaghe and his two sonnes.
Donalde Oge Mc Kighane in Tomonde.
Thomas Roo Fitz Geralde, brother to the erle.
William Bourke Fitz Edmunde.
The White knight.
Shane McCrahes three sonnes, namely: Thomas, Teige and Dermode Downe.

There rest some other that be not yet named: Thomas Ormounde and Ossorie.

fol. 142*b*. Geven in at Waterforde, the 30 of July, 1560.—Post meridiem:

Thiese are the names of suche persons of Butlers countrey as have praied, spoilled and robbed the erle of Desmoundes countrey, as appeareth perticularly by a boke redy to be shewed of the day yere and facte thiese foure yeres past:

John Butler, the erles brother.—Walter Butler.—James Butler.—Piers Butler, the sherife.—James Tobyn.—Thomas Purcell, baron of Loghmoye.—William Burke Fitz Tybbode of Ballylogan.—John Butler, bastarde brother to the baron of Donboyn.—Tybbod McRic[hard] of the Grenan, and his three sonnes, William John and Davy, servauntes to the saide Tybbod.

William, Redmond and Tybbod, servauntes to the saide Tybbod

Mathewe [and] Donogh Hogan, sonnes to William Hogan, servauntes to Tybbode.

Richarde, Mathewe and Edmunde, sonnes to William Nynaghe of the Grenan.

Hughe McThomas and Thomas Bakaghe O Hogan, servauntes to Tybbode, aforesaid.

Thomas Comen, servaunt to Piers Butler.
Shane McPiers Keaghe, servaunt to the sherife of Tipperary.
Shane McTeige gaynke, servaunt to the saide sheryfe.
Nevan Duff Mc e Taggarde.
Thomas Vale Fitz James.
ol. 143. Thomas Leester, horsman, servaunt to therle of Ormounde.
John Dullarde, horsman, servaunt to the said erle.
Thomas Shortall, horsman, one of the said erles men.
Patricke Duffe Comerforde, horsman.
Thomas Comerton, son to the sherife.
Richarde Comerforde of Killogho [h]is son.
James[1] Fitz John Grace, capitain of the erles gonners.
John Glasse McTeige McShane and his brother.
The two sonnes of William Purcell of Ballycormoke.
Philippe O Dwere, capitain of his countrey.

These persones afore mencioned are the chief and ringleaders of suche injuries as was doon and commytted upon the erle of Desmounde, beside their bande, retynnue, and dyverse other persones whose names are not presently remembred.—Gerot Desmounde.

fol. 143*b*. [CV.]—By the Lorde liewtennaunt and counsaill, xxv[to] Julii, 1560:

Forasmuche[2] as it standeth with reason and equitie that sesses and imposicions chardged upon any countie or countrey should be indifferently

---

[1] In margin: "My lord of Upper Osserie to bring him furthe."
[2] In margin: "Vacat."

and eqally layed and borne throughoute the whole countie or countrey among them all: and that it is complayned unto us by the lorde Power and other the gentilmen and freholders of that parte of the countie of Waterforde neere and aboute the citie of Waterforde that in all sesses appointed to be levied and taken up in the countie of Waterforde for the fortes or elleswheare the burden and chardge therof hath wholy rested upon them withoute imparting of the same upon any other parte of the saide shire, to thier greate over chardge and detrymente. 1560.

It is therefore nowe ordered by us, the lorde liewtennaunte and the rest of the quenes majesties counsaill of this realme, whose names are under this ordre subscribed that all and whatsoever sesses or imposicions concernyng the quenes majesties affaires or service chardged or sessed upon the countie of Waterforde shalbe indifferently sessed levied and borne equally thoroughe out and upon all the whole countie of Waterforde by the reverende father in God the bushop of Waterforde, the lord Power, sir Morice Fitzgarrett and the sherife of the saide countie for the tyme being, whom we aucthorise by vertue herof to call before them from tyme to tyme for that affaire the gentlemen and freholders of the said countie and with their advice and consentes to lay and chardge the said sessors indifferently upon the whole countie of Waterforde and therin from tyme to tyme to use suche ordre and meane for the levieng thereof by pledge, distresse and otherwise as the use and custome of the said countie with equitie will beare.

Yeven under her majesties signet, at Waterforde, the xxvth of Julye, 1560.

[CVI.]—By the lorde liewtennante and counsail:[1] fol. 144.

T. Sussex.—Trustie and right welbiloved we greete you well, and whereas at our laste being at Waterforde the tyme served us not for to determyne the sutes and complaintes whiche were there exhibited unto us, we sende unto you herewith bounde togedther suche of the saide billes as were not by us there determyned: Willing and requiring you to see justice mynistred unto the parties so compendiously as you may in that bihaulf and of your doing therin to certifye us in due tyme.

Yeven at Rosse, the thirde of Auguste, 1560.

To our trustie and right well biloved the lorde bushop of Waterford; the lord Power, sir Morishe Fitz Garret, knight, the maiour of the citie of Waterforde, for the tyme being, and the sherife of the countie of Waterforde, for the tyme being, and to any two of them, of whom the said bushop or maiour to be alwayes one.

The like letters to the seneschall, justices and sherife of the countie of Weixforde. The lyke letters to the commyssioners at Clonmel and Lymeryke; and the lyke letteres to therle of Ormounde, at one instante.

[CVII.]—By the lorde liewtennant and counsaill,[2] at Dublin, the xxv[th] of January, 1560[-61]: fol. 144b.

T. Sussex.—Where there hathe been complaynt exhibited before us, the lorde liewtenant and counsaill that there is muche money due as well to the inhabiters of the counties of Methe, Dublin, Kildare, Westmethe and Lowthe for cesses of corne appointed for the furniture of the fortes the foure yeres last paste, as also to dyverse Irishemen for beves cessed for the like cause, notwithstanding that the quenes majestie

---

[1] In margin: "Copia."

[2] *See* entry on fol. 163b., p. 113.

1560. hathe delyvered money out of her treasurye to the victuaillers appointed for the paymente and receipte thereof sufficient for the payment of the whole, saving certain sommes of money that be due unto them uppon their accompte for the last yere only.

It is therefore ordered and agreed by us, the lorde liewtennant and counsaill, that as well for the true payment of the countrie as also for the better and more spedy delyvering of the cesse appointed for this yere there shalbe present paymente made to the victuaillers not only of all suche sommes of money as be due unto them upon their accompte for the laste yere but also that there shalbe delyvered to the victuallers so muche money out of her majesties treasure as shall pay presently for the proporcion of corne and bieffes cessed for the furniture of the
fol. 145. fortes for this yere as be conteyned only in a bill rated by the quenes majesties auditor of this realme and subscribed with his hande whiche some of money shalbe delyvered by the victuallers in forme folowing, videlicet:

The victuailler appointed to receyve the corne of Methe shall, upon the xxix[th] of this present January, delyver in the presence of sir George Stanley, justice Dillon,[1] and sir Thomas Cusake, to the severall cessoures of every barony within that countie so muche money as shalbe due to the inhabitantes of that barony for the sesse for this yere, at whiche tyme the forenamed commissioners shall gyve straite commaundemete to the cessours that the whole proporcion of corne be brought to the place appointed by the xth of February next.

The victuailler appointed for Westmethe shall do the lyke at Molyngar, the first of February, before the said sir George Stanleye, sir Thomas Terrell, and sir Richarde Tute.

The victuailler appointed for Lowthe shall do the lyke at Ardie, the firste day of Februarye, before the lorde of Lowthe, sir James Garlande and capitain Warren.

The victuailler appointed for Dublin shall do the lyke the xxix of
fol. 145b. Januarye at Dublin, before justice Pluncket, baron Bathe, and Fruuncis Agarde.

The victuailler appointed for the countie of Kildare shall do the lyke at the Nasse the first of Februarye, before the viscounte of Baltinglas, sir John Allen, sir Morishe Fitz Thomas, and Ewstace of Castell Marten.

All which commyssioners before reherced shall straitely chardge all the cessours to see the proporcion of corne brought to the places appointed by the xth of Februarye, at whiche daies the forsaide victuaillers shall also make paymente to the countie of all things they can demaunde of them:

And if the foresaide commissioneres shall perceyve the whole countie shall not those daies repaire fully to demaunde the payment, then they shall by proclamacion appointe another day within fyve daies after, where the victuailler shalbe and not departe till the counties by the judgement of the commissioners shalbe fully paied and shall also cause every cessour
fol. 146. to make lyke proclamacion within every barony that the people may have perfite knowledge of the place and tyme of their repaire for the paymente.

And touching biefes cessed upon the Irishemen, the victuaillers appointed to receyve them shall make payment to the capteins of the countres at the daies before reherced, and if it shall appere to the saide commyssioners that there be any other victuaillers nowe dischardged, that do owe any thing to the countrey for the forsaide fowre yeres, that then they shall by their letteres commaunde them to be at the places and daies

[1] Dillon] Dillonde, MS.

appointed and shall not suffer them to departe till they shall have fully satisfied and paied [all] that can be justly demaunded of them. 1560.

H. Dublin, canc.—Christofor Donsene.—Crystofor Howthe.—George Stanley.—Jo. Plunket.—T. Lokwod, dean.—John Parker.—Robert Dyllon.—James Bathe.—John Alen.—Francis Agarde.—Jaques Wingfeld.[1]

[CVIII. 1.]—Thomas Sussex, comes, vicecomes Fitz Wauteres, fol. 149. dominus de Egremounde et Burnell, prenobilis ordinis garterii miles, omnium pencionariorum et generosorum illustrissime principis ac domine Elizabeth, Dei gratia, Anglie, Francie et Hibernie regine, fidei defensoris, etc. et ad arma in regno Anglie capitaneus, capitalis justiciarius omnium forestarum, parcorum, warenarum et chacearum ipsius domine regine citra Trentam, ac generalis locumtenentis dicte domine regine dicti regni sui Hibernie, ceterique sue majestatis in eodem regno a consilio, universis et singulis presentes litteras nostras visuris vel quorum intererit salutem:

In veritatis ac rei perpetuam memoriam certificamus quod quum circa mensem Decembris, anno Domini millesimo quingentesimo quinquagesimo nono, quedam navis nuncupata the Turtelldove de Purmaren in Sellandia, cujus gubernator et patronus Petrus Clarsson de Purmaren predicto tunc extitit, economus, vero seu dispensator, scriba vel bursarius, Jacobus Jacobson, alias Skutes, factor vero pro Alvero de Abrigo, Hispanici mercatoris in Antwerpia degentis, ac oneratoris ejusdem navis, Diego Diavus, onusta mercibus Hispania fol. 149b. versus Antwerpiam ex Hispania vi tempestatis adacta, in vadosum littus de Fidderthe, provincie seu comitatus Wexfordie predicti regni Hibernie, adeo periclitabatur ut iidem gubernator et patronus, bursarius et factor, sponte sua, pepigerunt cum Alexandro,[2] Fernensi episcopo, Davide Power, Petro Purcell et Patricio Browne, ejusdem littoris accolis et generosis, quatenus eorum auxilio et presidio quantum navis predicta bonorumque et apparatus ejusdem necnon mercium et bonorum omnium et quorumcunque in eadem navi onusto, recolligi et salvari quiverat omnium eorundem terciam partem dicti quatuor accole prenominati ipsismet ad usum suum proprium retinerent et haberent quiete et solute ab omni posteriori vendicione seu clameo cujuscunque cujus interesse vel referre poterit:

Itaque nave, bonis ac mercibus predictis (quam maxime fieri potuit) illorum ope et summa diligentia ad sinum reductis et salvis, tertiaque parte omnium eorundem ipsis in mercedem ejusdem auxilii secundum pacta retenta et habita:

Tandem supervenientibus Johanne Furlong de Horetone, generoso, Johanne Archer et Georgio Conwey, mercatoribus oppidi de Rosse, habitaque tractacione cum prenominatis patrono et gubernatore, bursario et factore de empcione reliquarum duarum partium navis apparatus, bonorum ac mercium predictorum universorum, vendiderunt illi ea fol. 150. omnia et singula dictis Johanni Furlong, Johanni Archer, et Georgio Conway (anteriori illo pacto excepto) pro summa centum et sexaginta librarum sterling'., quarum centum quinquaginta libre secundum singraphum ejusdem pacti juxta ratum monete Anglicane persolverentur eis vicesimo die mensis Decembris predicti decemque libre pre manibus in moneta sterling' regni Hibernie, quod si solucio predictarum centum et quinquaginta librarum sterling' monete Anglicane in promisso die

---

[1] Ff. 146b., 147, and 148 are blank.

[2] Alexander Devereux, bishop of Ferns.

1560. non soluta fuisset, quod tunc dicti emptores roborarent securitatem dicte solucionis ejusdem summe duplici pignore vasorum argenteorum in sequestracione virorum indifferentium donec persolveretur summa predicta :

Persolverentque interim expensas predictorum vendencium suorumque consortum prout per singraphum inde confectum et manibus tam predictorum vendentium quam etiam predictorum emptorum subsignatum et a nobis visis perlectum et examinatum, presentibus eisdem partibus, pro certo stetit.

Sed quum postea predictus Alverus de Abrigo graviter ad majestatem predicte domine nostre regina querelatus est quasi de injuria premissorum quoad se, vendicans ad se spectare proprietatem omnium mercimoniorum in navi predicta onustorum nec quoad vendicionem, eorundem, quemvis vendentium vel donantium prenominatorum, aliquod
fol. 150*b*. potestatis seu juris habuisse, atque ideirco litteras ex Anglia a sue majestatis consiliariis, jussu sue excellentie, obtinuit nobis, predicto locumtenenti sue majestatis in Hibernia, directas, gerentes datum septimo die Junii, anno 1560, mandantes quatenus querelam dicti mercatoris in eisdem litteris transmissam, adverteremus, ceterasque que in causa illa ad equum et jus spectarent satagere curaremus :

Quibusquidem litteris per dictum Jacobum Skute ad nos prolatis circa vicesimum diem ultimi mensis Julii, illico auditis allegationibus suis, quas nomine predicti mercatoris Hispani vel ejus factoris procurator exposuit adversus emptores supradictos, mandata summonitionis direximus, ipsisque comparentibus qer aliquot dies aures nostras attentas illorum interlitigationibus prebuimus, visoque et perpenso singrapho supradicto predictos emptores seu reos ad eorum causam honestandam prolato, contraque ad illorum instanciam, percunctati actorem seu procuratorem predictum qua auctoritate fretus causam predictum mercatoris Hispani prosequeretur et an valeret et sufficeret cuncta que in judicio seu terminacione litis predicte competerent vice predicti mercatoris Hispani gerere et peragere, protulit quoad eam rem coram nobis instrumentum quoddam manu et sigillo privato Francisci Winter, factoris, et procuratoris predicti mercatoris Hispani, sufficienter fulti, firmatum
fol. 151. signoque Henrici Broke, unius scribarum publicorum civitatis Londini seu notarii publici, (ut semetipse scribit) testificatum et roboratum, cujus verum exemplar presentibus annexavimus.

Quumque ulterius super ea de lite judicialiter processuri eramus post dies aliquot dictus procurator sive actor presentibus ipsis adversariis seu reis coram nobis fassus est, nempe apud oppidum de Rosse, predictum, tercio die Augusti, anno Domini 1560, se nimirum fretum auctoritate predicta unacum consensu predicti Petri Clarson, patroni et gubernatoris navis predicte actum demum fassi et profitentis, non solum navem predictam et apparatus ejusdem verum etiam quamplurimam porcionem mercium in eadem navi onustorum suamet propria bona esse; de nova convenisse et pepigisse cum predictis Patricio Welshe, Georgio Conway et Michaele Archer sibi vendicanti interesse et jus predicti Johannis Archer, de vendicione et quieta clamacione omnium et singulorum premissorum ipsis de cetero et preterito imperpetuum pro summa centum et sexaginta librarum sterling' currentis monete Anglie solvendarum ante vicesimum diem presentis mensis Augusti deducend' ut inde percellas summas illas que antea persolute sunt. Necnon quod restituent et permittent predictis patrono et gubernatori, ab omni clameo seu vendicacione liberam et extricatam navem predictam prout in presens super littus predictum solo adcumbit quodque quoad expensas dicti patroni ac gubernatoris, borsarii et consortium eorum, et

expensas et dampna predictorum mercatorum, utraque pars ab altera 1560.
restaret exonerata et quieta. fol. 151*b*.

Quodque dicti patronus et bursarius ex parte una (antequam receperunt navem predictam) predictique mercatores ex parte altera, utraque pars alteri, sufficienter exonerant et acquietant, signabunt, sigillabunt, et tradent, quodque utraque pars pro observacione et perimplecione premissorum se obligat alteri in ducentis libris sterlingorum currentis monete Anglie levandis et exigendis de bonis partis transgredientis ut merum et verum debitum parti observanti. Quibus omnibus et singulis non solum in scripto ita confecto et manibus utriusque partis subsignato in presentia nostra ostenso et perlecto verum etiam ejusdem scripti verbis per utramque partem coram nobis ore confessis requirentibusque publicum sibi instrumentum inde confici prioraque omnia scripta et causarum actionis quoad omnia et quecunque premissorum in presentia nostra abrumpi et deleri.

Nos, ad eorum omnium requisicionem, dicta hec in scriptum hoc publicum redigi jussimus, ac non tantum ad scriptionem signorum nostrorum qui presentibus interfuimus, nostro scripta hec firmavimus, sed insuper sigillo illustrissime regine domine nostre quoad causas publicas
actorum consilii suis majestatis utimur, in majorem fidem et testimonium fol. 152.
omnium et singulorum premissorum roboravimus.

Data in villa de Rosse predicta, in regno Hibernie, tercio die Augusti, anno Domini millesimo quingentesimo sexagesimo, et anni regni predicte illustrissimme regine, domine nostre, secundo [1560].

[CVIII. 2.]—Universis et singulis Christi fidelibus ad quos presentes fol. 152*b*.
littere pervenerint Franciscus de Winter, mercator de Antwerpia, London commorans, salutem in Domino sempiterna: Cum honorabilis vir, Alberus de Brien, mercator Hispanus, in Antwerpia residens, sponte omnibus modo, via, jure, causa et forma quibus potuit melioribus fecit ac solemniter ordinavit et decrevit me, prefatum Franciscum de Winter et Adrianum de Grote in Hibernia residentem, conjunctim et quemlibet nostrum in solido actores, factores ac nuncios generales et speciales, ita tamen quod generalitas specialitati non deroget, ad vicem et nomine dicti Alberi et pro eo petendi, exigendi, recuperandi, habendi et recipiendi ab omnibus et singulis persona et personis commune societate, collegiis et universitatibus quibus intererit tradere, consignare et restituere, tenebuntur, omnes et singulas illas merces, res, bonaque que nuper salvata et recuperata fuerint Waterfordie in Hibernia ex nave nuncupata Turtur, cui prefuit magister seu patronus Petrus Incolai ex Purmerenda Hollandie que ibi naufragio periit aut per ventum eorundem. Et de hiis que habuero recipero et recuperavero acquietanciam sive scedulas, exoneraciones una seu plures, dandas et concedendas cum pacto solempni et valido rem semel habitum amplius non petendam. Et super quibuscunque dubiis, differentiis et difficultatibus motis et movendis quomodolibet cum ipsis occupatoribus dictorum bonorum aut aliis quibuscunque fol. 153.
concordandis, paciscendis, transigendis et compromittendis in arbitros, arbitratores et amicabiles compositores semel et pluries, ac quotiens mihi, dicto Francisco et Adriano de Grote predicto et alteri nostrum ac coram quibuscunque judicibus et justiciis ecclesiasticis et secularibus cujusucuque qualitatis existunt experiri et comparandi unum seu plures alios procuratores cum simili aut limitata potestate substituendos cumque sive eos revocandos et insuper omnia alia facienda que causarum merita postulant et requirunt usque ad realem execucionem ac demum generaliter seu specialiter in premissis et que inde dependerint omnia et singula alia facienda, dicenda, procuranda et administranda que

1560. dictus Alberus faceret seu facere posset dum omnibus et singulis premissis presens personaliter interesset et negocium exigeret presentiam personalem aut mandatum specialius presente prout per instrumentum procuratorium desuper confectum, gerens dâtum apud Antwerpiam vicesimo tercio mensis Februarii ultimi preteriti, ac stipulatum coram perito viro Antonio Amala, notario publico, cui habeatur relatio, plenius liquet et apparet, vigore, virtute et auctoritate cujusquidem procurationis: Noveritis me, prefatum Franciscum de Winter fecisse, ordinasse, constituisse et in loco meo substituisse dilectos mihi in Christo Inegum de Baldaram, Franciscum de Baldaram de Hispania et Jacobum Escute de
fol. 153b. Pomaren in Hollandia, scrivanum navis, conjunctim et divisim ac quemlibet eorum per se et in solido meos veros, certos, legitimos et indubitatos procuratores et substitutos ad predictas merces, bona et mercimonia petendum, exigendum, levandum recuperandum et recipiendum ac detentores inde et quemlibet eorum si necesse fuerit arrestandum, attachiandum, imprisonandum et extra prisonam deliberandos ac coram quibuscunque dominis judicibus et justicie ministris comparendos agendos petendos et respondendos, generaliterque omnia alia et singula in et circa premissa requisita et oportuna facienda, agenda, dicenda, procuranda, solicitanda, et perficienda que egomet facere possem sive deberem si presens et personaliter interessem. Ratum et gratum habentem et habiturum totum et quicquid dicti mei attornati sive substituti fecerint, et eorum aliquis fecerit, in premissis per presentes.

In cujus rei testimonium presentibus sigillum meum opposui. Data duodecimo die Junii, 1560, anno regni serenissime domine nostre Elizabeth, Dei gratia Anglie, Francie et Hibernie regine, fidei defensoris, etc. secundo [1560].—H. Broke.—Per me, Franciscum Winter.—Sigillavit, subscripsit et deliberavit in presentia predicti notarii publici.

[Letter to Shane O'Neill.]

fol. 154. [CXIX. 1.]—Per dominum locumtenentem consiliariosque regios:

Accepimus literas tuas ex xvi^{to} hujus mensis, quibus et nostras tibi traditas fuisse intelleximus. Nostris autem diem tibi indiximus, videlicet, xx. hujus mensis, quo ad nos ad Drogheda venias ut ibi de tuis rebus quid statuerat regia majestas significare possimus. Ad quas respondes te certas peticiones misisse ad regiam majestatem et inter alia quæsivisse ut sua majestas tibi mitteret protectionem perpetuam pro te tuisque ut non liceret nobis vel alicui alii gubernatori vel locumtenenti hujus regni te tuosve arestare aut detinere pro aliquibus actionibus quoties ad nos accederes, sed solo modo tenere pignora tua in rebus mobilibus et quod regine majestas ad te scripsit commisisse se determinacionem et concessionem tuarum peticionum nobis, ideoque hortaris nos ut scribamus tibi qualiter agemus tecum quantum ad illam perpetuam protectionem antequam accedas ad nos ut desideramus, et quas ex aliis peticionibus concessuri sumus et quas negabimus igitur litterarum tuarum intentionem quoad predicta considerantes hiis prout se res habet respondere duximus: regiam celsitudinem nobis quidem in mandatis dedisse ut prius cum te ipso presente tractaremus non minus quoad protectionem illam perpetuam tibi tuisque concedendum quam quoad ceteras omnes illas peticiones tuas perticulatim et articulatim deinde quid in omnibus aut singulis illis annuerit aut velit sua majestas tibimet coram et presenti responderemus. Proinde aliter quoad illorum quidquam nisi te presente neque resolvere neque respondere commissionem ullam habemus.

Hortamur ergo te, ut beneplacitis et resolutionibus sue majestatis excipiendis, prout decet, te expedias ut adsis nobiscum apud Drogheda xxx. die hujus mensis Augusti, ubi te in tempus illud expectamus : 1560.

Quod si quidvis hesitas aut dubitas de quærelis ullis corporis tui libertatem veniendi vel redeundi illo dumtaxat tempore impetentibus, nos ea in parte protectionem tibi concessuri sumus sub scriptis et auctoritate nostris sufficientibus que tibi venienti ad Carik Bradaghe occurrent et tradentur xxviii hujus mensis quatenus tollatur circa hujuscemodi cautiones omnis occasio timendi aut excusandi, quominus te in omnibus geras bonum atque humilem sue majesttatis subditum secundum spem illam bonam quam sua majestas de te concepit. fol. 154*b*.

Et quantum attinet ad illas injurias unde nobis conquæris de Oregaly, quandoquidem ipse Oregaly erga majestatem dominæ reginæ omnesque suos ligeos se bonum subditum et ligeum exhibet, profiteturque ac firmiter promisit in omnibus se sisti et staturum ordini et judicio nostro de restitucione et satisfactione super quibuscunque injuriarum quærelis tum tibi tum aliis : idcirco illum sub majestatis suæ protectione et justicia vim pati indignum fore concessemus.

Itaque te serio hortamur ut violenter ulciscendi omnem ansam et occasionem abjicias, referasque nostro judicio causas illarum quærelarum tuarum terminandas et componendas quum tute presens nobis aderis, ubi eundem Oregaly tum quoque coram nobis adesse jubebimus, non dubitans quin in omnibus tibi justiciam exhibebimus :

De illo vero quod scribis te Scotorum quendam numerum recipisse ac retinere, admiramur certe presertim cum tam serio et data fide professus es ac promiseris in contrarium, cujus rei tandem memorem admonitum optamus, ut dismissis Scotis illis omnes occasiones suspicionis exuas et deleas, exemplumque illud boni et bene animati subditi prestare ne omiseris.

Atque ita te valere volumus. E Drougheda, xx° Augusti, 1560.

[CIX. 2.]—Per dominum locumtenentem consiliariosque regios :[1] fol. 155.

Omnibus ad quos præsentes litere pervenerint salutem :—Sciatis quod quum Johannem Oneyll, primogenitum comitis Tironie, ad nos accedere et coram nobis adesse apud Drougheda, xxx° die hujus mensis Augusti, volumus ac jussimus, idcirco dictum Johannem Oneyll libere atque absque ulla impeticione, impedimento seu molestacione accedere et recedere concedentes ac volentes eundem Johannem omnesque suos homines et sequaces itineris sui predicti comites et necessarios in protectionem et tutelam nostram pro hac vice et itinere suo predicto suscipimus, dantes ipsi et dictis suis hominibus comitibus et necessariis libertatem et liberam facultatem, potestatem et veniam huc ad Droughedam predictam in diem predictam accedendi presentes esse, et ad suos consuetos lares redeundi absque ulla ligeorum subditorum domine regine molestacione, arestacione, remoracione, impeticione seu impedimento.

In cujus rei testimonium hiis præsentibus nomina nostra adscriptimus. Data e Drougheda, xx° Augusti, 1560.[2]

[CX.]—At Drogheda, the xx[th] of Auguste, 1560 : fol. 156.

T. Sussex.—It is condescended concluded and [a]greed by us, the lorde liewtenant, the lordes spirituall and temporall of the realme and the rest

[1] In margin : "The copie of the protection graunted to Shane Oneyle, delyvered to the lorde of Louth to be geven to the said Shane if he come to Caricke Bradagho at the day lymyted."

[2] Fol. 155*b*. is blank.

1560. of the quenes majesties counsaill of the same, whose names be hereunto subscribed, assembled at Drogheda, the day and yere above written, in thabsence and bihaulf of the rest of the nobilitie and counsaill of the same being presently absent by excuse, and employed in her highnes affaires elliswheare, that for sundry ernest respectes and consideracions tending to the furtheraunce of her majesties service, there shalbe a generall hosting proclamed by writt, according to thauncient custome, for thirty dayes after the rate of three plowe lande to a carte.

The same to meete at suche place and tyme as shalbe upon eight dayes warnynge by proclamacion from us, the lorde liewtennaunt, ordered and appointed.

H. Dublin, canc.—G. Kyldare.—Christofer Donsene.—P. Barnewall, lord of T[rimletiston].—Alex. Darensis.[1]—W. Fytzwylliams.—John Plunket.—Robert Dyllon.—John Travers.—Jacques Wingfeld.—Thomas Lokwod, dean.—Fraunces Harbart.—Francis Agarde.—John Chaloner.

[CXI.]—At Drougheda,[2] the xxith of Auguste, 1560 :

The lorde liewtennaunt and counsaill at this present considering that the quenes majesties fortes and other her hieghnes holdes and garrisons are disfurnished of necessarie provision, chiefly wheate and other grayne, for their present relief, the tyme being nowe moost propice to put order for provision of the same, do will and straitely chardge that no grayne be bought and carryed conveyed or sent out of any countie within the Englishe Pale, in whiche the same is at this present growing or remayning, untill her majesties saide fortes holdes and garrisons be fully and sufficiently in that behaulf purveyd and furnished, upon payne of the seysure and forfacture of the same grayne so bought and carried, conveyed or sent, the one moytie to be to the quenes majesties use and thother unto the seysour himself :

Willing and straitely chardging and commaunding all and every her highnes officers mynisters and subjectes not only to have especiall eye and consideracion to the premysses, but also to be from tyme to tyme aiding and assisting to all those that shall put this our proclamacion in due execution. Not failing hereof as you and every of you do tendere your duties, the service of her majestie and the furtherance of the publique weale and will further answere for the contrary at your perill.

W. Fitzwilliams.—Jaques Wingfelde.—John Chaloner.

fol. 157*b*. [CXII.]—At Drougheda, the xj[th] of September, 1560 :

T. Sussex.—Memorandum : We, the lorde liewtenant, the lordes and nobilitie of this realme with the rest of the quenes majesties counsaill, assembled at Drougheda, and considering as well the disfurniture of her hieghnes fortes in Leix and Offally and other her majesties holdes as also the tyme of the yere to be moost propice for the victuelling of the same, concluded upon a generall sesse as well of wheate and malte as bieffes, swyne and other provysion for the whole yere, the same to be levied in maner and fourme folowing, that it is to saye :

In the countie of Methe, one thowsaunde fortye-sixe peckes wheate and one thowsaunde eight hundredthe threschore sixtene peckes malte, whereof the thirde parte to be beare malte. The wheate and beare malte

---

[1] Alexander Craik, bishop of Kildare.
[2] In margin : "Copia."

at foure shillinges, sterling, the pecke and the ote malte at two shillinge eight pence, sterling, the pecke. 1560.

In the countie of Dublin: sixe hundrethe fouretene peckes wheate, and one thowsaunde eight peckes malte, after lyke rate, price and division as before.

In the countie of Kildare: sixe hundrethe, threschore peckes wheate, and seven hundreth foureschore peckes malte, after the like rate and division.

In the countie of Uriell[1]: sixe hundreth tenne peckes wheate and eight hundreth three schore peckes malte, after lyke rate and division.

In the countie of Westmethe; three hundrethe thirty and nyne peckes fol. 158. wheate and fyue huudrethe tenne peckes malte, after the same.

The whole proportion to be brought in to the places by ——[2] next at the furthest, that is to saye, the corne of Methe to the towne of Trymme, the corne of Kildare to Athye. The corne of Uriell to Drougheda, the corne of the countie of Dublin to the towne of the Nasse, and the corne of Westmethe to suche places as by commyssion hereafter shalbe appointed.

And for the sesse of beofes and swyne, to be levied in Irishe mennes countreyes and upon parte of the shires west warde, there are letteres to be writtin:

To ORailly for biefes two hundrethe and one hundreth swyne.

To the Annally: one hundreth beofes and fyftye swyne.

To Magoghegane: fyftye beofes and twenty and fyve swyne.

To Macoughlane: thirty beofes and fyftene swyne.

To OKelly: threschore beofes and thirty swyne.

The Birnes: one hundreth beofes, and fyfty swyne.

The Toles of Omaily: twenty beofes and tenne swyne.

The countie of Catherlaughe: one hundreth and fortye biefe and twenty swyne.

Upper Ossorie: one hundrethe beofes and fyftye swyne.

Ocarroll: one hundreth biefes, fyfty swyne.

The countie of Tipperarie: one hundreth beofes, fyfty swyne. fol. 158*b*.

The countie of Waterforde: one hundreth beofes, fyftye swyne.

Ferney: fyfty beofes twenty fyve swyne.

Hughe Oge of Dartrye: thirty beofes, fyttene swyne.

The Kellyes beyonde the Sucke: threschore beofes, thirty swyne.

McMahones countrey: one hundreth kyne, fyftye swyne.

The bief at twelve shilling sterling and the porke at two shillings eight pence sterling.

It is further concluded that in the countie of Weixforde there shalbe sessed fyve hundreth peckes otes at twenty pence, sterling, the pecke:

In the county of Kilkenny two hundreth peckes otes, at twenty pence sterling the pecke, the saide otes to be delyvered as followeth that is to saye: They of Weixforde at the towne of Weixforde, those of Kilkenny at the towne of Kilkenny.

And further, it is ordered that the saide corne shalbe delyvered at two severall tymes in equall porcions, that is to saye, the fyrste parte on this syde ——[3] next, the secunde and laste parte before ——[4].

And that the corne of the counties of Methe and Westmethe shalbe after the measure and pecke of Trymme, Dublin, and Kildare according the pecke of Dublin and Lowthe after the measure of Droghedn, and for fol. 159. the otes of Kylkenny according the measure of Kilkenny, and those of Weixforde after the pecke of Weixford.

---

[1] Louth. [2], [3], [4] Blank in MS.

1560. H. Dublin, canc.—T. Louithe.—Roland Baltynglas.—Jenico vic. of G[ormanston]. — W. Fitzwylliams. — Henry Radeclyff. — Christofor Kyllen —Jo. Plunket.—John Travers.—G. Gerrard.—Thomas Cusake.—John Parker.—Jaques Wingfeld.—James Bathe.—Francis Agarde.—John Chaloner.

Postscript: It is likewise ordered and assented unto by us, the saide lorde liewtenant and counsaill, that the said subjectes shall have allowance for the carriage of the saide corne to the fortes as ensueth: Kyldar countie for every pecke of those betwene the Liffye and the forte in Leix 6*d.* sterling; for every pecke in the rest of the countie of Kyldar to the forte in Leix 8*d.* sterling.

Countie of Dublin: For every pecke of the saide countie to the forte in Leix, excepte the barony of Balrothery, 10*d.*, sterling; for the barony of Balrothery, 12*d.*, sterling; to the forte in Leix. Countie of Methe, for every pecke of the barony of Donboyne and Ratothe to the forte in Leix, 10*d.* sterling, and all betwene Trymme and the forte in Offailley, 6*d.* sterling the pecke; betwene Slane and the forte of Offailley the pecke, 3*d.* sterling. And all beyonnde Slane to the forte 10*d.* sterling, for the pecke.

Postscript: Also we likewise will and chardge you to sesse on every plowe lande within the saide countie for the furniture of the howshoulde of the saide lorde liewtenant two peckes of wheate and three peckes of malte whereof the thirde parte to be beare malte, the same to be delyvered at suche place and tyme as ——.[1]

fol. 159*b*. [CXIII.]—At Dublin, the xxvii[th] of Septembre, 1560:

T. Sussex.—Whereas for dyvers consideracions it pleased the queenes majestie to sende over three hundreth souldiers unto the accrew of her highnes army and power in this realme, it is nowe thought meete and ordered by us the lorde liewtenant and counsaill, in consideration of an universall quietnes nowe in this realme, that her majestie be no further burdened with thentertaynment of them so sone as they maye receyve their full pay and be transported into Englande.

G. Kyldare.—Jenico vic. of G[ormanston].—P. Barnewall, lord of Trimletiston.—Roland Baltynglas.—Christofor Kyllen.—W. Fitzwylliams.—G. Stanley.—John Plunket.—John Travers.—James Bathe.—Thomas Cusake.—Jaques Wyngfeld.—Francis Agarde.—Humfre Warene.

fol. 160. [CXIV.]—By the lorde liewtenant and counsaill at Dublin, the xxvii[th] of September, 1560:

The forme of lettere ordered to be sent to the sessours of every barony within the Englishe Pale:

T. Sussex.—Sessours of the barony of ——[2]: Wheare complainte is made that the souldiours under the leading of ——[3] be not so placed within that barony as they maye have lodging and victuelles convenient and fitt for them, and also that the same souldiours do missbehave themselfe and oppresse thinhabitants with dyverse exactions and extorciens, we will and commande you for redresse of the premysses to see thiese our orders to be strictly observed within all that barony as ensueth:

[1] MS. cut away. [2], [3] Blank in MS.

[1.] Firste: the souldiours to be placed upon good and hable husbondmen, wheare they may have suche lodging victuelles and necessaries as shalbe fitt for them, videlicet, upon the fleshe daies, breade, drinke and fleshe; and upon the fishe daies, breade, drinke and fishe or white meates; and the rest of the towne to be contributorie thereto and not to suffre the hoste to agree with the souldiour for any money or lyke exaction for his lodging victuelles or other furniture whiche he ought to have but that he serve him of the same in suche sorte as is before declared. And upon any disordre in the premyses that ye see it yourselfe redressed yf ye maye and if ye cannot then to complayne to the capitain of that bande and the neixte justice of peace. 1560.

Item: That no woman, boye, dogge, ne horsse be sessed upon any hoste otherwise then for every horseman two horses and one boye.

[2.] Item: To allowe the souldiour for his horsemeat day and night only sixe sheafes of otes, double bande with hey and gley; and wheare there is no hay and gley, then twelve sheafes double bande for every horsse, day and night, and for every hackney eight sheafes double bande. And wheare there be noo sheafes made with double bande there tallowe them onlye the double of those sheafes for every horse and hackney.

And every sheafe of otes to be delyvered without stripping, beating or any other guyle, wherby there shalbe leafte any lesse corne in the sheafe then is brought out of the fielde and layed in the recke.

And if you, the sessours, shall suffre in that barony the breache of any of thiese our orders, or any enormitie or misbehaviour betwene thinhabitaunts of the barony and the soldiors there appointed to be placed, and do not forthwith see the same reformed or enforme and complayn therof to the capten and justice of peace, as aforesaide, and for lacke of redresse there, to sir George Stanley, knight, marshall of tharmy, and for lacke of redresse there to us, the lorde liewtenant and counsaill, then we will not only punnyshe you for the same your negligence and disobedience but also cause you to satisfye the partie greved.

Wherfore see ye faill not in this behaulf in any wise as ye will aunswere for the contrary at your perill.

G. Kyldare.—Jenico, vic. of G[ormanston.]—Christofor Kyllen.—Roland Baltynglas.—P. Barnewall, lord of T[rimletiston.]—W. Fitzwylliams.—George Stanley.—John Plunket.—John Travers.—Thomas Cusake.—James Bathe.—Jaques Wyngfeld.—Francis Agard.—Humfre Warene.

[CXV.]—At Dublin, the xxvii[th] of Septembre, 1560: fol. 161.

T. Sussex.—It is concluded and agreed by us, the lorde liewtenant and counsaill whose names be hereunto subscribed, that for certaine necessarie fortificacions to be buylded in Leix and Offalley there shalbe sessed in the countie of Dublin two hundreth men and fyftye garrans with carres, in the countie of Methe cccc. men and c. garrans with carres, in the countie of Kildare cc. men and l. garrans with carres, and in the countie of Westmethe cc. men and l. garrans with carres to be at the Blacke forde and the forde in Offalley every of them with an axe, pikaxe, spade or shovell, furnished of xiiii daies victuelles for the daies here assigned as hereafter particulerly ensuethe, that is to witt:

Of the countie of Dublin two hundreth men and fyftye garrans with carres to be at the Blacke forde the xiiith day of the neixt Octobre.

Of the countie of Methe two hundreth men and fyftye garrans with carres.

1560. And of the countie of Westmethe one hundrethe men and xxv garrans with carres to be at the forte in Offally the same xiii[th] day of Octobre.

fol. 161b. And more of the saide countie of Methe two hundrethe men and fyftye garrans with carres.

And also of the saide countie of Westmeth one hundreth men and xxv[ti] garrans with carres to be at the saide forte in Offalley the xxviii[th] of the saide Octobre, and of the countie of Kyldare two hundreth men and fyftye garrans with carres to be at the Black forde aforesaide the same xxviii[th] of Octobre [1560].

G. Kyldare.—Jenico, vic. of G[ormanston.]—Roland Baltynglas.—T. Darensis.—Christofor Kyllen. —P. [Barnewall], lord of T[rimletiston.]—W. Fytzwylliams.—George Stanley.—John Plunkett.—John Travers.—James Bathe.—Thomas Cusake.—Francis Agarde.—Jaques Wingfeld.—Patryke Whyte.—John Chaloner.

fol. 162. [CXVI.]—By the lorde liewtenant and counsell :[1]

T. Sussex.—Where upon the fall of the base coynes in England there semethe to arise some doubt for paying and receyving within this realme of those kyndes of coynes and howe they shulde be currant here in this realme: It is for the decyding thereof thought fytt to us the lorde liewtenant and counsell to gyve notyce to all the quenes majesties subjectes by this our proclamacion that all those kyndes of base coynes be and ought to be currant within this realme of Irelande in suche sorte and at suche rates as heretofore by proclamacion was appointed: That is to say, every teston that was the fourth of October in the furst yere of the quenes majesties raigne currant in Englande at six pence shulde be from hensforthe and so still is currant within this realme of Irelande for and at eightpence, sterling; and that all other the base coynes of Englande shulde from hensforthe and so still be currant within this realme after lyke value in suche sorte and forme as in the said proclamacion for the rating of those coynes is specified and declared.

Wherefore we straightly chardge and commande all the quenes majesties subjectes within this realme that no man presume to pay or receyve any kynde of those forsaid base coynes nowe proclaymed downe in Englande at other rates then by the said former proclamacion was
fol. 162b. appointed and in this is rehersed upon payne by the lawes in suche cases provided.

And for thadvoyding of the gredynes of sondry persons that wolde take occasion hereby to rayse and enhanse the prices of all thinges to the grete discomodyte of the [w]hole body of the realme, we will and commande all mayors, justices of the peace, bayliffes, shrieffes, constables and all other the quenes majesties officers that they according to ther vocacions and trust commytted to them be carefull and diligent as well in seing of the markettes furnyshed with all victailles and other thinges necessary as also to see that the same be solde at prysos reasonable that by the insatiable gredynes of a fewe the [w]hole comonwelthe of this realme be not hyndred.

Dated at Dublin, this xxix[th] of October, in the secounde yere of the quenes majesties most prosperous raigne [1560].

The true copy of this proclamacion for the contynuance of the base coynes of Englande to be currant here at viiid., sterling, le pece. Signed by the lorde liewtenant and counsell, videlicet:

---

[1] In margin: "A proclamacion upon the fall of the base coyne of Englande, declaring how those coynes should be valued here."

Hugh Dublin, canc., G. Kildare, Rowlande Baltinglasse, Christofer Houthe, W. Fitzwilliams, G. Stanley, H. Radeclif, J. Plunkett, R. Dillon, James Bathe, J. Wyngfield, T. Cusake, F. Agarde, Mr. Deane,[1] F. Harbarde, H. Warren, J. Challoner. 1560.

[CXVII.] By the lorde liewtenant and counsaill: fol. 163.

T. Sussex.—We grete you well: And whereas upon sute made to the quenes majestie by Water Hope, it was her highnes pleasure that he shulde have in lease for terme of yeres certain parcelles of landes lyeing in Conaughta, bilonging to the howse of Kylmaynan, nowe annexed to her majesties crowne imperiall, videlicet, the howse of Saint Johnes of Randone with thappurtennces; the parsonage of Ballanclare, the towne of Clowne Mackanyn, the personadge of Kynneleghin, the personadge of Kyltaraughta and Kilvekena, the howse of Saint Johns in Gallwaye, with all their appurtenances, in consideracion that he hath reveled and brought to light the saide landes heretofore concealed and not aunswered to her highnes or her progenitoures:

We lett you witt that because presently we cannot take ordre for the survey therof we are contented and pleased that the saide Walter Hope shall have holde and enjoye the saide percelles of landes with their appurtenances with all profittes and commodities belonging to the same during our further pleasure for the which he shall answere rent to her majestie according to suche survey as shalbe made therof.

Wherefore we chardge and commaunde as well all suche as be occupiers and inhabiters of the saide landes to permitt and suffre him quietly without any your lettes or impedimentes peasibly to enjoye the same; as also all other her highnes officers mynisters and loving subjectes to be aiding and assisting to put him in possession therof and to mayntayne fol. 163b.
him therin till our further pleasure be otherwise knowen.

Yeven at Laughlin the xviii[th] of November, 1560.

H. Dublin, canc.—W. Fitzwilliams.—John Plunket.—James Bathe.—John Travers.—Thomas Lokwood, deen.—Fraunces Agarde.—John Chaloner.

To our verie good lorde the erle of Claricarde; Okelle, capitain of his countrey; the mayor of Galwaye, and all other her majesties officers, mynisteres and loving subjectes, to whom it shall apperteyne.[2]

1560–61.

[CXVIII.]—By the lorde liewtenant and counsaill at Dublin, the xxvii[th] of Januarye, 1560[–61]: fol. 164.

T. Sussex.—It is concluded and agreed by us, the lorde liewtenant and counsaill, that Kedaghe and Calloughe, the sonnes of Rory Omore, in respecte that their late father of the countrey of Leix, was a man of faithfull and good service there to her majesties late brother and father and was a gentilman comyn of the best lynage of that countree: and to thende that they may be so provided for their relief as they be not occasioned by desperacion or necessitie to geve themselfes to fall unto any evill waye that shulde not become them: They shalbe therefore

[1] Lockwood. *See* page 3.

[2] "Memorandum: That a proclamacion bearing date the twenty-fifth of Januarye, 1560[–61], for payment to be made by the victuaillers to the countrey was by error of haste entred in the twentyeth leaf [fol. 144b], next before written and signed by the counsaille whiche shulde have comen in in the next leafe before the matter ensuying."—*See* p. 101.

1560-61. allowed and paied out of such her majesties treasure as shall remayne in chardge of her majesties vice-treasourer and treasourer at the warres in this realme for the tyme being xx.*li.* sterling money of Irelande by yere for every of them during the space of three yeres neixt ensuying towardes their exhibicion at the schole in her majesties universitie of Oxforde or elleswheare within the realme of Englande and the erle of Ormounde and sir Morice FitzThomas, knight, do stande bounde in recognisaunce to her majesties use in 500*li.*, sterling, that they shall
fol. 164*b*. contynnue during the saide terme of three yeres within the saide realme of Englande, within whiche tyme meanes may be made unto her highnes for considering of them with some other convenient stay of lyving within the English Pale.

H. Dublin, canc.—Thomas Ormonde, Ossory.—Roland Baltynglas.—Christofor Dousene.—Crystofor Howth.—W. Fitzwylliams.—George Stanley.—John Plunket.—Robert Dyllon.—James Bathe.—Thomas Cusake.—Jaques Wingfeld.—T. Lokwod, deen.—John Chaloner.

fol. 165. [CXIX.]—By the lorde liewtenant and counsaill:

T. Sussex.—We grete you hartely well: And wheare we be enformed that some disordre doth growe within that countie for that some evill disposed persones as well within the corporate townes as in the countrey do refuse to receyve the coignes of England at suche rates and values as they were proclaymed to be current within this realme in the first yere of the quenes majesties moost prosperous reigne, and so by virtue thereof still current here, and so muste and ought to be, untill suche tyme as her majestie shall by proclamacion publishe the contrary:

Althoughe we do not doutte but every of you do as ye ought to do [and] understande what your partes vocacions and offices be to do herin; yet for the better advoiding of all dowttes and argumentes that by sedicious persones might be moved, we have thought fitt to require you and in her majesties name straitely to chardge and commaunde you, for that by her majesties letteres we have receyved suche commaundement, that ye do immediatly not only cause all maner of people of what degrees so ever they be to accepte, take and pay all coignes of Englande at suche rates and vallewes as they were proclaymed to be current within this realme by a proclamacion sett furthe in the firste yere of her majesties reigne,
fol. 165*b*. but also yf ye fynde any disobedient or stoberne persones that shall refuse so to do that then ye cause them to be apprehended and punnyshed according the lawes and statutes of this realme in suche cases provided, and if any of you be ingnoraunt or dowtfull of the lawes and statutes of this realme that then ye advertise us of your doinge and deteyne them in prison till you shall receyve further ordre from us.

Dated at Dublin, the xxiii^th^ of January 1560[-61].

H. Dublin, canc.—Christopher Howth.—John Plunket.—James Bathe.—Robert Dillon.—John Allen.—T. Lokwod, deane.—Fraunc is Herbart.—John Parker.—Fraunc is Agarde.—John Chaloner.

fol. 166. [CXX.]—By the lorde liewtenant and counsaill at Dublin, he xxiiii^th^ of January, 1560[61]:[1]

T. Sussex.—Wheras it hath pleased the quenes moost excellent majestie, by her gracious letteres to gyve comaundemennt to us, the lorde

[1] In margin: "A proclamation inhibiting the bringing of the base coines of England into this realme."

liewtenant and counsaill, not only to make diligent serche for all suche 1560–61.
persones as shall convey any of the base coignes of Englande into this her realme, contrary to the proclamation in that bihaulf sett furthe in Englande, and to see them straitely and severely punnyshed for their offences, but also, if occasion shulde serve, to advertise their doinges to her majestie, or to her honorable pryvie counsaill, wherby further inquisicion might be made of suche persones and therby further punnyshement taken of them to the terrour of others.

Althoughe it be not unknowen to the subjects of this realme that her majestie hath sett furthe proclamation in Englande, according the statutes of that realme, that every person that shall transporte any money out of that realme shalbe adjudged a fellon, and that we also have geven ordre to all serchours and other suche officers within this realme to make diligent serche of all suche offendours as shall bring into this realme any of the base coignes of Englande, yet some evill disposed persones daily do bring over secretly those kindes of coignes, contrary to the quenes majesties proclamacion, the lawes of that realme and orders taken here by us, by her highnes speciall commaundement, we have thought fitt for the bettre meting with the lewd doinges of suche evill disposed persones and for the bettre execution of her majesties pleasure and strayte commaundemente, to devyse suche remedyes as may seeme to us moost likely either to avoide from hensfurthe further transportacion fol. 166*b*.
of those base coignes out of that realme of England into this realme of Irelande or elles to cause to be returned into the realme of England suche portion of those base coignes as may appeare to us by any likelihode to have been brought into this realme synce the proclaymyng of them downe in England.

And considering that the quenes majestie did with all expedicion after the fall of those coignes in Englande sett furth a proclamacion that all the testones rated at iiii.*d.* ob. shulde be marked with a perculles[1] before the image of the king, wherby the moost parte of those coignes were marked with the one or the other marke.

Forsamuche as it appearethe manyfestly that all those base testomes within this realme bearing any suche marke were brought into this realme synce the fall of those coignes in Englande, contrary to the proclamacions in that bihaulf sett furthe, contrary to the quenes majesties pleasure therin signified to us, and contrary to suche orders and comaundemetes as thereupon were by us geven in this realme, we have thought fitt by this proclamacion to aucthorise every person within this realme, of what sorte soever he be, to stay and arreste the body of any person that shall offre to make paymente of any suche marked testone within this realme.

And further, we straitely chardge and comaunde all justices of peace, fol. 167.
maiors, sheriffs, bailliffs and other officers of corporate townes not only to comytt to straite prison the bodies of any suche persones as they shalbe justly enformed shall make offre to pay any suche marked testone, but also to be themselfes diligent and carefull in the serching owte and tryeing of the premysses and every parte thereof, and of your doinges to advertyse us, to thentente we maye see the parties offending punnyshed according their desertes.

H. Dublin, canc.—Cristopher Howthe.—John Plunket.—Thomas Lokwod, deane.—John Allen.—Robert Dillon.—James Bath.—John Parker.—Jacques Wingfeld.—Francis Agarde.—John Chaloner.

---

[1] Portcullis.

1560–61. fol. 167b. [CXXI.]—By the lorde liewtenant and counsaill at Dublin the xxiiii. of January, 1560 [–61]:[1]

T. Sussex.—Wheare it is geven to understaude to us, the lorde liewtenant and counsaill, that dyvers gredy and ill disposed persones within this realme do in the uttering of their wares victuailles and other kynde of thinges vendable indente and bargaine afore they make any price of suche thinges as they will sell what kynde of coignes they will receyve for payment, wherby they procure with their unsaciable gayne, great disquiet and trouble to many of the good subjectes of this realme a greate disfurniture of all markettes and in effecte a commen and universall disordre:

We have thought fitt for redresse of suche enormyties as already do and hereafter might aryse by the covetuousnes of suche unbridled appetites, not only to geve ordre and commaundement in the quenes majesties name by this proclamacion that no man shall from hensfurth indent or bargayne, what kynde of coignes he will receyve for any kynde of thing that he shall sell within this realme; but also to geve all her majesties true and loving subjectes to understande that if any gredy persones have heretofore, sithens the xx[ti] of Octobre laste, at what tyme the knowleage of the fall of the coignes came to us, made sale of any thing, whatsoever, and have in his bargaine indented or agreed to receyve paymente in any speciall coigne currant within this realme, then he who standethe bounde by any suche bargayne or agrement to make payment after any suche sorte, shall and may offre payment in any kynde of coigne currant within this realme, and that all justices of peace, maiours, sheriffes, bailiffes and all other the principall officers of any corporate
fol. 168. towne shall and may force every man within their severall precinctes, lymyttes and rules to receyve payment in the sorte before specified.

And if any man shall hereafter, contrary to this proclamacion, indent or bargaine what coigne he will be paied in for any thing that he shall sell, then the forsaide justices of peace, maior, sheriffes, bailliffes, and other officeres of corporate townes within their severall precinctes, lymyttes and rules shall not only force the partie so indenting and bargayning to receyve paymente in any kynde of coigne current within this realme, wherin the partie that shulde make the payment shall offre him paymente, but also shall commytt the partie so offending and indenting to pryson and therupon shall advertyse us, to thentent we may cause suche punnyshement to be geven to suche offendors as by the terror therof others may take example:

And like as we woulde be very sory that any of her majesties subjectes shulde incurre the daunger of suche punnyshement, so, considering the great disordre that may aryse by suche evill practyse, we ernestly require and in her majesties name straitely chardge and commaunde all her majesties officers of truste, before reherced, to be according their place and vocacions diligent and carefull in thexecution of the premysses.

H. Dublin.—T. Louth.—Christofer Donsane.—Christofer Howth.—George Stanley.—John Plunkett.—John Parker.—James Bathe.—T. Lokwod, deane.—John Allen.—Robert Dillon.—Jaques Wingfielde.—Frauncis Agarde.

[1] In margin: "A proclamation for punishinge of merchants and suche others as have any thinge to sell that do indent and bargain before they make price of that which thay would sell, what coyne they will receave for payment."

[CXXII.]—By the lorde liewtenant and counsaill : 1560–61.

T. Sussex.—We grete you hartely well: And wheare there is fol. 168b.
enformation geven to us, the lorde liewtenant and counsaill, that of late dyvers of the merchauntes of this realme have in their bargayns with the merchaunt straungiers for wynes, iron, salte and other merchauntdyse brought into this realme, covenanted and agreed to make the payment partly in wares and partly in money, wherby great sommes of money have of late come to thandes of dyvers merchantes straungiers repairing to this realme, and by them been secretly conveyed and transported oute of this realme, contrary to the lawes and statutes of this realme, to the greate diminishing of the quenes majesties coigne within this realme, we have thought fitt for redresse hereof not onely to sett furthe straite proclamation for diligent serche to be made within all portes in this realme that no money may be conveyed out of this realme, as by the same herewith sent to you to be proclaymed may better appeare. But also straitely to chardge and commaunde you to take ordre immediatly upon the receipt hereof that no merchaunt or other within your liberties and rules do make any payment of any sommes of money to any merchaunte straungier for any wares he shall buy of him before every suche merchaunt straungier shall have put in suerties sufficient before you to bestowe and disburse that somme whiche he shall so receyve in buyeing of other wares within the presincte of your liberties and rules, not forbidden by the lawes of this realme to be transported out of this realme. And if any merchaunt or other within your liberties and rule shall make any payment of any somme of money to any merchaunt fol. 169.
straungier contrary to this our ordre, then we straitely chardge and commaunde you that immediately upon the true knowledge thereof ye do seyse to the quenes majesties use all suche goodes as any suche merchaunt or other shall have bought of any suche merchaunte straungier and thereof advertise us or make certificate to the vice treasourer and barones of the eschequier in this realme, and like as for your well doinge herein ye shalbe rewarded with the moytie of that whiche thereby shall accrewe to her majestie so if we shall perceyve you to be negligent or remysse herin we shall see you to be punnyshed to the example of others :

And if any merchaunt straungier after he shall have entered bande, as aforesaide, shall in not bestowing and disbursing the sommes of money by him receyved breake his bande, then we will that you make certification thereof to us or to the vice treasourer and barrons of thexchequier, to thentente the forfaiture may be levied to the quenes majesties use.

Dated at Dublin the xxvi[th] of Januarye 1560[–61].

H. Dublin, canc.—Christopher Donsane.—T. Lowith.—Christopher Howth.—George Stanley.—Robert Dillon.—James Bath.—John Plunkett.—Jaques Wingfeld.—John Allen.—Fraunceis Agarde.—T. Lokwood, deane.—John Chaloner.

[CXXIII.]—By the lorde liewtenant and counsaille : fol. 169b.

T. Sussex.—Wheare there is informacion geven to us, the lorde liewtenant and counsaill, that of late tyme dyvers great sommes of money have been secretly conveyed and transported out of this realme, contrary to the lawes and statutes of this realme, and to the great diminishing of the quenes majesties coignes within this realme :

We have thought fitt for the redresse thereof to comaunde straitely, in the quenes majesties name, all serchours [and] other officers and

1560–61. subjectes whatsoever, within this realme of Irelande, to whom in case it shall appertayne, to be carefull and diligent in serching of all shippes that shalbe fraught out of this realme, to see whether there be any money laden in them; and if they shall fynde any money so laden in any shipp then to arreste the money and the parties that have laden the saide money, and to advertise us therof, that the parties offending may be punnyshed to the terror of others.

And for the rewarde of the partie travailing herin, he shall not only have that whiche by the lawes of this realme is due to him in suche cases, but also shall have at our handes any reasonable sute he can require whiche shall lye in us to graunt; and shall have our good favor in all other thinges that he can reasonably require to the better encouradgement of him and all others in that and the lyke case.

And if it fortune any merchaunt straungier evill disposed to incurre the daungier hereof we do not doubte but the other good and well dis-
fol. 170. posed merchaunt straungiers repairing to this realme (wherof there be great numbre) will with their good contentacion beare with the juste punnyshemente of suche offendors.

Yeven at Dublin, this xxv[th] of January, 1560[–61].

H. Dublin, cancell[arius].—Christofer Donsane.—T. Lowith.—Christofer Howth.—George Stanley.—John Plunket.—James Bathe.—Robert Dillon.—John Allen.—Jaques Wingfeld.—T. Lokwod, deane.—Humfre Warne.—Fraunceis Agarde.—John Chalouer.

fol. 170b. [CXXIV.]—The true copie of the quenes majesties letteres sent for the admyssion of sir William FitzWilliams, knight, into the office of the lorde justice during the absence of the lorde lieutenant:

By the quene:

Elizabeth.—Right trustie and right welbiloved, and trusty and welbeloved we grete you well:

And wheras we have presently licenced our right trustie and right welbeloved cousyn therle of Sussex, lieutenant of that our realme of Irelande, to make his repaire hither unto us for thexpedicion of certain his owne pryvate affaires, and have appointed our trustye and welbiloved sir William FitzWilliams, knight, our vice treasourer there, to be lorde justice of our saide realme during thabsence of our said lieutenant, we have thought good by thiese our letteres specially to require you that as you have bothe faithfully and lovingly geven your aydes and advises unto our saide lieutenant there for our service heretofore (for the whiche we geve you our hartie thankes) so you wilbe likewise aiding and assisting into our saide justice during thabsence of our saide lieutenant for thadmynistracion and execution of justice accordingly, and thiese our letteres shalbe your sufficient warrant in this bihaulf.

Yeven under our signet at our pallace of Westmynster, the ix[th] of Januarye, the thirde yere of our reigne [1560–61].

To our right trustie and right welbiloved, and to our trustie and welbiloved our counsaillors and states of our realme of Irelande.

fol. 171. [CXXV.]—At Athboye, the xii[th] of March, 1560[–61]:

W. Fitzwylliams.—It is concluded and agreed by us, the lorde justice and councell whose names be herunto subscribed, that for certen necessarie fortificacons, trenches and tcughers to be bildid and made in Leix and Offalley ther shalbe cessed in the counties under-specified for one monthe as foloweth, videlicet:

In the countie of Dublin fiftie garrons with fiftie carres and their drivers or leaders, and also wages for two hondreth laborers after viii.*d.* sterling per diem the laborer; 1560-61.

The lyke and asmoche in the countie of Kildare;

The lyke and asmoche in the countie of Catherloughe;

The lyke and asmoche in the countie of Lowthe;

The lyke and asmoche in the countie of Westemethe;

The lyke and asmoche in the countie of Wexforde and Fassaghe or Beyntree;

And the doble of suche and somoche in the countie of Methe;

All the premisses to be levied and sent by the severall cessors of every of the seid counties, unto capten Henry Cowlley and capten Francis Cosbye or to eyther of them as they or eyther of them shall by their or his handwriting require and appoynte the same. And the same to be executed with such ernest diligence as they ne eyther of them be in nowise disappoynted therof at the tyme and place which they shall appoynte. fol. 171*b*.

Post scripta: The men appoynted for the driving or leading of the garrons and carrs aforseide are parcell of the nombres of the aforseide laborers.

H. Dublin, canc.—G. Kyldare.—Christoffor Kyllen.—Jenico, vic. of G[ormanston].—Christofor Donsany.—T. Louithe.—John Plunket.—Robert Dyllon.—James Bathe.—George Stanley.—John Parker.—Jaques Wingfeld.—Thomas Cusake.—Francis Harbart.—Francis Agarde.—John Chalouer.[1]

[CXXVI.]—The true copie of the proclamacion for the fall of the coignes: fol. 173.

W. FitzWilliams. — The quenes most excellent majestie, understanding as well by her highnes deare cossen, the erle of Sussex, her graces lieuetenant generall of this her realme of Irelande, who in this behalf hathe bothe ernestly and carefully traveled with her majestie as by other dyvers wayes, that the dyversytie of standerdes of her highnes moneys currant within this realme as well Englishe as Irishe, with the unequall valuacions thereof, dothe gretely annoye her majesties commen weale here as a matier whereby, besides sondry other myschieffes, all maner of pryses of thinges bothe growing in this realme and brought and conveighed into the same from forren partes, growe dayly excessyve, to the manifest hurte of her crowne, grevous detryment of her nobylyte and lamentable opression and ympoverishement of her subjectes of this her realme, specially suche as lyve upon her highnes pay ether in cyvill or marshall offices or services. And being no less carefull to see to the admendement hereof for the relief and good compforthe of her most loving and obeadyent subjectes, then the naturall father wolde be over his deare childe, her majestie of her tender zeale and princely affection that she bearethe to this her realme and to her subjectes therein, after grete delyberacion had as well with her said lievetenant as with others, which in the helpe of thies matiers be most wise and experte, hathe for reformacion of the said evillis resolved and determyned, by thadvice of her right trustie and welbelouved counsellor sir William FitzWilliams, knight, vicethesaurer of this realme of Irelande, and lorde justice of the same, and of the rest of her highness counsell here, to reduce the said moneys coigned and nowe currant

[1] Ff. 172 and 172*b*. are blank.

1560–61. within this realme, as well Englishe as Irishe, as neighe to ther values as may be in lyke manner as her majestie hathe already attempted within her realme of Englande, having therein respecte to the antient accustomed valuacions of the moneys of bothe her highnes realmes of Englande and Irelande being compared together as hereafter followythe:

fol. 173*b*. Furst her majestie dothe, by thadvice of the said lorde justice and counsell, ordeyne proclame and value that all testons of her realme of Englande which be nowe currant at iiii.*d*. ob. in her saide realme of Englande, shalbe from the tyme of this proclamacion valued and currant here for six pence of moneys currant in this her realme, and so shall contynue currant untill the last of Aprill next commyng:

And that from the same last of Aprill all the said testons of iiij.*d*. ob. and every of them shalbe taken as bullyon and brought to her majesties mynte in England, where the bringer thereof shall have for every teston iiij.*d*. ob., currant money of England, or elles the same testons shall from the said last of Aprill be brought to her treasury in this her realme of Irelande where they shalbe receyved for vi.*d*. of currant money of this realme.

Item: Her majestie, by the advice aforesaid, doth ordeyne, proclame and value that the other base testons of Englande, late valued at ii.*d*.q. Englishe, shalbe valued in this realme from the tyme of this proclamacion for and at three pence of currant moneys here, and so shall contynue currant untill the said last of Aprill, and from thenceforthe shalbe taken for bullyon in her said mynte of Englande or in her treasury in this realme, according to the rates of the value.

Item: That every pece of the base moneys of Englande now valued in that realme at i.*d*. ob., shalbe currant in this realme from the tyme
fol. 174. of this proclamacion for and at two pence of moneys of Irelande and so shall contynue during her majesties pleasure.

Item: That the teston of this realme, stamped with the harpe, being nowe currant in this realme for vii.*d*. ob. sterling, shalbe valued from hensforthe for and at vi.*d*. of currant money of this realme.

And that the pece of a grote, stamped with the harpe, shalbe currant from hensforthe at ii.*d*. of the currant moneys of this realme and so to contynue.

And as her majestie hathe in this behalf most graciously seen to her loving and faithfull subjectes, and ordeyned for ther relief and compforte this present rate and valuacion, the dyrecte and onely perfecte good meane to reforme the grete enormyties and darthes that have bene in growing this long tyme by reason of abasing of the moneys and of the varyacions and inequalyties of the standerdes thereof, so her highnes wysshethe and ernestly dothe will her subjectes of all sortes to understand and conceyve that althoughe even presently with this her most godly and beneficiall order the full redresse and ease of derthe and other myschieffes shall not seme to followe, yett within very shorte tyme the fruyt and proffytt thereof is to the commen and universall joye of her people to be undoubtedly loked for.

And as nature gyvethe the fruytt in due season and not forthwith upon the seede or plant commytted to the erthe, so of this her gracious and princely order must of necessyte in the due tyme followe, and that with spede, the good and prosperus state of this commenweale, which all honest hartes have long expected.

And therefore to thende that malyce of the ill membres shall not gyve ympedyment hereunto, her majestie chardgethe all manner of justices, mayors, shrieffes, and other publique officers and mynestres that have by any manner way jurisdiction or auctoryte to see markettes and fayres governed or victailles to be reasonably assised, that they attende upon ther offices and prevent and staye the malycious covetuousnes of any suche as upon this proclamacion shall seke to advaunce or enhance thaccustomed prises of any manner of victailles or suche other necessary thinges. 1560-61.

And if nede shall requyre to ponnyshe thoffendors herein with spede and severyte. And therein to use no delay as they will answere at ther perill.

Yeoven at Dublin, this xxiiiith of Marche in the thurde yere of her majesties most prosperus raigne, 1560[-61].

H. Dublin, canc.—James Bathe.—Jaques Wingfielde.—Francis Agarde.

[CXXVII.]—The true copie of the proclamacion for keping the coignes within the realme: 1561. fol. 174b

Where by sondry lawes and ordynances made and establyshed in the tymes of the most worthie progenitors of the quenes majestie, yt was provided within the realme of Englande and after ratified and confyrmed by auctoryte of parliament in this realme, that no golde nor sylver shulde be caryed out of the realme, upon payne of forfayture of the value of the somme of money or golde so caryed out of the realme, to be leavyed of hym that the same shall conveighe, carry or sende out of the realme; and that he that the same espiethe and therof gyvethe knowledge to the counsell or to the treasurer of the realme, shall have the fourth parte of the forfayture.

Where also yt hathe bene likewise establyshed that if any serchor of the king may fynde golde or sylver in coigne or masse in the keping of any that is passing or upon his passadge in any shippe or vessell for to goo out of any porte, havon or creke of the realme without the kinges speciall lycence, that golde or sylver shalbe forfayte to the kyng, saving his reasonable expences which he shalbe bounde to confesse and discover incontynently after that he that so to do be warned and chardged by the same serchor, or elles all the saide money so conceyled shalbe forfayte to the king; contrary to which good provisions certayne wilfull persons, as well subjectes and denyzens as aliens, having more ernest eye to ther pryvate lucre, then to the universall state of this realme, and in respect thereof lytle weing the distruction of the same, do dayly carry and conveigh out of this realme the moneys and coignes thereof, to the grete ympoveryshing of this realme and fynall consumpcion of the treasure thereof, if spedy remedy be not provided.

Her most gracyous majestie, mynding to brydle the dysordered greadynes of suche singuler apetytes, do straightly chardge and commande that all and every the saide lawes, statutes and ordynances heretofore made for keping the coignes of this realme within the same, shalbe hensforthe fyrmely and inviolably observed and kepte according fol. 175. to the tenors of them.

And that no manner of person or persons subject, stranger or alien of what estate degree or condicion he be, shall hereafter attempte to conveigh, carry or sende, or do to be conveighed caryed or sent out of this her highnes realme of Irelande, any manner money of coigne of this realme, nor of the coigne of other realmes landes or seingnoryes, nor no plate, vessell, masse, bullyon, nor juelles of golde or sylver, wrought or unwrought, without her majesties lycence, contrary to the tenors and provisions of the antient statutes made in that behalf, upon forfayture to her majestie of the just value of the money, plate, vessell, masse, bullyon or juelles so conveighed, caryed or sent out of this realme contrary to

1561. the said ordynances, of which forfeyture he that espiethe and gyvethe knowledge, as ys appointed by the same statutes, shall have the fourthe parte.

And for the furder terror of suche dissobedient persons her majestie willethe and dothe order that thoffendor in any the premisses shall for every his offence, over and besides the same forfayture have and suffer themprisonement of his body by the space of thre monnethes, without bayle, myinprise or other kind of enlardgement.

Moreover her majestie, to thende the said lawes and ordynances shalbe the better observed, dothe gyve straight chardge and comaundment unto all serchers of her portes in this realme, and others to whome in this case yt shall appertayne, that they be ernest, careful and vigilant in and aboute the full and due execucion of all and singuler the same lawes and ordynances, according to the purporte of them, as they tender ther duties to her majestie and to this her realme, and will answere to the contrary at ther perilles.

Yeven at Dublin this ——[1] of ——[2] 1561. God save the quene. Vivet regina.

fol. 175*b*. [CXXVIII.]—By the lorde justice and counsell:

Memorandum: That where there hathe rysen doubt and question amonge the quenes majesties subjectes upon her majesties late proclamacion for calling downe her moneys in this realme towching the rate of thies moneys ensuing, videlicet: one pece commenly called the Reade Harpe and one other pece commenly named the Rose half peny:

It is by us, the lorde justice and others of her hignes counsell, whose names be hereunto subscribed, as well upon good delyberacion of her majesties letteres, addressed to us for that purpose, as also upon mature consideracion of her majesties meaning, and for other weightie purposes, agreid and concluded that from hensforth the said moneys shalbe receyved and taken in her highness exchequier and so universally in this realme, after and according to the rates following, that is to say:

The said pece called the Reade Harpe shalbe taken and receyved onely for and at two pence currant of this realme; and the said pece called the Roose Halfpeny shalbe taken and receyved only for and at one halfpeny currant of this realme.

This to contynue till her majesties pleasure shalbe signified unto us in this behalf.

Yeven at Dublin, this xxiiith of Aprill, 1561.

fol. 176. [CXXXIX.]—Apud Dubliniam, viii° die Junii, anno tercio regni regine Elizabeth:

T. Sussex.—It is concluded by us, the lorde liewtenant, the lords spirituall and temporall of this realme and the rest of her majesties counsaill of the same, whose names be hereunto subscribed, the rest being upon reasonable excuses and otherwise in service of her majestie absent:

That for the service of her hieghnes and quiet and defence of this realme, and of her majesties subjectes of the same, there shalbe a generall hosting proclaymed after the olde custume by writt for sixe

[1], [2] Blank in MS.

wekes, at the rate of three plowlande to a carte, the same to begynne the firste day of July next to come, and to assemble the saide daye at the Roche in the countie of Lowthe. 1561.

H. Dublin, canc.—Jenico, vic. of G[ormanston].—Roland Baltynglas. —Christofor Donsany.—Rychard Montgarrett. — J. Slane. — Jamys Kyllen.—W. Fizwylliams.—George Stanley.—Robert Dyllon.—James Bathe. — Henry Radeclyff. — Thomas Cusake. — John Plunket.— Francis Agarde—Thomas, dean.[1]—John Parker.—Jaques Wingfeld.— Fraunsis Harbart.—John Chaloner.

[CXXX.]—At Kilmaynan, the xvii[th] day of June, anno Domini 1561 : fol. 176b.

T. Sussex.—Memorandum: That wheare contencion hath growen betwene the three seiptes of the capitaynes of the quenes majesties galloglasses synce the deathe of Donoghe McOwen, late chief capitaine of the same galloglasses, which of them ought to be chief capitayne of all the three septes, and therupon either of them hath produced suche mattier as they had to shewe for them:

It is upon deliberate debating and consideracion therof and by consent of all the capitaynes of the three seiptes, fynally agreed ordered and concluded by us, the lorde liewtenant and counsaill, that from hensfurth there shalbe no more any chief capitayne of those three seiptes of galloglasses, but every of them to be ledde and governed by the chefe capten of their owne seipte:

And that for the more eqall distribucion of suche bonaght as is or shalbe by warraunt graunted to them to be eqally devided into three partes, videlicet, for every seipte one parte, and to avoide debate that in the levyeng thereof might arise they shall caste dyce for every countrey whiche of them shall firste chose his parte, whiche of them shall chose secunde and whiche shall have the thirde parte:

This ordre to stande in force for ever and never any other division to be made hereafter.

H. Dublin, canc.—W. Fitzwylliams.—Henry Radeclyff.—G. Stanley. —James Bathe.—John Plunket.—Jaques Wingfeld.—John Travers.

[CXXXI.]—At Dublin, the xxx[th] of Octobre, 1561 : fol. 177.

T. Sussex.—Memorandum : That we, the lorde liewtenant, the lordes and nobilitie of this realme with the rest of the quenes majesties counsaill assembled at Dublin, for the furniture of her majesties fortes in Leyse and Offailly and other her majesties holdes, have concluded upon a genrall sesse as well of wheate and malte as also of bieffes, swyne and other provision for the whole yere, the same to be levied in maner and forme following, that is to saye :

In the countie of Methe : two thousaunde foureschore peckes, whereof sixe hundrethe foureschore and fourtene peckes to be wheate, and one thousaunde three hundrethe foureschore sixe peckes to be malte, wherof the thirde parte to be beare malte. The wheate and beare malte at foure shillinges the pecke and the otte malte to be at two shillinges eight pence the pecke.

In the countie of Westmeth : one thousande forty peckes, whereof three hundreth forty and seven peckes wheate and sixe hundreth foureschore and thirtene peckes to be malte, after the like rate, price and division.

---

[1] Lockwood. *See* p. 3.

1561. In the countie of Dublin: one thousaunde forty peckes, whereof three hundreth forty seven peckes to be wheate, sixe hundrethe fourschore thirtene peckes to be malte, aftre the like rate, price and division.

In the countie of Kildare: one thousaunde forty peckes, whereof three hundrethe forty seven peckes to be wheate and sixe hundrethe foureschore and thirtene peckes to be malte, after the like rate, price and division.

fol. 177b. In the countie of Weixforde: foure hundreth peckes, whereof one hundreth thirtye and three peckes to be wheate, and two hundrethe threeschore and seven peckes to be malte, after the same rate, price and division.

The whole proporcion to be brought into the places hereunder specified, the one halfe by the twentieth day of November neixt at the furtheste and the other halfe by the first of february neixt at the furtheste, that is to saye:

The corne of the countie of Methe to the forte of the Dinghan in Offailly, excepte the baronyes of Ratothe and Donboyne, whiche are appointed to the newe forte in Leix; and to have for the cariage therof from the baronyes of Donboyne and Ratothe to the saide newe forte in Leix after tenne pence the pecke. And all betwene Trymme and the forte of the Dinghan, in Offailly, after sixe pence the pecke. And all the rest to the saide forte in Offailly after eight pence the pecke.

The corne of the countie of Kildare to the newe forte in Leix and to have for the carriage of every of those peckes betwene the Lyffy and the saide forte after sixe pence the pecke; and for the rest of the saide countie to the saide forte after eight pence the pecke.

The corne of the countie of Dublin to the said newe forte in Leix. And to have for the carriage of every pecke to the saide forte from the barony of Balrothery after twelve pence the pecke, and for the rest of the saide countie after tenne pence the pecke.

The corne of the countie of Westmethe to suche places as hereafter shalbe by commission appointed.

The corne of the countie of Weixforde to the new forte in Leix and to have for the carriage of every pecke to the saide newe forte after twelve pence the pecke.

fol. 178. And for the sesse of bieffes and swyne to be levied in Irish mennes countreys and upon parte of the shires westwarde, there are letteres to be written:

To ORaily for bieffes too hundreth and one hundreth swyne.
To the Annally: one hundreth bieffes and twenty-fyve swyne.
To MacCoughlane: thirty bieffes and fyftene swyne.
To OKelly: threschore bieffes and thirty swyne.
The Birnes: one hundreth bieffes and fyfty swyne.
The Tooles of Omailly: twenty bieffes and tenne swyne.
The countie of Catherlaghe and the Kevanaghes countrey: one hundrethe and forty bieffes and twenty swyne.
Upper Ossorie: one hundreth bieffes and forty swyne.
Ocarroll: one hundreth bieffes and fyfty swyne.
The countie of Tipperarie: one hundreth bieffes and fyfty swyne.
The countie of Waterforde: one hundreth bieffes and fyfty swyne.
Ferney: fyfty bieffes and twenty fyve swyne.
Hughe Oge of Dartry: thirty bieffes and fyftene swyne.
The Kell[y]es beyounde the Sucke: threschore bieffes and thirty swyne.
Mc Mahownes countrey: one hundreth bieffes and fyfty swyne.

The bieffe at twelve shillinges and the porke at two shillinges and eight pence. 1561.

And further it is ordered that the measure of the corne of Meth and Westmeth shalbe after the pecke of Tryme; Dublin and Kildare after the pecke of Dublin: and Wexforde after the pecke of Weixforde. Every pecke to be delyvered by strike.

H. Dublin, canc.—G. Kyldare.—Roland Baltynglas.—T. Louithe.—Edmond Dunboyne.—J. Slane.—W. Fytzwilliams.—Henry Radeclyff.—Thomas Cusake.—George Stanley.—John Plunket.—James Bathe.—J. Wingfelde.—Humfre Warne.—John Chaloner.[1]

[CXXXII.]—At Dublin, the xxiith of October, 1562: fol. 179.

T. Sussex.—Memorandum: That we, the lord-lievetenant, the lordes and nobylyte of this realme with the rest of the quenes majesties counsell assembled at Dublin, for the furnyture of her majesties forte in Leyce and Offaly and other her majesties holdes, have concluded upon a generall cesse as well of wheate and malte as also of byeves, swyne, and other provision for the whole yere, the same to be leavyed in manner and forme following, that is to say: 1562.

In the countie of Methe: twoo thowsande foureskore peckes, whereof six hundrethe foure skore and fourtene peckes to be wheate and one thowsande three hundrethe foure skore sixe peckes to be malt, whereof the thurde parte to be beare malt. The wheate and beare malt at iiii*s*. the pecke, and the otemalt to be at ij*s*. viij*d*. the pecke.

In the countie of Westmethe: one thowsande fourtie peckes, whereof three hundreth fourtie and seven peckes wheate, and sixe hundrethe foureskore and thyrtene peckes to be malt, after the lyke rate, pryce and dyvision.

In the countie of Dublin: one thowsande fourtie peckes, whereof thre hundrethe fourtie seven peckes to be wheate, six hundrethe foureskore thyrtene peckes to be malt; after the lyke rate, pryce and dyvision.

In the countie of Kyldare: one thowsande fourtie peckes, whereof iij. c. xlvij. peckes to be wheate, and six hundreth foureskore and thyrtene peckes to be malt; after the lyke rate, pryce and dyvision.

In the countie of Wexforde: foure hundrethe peckes whereof one hundrethe thyrtie and three peckes to be wheate, and twoo hundrethe threskore and seven peckes to be malte; after the same rate pryce and dyvision.

The [w]hole proporcion to be brought in to the places hereunder specified, whereof twoo partes to be leavyed and sent in out of hande without any delay, and the thurde and laste parte to be in readynes to be sent in at suche tyme and place as we, the lorde lievetenant shall appoint:

The corne of the countie of Methe to the forte of the Dyngan in Offaly, excepte the baronyes of Rathtowthe and Donboyne which ar appointed to the newe forte in Lex, and to have for the carriadge fol. 179*b*. therof from the baronyes of Donboyne and Rathtowthe to the saide newe forte in Lexe after tenne pence the pecke. And all betwene Trym and the forte in Offaly after sixe pence the pecke. And all the rest to the saide forte in Offaly after eight pence the pecke.

The corne of the countie of Kildare to the newe forte in Lex, and to have for the carriadge of every of those peckes betwene the Lieffie and the saide forte, after sixe pence the pecke. And for the rest of the saide countie to the saide forte after eight pence the pecke.

---

[1] Fol. 178*b*. is blank.

1562. The corne of the countie of Dublin to the saide newe forte in Lexe, and to have for the cariadge of every pecke to the said forte from the barony of Balrothery after twelve pence the pecke and for the rest of the said countie after tenne pence the pecke.

The corne of the countie of Westmeth to suche places as hereafter shalbe by commyssion appointed.

The corne of the countie of Wexforde to the newe forte in Lexe, and to have for the cariadge of every pecke to the said newe forte after twelve pence the pecke.

And for the cesse of bieves and swyne to be leavyed in Irishe mens countreys and upon parte of the shyres westwarde there are letteres to be wrytten:

To ORayly: for bieves twoo hundrethe and one hundrethe swyne.

To the Annally: one hundrethe bieves and fiftie swyne.

To Magoughegan: fiftie bieves and twentie fyve swyne.

To McCoughlan: xxx. bieves and xv. swyne.

To OKelly: lx. bieves and xxx. swyne.

The Byrnes: one hundrethe bieves and fiftie swyne.

The Tooles of Omaile: twentie bieves and tenne swyne.

The countie of Catherlaugh and the Cavanaghes countrey: one hundrethe and fourtie bieves and twentie swyne.

fol. 180. Upper Ossory: one hundreth bieves and fourtie swyne.

Okarwell: one hundrethe bieves and fiftie swyne.

The countie of Tipperary: one hundrethe bieves and fiftie swyne.

The countie of Waterforde: one hundrethe bieves and fiftie swyne.

Ferney: fiftie bieves and twentie-fyve swyne.

Hugh Oge of Dartry: xxx. bieves and xvth swyne.

The Kellyes beyonde the Sucke: lx. bieves and thyrtie swyne.

McMahons countrey: one hundreth bieves and fyftie swyne.

The bief at xii*s*. and the porke at ii*s*. viii*d*.

And furder yt is ordered that the measure of the corne of Methe and Westmethe shalbe after the pecke of Trym; Dublin and Kyldare after the pecke of Dublin; and Wexforde after the pecke of Wexforde. Every pecke to be delyvered by strycke.

There is also contributory to this cesse in wheate and malt as followethe, whereof the thurde parte to be beare malt:

Upon the countie of Lymericke: fyve hundrethe peckes.

Upon the countie of Kilkenny: fyve hundrethe peckes.

Upon the countie of Corke: fyve hundreth peckes.

In Leyce one hundrethe peckes, and in Offaly one handreth peckes, which is cessed for the provision of the same fortes over and above the cesse before wrytten.

There is also to be cessed upon the countie of Louthe, in wheate and malt butt v.c. peckes for respectes to be eqally dyvyded, the same to be deducted out of suche porcions of this cesse as ys appointed upon the counties of Dublin, Kildare, Methe, and Westmethe.

And yt is furder ment that if the proporcions cessed upon the counties of Kilkenny, Lymerycke and Corke be brought in, that then the counties of Dublin, Kyldare, Westmethe, Methe and Louthe shalbe dischardged after eqall porcions of so moche cessed upon them as shalbe upon the forsaid counties leavyed.

H. Dublin, canc.—G. Kyldare.—Roland Baltynglas.—Crystofor Howthe.—W. Fitzwylliams.—Henry Radeclyff.—George Stanley.—John Plunket.—Robert Dyllon.—James Bathe.—Thomas Cusake.—Francis Agarde.[1]

[1] Fol. 180*b*. is blank.

[CXXXIII].—T. Sussex.—Memorandum: It is by us, the lorde leutenant and councell, upone good and deliberate consideracone, and for the suertie of the state of this realme, resolved that the souldiers appointed by the quenes majestie to be dischardged in the lewe of Mr. Brian Fitzwilliams bande, appoincted to be placed here, shalbe together with the said Mr. Brians band, continewed untill her majesties pleasure be further knowen, in consideracione that if Shane Onele, with his complices shulde at this tyme of the yeare attempte to make warres upone her majesties Englishe subjectes tharmy remayninge owte of the fortes after the dischardge of thes souldiers will not be sufficient to encounter with him and garde also the Englishe Pale to her majesties honor and the suertie of the realme. 1562. fol. 181.

Dated at Dublin, the xxvi[th] of Octobre, 1562.

H. Dublin, canc.—G. Kyldare.—Roland Baltynglas.—W. Fytzwilliams.—Henry Radeclyff.—George Stanley.—Thomas Cusake.—John Plunket.—Robert Dyllon.—James Bathe.—Francis Agarde.

[CXXXIV.]—At Dublin, the xxiv[th] of November, 1562: fol. 181b.

Copie of the queens majesties commission showed by Sir Nicholas Arnolde and the rest of her majesties commissioners for the musters before the lorde livetenante and counsell of Irlande under the signature of her majesties hande, in hec verba:

Instructions geven to our trustie and welbeloved sir Nicholas Arnolde, knighte, sent into Irelande:

Elizabeth R.—You shall lett our cousen of Sussex, our livtenante there, understande that our pleasure is you shall joigne with certen lordes and other men of worship in that realme to mustre all our guarrisons in that our realme of Irelande, and therin shall require him that he shalbe aydeing and assisting to the beste of his power.

Item: We be enformed by one William Bermingham, sergeant, of Methe, that we have bene greatly deceved, in our mustres there for lacke of nombres, and for other abuses in supplyeng of soldiors at the mustres with hired men of that contrie and suche lyke, not only to the hynderance of our service, but also to the great deceipte of us, as the enformor saithe, to the valor of x.m. li., and for triall therof he requireth that certen of the nobilitie of that contrie and others of worshipp mighte suddeynlye make the mustres therof: we have for more assurance of the truthe, and to avoyde all partialitie, apon speciall truste in your uprightnes, thoughte mete to send you thither to joigne with them in the saide mustres, and therfore will and authorise you, to conferr with suche parsons as herafter be named, or as many of them as convenientlye you maye, concerning the saide mustres and procede therunto as circumspectlye as you may for the juste triall of the truthe therin, examynyng dulye the doyngs of our captaynes there ever sence the begynnyng of our reigne.

And if you shall see needfull, bycause of the diversitie of the places, to have any other to assiste you, we geve you leve to make choice of any one or two of our counsell there, folowing therin as neere as you maye the advise of the enformor.

The persons whiche the enformor requireth to have the charge to see to the mustres be theise:

In the countie of Kyldare: fol. 182.

The viscount of Baltinglasse, John Eustas of Castellmarten, Gerrard Sutton of Connall, Patrike Sarsfelde of Desertdelan.

1562. In the counties of Methe and Lowthe:

The baron of Dunsane, the baron of Lowthe; the cheef justice of our comon place; James Dowdall, our sollicitor; sir Cristofer Chiver, knighte, Barnewell of Crikston.

In the countie of Dublin:

The cheef baron of our exchequer; Cristophor Barnewell of Gracediew, Tallbott of Malahyde, Richard Fynglas, our sergeant-at-lawe.

fol. 182*b*. With whiche persons or with as many as you convenyentlye maye, our pleasure is, you shall conferre for the furtherance of our service herin, to whome we have according to the distinction of the counties, written that they shall herein serve us, and assiste you, according to the credite we have given you, and as sone as you have fynyshed theis mustres, and shall fynde any notable defaltes in any of our captaynes or soldyors, our pleasure is that you shall require our lieutenant to see that eyther by committeng to safe custodye, or by taking bande with surties, the same be redye to answer to their demerites; so as bothe we may be satisfied for our losses, and the enformor rewarded, as reason is.

And if you shall fynde no suche defaltes as the enformor hathe geven us cause to mistruste, but that it shall appeer to you that eyther malice or partialitie hathe moved him, to make a sinistre informacion, you shall then cause him by ordre of our lieutenaunte to put in good surties to be answerable to his faltes, and in that case to declare to our lieutenaunte and our thresurer, that if they knowe no cause to the contrarye they may cause our soldiors to be payde in lyke maner as they ment to have done before your commyng.

1563. [CXXXV.]—At Dublin, the xixth of Maye, 1563:

fol. 183. It is condescended, concluded and agreed by us, the lord lieutennante, the lordes spirituall and temporall of the realme, and the rest of the queens majesties councell of the same, whose names be herunto subscribed, assembled at Dublin, the day and yere above written, in the absence and behalfe of the rest of the nobilitie and councell of the same, beeing partlye written for to have assembled there that daye and not come and partlye employed in her highnes affaires ellswhere:

That for sondrie respectes and consideracons tending ernestlye to the furtheraunce of her majesties service there shalbe a generall hosting proclaymed by writt according to the auncient custome for fortie dayes, after the rate of three plowlande to a carte, the same to meete at Dondalke, the xiiiith day of June next comyng. The said cartes to be converted into garrons after the rate of five garrons for every carte.

H. Dublin, canc.—Adam Armacanus.—G. Kyldare.—Christofer Donsany.—Jo. Plunket.—James Bathe.—John Parker.—Thomas Lokwod.—John Chaloner.

1563-4. [CXXXVI.]—Resolucions[1] agreed on by the lorde livtenante and
fol. 183*b*. councell at Killmaynam, the xvth of Marche, 1563-[4], anno sexto regni regine Elizabethe, as followith:

T. Sussex.—The erle of Ormounde and Ossirie, lorde treasowrer of this realme, the erle of Kildare and sir Henry Radclyf are apoyncted commyssioners to parle with the Moores on Monday nexte, which shalbe the xxth daie of this monnethe, and to offer them theis condicions, videlicet:

---

[1] In margin: "A copie."

[1.] First: That everie septe of theym shall delyver suffycyent pledges for the perfourmaunce of all the underspecified articles to be concluded with them, and the pledges must be theis: 1563-64.

Neill McLyse or Onye McLyse of that septe;

Of Keddowe Omores septe: Lisaghe McKeddowe, or Kayer McKeddow;

Of Rowrye Omoores septe:—[1]:

Of Patrik Omoores septe:—[2] ;

Of Conell Oges septe:—[3] ;

Of Donell Moores septe—one;

Of the Dowlyns—one;

Of Lisaghe McKeddow Omores septe—one;

Of Davy Omores septe—any two;

Of Clanmalaghlyn—one;

Of the McDavyes—one;

Of the Kellyes—one;

Of the Claneboyes—one;

Of Poble McFaghney—one;

Of the Lallors—one;

Of Tirlagh McShane—one;

Of the septe yn Galyn[4]—one.

[2.] Item: That they shall putt away all their men, savinge suche as they shalbe lycensed to kepe, whose names shalbe written, and they shalbe bounde to aunswer for theire doynges.

[3.] Item: They shall muster and showe themselves and their saide men the fyrst day of everye monneth at the queens majesties forte of Maryboroughe before the pryncipall governor of the countree, or his deputie yn his absence.

[4.] Item: They shall not take meate nor drynke forceablie of any of the queens majesties subjectes, neyther shall goo reyotowsly yn grete companyes where the queenes subjectes shall have cawse to be afrayed of them.

[5.] Item: They shall from tyme to tyme delyver to the principall minister of that countie or his deputie, suche of their men as shalbe demaunded to aunswer to anny facte that shalbe objected agaynst theym. fol. 184.

And if they refuse theis condicions or shall stande apon demaundes not thought fytt, then the saide commyssioners shall use their best meane to enduce them to sende two of their chiefest as of eche of their principall septe one, videlicet, ——[5] and ——[6] to open their owne requestes before the lorde livtenante and councell, with aucthoritie to conclude for themselfes and the rest apon whatsoever shalbe theare condescended on; and shall promyse them protection for the meane tyme; they behaving themselfes therwhiles accordinge the laste conclusyon of peace taken with them.

And if they shall also refuse to sende suche two, then the said commyssioners shall take a further day of parle with them, videlicet, the ——[7] of ——[8] to thend they may make relacion to the lorde lewtenante and councell of all suche peticions as they shall have moved at that parle now appoyncted and then lastlie bring them a finall and resolute aunswer, they in the meane tyme observing the articles of the last conclusion of peace taken with them.

---

[1], [2], [3], [5], [6], [7], [8] blank in MS.

[4] Galyn or Galin, now a portion of the southern part of the Queen's county, and sometime appropriated to the rectory of Dysert Galen, in the diocese of Leighlin.

1563-64. And if thereapon theare appeare sufficient securitie for the contree in the meane tyme, then it is concluded that the extraordynarie horsemen and fotemen nowe placed at the said forte may for the tyme (untill further necessitie apparent) be brought away from thence, for the minisshing of the queens majesties chardges theare.

And further it is thought fytt and agreed that sufficient provision and furnyture shalbe putt into the queens majesties fortes in Leix and Offailley betwene this and the foresaide day appoyncted for the latter parle, according to a schedule agreed apon by us the lorde lewtenante and councell.

And it is further agreed that betwene this and the same daye, the Oconors shalbe treated with, to be reduced unto like articles.

H. Dublin, canc.—Adam Armachanus.—Thomas Ormounde et Ossorie. —G. Kyldare.—H. Midensis.—Richard Mountgarret.—Christoferus Tuamensis.—Robart Trimledston.—C. Donsany.—T. Lowthe.—John Plunkett.—Edmond Dunboyn.—George Stanley.—Henry Radeclyff.—James Bathe.—Thomas Cusak.—Francis Agarde.—John Chaloner.

1564. [CXXXVII.]—Resolucions[1] taken at Kilmaynam, xth Aprilis, 1564:

fol. 184*b*. [1.] Fyrst: For that it appearith the queens majesties pleasure is the rebellion lately attempted by the Omoores sholde be spedelie depressed in sorte as it shoulde geve occasion of feare unto others to attempte the like: it is therefore concluded that a sufficient masse of victuelles shalbe presentlie put into the forte in Leix for the sustenance of so many soldiers of all sortes as shalbe appoyncted to prosequute them, and that ootes shalbe sent out of the countie of Kildare to the forte in Leyse for one monnethes provysion for sir Henrye Radclyffes band of horsemen, to begynne the xviiith of Aprile.

[2.] Item: It is concluded that there shalbe cessed for sixe weekes apon the countie of Caterlaugh cxx kerne for the garde of those counties.

And letteres shalbe wrytten to the erle of Ormounde to garde sufficientlie all places within his rule; and lyke letteres shalbe wrytten to all Yrishe borderers apon Leise and Offaley to garde their countreys.

[3.] Item: It is concluded that letteres shalbe wrytten to all persons that shalbe apoynted to have any chardge of men for offence and deffence to be in a redynes at certeyn places with their force and eight daies victuelles, the xviiith of Aprill and then to doe as they shalbe hereafter directed.

[4.] Item: It is concluded that letteres shalbe wrytten to grete men Englysh and Iryshe, and to all captens of countries to apprehende all suche persons as be or shalbe proclaymed rebelles from tyme to tyme and specially suche whose names shalbe wrytten in those letteres, as they will avoide to be taken as favourers of rebellyon.

[5.] Item: It is concluded that all suche of the Omoores as shall not submytt themselves apon condicions folowyng before the xviiith day of Aprile shalbe proclaymed rebelles and sutche as will before that day submytt themselfes yn suche sorte shalbe receyved unto mercy, videlicet:

They shalbe hereafter true subjectes to the queens majestie and obedient to the principall governor.

They shall putt yn suche pledges as shalbe demaunded of them.

They shall obey the governor of Leise for the tyme beinge.

They shall aunswer all parlees and orders for the countrey as other thenhabytauntes thereof.

---

[1] In margin: "A copie."

They shall with all their menne repaire to the governor of Leise for the tyme beinge for all services comaunded by hym. 1564. fol. 185.

They shall kepe no men but suche as shalbe lycensed by a biil subscribedd with his hande.

They shall delyver such of their men as offend or satisfie for the offence; and if there be any notable offender, they shall delyver his persone.

And they shall take forcibelie no meate, drynke, or other exaccion or extorcion of any the quenes subjectes.

And beinge conformable to theis condicions they shall have apoynceted to them in the countrey sufficient to fynde them and their men of suche lande as if not alredy bestowed, to holde the same of the queens majestie by patent as others in the countrey doo.

[6.] It is also concluded, for the more securitie of Offaley, lest the Oconnors might happen to rebell (whereof there ys some lykelihode) that like provysion shalbe made for the forte in Offalley. And that capten Gyrtons bande of horsemen lieng in Westmethe shalbe furnyshedd with ootes for one monneth owt of Westmethe, to begynne the xviiith day of Aprile, and the same to be brought to the forte in Offaley, and that the chardge of all victuelles for the guarrisons in Leix and Offayle, synce the begynnynge of the rebellion to thende thereof, above the prices paiable by the souldiors, shalbe cessed apon the countrey.

[7.] Item. It is concluded that for the garde of the borders of Methe there shalbe cessed cc. kerne apon the whole countie of Methe and ccc. kerne apon the countie of Westmethe for the garde of Westmeathe.

And that sir George Stanley, knight, marshall of the army, shall have the orderynge and commaunding of the borders of Methe, and of the kerne cessed for that defence; and that the lorde livtenante shall hereafter appoynete sufficient persons to take the chardge of Westmethe.

[8.] Item: It is concluded that the lorde livtenante shall from tyme to tyme geve commyssyon under the greate sealle, or by his handwrytinge to suche persons as he shall thynke fytt to prosequute suche of the Omoores and Oconnors with their ayders and succorers as shall rebell.

And nevertheless there shalbe done what may be to deteyne all the Oconnors yn obedience and such of them as will receyve lande apon the condicious before specified, shall have sufficient lande appoyncted to them as aforesaid. fol. 185b.

[9.] Fynally: For that the maner and order of thexecucion cannot in all partes be expressed, and yet it is here sufficiently declared what is ment shoulde be done: the whole order in the execucion is lefte to the discression of the lorde liutenante and such others as he shall appoynete.

And for the better furnysshyng of victuelles, carriadges, horsemeat and all other thinges ordered for this service, the sheriff and certeyn principall persones in everie countie shalbe appoyncted to take the care and chardge to see all orders apoynted by the lorde livtenante and councell to be putt in execution acording the trewe meanyng thereof, as they wyll aunswer for the lackes, which persons shall have auctoritie, to punnyshe eny that shall disobey in these cases videlicet:

In the countie of Kildare: the erle of Kildare, and under him the vicounte of Baltinglas, the sheryff; Patricke Saresfilde, Aylmer of the Lyons and Garrett Sutton:

In the county of Methe: the sheryff, the baron of Galtrim, sir Christofer Chevers; the queens majesties sollycitor, and Symon Barnewell.

1564. In the countie of Westmethe, the sheriff and every person that hathe a chief chardge within his chardge.

In the countie of Catherlaugh, the sheriff; sir Edmonde Butler, Fraunncis Randall, and John a Barre.

And in the countie of Dublin, the lorde chauncelor; Justyce Plonkett, baron Bathe; the sheryf and Barnewell of Gracedieu.

H. Dublin, canc.—Adam Armachanus.—H. Midensis.—G. Kildare.—Henry Radclyff.—George Stanley.—Thomas Cusake.—Jo. Plunkett.—John Parker.—Francis Agarde.—John Chaloner.

fol. 186. [CXXXVIII.] By the quene.[1]

Elizabeth R.—Right trustie and right welbeloved cosin, and trustie and right welbelovedd wee greete you well: Upon earnest request made unto us on the behaulf of you, our livtenante, wee are pleased that yow shall retorne hither.

And for that in your absence it is mete some person shulde holde the place as justice of our realme we will and commaunde you that according to the ancient custome therein usid, ye will make choice of one to be our justice there. And for significacion of our meaning and opinion, we shall best be content to have sir Nicholas Arnold appointed thereunto, whom we wolde have auctorizid as other justices in lyke tymes have there bene, and so wee do require you to have thereof due consideracion.

And although yowe, sir Nicholas Arnold, shall thinke the burden of such an offyce very greate, yet considering yow have there so good assystance of your colleague, sir Thomas Wrothe, and that presentlie we are come to peace with the Frenche, and no perill seene to us in that realme, we doubt not but the burden hereof shall dailie wax lesse and lesse.

Fynally wee will and require yowe all to consult and accord how to demynishe our excessive charges there, wherewith bothe our threasure is unnecessarily wasted, and for lacke of expedite payment our people there burdenid, to their grete hinderaunce and agaynst our disposicion.

Yeven under our signet at our castell of Windsor the xxiith of Aprill, the sixth yere of our reign, 1564.

Copie of direction: To our right trustie and right welbeloved cosin earle of Sussex, our lieutenante in our realme of Irland, and to our trusty and right welbelovid the rest of our counsell there.

fol. 186b. [CXXXIX.][1]—After our right hartie commendacions: Where it hathe pleasid Almightie Godd to restore to this realme and all other the quenes majesties domynions, by the meanes of her highnes, a good and honorable peax with France, which was concluded the xith of this month in France; and that it is among other thinges accorded, that it shalbe published on both partes before the xiiith hereof, as it shalbe. After which day it shall not be lefull for any subjecte of either parte to use any hostilitie but yf they shall the same shalbe accompted as a brech of peax on their parte, and shalbe aunswerable, wherof wee thought mete to advertyse your lordshippe.

And albeit this our advertysment may happen to come unto you longe after the daie, yet if any shall in the meane tyme attempt to the contrary to take order therein as shall apperteyn.

---

[1] In margin: "Copie."

And so fare your good lordshippe right hartelie well. Your good lordshippes assured loving freendes: 1564.

W. Northampton. — Pembroke.—R. Duddley. — E. Clynton. — E. Rogers.—W. Cecill.—F. Knollys.

Copie of direction: To our very good lorde the earle of Sussex, the quenes majesties lieutenant of her realme of Irland:

Hast, hast, hast, hast, hast, post hast, with all diligence.

[CXL.]—At Dublin, in the castell chamber, xiii° die Maii, 1564: fol. 187.

Memorandum: The said day and place the right honorable erle of Sussex, lord livtenante of this realme, delivered unto the hands of sir Thomas Cusake, knighte, to have in redynes to be showed unto the erle of Desmonde, at the seid sir Thomas his repayre into the weste partes, as well the articles signed by the queenes majestie, nono Augusti 1563, wherunto the erle of Desmonde hath voluntarylye agreed to be observed; as also other articles signed by the erle of Desmonde himself, dated the xxiith day of Februarye, 1563, intituled in hec verba Thaunswer of therle of Desmonde to sir Thomas Cusake, aswell for the performaunce of the articles condescended unto in Englande as for other matters required of him by my lorde livtenante and councell. Bothe the which articles the seid sir Thomas hath promised upon his retorne from the weste partes to sende unto the handes of the seid erle of Sussex now lorde livtenaute of this realme.

Memorandum: Also the said xiiith day of May, 1564, in the sayd castell chamber, the seid erle of Sussex, lord livtenante of this realme, delivered unto the handes of sir Nicolas Arnolde, knighte, the queenes majesties lettere addressed to the seid erle, her majesties livtenante here, dated at her castell of Wyndsor, the xviith of January, the sixth yere of her reigne, for the consideracion of the entreteynyng of Cormok Oconor by some lande and pencion, amounting to one hundred markes or therabontes, and letting her majestie to know the seid erles oppynyon her majestie wolde signifye her determynacion.

And therin, bycause sir Thomas Cusake hath delte with him, her majestie wolde the seid erle sholde take his advice, as in the seid lettere more fully aperith.

[CXLI.]—Copie of a lettere from the lorde livtenante and councell, addressed to the erle of Kildare, touching certayne bonnaughtes under his rule, due and to be paid to the queens majesties capteyns of the gallowglasses: fol. 178*b*.

After our right hartie commendacions to your good lordeshippe: Where the captens of the queens majesties gallowglasses have nowe and sondry tymes before complayned of the nonpaymente of their bonaghte due and behinde in the Annallye, wherin wee heretofore wrote unto your lordeshippe our resolucion that they ought to be satisfiedd the haulf of the same in victuelles; and that forasmoche as they for wante of such paymente were fayne to furnyshe them selfes of their owne chardges for that service, they shoulde therefore be paide for the same in money, acccording to suche prices as victuelles were then solde for in the markettes, the which (as they saye) ys notwithstanding unsatisfied, and they are sued here for soudry dettes by them owing, which Mr. Marshall and Mr. Livtenante have, by our order, become suerties for to see satysfied by a day lymytted; we shall eftsones requyre your lordeshippe to geve order that they may have satisfaccion of their said

1564. bonaghte in the Annalye, according to our said former lettere, before the xth of Julye nexte. And if they faille of such satisfaccion at that day, then we pray your lordeshippe not to faille to delyver into the handes of Mr. marshall and Mr. livtenante the captens of the Annaley untill they shall have paide all the dewties as before saide. Wherof wee pray your lordeshippe not to faille in any wise in respecte of the queens majesties interest therein.

And so wee bydd your lordesshippe well to fare. From Dublin, the xixth of May 1564,—Your lordeshippes loving freendes:

T. Sussex.—H. Dublin, canc.—R. Darensis.[1]—N. Arnold.—W. Fitz-williams.—John Parker.—James Bathe.—Francis Agarde.—John Chaloner.

Copie of direction: To our very good lorde, the erle of Kildare.

ol. 188. [CXLII.]—Copy of another lettere from the lorde livtenante and counsell touching the levyeng of the bonnawghtes due to the captens of the gallowglasses:

T. Sussex.—After our hartie comendacions: Whereas the captens of the queens majesties gallowglasses being sewed here at the lawes for sondrie their debtes owing to dyverse persons, for the which yowe, sir William Fitzwilliams, sir George Stanley and sir Henry Radeclyff, by our order, have undertaken the parties shalbe satisfied by a day, which they have at our request consented unto and forborne further sewte agaynste them, to thende that by that respecte, the said captens maye yn the meane tyme levie tharrerages of ther bonnaghtes which are in sundrie Yrish countreys yet unpaid unto them, wee do by tenor of theis our letteres auctorise yowe and every of yowe yontlie and severallie to ayde the saide captens for the levieng of the arrerage of the saide bonnaghtes in every countrey where the same is owing, excepte those countreys whereof any Englyshman ys capten.

And so we bydd you hertelie well to fare. Yeven at Dublin, the xixth of Maye, 1564.

Your loving freendes: H. Dublin canc.—R. Darensis.—N. Arnold.—John Parker.—James Bathe.—Francis Agarde.—John Chaloner.

Copie of the direction: To our loving freendes sir William Fitz-williams, knight, vicetreasurer and treasowrer at warres of this realme, sir George Stanley, knight, marshall of the queens majesties army, and sir Henry Radeclyff, knight, livtenante of her majesties fortes in Leix and Offaley.

fol. 188*b*. [CXLIII.]—At Dublin, the xxiiiith daye of Maye, anno sexto regni domine nostre regine Elizabeth, Anno Domini 1564:

Memorandum: Forsomoche as the queens majestie, by her highnes lettere, dated under her privie signett at her castell of Wyndsor, the xxiith of Aprill, the vith yere of her raigne, 1564, directed in hec verba: To our welbeloved cosen the erle of Sussex our livtenante in our realme of Irland, and to our trustie and welbeloved the rest of our councell there, hathe bene pleased that her saide livtenante shoulde repayre into Englande. And for that it is meete some person shoulde holde the place as justyce of this her majesties realme, her majestie willeth and commaundeth us the rest of her majesties councell here,

---

[1] Robert Daly, bishop of Kildare.

that according to the auncyent custome therein used wee will make 1564. choyce of one to be her majesties justyce here. And for signyficacon of her majesties meanyng and oppynyon [she] writeth that her highnes shalbe best contente to have sir Nicholas Arnolde apoyncted thereunto, whome her majestie woulde have aucthorised as other justyces in lyke tymes have here bene, And so requyreth us to have thereof due consideracion. The lorde channcelor, according thauncyent custome in this behaulf here used, hath directed the queens majesties wryttes to the lordes and others having to do with the saide election to appere here at Dublin for the same purpose the aforesaide xxiiiith day of May, in the yeare aforesaide.

At which day and place have appered wee, whose names are hereunto subscrybedd, wee proceadinge accordingly, by vertue of her majesties saide letteres unto the election of one to holde the place of justice of this her majesties realme, have elected and chosen sir Nicholas Arnold, knighte, to be her majesties justyce of this realme during her majesties pleasure, as well observing therein our owne election and choyce. accordinge thauncyente custome therein used, as also havinge especiall consideracion of him in our saide choyce, accordinge the tenor and meanynge of her majesties saide letteres. And do by like assent conclude determyne and order that the said lord chauncelor shall make, fol. 189. seale, passe and delyver unto the said sir Nicholas Arnolde letteres patentes in her majesties name under her highnes greate seale of this realme of and upon the said offyce and roome ef justyce: to have, exercyse, holde and occupie the said offyce and roome of justice unto the said sir Nicholas Arnolde during our said soveraigne lady the queens majesties pleasure.

Yeven at Dublin, under the testymonye of our handes, the abovesaid xxiiiith day of Maye, in the said vith yere of the raigne of our soveraigne lady, queene Elizabeth.

H. Dublin, canc.—Adam Armachanus.—G. Kyldare.—Roland Baltynglas.—Christofor Donsany.—R. Darensis.—R. Trimileston.—Crystofer Howthe.—W. Fitzwylliams.—Jo. Plunket.—James Bathe.—Thomas Lokwod, dean.—Henry Radeclyff.—George Stanley.—Robert Dyllon, justice.—John Parker.—Francis Agarde.—John Chaloner.

[CXLIV.]—At Dublin, the xxixth of May, anno sexto regni fol. 189b. domine nostro regine Elisabeth, anno Domini 1564:

N. Arnold.—Forsomoche as generallie the wholle realme is in quiett, no rebellion beeng presentlie within the realme (the Moores excepte, and some parte of strife betwene the erle of Thomond and sir Donogh Obryne); and the next neighbors to the Englishe Pale, the Birnes, the Towlles, and the Kavenaghes beeng helde in obedience; Upper Ossorie at commaundement, Ocarrolls, the Foxes, Odwyns, McCoughlanes, McGougheganes, Omollaghlynes, Omolloyes contries beeng quiett and at commaundement; the rebells which are the Moores of Leixe so sparkled[1] as allthoughe they may by suddeynes do harme, yet are they not liable to keepe together nor indeede of them selfes to withstande any small force; and the Oconors of Offaillye have so submitted themselfes, as there is now no great dowbte of hurte by them: so as from the Shenon sowthe and este there is now no greate perill; and that Oreiglye with that side are not lyke moche truble; Oneill holding his obedience:

[1] Dispersed.

1564. We thinke that the queens majesties garrison of soldiors in her sold within this realme for her ffortes and all may be abated for the present till further neede appere, the queens majestie first being advertised therof and her pleasur therin knowne, unto the nombre of two hundreth horssemen, comprehending therein the lxxxxi horssemen which are graunted by letteres patentes unto officers; and of five hondreth footemen, to remayne still within this realme in her majesties fol. 190. entretaynement of solde untill her highnes further pleasure knowne.

For wittnes of which our oppynyon apon deliberate arguyng and debating emongest us agreed apon we that were at this resolucion have herunto subscribed, the day and yere afore written.

H. Dublin, canc. — G. Kyldare. — Adam Armachanus. — Roland Baltynglas.—Crystofer Howthe.—R. Trimletston.—T. Lowthe.—Cristofor Donsany.—Jo. Plunket.—Robert Dyllon.—James Bathe.—John Parker.—Thomas Lokwod, dean.—John Chaloner.

fol. 190*b*. [CXLV.]—By the lorde justice and councell:[1]

N. Arnold.—Whereas Arte Oneill, the basse sonne of the late baron of Dungannon, having served the queens majestie in her late warres in the Northe trewly and valyantly, as those of creditt which have bene thereat presante do crediblie reporte, and synce the quyet of those borders establyshed, maye not convenyentlie dwell ne remayne theare, and therefore hath made humble sewte unto us to be considered with some enterteynement in her majesties service havinge himself and his three horsemen which he offerith to serve with as he shalbe placed and apoyncted, wee have thought fytt in consideracion of his saide trewe and faithfull servyce and for the encoragement of others to do the lyke, to enterteyne him in her majesties service with his said three horsemen, as parcell of the retynewe of her majesties armye in this realme, with the wages of three shillinges current money of this realme by the daye untill her highnes further pleasure therein knowne, and that he, with his saide three horsemen, shalbe from tyme to tyme emploied in her majesties service, as we or other the chief governor of this realme for the tyme beinge shall thinke fytt. And do therefore requyre yow, Mr. Treasowrer, of suche her majesties treasure as remayneth or shall remayne under your custodie to make payment of the saide dailie wages unto him from tyme to tyme for and during his remayneng enterteyned yn her highnes service, as aforesaide, untill her highnes further pleasure therein knowne and signyfied unto us.

And taking from tyme to tyme the said Artes acquytance, confessing the receipte therof, this shalbe your sufficient warraunte for the same.

Yeven at Dublin, the vth of June, 1564.

H. Radeclyff.—John Parker—Thomas Cusak.—Francis Agarde.—John Chaloner.

To our right trustie and welbeloved sir William Fitzwilliams, knighte, vicethreasorer and threasorer at warres in this realme.

fol. 191. [CXLVI.]—At Dublin, xii° Junii, 1564:

N. Arnold.—Upon Odoneills peticion, that daye exhibited to the lorde justice and councell by Odoneill himself, day was geven him to have his answer the next daye, And so he beeng for that tyme dismissed; his

[1] In margin: "A copy."

peticion beeng considered by the lorde justice and counsell it was by them condescended and resolved, that Odonell sholde be answered in this forme ensueng, videlicet: 1564.

That no promise was made by the lorde livtenante and counsell nor synce, for ayde to be geven him agaynst his kynnesmen that usurped his castells, but that the queens majestie was written unto towching that and other his peticions, with truste to receive her majesties gracious resolucion therapon; and that if the same were so signified from her majestie, he sholde fynde every of the councell redye to further him, which is not yet signified over from her majestie; neyther yet for his licence to repaire unto her majesties presence, withoute the whiche it is not thoughte fitte for the lorde justice and councell nor expedient for the furtherance of his sutes unto her majestie that the lorde justice and fol. 191*b*. counsell sholde licence him afore to repaire over unto her majesties presence.

And for his sonne, Conn Odonnell, there is a lettere written to Oneill, according Odonells request, and therin a relacion of commission geven to the deane of Armaghe, the chauntor of Armaghe and Symon Barnewell, gentleman, to commen with Oneill upon the controversies betwene him and Odonell and to make relacion thereof if they cannot be there with both their contentemtes componed; as by the minutes of that lettere and comission apereth.

Dated xiii° Junij, 1564.

H. Dublin, canc.—Roland Baltynglas.—W. Fytzwylliams.—James Bathe.—Francis Agarde.—Henry Radeclyff.—John Chaloner.

[CXLVII, CXLVIII.]—At Dublin, the xiiiith of July, 1564: fol. 192.

It is by us, the lorde justice and others of the counsell of this realme, whose names be signed hereunto, thought expedient and agreed on for the quiett and suertie of the Englishe Pale which swarmeth full of idle men, daylie doenge harme, robberies and spoille on the queens majesties good subjectes within the same, and when longe nightes shall come are very like then to joigne with suche as are proclaymed in open rebellion and hostilitie, that there shalbe commissions made owt under the grete seale of this realme by the fourme of president commissions in suche behaulf unto the persons undernamed for to execute during the queens pleasure the lawe marciall within the shires and countrees underspecified upon all suche idle and suspecte persons as they shall take within the same, not having of freholde in possession the yerelye value of forty shillinges above all chardges or not worthe of substaunce in goodes and cattalles within the Englishe Pale or other the contrees underspecified the value of ten poundes, and not beeng of good and honest name and fame within the lymytes of the county or countree wheare they shalbe so founde idle or taken suspecte.

And neverthelesse yf the partie so taken beeng not of the possessions or value of substaunce aforesaid but yet of honest name and fame as aforesaid, be found or taken withe the manere in evell doyng or be dewly convicte, then every suche person so founde or taken, or dewlye convicted, to be ponyshed and executed by the lawe marciall, according the qualitie and quantytie of his offence or offences, videlicet:

To Mr. Marshall, solely, for all the counties and places undermencioned:—

For the countye of Dublin: fol. 192*b*.

To the lorde Howthe, Mr. Thresurer, Fruncis Agarde, Jacques Wingfelde, John Chaloner, Robert Pyfolde, sherife to the countie of

1564. Dublin, Christofor Barnewell of Gracediew, and James Barnewell and William Talbott of Malahide, Thomas Fitzwilliams, Roger Fyngles, —Luttrell of Luttrellston, Patrik Sarsfield, William Basnett, Edward Barnewell.

For the countie of Methe :

To the lorde Trymledston, the lorde of Slane, sir Oliver Plonket, sherif, sir Christofer Chevers, Barnaby Shurlock and Henry Draycott, or any two of them.

For the county of Westmeth :

To Mr. Thresurer—a comission speciall for the county of Westmeth and the Irish contrees adjoynyng sir Garet Petyt, James Nugent, Thomas Le Strange, John Bryan and Richard Tute or any two of them.

For the county of Uryell.

To the lorde of Lowthe—a comission speciall for the countye of Uriell, sir John Bedlow, James Barnewell, Edward More of Mellyfonte, and the sherif or any two of them.

For the countye of Kildare :

Richard Manoring, Robert Manoring, Garett Sutton, John Sutton of Tippar, James Flattisburye, sir Fruuncis Harbert, John Eustace, of Castlemartin, and Thomas Aylmer, of the Lyons, Patrik Sarsfelde, or any two of them.

For the countye of Catherlaughe :

Sir Edmonde Butler, Nicholas Heron and Fraunces Randall, or any two of them.

For the countye of Kylkenny :

Sir Edmonde Butler, Nicholas White, Patrick Shurlock, William Sweteman, sherif, and Thomas Masterson, or eny two of them.

The erle of Ormonde : a comission speciall for the countyes of Kilkenny, Tiperary and another comission for all those Yrish contres under his rule withoute excepcion, etc.

fol. 193. For the countye of Wexforde :

The senesshall, the vicount Mountgarret, the sherif, sir Nicholas Deveroux, Patrick Browne of Malrankan, and Anthony Cockeley or anny two of them.

For the countye of Waterforde :

To the lorde Powre, John Cuff, Anthony Powre, and Mathew Wise of Waterforde, or anny two of them.

For the Queenes countie and the Yrish contrees adjoyninge :

Sir Henry Radclyf—a comission speciall for the Queenes county and Kinges countie and the Irishe contrees adjoynyng, Fraunci Cosbie, the sherif, and William Portas or any two of them, of whome sir Henry Radclyf to be one, from tyme while he shalbe there remayning.

For the Kynges county and the Yrishe contrees adjoyninge, and also Brimighams contree :

Henry Cowley, Nicholas Harbert, and Robert Cowley, or anny two of them, of whome sir Henry Radclyf to be one, from tyme to tyme while he shalbe theare remaynynge.

1564.

For Omeylle and the Towlles and freholders of that contree :

Richard Manoryngc.

The vicount of Baltinglas : a comission speciall for the countyes of Kildare and Catherloughe and for the contree of Omeill.

The erle of Kildare : a commission speciall for the countyes of Kildare, Methe and Westemeth.

Also an other commission for the Annaly and Ferbill and other Irishe countres under his rule.

For the other Towlles and Byrnes contree : fol. 193*b*.

To Jaques Wyngefyld, solely.

[CXLIX.]—At the Castle of Dublin, the xiii° of July, 1564 : fol. 194.

Whereas David Hay, of Slead, in the barony of Forth and county of Wexford, and his sone, James Hay, esquires, being, the xiii° January last past, accused before us, the lorde deputye and counsaill, here assembled as well off felony as high treason towching the queenes majesties most royall person, were, by order of this board, committed forthwith to close prison within the Castle of Dublin, and now having remained and continued prisoners there for the space of xxv weeks to abide their trialls, have not in the mean time either by their accusers or any other men bene detected of any matter arreignable or any other cause whereby they might have further triall, as by the judges and the rest of her majesties learned counsaill of this realme we be enformed, to whom we referred the hearings, examinings, discussinge and judginge of the matter :

Forasmuch as the said David and James Hay have made sundry times humble sute and petition unto us for that there is no matter fownde to charge them withall, whereby they ought to be deteined any longer in prison : and also for that duringe the time of their imprisonment and by occasion thereof (as they alledge) they have bene robbed and spoiled by the rebells and traitours, sir Edmund Butler and Piers, his brother, with ther complices, and lost by them all their goodes and cattles, their tenants are fledde and run away, their growndes lie wast and unmanured :

It is therefore condescended, concluded, and agreed by us, the lorde deputy and counsaill, whose names be hereunto subscribed, that the said David and James Hay, esquires, shalbe enlarged and put at liberty conditionallye, that is to say : that they the said David and James Hay, fol. 194*b*. with sufficient suerties with them shall first enter into good and sufficient bonds of recognizances of five thousand pounds currant money of England before the lord chancellor for their forthcoming and personal apparance at any time within twentie daies after notice given unto them or any one of their suerties either by or from the lorde deputy or in his absence from the lorde chancellor and counsaill betwixt this and the last day of Michaelmas terme, next ensuing to answer any matters of accusation that may be apposed or laid against them.

And in the meantime if no further matter may be objected and laied against them betwixt this and the said last day of Michaelmas terme, before specified, then presentinge themselves before us, the lord deputye, or in our absence the lorde chancellor and counsaill ther bondes to be cancelled and they fully discharged and set at libertie.

H. Dublin, canc.—John Chaloner.[1]

---

[1] Folio 195 is blank.

1564. [CL.]—At Dublin, tercio Augusti, 1564:

fol. 196. N. Arnold.—Upon deliberate consultacion and consideracion of the maliciowse conspiracie, detestable rebellion and most cruell and heynowse offenses of suche of the natyons of the Omores and Oconnors, their followers, servantes, abbettors, counseillors, receyvors, relievers and succurrers, as lately within this yeare have conspyred in rebellyon and disobedience agaynst the queens majestie and to the distruccion or harme of her majesties good subjectes.

It is by us, the lorde justice and the rest of the nobylitie and counsell of this realme whose names ar signed hereunto, fully determyned and resolved that they and every of them (excepte suche as heretofore upon their humble submission ar receved into her majesties protection) shalbe pursewed and revenged upon by sharpe warr with fyar and swourde, and none of them to be received unto the queenes mercy, neither wholie nor parte of them, excepte her majesties expresse pleassure signified to the contrary:

And that suche of them as are received yn or have remayned as her majesties good and obedient subjectes without offendinge shalbe used and conserved as her majesties good subjectes:

And that suche of them as hereafter shall conspire or rebell, from the tyme of their rebellion or conspiring with the others shalbe reputed banyssbed and persecuted as the rest of the said rebelles:

And whereas for the better persecuting of them the soldiars of the queens majesties army in retynewe are removed out of suche places of the English Pale as they before were cessed yn unto the border and other more fyt places for her majesties saide service for whose victelling provision must be made for redy mony as the markett and bargaynes in that behaulf will serve, it is further concluded and condiscended by us that the baronyes and other places where before they were cessed and placed shalbe cessed and contribute to beare and satisfie emonge them the overplus of the price of all and singler the said provisions, achates and bargaynes employed in and for theire said victuelles above the ordinary rates and prices heretofore ordeyned and used for those of her majesties army and retynewe in such case to pay.

H. Dublin, canc.—J. Slane.—G. Kyldare.—R. Trimletiston.—Henry Radeclyff.—W. Fytzwylliams.—Jo. Plunket.—George Stanley.—Francis Agarde.—James Bathe.—John Chaloner.

fol. 196*b*. [CLI.]—At Dublin, the xxixth of August, 1564:[1]

It is concluded and agreed by us, the lorde justice and counsaill, whose names are hereunto signed, the rest being absent partely in the quenes majesties service and partely otherwise in their necessarye affaires, that while we, the lorde justice, and suche other as are appointed to repaire unto Ophailley and Leix and the Irishe borders there for her majesties service against the rebelles of the Mores and Oconnors, are absent; considering the dowbtfull bihavior of the Birnes and Towelles, the lorde chauncelor, the lorde of Howthe, justice Plunkett and baron Bathe shall remayne to geve ordre and directe, aswell for all suche matters touching the state as we the lorde justice shall write or sende unto them in, as also they and Jaques Wyngfielde, esquier, and the sherieffe of the countie of Dublin or any three of them to geve ordre for the defence of the borders of the saide countie against

[1] Fol. 195 is blank.

the Birnes and Towles by the power of the saide countie and by suche 1564.
other of her majesties kerne and horsemen appointed or to be appointed thereunto.

[CLII.]—Consultacions at St. Patrickes,[1] xvii Septembris, 1564: fol. 197.

[1.] The cattail and goodes of those whiche are suspected or likely for the rebelles to be releved of to be brought further into the Englishe Pale and the owners and their tennauntes and folowers to come in and lyve thereon.

[2.] Those that have slipted awaye and be come home agayne to be demaunded of their maisters and executed, and their maisters also put to aunswere, etc.

[3.] No holding kerne to be taken to serve but to bill their names with caution that they shall not be chalenged at their handes for former offences being not the offence nowe prosecuted; nor for the same neither yf it be a partie taken in for a speciall service by vertue of the commyssion to him graunted that hath taken him in.

[4.] The corne of Leix to be gathered into some one or mo[re] saulf places by a common chardge and rather serve for the common defence of the countrey then to be leaft to be distroyed by thennemye or for relief of thennemye.

[5.] Those that for service against thiese rebelles are taken in by vertue of commyssion for a tyme whiche are within daungier of the proclamacion to be certified by those whiche take them in, and notice to be geven what bihaviour they thinke those wilbe of after the expiring
of their protection. Whoso hath either son or folower for whom he is fol. 197b.
holden to aunswere and woulde be excused to be no longer holden to aunswere for him, shall not be excused to have put him from him onles he have first brought him furthe in open assembly and there dischardge himselfe of him before them all, the partie being present.

[6.] The cesse of the holding kerne on the counties of Westmeth, Dublin, Kildare, and Wexforde and McVadoges countrey, McDamores countrey and McEdmunde Duffes countrey to be contynued in suche forme from tyme to tyme as the former warrauntes purporte untill the service aforsaide accheved.

[CLIIA.]—18 Septembris, 1564:

Our newe commyssion to John Tirell, capitaine of Fertullaghe, for the renewing of the cesse of the sixe schore kerne in that countrey for other sixe wekes:

Hughe Boy Orowrke his mocion and offre to be accepted, whiche is moved by him to Mr. Marshall, videlicet, his castell to be recovered with the quenes majesties ordennaunce and aide, and delyvered to him and he to receyve the same and his land and tenure of her majestie, and to put in good pledges to be her good subjecte and not only not to receyve nor succor any the rebelles but also to plague them and their receyvors and maynteynors within his rule.

[CLIII.]—At Dublin, the xi[th] of Octobre, 1564: fol. 198.

It is concluded and agreed by us, the lorde justice and the rest of her majesties counsaill, whose names are hereunto subscribed, that the cesse

---

[1] Dublin.

1564. of an hundreth holding kerne and fyftye boyes, for the defence of the countie of Kildare, shalbe contynued upon the countie of Dublin for three weekes, to be ending at the ende of the last cesse of holding kerns cessed for sixe weekes by our former warraunt.

fol. 198*b*. [CLIV.]—At Dublin, the xxvi[th] of Octobre, 1564:

[1.] The Plonkettes and Newgentes who were written for to be at the castle chamber,[1] in crastino animarum, are eftesones written for by an other lettere xxiiii[th] Octobris, to apere upon the sighte thereof: And upon their commynge order is to be taken with them by good bondes for their better concorde and joigninge together for the deffence of the borders agaynste the Oreiglies, etc. And also some of the said Plonkettes and Newgentes, suche as are the notableste offendors of those enormyties theare, to be ponysshed for example, accordinge their demerites.

[2.] The order for the watche and rising owt and folowing every hewghe and crye there; to be relyed unto, and more dewlie followed and executed; and also order to be taken with that countye for the garde of their borders.

[3.] The lorde of Hoothe, the lorde of Trymbledston, and sir Thomas Cusake to speke with Oreiglye upon the borders, and the sherif of Methe to be written under and comaunded that the commissioners be wayted on with the force of the countie from day to day duringe the parlee.

[4.] Horsemen of the army to be placed on those borders agaynst Oreiglie:—Gyrtons bande.

[5.] Oreiglye is to be written unto to mete with the commissioners at the Blackwater, on Wednesday the first day of November.

[6.] Oneyll is to be written unto from the boorde, touchinge sir Thomas Cusakes metynge with him, with also wordes of creditt unto his relacion concerninge Odonels goyng over.

fol. 199. [CLV.].—At Dublin, the xxviiith of Octobre, 1564:

It is thoughte fytt nowe for deffence of the borders agaynst the Occonnors, for six wekes to begynne the last of October.

Westmethe:

Six score gallowglasses to live of their owne bonnaghter for a quarter of a yere, to be placed and ordered by the erle of Kildare, also sir Nicholas Bagnals bande of fortie horsemen to be layde in that countie beyonde Molyngar, in twoo townes or more where the saide erle shall appoyncte and to be ordered by his lordshippe and the whole countie to contribute to the victelling of the horsemen at the ordinarie rate and the accustomed holdinge kerne of Tirrelles contre and Ferbill, and the rest of Westmethe.

Methe:

Four score holding kerne to be cessed for the garde of the borders of that countie agaynst the Occonnors, and those to be at the placing and order of the said erle of Kildare and for every two kerne one boye. This to be besides Gyrtons bande of horsemen and force of that countie, as must garde the borders agaynst Oreiglye.

---

[1] At Dublin.

Kildare : 1564.

Fourscore holding kerne to be cessed for the garde of the borders of that countie, to be likewise at the placing and order of the saide erle of Kildare, and every two kerne one boye.

For the pursute of the Oconnors :

Moreover, the saide erle of Kildare to have yn mony the enterteynemente of twoo hundreth kerne of his owne chusinge for to pursue the rebelles of the Occonors, the said enterteynment to be devided, cessed and levied on theis counties and contrees, viz. :—

Offailey for xxx kerne. fol. 199*b*.

McDamores, McVadockes, McEdmund Duffes contrees and the countie of Wexford and Fassaghe Bayntre, lx kerne.

The countie of Westmethe, xxx kerne.

" " Lowthe, xl "

" " Dublin, xl "

Two hundreth kerne to be levied in money and for every two kerne one boy.

Moreover, for the said erle of Kildares satisfaction of the enterteynment in mony alredy growen dewe to his lordshippe for the former holdinge by the former warrantes, and for his new holdinge also : It is agreed it shall be levyed and his lordshippe thereof satisfied by this day fourtene daies, videlicet, the xith of November.[1]

[CLVI.]—At Dublin, the xxviiith of Octobr, 1564 : fol. 200*b*.

It is thoughte fitt nowe for deffence of the borders agaynst the Omoores for six weekes to begynne the last of October :

That the countie of Carloghe, with the rest of the Cavanaghes, to be cessed withe four score kerne for six wekes for garde of their borders.

Letteres to be sente to the freholders of Leix to be resident on their holdes with their furnyture dewe by their tenures.

Moreover, for to garde the forte and contree of Leix, etc. :

Soldiers : cxxx fotemen and xx horsemen ; six skore gallowglasses, and nine skore of the queens kerne.

Victells to be provided for the furnyture of the forte in Leix, videlicet, for every monneth :

Bieffes, lx ; wheate, c peckes ; mawlte, cc peckes, whereof the thirde parte to be beare mawlte.

[CLVII.]—At Dublin, the xxixth of October, 1564 : fol. 201.

It is agreed that letteres shall be written to the Irish captens for beefes and porkes for the victelling of the soldiars in the fortes for the yere ensueing, viz. :

To Oreiglie for 200 fat beefes and an 100 swyne.

" The Annaly for 100 befes and 50 swyne.

" McGoghegan for 50 befes and 30 swyne.

" McCoghlan for 30 befes and 15 swyne.

" OKelly for 60 beefes and 30 swyne.

" the Birnes for 100 befes and 50 swyne.

---

1 Fol. 200 is marked as cancelled, with the following note in margin : "Vacat hic, quia postea in ordine." The matter on fol. 200 marked as cancelled is re-entered on fol. 200*b*.

1564. To the Towles of Omayle for 20 befes and 10 swyne.

„ the countie of Catherlaghe and the Cavanaghes contree for one hundreth and fortie beefes and twentie swyne.

Upper Ossorie : one hundreth beefes and 40 swyne.

To Occarrall : one hundreth beefes and fiftie swyne.

The countie of Tipperarie 100 befes and 50 swyne.

The countie of Waterforde : 100 beefes and 50 swyne.

Farney : fyftie beefes and 25 swyne.

Hughe Oge of Dartrie : 30 beefes and 15 swyne.

The Kellies, beyonde the Sucke, for 60 beefes and 30 swyne.

fol. 201*b*. McMahones contree : 100 beefes and 50 swyne.

Every beef at twelve shillinges and every porke at twoo shillinges and eight pence.

Beeffes—1340. Swyne—610.

fol. 202. [CLVIII.]—At Dublin, the xxixth day of Octobre, 1564 :

Sir Henry Radcliffe, knight, lieutenant of the counties called the Kinges countie and the Quenes countie and of the fortes of Philippistowne and Marybowroghe, within the same counties, etc., hathe the saide day and yere made request unto the lorde justice of this realme, in the presence of us whose names are hereunder signed, that the same lorde justice will from this day furthe appoint suche person or persones as his lordeshippe shall thinke fitt for to take the chardge and government of the saide fortes and counties and of the souldiors and other inhabitauntes and people within the same ; forasmuche as he the saide sir Henry is licenced to repayre over into Englande by the quenes majestie and cannot neither will constitute a deputie to supplye his saide chardge.

fol. 202*b*. [CLIX.]—At Christes Churche,[1] xvii° Novembris, 1564 :

It is agreed by the lorde justice and counsaill that the lorde Barrimores and the lorde Roches childerne, whiche were put in as their pledges at the going over of the erle of Desmounde for the keeping of the peace during his absence, shalbe enlarged forasmuche as nothing hath been chardged in that behaulf by the erle against them ; and forasmuche as they themselfes are aunswerable in case any suche matter be.

fol. 203. [CLX.]—Apud Dublin, xx° Novembris, 1564 :

It is agreed by the lorde justice and counsaill that the erle of Ormounde and Ossorie, lorde thresurer of Irlande, shall have the quenes majesties commyssion under the great seale of this realme for the saulfgarding of the countreys of Leix, Irry, Glanmalirry and Slewmarge, and of the fortes, garrisons and other the quenes majesties good subjectes within the same, and also of and in the counties of Catherlaghe and Kilkenny, and of and in the countreys of thiese Irishe lordes and capitaynes bordering upon the same, videlicet, Upper Ossorie, Occarrowlles countrey, OMulrianes countrey, ODonnes countrey, Omaghers countrey, against the proclaymed rebelles of the Omores and the Occonnors, their ayders succourers releyvers, counsaillors, abettors, folowers and adherentes and to pursue them with fyre and swerde in and throughe all and singuler the countreis and counties aforsaid besides the folowing and pursuying them elliswhere in whatsomever the countreys adjoynyng, as his lordeshippe shall understande them to have repaired

[1] Cathedral, Dublin.

or be receyved in, conferring in that case with the erle of Kildare, yf it concerne Ophailley or the borders thereof or any other the countreys or counties whiche the lorde justice and counsaill have unto his lordeshippe appointed a lyke especiall aucthoritie and chardge, and for the better execution of the premysses a letter to be written to the saide lorde threassourer from the saide lorde justice and counsaill as here ensueth: 1564.

Our very good lorde: After our right hartie commendacions: The quenes majesties commyssion under the great seale of this realme is presently addressed unto your lordeshippe with generall aucthoritie for the pursute of the proclaymed rebelles of the Moores and the Occonnors, their folowers adherentes and succourers, as in the same is more at fol. 204. large expressed.

And for the better executing thereof, we have appointed unto your lordeshippe the entretaynement of two hundrethe holding kerne of suche as your lordeshippe shall thinke fitt to choose and employe in that her majesties service for one quarter of a yere, to begynne the ——[1] of this Novembre, to be levyed in money and delyvered unto your lordshippe, the one haulf upon the countie of Waterforde and the other haulf upon the countie of Lymericke. And also that as well sixe schore of her majesties galliglasses and their capitaynes appointed for defence of the countries of Leix, Irry, Glanmalirry and Slewemarge, nowe called the Queenes countie,[2] Frauncis Cosbye, with his hundrethe of her majesties kerne; your brother, sir Edmunde Butler, with his forty of her majesties kerne, sir Barnaby Fitzpatricke, with his forty of her majesties kerne, capitayne Portas, with his fortie and fyve souldiors, and John Fitzwilliames, with the hundreth souldiors in the forte of Leix and the sheriffe and forces as well of holding kerne, inhabitauntes and other her majesties garrysons as well in that countie called the Quenes countie as also in the counties of Catherlaghe and Kilkennye, and also the Irishe lordes and capitaynes, with the forces of Upper Ossorie, Occarrowlles countrey, Omulrians countrey, Odonnes countrey, and Omaghers fol. 204b. countrey, shall, from tyme to tyme, aunswere your lordeshippe in and concernyng her majesties saide service according as your lordeshippe shall will and ordre them.

And hitherto have we thought fitt besides the generalitie of her majesties aforsaide commyssion to appointe and aucthorise your lordeshippe, especially by the tenor hereof, unto the saulfgarding and defence of all her majesties goode subjectes and repressing and correcting of thoffendors and transgressours aforsaide, their aydours, succourers, relevers, counsaillors, abettours, folowers, and adherents in and throughe all and singuler the counties and countreys aforesaide, besides the folowing and pursuyng them elliswheare in what soever the countries adjoyning as your lordeshippe shall understand them to have repayred or be receyved. In whiche case we require your lordeshippe to conferre with our very good lorde the erle of Kildare, if it concerne the countie called the Kinges countie otherwise called Ophaillie, or the borders thereof or any other the countreis or counties whereof we have appointed unto his lordeshippe a like especiall aucthoritie and chardge.

And also, whereas your lordeshippe shall conceyve any cause of suspicion in the premysses there at your discrecion to take pledges, and sequestre the possession of any castell, howse or place to your lorde-

---

[1] Blank in MS.

[2] *See page* 32.

1564. shippe thought in that behaulf expedient, and therein to put suche warde as your lordeshippe shall therefore thinke fitt.

And moreover to take, from tyme to tyme and place to place, meat for your saide kerne and the rest of your company in what so ever place as often as they shall repayre in and aboute the saide service in chace and pursuite of the saide offendors.

fol. 205. And moreover to take upp wyne, grayne, beeffes, porkes, muttons, and all other victuailles of meate and drinke and cariage for the same by lande and by water, at reasonable prices therefore to be paied in reddy money, that is to saye, for the first price it coste and the reasonable chardges thereon bestowed in whatsoever place or places within liberties or without, for the furniture of her majesties service aforesaide.

Straitely, in her majesties name, chardging all and singuler persones to whome it shall appertayne to be unto your lordeshippe and your mynisters in and aboute the execution of all and singuler the premysses, obedient, ayding and assisting, as they and every of them will aunswere for the contrarye at their uttermost perilles:

And therefore we heartely require your lordeshippe in her majesties saide service and in all thinges concernyng the same to employe your best endeavor and diligence to the satisfaction of her hieghnes ernest expectacion theron.

And so we bidde your good lordeshippe right hartely well to fare.

From Dublin, the xxith of Novembre, 1564.—Your lordeshippes loving frendes ——.[1]

fol. 205*b*. Moreover, a letter of commyssion to the sheriffe and gentilmen of the countie of Waterforde for the cesse in money of one hundreth holding kerne and their fyfty boyes, at suche entretaynement as the erle of Kildare hath for the like.

A like to the sheriffe of the countie of Lymericke for the lyke for one hundreth holding kerne and their fyftye boyes, at the like entretaynement.

fol. 206. [CLXI.]—Resolucions agreed on by the lorde justice and counsaill, at Dublin, ix°, x° et xi° diebus Decembris, 1564:

[1.] The olde cessoures to remayne in their offices unchaunged unto the begynnyng of the neixt terme, that in the meane tyme they may levie the money whiche they have warrantes to levye and also make theire accomptes, etc.

For the greeffes of the Englishe Pale as over chardged by reason of freedomes[2] graunted by the principall governor and counsaill more then are allowed by the statute, to make their complaynt and name those freedomes, and thereupon the same to be considered and remedied as shalbe thought expedient.

Capitayne Heron is commaunded for the cesse of beeffes and corne of the countie of Catherlaghe to cesse the whoalle upon the landes that ar cessable and have no freedomes, and therby to dryve them to complayne if they be greved at the graunting of freedomes to suche landes as weare wont to beare with them and thereupon the validitie of those late graunted freedomes (more then allowed by the statute) to be considered, etc.

For Knockefergus capitayne Pieres his accompte to be taken and he to be holpen with suche parte of his paye as may suffyce for the provision of bieffes and grayne for that forte, etc., videlicet, xl. *li.*

---

[1] Blank in MS. [2] In margin: "The newe fredomes."

A lettere to the cessours of the counties of Dublin and Methe to certifye howe every barony of those counties are chardged with cesse of souldiors and horsses upon Friday neixt, the xvth of Decembre, and then to remembre the erle of Kildares money for the cesse of the kerne to him graunted. 1564. fol. 206b.

Souldiours to remayne in retynnue:

200 horssemen and 500 footmen,—700.

Whereof to be at bothe the fortes: 200 footmen.

With Mathewe King: 10 horssemen.

At Knockefergus: 20 footmen.

At Athlone: 20 footmen.

At Catherlaughe: 8 footmen.

At Monaster Evan: 8 footmen.

At Leighlyn: 20 horssemen, 30 footmen.

At Dungarvan: 6 horssemen, 6 footmen.

Summa hucusque in the fortes: footmen 292, horssemen 36—328.

Reste, to be placed upon cesse: footmen 208, horssemen 164.

1564.—The countie of Dublin: 30 footmen and 24 horssemen.

The countie of Kildare: 30 footmen and 24 horssemen.

The countie of Methe: 60 footmen and 48 horssemen.

The countie of Lowthe: 30 footmen and 24 horssemen.

The countie of Westmeth: 30 footmen and 24 horssemen.

The countie of Wexforde and Fassaghe Bayntree: 30 footmen and 24 horssemen.

[2.] Decimo die Decembris, 1564:[1]

Wheare there were cessed two hundreth kerne and their hundreth boyes with his lordeshippe, to followe the rebelles, and foure schore kerne, with their forty boyes, for the garde of the borders of Meth and foureschore kerne with their forty boyes for the garde of the countie of Kildare, his lordeshippe to have nowe for this cesse folowing for and untill the begynning of Marche neixt ensuying bothe for the folowing of the rebelles and saulfgarde of those two counties twelve schore kerne and their sixe schore boyes. This new cesse to begynne on Thursdaye, the xiiiith of Decembre, 1564. fol. 207.

To be cessed in money, videlicet:

Upon	the countie of Methe,	54	kerne	and	27	boyes.
„	the countie of Kildare,	54	„	„	27	„
„	the countie of Westmethe,	20	„	„	10	„
„	the countie of Lowthe,	26	„	„	13	„
„	the countie of Dublin,	26	„	„	13	„
„	Offailley,	20	„	„	10	„

„ McDamores, McEdmunde Duffes, McVadoges countreys and the countey of Wexforde and Fassaghe Bantree, 40 kerne and 20 boyes.

A proclamacion to be made that wheare it is complayned that dyvers of the Birnes and the Towlles and other their associates take mente perforce and commytt other spoilles upon the quenes good subjectes of fol. 207b.

[1] In margin: "In the erle of Kildares chardge against the Occonnors of Offailly and defence of the borders of the countie or Meth and the countie of Kildare against the said rebelles."

1564. the Englishe Pale bordring on their countreys, it shalbe lawfull for her majesties subjectes to resist them in those attemptes and fynding them with the attempt or doyng of the premysses, to apprehende them or kill them yf they resist the apprehension.

[3.] Furthermore the pynnysse,[1] with her ordennance tackling and furniture, whiche Jasper Horssey and other his complices, suspected of piracye, have brought to Howthe to be viewed, inventoried and praysed[2] by suche as the lorde justice shall appointe and the ordennance and municion and other suche kynde of furniture to be put in the master of the ordennances keeping untill they be tryed or otherwise by due ordre enlarged and the certaintie knowen to whome of right the same ought to appertayne. And the pynnysse, with her tackling and furniture so being inventaried and praysed to be delyvered to Patricke Tirrell to occupye in the quenes majesties service, keeping the same alwaye from tyme to tyme repayred and in as good plight as he receyveth the same, he being bounde to delyver the same hereafter to those of suche as upon the triall aforsaide shalbe knowen to have just right thereunto.

fol. 208. [CLXII.]—A warraunt also graunted out to Mr. Treasourer, the double whereof here ensueth verbatim:

By the lorde justice and counsaill:

Mr. Threasourer: For that we understande you are not only by warraunt from the quenes majestie restreyned from paieng or yssuyng any of her majesties threasoure here in Irelande under your chardge, otherwise then by warraunt, only under sir Thomas Wrothe and sir Nicholas Arnolde their handes togedther, her majesties comyssioners for causes here in Irlande, but also receyved from them bothe commaundement so to do, they chardging you therewith in her hieghnes name and bihaulf. And nowe, knowing sir Thomas Wrothe to be departed hence into Englande, by vertue of her hieghnes pleassure in her majesties lettere to him signified in that bihaulf, and sir Nicholas Arnolde still abiding here in Irlande, lorde justice of the same realme, wherebye you cannot have any warraunt to make any payment of suche sommes of money as shalbe meet and needfull to be paied and yssued for the services of her hieghnes here untill suche tyme as her hieghnes shall in that bihaulf signifie to us, the lorde justice, or to yourself her further pleasure therein:

We have thought good for thadvauncement of her hieghnes service here and to avoide suche chardges as mought growe to her majestie by contynuuyng some of the saide souldiors in a daily pay till then, not
fol. 208b. only to require you but also in her majesties name do chardge and commaunde you hencefurthe, from tyme to tyme, to make suche paymentes upon warrauntes as shall come to you signed by us, sir Nicholas Arnolde, lorde justice of Irlande, and the counsaill of the same; so as there be at every warraunt fyve counsaillors handes at the leste, and that the same warrantes be for suche sommes of money, as shalbe to pay the handes of footmen or horssemen or either of them whiche shulde be dischardged presently out of wages, the reckonynges of whiche bandes dischardged to be made upp by Mr. William Dixe, auditor put in truste by her majestie for the same, with his hande sett thereunto, and was also further agreed upon to be so donne by us, the lorde justice and sir Thomas Wrothe, under our handes before the saide sir Thomas his departure

[1] Pinnace. [2] Appraised.

out of Irlande, and is expressed in writing remaynyng with you, sir William Fitzwilliames, bearing date the xxiith of Novembre, 1561. 1561.

And further weyeng what other great occasions maye daily happen aboute her majesties services in this realme, for the whiche money shall also be very nedefull to be presently occupied and disbursed, we do also require and commaunde you, upon warrauntes in like sorte as for the other parte before us expressed, to delyver suche sommes of [money] as shall in them be named and appointed. fol. 209.

And this our concordatum shall testifye our ordre and commaundement to you geven in this bihalf.

Yeven at Dublin, the xth of Decembre, 1564.

Hereafter ensueth such the conclusions and resolucions of counsell in this realme, as for the good government and securytie of the state thereof, have been concluded and resolved on, in the tyme of the right honorable syr Henrye Sydney, knight, of the noble order of the garter, lorde president of the queens majesties counsell in Wales and the marchesse thereof, and lorde deputy of this realme of Ireland, who toke his othe in Christchurch,[1] and entred into the government of this the queens highnes realme, the xxth of January, in the eight yeare of her majesties moost prosperous raigne, anno, 1565[-6]: fol. 209b. 1565-6.

[CLXIII.]—At Dublyn, octavo Februarii, 1565[-6]:

It is ordered[2] and concluded by us the lorde deputy and counsell; with the expresse consentes and assentes of Tirrelagh MacDonell, Tirrelagh McAlexander, Molmory McEdmond, and Callagh Mac Tirrelaghe, captens of her majesties gallowglasse, uppon their sewte and demaunde for foure skore sparres[3] for their last yeres bonaght, graunted to be levyed on the Obyrnes countrey, and then also beeng present Obyrn, chief of his nacyon, Donogh MacBrenyn, Teig Oge Obyrn, and Bryan MacCalagh:

That the said fowre skore sparres after the rate of tenne markes, current mony of this realme for every sparr, shall be paid in maner folowing, that is to say, haulf thereof in victels and mony, according thaccustomed maner, at Lammas next coming; and the other haulf in lyke manner at Alhalontyde, then next ensueng. And that in defalte of payment at either of those dayes, the said gallowglasse and their forces to entre the said countrey and levye there their said whole bonaght.

[CLXIV.]—At Saynct Sepulchrès,[4] nigh Dublin, the xxth of February 1565[-6]: fol. 210.

Uppon the severall complayntes this daie moved and harde before us, the lorde deputie, as well on the behaulf of Occarall, chief of his nacion, against the baron of Upper Ossorie, then absent, and, sir Barnabe Fitzpatricke, knight, his sonne, here then present, as also on the behaulf of the same sir Barnabe and by him for his said fathers behaulf against the said Occarall:

It is accorded concluded and agreed before us the said lorde deputie by the mutuall assentes and consentes of the saide Occarall, and also of the saide sir Barnabe, for himself and undertaking also for his saide father

[1] Dublin.
[2] In margin: "Towching the galloglasses for their bonaghe."
[3] *See* Introduction.
[4] *Sepulchres*] Pulchers, MS.

1565-6. that all maner variaunces, greves strifes and all other damages or matters whatsoever betwen the saide parties from the begyning of the wourld untill the daie of the date hereof in eny wise styrred arrysen moved, attempted or betwene them depending (the right of the castle of Ballaghmore and the appurtenances thereof, now in the possession of the saide sir Barnabe and in variance betwene him and the said Occarall, onely excepted) shall be herd ordered and determyned by Fraunçis Cosby, esquier, and John MacGilpatrick, gentleman, arbytrators indifferently chosen with thassentes of the saide Occarall and the saide Barnabe, to here order and determyne the controversies variances and greffes aforesaid.

And that the said Occarall and the said Barnabe for the better perfourmance of such order as touching the premisses shall be taken betwene them by the said arbitrators shall on either partie on this side the fifth of March next comyng, put into thandes of the said arbitrators such and so many pledges as the same arbitrators shall nomynate, requier and accepte as sufficient on either partie, and advertise if eny defaulte shall be then made by eny of those parties in not bringing those pledges on this side the daie afore prefixed.

And uppon the pledges as aforesaid beeng receyved, the said arbitrators to fynyshe and publisshe theire order made in the premisses betwene the saide parties by the xxth of Marche, next comyng, and furthewith then to certifie us the lorde deputye of the same.

And where there is clayme made by the saide Occarall to the saide castle of Ballaghmore, nowe in the possession of the saide sir Barnabe, it is also ordered by us, the saide lorde deputie that the said sir Barnabe shall contynewe in the quiet possession thereof without eny the interrupcion, molestacion or impediment of the said Occarall or eny of his or eny other by his or theire procurmentes till uppon the further openyng of that variance by the saide Occarall at this bourde and the matter throughlie herd and discussed the right and title of that castle
fol. 210*b*. with the appurtenances so in variance maie be by us, the saide lorde deputie and the rest of her majesties counsell here, further ordered and adjudged.

And that furthermore as well the saide Occarall, for him and his servauntes tenantes and followers or eny others to be by him or them procured, as also the saide sir Barnabe, for his owne behaulf and for his fathers partie and theire servauntes, tenantes and followers or eny others by his or theire procurementes, shall well and trewlie on eche syde one to the other observe and kepe her majesties peace and not to attempte on either syde eny revenge or breche of that her majesties peace for eny cause or matter whatsoever.

And to the dewe and faithfull observacion thereof the said Occarall and the said sir Barnabe have undertaken the same before us, the saide lorde deputie, by theire handes layed or geven in the hande of us, the lorde deputie, aforesaide.

[CLXV.]—At Sainct Sepulchres, nigh Dublin, the xxth of February, 1565[-6]:

The said daie and yeare appered before us, the lorde deputie, Nicholas Harbart, esquier and Heugh MacShane, chief of his nation, against whome the same Nicholas objecting the matters of the praye lately taken from sir Fraunces Herbert, knight, deceased, father to the saide Nicholas, and the murthering of certeyne the same sir Fraunces men and chardging further the said Heugh MacShane with other sondry injuries and wronges:

It is with thassent of those parties, indifferentlie electing and chosing arbitrators, that is to saie the said Nicholas, for his parte, chusing Henry Cowley, esquier, and Meilor Hussey, gentleman, and the said Heugh Mac Shane electing for his parte Fraunces Cosby, esquier, and Ony Mac Heugh that the same arbitrators or eny two of them, whereof one to be of the saide Nicholas parte and the other of the parte of the said Hugh MacShane, meting togethere on this side the last of Marche next comyng, at Carikyn Earle, shall order and determyne so muche of the said matters in variance as shall by them be founde knowen or proved to touch or concerne the person only of the said Hugh. Whereunto the same Hugh hath fyrmely promised to stand and the same order to performe : 1565-6.

And what further in the behaulf aforesayd shall be found knowen or proved by the said arbitrators against eny others under the same Hughes fol. 211.
rule the same to be certified by the daie aforesaid to us, the said lorde deputye and counsell, that we maie thereon take suche further order as to us shall be thought expedient.

[CLXVI.]—At Saynct Pulchers, the xxth of February, 1565[-6] :

Uppon the variances herde before us, the lorde deputie, as well on the behaulf of Arte Omolloy, chief of his nation, toutching the taking of a certeyne distresse of late in the saide Omolloyes countrey by Callagh MacTurelagh, one of the captens of her majesties gallowglasse (in respecte of bonnaght then by him demaunded) and not denyed by the said Callagh :

As also on the behaulf of the said Callagh complayning also against the said Omolloye for a prey by him lately taken from the said Callagh, and likewise by the said Omolloy not denyed :

It is ordered by us, the said lorde deputie, with thassentes of the said Omolloy and the said Callagh, that the matters of those two causes betwene the said Omolloy and Callagh some variance and the restitucions and recompences on eche of theire behaulfes to be made one to the other shall be ordered and determyned by Fraunces Cosby, Henry Cowley, and Nicholas Harbert, esquiers, joyntly, on this side the viith of Aprill next comyng. And for that purpose then to assemble themselves and mete at Castle Gasshill in Ophalye, and there diligently to employe there best endevors and travaile to the ordering and determyning of those variences and to advertise us, the lorde deputie, of theire order therein to be taken by the feast of Ester next comyng.

And that furthermore, if they the said commissioners shall fynde that the said Callagh for eny respecte or cause shall, over and above the distresse by him taken from the said Omolloy, be ordered to make eny restitucion or recompence, that the same shall be defaulked uppon suche
the bonnaght as the same Omolloy is ordered by us to pay unto the said fol. 211b.
gallowglasse.

[CLXVII.]—At Dublin the xxith of February, 1565[-6]:

Wheare Occarrall, chief of his nation, hath by former warrant to him addressed from the late lorde justice and counsell been willed and commaunded to yeld and paie unto the captens of her majesties gallowglasse one quarter of a yeares bonnaght, the last year graunted for sixe skore sparres of gallowglasse, so rated uppon the said Occarall and his countrey, by warrant as aforesaide :

1565-6. And the same Occarrall, being nowe present here before us, the lorde deputie, and alleging himself and those under his rule inhabiting to be farr unhable, in respecte of theire greate povertie and decayes in the same his contrey happened, to satisfie that bonnaght according as the same was by the said warrant graunted and humblie prayeng a mytigacion thereof:

It is ordered by us the lorde deputie with the expresse consentes and assentes of the captens of the saide gallowglasse, here also present, for the causes above rehersed and their good consideracions moving us, the
fol. 212. said lorde deputie, hereunto that for this one tyme onely the said Occarall, in full satisfaction of the bonnaght aforesaid, shall content and paye to the saide captens of the gallowglasse onthis side Whitsondaie next comying, at the forte in Leix, seaven hundreth markes current money of this realme to be annswered and paid in kyne by the same Occarall in maner following, that is to say:

The one haulfe thereof incalf kyne, at the rate of twentie sixe shillinges eight pence for every of those incalf kyne, and the rest in other kyne not being in calf kyne, at the rate of thirten shillinges fower pence for every of the same kyne not being incalf kyne. Provyded alwaie that the said Occarall shall not by this our order hereafter in eny wise ——[1] to paye bonnoght at eny lesse quantitie or other lesser rate then as by indenture of recorde remayning he hath covenaunted and is holden to paie and annswer to her majestie xxiv. of February 1565:

A lettere issued to Omagher to contribute to Occarall, as hath been wonted, the thirde parte of the said bonnaght as the said rates are for this tyme rated and mitigated.

fol. 212b. [CLXVIII.]—At Saynct Pulchers, nigh Dublin, the xxvth of February, 1565[-6]:

Uppon the hering of the complaintes of sir Edmund Butler, knight, and of Oliver Fytzgarald, gentleman, one against the other, put upp before us, the lorde deputy, beeing for the present occupied with other matters of weightie importance and entending shortely to traivell on our apoyncted journey to the parties of Leynster and others the shires nere adjoyninge, for the causes of her majesties service:

It is therefore consydered and ordered by us, the said lorde deputie, that those complaynntes so moved by the parties aforesaid one against the other, and before us depending; shall have contynuance in the same state as now they stand untill the fyrst day of the next terme, and then to be further herd, consydered and ordered as justice shall requier:

And that presently as well the said sir Edmonde Butler as also the same Oliver Fitzgarald shall be bounde severally with good suerties in recognizance of fyve hundreth poundes to be knoleged by them severally to her majesties use, that is to say, the said sir Edmond with condicion to appere here before us, the saide lorde deputie, on the said fyrst daie of the next terme, and in the meane tyme to observe her majesties peace for him and his or eny others by his procurement as well towardes the said Olyver, his servauntes, tenantes and followers as also towardes Fraunces Randall, gentleman, and that the same sir Edmond furthermore presentlie, uppon his repaire home, shall without delay make full restitucion to the said Oliver of the demaundes by him complayned on and not denyed by the said sir Edmond or so satisfie him for the same as no further complaynt be thereon made before us:

---

[1] Blank in MS.

And the said Oliver with condicion also for like apparance on the daie aforesaid and to observe for him and his or eny others by his procurement likewise her majesties peace towardes the said sir Edmond, his servauntes, tenantes and followers and to make such restitucion to the said sir Edmond of his demaundes which he by his complaynte demaundeth against the said Oliver and by him denyed; as uppon further proof to be made before us the said sir Edmund shall by us, the said lorde deputy, be ordered or adjudged. And that as well the said sir Edmonde as the said Oliver after their appearaunce so made shall not departe the cittie of Dublin withoute the especiall lycense obteyned of us, the said lorde deputye. 1565–6.

[CLXIX.]—At Arcloo,[1] the xiith of March, 1565[–6]: fol. 213.

Wheare advertisement hath been geven us, the lorde deputie, that contrary former order taken betwene Hugh MacShane, beeng here then present, and Nicholas Harbert, esquier, the same Heugh hath made defaulte, and hath not brought in by the fyrst of March, according that former order, Feagh MacHugh, Shane Coge Bewrke, Tirrelagh MacTeige etroda and Cahir Carragh MacDowlen Oburne, as pledges to the handes of the arbitratours betwene them chosen, by the fyrst of March last past, and the said Heugh MacShane, uppon that advertisement, cauled to aunswer and alleging that he understode those pledges to have been brought to us, the lorde deputie, when we should requier them and not otherwise and so thereby mistoke the order aforesaid:

It is therefore nowe ordered that the said Hugh MacShane shall by Lowe Sonday, next comyng, bring to us, the saide lorde deputie, at Dublin, the pledges above named to abyde such order as then we, the lorde deputie, shall take with them in the behaulf aforesaid.

[CLXX.]—At Arcloo, the xiith of March, 1565[–6]: fol. 213b.

Uppon the hering of the complaynt before us exhibited by Owen ODowle MacBryan, sonne to Bryan O'Dowle McYnerse against Morrough McDowle, of Ballenvallagh, for the killing of the said Bryan, father to the said complaynant, and other matter of losses, damages therein demaunded against the said Morrough: and the said Morrough humblie submytting himself to us, the lorde deputie, and being receaved into her majesties grace:

It is ordered and agreed by thassent of both the said parties and the playntif, both as touching the advauntage of any appele for his fathers said death to be prosecuted against the said Morrogh, and also for all other matters, controversies, strives or demaundes from the begynning of the world unto the daie of the date hereof, moved, arisen, styrred or depending betwene either of the said parties ech against the other that they shall abide, perfourme, and obey therin such order, arbitrament, or determynacion as Robert Pipho, William Basnett, Hugh MacShane, and Tibbott MacMorrishe (arbitrators indifferently chosen betwene the said parties) shall arbitrate, order or determyne on this side the feast of Penthecost next comyng:

And it is further ordered that Lucas Othowle and the saide Tibbott Mac Morrishe shall furthwith be bounde to her majestie by waie of recognizaunce before her majesties justice of her chief bench, to be taken in one hundreth poundes, aswell for the good behaviour and

[1] Arklow, Wicklow.

1565–6. abering of the said Morrogh hensfourth towardes all her majesties liege people, as also to bring fourth the body of the said Morrogh on the day of the feast aforesaid, or soner if they shall so be required before us, the said lorde deputie and counsell, whereby the said Morrogh shall thereuppon take knowledge of the order passed by the arbitrators aforesaide and further assure the playntiff for the performaunce of the same.

fol. 214. [CLXXI.]—Apud Droghedam, die Martis, decimo sexto, videlicet, die Julii, 1566, anno regni regine Elizabeth octavo:

1566. H. Sydney.—It is concluded by us the lorde deputye, the lordes spirituall and temporall of this realme and the rest of her majesties counsell of the same, whose names be hereunto subscribed, (the rest beeng uppon reasonable excuses, and otherwise in service of her majestie absent): That for the service of her highnes, and quyet and deffence of this realme and of her majesties subjectes of the same there shall be a generall hostyng proclaymed after the old custome by wrytte, for six weekes at the rate of three plowland to a carte. The same to begyn the xvth of Auguste next to come, and to assemble the same daye at such place as the lorde deputye shall apoynte, with the risyng owt of the countrey requysite to the same.

Adam Armachanus.—H. Midensis.—Jenico, vic. of Gormanston.—Christopher Delvyn.—R. Trimletiston.—T. Louithe.—Crystofer Howthe.—Jo. Plunket.—Robert Dyllon.—Thomas Cusake.—N[icholas] Bagenall.[1]—Henry Draycott.—Francis Agarde.

fol. 215.[2] [CLXXII.]—At Dublin, the ixth of Aprill, 1566, in the castell chamber there:

Memorandum: That day appering before the lorde deputie and counsell as well the right honorable Gerald, erle of Desmound, as also sir Morrice Fitzgerald of the Deassy, knight, lately in this realme arryved, and after delivery made by the said erle of her majesties letteres to the said lorde deputie and counsell, wherein her highnes pleasure is signified as touching the variaunces and demaundes betwene the said erle and the said sir Morrice:

It is for the present ordered that as well the said erle as also the said sir Morrice shall be bound presently in recognizance severally to be taken of them to her majesties use in the somme of one thousand poundes currant money of this realme, to observe her majesties peace eche of them to and towardes the other and to and towardes the servauntes, tenantes and followers belonging to either of them:

And that as well the said erle as also the said sir Morrice, within xiiii daies next ensueng the date hereof shall inlardge and sett at libertie all such prysoners as hath been at eny tyme within twelve monnethes last past, taken aswell on the behaulf of the said erle or eny others under his rule, being the said sir Morrice[s] servauntes, tenantes or followers, as also on the behaulf of the said sir Morrice or eny other for him, beeng servauntes, tenantes or followers to the said erle and to accquite and dischardge presently all and every such the suerties and theire bandes as have been or are bounde or have undertaken for eny rampson of eny those prysoners on ech partie or behaulf to be paid or aunswered. And if such rampson as allredy hath been exacted or receved by any of those parties on eny prysoner so taken within the

[1] Marshal of the army in Ireland. [2] Fol. 214*b*. is blank.

tyme aforesaid, to abide thereapon the further order of the said lorde deputy in that behaulf hereafter to be taken. 1566.

And that aswell the said erle as also the said sir Morrice shall personally appere at Youghell, before the said lorde deputy uppon his lordeshippes next repaire thither and there not to departe without the speciall lycense of the said lorde deputie, till that there uppon the further hering and debating of the originall causes of the variances between the fol. 215*b*. parties aforenamed, growen and arisen within the tyme before lymyted and their proffes on eche syde also herde which are ordered by this our order to be in the meane tyme produced and examyned before sir Warham Scintleger, knight, and the rest of her majesties commissioners, beeng presently repared into the parties of Mounster for the stablishement of the good order and quiet in those parties.

Further order uppon those variances may be taken and established as by the lorde deputy and counsell shall be thought mete according her majesties said pleasure signified unto them in that behaulf.

[CLXXIII. 1.]—At Kylkenny, on Saturday the xxiii[th] of Marche, 1565[–6]: M. 1565–6. fol. 216.

It is ordered by the lorde deputie and counsell, uppon the hering of the complayntes as well on the behaulf of the lorde baron of Donboyne against Piers Butler of the Grallagh, his brother and Patricke Shurlog, esquier, as also on the behaulf of the same Piers, the said Patrick and others, the freholders or inhabitants of the cantred of the Tryemneanaghe against the said lorde baron of Donboyne, there severally exhibited, and the severall aunswers thereon then also beeng redd, that bothe for because the shorte abode of us, the said lorde deputie, here and the conveniencie of tyme and place hath not served to the orderly fynisshing or deciding of those variaunces that the same complayntes with the said severall aunswers thereunto shall be further referred uppon the further proof thereon to be had on eche parties behaulf to the order and determynacion of sir Warham Sentleger, knight, and the rest of the commissioners nowe aponcted to repaire into Mounster for the establishment of the better good quiet in those parties:

And that aswell the said lorde baron of Donboyne, for the good observacion of her majesties peace to be well and trewly observed and kepte by his lordshippe, his tenantes servauntes and followers to and towardes the erle of Desmound, his servauntes, tenantes, and followers and the freholders under his lordeshippes rule, and likewise that the same lorde baron shall quietly permytt the said Patricke Shurlog or his sufficient deputie to exercise his office as sheriff within that the countie or libertie of Typperarie so long as he shall be thereunto aucthorised and that the same lorde baron hensforth shall not use or enterteyne any other or more nomber of gallawglasse, harquebuters, horsemen or kerne then by former order hath been appoynted and allowed from this bourde to be kepte enterteyned or used by his lordeshippe excepte hereafter by this bourd he shall therein further be lycensed uppon especiall occasion:

As also that the said Peires Butler and the sayde Patricke Shirlogo and either of them for them selfes their servantes tenantes and followers, for the like observacion of her majesties peace to and towardes the said lorde baron of Donboyne, his kynesmen, servantes, tenantes and followers and the rest of the freholders and the inhabitantes under fol. 216*b*. his lordeshippes rule shall be also severally bounde to her majestie in fyve hundreth poundes apece by recognizance, orderly to be recognized for that purpose.

1565-6. And further that either personally shall appere at Dublin on the fyrst day of the next terme and thence not to depart without lycense of us the said lorde deputie but to attend the further order of this bourde to be taken for the further quiet and reducing to good agrement and confirmytie the above named the baron of Donboyne and the said Pires and Patrick, nowe at this present resting so in variance and as yett unreconsiled, and that the said lorde baron, Piers Butler and Patrick Shurloge ne eny or either of them shall departe the saide towne of Kilkenny till they have orderly, as afore is ordered, recognized severall the recognizance as afore expressed before her majesties commissioners here now remayning.

[CLXXIII. 2.]—xxiiiith March, 1565[-6]:

The within named lorde baron of Donboyne, Piers Butler of the Grallagh, esquier, and Patrick Shurloge, esquier, hath confessed severally to owe her majestie fyve hundreth poundes, as within ys ordered, uppon condicion to performe on either their behaulfes the order of the lorde deputy and counsell within specified before her Majesties commissioners.—

John Plunckett.—Henry Draycott.—Luke Dillon.

fol. 217. [CLXXIV.]—The true copie of the lettere sent unto the lorde deputy:

1566. My humble duty premissed: I have received your lordshippes lettere on Monday last past, which daie, being ryding one of my young horsses, had a falle and strayned my legge and thingking that I had no harme thought a rodyn yesterday to accomplishe your lordeshippes will but for that my leige is not as yet well recovered I have sent your lordeshippe my servaunt Hossey to understand your lordeshippes further pleasure and if it be for eny weightie matters as sone as I fele myself well at eyse, I will do your lordeshippes commaundment.

I have sent your lordeshippe Lysagh Omore and Caeyr Omore, whereof one of them is to be deliyverid unto your lordeshippe in a hand lock, which your lordeshippe maye retourne unto agayne, and, God willing, he shall be saffly kept.

And so I take my leave, wisshing your lordeshippe helth with increase of honor.

From Rathehangann the xth of Apprill, 1566, your lordeshippes assuryd to commaund, G. Kyldare.

To the right honorable and my very good lorde, my lorde deputy, gyve this.

fol. 217b. [CLXXV.]—At Kylmayneham, on Thursday the xith of Apprill, 1566:

The same daie and in the place aforesaid came before the lorde deputie Lysagh MacKedagh Omore, the elder brother, and Kahier MacKedagh Omore, the younger brother, humblie uppon theire knees submytting themselves to the said lorde deputie and made humble peticion to be receved under her majesties grace and protection, and promising and understanding hensfourth to become of good behavior and lyve as her majesties good and loyall subjectes:

The said Lisagh, the elder brother, with the expresse assent and consent of the saide Cahier, his younger brother, both in perfourmaunce of the said promise and undertaking and also that the same Lisagh

during his libertie nowe graunted and that such his servauntes or late 1566.
followers as he shall allure bothe to dwell with him or to manure and bring goodes and cattells to suche porcion of land as the said lorde deputye, uppon further deliberacion and advise, shall assigne unto the said Lisaghe, shall likewise be and contynue of good behavior; and the same Lysaghe to aunswer also for eny their factes hensfourth or to present theire bodies before the said lorde deputie, did put the same Cahier into the handes of the said lorde deputie into a hand locke to remayne as pleadge for the trewe observacion of the premisses and uppone eny defaulte or breche to happen in the behaulf aforesaide the same Cahier to be ordered at the will and pleasure of the said lorde deputie:

Whereuppon the said Cahier was receaved as pleadge in hand by the said lorde deputie for perfourmance of the premisses aforesaid, and for the advoyding of the said Cahiers further chardges if he shulde have been commyted to the castell of Dublin, there to be kepte in safetie, (and former request in this behaulf beeng made by the erle of Kyldare to have the custody of him) the same Cahier was presently by the said lorde deputie delyvered in hand to Meylor Hussey, gentleman, steward to the erle of Kyldare), who receved him in charge as her majesties prysoner, ymmediately to be brought and presented to the sayd erle and under his lordeshippes chardge and saulf custody to remayne and be fol. 217*
kept as pledge for the causes aforesaid and to be forthcoming when the said lorde deputy shall demaund him.

[CLXXVI.]—By the lorde deputy and counsell:

Uppon the hering of sondry complayntes aswell on the behaulf of Teyg MacWilliam OKelley agaynst the right honorable Richard, erle of Clanricard, as also on the behalf of the same erle against the said Teige, one against the other, severally propounded and especiall of the matter of the praye lately taken by the said erle from the said Teige of the valewe, as he complayneth, of two hundreth poundes, besydes the imprysonment of the same Teiges wiffe and his eldest sonne, now beeng in hand with the said erle:

It is ordered and decreed, with thassent of the said erle, that ymmediatly uppon his repaire home from this the towne of Dondalk he shall release and putt at libertie Sabyne,[1] the wiffe of the said Teige, and make restitucion of the said praye so as aforesaid taken from the same Teige MacWilliam OKelly, to the handes of the said Teige or such fol. 217*b.
other person as he shall appoynete to the receipte thereof:

And for the more better deciding and ending of the rightfullness of the taking of that praye aswell as all other matters of complaynte, challenge and demaunde, which on the partie or behaulf of the said erle against the said Teige, or on the behaulf of the same Teige against the said earle, or to be objected, challenged or demaunded: it is agreed, with the assent of both the said parties that the same shall be decided and ended on this side mydsomer daye next comyng after the date hereof by the archbisshopp of Tuam[2] the bisshopp of Clonforte and the maior of Galwaye, nowe being, yf they so can do or then indelaydly to advertice us in whome the default is why they cannot so end or fynnyshe those variances:

That thereuppon to prefix to the said earle and Teige a certen daie to appere before us to abide our further order to be taken for the fynyssh-

---

[1] Sadhbh, Sabina.

[2] *Tuam*] Thomond, MS.

1566. ing of those variances. And that the commissioners certifie us of that daie if any shall by them be so prefixed:

And it is furthermore ordered by us, the lorde deputie and counsell, that for the better assurance and performacion of such the orders as either by the said commissioners or as aforesaid otherwise by us shall fortune to be taken touching eny the said earles challenges or demaundes against the said Teig that John MacTeige OKelly, sonne to the said Teige, nowe beeng in hand with the said earle, shall be by the said earle uppon his said repaire home furthwith delivered and putt into thandes and under the custody of the maior of Galwaye, to be remayning as one pledge in that behaulf till order be further addressed from us for his release.

And that also Hugh MacTeige OKelly, another sonne of the said Teiges, for the like purpose as herein the earle of Kildare also hath undertaken before us, shall likewise be delivered as a pledge in like maner into the handes of us, the said lorde deputie, when we shall demaunde the same pleadge in like manner into the custody for cause aforesaid.

Yeven at Dondalke, the third of May, 1566.

fol. 218.

[CLXXVII.]—By the lorde deputye:

Uppon the hering of the complaynte of Bryan OKelly of Connaght, gentleman, against the right honorable Richard, earle of Clanricard, before us exhibited and the same earle, here then beeng present and cauled to the aunswering thereof, hath for aunswere said that as toutching the matter therein charged on Ullyke Bourke, the said earles sonne, for the killing of Hugh OKelly, sonne to the said Bryan, albeyt the same Ullike happened to be in the company of the malefactors whiche commytted that facte, yett the same Ullike with his owne handes commytted not that acte nor was, the said earle alledgeth, assenting thereunto, and neverthelesse the pryncipall malefactor by the earles meanes apprehended and executed for that facte, whose aunswer for that parte no mattereall matter on the behaulf of the said Bryan beeng alleged before us to the contrary, we have accepted [1] as sufficient to the dischardge of the said Ullike for that facte onely.

And forasmuch as the pray taken by the said Heugh from Occonnor Dune, mencioned in the saide complaynt, is not denyed by the said erle to be reskued and taken by the said Ullike and his company from the said Hugh, before the tyme he was so killed, and also three horsses and three habergyns:

And that moreover the rest of the matter of the said complaynt touching the praye taken by the said earle and other the burninges and spoyles by him done uppon Koghe Offallon, a tennant of the said Bryans, and averred by the said earle to be well taken by reason of slanty broken [2] by the said Bryan towardes the said earle, and the said Bryan protesting contrarywise that no such slanty was by him broken but was and is to be warranted at the tyme of the supposed breach thereof by vertue of commission then adwarded from the late lorde

fol. 218b. justice in the causes of her majesties service with the underconstable of Athlone remayning, is presently with the assentes of the said earle and Bryan, putt to the saieng of the said Koghe Offallon himself, for the more manyfest declaracion of his certen losses, and the certen of the praye so from him taken by the said earle:

---

[1] *Accepted*] excepted, MS.

[2] In margin: "Justification of burnings and spoyles by reason of slantie broken."

It is therefore by us ordered and decreed that the said earle shall make present restitucion to the said Bryan of the foresaid praye so reskued and taken from the said Heugh OKelly by the said Ullike, togethers with the three horses and the three habergynes aforesaid. And our further order as toutching the matter of the said Koghe Offallans preye to depend in suspense [1] till the repayer of us the said lorde deputy into those parties and the sayeng knowen in that behaulf of the said Kogh Offallen. 1566.

Yeven at Dondalke, the third of May, 1566.

[CLXXVIII.]—By the lorde deputie and counsell : fol. 219.

Wheare of long contynuance aswell in the tymes of the severall governementes of sondrye the governors of this realme, predecessors to us, the said lorde deputye, as also synce we, the same lorde deputie, have had the governement here, sondry grevouse complayntes have arrisen, and been moved as touching the placing and victelling of the soldiars reteyned in garrison in this realme, and divers variaunces by reason thereof growen betwene the same soldiars and such other persons on whome they were in tymes past and nowe are so cessed and placed, (over and besydes the gret unredynes and discomoditie for reddy service) insomuch as beeng at cesse and dispersed in sondry countres, farr distant one from another, they mought not easely, aptlye or comodiously (eny sodeyn or present occasion serving for service) be togethers in redynes assembled; whereby greate hindraunce hath arisen and doth accrewe in the marshall service and affaires of this realme :

It ys therefore condiscended concluded and agreed by us, the said lorde deputie and those of her majesties said counsell, whose names are hereunto signed, for the better ease of the parties so greved, and the soldiers for her majesties service to be in the more and better redynes, that two hundreth and fyfty fotemen of her majesties retynue here, such as the said lorde deputie shall please to appoynt, shall be placed and cessed in suche townes nigh to the borders for occasion of her majesties service as to the said lorde deputies discretion shall seame fyttest, and so to remayne and contynue from the fyrst day of May last past till the last of September next comyng.

And for that the exilitie of those soldiers interteynementes is such as with respecte had of payeing owte thereof for theire victelles, and otherwise therwithall also to furnishe them selffes with competent apparrell and munycion, will not suffice or arrise to the aunswering of that charge so long as they shall be so remayning and placed in the townes nigh the borders, as aforesaid, wee have agreed and concluded also for the better ease of the countrey which shuld so have borne them to cesse, that a certeyne overplus [2] of fower pence per diem for the better mayntenaunce or increase of thentertaynement or wages of every the aforesaid two hundreth and fyftie fotemen so being placed on the borders aforesaid, fol. 219b. whilst during the tyme as aforesaid, they shall be there remayning, shall be rered, levied, and contributed on the severall counties of Wexford, Kildare, Dublin, Meth and Westmeth, on this syde the fyrst of October next commyng by such person and persons as thereunto the said lorde deputie, [by] warrant under his hand signed, shall apoyncte and aucthorise :

The devicion or allotment whereof is by us referred to sir John Plonkett, knight, sir Robert Dillon, knight, sir Thomas Cusacke, knight, and

---

[1] *Suspense*] suspecte, MS.

[2] In margin : "An increase of fourp ence per diem upon the country to eche of the souldiers lying upon the borders."

1566. James Barnewell, esquier, or eny thre of them, to be made and fynysshed by the twelveth daie of July, next ensueng:

And the county of Lowth, whereon the marshall with his band of horsemen and theire horsses, are presently cessed and placed; and also the countie of Catherlagh, which also is chardged with the cesse of horsemen under the leading of capten Heron, and belonging to the howse of Lawghlyn, clerely to be exempted owt and from the same contribucion and therwithall in enywise not to be chardged, for the considerations before rehersed.

Yeoven at Dublin, the xxii[th] of May, 1566.

fol. 220. [CLXXIX.]—Hec indentura, facta decimo septimo die Junii, anno Domini, secundum computacionem Anglicane ecclesie, millesimo quingentesimo sexagesimo sexto [1566], inter Omolaghlyn, sue nationis principalem, ex una parte, et Johannem MacCoughlan, filium Macoughlan, sue nationis nunc etiam principalis, partem se facientem pro eodem patre suo et liberis tenentibus patrie sue, ac de ad infrascripta sistendo, ex parte altera, testatur qualiter prefati Omolaghlyn et Johannes MacCoughlan, die et anno predictis, coram nobis personaliter constituti, eidem Omolaghlyn conquestus est quod prefatus Maccoughlan, ejus ut pretendebatur sequax, vi atque injuria ab eo per longum temporis cursum detinuit non solum quendam annualem redditum duodecim marcarum,[1] (quem redditum antecessores predicti Maccoughlan, prefati conquerentis, antecessoribus solvere usitati sunt) verum etiam expensas patrie predicte pro victualibus ibidem sumendis quolibet anni quarterio pro viginti et octo horis, totiens quotiens, ejusdem Omolaghlyn antecessoribus vel sibimet ipso visum fuerat:

Necnon surreccionem sive evocacionem centum turbariorum super et extra eandem patriam ad libitum conquerentis evocandorum:

De quibus premissis antecessores prefati Omolaghlyn, tempore a quo memoria hominum non existit, possessionati fuere et per eundem Omolaghlyn coram nobis adhunc allegatum fuit:

Ad que predictus Johannes MacCoughlan, ex parte predicti patris sui aliorumque dictorum liberorum tenentium patrie predicte, pro quibus idem Johannes in hac parte stare et respondere coram nobis aucthorisatus est, ut adtunc affirmabatur respondendo dixit clameum prefati Omolaughlyn in premissis minus justum fore, allegans initium demandorum predictorum hactenus vi et injuria atque manu forti antecessorum prefati Omolaghlyn inceptum usurpatoque titulo usitatum fuisse et esse, neque enim aliquo recto jure stabilitum, quodque eo pretextu et occasione predictus Maccoughlan, pater predicti Johannis,
fol. 220b. redditum predictum, ut prefertur per dictum Omolaghlyn clamatum per spacium sexdecem annorum ultime preteritorum solvere renuit et omnino recusavit:

De quibus tamen controversiis et demandis omnibus et singulis partes litigantes prenominate ex suis unanimis et voluntariis consensubus et assensubus submiserunt se arbitrio sive ordinacion nostri domini deputati reliquorumque hic sue majestatis a consilijs quoque modo fiendo: et habita superinde per nos dictum dominum deputatum et consilium matura deliberacione, perpendentesque consuetudinem predictam de expensis patrie predicti Maccoughlan sive victualibus super eandem modo et forma prerecitatis sumendis, irritam, invalidam, cassam et anno vacuam et vetitam de jure hujus regni fuisse et esse sicque fore debere:

---

[1] In margin: "For Omolaghlin, for nine markes, Irish, chiefe rent upon Macoghlan."

Necnon surreccionem sive evocacionem turbariorum dictorum in forma predicta per ipsum Omolaghlyn clamatum et petitum alicui tali subdito sue majestatis haud convenire seu aliquem talem regalem usum vendicare et propterea quod predictus Johannes Maccoughlan haud negare nequivit, quin quod predictus redditus aliquibus temporibus predictos sexdecim annos precedentibus solvebatur predictei Omolaghlyn predecessoribus, quamvis tamen (ut idem Johannes asserit) minus juste. 1566.

Nos, dominus deputatus, ac reliqui sue majestatis a consiliis, quorum nomina presentibus subscribuntur, ad refellendum controversias quascunque circa premissa inter partes predictas quomodolibet exortas, motas, sive pendentes indiscussas, per hanc nostram senteuciam sive hoc nostrum finale decretum quam sive quod ferimus et pro mulgamus in hiis scriptis:

Decernimus, declaramus et pronunciamus et adjudicamus predictam Macoughlan, sue nationis nunc principalem, et successores et heredes suos de cetero et imperpetuum ab omni et omnimodo servitio prefato Omolaghlyn, nunc sue nacionis principali, seu successoribus vel heredibus suis quovismodo impendendo et ab omni clameo pro eodem liberos et immunes imperpetui fore et esse, atque ab omnibus impositionibus preantea specificatis:

Quodque prefatus Omolaghlyn seu successores vel heredes sui prefatum Maccoughlan, heredes seu successores suos, racione alicujus prescripcionis sive preteriti consuetudinis ut sequacem sive sequaces suos vel aliquas imposiciones prelibatas seu aliquam partem eorundem exigere, clamare sive vendicare minime debeat aut debeant aliqualiter, sed ab omni clameo inde totaliter sint exclusi:

Et quod solummodo prefatus Maccoughlan et successores sui tenentur imperpetuum per presentes solvere prefato Omolaghlyn, seu heredibus fol. 221. vel successoribus suis, quandam annuitatem sive annualem redditum novem marcarum legalis monete Hibernie, ad duos anni terminos, videlicet, ad festa Sancti Michaelis Archangeli et Pasche annuatim per equales porciones, intra unum mensem proxime sequentem quodlibet festum festorum predictorum solvendam, prima enim solucione inde incipienda ad festum Sancti Michaelis archangeli proxime futurum, pro omnibus servitiis, clameis et demandis quibuscunque.

In cujus rei testimonium tam partes predicti hisce indenturis sigilla sua alternatim apposuerunt, quam etiam nos, dominus deputatus, et reliqui a consiliis presentibus nomina nostra subscripsimus in majorem fidem et testimonium omnium et singulorum premissorum:

Apud Dublin, die et anno prius prerecitatis.

[CLXXX.]—The generall hostyng northwarde agaynst Shane Oneill, sett fourth by the right honorable sir Henry Sydney, fol. 221*b*. knight of the noble order of the garter, lorde president of Wales and marchesse thereof, lorde deputy generall of this realme of Irelande the — [1] of — [2] and contynuyng for — [3] dayes:

A note wheareby the shireff of the countie of Dublin shall knowe and warne suche persons as shall sett fourth to this hosting and howe:

Dublin :—The barony of Balrothery:

John Cardiff of Turvy	- - - -	i archer on horseback.	
James Barnewell of Brynmore	- -	ii archers	,,
Christofer Barnewell of Gracediew	- -	iv ,,	,,
Richard Fynglasse of Westplestone	-	i archer	,,

[1], [2], [3] Blank in MS.

1566. Robert Prestone of Balmadon, to sett fourthe - - - - - ii archers on horseback.
Walter Cruce of the Nall - ii " "
Travers of Ballykey in person, and - - ii " "
Nicholas Stokes of Knockengen in person, and - - - - - - i archer "
Thomas Fitzsymondes of Curduff - - ii archers "
Bartholomewe Bathe of Laundeston in person - - - - - i archer "
Mathewe Begge of Boranstone - - i " "
William Conran of the Corragh, in person i " "

The summe of this baronye amounteth to —[1] cartes, which cartes were converted into garrons, after the rate of five garrons to every carte and to every five garrons three hable men to dryve them.

fol. 222. The barony of Cullocke:

The lorde of Howth in person - - vi archers on horseback.
William Talbot of Malahide, in person - iv " "
The baron Bathe of Dromconragh - - iii " "
John Plunckett of Donshoghelcy - - iii " "
Nicholas Hollywood of Tartayne - - iii " "
Robert Taillor of Swerdes, in person - ii " "
Patricke Russell of the Seaton - - i archer "
Bartholemewe Russell of Feltrym and his brother, James Plunckett, in person - i " "
Thomas Wicombe of Drynan in person - i " "
William Blackeney of Rigkynehorde, in person - - - - - - i " "
Patricke Caddell of Caddlestone - - i " "
Christopher Foster of Killogh - - i " "
Emery Howthe of Killester - - i " "
Markes Barnewell of Donbroo - - i " "
Walter Golding of the Grange, in person - i " "

The summe of this baronye amounteth to —[2] cartes (fredomes except) which was converted into garrons, as is aforesaid.

The barony of Newcastell.

The archbisshopp of Dublin - - viii archers on horseback.
Edward Barnewell of Dromnagh, in person i archer "
William Sarsfeld of Lucane - - i " "
Robert Talbott of Belgar, in person - ii archers "
Alen of Palmerston - - - i archer "
Richard Talbott of Templeoge - - i " "
The portreff of the Newcastle - - i " "

The somme of this baronye amounteth to —[3] cartes converted as aforesaid into garrons.

fol. 222b. The barony of Castell Knocke:

Symond Luttrell of Lutrelston - - ii archers on horseback.
Bartholmew Dillon of Cappoke - ii " "
Thomas Bealing of Stradbally - - ii " "
Roger Fynglasse of Porterston in person - ii " "

The summe of the cartes of this baronye amounteth to —[4] the same converted as aforesaid into garrans.

[1], [2], [3], [4] Blank in MS.

The barony of Rathedowne: 1566.

The Lady Travers[1] of Monkton - - iv archers on horseback.
Thomas Fitzwilliams of Meryon, in person ii " "

This barony amounteth to cartes levied alwaies in money and to this hosting was not cessed but did answer the marche cariage.

Meith.—The barony of Dulike:

The lorde viecounte of Gormauston - viii archers on horseback.
Darcy of Platen, in person - - iii " "
James Aylmer, in person, of Dolardston - ii " "
Oliver Darcy, in person - - - i archer "
Talbott of Dardeston - - - iii archers "
Caddell of the Nall, in person - - ii " "
Bryte of Tullocke, in person - - ii " "
Feld of Payneston, in person - - i archer "
Thomas Darcy, in person - - i " "
Hamling of Smythstone, in person - i " "
Whyte of Flemyngton - - - i " "
Sarsfild[2] of Sarsfieldstone - - i " "
Bathe of Colpe - - - - i " " fol. 223.

The summe of this barony amounteth to —[3] cartes and the same, converted as aforesaid, into garrans, after the rate above lymyted.

The barony of Skryne:

The lorde of Killene, the lorde of Donsany, with the rest of the Plunckettes, in person - - xxiiii horsemen.
Nicholas Nugent - - - iii archers on horseback.
Mr. Draycott - - - - i archer "
Sir Thomas Cusacke of Lesmollen, in consideracion of his absence, but - iii archers "
Sir Christofer Chever of Maston - iiii " "
Bathe of Raphecke, in person - iii " "
Kent of Daneston - - - ii " "
Cusake of Gerardeston, in person - ii " "
Thomas Dillon of Ryverston - - iii " "
Peter Dillon - - - - i archer "
Tancarde of Castelton, in person - i " "
The portriff of Skryne - - i " "

The summe of this barony amounted to —[4] cartes to be converted into garans, as aforesaid.

The barony of Ratowthe: fol. 223*b*.

Barnewell of Kilbrye, in person, with - i archer on horseback.
Berforde of Kilrowe " " - i " "
Talbott of Robarteston " " - ii archers "
Ivers of Donshaghlen " " - i archer "
Weasely of the Blackehall " " - i " "

The summe of this barony amounteth to —[5] cartes, converted as aforesaid into garrons.

---

[1] *See* Chartularies of St. Mary's Abbey, Dublin, Rolls series, 1884, ii. xxxviii, xliv.
[2] In margin: "Within adge."
[3], [4], [5] Blank in MS.

1566. The barony of Donboyne:

Phepo of the Rowan, yf he have a fredome - - - -	i archer on horseback.
Fraunces Delahide - - - -	i „ „

The barony is in the [w]hole but three cartes, which, converted into garrans, after the rate abovesaid, make fifteen garrans.

The rysing owte of Westmeth:

The lorde of Delven; the Nugentes of the half baronye of Fower - - - - -	xx horsemen.
The Tuites[1] - - - - - -	vi „
The Tirrelles - - - - -	vi „
For Ferbill - - - - -	vi „
Petites - - - - -	iiii „
Dallamares - - - - - -	iiii „
The Nangelles and Ledwidiches - - -	ii „
The Daltons - - - -	vi „
The Dillons - - - - - -	vi „

fol. 224. The baronys of Dece and Moyfenraghe:

The baron of Galtrym, in person -	iiii archers on horseback.
Barnewell of Arrotesten, in person -	ii „ „
James Dowdall - - - - -	ii „ „
Delahide of Moyglare, in person -	ii „ „
Wesley of the Dengen, in person -	iii „ „
Bartholemewe Cusake - - -	i archer „
Flemyng of Derpatricke in person -	i „ „
Meiler Hussey - - -	ii archers „
Delahide of Asye in person - -	i archer „

The summe of theise two baronyes amounteth in the hole to [2] cartes as aforesaid.

The barony of Lune:

Lynch of Dunnore - - - -	i archer on horseback.
Rocheford of Kerauston in person -	i „ „
The porteriff of Atheboye - -	iiii archers „
Barnabe Skurloke - - -	ii „ „

The summe of this barony amounteth to [3] cartes converted as aforesaid.

The barony of the Novan:

The bisshopp of Meth - -	viii archers on horseback.
The lorde of Trymleston - -	vi „ „
The baron of Novan - - - -	iii „ „
The baron Dillon - - -	ii „ „
Rocheforde of Kilbryde - -	iiii „ „
Michell Cusake, in person - -	ii „ „
Ivers of Ratayne - - -	i archer „
The portriff of Trym - -	iii archers „
fol. 224b. The portriff of the Novan -	iiii „ „
Teling of Mullagha, in person -	i archer „
Hill of Alenston, in person - - -	i „ „
Missett of Laskartan - - -	i „ „
Eustace of the same - - -	i „ „

The summe of this barony amounteth to —[4] cartes, converted into garrans, as aforesaide.

---

[1] In margin: "This sholde have bene entred after all the baronyes of the countie of Methe."

[2], [3], [4] Blank in MS.

The barony of Kenlis : 1566.

Alexander Barnewall, with the horsemen - - iii horsemen.
Everarde of Randelston, in person - - - - ii „
Mape of Maperath, in person - - - i horseman.
Drake of Rahode, in person - - - ii horsemen.
Betaghe of Moynaltie, for his contrey - - - vi „
Ledwiche of Cookestone - - - i horseman.
FytzJohn, Fyanston, in person - - - i „
The sofferaigne of Kenlis - - ii archers on horseback.
The summe of this barony amounteth to —[1] cartes converted as afore.

The barony of Slane:

The baron of Slane to serve to the hosting but sixe horsemen for himself, besydes the leading (if he go to the hosting) of the baronyes of Slane and Margallen, and nowe for the defence of the contrey to have but his owne horsemen and his owne kerne, and the leading of the barony of Slane and to make upp sixteene horsemen and twenty-four kerne to attend uppon Thomas Flemynge of Sydone and such one as the said baron shall appoynete to wache night and daie for defence of the contrey with theire victells. fol. 225.

Barnewell of Stockallen, in person - - - iiii archers.
Barnewall of Roweston - - - - - - ii „
Netterfeld of Dowth, in person - - - ii „
All the archers to be ahorsebacke.

The halff barony of Fower :

The Plunkettes - - - - - - xxiiii horsemen.
Balffe of Galmoweston, in person - - ii „
Barneweil of Moylagh, in person -- - - i „
Tuyte of Baltrastyn - - - - - - i „
Summe of this barony amounteth in the whole but to —[2] cartes, converted as afore, etc.

The gentlemen of the baronye of Kells and the half baronye of Fower to attend uppon the Plunkettes, to serve to the hosting thirty-one horsemen and serving at home four score horsemen.

The baronye of Margallen to attend upon the sheriff and Patricke Cusake in the contrey double there nomber with their vituelles to lye owte night and daie, where it shall be thought requisite for the defence of the contrey.

The barony of Margallen :

Thomas Flemyng of Stephenson, sherif, in person - iii horsemen. fol. 235b.
White of Clodgell, in person - - - - ii „
Veldon, in person - - - - - - ii „

A note whearby the sheriff of the countie of Lowth shall knowe and warne suche persons as shall sett fourth to this hosting and howe :

County of Louth :[3]

The lorde Prymate - - - vi archers on horseback.
The lorde of Lowth, in person, with the Plunckettes - - - vi „ „
Taff of Cookeston, in person - - ii „ „

---

[1], [2] Blank in MS.

[3] In margin : "The rising owte of Uriell, at the leading of the lorde of Lowth, xxiiii horsemen to the hosting and at home double the nomber. This xxiiii horsemen is besyd the prymates companye, the townes of Dondalk and Arde."

1566.			
	The Dowdalles, in person	iiii	horsemen.
	The Garrnons, in person	vi	,,
	The Bedlowes, in person	v	,,
	The Taffes, in person	vi	,,
	White of Balregan	i	,,
	Hadsor	i	,,
	Moore of Barnemeth, in person	i	,,
	White of Rochefordeston	i	,,
	Clynton of the Water, in person	i	,,
	Clynton of Dromcasshell	i	,,

This sheire hath no cartes but the plowelandes are alwaies accustomed to be levied in money, saving onely fower cartes owte of the barony of Ferrarde.

fol. 226.

Kildare:

The countie of Kyldare did not aunswer the accustomed cartes to this hosting, for that the erle of Kildare, with the vicecounte of Baltinglas and the rest of the gentlemen of the same shiere, were appoynted to attend uppon the lorde deputie.

City of Dublin:

The cyttie of Dublin sett fourth to this hosting with threscore archers and gonners, well appoynted, who nevertheles went not but remayned for the deffence of the borders.

Town of Drogheda:

The towne of Drogheda did likewise sett owte to this hosting with fortie tall fellowes, well appoynted, who nevertheles went not but remayned for the deffence of the borders.

The rysyng owte of the Iryshe lordes and captaynes to this hosting:

Fraunces Agard, esquier, senesshall of the Byrnes contrey, with the gentlemen of the same, xii horsemen, xxiiii kerne.

Nicholas Heron, esquier, capten of the Cavennaghes contrey, with the gentlemen of the same, xii horse, xxx kerne.

	Okarwell, with	xii	horse,	xxiiii	kerne.
	Magoghegan	iiii	,,	xxiiii	,,
	Omolmoye, with	vi	,,	xl	,,
	Omolaughlyn, with	iiii	,,	xxiiii	,,
	Omadden, with	iiii	,,	xii	,,
	Hugh Omadden	—	,,	—	,,
fol. 226*b*.	Magennesse	xii	,,	xxiiii	,,
	MacMaghon	viii	,,	xv	,,
	Capteyne of Ferney[1]	x	,,	xxx	,,
	Savage	iiii	,,	xiiii	,,
	Oraley	xl	,,	c	,,

Phelym Roo, with his accustomed owte rysing.

Ohanlan, with his like rysing owte.

Magwyer, in the same sorte.

Omagher, with his accustomed rising owte.

Sir Edmond Butler, knight, for the erle of Ormounde, his brother, in person, with the same erles rising owte of horsemen and kerne, and her majesties forty kerne under the same, sir Edmondes leading.

---

[1] In margin: "By later presidentes, 8 h[orse] 15 k[erne]."

The baron of Donboyne, in person, with his horsemen and kerne. 1566.

The baron of the Cahier to send his sonne or his brother to the hosting, with his accustomed rising owt of horsemen and kerne.

The baron of Upper Ossories sonne, with his horsemen and kerne, together with her majesties forty kerne under the same barons sonne, sir Barnabe Fitzpatrickes leading.

[CLXXXI.]—After our hartie commendacions to your lordshippes : fol. 227.

For the better deffence of the severall baronys of Mergallen, Kelles, and the haulf baronye of Fower, and all the whole borders of the countie of Westmeth agaynst eny of the Irissherie which hensfourth shall happen to make incursions within those lymyttes, or the which otherwise do or shall annoye her majesties good subjectes inhabiting or bordering on those confynes, we have thought fitt by tenor hereof to apointe and aucthorise you, Chistoffer, lorde baron of Delvin, James Plunkett, lorde of Killyne, sir Oliver Plonkett, knight, Thomas Flemyng of Stephenson, gentleman, sherif of the county of Meth, Garrett Fay, gentleman, sherif of the countie of Westmeth, Thomas Le Strange, gentleman, Patrike Cusake, gentleman, and John Plonckett of Lowgherewe, gentleman, or eny twoo of you, of the which alwaies we woll your lordeshippe, the barone of Delvyn, to be one, as well to forsee and cause contynuall watche by daye and night, bothe by horsemen and footemen, to be kepte according your good discressions in the townes and villages and other the streightes within the severall baronyes and borders aforesaid for the deffence thereof and the good salfetie of her majesties subjectes in the same, as also for your better ease whilest ye shall intende thexecucion of the said affaires, aswell as for the apprehending of eny suspectes uppon occasion so serving, and for your good safeties, to resorte or enter into any castle, scituated within the lymyttes of your said aucthorisement :

And suche person or persones as you shall fynde in behaulf aforesaid offending, with your power and forces, and the power and forces within the said baronyes and lymites aforesaid to resyst, prosequute, chase or followe eny the same offendors into the Yrishe contres and them or eny of them by yowe taken to ponyshe, correcte and plague according your discressions or according suche aucthoritye as eny of youwe alredy hath for thexecuting of the marciall lawe, and also the goodes and cattells by eny of the Yrishrie to be hensfourth preed or taken from eny her majesties good subjectes out of the Englishe Pale, dwelling within the lymyttes fol. 227b.
aforesaide, to reskewe and recover the same, that restitucion thereon may accrue to the parties greved accordingly, as to the uttermost of your powers yt maie therein belonge.

And furthermore for your better furtherance in this her majesties service and the better deffence and securitie of the countrey and places aforesaide, we do also by tenor hereof geve full power and aucthoritie to you or eny two of yowe (of whom alwaie we woll the said baron of Delven to be one) to apoyncte and commaunde aswell suche archers as shall be assigned to the defence of Kelles and the Nobber, as also all horsemen and fotemen within the circuite of your said aucthoritie, to be attendant on you or eny twoo of you (of whome the said barone of Delvyn alwaie to be one) from tyme to tyme, and by you to be ordered, guyded and governed as to and for the dewe executing of our aucthorisement in theis our letters specified maye be most behovefull and expedient :

1566. And suche as shall be founde in that behaulf disobedient to punyshe the same according your discressions or eny twoo of yowe, the said barone of Delven or the lorde of Killyne alwaye beeng one, willing and streightly also chardging in her majesties name all and singuler her majesties officers, ministers and loving subjectes to whome in case it dothe shall or maye appertayne, as well within liberties as withowt, to be unto you or eny two of you (of whome the saide barone of Delven alwaie to be one) from tyme to tyme attendant, ayding, helping and assisting as ye shall requier them, withowt failing thereof as they and every of them will be aunswerable to her majestie, and will avoyde her high indignacion for doeng of the contrarie:

Wherefore we requier and ernestlie charge you on her majesties behaulf that ernestlie, diligently and carfuly ye intend and applie this her majesties especiall service and to employ therein the uttermost of your good endevoyers and trayvell, according your discressions as our ernest and very trust is reposed in you in this behaulf.

fol. 228. Yeven at Drogheda, the 17th of July 1566.

To our loving freendes Christopher, lordeof Delvyn, James Plunket lorde Killine, sir Oliver Plunket of Rathmore, Thomas Flemyng of Stevenson, sherif of Meth; Garet Fey, sherif of Westmeth; Thomas le Strange, Patricke Cusack, John Plunkett of Lowgherewe, to eny twoo of them, quorum the lorde of Delvyn to be one.

A like to the barone of Slane, Thomas Flemyng of Syddan, and a thirde to be nomynated by the baron and the barone to be of the quorum only, for the barony of Slane and the borders there.

A like in effecte to the barone of Lowthe, so[le]ly for the countie of Lowth and the borders there, with clause for defaite of every gentleman xl.*s*; of every horseman, xx.*s*; of every foteman, vi.*s* viii.*d*; every towneshipp xx.*s*; and the lorde of Lowth to certifie these defaultes from tyme to tyme that the forfeitures maye be levied and aunswered to the quene.

fol. 229.[1] [CLXXXII.]—At Drogheda, the iiiith of November, 1566, anno regni regine Elizabeth viiii°:

H. Sydney.—It is concluded by us, the lord deputy, and the lordes spirituall and temporall of this realme, with the residue of her majesties counsaill, whose names are subscribed, the rest being absent uppon occasion of the queenes majesties service, that a generall contribucion or sesse be made of corne and befes, to be devided uppon the sheris and countrees as hereafter followith:

First: The countie of Dublin to pay in wheat 400 peckes, and in malt 600 peckes, in otes one thousand peckes.

Kildare:	wheat,	400	peckes.	Malt,	600	peckes.	Otes,	1000 peckes.
Westmeth:	,,	400	,,	,,	600	,,	,,	1000 ,,
Methe:	,,	700	,,	,,	1100	,,	,,	1800 ,,
Kilkenny:	,,	100	,,	,,	150	,,	,,	250 ,,
Waterforde:	,,	100	,,	,,	150	,,	,,	250 ,,
Tipperary:	,,	100	,,	,,	150	,,	,,	250 ,,
Kinges countie:	,,	200	,,	,,	300	,,	,,	500 ,,
Queens countie:	,,	200	,,	,,	300	,,	,,	500 ,,
Caterloughe:	,,	100	,,	,,	150	,,	,,	250 ,,
Wexford:	,,	300	,,	,,	400	,,	,,	700 ,,

[1] Fol. 228*b* is blank.

And forasmuch as it is alleagid to be doubtfull whether the said graine can be levied in eche of these counties according the proporcion, it is condiscendid that, at the election of the counties, they shall ether deliver the corne or elles for every pecke of wheat three shillings sterling, and for every pecke of beare malt the like rate. And for every pecke of ale malt two shillinges sterling, and for every pecke of otes twelve pence sterling. The same money to be delivered to the handes of Thomas Might, at or before the first day of February next, in maner and forme following, videlicet: 1566. fol. 229b.

The counties: Of Dublin at Dublin:[1]—Methe at Navan:—West Methe at Aboy:—Kildare at Naas.

Caterlough, Tipperary, Kilkenny, at Laughlin:—Waxforde, Waterford.

The Kinges county at Trimme.

The Queenes county at the Naas.

Allso it is agreed that the third part of the malt shall be beare malt, and every person that shall deliver corne shall receive of the said Thomas Might four shillinges, Irish, for every pecke of wheat and beare malt, and two shillinges, eight pence, Irish, for every pecke of ote malt, and sixteen pence, Irish, for every pecke of otes.

Yt is farder agreed that their shall be befes paid by the severall captaines of the Irish cuntries according to the proporcion insuing, to be deliverid to the handes of Thomas Might, at the rate of twelve shillinges, Iryshe, for every beafe and in such places as followethe: The price of every porke allso two shillinges eightpence Irish.

BEFES. fol. 230.

First: Oreighlie to deliver at Kellis	160	beefes,	160	porkes.
The [w]hole Annaly to deliver at Aboy	100	„	100	„
Maccoughlan	20	„	20	„
Omilaughlin	20	„	20	„
The Okellies	80	„	80	„
Magouigan	20	„	20	„
Omiloy	10	„	10	„
Occarroll	30	„	30	„
The baron of Upper Ossory	20	„	20	„
The Cavanaughes	20	„	20	„
The Birnes	20	„	20	„
Omaddin	20	„	12	„
Upon those of Mointerconnought	12	„	12	„

G. Kyldare.—H. Midensis.—C. Delvyn.—R. Trimletiston.—T. Louithe. —Jo. Plunket.—N. Bagenall.—Robert Dyllon.—Thomas Cusake.—Warhame Sentleger.[2]

[CLXXXIII.]—Fiant indenture dupliciter indentate, in debita forma, sub tenore verborum sequentium inter serenissimam dominam nostram reginam, ex una parte, et Hugonem MacMolaghlin Ballagh OMadden, filium primogenitum sive heredem Molaghlyn Ballagh OMadden, capitanei sive sue nationis principalis, de le Longegorte cum Shelamwhie communiter nuncupate OMaddyns controy (extendentis in parte usque rivulum de Shenan atque in parte ultra eundem rivulum) nuper defuncti, ex parte altera, etc., testatur concordatum, conventum et concessum esse fol. 231.

[1] Athboy, co. Meath. [2] Fol. 230b is blank.

1566. inter dictam illustrissimam dominam reginam et dictum Hugonem, de et cum assensu predilecti et fidelis consiliarii nostri, Henrici Sydney, prenobilis ordinis garterii militis, presidentis consilii nostri Wallie ac marchiarum ejusdem, ac deputati nostri generalis regni nostri Hibernie, ac de advisamento consilii nostri ejusdem regni nostri, modo et forma sequenti videlicet:

In consideracione et pro eo quod idem Hugo (nunc suo patre predicto defuncto) nobis humiliter supplicaverit ut pro bono et meliori regimine patrie predicte ipsum Hugonem ad capitaneatum sive gubernamen prefate patrie ac sue majestatis subditorum in eadem per nos admitti sive nominari dignaremur:

Nos de vera obedientia ejusdem Hugonis deque ejus promptitudine ad fideliter serviendum nobis adque patriam predictam decenter gubernandam et tuendam plurimum confidentes, eundem Hugonem capitaneum patrie predicte per presentes nominamus et constituimus, atque bonum gubernamen subditorum nostrorum in eadem patria degentium eidem Hugoni contulimus etiam per presentes:

Item: Conventum est per hasce indenturas quod predictus Hugo inveniet quolibet anno de anno in annum octoginta Scoticos sive galloglassos ad desserviendum nobis juxta mandatum nostrum vel heredum seu successorum nostrorum pro quatuor hebdomadis atque in qualibet
Fol. 231b. generali expedicione (vocata Anglice an hosting)[1] inveniet similiter octo equestres et viginti quatuor turbarios sumptubus suis propriis et expensis cumque victualibus promptos et paratos ad nobis ser viendum pro quadraginta diebus. Solvetque nobis heredibus et successoribus nostris annuatim ad festum Sancti Michaelis, archangeli, duodecim denarios de qualibet carucata terre infra patriam predictam ad manus subthesaurarii sive generalis receptoris nostri infra hoc regnum nostrum Hibernie vel talibus quibus ille ordinabit pro recepcione ejusdem ad usum predictum.

Item: Preterea idem Hugo obviam dabit (intimacione prius ei facta) domino deputato hujus regni pro tempore existenti sive alio gubernatori ad patriam predictam quandocunque accedenti sive itineranti cum omnibus irribus atque copiis suis cum victualibus pro eis pro tribus diebus:

Conventum est insuper quod prefatus Hugo fideliter persolvet moderno deputato nostro pro nominacione ejusdem Hugonis ad capitaneatum predictum centum bonas et pingues vaccas deliberandas ad quemcunque locum infra comitatum de Westmeth ad sive ante festum Omnium Sanctorum proxime futurum, sicut idem deputatus noster ordinabit:

Habendum, tenendum et gaudendum capitaneatum predictum eidem Hugoni quamdiu se bene gesserit veluti fidelis subditus, et accedat ad dictum deputatum nostrum seu aliquem alium gubernatorem regni nostri predicti pro tempore existentem et ad consilium regine regni predicti quandocunque habuerit in mandatis ad eos accedere. In cujus rei, etc.

Fol. 232. [CLXXXIV.]—By the lorde deputie and counsell:

Wheare we are infourmed that the villages or towneshippes of Acregar, Derikill, Kilmolgan, Bally Cowleu, Clancosney and Shanebally Moortagh, the which were lately demised to Hugh MacCallowe and his heires males, conteyning by estimacion three hundreth and twelve acres

[1] In margin: "Omaddens rysinge out in hostinge jorneis."

arrable land and pasture, are nowe remayning in her majesties handes and possession by reason the said Hugh MacCallow, uppon treason latly by him commytted, is fled, as it is alledged, owte of this realme, and for that offence against her majestie, her crowne and dignitie stondeth presently owtlawed by the due course of her majesties lawes: 1566.

It is concluded and agreed by us, the said lorde deputie, and the rest of her majesties counsell, whose names are unto this our concordatum subscribed, uppon the humble sewet to us made by Thomas Leke, gentleman, in respecte bothe of the better manurance of the said landes remayning presentlie as wast, and for other consideracions us hereunto moving, that the said Thomas Leke shall have, hold and enyoy by vertue of this our concordatum, the custody, keping, use occupacion and manurance of all and singuler the landes afore specified with the appurtenaunces whatsoever thereunto belonging during and for so long tyme as the said landes do or shall remayne in her majesties handes by occasion aforesaide the said Thomas Leke yelding and payeng for the same yearely at the receipte of her majesties exchequier in this realme to the handes of her majesties vice treasourer and treasourer at warres of this realme or other her majesties receivor generall of the same for the tyme beeng, at the feastes of Michaelmas and Ester, by even porcyons, so long as the same shall so remayne in her majesties handes suche rent or rentes, and further fynding and doeng such services to her majestie as in the demise made of the premisses to the saide Hugh MacCallowe, and bearing date the last of February in the sixte year of the queenes majesties reigne that nowe is, is expressed and reserved.

Yeven at Drogheda, the xvith of July, 1566.

[CLXXXV.]—By the lorde deputie and counsell: ol. 232b.

Wheare we are infourmed, that [the] townes and villages of Kilmagood and Clonestlyne, Bollybegge Creig, Ballacaslyn, Bollenebayne, Kiltebrennan, Clancolyna, Kylneshyan, and Kilcronan, in the Queenes county, commonly called Leix, together with the landes bothe arrable and pasture thereunto, with the appurtenances thereof, are remayning presently in her majesties handes and free disposicion: It is concluded condiscended and agreed by us, the said lorde deputie, and the rest of her majesties counsell whose names are unto this our concordatum subscribed, in consideracion of the late submission to her highnes made by Lysagh MacKeddowe Omoore and Kahier, his brother, for theire former offenses and beeng receaved into her majesties mercie and free pardon uppon theire faithfull promise to contynewe hensfourth in theire dewe obedience and loyaltie to her highness and observe dewtifully and obediently suche orders and ordenances as we, the lorde deputie, have alredy synce our arryvall sett fourth and published or shall hereafter sett fourth or publisshe in the countie or contrey aforesaid and other like places of this realme for the better good order and government of the same:

That the saide Lysagh and Kahier shall have, hold, use, occupie and enjoye in theire custody the aforenamed townes and villages together with the said landes arrable, pasture and the appurtennances thereunto belonging, for the better manurance and tillage thereof during her majesties pleasure (those landes are nowe remayning for the most parte bothe as waste and unenhabited and yeldeth no proffett to her majestie) and that during theire custody of the premisses by this our concordatum graunted the said Lysagh and Cahire ne eny or either of them shall be chardgeable or chardged by vertue of this our concordatum for eny the

1566. said landes to theire custody as aforesaide graunted, with eny maner of cesse or imposicion of the contrey but thereof to be free and dischardged for the tyme afore expressed for the consideracions and causes aforesaid :

Provided alwaies that no ydell person shall be receaved or admitted by the said Lysagh or Kahire to be planted or dwell in or uppon eny of the said landes, but that they and either of them within tene-daies after receipte or addmytting eny suche ydle person shall gyve notice thereof to the senesshall of the said countie for tyme beeng and shall be aunswerable for every such person so by either of them to be taken into inhabite on the landes aforesaid or eny parte thereof. For the which and other lyke reasonable causes condicions and covenantes the said Lysaghes pledge is alredy in hand remayning.

fol. 233.

Yeven at Drogheda, the ——[1] of ——[2] 1566.

fol. 233*b*. [CLXXXVI.]—By the lorde deputie and counsell :

Trustie and welbeloved we greet you well : And albeit the quenes majesties writtes are alredy addressed aswell into those your parties as elswheare within this her highnes realme, signifieng a generall hosting to begynne the xvth of August next, whereuppon the accustomed rising owt of that the countie of Waterforde ought dewlie to arrise owt and be aunswered to this service of this hosting :

Yett nevertheles having thought fytt and considering the harvest season and other like busy tyme nowe being at hand that it woold be no lytill hindrance to nude or barreyn that countie with horsemen or cariages or other like imposicions, whatsoever necessitie shoulde happen in the same, but that in respecte thereof the rather for your better ease and quiet ye maye and shall entend your owne defence in that countie withowt your accustomed rysing owt for the present to this hosting :

That therefore, on her majesties behaulf, theis shall be to will and commaunde you that uppon sight hereof ye faile not indifferently eqally and ratablye to cesse on that whole countie so muche money as after the rate of threepence by the daie shall sarve to and for the enterteyning and furnyture of thirtie kerne for one quarter of a yeare begynning the saide fyftene daie of August :

And that the same monney be levied and sente unto us on this side the same xvth daie without any further tracte of tyme or frustratory excuse or delaye, for the payment of the same kerne accordingly, whome we have alredy prepared for that purpose wherein we straightlie chardge you in her majesties name not to faile as ye tender the dewties of your allegiance and the furtherance of theis her majesties affaires, importing (as they do) so weightely the benefitt, wealth and good state and deffence of this realme. Yeven at Dondalke, the xxviith of July, 1566.

A lyke for Wexford, for 60 kerne.
 „ Tipperarie, for 60 kerne.
 „ Kylkenny, for 60 kerne.

fol. 234. [CLXXXVII.]—A proclamacion set forth at Drogheda by the lorde deputie and counsell, the seconde of August, 1566, against Shane Oneill and his adherentes standing with him in open hostilitie against our soveraign lady :

Albeit the actions and doynges of Shane Oneill are at this present so manyfest rebellious and traiterous agaynst the quenes most excellent

[1], [2] Blank in MS.

majestie, her estate crowne and dignitie, as eche member of this commen 1566.
wealth and kingdome, hathe seene and felt a number of argumentes of his[1] arrogant unduetifull and traiterous attemptes, yet for the more evident declaracion of her majesties clemencie, and of his unnaturall ingrate and detestable conspiracies and treason, the lorde deputie and counsell have thought meete to publishe and denounce by this present proclamacion, what hope her highness had of this[2] ductifullnes and conformytie and howe worthelie his desertes hath hepid uppon him her highnes utter indignacion and corrections and her uncurable displeasure:

And namely sence we, the lorde deputie, accepted the deputacion and governement of this kingdome, before which tyme his dissimulacion and hypocrisie was such as in humble and repentant maner he promised his loialtie and faithfull obedience with suche subjection hereafter, as he obtayned at her majesties handes, not onely peace, but pardon to his offences agaynst her highnes and her crowne, and after that exhibiting certeyne peticions in Englande by the deane of Armagh, the same deane was returned with letters from the queue to the lorde deputie, wherein the most parte of his demaundes were yelded to condiconaly that it maght appeare to the worlde, that he ment faithfully, effectualy and truly to observe and perfourme his humble and loyall promis: Which being dissimbled tyll the fyrst of Maie last, at which tyme he craved a meting and a conference in the confynes, bysydes Dundalke, the said lorde deputie and counsell, both for his benefit and the quiet estate of this countrey, repaired thether, and there contynued by the space of ten fol. 234b.
daies, where in all that space he could not be perswaded or allured by his best frendes either to repaire to the lorde deputie, according his bounden dewtie, or to meete in convenient place where by speech and conference, his loyaltie and good meaning (if there had been any) might have ben wittnessed and dissiphered by the lorde deputie and counsell, and by them for his benefitt pronounnced to her highnes:

At his returne from thence, the malice of his traiterous hart, waxing as it were to a ripenes, and not any longer able to be conteyned repressed or hidden in yt self, he hath not onely ruynyd, broken downe, and defaced the metropolitayne church of Armagh in the countie of Ulster, most unnaturaly irreligiously and contempteously, but also hath raysed dyvers holdes, fortes, houses and castells, within the same countie, detayning and imprysoning her majesties good and obedient subjectes without eny cause offered of offence. And besydes invaded the countrey of Farmanagh and from thence expellid Maguyre, her majesties loyall and faithfull subject, exempted from all rule and aucthoritie of Oneill and his auncesters, as maye appere by sufficient testimony and recorde:

And when, as after all theis tyranous, fellonyous, and traiterous attemptes, he urgid agayne a parlement and meeting the xxvth of July, professing by the humilitie of his letters as though he could have been glad of peace, forasmuche as the lorde deputie and counsell were trewlie adverticed that he repaired to the confynes and [in] warlike manner with all the force and power he was able to make, yt was thought meete that a convenient force to resyst his invacions shulde at that daie be assembled at Dondalk aforesaid:

And albeit that by the space of two daies the lorde deputie remayned in the frontiers of Ulster, redy to have herd any request that he shuld humblie have offered, yet he not onely refused to repaire unto him, or to

[1], [2] *His*], this MS.

1566. send any man instructed in his grieffes, but caused his people to begyne warre, and skyrmishe, contrary to his othe and duetie of a subjecte:

fol. 235. And after such tyme as the lorde deputie had dispersed his force for the commoditie and ease of the people, the same Oneill hath, with banners displayed, as an open enemye, traitour and rebell, entred into the Englesshe Pale, and with fier and sworde wasted parte of the countrey and slayne of her majesties subjectes:

And lastly hath besegid Dondalke, where the pryde and treason of his arrogant rebellous mynd, was justlie scorged by God and the valiant defence of the soldiers, and inhabitantes, where he lost no small number of his people, with theire capteynes, ensignes and leaders:

And for a furder declaracion of the malice of this traitour yt is evident that he hath practiced with forayne prynces to bring into this realme a power of strangers, to the disherison of her majestie and the utter ruyne and spoyle of this her highnes countrey and people:

For all which causes the said lorde deputie and counsell doth pronounce him a rebell, and a most unnaturall, vile and corupte traitour to the queene, her crowne and dignitie, to be prosequuted as the lothsomnes of his treason and rebellyons deserveth at her majesties handes:

And further that all suche, as ayde, assist, helpe, and maynteyne him be accounted traitors and rebelles to her majestie, unles it be such as before the xxiith of this moneth shall personally come before the lorde deputie and receave pardon, with such condicions as the said lorde

fol. 235b. deputie and counsell shall thingke good to offer for the assurance of theire fidelitie hereafter:

And further the said lorde deputie and counsell promyseth by theire woord and honor, and thereunto fyrmly bynd themselfes by this present testymonye, that what person soever shall bring unto the said lorde deputie the body of the same rebell and traitor, Oneill, alyve, shall receave for his rewarde one thowsande poundes and free pardon of his goodes, landes and lyfe, if he have been an ayder, helper, assister, mayneteyner, follower, or abetter of the said traitor and rebell:

And whosoever of what nacion, contrey, estate, degre whatsoever shall bring unto the said lorde deputie the dead body, or the head of the same Oneill shall have for his rewarde, one thousande markes, and free pardon of his goodes, landes and lyf in maner and fourme aforesaid:

And whosoever shall by meanes directe or indirecte slaye [or] kill the saide traitour, though he neither bring the head nor the body, yet beeng justly proved, shall receave the somme of fyve hundred poundes, fourthwith uppon the proofe so made:

And therefore the said lorde deputie and counsell wissheth and perswadeth that every true, loyall and naturall subject, shall endevor himself to slay, cut off and utterly extirpe this unnaturall traitour and corupt member of the body of this comenwealth, whereby they shall no doubt deserve well of God, the queene and this countrey, and procure to them selfes wealth, fame and estimacion.

God save the queene. Amen.

fol. 236. [CLXXXVIII.]—A proclamacion set fourth at Drogheda by the lorde deputie and counsell, the seconde of August, 1566, prohibiting powder, shott, or other munycion, or eny other relief of victuelles to be solde, sent, or conveyed to Shane Oneill, or eny his adherentes standing with him in open hostilitie agaynst our soveraigne lady the queenes majestie:

Wheare of late Shane Oneill, careles chiefly of his dewtie to Godward and of his allegiance and obedience to her majestie, hath manifested him self in open hostilitie and rebellion against her highnes imperiall crowne and dignitie, to the subversion of the good estate of this realme and of her majesties good subjectes of the same: And that moreover it is geven the said lorde deputie and counsell to understande, that nevertheles dailye the same Oneille, and his saide adherentes, have been ayded, mayneteyned and succored with victuelles, powder, shott, and other kyndes of munycion, and other succours and relief, which have been solde, conveied, and brought unto them from owt this her majesties Englisshe Pale, whereby the rather they have endured and persevered in theire rebellious attemptes of late commytted: 1566.

Therfore the said lorde deputie and counsell have thought fitt, in her majesties name, to publishe and denownce by this present proclamacion, that all and every suche person or persons, of what estate degre or condicion soever he or they be of, as after this proclamacion shall be founde or knowen either by sale as aforesaid or otherwise directly or indirectly to be ayding, helping, comeforting, or relyving the forsaid Oneill, or eny his rebellyous adherence with eny kynd of victells either of meate or dringke, powder, shott, or eny other whatsoever kynd of munycion or armour, or by eny meanes or waies shall otherwise succour fol. 236b. or relief the said Oneill or eny his aforesaide adherentes, to be taken, accepted and reputed as open and manyfest rebells and traitours, to her majestie, her crowne and dignitie, and to be exequuted or hanged for commytting that offence, as in cases of rebellyon hath been accustomed.

God save the queene.

[CLXXXIX.]—Per dominum deputatum: fol. 237.

Quandoquidem curavimus Johannem Oneill, ex demeritis malefactorum suorum id poscentibus, juste proclamari et proscribi traditatorem ac rebellem odiosum contra reginam, majestatem, statumque universum hujus sue majestatis regni, supponimusque te inter alios eidem Oneill in hujuscemodi suo rebellione secum violencia atque metu ductum astrictum esse:

Atque item eandem rem in animo habentes, curavimus insuper in proclamacione predicta ut quivis sic astrictus et cupide volens suam veram obedientiam majestati sue agnoscere, nec volet ulterius eidem Oneill adherere valeat et possit infra quindecim dies proclamacionem predictam hodie publice proclamatam sequentes ad nos aggredere libere et quiete colloquii gratia sive fedus subjeccionis sue majestati subeundi, veluti nos, dominus deputatus, superinde consideraverimus ordinare alioquin ad consuetos lares pacifice revertere absque impedimento sive nocumento alicujus:

Nos, respectu quod majestatis subditus reputaris, subtusque tutelam suam solummodo dependere decorum sit et non subtus alium quemcunque hoc in regno sue majestati inferiorem, te de hiis premonisse duximus, ea autem intencione ut temet in tempore opportuno revoces caveasque eidem traditori Oneill ulterius adherere, submissione autem tua nobis oblata de sistendo ordinacioni nostro evitabis temet rebellem versus celsitudinem reginam reputari, atque famam bonam et firmam pacem sue majestatis demerere. Data ex Drogheda, tercio Augusti, 1566.

Dilecto nobis MacMahon, sue nationis principali.

A like to McGynnysse.

" " to Ohanlan.

" " to Collo MacBren, capten of Ferne.[1]

[1] Farney, Co. Monaghan.

1566. fol. 238.

[CXC.]—By the lorde depatie and counsell:

It is concluded and agreed that for the better and reddy victelling for xxii daies of her majesties army appoyncted to proced to the late proclaymed hosting, and remayning on the borders here, a hundreth fyftie fower beeffes at the rate of xiis., Yrisshe, the pece, shall be taken upp to her majesties use and levied by waie of cesse, in manner following:

Upon the countie of Dublin 30 beffes:
Uppon the countie of Methe 60:
Uppon the countie of Kildare 30:
And uppon the countie of Westmethe 33:

For the proporcion of the nomber of horsemen and fotemen as ensueth, that is:

Summe of beeffes—154, to be delivered at Melyfont to Mr. Edward More by the fyrst of September next commyng, and the overplus that is for every beef ——[1] above the rate aforesaide to be eqally contributed, borne and levied uppon the said severall counties on the plowlandes there not beeing free or wast.

Yeven at Drogheda, the seconde of August, 1566.

Mr. Marshall - - - - -	c horsemen.
Capten Agard - - - - - -	c ,,
Master of the ordynaunce - - -	xxx ,,
The Treasourer - - - - - -	xx ,,
	Summa ccl.

At two beefes the daye for every hundreth for and from the 29th of July, 1566, unto and for the 20th of August, amounting to 22 daies: In beffes, cx.

Capten Fludde: fotemen, c.
,, Horsey: fotemen, l.
,, Bryan Fitzwilliams: l.—Summa cc.

At two befes a daie for the [w]hole nomber for 22 daies, begynnyng and ending ut supra, in beffes xliiii. Summe of beefes—cliiii.

fol. 238b.

[CXCI.]—At Drogheda, the second of August, 1566:[2]

It is agreed and concluded, in consideracion of the more safetie of the corne of that countie of Lowth, alredy howsed, and the better deffending of the same from eny the spoiles or attemptes of Oneill, that the corne or grayne of the contrey there shall be stapled, placed and remayne in the places or townes undermencioned, beeng thought most fyttest for that deffence, that is to saye:

The barony of Dundalke:

The parisshe of Machorconell: to Castelltowne and the Roche.
The Haggard and Dunbenne: to Dundalk.
The parishe of Heinestowne: to Dunmowghan.
The parisshe of Rosmaha Stevenson: to Allarstone.
Ratheddy, Rathwill: to Allarstone.

The barony of Louthe:

The parisshe of Louth, Killencoule, Darver, and Talestowin: to Killencoule or Taliston.

---

[1] Blank in MS.
[2] In margin: "Orders for the safe keping of the corne of the county of Lowth."

The parisshe of Mounfelston and Clonkyffan : to Ballibragan. 1566.
The parisshe of Dromiskin : to Drumiskyn.

The barony of Ardee :

The parisshes of Killemoge, Smerymor, Shenles, Stackellen, Mapelston : to Ardee.

Richardstowne : to Richardstowne itself. fol. 239.

Sherleston and Clonkyen : to Tallinston and Cookestowne.

Ardee :

The parisshe of Phillistowne . . Ineselerafe. Cremarten : to Ballihowe.

The parisshes of Dromcarre, Salthous, Dunhany, Clonmore : to Warenstown.

The parishe of Kylsarran : to Kyllsarran.

The parisshes of Drumyn and Dunlier : to Rathehesker.

The parisshe of Stabanam : to Rowthiston.

Ferrarde :

The lordshipp of Mellefant within the countie of Louthe : at the sherifes discretion, in one place.

The parisshe of Dunleir : to Rehaskath.

The rest, at the discretion of the commissioners, to Drogheda, Lyskyn, Glaspestell and Barremeth.

A commission also to be directed to the persons folowing for stapleng the said corne of the said countye in manner aforesaid : fol. 239b.

To the lorde of Louth,
The sheriff of Uryell,
Sir John Bedlowe, and to
Robert Taft,
Thomas Plunkett,
Nichollas Dromgold and
John Fey.

[CXCII.]—Articles of agreement betwene the lorde deputie and the captaynes of the galloglas for the service of the queenes majestie when they shall be callyd :[1] fol. 240.

[1.] Fyrst : The saide galloglas to bring to the hill of Tarragh the 15th of August next three hundreth armyd men furnished for six weekes.

[2.] Item : That if the daie be deferred then to be in rediness to come to the same place uppon ten daies warning.

[3.] Item : Every septe of them to receive inprest of the queenes majestie, to be defalked upon theire bonnaght, three hundreth markes, currant money of Ireland.

[4.] Item : Every septe shall have inprest to be repaied uppon theire bonnaught forty markes of this money for the hiering of fortie garrans, the money to be devided to such captaynes as goe in the journey from every sept.

---

[1] In margin : "Concerning the captens of galloglas, what nombre of men they shold bring to serve and what ympreſt they should have."

1566.
fol. 240*b*.

[CXCIII.]—At Drogheda, the second of August, 1566:

A note of the bonaghtes graunted to the galloglas for three hundreth armyd men to be brought to the filde, which maketh with their allowaunce eighteen score and fifteen sparres for one [w]hole quarter of a yeare to be cessed and levied, half in victells and the other half in money uppon such landes as are not wast, uppon the Irishe lordes and theire contres, as followith with the assentes of the said galloglasses:

Item: Uppon Occarroll	xl sparres.[1]
„ The Annaly	cx „
„ Omadden	xl „[2]
„ Macoughlan	xx „[3]
„ The baron of Upperosserie	lxxx „
Uppon the Morowes	xl „
Edmond Duff MacDavy More McVadacke The four septes of the Cavenaghes	xxxv „[4]

And yt shall be at the choyses of the contreys severally to pay the above specified bonnaght, haulf in victels and haulf in mony, according the accustomed maner, or else tenne markes in mony only for every sparr of the said eighteen score and fifteen sparres for this one quarter graunted with the assent above mencioned.

fol. 241.

[CXCIV.1.].—By the lorde deputie and counsell:

Trustie and welbeloved we greet you well. Where for the better deffence of the northern borders against eny the attemptes of Oneill or his adherentes and for the supplie of suche as by our order do presently garde the same borders, we have ordred that fower hondreth hable men bowemen, billmen and gonners shall be presently chosen owt of that the countie of Dublyn, whereof one hondreth and tenne men to be chosen out of the barony of Balrothery, Crosse and countie to be assembled togethers yn warlike redynes and to make theire repaire to the towne of Kelles by the xviith of this present mouneth of August, and there to be remayning during tenne daies.

We, having especiall trust of your trustynes, diligences and circumspection in this behalf, have apoyncted and aucthorised yowe by tenor hereof to electe and make choyse of those one hundreth and tenne men within the barony before mencioned, the which we have commytted to the leading of John Howth, gentleman:

Requiring yowe ernestly, as ye tender the advancement of her majesties service in this behaulf, that furthwith meting togethers for the purpose aforesaid ye employe hereyn your spedy trayvell and diligence and without faileing to advertise us spedely of your whole doeing herein:

Willing also and commaunding by tenor hereof the sherif and suche other her majesties officers of the said countie, to whome it may apperteyne, to be unto you it the executing of this our aucthorisment, ayding, helping, obedient and assisting as you shall requier them.

Yeven at Dublin, the xith of August, 1566.

[1] In margin: "Of cld, 120."
[2] In margin: "Of old, it is more."
[3] In margin: "Of old, forty."
[4] In margin: "Of old, nine score."

[CXCIV. 2.]—By the lorde deputie and counsell : 1566.

Trustie and welbeloved we greet you well: Where for the better defence of the northern borders against eny the attemptes of Oneill or his adherentes and for the supplie of suche as by our order do presently garde those borders, we have appointed one hundreth and ten men, parcell of four hundreth men out of the countie of Dublin, to be chosen out of the barony of Balrothery, Crosse and countie, and to make theire repaire under the leading of John Howth, gentleman, to the towne of Kelles, by the xvith of this present monneth of August, there to be remayninge during tenne daies, and eche of those one hundreth and ten men to have twelve pence by the daie for meate, drincke and wages, to be aunswered out of the said baronye, Crosse and countie, and to be levied uppon the freholders not chardged to journies and uppon the farmers, cottiers, and houshold servauntes, receiving wages. And that the said capten shall likewise have two shillinges by the daie, to be levied as aforesaid : fol. 241b.

We having good confidence of your uprightnes and indifferencies have apointed and aucthorised you by tenor hereof to cesse and devide on the said barony, Crosse and countie the aforesaid wages for the said one hundreth and ten men and theire said capten and to cause the same furthwith to be levied and aunswered, as is fytt for the better and redy furnishing and victeling of them for the better and redy furnishing and victeling of them for the said tenne daies.

Requiring you therein to employe your spedy trayvell and diligence as ye tender the specyall advauncement of this her majesties service and with aunswer for the contrary.

Yeven at Dublin, the xith of August, 1566.

[CXCV.]—By the lorde deputie and counseil : fol. 242.

Trustie and welbeloved we greet you well: Wherefor the better deffence of the northern borders against eny the attemptes of Oneill or his adherentes and the good supplie of suche as by our order do presently gard those borders, we have appoyncted the nomber of one hundreth and tenne men to be chosen by ——[1] Fynglas and James Barnewell, esquiers, owt of that the barony of Balrothery, and to repaire in redynes with tenne daies victells to the towne of Kelles by the xviith of this present August :

We, having good trust of your skill, activenesse and pollicye, have appoincted, like as by tenor hereof, we do apoincte you capten and leader of the said hundreth and tenne men with the allowance and wages for yourself of two shillinges by the day, and for every other of the saide hundreth and tenne men twelve pence by the daie for theire meate, drinke and wages for every of those tenne daies, to be cessed devided and levied on that barony in suche maner and fourme as therein we have prescribed order and geven warrant to our loving freendes ——[2] Fynglas, James Barnewell, Christofer Barnewell, esquiers, and the cessors of the barony of Balrotherye, Crosse and countie aforesaid :

Requiring you ernestlie, on her majesties behaulf, therefore to put yourself in full redynes to intend this chardge by us commytted to your trust without failing to be with your said company at Kelles on the day aforesaid for cause of her majesties service as afore rehersed.

Yeven at Dublin, the xith of August, 1566.

---

[1], [2] Blank in MS.

1566. [CXCVI.]—Ordinaciones capte apud civitatem Dublinensem,
fol. 242b. decimo tercio die Augusti anno Domini millesimo quingentesimo sexagesimo sexto [1566] per dominum deputatum et consilium inter prenobileum virum, comitem de Clanricard, et MacWillelmum Ewghter ac inter eundem comitem ac Donagh Reaghe Okelly, Walterum FitzJohn Burgk, dominum Brimidgham de Anrye,[1] atque dictos Walterum et Jacobum Brimidgham de septu sive natione Thome Brimidgham :

[1.] Item : Idem MacWillelmus Ewghter, personaliter, dictis die et anno coram nobis constitus et comparens humiliter sese submisit sue excellentisine regie majestati, agnoscens suam celsitudinem super illum dominam suam supremam et super regnantem reginam cui solummodo-fatetur et agnoscit servitium suum atque debitum alligeancie sue exhibere omnesque alii prenominati partes litigantes sive inter se discrepantes coram nobis, domino deputato et consilio, similiter personaliter comparentes, atque auditis hincinde per nos eorum objectionibus et responsionibus submiserunt etiam semetipsos de sistendo arbitrio ordinacioni et determinacioni nostris super eorum controversius quam ordinacoem sive decretum nostrum quoad easdem controversias modo sequenti ferimus et promulgamus :

[2.] Item : Ordinamus per presentes quod quilibet partium prenominatorum sue majestatis pacem colcat versus alterutrum ac omnes alios sue majestatis subditos tam infra separales eorum diciones sive gubernamina quam etiam versus Morghue Toow Offlartye, Occonor Rowe, MacCostillo, MacShurtan et Okelly et reliquos generosos patrie de Imanny[2] omnesque alios capitaneos infra provinciam de Connaght constitutos, qui de presenti sue majestati pacem colent colereve debent aliqualiter :

fol. 243. [3.] Item : Quandoquidem predictus MacWillelmus instanter petierit quendam Occonnor Rowe per Occonnor Dunne, sue nationis principalem, nuperrime, ut asseritur, captum ac subtus ejus custodiam in prisona detentum elargari, quemque etiam allegavit captum fore tempore pacis concluse inter prefatum comitem de Clanricard et predictum Mac
fol. 243a. Willelum in Ballyloughreaghe, coram Willelmo Tirrell, uno nunciorum predicti nostri domini deputati, quodque itidem idem Occonnor Dunne subtus pacem dicti comitis ad tunc temporis existens predictusque Occonnor Rowe subtus pacem dicti MacWillelmi idem Occonnor Rowe, ut prefertur, captus fuerat, quod quidem per dictum comitem expresse denegatur :

Ordinatur per nos igitur, de et cum consensu partium predictarum, quod si per eundem nuncium fuerit affirmatum pacem eandem sic conclusam fuisse, quod tunc ipsemet comes totis viribus quoad posse suum (semota simulacione uliqua) prefatum Occonnor Donne pro elargatione predicti Occonnor Rowe prosequetur. Et si fortassis idem nuncius quendam Willelmum Petit, generosum, etiam presentem tempore pacis predicte concluse affirmaverit sive attestatus sit, assentimus eundem Willelmum Petit superinde examinandum fore ut ejusdem rei veritas melius erui poterit et inquiri :

[4.] Item : Ordinatum est insuper quod predictus comes de Clanricard ac predictus MacWillelmus, atque relique prenominate persone amanter et unanimiter sese conjungant ad fideliter serviendum sue majestati, sicuti nos, dictus dominus deputatus vel aliquis alius hujus

[1] Athenry. [2] Ui Maine, Hy Many.

regni gubernator pro tempore existens, de tempore in tempus assigna- 1566.
verimus in quibuscunque locis tam inter seperales gubernaciones suas quam extra cum talibus suis viribus atque copiis, victualibusque talique tempore, prout predicto nostro domino deputato vel gubernatori hujus fol. 243b.
regni cuicunque pro tempore existenti rationabiliter visum fuerit.

[5.] Item: Ordinamus preterea quod si deinceps contingat aliquem eorundem prenominatorum partium incursiones aliquas seu predas versus alterutrum attemptare vel aliquas injurias seu molestias hincinde inferre, quod ille sive illi versus quos hujuscemodi incursiones vel prede seu alique alie injurie sic attemptantur nullam nichilominus superinde vindictam propriis copiis seu captant pro reformacione injuriarum illarum; sed prius nos, dictum dominum deputatum seu aliquem alium hujus regni gubernatorem pro tempore existentem, certificare per querelam suam non omittant, quo facto, et nullo habito super eandem remedio, archiepiscopoque Tuamensi pro tempore existenti per litteras gubernatoris in hac parte ei mittendas certiore existente de responso dicti gubernatoris, evocatoque coram eodem archiepiscopo parte rea sive querelata et in obstinacia sua perseverante, quod tunc pars gravata in casu hujusmodi omnibus melioribus quo poterit viis et modis remedium suum versus partem ream sive querelatam libere prosequi valeat.

[6.] Item: Quandoquidem Donogh Reaghe Okelly conqueritur coram nobis quod predictus comes de Clanricard vi ipsum a possessione castri de Garvally, in patria de Imanny, expulerit, eoque facto per dictum comitem negato, diceenteque se nihil interesse in castro predicto habere etc., aliter quam quod quidam Thadeus OKelly castri predicti verus fol. 244.
possessor pro certis injuriis, predis, latrociniis, murdris et furtis versus eundem comitem et suos perpetralis possessionem castri predicti liberavit eidem comiti in pignus usque dum idem comes plenarie satisfactus esset de dampnis predictis, ad que idem Donoghe dixit quod diu ante impignoracionem castri predicti prefato comiti per antedictum Thadeum, expulsus ab eodem idem Thadeus Molaghlin et Connor patres sui, de eodem castro rite seisiti existentes, totum jus, titulum et interesse sua in eodem eidem Donogh Okelly vendiderunt, pretextu cujus possessionem ejusdem aliquod tempus occupavit absque impeticione vel interruptione alicujus usque dum per eundem Thadeum expulsus ab eodem, atque castrum illud sic vi adipiscens impignoravit illud prefato comiti modo et forma prerecitatis.

Unde, ex assensu partium predictarum, ordinatum existit quod reverendissimus in Christo pater, Tuamensis archiepiscopus, reverendus pater, episcopus Clonfortensis, maior sue majestatis oppidi de Galway nunc existens atque Omanning,[1] sue nationis principalis, seu aliqui tres vel duo eorundem, quorum predictum episcopum Clonfortensem ac dictum Omanning semper duos esse volumus, commissarii nostri existant ad audiendum, recipiendum et examinandum testes quoscunque hincinde coram eis producendos pro probatione et meliori sive certa noticia contentorum in hoc articulo, et depositiones easdem sic captas sub eorum manibus et sigillis inclusis et sigillatis in festo Sancti Andree, Apostoli proxime futuro post datum presentium, nobis transmittere, unacum opinionibus suis quid de sufficienciis testium hinc inde coram illis producendorum et examin- fol. 244b.
andorum senticrint ex quo nos, prefatus dominus deputatus, ordinem superinde sumere secundum justiciam et equitatem valeamus.

[7.] Item: Cumque preterea prememoratus MacWillelmus coram nobis conquestus sit quod antefatus comes possessionem castri de Moyne

[1] O'Mainnin, chief of a cantred in the district of Hy Many.

1566. quod idem Willelmus jure hereditario sibi devoluto intraque limites patrie sue scituatum clamat sibi attinere, atque illud per nos restitui petierit: ad quod comes predictus respondendo dixerit quod pater suus Ullickus Burgk de castro predicto seisitus existens inde seisitus obiit et sic eidem comiti descendebat ut vero heredi predicti sui patris vultque ea verificare quandocunque per nos, dominum deputatum et consilium ante dictum requisitus erit, ac medio tempore pro meliori promovendo sue majestatis servitio atque ad illud animandum prefatum MacWillelum utque satius intelligat ut nihil aliud de eo sentierimus quin justitiam et equitatem ei tribuere, ordinamus ex assensu predicti comitis quod castrum illud de Moyne liberetur intra quindecem dies proxime sequentes datum predictum in possessionem nostri dicti domini deputati, quo pretextu castrum predictum idem dominus deputatus liberare possit ad manus cujuscunque talis persone sive talium personarum sicut nostro domino deputato visum fuerit ad illud indifferenter et salvo custodiendum atque redeliberari secundum equitatem.

[8.] Item: Quoniam Thomas Burgk, filius predicti Mac Willelmi, Thomas MacRichard Boye MacJohannis, Meilor Mac Richard Mac Johannis,
fol. 245. et Richardus Mac Edmond Boye Mac Johannis per dictum comitem detinentur pro certis denariorum summis eidem comiti, ut asserit, debitis super propriam composicionem earundem partium, ordinatur nichilominus per nos dominum deputatum et consilium antedictum, ex diversis bonis causis et consideracionibus nos ad id moventibus, quod comes predictus omnes dictas personnas in hoc articulo prenominatas ante primum diem Septembris proxime futurum liberabit in manus nostras ut liberentur salvo custodie constabularii de Athlone ac redeliberari per ordinacionem nostram.

Et cum quidam Cahir Mac Donyll Mac Conyll captus in fuga per Edmundum, fratrem dicti comitis, atque ad largum existens super fideiussoribus pro fine sive redempcione sua obnixis, Johannesque Mac Richard Mac Meilor extra prisonam evaserit ut idem comes allegat, ordinamus finem illum sive redemptionem illam ad usum dicti comitis solvendam esse si per nos vel tales commissionarios quos nos ad id considerandum assignaverimus sic fuerit visum personamque illam qui sic evaserit (si enim constaverit ipsum intra potestatem gubernaminis dicti mac Willelmi devenisse) per eundem mac Willelmum deliberari ad manus prefati constabularii ibidem salvo custodiri, ut de aliis prescribitur, alioquin quod prelibatus comes personam illam sic evadentem producere ordinamus et ipsum predicto constabulario liberare in forma predicta.

[9.] Item: Quoniam dominus Brymigham de Anrye, simili modo est coram nobis querelatus quod predictus Walterus FitzJohn Burgk vi castrum de Dunmore in Conacia ad predictum dominum Brymudgham, ut asserit, altinens detinuerit, quod enim dictus Walterus haud fatetur sed dixerit quod Jacobus Brymughan, filius Edmundi Brimugham, Thomas ac Meilor filii Richardi Brimigham, veri heredes castri predicti existunt, ipseque Walterus nil clamei in eodem habuerit, ordinatur ut evocentur partes illi coram nobis per litteras nostras eis dirigendas ad interesse sive titulum suum in eodem proponendum ac interea temporis ut castrum illud sub sequestro nostro custodietur, delibereturque salvo custodie talis persone sive talium personarum quam sive quas ad id nos custodiendum assignaverimus, et illis nunc inde possessoribus hoc refutantibus quod tunc predictus mac Willelmus atque item dominus Walterus necnon itidem comes antedictus constanter promittunt omnibus viis et mediis pro toto posse suo quibus poterint eos ad id faciendum constringere.

[10.] Item: Quod cotenciones indecisas pendentes inter predictum comitem et dictum mac Willelmum omnesque alios ex utraque parte servientes suos sequaces vel generosos sub alterius eorum gubernamine degentes, pro aliquibus predis, furtis, occisionibus et aliis magnis offensis atque enormitatibus ex utraque parte commissis. Quandoquidem nos, dominus deputatus atque ceteri sue majestatis consiliarii ex diversis causis urgentibus bonamque hujus regni utilitatem sueque majestatis speciale servitium tangentibus, ad illas contenciones decidendas opportunum tempus de presenti minime nobis inservierit; statuimus nihilominus ut, opportuno inserviente tempore, quod speramus breviter futurum partes illas coram nobis comparere ac finem debitum in contenciomibus illis imponere sicuti equitas et justicia persuadebunt. 1566. fol. 245*b*.

[11.] Finaliter, pro meliori observacione et performacione omnium et singulorum contentorum in articulis predictis tam ex parte dicti comitis et Mac Willelmi dictique Walteri Burgk quam ex parte reliquarum predictarum partium litigantium respective perimplendorum dicti comes ac Mac Willelmus dictusque Walterus Burgk et reliqui partes predicti, ultra duas mille libras quas eorum quilibet recognovit se debere domine regine, per recognicionem in cancellaria de recordo remanentem, si defecerit eorum aliquis in premissis sacramentum prestiterunt corporale ad sancta Dei evangelia jurati, conceduntque per presentes omnia sua bona et cattella terras et tenementa ubilibet infra hoc regnum inventa seu invenienda forisfacta esse et ad usum sue majestatis heredum et successorum suorum levanda si contenta aliqua in precedentibus articulis specificata et que respective per eorum quemlibet sunt perimplenda adimplere defecerint.

In cujus rei testimonium, tam nos dominus deputatus atque reliqui de consilio predicto quam dicti comes, Mac Willelmus et ceteri partes litigantes hoc scriptum manibus suis signaverunt, die, anno et loco superius specificatis.

[CXCVII.]—At Drogheda, the viii[th] daye of September, 1566: fol. 246.

It ys agreed by the lorde deputye, the earle of Desmounde, and the rest of the queenes majesties pryvye counsell there assembled: that the saide erle of Desmounde and the baron of Donboyne, the baron of Coraghmore, sir Warham Sentleger, capten Herón and others to attende on the said erle shall repayre from hence. And the said erle, with those and such other as he shall bring with him owt of his countrey of his forces to be at Trym, in the countye of Med, the xxiiith daie of this Septembre, with the nombre of one hundreth furnished horsemen, at the lest, there to mete with suche of her majesties pryvye counsill and of the forces of the Englishe Pale as the lorde deputy, entring into Ulster shall leve behynde to joyngne with him, and he with them for the deffence and saulfgarde of the Englishe Pale and borders agaynste Oneill and his adherentes, and he with those said forces and companye or more comyng with him to serve her majestie to have victuelles and horsemete during their commyng, abode and retorne.[1]

[CXCVIII.]—Articles of submission offred by Coll MacBryan, captayne of Ferney, and taken by the lorde deputy in the campe at Raskeath, the xxth of September, 1566: fol. 249.

[1.] Fyrst: The said Coll submytteth himself as symple and obedyent subject to the queenes majestie without being servant or follower to eny

[1] Ff. 246*b* to 248*b*, inclusive, are blank.

1566. other, and to hold his rule and capteynry with all his landes and goodes under her highnes and her majesties protection.

[2.] Item: He submytteth himself to stande to the arbytrement and order of indifferent persons, agreed upon betwene the Englyshe Pale and them of Ferney, for all such gryfes as shall be objected by ether of the same countreys.

[3.] Item: He shall delyver in the names to the lorde deputy of all such persons as he will undertake for at or before the xxvi[th] of this month. And all suche as he will not undertake for, he shall doe his uttermost to bring in and not to suffer to take eny meate or dryncke in his countrey but if yt maye be proved that they take anye meate or dryncke that then he shall be answerable for all hurtes done by them.

[4.] Item: He shall before the xxvith daie of this month gyve in the bodies of Bryan MacCollo, sonne to the saide capten, and Patricke Mac Mahound, sonne to Hughe MacCarte, and one of the sonnes of Remonde MacRorye to the lorde deputye, to remayne as pledges for the observacion of theis articles.

[5.] Item: That if the said Collo or Hugh MacCart, or eny of them that he shall aunswer for, shallhere after declyne from theire obedyence and yoyne with the rebell Shane Oneill, or eny other traytor, then the pledge before named to be hanged ymediatlye.

[6.] Item: Yt ys agreed that no griffes shall be demaunded of ether parte being done above four yeres past.

[7.] Item: Yt is agreed that after the saide capten shall have delyvered all suche damage as shall by the arbytrators be adwarded, the damage which shall by the same commissioners be also awarded to them for Ferney shall be payed for the Englishe Pale by the handes of the lorde Lowthe and the sheryff of the countie.

fol. 249*b*. [8.] Item: The same Coll ys contented to paie and contribute to the queenes majestie and her successors all such rysinges out of horsemen and footmen and bonnaght for galloglasse in as ample maner as Patrick McRowrye or eny other capten of Ferney hath yelded in tymes past.

[9.] Item: That the said pledges be delyvered to Robert Tate of Cookestowne and Nicholas Tate of Ballybragan, to be salfely kepte during the pleasure of the lorde deputye, and to gyve a bill to the lorde of Lowth touching the receipte of the same.

[9.] Item: He shall delyver to my lorde of Lowth the xxvith of this monneth to the use of the lorde deputye twentie fatte beefes.

[10.] Item: That the saide Coll shall not after the said xxvith daie of this month foster and kepe eny catell or creates of Shane Oneile or eny other rebelles. And if the same be founde and approved then the pledge to be hanged and the same Coll to lose the benefitt of her majesties protection.

[11.] Item: Yt is agreed that the commissioners for the Englishe Pale shall be the lorde of Lowth and Mr. justice Dudall, and for them of Ferney Hugh MacCarte and Phelym MacCrayen; and thes causes to be determyned by them at or before the xvth of November next.

Pilip MacChraige.

Signed in the presentes of us: Lowth:—by me, Thomas Flemyng.

[CXCIX.]—Hec indentura, facta, vicessimo die mensis Octobris, anno regni serenissime et invictissime principis Elizabeth, Dei gracia Anglie, Frauncie et Hibernie regine fidei defensoris, etc octavo [1566] inter honorabilem vinum dominum, Henricum Sydney, ordinis garterii militem, presidentem consilii Wallie et marchiarum earundem, deputatum suum in Hibernia generalem, ceterosque de consilio in eodem regno quorum nomina subscribuntur, ex una parte, et dominum Calvatum[1] Odonell, ex altera parte testatur quod predictus, dominus Odonell concessit, promisit et per presentes se obligavit firmiter teneri et perimplere dicte domine regine et successoribus suis tenorem et formam articularum subsequmtum : 1566. fol. 250.

[1.] Primum : Confitetur se magnopere devinctum esse Deo Optimo, Maximo et serenissime regine, cujus justicia et misericordia post tantam miseriam, et exilium, restauravit eum omnibus suis hereditamentis, castellis, honoribus et regiminibus nec parcit immensis sumptibus nec laboribus sue majestatis deputati nec non exercitus istius regni :

Euaquidem racione novit quid sit tam juste ei excellenti principi adherere et appellare et igitur cum omni graciarum actione promittit pro se et omnibus aliis suis successoribus, dominis Odonellis, favores hos remunerare suorum serviciis sicut fidelium subditorum est et semper obedientes erunt sue majestati et sue majestatis deputato et omnibus aliis locum predictum tenentibus in hoc regno Hibernie.

[2.] Item : Confitetur reginam serenissimam suam solam et naturalem dominam supremam et quod in omnibus causis tam spiritualibus[2] quam temporalibus sua majestas est et esse debet sola et suprema gubernatrix in hoc regno, et quod ad posse suum adjuvabit et supportabit auctoritatem predictam et expellabit et eradicabit omnes hos qui in Connalia[3] contradictores erunt :

Et ulterius dictus dominus Odonell pro se et successoribus suis dat et sursum reddit in manus serenissime regine omnia servitia et jura regalia in Connalia appertinentia corone hujus regni imperiali.

[3.] Item : Dictus dominus Odonell promittit pro se et omnibus aliis fol. 250b
dominis Connalie quod nunquam confederabunt cum aliquibus inimicis vel rebellibus sue majestatis, vel suorum successorum, nec in amicitiam vel servitium suum accipiant aliquos Scotos vel ullos alios alienos sine licentia sue majestatis vel successorum suorum vel eorum deputati et consilii in hoc regno, et ulterius ad posse suum obediens erit ad mandatum deputati et consilii et prosequetur pro virili rebellem, Johannem Oneill, et omnes sibi adherentes.

[4.] Item : Dictus dominus Odonell consentit quod quoties ipse Odonell vel successores sui rogati vel mandati erunt per litteras domini deputati vel sue majestatis locumtenentis in hoc regno veniet in propria persona (si modo validus fuerit) ad omne magnum et generale viagium in hoc regno et secum adducat sexaginta equites et centum viginti turbarios et tercentum Scoticos[4] vel (si non validus erit) mittet saltem principalem generosum de Connalia, ad electionem domini deputati cum totidem equitibus, turbariis et Scoticis, cum victualibus pro quadraginta diebus.

[5.] Item : Dictus dominus Odonell consentit quod quoties dominus deputatus hujus regni et ejusdem regni consiliarii mittent

---

[1] Calbhach.

[2] In margin : "Supremacie."

[3] Tirconnell, now Donegal.

[4] In margin : "Risinge out of Odonell, 60 horsemen, 120 galloglas and 300 Scotts."

1566. litteras suas pro dicto domino Odonaill veniet tociens ad omnes locos et parlementa in illis litteris specificata et nominata.

[6.] Item: Consentit dictus dominus Odonell perimplere omnia decreta publicata vel publicanda per dictum dominum deputatum et consilium inter predictum dominum Odonell et patrem suum, Hugonem MacManus Odonell, vel avunculum suum, Hugonem Duff Odonell, tam pro divisione hereditamentorum quam pro aliqua alia causa vel materia.

[7.] Item: Dictus Odonell, pro se et omnibus aliis dominis de Connalia in futuro, confitetur se tenere patrias, terras et tenementa de majestate serenissime regine solum. Et si imposterum suo majestati
fol. 251. placuerit, usus et ritus hujus patrie commutare et eam reducere ad ordinem civilem et gubernandam per leges suas sicut in Anglicanis partibus hujus regni, vel si sua majestas honorabit titulo aliquo honoris predictum dominum Odonell vel aliquos generosorum de Connalia, predictus dominus Odonell ad posse suum adjuvabit et suppetias sue majestati dabit.

[8.] Item Predictus dominus Odonell consentit, pro se et omnibus aliis dominis de Connalia, quod quando et quotiescunque visum est sue majestati castra aliqua erigere et componere, vel exercitus in Connaliam mittere pro defensione suorum subditorum, sicut jam agitur, predictus dominus Odonell et successores obedientes et morigeri erunt ad perimplendum pro virili mandata et voluntatem regine.

[9.] Item: Consentit et affirmat quod majestas sua habebit donacionem omnium episcopatuum et nominacionem omnium episcoporum Connalie, sicut in ceteris partibus hujus regni, ac presentacionem omnibus beneficiis ecclesiasticis quibus majestas sua titulum habet aut imposterum habere poterit, ac etiam liberam dispositionem omnium terrarum quibus majestas sua investiri poterit.

[10.] Item: Quoad potest supportabit omnes tenentes regine infra dominaciones suas existentes, et eos, terras suas et tenementa ac commoditates eorum tenere ac possidere quietos patietur, nec predictos depredabit nec ab hiis accipiet coyne et livery, vel aliquos alios usus, impositiones aut exactiones quascunque per ipsum aut predecessores suos usitatas, in contrarium non obstante aliquo usu.

[11.] Item: Bene supportabit et supportari faciet quoad potest exercitum tam equitum quam peditum nunc relictum apud Derry,[1] sub conductione Edwardi Randall, armigeri, ——[2] peditum in Hibernia existentium ac etiam dabit aut dare faciet eidem coronello quamdiu in Connalia manebunt aut prope eum numerum quadraginta martarum singulis septimanis, prima autem solucio incipiet primo die Decembris,
fol. 251b. quo tempore etiam predictus Odonell dabit vel dari faciet pro tribus mensibus, videlicet, quatuor centum et octoginta martarum precii sex solidorum et octo denariorum sterlingorum, pro unaquaque marta, et pro defectu ——[3] marte dabit aut dari faciet sex oves aut quatuor porcos unius anni etatis et ultra.

[12.] Item: Dabit aut dari faciet eidem coronello avenas in stramine sufficientes ad victum centum equorum, videlicet, unoquoque equo quatuor onera pro die, et in singulis oneribus viginti quatuor manipulos aut in loco ejusdem duas mensuras avenarum, nuncupatum a mether.[4]

---

[1] Colonel Edward Randolfe. In margin: "Force at the Derry with corronell Randall."

[2], [3] Blank in MS.

[4] *A mether*] or mether, MS. In Irish, *meadar*, a pail or drinking vessel.

[13.] Item: In consideracione gratuitatis et benevolentie sue majestatis et ob magnos favores ac copiosa beneficia per protectionem ac magnam clementiam majestatis sue accepta, contentus est et concedit dare et solvere in scaccarium majestatis sue Hibernie pro se et heredibus vel successoribus suis, dominis Odonellis, in perpetuum ducentas marcas sterlingorum solvendas annuatim[1] ad festum Sancti Michaelis archangeli et Phillipi et Jacobi, Apostolorum, per equales porciones, aut in loco ejusdem, ad electionem suam ipsius Odonell, tres centas martas quas dabit aut dari faciet ad festa predicta in villa de Kellis in comitatu Midie. 1566.

In cujus rei testimonium, predictus dominus Odonell has indenturas manu sua propria subscripsit et sigillum suum posuit, in presentiis Hugonis MacManus Odonell, fratris sui, Hugonis Duff Odonell, avunculi sui, Donallei Magonii,[2] episcopi Rapotensis, Odohorti, cognominis sui principalis, MacSwine Fannade, sui cognominis principalis, MacSwine Banaugh, MacSwine Duine[3] et ceterorum generosorum Connalii, quiquidem his predictis consensias suas dederunt et affermaverunt apud Ballcshein,[4] die et anno predictis. Adfuerunt quoque fol. 252.
Johannes Oghalloher, capitaneus de Bondroies,[5] et Hugo Odonell, officialis Rapotensis.

[CC.]—Hec indentura, facta vicesimo quarto die Octobris, anno fol. 252b.
serenissime principis Elizabeth, Dei gracia, Anglie, Frauncie et Hibernie regine, fidei defensoris, etc. octavo [1566], inter honorabilem virum, dominum Henricum Sydney, ordinis garterii militem, presidentem concilii marchiarum Wallie, deputatum suum generalem in Hibernia unacum concilio ejusdem regni quorum nomina subscribuntur, parte ex una, et Donaldum Oconnor, ———[6] nuncupatum Oconnor Sligo, ex altera parte, testatur quod predictus Oconnor concessit et promisit et per presentes se obligavit tenere et firmiter perimplere dicte domine regine et successoribus suis tenorem et formam articulorum subsequentium:

[1.] In primis: Recognoscit et acceptat predictam dominam reginam in suam solam naturalem et legitimam dominam et reginam, illique et successoribus suis adherebit sicut fidelis subditus et sicut ceteri hujus regni subditi soliti sunt obedire et servire.

[2.] Item: Recognoscit predictam dominam reginam solam et supremam tam in causis ecclesiaticis quam temporalibus, et quod nullus princeps alienus habet vel habere deberet ullam potestatem vel auctoritatem in hoc regno, et hanc suam auctoritatem regalem defendebit et manutenebit ad posse suum durante vita sua.

[3.] Item: Promittit nec confederare nec adherere aliquo rebelli vel inimico domine regine sed eos pro virili prosequetur et presertim Johannem Oneill. Et obediens erit de tempore in tempus sue majestati et sue majestatis deputato, et omnibus mandatis et letteris suis sicut bono subdito decet:

Et ulterius cum predictus dominus deputatus, ex parte domino regine, intravit in castellum de Sligo et petiit quendam annualem redditum

---

[1] In margin: "A rent of 200 markes per annum reserved out of Odonells countrey."

[2] Donald Magongail or MacCongail, bishop of Raphoe. He was present at the council of Trent in 1563.

[3] In Irish—Na-dtuath.

[4] Ballyshannon, co. Donegal.

[5] Bundrowes, near Ballyshannon.

[6] Blank in MS.

1566. de predicto Oconnor, et prenobilis vir, comes Kildarie, posuit clameum et demandum suum pro castello et redditu predicto, allegitque jure hereditario redditus et castellum predictum possidere debet, et quandoquidem etiam dominus Calvatius Odonell, capitaneus et principalis de Tireconell, petiit quoque redditum predictum, dicens se in hoc pacifice investiri per prescriptionem temporis longe preteriti, et hoc annuatim recepisse de tempore in tempus usque ad purificacionem Beate Marie Virginis ultimo preteriti: Concordatum est igitur quod quia nullus antehac petiit redditus et servitia predicta ad usum serenissime regine
fol. 253. vel ad usum comitis Kildarie, quod predictus dominus Odonell habebit dimidium unius anni redditus de predicto Ochonnor:

Et in consideracione belli et defencionis sue patrie (jam restitute) ab invasionibus rebellis Johannis Oneill predictus dominus deputatus et consilium in nomine regine majestatis ut de celsitudinis sue mero motu et dono concesserunt domino Odonell pro suo majori auxilio alteram partem sive dimidium unius anni redditus solvendi in festo Purificacionis Beate Marie proxime sequenti per ipsum Ochonnor:

Proviso semper quod salva sint omnia demannda et jura tam serenissime principis quam predicti comitis post diem et festum jam nuperrime nominatum.

Et ultra, dictus dominus deputatus promittit ante primum diem Maii proximum sequentem jus et titulos tam invictissime regine quam comitis et domini Odonell discutere et adjudicare:

Et predictus comes et Odonell promiserunt scripta et evidencias suas ante predictum primum diem domino deputato ostendere:

Et predictus Ochonnor contentus est stare ordinacioni et judicio domini deputati pro omnibus hiis adjudicandis:

Ordinaverunt quoque dictus dominus deputatus et consilium quod predictus Ochonnor pro hac hieme et vere appropinquante tantum suppetias dabit predicto domino Odonell contra rebellem Johannem Oneill, cum equitibus et turbariis, et hoc non jure aliquo (donec, ut predicitur, judicaverit dominus deputatus de lite et titulis) sed virtute autoritatis et mandati domini deputati pro servitio regine et bono statu reipublice factum.

In cujus rei testimonium partes supradicti hiis indenturis alternatim subscripserunt, apud monasterium de Aboile,[1] die et anno predictis.

fol. 253*b*. [CCI.]—Here followyth the thoroughfare townes agreed by the lorde deputie and counsell to be dischardged of all horses to contynue there to sojorne, in consyderacion that they must receave all men and horses to theire ——[2] that shall passe thorough the same when passengers shall lodge there:[3]

Countie of Dublin:

The Newcastell,—Rathcowill,—Balrothery,—Ballymore.

Meeth:

Trym, Athboy,—Novan,—Kelles,—Slane, Rathtouth, Grenock,—Donboyne.

Kyldare:

The Naas,—Kildare,—Rathmoore,—Castledermot.

---

[1] Boyle, co. Roscommon. [2] Blank in MS.

[3] Transcript of undated order, made apparently during government of sir Anthony St Leger, 1553–4.

Countie of Lowth :—Arde,—Dondalke.

Anthony Sentleger.—George Dublyn.—Edward Midensis.—Gerald Aylmer, justice.—Thomas Luttrell, justice.—James Bath, baron.—Thomas Cusack, magister rotulorum.—Thomas Howeth, justice.—Edward Basnet, deane.[1]—John Travers.—Osborne Echingham.[2]

[CCII. 1.]—After our right hertie comendacions: We have receved your letterres of the 26th of May fourth of June, touching two severall suetes made unto you there by Water Hope of Dublyn, the one for the obtayning of a pencion graunted unto him of late years by Oswald Massingberde, late pryor of Kylmayneham, for service by him done unto the said pryor and howse, as he alleageth; and the other concerning the fee farme of the late dissolved monastery or howse of fryers in Mollingar in the countie of Westmeth, heretofore graunted by the queenes majestie unto one Robert Gory, together with the parsonage of Westyna and Churchtowne, in the said countie, with condicion that he should erecte a gaole in Mollingar, aforesayde, the interest and right of whiche graunt the saide Gory hath passed and conveyed over unto the said Walter Hope: 1566. fol. 254.

For aunswer unto bothe which sutes you shall understande that like as in the fyrst we thinke yt veary resonable yf in the acte of parlyament made for the uniting of the landes and possessions of the said howse of Kylmayneham [to] the crowne there be any suche clause or provision, as he alleageth, for the allowing of all those grauntes that passed bona fide from the said pryor before the dyssolucion of the said howse, and that it shall also appere unto you that the graunt passed unto him for his said pencion ys of that nature, and made bona fide, without fraude or covyn; and farther, that the landes graunted unto him in Connaght by a concordatum of our very good lorde the earle of Sussex, and the counsell then beeng, were not allotted unto him in recompence of his said pencion, but for other respectes and consyderacions that then he be allowed his said pencion according to equitie and justice, together with the arrerages due unto him uppon the same:

So for his other sute, consydering that the havinge of a gaole at Mollingar is of suche importance and necessitie for the good estate and quietnes of the countrey as ys reported by your letteres and that he shall be at greate chardges with the buylding of the same, we thinke convenyent he have in respecte thereof the benefite of the said graunte and doo enjoye the feefarme of the aforesaide dissolved howse of fryeers in fol. 254b. Mollingar, together with the parsonage of Westyna and Churchtowne, and the constableship of the said gaole; yelding and payeng unto her majestie for the same the yerely rent of tenne poundes, Iryshe, in the whole, that ys to saie, for the saide parsonage eight pounde, as yt hath been heretofore surveyed, and for the said fryerhowse fortie shillinges, yn consyderacion as well of his chardges of buylding the saide gaole as for that you write that the saide frierhowse, although yt were surveyed at fower pounde, Irishe, by the yere, hath nevertheles yeldyd nothing unto the queenes majestie synce the dissolucion of the same; for your better direction wherein we have byn meanes unto her highnes to addresse unto you her majesties letteres and warraunt for that purpose, as by the same which you shall receve herewith you maye at better length, perceve, according whereunto you maie procede with the sayde Hope in such sorte as by her majesties said letteres ys prescribed unto you.

---

[1] Of St. Patrick's cathedral, Dublin.

[2] *See* "Chartularies of St. Mary's Abbey, Dublin," Rolls series, 1884.

1566. And so we byd you right hertely well to fare. From St. James, the seconde of July, 1566. Your loving freendes:

N. Bacon, c.—E. Clynton.—W. Howard.—Ed. Rogers.—Fraunċis Knolles.—W. Cecill.—Amb. Cave.

The direction: To our assured loving freendes: Sir Henry Sydney, knight of the order of the garter and deputie of the queenes majesties realme of Ierlande, and to the rest of her highnes counsell there.

[CCII. 2.]—By the queene;

Elizabeth.

fol. 255. Right trustie and welbeloved we greet you well: We perceve by your letteres of the iiiith of the last mounethe, addressed unto our pryvie counsell, the sute that hath been moved of late unto you there by Walter Hope, one of our subjectes of that our realme of Ierlande, touching a graunte heretofore passed from us unto one Robert Gory, for the feefarme of the late dissolved monastery or fryerhowse in Mollingar in our countye of Westmethe, with the parsonage of Westyna, and Churchtowne in the said countie, the said frierhowse having been heretofore surveyed at fower poundes, Irishe, by yere, and the said parsonage at eight poundes, Irishe, as appeareth by your said letteres, which graunt being nowe conveyed over by Gory unto the said Hope, he desyreth maye be passed unto him by your letteres patentes in due forme, according to the effecte and meaninge of our saide former graunt:

And because we perceyve by your said letteres that the havinge of a gaole at Mollingar, aforesayde, which, by the condicions of our said graunte, Gory was bounde to buylde, and Hope will take uppon him nowe to performe, ys very necessarie for the suerte and quiet estate of our country and subjectes thereaboutes, we are well pleasyd that the saide Hope shall have in feefarme to him, his heyres and assignes, the saide frierhowse in Mollingar, with the parsonage of Westyna and Churchtowne aforesayde, and the conestableshipp of the sayd gaole, yelding and payeng unto us, our heyres, and successors for the same, the yerely rent of tenne poundes, Irishe, that ys to saye for the sayd parsonage eight poundes, as yt hath byn heretofore surveyed, and for the saide late monasterie or fryerhowse fortie shillinges, Irishe, in consyderacion as well of the chardges he shall be at in buylding of the said gaole there, as for that also yt appereth by your letteres that allthough the saide fryerhowse were heretofore surveyed at fower poundes Irishe by the yere, yet hath yt not hitherto, by reason of the contynuall wast thereof, yelded any thing unto us, synce the dissolucion of the same:

fol. 255*b*. We therefore will and requier you to cause our letteres patentes, under our greate seale of that our realme, to be in due forme made unto the saide Walter Hope for the premisses, in forme aforesaide, taking sufficient bandes of him, not onely that he shall buylde and perfourme the saide gaole within such reasonable tyme as you shall thinke convenient to appoint, but also that he and his heires shall, from tyme to tyme, keepe and maintayne the said gaole in good and sufficient reparacion and strenght. And theis our letteres shall be your sufficient warrant for the same.

Yeven under our signet, at our manor of St. James, the thirde daye of July the eighth yere of our reigne, 1566.

The direction:—To our right trustie and welbeloved Sir Henry Sydney, knight of our order, and deputie of Ierlande.

[CCIII. 1.]—Depositions of wittnesses taken at the Naas before John Sutton, John Wedgewoode, and Readmonde Oge, esquiers, by vertue of commission to them directed from the right honorable the lorde deputie and counsaill, the iiiith of October anno regni reginæ Elizabeth, etc., octavo [1566]: 1566. fol. 256.

[1.]—Patrick White, clerke, vicur of the Naas, of the age of lxii yeares or thereaboutes, sworne and examyned, deposeth and saieth: That he knewe sir Morrice Eustace, knight, and Christofer Eustace, his sonne and heire, by the space of theis fiftie yeres last past, and that they by all the saide space were lawfully seised of Cottlanston,[1] with all and singuler the landes thereunto belonging, and that they dyd oftentymes resorte to his mothers howse, then dwelling in the Naas and tenaunt to the said sir Morrice and his said sonne after him, at which tyme he harde the saide sir Morrice often tymes saie that Cottlanston with all the landes thereunto belonging was free from all imposicions and cesses:

And furder being examyned whether Fyaston be a parcell belonging to Cottlanston or not, saieth that he is therein ignorant, and saieth that he never harde of any imposicions or cesses taxed uppon Cottlanston untill the same came to the princes handes; and further cannot depose.

[2.]—William Odyvie of the Naas, aforesaide, in the countie of Kyldare, of the adge of lxx yeres or thereaboutes, sworne and examyned: Deposeth and saieth that he was a howseholder dwelling in Bayly Moore by the space of xlviii yeres, by all which space he saieth that Cottlanston with the landes thereunto belonging was free and cleere from all imposicions and cesses:

And further saieth, uppon his oothe that he dothe very well knowe that Fyaston ys and tyme out of mynde have byn parcell of Cottlanston. And furder cannot depose, saving that he saieth as well Fyaston as Cottlanston hath byn allwaies free from all imposycions and cesses, as one thing.

[3.]—Patricke Edwarde, of Bellarture, of the age of lx yeres or thereaboutes, sworne and examyned, deposethe and saieth that he was borne and brede in Cottlanston, and that he hath knowen the same eversythens he hath any remembrance. And that the same, during his remembrance, hath alwaies byn free from all imposicions and cesses, and saieth that he never hard any questyon to the contrarye: fol. 256b.

And furder saieth that the lande of Fyastone, the lands of Grage, and the lande of the Hookes, and the lande of the Rayne ys parcell of Cotlanstone, and that the same hath allwaies been free from all imposycions and cesses as Cotlanstone, untill the same came to the princes hand and possession. And furder cannot depose.

[4.]—Thomas Ewstace, of Ballymoore, gentilman, of the age of lii yeres or thereaboutes, beeng sonne to sir Morryce Ewstace, knight, who was lorde of Cotlanston aforesaide, deposyth and saieth in every poynte and article as Patricke Edward, the former deponent, hath saide. And also saieth that Johnson and Cowlocke, with the other parcelles aforenamed, are parcelles of Cotlanstone, and also have byn free from all imposicions as Cotlanstone. And furder cannot depose.

[5.]—James Dowding, of Ballymoore, of the age of lx yeres or thereaboutes, being a freholder, of Bayllymoore, aforesaide, and sworne and examyned, deposeth and saieth in every point and article as Thomas Ewstace, the former deponent, hathe said: And furder saieth that he

[1] Cotlandstown, co. Kildare.

1566. knoweth that the said lande of Cotlanstone hath ben free from all imposycions and cesses during all the tyme of sir Morrice Eustace and Christofer, lordes of the same, and one Christofer Ewstace, fermor thereof, and also saieth that the same hath also byn free as well from all subsydies as imposicions and cesses during the space aforesaid; and furder cannot depose.

fol. 257. [6.] Davy Donell of Ballymoore of the age of xlii yeres or there aboutes, being sworne and examyned in every pointe deposeth and saieth as Thomas Ewstace, the former deponent, hath saide; and furder cannot depose.

[7.] Patrick Denys, of Baillymoore, of the age of fyftie yeres or there aboutes, deposeth and saieth as Thomas Ewstace the former deponent hath saide; and furder canot depose.

[8.] Edmound Arthure, of Ballymoore, of the age of lx. yeres or thereaboutes, deposeth and saieth in everye pointe and article as Thomas Ewstace, the former deponent, hath saide. And furder saieth that after the said land of Cotlanstone came to the princes handes, one Robert Husseye being fermor thereof suffred certen cesses to be taken out of the land of Cotlanstone as he thinketh to ease certen other land that he had of his owne within the same baronye, and also sayeth that all the people of the countrey dyd make exclamacion uppon him for suffering the same to be theus taken; and furder cannot depose.

[9.] Shane MacThomas of Ballymoore, of the age of lx. yeares or thereaboutes, deposeth and saieth yn everye point and article as Thomas Ewstace, the former deponent, hath said; and furder cannot depose.

[10.] Teige Arthure of the age of fyftie yeres or thereaboutes, John MacPhellym, freholder, of the age of fyftie yeres or thereaboutes, Teig Offollowe, of the age of lx. yeres or thereaboutes, Nichollas Cosgrave of the age of lxx. yeres or thereaboutes, Patrick MacKellyn of the age of xl. yeres or thereaboutes, and Jennet ne Morrice, being all six of
fol. 257*b*. Ballymoore, and Teig MacDavy of Ballyflemyng, being sworne and examyned, depose and sayeth in every point and article as Edmounde Artyre, the former deponent, hath sayd and furder cannot depose.
John Sutton.—Redmound Oge.—John Wedgwoode.

[CCIII. 2].—By the lorde deputie and counsell:

We greet you well: Requiring and commaunding you and everie of you, in her majesties behaulf, all excuses set apart, that you make your personall appearaunce before John Sutton of Tipper, esquier, justice of peace, John Wedgwoode, esquier, controller to us, the lorde deputie of Ireland, and Readmound Ooge of Cloinblock, esquier, or eny two of them, whereof John Wedgwoode to be one, at such daie and place as you and every of you shall be appointed by them betweene this and the fyrst daie of the next terme, there to declare before them, by vertue of your booke othes, severally deposed, unto them what knowledge you and every of you have of the usuall contynuance of the antique fredome of the demeanes of the lande belonging to the howse of Cotlanston, and whether any parte of the land of Cotlanston or Fyanstone was chardged with cesse in sir Morrice Ewstace tyme and in the tyme of Christopher Ewstace, his sonne and heyre after him, sometyme lordes of that howse of Cotlanstone; and by whome thos landes were fyrst suffred to be ymposed and chardged with cesse after they came to the princes handes, and by whose meanes. Hereof you maie not faile at your perilles.

Yeven at Kylmayneham, the xxvii[th] of June, 1566. 1566.

The direction : To our loving freendes, Nicholas Ewstace, of Yagogston, gentleman, sir Patrick White, vicar of the Naas, William Mac Davy, and Owene Conwaye of the same, Patrick Edwarde of Bellyarture, Thomas Ewstace of Bellymoore, James Dowding, John Ewstace Fitz Edmounde, of the same, Davy Donell, Patrick Dempse, Edmound Ohartyerne, Teige Ohartyerne, John MacPhillipp, Teige MacDavy, Teige Ofole, Morrowgh OConwaye, Richard Mac a Clere, Nicholas Cosgrave, Patrick MacCollyn, Shane MacThomas, Jenet ne Morrishe, John Gomast of Ballymoore, Morryarte MacThomas, nyne Thomas of Cotlanston, Richard MacCormock, and Thomas Bane of Surdwalstone, and to every of them geve theise. fol. 258.

[CCIII. 3].—By the lorde deputie and counsell :

Welbeloved we greet you well : Wheare Nicholas Harbart, esquier, hath alleadged before us how that usually in tymes past, whereof the mynde of man doth not remember, the howse of Cotlaustone and all the demeanes to the same belonging, sometymes being in the handes and possession as well of sir Morrice Eustace, knight, then lord thereof, as also of Christofer Ewstace, gentleman, his sonne and heire, deceased, have remayned free from all ymposicions of the countrey and yet nevertheles, as the saide Nicholas hath alledged, part thereof lately, through the default and exaction of the cessor of that baronye, hath been ymposed, which cesse and that latly sir Fraunces Harbart, knight, deceased, father to the saide Nicholas, was also distrayned for the aunswering of that cesse; whereuppon the said Nicholas hath prayed remedy and redresse at our handes :

We, mynding therefore to be trulye assarteyned of the antiquetie and contynuance of the said freedome, and having good confydence of your uprightnes and indiffencye in that behalf have by tenor hereof appointed and authorysed you three joyntly or eny two of you, whereof John Wedgwood to be one, by all such wayes and meanes as shall seme fyttest to your good discretions, diligentlie and trewly to inquier of the certeyne truth of and in the premisses and what ye shall knowe or
fynde or try owt uppon that your inquirye in the behalf aforesaide to fol. 258b.
certifie us on the fyrst daie of the next terme under your handes and seales, close sealed with theis our letteres, to the end that uppon your certificat theirein such further order may be taken in the matter aforesaide as with right and iustice ys apperteyning.

Yeven at Dublyn, the xxvi[th] day of August, 1566.

[CCIV.]—Hec indentura facta inter honorabilem virum, dominum Henricum Sydney, ordinis garterii militem, presidentem consilii Wallie, et deputatum in Hibernia generalem, unacum concilio, quorum nomina subscribuntur, ex una parte, et Hugonem Oreigly, sue nationis capitaneum, et Edmundum, fratrem suum, tanistam[1] patrie de Brenny,[2] ex altera parte, testatur quod predictus Oreigly obligat se tenere et perimplere tenorem et formam articulorum subsequentium : fol. 259.

[1.] Primum : Promittitur quod ad posse suum prosequetur fratres suos, Caier Oreigly, Owinum Oreigley et Johannem Oreigly, nunc

[1] Tanist, successor under Irish law.

[2] Breifne O'Raighilligh, now county of Cavan.

1566. rebelles serenissime regie majestati, et eos et sequutores eorum ferro et flamma puniet, nec patietur eos terras et tenementa sua possidere tenere vel arare et colere sed eos omnes ut inimicos suos castigabit, cum fuerint per predictum dominum deputatum adjudicati rebelles et inobedientes subditi.

[2.] Item: Promittitur quod quicquid commissarii dicti domini deputati, nominati vel nominandi per ipsum dominum deputatum, adjudicaverint pro injuriis finendis et bonis restituendis inter Anglicanas partes, et habitantes in Le Brenny quod ipse Oreighly articulos et judicia eorum perimplebit et observabit.

[3.] Item: Promittitur quod ubi lis est inter honorabilem virum, baronem de Delvin[1] et predictum Oreiglie pro titulis et demaundis inter ipsos et patrias suas, quod ipse Oreigly observabit omnia decreta et judicia que in futurum adjudicabuntur per commissarios domini deputati secundum morem et observaciones patriarum suarum per prescripsionem temporis preteriti.

[4.] Item: Similiter observabit et perimplebit omnia judicia et decreta que in futurum comissarii predicti domini deputati decreverint inter habitantes patrie de Annaly[2] et patria de Brenny, pro injuriis tam futuris quam preteritis.

[5.] Item: Ubi predictus Oreigly obligatus est solvere honorabili viro, comiti Sussexie, mille et centum martas, quorum magna pars non
fol. 259b. est hactenus data, ad usum predicti comitis, predictus Oreighly dabit et deliberabit numerum predictum vel reliquum, sive martas non adhuc solutas, ante festum Sancti Johannis Baptiste proximum futurum ad manus dicti domini deputati.

[6.] Item: Ubi filius dicti Oreighly, videlicet, Johannes, accepit predam rebelliam usque ad numerum trecentarum vaccarum, predictus Oreighly promittetur quod infra quindecim dies jam proxime futuros dabit dicto domino deputato predictas tricentum martas, vel suo certo atturnato, in villa de Kellis in comitatu Midie, vel predictum filium suum, Johannem, mittet domino deputato custodiendum donec de martis predictis solucionem fecerit.

[7.] Item: Ubi dominus deputatus in manus suas ad usum regie majestatis accepit castrum de Tulleyvin nuper in possessione Owini Oreigly, et jam comisit hoc castrum Edmundo Oreigly, ad usum regine, predictus Oreighly observabit et curabit quod predictus Edmundus non nutriet vel sustinebit predictum Owinum vel aliquem alium rebellem sive bona eorum in castro predicto vel alibi. Et ulterius (hac lege) ——[3] Edmundum in possessione castri predicti.

[8.] Item: Dictus Oreigly promittitur habitare in confinibus patrie sue et Anglicanarum partium ad placitum domini deputati durante bello et rebellione fratrum suorum et Johannis Oneill, ut inde eveniet securitas bonorum Anglicanarum partium per protectionem suam contra rebelles predictos.

Et pro hiis omnibus articulis observandis predictus Oreighly dabit in manus predicti domini deputati intra quindecim dies proxime sequentes eum obsidem quem secreto inter ipsos concordatum est dari et deliberari, et interim obsides jam in custodia Patricii Cusack, armigeri, remanebunt tam pro hiis quam omnibus aliis articulis finiendis et perimplendis.

---

[1] *See* pp. 142, 167.
[2] Anghaile, Annaly, co. Longford.
[3] Blank in MS.

In cujus rei testimonium, tam predictus dominus deputatus et consilium quam predictus Oreigly alternatim hiis indenturis subscripserunt. 1566.

Data in campo apud Loghfillen, xxviii° Novembris, anno nono [1566] Elizabeth.

X., the signe manuell of Oreigly.

X., Edmund Oreighly, sygne manuell.

[CCV.]—Invictissimo nostre regine meritissimo in Hibernia deputato, Henrico Sydney, obedientia perpetua, fidelis atque indubitata: fol. 260.

Non possumus non meminisse tuam erga nos benevolentiam cui condignam recompensationem non posse nos exhibere fatemur, verumtamen id palam protestamur quod nosmetipsos nostra maneria et castra, terras insuper universas et singulas nostre ditioni subjectas serenissime nostre regine tibique suo nomine voluntarie ac libenter immediate submissimus, prout per presentes libentius submittimus atque quecunque in campo tuo de Belinathafada tue reverendissime dominationi polliciti sumus ex hiis, duce Deo Optimo Maximo, nec unum iota preteribit quin omnia adimpleta fuerint; majorem quidem et firmiorem fidem in nostro (ut reor) Israell non reperies, et si quos Zoilos aut emulos, qui michi male volunt, aliud tibi persuaderent id ex fomite invidie processisse non dubitabis.

Quod ad marthas quas tue dominationi promisimus attinet, domino comiti de Clanricard ut jussisti si lubet indilate persolvemus et mandatum tuum hic introclusum transmittimus ut scire possimus an comiti predicto predictas marthas persolvere debemus an non. Porro dominus Odonnayll, qui jam decessit, cujus totum dominium seu territorium ad indescriptibilem paupertatem deductum est cum vivebat, omnia sibi necessaria ex me et ex meis (per fas, nefas) habere volebat, subsidium vero hominum quod contra rebellem illum ac regialis majestatis hostem, Johannem Oneill, promissimus id non habere potius quam habere desiderabat ut sibi aut coram vobis querele ansa seu occasio aperta esset aut nos nostrosque homines expoliandi seu depredandi :

Et scire digneris quod subsidium hominum quod sibi pollicitus eram paratum omnino habebam antequam ipse Johannis Oneill, proditoris, patriam seu porciunculam terre adibat, verum quum ipse prius accessit meos ob itineris discrimen accedere nullo pacto valuerunt, ipsius defuncti domini Odomnaill, subdito attestante Henrico Odueayn, videlicet.

Insuper iste Hugo, qui nunc regnat, magis dominari desiderat et plures exactiones exigit quam aliter. Tuam colendam tremendamque dominationem vehementer efflagito ut unum e duobus facies aut me per tuum mandatum omnino liberum ab illis exactionibus facies donec tuam adibere presentiam aut me hic ab emulis et inimicis defendes. Nam si me vel meos absentarem, nunc dominus MacWilliam Burk, nunc Bernardus Orwerke meam devastarent seu destruerent patriam.

Dictum dominum Odonnaill personaliter adire nequaquam audeo. fol. 260b.
Verumtamen hiis omnibus nequaquam obstantibus pro serenissime regine nostre majestatis nomine vivere et mori cupio, et quidquid horum suo nomine velis me facere cum vestro nuncio seu latore ad me scribere non pigriteris et id pro posse libenter agam.

Vale ex nostro manerio ——[1] vero Decembris vicesimo secundo, 1566.

---

[1] Blank in MS.

1566. Salutat vos in Domino et intimius quo valeas germanus meus, Eugenius Ororcus, et multum optat vestram prosperam et bonam fortunam.

Vale, illustrissime Domine, in Eo qui recte volentibus defuit nunquam—
Oconnor Sligo.

Henrico Sydney, nostre invictissime regine meritissimo in Hibernia deputato, cum reverencia et obedientia, tradatur in Dublin vel alibi.

fol. 261. [CCVI.] After our verie hartie commendacions to your good lordeshippes: We have receaved your letteres of the xxiith of the last monneth, whearby you recommend unto us the case of this poore man, the bearer hereof, and certeyne other mayned soldiors, who having of late for theire impotencie and disabilitie to serve ben cassed and lost theire intertaynement, and nowe lefte without any meanes to maynetayne themselfes withall:

And albeit we woold be verie gladd to further this bearer and the rest with any convenient meanes that might be devised here for theire relieffe and sustentacion, yett consydering that the same cannot well be doon without some extraordinary chardges to the quenes majestie, no beadmens roomes being presently voyde to be bestowed uppon them, we have thought fitt, seing this man hath the use of his lefte arme, and can as he affyrmeth, weld the same as well as he was woont to doo his right arme, whereby he maie be able to make sume shewe and do some service, though not in suche degree as yf he hadd the use of his whole lymes, to pray your lordeshippe to cause him to be placed in the roome of sume porter, warder, or other like officer within sume of her majesties holdes or castles there that stand farthest from danger, and be of least importance, wheare he maye have sume reasonable interteynment and be also hable at a brunt to doo summe service yf need be.

The like order we think good your lordeshippe doo cause also to be taken with the rest of his company, for better were yt, in our opinions, seing none other meanes can presently be founde for theire relief, that her majestie shoold be at sume extraordynary charge with the intertaynement of these men there where they have heretofore served, then to be burdened with provydinge for them here, which cannot, we suppose. be so well nor so conveniently doon as yt maye be there, and therefore we comett the ordring thereof unto yoor owne wisdome and consideracion to be used either in the sorte before remembred, or in such other, yf you knowe eny, as may best serve to relieve the poore men and be lest burdenous to her majestie.

And so we byd your lordeshippes right hertely well to fare.

From Kymbolton castell, the xxith of July, 1566.

Your lordeshippes assured loving frendes, E. Clynton.—E. Rogers.—W. Cecill.—W. Howard.—F. Knowelles.

1566–7. [CCVII.]—By the lorde deputie and counsell:

fol. 261*b*. Wheare uppon the letteres addressed by us, the lorde deputie to her majesties right honorable pryvie counsell in Englande, bearing date the xxiith of June last past, and sent thither by us by Walter Pott, a maymed soldior, late serving her majestie in this realme, declaring thereby the indigent and poore estate as well of the same Walter Pott as also of sondry others bothe aged and maymed soldiars, which have ben here cassed and lost theire intertaynement through theire impotencie and dishabilitie to serve, to the ende some consyderacion and order by her maje-tie or their lordeshippes might have been there taken for the better relief and staie of lyving.

In which behalf we, the lorde deputie, receiving resolucion from theire lordeshippes by their letteres of the xxith of July last and redd at this bourde, yt ys hither signified theire pleasures that the same Walter Pott and the rest shold be placed severally in the romes of sume porter, warder, or other like officer within such of her majesties holdes or castelles here that stand furthest from dauger and be of lest importance and there to have some reasonable interteynement: 1566–7.

And seeing none other meanes coold presently be founde by the said lordes to relieve the saide poore men but that her majestie shoold be at sume extraordynarie charge with the interteynement of those men here, where heretofore they have served then to be burdened with the providing for them there, have thought by those theire letteres commytted the ordering thereof to the consyderacion of us, the lorde deputie, to be used either in the sorte before remembred or in such other as maie best serve to the relief of the poore men and be lest burdenous to her majestie. And consydering that in this tyme of the present warres here yt were not fitt to disfurnishe eny of her majesties said holdes or castells with placing therein such dishable and maymed men but rather the same to be replenished for the better and urgent deffence thereof with men of hable service:

It ys therefore by us ordered that as well the said Walter Pott, as also Thomas Barrett, William Bowtcher, William Vicarman, William Dixson, Edmond Penanga, William Bell, Thomas Alee, Mathewe Bell, John Alee of Ballyna, William Hickye, Randall Blackburne and William Wolverston, every of them from the fyrst daie of January last past shall have her majesties wages and enterteynement in the consyderacion afore rehersed of syxe pence by the daie, current money of this realme, during every and either of theire lyves, to be had and receyved without check or eny service, doing for the same, at the handes of her majesties vicetreasourer or treasower at warres or other receivor generall, for tyme being in this realme.

Willing and commaunding as well you the said treasourer, vice-treasourer or other receivor generall for the tyme being by warrant hereof or uppon the enrolement of theis our letteres to make due payement from tyme to tyme to the severall persons above-named of theire sayd severall wages. As also you, the barons, audytor, and others her majesties officers and mynisters of her saide courte of exchequyer to geve thereof due allowance from tyme to tyme to the said treasourer or receyvor generall, for tyme being, as apperteyneth to either of your offices in this behaulf. fol. 262.

Yeven at Dublyn, the xx[th] of January 1566[–7].

[CCIX.] The humble submission of Tirlaghe Oneile alias Tirloghe Lenaghe, made unto the right honorable sir Henry Sidney, knight of the most noble order, lorde president of the counsell and marches of Wales, and lorde deputie generall of this her graces realme of Irelande, in his camp at Castell Corkra in Tirone, xviii[th] day of June, 1567: 1567. fol. 262b.

First: The said Tirlaghe Oneil, alias Tirlaghe Lenaghe, confesseth himself to have offended the queenes most excellent majestie in that he hathe adhered abetted and served the late archerebell, and most notorious traitor, Shane Oneill, in his most cruell and shamefull rebellion against her most excellent highnes, for the which as he is most hartelie sorie, so doithe he most humble submitt himself, his life landes and goodes to her highnes grace and mercie, and in like maner cravethe her gracious pardon for the same:

1567. 2. Item: Whereas after the deathe of the foresaide rebell certein of the countrie of Tiron, accordinge to the auncient custome of the same, elected and nominated the said Tirlaghe Oneill, alias Tirlaughe Lenaughe to the name and jurisdiction of Oneill: the which he rather ignorantlie than arrogantlie took upon him:

The said Tirlauge doithe now utterlie refuce the said name, and all auethoritie that may by the same growe unto him, protestinge that he will never take upon him either that name or any auethoritie or dignitie but suche as shall please her most excellent majestie to bestowe upon him, at suche time as it shall seme best to her gracious pleasure and grave wisdome:

3. Item: He covenantethe duringe his lief to be a trewe subject to her most excellent majestie and to the crowne imperiall of Englande and Irelande, and that he will never assist any forren ennemy or proclaimed rebell against the same:

4. Item: That he will to his power defende the holy churche, the ministers landes and jurisdictions of the same, and shall not encroche
fol. 263. nor exacte any thinge or parte thereof, nor suffer any under him to doe.

5. Item: He covenantethe that he will never enterteigne any Scottes or Scottisheman, beinge a man of warre, without speciall licence graunted unto him of the governor for the tyme beinge:

6. He covenantethe to make dew restitucion and amendes to any the good subjectes of the Englishe Pale for any hurtes done unto them by him or any of his, or other by his procurement, not beinge done in the tyme of the actuall rebellion of the aforenamed traitor and rebell, Shane Oneill, accordinge to the arbitrement and sainge of indifferent men chosen and agreed upon by the partie greved and him.

7. Item: He shall deliver unto the handes of the lorde deputie all suche pledges as he hathe which were taken by the forenamed rebell of any either of Tirone, or of any other parte of Irelande.

8. Item: He shall make immediat deliverie of all suche juells, plate, money, gold, coined or uncoined, artillerie as well brasse as yron, stoddes all kinde of horses, and creaghes[1] of kine, as also all maner of apparell which are come to his handes, or hereafter shall come, which were the late rebells, either in his possession or in any other mannes to his use. And if he shall knowe where any of the forenamed goodes or cattell doe remaine in the handes of any other man he shall reveile the same, unto the said lorde deputie.

9. Item: He shall suffer the tenantes and occupiers of all suche landes as merely apperteined and of right ought to apperteigne to the capitaine of the countrie, quietly to occupie and enjoy the same untill Hallontide next.

fol. 263b. 10. Item: He covenanteth to observe the peace against all the Englishe Pale, and all the inhabitantes thereof.

11. Item: He covenantethe to suffer any of Tirone, now in possession of any landes, lienge in the same countrie, quietlie to enjoy it without interruption, untill suche tyme as further order (upon his complaint) be taken by the lorde deputie and counsell.

12. Item: He covenantethe to performe observe and accomplishe all suche orders and decrees as are alredie past unto all her majesties subjectes, thei of their partes performinge the like unto him.

[1] Herds.

13. Item: For the obtaininge of his pardon aforesaid he covenantethe to paie unto the lorde deputie suche nomber of kine as the lorde deputie, and the erle of Kildare shall appointe. 1567.

14. And for the performance of all and everie the abovewritten articles he offerethe to deliver unto the handes of the said lorde deputie, suche pledges or hostages, as the saide lorde deputie shall demannde of him; and further dothe offer to take his corporall othe upon the holie evangelist in the presence of us the lorde deputie and others whose names are subscribed: and manye moe.

This under signe is the marke of Tirlaghe Oneill, alias Tirlaghe Lenaghe, ×.

G. Kyldare.—Christopher Delvin.—N. Bagenall.—Lowthe.—W. Fitzwilliams.—Warhame Seintleger.

[CCX.]—The humble submission of one Tirlagh Oneile, alias Tirlagh Brassellagh, made unto the right honorable sir Henry Sidney, knight, of the most noble order of the garter, lorde president of the counsaile and marches of Wales, lorde deputie of this realme of Irelande, in his campe of Castell Corkera in Tyrone, the xviiith daye of June, 1567: fol. 264.

1. Furst: The said Tirlagh Oneile, alias Tirlagh Brasillagh, confesseth himself to have offended the queenes moste excellent majestie in that he hath adhered, abetted and served the late archerebell and most notorious traitor, Shane Onele, in his most cruell and shamefull rebellion, against her most excellent highnes, for which, as he is most hartly sorie, so doth he most humbly submitt himself, his liffe, landes and goodes to her highnes grace and mercie, and in like maner cravith her gratious pardon for the same.

2.—Item: He covenanteth duringe his life to be a trewe subjecte to her most excellent majestie and to the crowne imperiall of England and Irelande, and that he will never assist anye foraine enemie, or proclaymed rebell against the same.

3. Item: That he will to his power defende the holie churche, the ministers landes and jurisdiccions of the same, and shall not encroche nor exacte eny thinge or parte thereof, nor suffer any under him to doe.

4. Item: He covenanteth that he will never entertayne any Scottisheman, beinge a man of warre, without speciall licence graunted unto him by the governor for the tyme beinge.

5. Item: He covenanteth to make dewe restitucion and amends to any the good subjectes of the Englishe Pale for any hurtes don to them by him or any of his or other by his procurement, not beinge don in the tyme of the actuall rebellion of the aforenamed traitor and rebell, Shane Onele, accordinge to the arbitrament and sainge of indefferent men, chosen and agreid upon by the partie greved and him. fol. 264b.

6. Item: He shall delyver into the handes of the lorde deputie all suche pledges as he hath which were taken by the forenamed rebell of any either of Tirone or of any other parte of Irelande.

7. Item: He shall make imediat delyverie of all suche juells, plate, money, golde, coyned or uncoined, artillerie, as well brasse as iron, stodes all kindes of horses and creaghtes[1] of kyne, as also all maner of apparell which are comen into his handes or hereafter shall come, which were the late rebells either in his possession or in any other mans to his use,

[1] See p. 198.

1567. and if he shall knowe where any of the forenamed goodes or cattells do remayne in the handes of any other man, he shall revell the same unto the lorde deputie.

8. Item: He shall suffer the tenantes and occupiers of all suche landes as merely appertainith and of right ought to pertaine to the capten of the countrie, quietly to occupie and enjoye the same untill Haloutyde nexte.

9. Item: He covenauntethe to observe the pece against all the Englishe Pale, and all the inhabitantes thereof.

fol. 265. 10. Item: He covenaunteth to suffer any of Tirone nowe in possession of any landes lienge in the same contrie quietlie to enjoye it without interrupcion, untill suche tyme as further order upon his complaint betaken by the lorde deputie and counsaile.

11. Item: He covenaunteth to performe, observe and accomplishe all suche orders as are alredie past unto all her majesties subjectes, they of their partes performinge the like unto him.

12. Item: For obtaininge of his pardon aforesaid he covenanteth to pay unto the lorde deputie suche nomber of kyne as the said lorde deputie and the earle of Kildare shall appointe.

13. And for the performaunce of all and everie the above written articles, he offreth to delyver into the hands of the said lorde deputie suche pledges or hostaiges as the said lorde deputie shall demaunde of him, and further doth offer to take his corporall othe upon the holly evangelist in the presence of us, the lorde deputie, and others whose names are subscribed and many more.

+ the marke of Tirelagh Oneile alias Terilagh Brasellagh.

G. Kildare.—Christofer Delvin.—T. Lowth.—W. FitzWilliams.—Nicholas Bagnall.—Warham Sentleger.[1]

fol. 266. [CCXI.]—The humble submission of one Tirlagh Onele, alias Tirlagh McHenrie McShane, made unto the right honorable sir Henry Sydney, knight, of the most noble order, lorde president of the counsaile and marches of Wales, and lorde deputie generall of this her graces realm of Irelande in his campe at Castell Corkera, in Tirone, the xviiith daie of June, 1567:

[1.] Furst: The said Tirlagh Onele, alias Tirlagh McHenrie McShane, confessith himself to have offended the quenes moste excellent majestie in that he hath adherid abetted and servid the late arche rebell and most notorious traitor, Shane Onele, in his most cruell and shamefull rebellion against her most excellent highnes, for which as he is moste hartlie sorie, so doth he most humbly submitt himself, his life, landes and goodes to her highnes grace and mercie; and in like maner craveth her gracious pardon for the same.

[2.] Item: He covenanteth, duringe his life, to be a trewe subiete to her most excellent majestie and to the crowne imperiall of England and Irelande, and that he will never assiste any foren enemie or proclaymed rebell against the same.

[3.] Item: He will, to his power, defende the hollie churche the ministeres landes and jurisdictions of the same, and shall not encroache or exacte any thinge or parte thereof, or suffer any under him [soe] to doe.

[1] Fol. 265*b*. is blank.

[4.] Item: He covenantith that he will never entertaine any Scottisheman, beinge a man of warre, without special licence graunted unto him by the governor for the tyme beinge. 1567.

[5.] Item: He covenanteth to make due restitucion and amendes to any the good subjectes of the Englishe Pale for any hurtes don unto them by him, or any of his, or others by his procurement, not beinge don in tyme of actuall rebellion of the forenamed traitor and rebell, Shane Onele, accordinge to the arbitrament and sainge of indifrent men chosen and agreid upon by the partie greved and him. fol. 266*b*.

[6.] Item: He shall delyver into the handes of the lorde deputie all suche pledges as he hath which were taken by the forenamed rebell of any either of Tirone or of any other parte of Irelande.

[7.] Item: He shall make imediat delyverie of all suche juells, plate, money, golde, coined or uncoyned, artillerie, as well brasse as yron, studds, all kinde of horses, and creaghtes of kyne, as also all maner of apparell which are come to his handes, or hereafter shall come, which were the late rebells, either in his possession or in any other mans to his use, and if he shall knowe where any of the forenamed goodes or cattell do remayne in the handes of any other man he shall reveale the same unto the said lorde deputie.

[8]. Item: He shall suffer the tenantes and occupiers of all suche landes as merelie appertayned and of right ought to appertaine to the capten of the contrie quietlie to enjoye and occupie the same untill Haloutyd next.

[9.] Item: He covenanteth to observe the peace against all the Englishe Pale, and all the inhabitants thereof. fol. 267.

[10.] Item: He covenanteth to suffer any of Tirone nowe in possession of any landes livinge in the same contrie quietlie to enjoy it without interupcion, untill suche tyme as further order upon his complaint be taken by the lorde deputie and counsell.

[11.] Item: He covenanteth to performe, observe and accomplishe all suche orders and decries as are alredie paste unto all her majesties subjectes they of their partes performinge the like unto him.

[12.] Item. For the obtaininge of his pardon aforesaid he covenanteth to pay unto the lorde deputie suche nomber of kyne, as the said lorde deputie and the erle of Kildare shall apointe.

[13.] And for the performaunce of all and everie the above written articles, he offerith to deliver into the handes of the said lorde deputie, suche pledges or hostages, as the said lorde deputie, shall demaunde of him, and further doth offer to take his corporall othe, upon the Holy Evangeliste, in the presence of us, the lorde deputie and others, whose names are subscribed, and many more.

+ The marke of Tirlaghe Oneyle Mc Henry Mc Shane.

G. Kildare.—Christofer Delvin.—T. Lowth.—William FitzWilliams.—N. Bagnall.—Warham Sentleger.[1]

[CCXII.]—The copie of a lettere sent from the lord president and counsaill of Connaght, touchinge the disorders and lewde proceedings of the earle of Thomonde: 1569–70.

May it please your lordship to understande the whole course of our journey and our presente state: Since wee wrote laste from Clonferte fol. 268

[1] Fol. 267*b*. is blank.

1569–70. the xx[th] of this moneth, we came that night to Loghereaghe, from thence the next day to Oshaughnes[1] and so uppon Sondaye, being the xxii[th] day, wee came to Inishe,[2] whether came to us that night Mr. Apsley and under him xl[tie] of his bande.

When wee came thither wee neither founde provision for man nor horse, savinge a litell that the sherief had broght in of his owne peculiar chardge, althoughe both the earle, the sherief and a nomber of gentlemen besydes that were at Galwey before were warned to levie and bringe in againste this tyme both mans meate and horse meate and the earle, writte to us that it was done accordingly: Neither herde wee any thinge of the earle afore yesterdaye about iii of the clocke in the afternone, savinge that a man of his named William Nailande came to us but not from the earle aboute a myle shorte of the Inyshe, whom we committed for not providinge horsemeate, havinge speciall chardge thereof from us. And uppon the earles cominge wee thought good to estrange ourselves from him that night because of his undutifull behaviour in neither sending unto us nor meeting of us in any parte of the waye; and allso for his slacke dealinge concerninge our provisiones, and not so only but all the people under his rule in the countrey were fledd away, bothe man and beaste, as thoughe wee had beene ennemies. Neverthelesse we gave him no evill wordes, but thinckinge better to reprehende him openly in the morninge to the example of others, sente him woorde wee were busie and willed him to take his ease for that night.

The earle of Clanricarde beeing presente with him he neither seemed to excuse his doinges nor talked one worde with him of our beeing heere nor any suche like matter but when the said message was brought to the earle of Clanricarde who reported it unto him, he said he woulde goe to his nexte howse being but halfe a myle from thence and come

fol. 268*b*. againe in the morninge, and sent worde by Martin to us, requiringe that he might goe home and fetche his Englishe appareill, but wee answered him that in no case wee woulde consente he shoulde departe the towne, neverthelesse and notwithstanding allso all the persuacion my lorde of Clanricarde coulde make unto him he soddenly toke his horse and went his way, which when wee hearde wee sente William Martin after him, comandinge him that uppon his allegiance he shoulde immediatly come unto us. Martin founde him at his castle of Clare, and by occasion of the fludd he coulde not gett in till aboute midnight, who then was well used at his handes and promised answere in the morninge, which was that he was ashamed to tarie heere havinge no provision to bestowe upon the souldiours and others, and also reciting the greate injuries that Teig McMoroughe, the sherief, had done unto him saying plainly that he woulde not be earle if he were sherief, and allso taking some occacion of our strange dealinge with him, whereby he gathered wee were displeased:

He concluded plainly that he woulde not come at us without proteccion and allso that the earle of Clanricarde shoulde meete him a myle oute of this towne, which consideringe his behaviour before wee thought good to deny him bothe and agreed to sende unto him the sergeante at armes, and yett not daringe to venter him alone, sent M[r]Apsley and his bande with him to guarde the Mase if any injurie shoulde be offered, and doubtinge that the warde in the castell woulde denie the earle to be theare when the sergeante came wee sente Martin before them under pretence of bringing him answere from us, that he might justifie the

---

[1] O'Shaughnessy. [2] Ennis, co. Clare.

earles presence there the same tyme. But your lordeshippes shall understande his dealinge with us: he hath not only taken Martin in hande and keepeth him, but also sendinge to Apsley to come in, promising him suche cheere as was there, overcame the gentleman (contrarie to our precise commaundement and also contrarie to thadvise of moste of his owne companie) to enter the castell and a nomber of his souldiours allso to the nomber of tenne, as wee can learne, were entysed likewise to goe in, whereof some were killed, and some taken, amongst them that were slaine olde John McRobin was one by name; whereuppon the sergeante and the reste of Apsleyes companie who had grace to doubte the worste retorned hither to us againe saulf. The newes amased us greatly, and wee resolved to goe to the castell ourselfes and did so of purpose to speake with the earle and perswade him if wee coulde, but comming thither and sendinge our trompett and messenger to the castell requiring the erle to come forthe and speake with us uppon oure worde saulfe to retorne wee were answered the erle was not there; and demanding wheare Apsley, Martin and the reste weare, answered that the earle of Thomonde coulde tell, and that the erle himselfe woulde meete us to morrowe, but it is plainly judged that the earle hath both Apsley, Martin and the reste with him and is gone to Bonrattie[1] and certaine it is that he is gathering power with all possible diligence and the Butlers are borderinge heere harde uppon Shanan by the erle of Thomondes procurement as it is thought for this pretended purpose and were sent for by two horsemen of the erles uppon Monday at night: 1569-70. fol. 269.

The premisses considered, together with our owne strenght, being but our owne ordinarie and a fewe of the erle of Clanricardes and nowe these xxv of Apsleies and never a footeman, wee have resolved to retyre ourselves as wee may to Gallwaye, there to waite for your lordeshippes further pleasure, which wee humble beseche you may be with speede. Wee heere also, but not credibly, that the earle of Ormonde was either yesterday or this day at his howse of Nenaghe, by the Shanan syde and there called an assemblie of gentlemen but to what ende wee can not learne.

And it is allso reported that the earle of Thomonde had letteres from him within these twoe dayes but of what effect wee knowe not.

And thus wee humble take our leave: From Inyshe, the xxiiii[th] of Januarie, 1569[-70], your lordshippes humble to commande

Edward Fitton.—R. Clanricarde.—Rafe Rokeby.—Robert Dillon.

Postscript: My lorde: A greater contempt and viler treason never was nor can be wrought, which if it be lefte unrevenged I beseche your lordshippe lett me never tarrie in Connaught, and I shall wishe myselfe I had never lived to come here, but I doubt not of your goodness and will expecte your pleasure, but not at Gallweye, as is written afore. For this night, lyinge upon my bedd, I have fully persuaded myselfe that it is more honorable to the queene and more commodious to the service to goe to Limericke for preparacion of the souldiours there. fol. 269b.

My lorde, I finde suche comforte and stay in the earle of Clanricarde both for advise and companie that I woulde not wante him for my whole interteinement. His chardge allso in interteininge of us at his howse nowe twyse hath beene passing greate. His cominge to us at all tymes even to the uttermoste limittes of his countrey and further sheweth a marvelous reverence to the prince, I beseche your lordshippe wryte him thanckes for all together and lett me heere from you with speede.

---

[1] In county of Clare.

1569-70. Some skilfull man to take chardge, nowe Mr. Gilbert and his lieutenant are both absente, are in my judgement needfull.

Ones againe I take my leave besechinge God to preserve the queenes honour and yours and my honestie which I hope your lordshippe will tender in this case.

At Inishe, this xxv[th] of [Januarie] at iiii. of the clocke in the morninge, your lordshippes humbly and assuredly to comaunde,—Ed. Fitton.

The earle doth accompanie me to Limericke.

fol. 270. [CCXIII.]—The copie of the firste lettere written to the earle of Thomonde:

Wee greete your lordshippe well. And allthoughe wee have received letteres of adverticement from our verie good lorde the lorde president of Connaght, subscribed allso with the handes of our verie good lorde the erle of Clanricarde and the rest of her majesties counsell of that province of a notorious misbehaviour in your lordeshippe, which, if it were not to be ascribed unto subdenesse and lacke of good advisement of your dutie, loyaltie and honorable callinge, were verie haynous and of perilous sequele to be suffered and permitted into example.

Yett wee have not hitherto conceived suche opinion of your lordeshippe that there coulde any suche thinge proceed from you as of any purposed rancour to fall from your due obeisance towardes the queenes majestie and the governement by her majestie in this realme established and apointed, but rather of some errour and lacke of due consideracion.

And therefore have thought fitt to require and in her majesties behalfe to will you to leave all suche partes asyde as perteine to the shewe of rebellion or keepinge of your selfe with force or your castells or countrey other then to permitt the same to her majesties defence, and to make your speedie and indelayed personall repaire unto us under the convoye of our verie good lorde the erle of Ormonde and Osserie, lorde threasurer of this realme, to the intent wee may take suche order with your lordeshippe as best shall apperteine. And thereof not to faile as your lordeshippe woulde be accompted her majesties loyall subjecte, and woulde avoyd the imynent incurringe of her majesties grevous indignacion and the juste sequele thereof.

Yeven at Laughlin, the laste of Januarie, 1569[-70].

fol. 270b. [CCXIV.]—The copie of the seconde lettere written to the earle of Thomonde:

Wee greete your lordeshippe well. And have received your letteres conteininge the manner of an excuse and the allegacions you lay for the answering of the disorders and disobedient behaviour heinously complained on to us by our verie good lorde the lorde president and counsaill of Conaght againste you, together with your earnest requeste and desire that the matter might be herde to the ende the truthe might rather appiere who justly is to be blamed and deserveth to be chastised for disorder, which your peticion, as wee muste needes like verie well of, and finde it not in any sorte reasonable that any man be he of never so base condicion shoulde be condemned before he be harde, muche lesse a man of your place and callinge, being one of the peeres of the realme, to whom greate respecte is to be borne, so on the other syde wainge the gravitie of the cawse, the queenes honour, and the credit of the state there represented, wee thinke it convenient to call the matter being of suche consequence before us, the lorde deputie and counsell, at whose handes you shall be assured to be indifferently harde and finde justice administred unto you with favour. 1569-70.

At which tyme, upon knowledge had of your repaire to us, wee will cause the said lorde president to make his appearance likewise. And further wee will take order with our verie good lorde the earle of Ormonde for his presence and assistance at the heering of the matter, under whose convoye wee woulde wishe your lordeshippe shoulde presently come without any longer delay.

And for your further contentacion and suertie, if you shall not thinke us for any respecte competent judges in your cawse, and suche indeed to whose judgment you will willingly submitt your selfe, you shall have free libertie with our good licence and consentes to addresse yourselfe and your cawse to the queenes majestie.

Both which offers if you shall seeme obstinatlye to refuse, wee can not then any longer perswade our selfes that you meane the dewtie and obedience of a good subject, as by your wordes you nowe seeme colorably to pretende, which your devise and practice wee will seeke to your further greefe to cutt off and prevent, not meaninge any more fol. 271.
henceforth to sommon you by letteres.

And therefore presently wee expecte your answere, what you intende, and even so bid your lordeshippe farewell.

From Dublin, the laste of Februarie, 1569[-70].

Postscript: Our meaninge is that suche answere as you meane and intend to make that you declare the same to our verie good lorde the earle of Ormonde, who knoweth our further resolucion in what sorte to proceed with you, which answere we woulde you shoulde make presently without delay.

[CCXV.]—The copie of the earle of Ormondes lettere: 1570.

My verie good lorde: As I did advertise your lordeshippe in my laste lettere howe ill I was furnished by the maior of this cittie with boates for conveing of her majesties ordinance towardes Bounratie,[1] so I thought good to lett your lordeshippe understande that since, he hath not taken any order for providing of any other, ne yett repairing those twoe boates by him delivered, which sounke at the key as sone as the ordenance was shipped, and the boate which sir Thomas of Desmonde promised never came:

And seeing no meane to carrie the ordenaunce by seae, for wante of boates, lieng heere at my greate chardge, I marched forwarde into Thomonde, wheare the earle came unto me uppon proteccion. And after longe speeche made to move him to his dutie in making of his submission simply to the queenes majestie and your lordeshippe, I demanded of him the prisonners which he kepte to be sett at libertie, which thoughe he was loth to doe when I entered the countreye, he condiscended thereto. And allso agreed to deliver unto my handes all his mannours to the queenes majesties use uppon certeine condicions, which I doe send to your lordeshippe heere inclosed, whiche I was contented to accepte for a tyme untill I had knowen your honours further pleasure, considering I coulde gett no boates for to carrie the ordenance thether, and thereuppon marched on further into the countrey till the prisoners were delivered to my handes and lefte warde at Clonerawd, the Clare and Bonrattie, from whence I came yesterday, so that if your lordeshippe doe mislike of his requestes, there is no good tyme

[1] Bunratty, in county of Clare.

1570. loste, for as yett can I not get one boate to carrie the ordenaunce heere hence unles my lord FitzMorishe doe helpe me to the same hereafter.

The service of these gentlemen of Thomonde that be inlardged are to be imployed againste the said earle.

fol. 271b. And allso I have taken viewe wheare to lay battrie to his castells if he shoulde be restored thereunto. And have made a good way thorowe the longe pace[1] that goeth to Bonrate, which was before all cutt and plashid.

Till retourne of your lordeshippes answere I meane to prosecute James FitzMorishe, againste whom I finde sir Thomas of Desmondes service with the rest of this countrey of small purpose notwithstandinge that at my going to Thomonde I gave him and the freeholders of this countrie and Connilaghe[2] speciall chardge to be verie carefull thereor till my retourne, who to this houre hath done nothinge therein.

I brought these gentlemen of Thomonde (that were prisoners) hither, where I meane to stay them till I have theire pledges both for theire trewe service to her majestie and for observacion of her majesties peace to all her faithfull subjectes in Thomonde or till your lordeshippes further pleasure be certified unto me in that behalfe.

I cannot but recommend unto your lordeshippe Mr. Dallawod, and Mr. Cruce, who verie diligently and painfully have traveiled with me this journey into Thomonde. Beseching the same to wryte unto them your comfortable letteres for theire further incurradginge therein. They complaine to me that they lacke 400 weight of ledd, which I pray your lordeshippe to send with the culverin shott and the holbardes I wrote to you for by my former lettere.

Thus wishinge to your lordeshippe muche increase of honor, I humble take my leave, praing you that I may with all speed understande your pleasure herein.

My lorde, the countrie heere sendeth in neither horsemeate nor mans meate, nor the sherief is hable to doe anythinge amonge them. So that what provision I have I am faine to buy the same heere as the markett goeth.

From Limericke, this x[th] of Aprill, 1570.

The good service that sir Thomas of Desmonde hath done since my departinge hath been the spoiling and prainge of sir William Bourke FitzEdmonde, so that to tell your lordeshippe myne opinion, with the judgement of all the countreies heereaboutes, I holde him of as little discression in service as any man, for that he seketh more the revenge of his private quarrells againste his countrey people then the revendge of her majesties cawse againste the rebell James FitzMorishe.

fol. 272. Your good lordshippes pleasure I only stay uppon and woll proceed presently uppon knowledge had thereof.

Your lordeshippes allwaies assured to commaunde,—Thomas Ormonde and Ossorie.

[CCXVI.]—The offers and humble requestes of the erle of Thomonde, made to the right honorable sir Thomas Butler, knight, earle of Ormonde and Ossorie, lorde of the liberty of Tipperarie, highe lorde threasurer of Irelande and generall of her majesties armie in Mounster and Thomonde, at the campe by Bellaghenefoilye,[3] the second of Aprill, 1570:

1. Firste: The saide earle doth offer to deliver presently unto the said earle of Ormondes handes all suche her majesties subjectes as he

---

[1] Pass. [2] Connello, Munster. [3] Baile an phoill—Piltown, Waterford.

hath nowe prisonners, as well Englishe as Irishe, and for accomplishment thereof was solemply sworne uppon the holy evangelistes. 1570.

2. Item: The said earl of Thomonde shall allso presently deliver unto the handes of the said lorde generall, to her majesties use, all his manors, lordeshippes and landes within Thomonde, uppon condicion followinge, videlicet: that if the lorde deputie and counsell doe agree that his attourney may have free recourse and licence to passe into Englande to exhibite his complaintes before her highnes, and to answere the objeccions of sir Edward Fitton, lorde president of Connaght. Then if the queenes majestie, uppon hering of these causes of both sydes, doe thinke him selfe worthie to loose his said manors and landes then he doth agree and consente that her majestie shall injoye the same at her owne will and pleasure, only grauntinge, unto the said earle of Thomonde pardon of his lyfe, with libertie and license that he may repaire in person to serve in her courte or ellswheare her majestie shall commaunde.

3. Allso: That the said lorde president and all other her majesties subjectes within his rule shall forbeare to prejudice the said earle of Thomonde or any of his followers till suche tyme as the queenes majesties pleasure be advertised oute of Englande. And allso that the fol. 272b. lorde deputie shall protecte the said earle his goodes, tennantes and followers till her highnes pleasure be knowen.

4. Item: The saide earle of Thomonde doth offer in the meanetyme to serve the queenes majestie againste James Fitz Morishe or any other rebell or traitour at any tyme he shalbe required thereto.

5. Item: The saide earle of Thomonde doth moste humbly request that it may please the lorde deputie to stande good lorde unto him, as hitherto he hath been, and to comforte him with his favorable lettere. And that if it shall please the queenes majestie to graunte him pardon, as aforesaid, and licence to repaire to her highnes that then it may please my lorde deputie to comaunde the erle of Ormonde to take speciall chardge of his countrey and followers in his absence, and them to defende from the spoyle of any man.

6. Item: The said earle requireth that Teige McMoroughe, nowe sherief, may be removed and some Englishman or other whom the lorde deputie will apointe to be sherief.

7. Item: The said earle requireth to borrowe some reasonable somme of money to beare his chardges into Englande of the queenes majesties treasure here in Irelande, for which he will mortgadge and pledge to her highnes use all his landes in the Englishe Pale and suche other castellis and landes in Thomonde as the lorde deputie shall thinke goode.

8. Finallie: If my lorde deputie doe not agree to the aforesaid articles, that then the said earle of Ormonde shall uppon retourne of my lorde deputies pleasure, accordinge his promese, redeliver to the said earle of Thomonde all suche his castells and landes as shalbe delivered to him, without breaking or weakninge of them or any parte of them. And after redeliverie thereof to give him five dayes respecte before he be proclaymed or prosecuted.

[CCXVII. 1.]—The copie of a lettere to the erle of Ormonde and therein inclosed certeine offers to be presented to the earle of Thomonde: fol. 273.

After our right hartie commendacions unto you, our verie good lorde: Your letteres of the tenth of this presente written to me the lorde

1570. deputie came to my handes the sixth of the same, delivered by Mr. Patrike Sherlocke, and the contentes thereof have beene debated amongst us with the articles of the offers and requestes of the earle of Thomonde which were inclosed in your said letteres, with as substanciall and grave consideracion as our skilles can reache unto:

And like as wee perceive of your lordeshippes parte, to our good contentacion and greate comforthe, howe you have proceded with diligence, greate care, paine, and coste so farre forthe as the opportunitie of thinges to serve your purpose would permitt and cannot but allowe and like well of the use and bestowinge of the intervall, whyles the state of the earles case may be debated and resolved, whereby the deliverie of the persons is absolutely gayned. So to answere your lordeshippe, our opinions judgementes and resolucions touchinge the said articles wee be all of one mynde, that thoughe it please him to call them humble requestes that they be without all humilitie verie skornefull, and so imperious, thoughe not in commaundement: yett in untowardenes to obey, as wee thinke it not for the queenes honour to allowe of them, nor for the dewetie of this state to yelde to graunte them.

The cawses for that he no manner of way offeringe to stande to or abyde the order and judgement of this state that her majestie hath placed for the governement of the whole realme, but that more is limitynge by his offers in what sorte he wilbe used, wee doe judge that it becommeth not us, with the referring of any matter brought to her majesties judgement, to abridge any parte of her highnes power to doe what her pleasure shall best like in justice nor to prevent by our assentinge that that her majestie may doe and is inclyned to doe, of her moste gracious clemencie and disposecion to mercie, and next wee thinke it verie inconvenient, seeing his disobedience hath beene chiefly in resistance of that auctoritie placed by her majestie in those provinces
fol. 273*b*. of Connaght and Thomonde, that he shoulde, during the tyme of his triall, exempt himselfe and all his from that rule and auctoritie and so winne and recover by the agreement that, that by his rebellion he hath attempted, for so muche wee take that that request doith implie, and importeth a sturringe of the others of that province that are unwillinge to be governed to evict and exempt themselfes by the like meanes:

The substance of the rest of his offers and requestes wee accompte not worthie to be spoken of more then wee expresse in suche articles of our offers as wee doe send your lordeshippe heere inclosed. And therefore in no wyse wee thinke it convenient to allowe of those his offers:

And yett, for that wee woulde all men shoulde knowe howe unwillinge wee be to mainteine warres where wee may conclude any good and honorable peace (presuming that your lordeshippe is of our opinion, as wee can gether no greate likinge that you have of his articles aforesaid, we be contented that your lordeshippe shall make him offer of our said articles, to be refuced or accepted within the apointed tyme of five dayes after redeliverie of his castells. And thoughe wee doe acknowledge therein to lessen the majestie of the queene in this state, committed to our government, and that it is more then he is worthie of that hath not only refused the accomplishment of our firste and second letteres, offeringe all reasonable indifferencie, but allso hath in the meane tyme (besides his delayes) committed many disorders and attempted detestable practises, yett for quietnes sake wee thinke meete to make apparante demonstracion that it shalbe his only faulte if those troubles goe further on. And, even as in makinge the agreement wee pray your lordeshippe to expounde all doubtes that may rise, as it may

sowndе to the speciall regarde of the roiall majestie of the queene, as 1570.
well in this governement as in that perticuler province, so if you finde that the earle will not yelde to this reasonable conformitie our whole truste and hartie desire is and (if in any) point wee may augment your aucthoritie, wee doe hereby geve you power that your lordeshippe fol. 274.
(imediately after the dayes paste that you stande bounde to him in honour) doe prosecute him, all manner of waies, accordinge to the intent of your former commission and that with as muche speede as you can, for that wee finde (and your lordeshippe seeth by profe) that delayes doe both increase her majesties coste, consume your lordeshippe and waste the countrie.

Like as wee meane no lesse then uppon advertisement from your lordeshippe of his in conformitie to proclayme him rebell and to proceed in the next session of parliament for his atteinder.

And so hopinge more in your lordeshippes towardnes then in our instruccions wee committ this weightie cawse unto your in forme aforesaid, and bid your lordeshippe most hertely well to fare.

From the castell of Dublin, the xxiii[th] of Aprill, 1570. Your lordeshippes verie lovinge frendes, ———.[1]

[CCXVII. 2.]—Offers of agreement graunted by the lorde fol. 274b.
deputie and counsell to be proponed by the right honorable the earle of Ormonde lorde highe threasurer of this realme of Irelande to the earle of Thomonde, to be accepted or refused by the said earle of Thomonde within five dayes after they shalbe published unto him by the said earle of Ormonde:

1.—Firste: That the said earle of Thomonde shall have free license and libertie for him selfe and suche nomber with him as the said earle of Ormonde shall thinke meete, to make his repaire and accesse unto us the lorde deputie and counsell, to declare his causes of mislikinge with the lorde president and counsell of Connaght, and to propone what he hath for the justifieing or excuse of his doinges thereon fallen owte and shall not faile at our handes to have therein justice with all indifferencie and favour, which if he any way dowbte of or shall thinke in the profe that he findeth it not he shall have free license and libertie for him selfe and suche other with him as the said lorde threasurer shall thinke meete, to passe into Englande to make his repaire unto the queenes majestie in person and there simple to submitte himselfe and all his causes to her majesties judgement and mercie, betwene this and the xxvi[th] of May next.

2. Item: If the saide earle of Thomonde within five dayes after the restoringe of his castells doe accepte either of the offers aboveaaid that then he shall yelde that those his castells and other his mannors and landes shalbe redelivered as afore and remaine in guarde to the queenes majesties use and all his mannors and landes to be and remaine in her highnesse proteccion till her pleasure be signified in that behalfe.

3. Item: That thenceforth the profittes of his landes shalbe sequestred fol. 275.
into the handes of the earle of Ormonde, to her majesties use likewyse, till she have declared her pleasure in the disposicion of it.

4. Item: That the said lorde threasurer, earle of Ormonde, shall have power and aucthoritie in the tyme of sequestracion lawfully to defend all wronges offered unto any of the tennantes of the said earle of Thomonde

---

[1] Blank in MS.

1570. and to followe the redresse thereof by order of lawe in as lardge and ample manner as the earle of Thomonde might lawfully have done if he had never offended.

5. Item: That for any offence committed in parte taking with the said earle of Thomonde since his said disobedience and rebellion untill the said earles acceptance of theise articles the lorde president, executinge the aucthoritie in that province according to her majesties commission, shall suspend to prosequute the executing of that her majesties commission uppon suche of the tenantes and followers of the said earle of Thomonde as the said earle before his departure into Englande, if he doe goe, shall in one booke give in theire names to the said lorde president, to witt, for any offence heretofore or in the tyme of his rebellion by any of them done and no otherwyse.

fol. 275b. [CCXVIII.]—The copie of the queenes majesties first lettere towchinge the erle of Thomonde:

By the queene.

Right trusty and wellbeloved, we grete you well: We have a good time now past intended to have sent thither to you the erle of Thomonde, to be hard and ordered by you and our councell there as should seme metest for the honor of the state which we have committed to you in the supreame government of that realme, and also for example of others of his condition in such like cases as his is, but his sicknes hath bene such in the meane time as he coulde not convenientlу departe in jorney thetherward untill now. And because we perceave by the letteres and informacion sent hither at this present to our councell by Rauffe Roockby, our justice then in our councell established in Connaght, that you have had some doubt that we ment to use him with such favor as his fawtes to our state there did no wise deserve, for that he himself by letteres sent from hence to you pretendeth that he hath found greate favor with us and our councell and by letteres to our cosen, the erle of Ormonde, that he was sent for honorably by us and our councell after his arivall into Fraunce without expressing any thing how he made greate labor and sute to our ambassador there, or how otherwise he hath bene used, we have thought mete to advertise you the very trought of our usage towardes him:

At the beginnynge that we hard of his beinge in Fraunce first by some intelligence privatly out of Normandye, where he landed, and next by our ambassador in Fraunce. And then we also harde of his being secretly about the French court. And how that although he made
fol. 276. meanes to our ambassador to recover our pardon and to retorne, yet he was also enticed to offer service to the king there, from whom he receaved some porcion of money, wheruppon our ambassador, upon his owne discretion, thought good secretly to stay him from desperacion of our mercy and advertised us of the same, whereuppon we commanded our ambassador to move him to come hither, where he should be hard to saye what he could for himself, if his offences were no greatter then he pretended, being, as he saide, non other but fleeing out of the realme for feare of the president, and intending to come hether by sea into England; which the master of the ship, being a freinde man would not let him do, and so forth, with other coulorable matters to induce us to thinke no default in his loyalte.

And though at the first he liked not of this kind of answere, still pressing to receave absolutely grace and pardon, yet in the end the ambassodor told him, that he had no commission from us to give him other answere; but because he had compassion of him, and trusted his owne assertions for his truth of allegiance to us, he wold thus much adventure, as to send one of his trustie servauntes with him to come into England and to make humble request, that he might be hard to alledige what he cold for himself. And if therby we shuld not be moved to pardon him that then it might be lawfull for him to retorne into Fraunce or where he wold. And so he was brought nere to our court, being then in Oxfordshire, where we wold not permitt him to come nere unto us but cawsed him to be committed to the custody of one of our servauntes in Oxford, where he remained a good space before he had accesse to any of our counsell, and after longe and humble sute made by him he was hard how he could answere sundry thinges wherewith he was chardged for his disobedience to our president and counsell in Connaught, making such answere therunto as nether appeared sufficient nor yet was credited, and so he found no other resolution at that time, but that he should be sent thither into Ireland to appeare before you and our counsell and theare to be hard and abide such order as to you should be found reasonable. And if it might appeare that ther was non other fault in him but his departing out of the realme for feare of the president, he was put in some comfort that then he should be favorably used by you, and if he liked not this it was said unto him, because the ambassador had offered him more then he had warrant to do, that he yet shold be suffered to departe the realme as he came : 1570. fol. 276b.

And therewith also he was roundly used with sharpe wordes and so reproved as he found no suche reputacion made of him, as wherby he might write or reporte of any such favor shewed unto him as by his letteres he reporteth.

Heruppon he continued still in his humble request to have favor with justification of his truth and allegiance, although he yelded to some oversight in his departing, and accepted the order ment to be sent into Ireland to be ordered by you, which being determined to be forthwith executed, he fell sicke, and so continued more then a moneth, whereof being recovered, upon long sute made by him to our councell, he was suffered to come to our presence to make his submission, havinge not before bene suffered to speke to us.

And there openly being on the first day of this moneth, notwithstanding his most humble submission, desire of pardon and offer of all kind of service he had no answere of us but with sharpe reprehention, in the best sorte we cold use it, both for abassing of himself, and for reputacion of our state there, with speciall allowances of you and our president and councell, concluding with him that he should repaire into Ireland, and submitt himselfe in all thinges to the order of you and our counsell there. Adding nevertheles for some comfort of him, uppon his very humble submission and token of repentance, that we wold write unto you that if he were not found culpable in any pointe of treason against us or our state there that then he shold be spared from the judgement of deathe, and otherwise he shuld receave such ponishment and order concerning himself his landes and living as to you shuld seme mete : fol. 277.

And otherwise then this he never receaved favor by any speche of us, whatsoever he or any other for his advantage have or shall reporte. And in this sorte we have thought good at length to explicate our usage towardes him. So as now our pleassure is at his coming to you, he be used by you as shall seme metest for the reputacion and benefitt of our service there, having also nevertheles regard that some difference be made in the sight of the world of him from others, being as we take him but simple in understanding and coming out of a foreine countre, where he was entised to have abiden not without some slander to our

1570. government and to submitt himself as he hath done to abide your order
fol. 277b. in that realm which we doubt not but ye will have in consideracion; and of your procedinge with him we require to be spedely advertised. We wold also have you in your ordering of him and his landes that payment and satisfaction may be made of sondry somes of money which have bene laied out bothe here by your order and also in Fraunce by our ambassador, whereof you shall receave a note from our secretary, by whom you shall forder understand our pleasure in that behalf.

Yeven under our signet at our honor of Hampton Court, the viiith day of November, 1570, in the twelfth yere of our reigne.

The direction: To our right trusty and welbeloved sir Henry Sidney, knight of our order our deputie of our realme of Ireland, and president of our councell in the marches of Wales.

fol. 278. [CCXVIII. 2.]—The coppie of the quenes majesties seconde lettere towching the erle of Thomonde, brought by himself:

By the quene:

Right trusty and welbeloved we grete you well: Although we have by our former letteres made full declaracion to you how we have proceded with the erle of Thomond and in what sorte we entended to send him thither to yow, yet now upon his humble and lowly submission renewed to us at his departure, with very ernest request for our favorable letteres to yow, we could not but after some sharpe reprehension of him for his greate follies and contemptes graunt him thus much by these our letteres, to be caried by himself, that not hearing of any attempt of treason towching our royall estate or person, we wold give yow knowledge that we ment not that he should be in danger of his lief, but that being saved to him, he shold be hard and ordered for all the rest by yow, our governor and deputie, as to yow and our counsell shold seme mete for our estate:

And so we require yow to deale with him in as favorable sorte, as may seme to be agreable and not prejudiciale to the authoritie that we have committed to yow or to our president in Connought:

For though his coming hither as he did, without any warrant from
fol 278b. us, and his continuall attendance and lowlines in submitting himself absolutely to us, might provoke us to shew furder clemency, yet we have more regard of our estate reposed in your handes then anywise to yeld any thing to him that might prejudice the creditt and reputacion of yow and our councell there in that realme.

Yeven under our signet at our honor of Hamptoncourt, the xx[th] of November, 1570, in the xiii[th] yere of our reigne.

The direction: To our right trusty and welbeloved sir Henry Sidney, knight of the order of our garter and deputie of our realme of Irelande, etc.

[CCXIX.]—The submission of the erle of Thomond:

To the right honorable sir Henry Sidney, knight of the honorable order of the garter, president of the councell in Wales and lorde deputie generall of the realme of Ireland:

Most honorable, gracious and mercifull lord, I, your humble suppliante, Conor, erle of Thomonde, here prostrat uppon my knees do in this honorable presens most humbly submitt my body, landes and goodes unto the quenes moste excellent majestie and her unspekable mercye and to your honorable estate representinge here hir most royall person:

And do acknowledge and confes that through evell and naughty 1570.
counsell, and withowt eny occasion ministred unto me, I traiterously and fol. 279
rebelliously have committed high treason against her majestie divers and soundrie times, and of late by beinge in open rebellion and ostilitie against her majestie and the lord president of Connought, representing her majestie, and by her established within the province of Connought and Thomond :

I do also acknowledge and confes the wilfull and traiterous morderinge of parte of her soldiars and taking other parte prisoners and kept them in captivitie. I confes the receite of letteres from James Fitz Moris, being in rebellion, to percever and joyne with him in his abhominable treason.

I confes also to have taken shipping into Fraunce withowt license of your honorable lordeshippe for evell purposes. These and many other disloyall offences, which I cannot remember, I have most traiterously committed, contrary to my bounden dutie of alegiance and to the disquietnes, so farr as laye in me, of that state of Connought and Thomond, for the which I am most hartely sory and greved in my consciens, wherby I have deserved to lose land, lief and goodes, and do most humblie, reverently and obediently yeld unto the queenes majestie
my lief, landes and goodes to be used in her majesties pleassure. fol. 279*b*.

Humbly beseching your honorable estate and my lordes of the counsell here present to be humble suters for me unto her excellent majestie that it may please her highnes of hir wounted goodnes to shew unto me her most gracious mercy and clemency which my undutefull actes hath nothing deserved.

And so shall I, according my bounden dutie, pray for the prosperous estate of her majestie and your honorable good lordeshippes longe to endure.

Your honors humble suppliant,—Conor Thomonde.

[CCXX.]—The surrender of the erle of Thomonde :

Omnibus Christi fidelibus ad quos hoc presens scriptum pervenerit Cornelius, alias Conor, comes Thomond, salutem in Domino sempiternam :

Noveritis me prefatum Cornelium, alias Conor, ex quibusdam causis justis ac racionabilibus animam et conscientiam meam specialiter moventibus, ac spontanea voluntate dedisse, concessisse et sursum reddidisse ac per presentes dare, concedere, reddere, deliberare, confirmare et sursum reddere illustrissime et invictissime domine nostre Elizabeth, Dei gratia, Anglie, Francie et Hibernie regine, fidei defensoris, etc. omnia et omnimoda maneria, dominia, messuagia, terras, redditus, reverciones, molendina, prata, pascua et pasturas silvas, boscos,
subboscos, domos, edificia, grangias, horrea, stabula, columbaria, piscaria, fol. 280
warrennia, gurgites, aquas, stagna, rectorias, vicarias, feoda militum, advocaciones, patronatus ecclesiarum, capellarum et cantariarum quarumcunque, pensiones, porciones, decimas, oblaciones, curias letas, visus franchi plegii, ac perquisiciones et proficua eorundem; ac omnia alia jura, possessiones et hereditamenta quecunque tam spiritualia quam temporalia cujuscunque generis et nature sunt et quibuscunque nominibus censeantur seu cognoscentur, cum omnibus et singulis eorum membris. juribus et pertinentiis universis in Clonraund, Clare, Bounrattie, Moaige, Castell de Banke, Daungebreake in comitatu Clare, alias Thomonde, ac alibi in dicto comitatu Clare, alias Thomonde, Drisshoke, Kylmacodricke et Newgraunge, in comitatu Dublin et alibi ubicunque infra terram dicte domine regine Hibernie predicto Cornelio, alias

1570. Conor, spectantia sive aliquo modo pertinentia; ac omnimoda cartas, evidencias, litteras patentes, scripta munimenta et jura quecunque dicti manerii dominia, terras tenementa et cetera premissa cum pertinentiis seu alicui inde percellas quoquo modo spectantes sive pertinentes; ac omnia bona et catalla mea, mobilia et immobilia, viva et mortua, tam realia quam personalia ubicunque sunt inventa infra dictam terram Hibernie:

Habenda, tenenda et gaudenda omnia predicta maneria, dominia, messuagia, terras, tenementa ac cetera premissa cum omnibus et singulis suis pertinentiis prefate illustrissime domine regine heredibus et successoribus suis imperpetuum.

Et ego vero predictus Cornelius, alias Conor, et heredes mei omnia predicta maneria, dominia, messuagia, terras, tenementa ac cetera premissa, cum omnibus et singulis suis pertinentiis prefate illustrissime domine regine heredibus et successoribus suis contra omnes gentes warrantizabimus, acquietabimus et imperpetuum per presentes defendemus.

In cujus rei testimonium presentibus sigillum meum apposui.

Datum vicesimo primo die Decembris, anno [1570] regni dicte domine regine tercio decimo:—Conor Thomonde.

fol. 280*b*. Memorandum: Quod vicesimo primo die Decembris, anno [1570] regni regine Elizabeth tercio decimo, infra civitatem Dublin, Cornelius, alias Conor, comes Thomonde, ex certa scientia et spontanea voluntate per ejus donacionem, concessionem, sursum reddicionem et alienacionem infrascriptum ut factum suum merum, liberum et voluntarium cognovit. Ac ut factum suum in manibus honorabilis domini Roberti Weston, cancellarii domine regine in terra sua Hibernie ad usum dicte illustrissime domine regine ultro et sponte tradebat. Et petierit instanter dictum dominum cancellarium ut factum suum hujusmodi ad perpetuam rei memoriam in curia cancellarie domine regine terre sue predicte irrotularetur, insumaretur et inscribi faceret.

Et rogavit hos testes subscriptos quatenus tam super ejus factum quam super sigillacionem, deliberacionem, recognicionem et peticionem predictorum testimorium perhiberent.

Sequuntur nomina: Adam, Dublin.—H. Midensis.—John Chaloner.—E[dmund] Tremayne.

[CCXXI.] Articles agreed upon by the lorde deputie and counsell for orders towchinge the erle of Thomonde:

1. First: That where the said erle hathe confessed himself to have committed treason, murder, etc. within the province of Conaught and Thomonde, and of his owne free will hathe submitted himself to her highnes mercie and surrendored all his landes, tenementes, hereditamentes, offices and other rightes to the queenes majestie to be disposed at her majesties will and pleasure: It is ordered that the same submis-
fol. 281. sion and surrender shall at the next generall sessions to be holden in Thomonde, be by the said erle openlie and solempnelie redde and published afore the people, to the terror and example of others that shall committ the like offence:

2. Item: It is ordered that the said erle shall not depart this towne of Dublin till he be delivered to the lorde president of Conaught and so remaine in compagnie of the said lorde president till he and the counsaill of Conaught goe into Thomonde to hold sessions, and then and there the said erle to say for himself what he can:

3. **Item**: Where the queenes majestie of her greate mercie is inclined to graunte the said erle pardon of his lief in some sorte, it is ordered that the same pardon shalbe delivered to the handes of the lorde president to remaine with him and the counsell till the said sessions and that the same to be delivered openlie to the erle upon suche condicions as to the lorde president and counsell shall seme good for the preservacion of the queenes honor and quiet of the countrie : 1570.

4. Item: For the better instructions of the lorde president and counsell yt is ordered that before the said erle have his pardon delivered or him self be discharged he shall surrender and deliver into theire handes to her majesties use all his letteres patentes and other evidences as well of landes as offices, and also deliver in his brother, Tirrelaughe, as pledge for his good behaviour, and also disarme and remove the warde of Moybrakan, and put the lorde president and counsell in quiet possession thereof to her highnes use.

[CCXXII.]—*Apud castrum Dublinii, xxii° Decembris, 1570, et anno regni illustrissime regine nostre Elizabeth, xiii°*: fol. 281*b*.

Memorandum : That where the erle of Thomonde had declared before the queenes majestie and her highnes most honorable privey councell in Englande that the cawse of his rebellion and declinacion from obedience proceded chieflie of the feare he had of the lorde president of Conaught, and the extorcion that the said lorde president and his used upon the poore people, and ther oppression of the countrie, whereby the state there was unjustely sklaundered and the lorde president and his in perticuler towched :

The said erle, beinge, at the especiall sute of the said lorde president, brought before the lorde deputie and counsaill to declare the cawse of the feare he conceived of the lorde president; and to showe what extorcion and oppression he or his had used upon the countrie, denied utterlie that there was any juste cawse geven him on the lorde presidentes parte to move him to that disorder, or to attempt that offence of the state there. Upon which his publique and manifest deniall, beinge urged by the lorde president to put away all vaine feare or imagenacion of dowbt that he might conceive of any intencion that was mente in any sorte to entrappe him by this demaunde but that the same was only sought at his handes for the simple declaracion of the trewthe and for no other cawse; and that by the openinge of the trewthe he shall in some parte repaire the greate and heinous offence he had committed against that governement, addinge further to encorage him not to hide any parte of the troth, that the queenes majestie had delt most mercifullie and graciouslie with him and had pardoned him his lief and thereof he might stande most assured for it was now resolved upon by the lorde deputie and counsaill that his pardon shulde be passed under fol. 282. the greate seale and delivered him and therfore he might now be bolde to declare the trewthe and stande no longer in feare, since order was taken bothe for his pardon and enlargement.

Whereunto the erle answered that if he had said any thing against the lorde president in those two pointes he was now charged with that he did recante it and utterlie renounce and denie it. Yet beinge further urged for the declaracion of the trothe what he could say against the said lorde president, answered: 'What will you have me 'say? I can say no more than I have said. I have grevouslie offended the queenes majestie, you, my lorde deputie and my lorde president, and I pray you forgeve me, and the next time I shall offende or decline from my dewtie of obedience and loialtie towardes the queenes

1570. majestie or the state, I pray God I may have no longer lief; and that he wold never crave pardon if he shulde henceforthe offende either the queene or the state, but that then the lorde deputie and counsell shuld doo with him as thei lest.'

[CCXXIII.]—A coppie of a lettere to the lordes of the counsaile in England for the lord president of Connoghte:

Maye it please your good lordshippes: By the last letteres of me, the deputy, written to the quenes majestie, in aunswear of those that wear sent, by hir highnes toutchinge the earll of Thomond, is advertised so muche as was at that time delt with the said earll, and somewhat also what was determined towardes him. Among which it was agreede that he should submitt himself to the lorde president of Conoghte, and proceedinge accordinge as was entended, we thoughte it convenient to
fol. 282b. send for the saide lorde president wyth whom having some consultacion we founde that notwithstandinge the earles offer of humble submission, he accounted himself agrevid that the earle had reported, as by hir majesties letteres did appere, that the fear of him was the cause of his first sturr, and his flyinge into Fraunce, and also that the said lorde president should oppresse his countrey and people, and thearuppon desiered that the saide earle, in presence of this lorde, mighte be heard, what he could saye toutchinge the same, which, beinge thought verey convenient, the earle was brought accordingly, and the matters aforesaid laid to his chardge:

He aunswered with great humility, uppon his knees, that he had sondry waies offended the quenes majestie, the lorde deputy, and the lorde president, for which he had submitted himself, and did now to them all and in perticuler to the lorde president, acknowledginge that the whole advertismentes and circumstances of his doinges sent by the lorde president and counsell to me, the lorde deputy, and from me to your honors wear and are true; callinge for mercy and refusing to stand to justificacion, praied us all to be good unto him:

And althoughe it wear pressed uppon him that he should freely expresse if he had eny cause of fear, or that thear was eny suche oppression offerid, yet did he not aledge any but still praied us all to be good unto him and that he moughte have his pardon for his liffe. So as on the one parte we be perswaded that he had no further cause of fear than proceded of his owne ymaginacion at the first and upon his desertes and gilty conscience at the last, nor that thear was eny oppression offered at all to him or his countrey, so on the other side seeing
fol. 283. how firmely he reliethe to mercy, desieringe nothinge but his liffe, havinge by substanciall instrument, under his hand and seale, surrenderid to hir majestie all his landes and goodes, wee have thoughte meete to comfort him with the assurance of his liffe, promessinge that it shalbe emediatly passed under hir highnes seale, and be deliverid unto him by the lorde president, in his countrey, at some generall sessions, wheare in like sorte in the face of his owne people he must submitt himself, openly knowledginge his offence to that state of justice being by us thought so to be moste necessarie, for that his first revolt disturbed the sessions then appointed:

We have presently graunted him the libertie of this cittie, uppon sufficient bond not to departe without lycence, and do porpose to consider of his further liberty and favor as we shall fynde increace of his good dispocision to obedience:

And thus muche have we thought convenient to signify unto your lordeshippes, as well in the satisfaction of my lorde president, that in this case is not to be spotted, as also to commend unto yow the state of this poore earle, that now altogeather dependeth uppon the queenes majesties goodnes, and praieth God to be no otherwise holpen then from hence-forthe he meanethe faithefully and truely to scarve hir. 1570.

And so, leavinge it to your lordshippes more grave conscideracions, we most humbli take owre leaves.

From Dublin, the xxiiith of December, 1570.

1570–1.

[CCXXIV.]—The copie of the commission togeather with the instructions for a parle to be had with Tirrillogh Leonaghe, given the viiith of Januarie, 1570[–1.]: fol. 283b.

Right trustie and welbeleved we greet you well:

Whereas greate disorders have bene and dailie are committed upon the borders of the northe, to the annoyance of hir majesties good subjectes, and to the continuall disturbance, of hir highnes peace, by Tirlogh Leonaghe and his folowers: And of his parte also complaintes hathe bene exhibited unto us, of some wronges done unto him and his people, in the time of truese appoincted and agreed betwixt us. Forsomuche as the saide Tirlogh Leonaghe hath desiered that a place of meetinge moughte be appoincted, and convenient comissioners assigned for the hearing and determining of all causses on bothe sides, like as he for his parte hathe promesed to send forthe suche as shalbe fully authorised to deale in all causes toutchinge himself and his people, and to come also in person to some convenient place near unto the borders for the same porpose:

Evin so wee, for hir majesties parte, beinge inclyned to embrace and mainteine peace so far forthe as it may stand with hir majesties honor, for the great trust and confidence that we repose in the wisdomes, discreacions, and assuerid fidelities of you, sir Nicholas Bagnall, knighte, marshall of hir majesties army, within this realme of Ireland, sir Thomas Cusake, knighte, one of hir majesties preavie counsaile, James Dowdall, esquior, second justice of hir majesties benche, Terrence Daniell, clercke, deane of Ardmaghe, and sir John Bedlo, knighte, wee have and doe by virtue of this our commission, appoincte, assigne, and authorice you fyve, foure, three, or eny two of you to meete, treate and taulke with the saide Tirrilloghe Leonaghe, and eny suche commissioners as he shall send, to eny place or places that you shall like of, and at what time soever you shall agree uppon. And doe further give you as aforesaide, full power and authoritie to heare and determin with the commissioners of the other parte, all causes in controversy, and to ordre restitucion and amendes to all parties agrieved. fol. 284.

And also to make truese and to conclude peace, or abstinence from warres by your discreacions, accordinge to suche instructions, as are heareunto annexed.

And whatsoever you fyve, four, three, or eny two of you shall doe, we do promes to hold it ratified and confirmed inviolable in as suer and substantiall maner and order as thoughe the same had beene done or concluded uppon by oure owne person with the consent of the whole counsaile.

And the same your doinges we doe also promes to confirme by eny further instrumentes at all times when we shalbe thearunto required uppon your honor, which we will mainteyne unspoted.

And this with our instructions folowinge, wee thincke sufficient to you, beinge of yourselves wise men and of good experience in thiese cases:

1570–1. Instructions:

1.—You shall procure Tirriloghe Leonaghe to come to the Newry or to Dundalke, or as near the borders as you can. But if you cannot, we refer to your discreacions to make choise of the place of meetinge as you shall thincke meetest; and evin so of the time and the alowance of suche persons as shalbe sent to taulke with you.

2.—You shall demaunde first what requestes hee makethe, what grieffes he hathe to complaine of, either toutchinge himself or his people and use yourselves so as thoughe this meetinge wear onely at his request and for his causes.

3.—Declare unto him oure disposcition to peace generally, and of our good will to peace with him, wheare it is and shalbe agreabie to the quienes honor; what inconvenience comethe of warres, specially uppon him when the army shalbe bent uppon him.

fol. 284*b*. 4.—Make knowen unto him in what reddines we have the whole garrison at this time abowte our person by the accesse of all the horsmen and footemen that wear in Mounster, whear thear is now no neede of them, with the provision of victualls and other necessaries, by the cominge of the victualler, sufficiently furnisshed with money.

5.—You may put him in dispair of all forraine helpe, the quiene of Skottes beinge prisoner in England, the kinge thear maynteyned by the quien, oure misteris power; Fraunce so wasted and weary of warres at home as they rather seeke friendship with our quiene, then eny way to annoy hir; Spaine vehemently afflicted with Moores, and otherwise in greate towardnes of amity with us.

6.—All this notwithstandinge, wee are contented to absteine from subduinge of him, till he may make his suite into England to the quienes majestie by suche agent or agentes as you shall thincke to be convenient, whearein it behovethe you to have regard to the quienes honor, and so shall it behove him, if he expect any grace to come thereof.

7.—Duringe which abstinence of our parte we loke to have him bounde bothe by othe and pleadge to keape peace to all suche as of our parte formerly composed onlesse we shall uppon eny occasion proclaime eny of them for enimies, then he to doe his pleassure againste all such.

8.—And duringe the same time of abstinence we will use no hostilitie againste eny in the Northe but for non payment of debtes already orderid and judged, or for hurtes that eny of them shall heareafter doe uppon eny of the quienes good subjectes.

9.—Yf he claimbe eny uriaghtes heaaretofore disclaimed by him you shall put him in rememberance of his othe uppon the holy booke, solempnely sworne and toutched, and his sonne in pleadge uppon losse of his liffe for performance of it, wheareof the quiene hathe bene fol. 285. advertised, and thearof we neither dare, can nor will dispence with eny parte, hir highnes not beinge made privy to it.

10.—Remember to alledge unto him the possession that the quienes majesty hathe by the act of parliament of the whole countrey, and the chardges already susteyned which may not be lost.

11.—That you heare, ordre and determin all controversies betwixt sir Brian McPhelem and him, and the barons sonnes and him, sins the first truese taken by the deane, and the causes of all others that shalbe contented to depend uppon the quienes majesties parte, callinge before you by virtue of this your commission all suche as you shall thincke necessarie, either as parties or witnesses to testify the trouthe, in which it is necessary that you give sufficient warninge of the time and place of your meetinge. 1570-1.

12.—And that you doe deliver your orders made in writinge to the parties betwixte whom the same is orderid, with streighte chardge in hir majesties name for performance thereof, as effectually as thoughe it wear done by ourselves, and as assuridly they shall aunsweor the contempte at their perills.

13.—If he will make particion with the barons sonnes of landes in Tirone, to accepte the same till hir majesties pleassure be knowen for further confirmacion.

14.—Finallie: If you finde him conformable, embrace it at your discreacions, if not yett as longe time of truese as you can and retourne in peix.

15.—That you demaund restitucion of Logh Sidney and the men that wear in the ward theareof, specially of the men and of the forte, also if you can, thoughe you doe undertake that you will obteine at our handes that the keepinge theareof shalbe graunted to Tirrilloghe Brasselloghe which shalbe performed if you so promes.

[CCXXV.]—Ordo concordie seu pacis facte et determinate inter commissarios regine majestatis, justiciarium Dowdal, et decanum Armachanum, authoritate domini deputati, ex una parte et Terrentium Oneile, principalem sue gentis et cognominis, ex altera parte, in campo dicti Terrentii, apud Dromgarra, xx° die Januarii, anno Domini 1570, et anno regine Elizabethe xiii°: fol. 285b.

[1.] Imprimis: Ordinatum et conclusum est quod dictus Terrentius Oneile, principalis sue gentis suique cognominis, observabit pacem generaliter omnibus Anglicanis subditis regine majestatis; et quod Odonill, Oreiley, Bernardus, filius Phelmei Oneile, Magnassa, Ohandlone, Filii baronis, et Arthurus McDonill dependent super pacem domini deputati:

Et quod dictus Terrentius propria authoritate nullum ex predictis invadat, sed si aliqua causa controversie inter eum et eos vel eorum aliquem oriri contingat, quod tunc querrellam suam proponat coram domino deputato vel gubernatore pro tempore existenti, et dictus dominus deputatus vel gubernator mittat comissarios ad determinandam causam earum controversiarum. Si qui autem qui dependent super pacem domini deputati hujusmodi pacem violaverint, ordinnatum est quod imediate tenebitur marascallus, authoritate domini deputati compellere partem restituere damna sic illata unacum quatuor animalibus in penam pro quolibet animali sic ablato:

Et similiter dictus Terrentius teneatur sic agere pro sua parte et omnibus sibi adherentibus: et hujusmodi forma pacis inviolabiliter observetur usque ad redditum nuntiorum dicti Terrentii a majestate regine quos mittet cum certis peticionibus.[1]

[2.] Item: Ubi dictus Terrentius desideravit habere McGwyre, fol. 286. McMaghone et Colla McBrian super sua pace, ut urrachus,[2] usque ad redditum suorum nuntiorum a majestate regine ex eo quod dicti ad eum voluntarie pendente bello venerunt prout secundum eum ex antiqua consuetudine debreannt. Hoc penitus sibi per commissarios negatum

---

[1] In margin:—"Onele to performe this order untill his messenger shall retorne from her majestie."

[2] In Irish: *Urrigh*,—sub-king.

1570–1. fuit attamen pollicitum sibi fuit ad humilem suam peticionem ex diversis consideracionibus quod dominus deputatus vel gubernator pro tempore existens eos neque aliquem alium in boriali parte invadat usque ad redditum dictorum nuntiorum a majestate regine, nisi propter licquida debita jam judicata vel propter malefacta in futurum committenda.

Et quantum ad probacionem predictorum debitorum, ordinatum est quod plene probentur coram commissariis, et eis probatis quod comissarii certum tempus limitabunt infra quod pars condemnata debita solvat ante aliquam invasionem vel pignora.

Demum quantum ad malefacta in futurum punienda, ordinatum est quod comittitur offensa determinationi commissariorum et si pars culpabilis non solvat secundum decretum commissariorum, tunc licebit eam hostiliter prosequi.

[3.] Item: Ordinatum est quod ubi plura damna fuerunt commissa per subditos dicti Terrentii his qui dependebant super pacem domini deputati, et simili forma damna fuerunt illata subditis dicti Terrentii per filios baronis et alios dependentes super pace domini deputati, pendentibus
fol. 286b. judiciis factis per dictum decanum et alios nomine domini deputati, quod fiat plena restitucio in omnibus, prout ordinatum fuerit per commissarios.

[4.] Item: Ordinatum est quod in determinandis omnibus controversiis emergentibus vel insurgentibus duo discreti viri ex hominibus dicti Terrentii astabunt commissariis.

In quorum omnium et singulorum fidem et testimonium dictus Terrentius juravit adimplere premissa per sacra Dei evangelia, presentibus hiis qui sequuntur, videlicet, magistro justiciario Dowdall, domino decano Armachano, Terrentio filio Henrici Ynele, Terrentio filio Phelmei, Arthuro filio Henrici, domino McGwire, domino McMaghoune et Collatio McBriene et aliis generosis nonnullis.

Hi omnes generosi quorum nomina hic subscribuntur, unacum suo uxore, solemniter jurarunt observare predictam pacem.

Ad humilem peticionem Terrentii Oneile, nos, dominus deputatus et regine majestatis consiliarii manus nostras ad hanc concordiam seu pacem determinatam et conclusam, ut supra, apposuimus: et sigillum hujus regni privatum apponi fecimus.

Datum tercio die Martii, 1570[–71], et anno regine nostre invictissime xiiio.

[1566.]
fol. 287. [CCXXVI.]—Hec indentura, facta xxiiiio die Octobris, anno serenissime principis Elizabethe, Dei gratia Anglie Francie et Hibernie regine, fidei defensoris, etc. octavo [1566], inter honorabilem virum, dominum Henricum Sydney, ordinis garterii militem, presidentem consilii marchiarum Wallie, deputatum suum generalem in Hibernia, unacum consilio ejusdem regni quorum nomina subscribuntur, parte ex una, et Donaldum Oconnor, vulgariter nuncupatum Oconnor Sligo, ex altera parte, testatur, etc. (as at p. 187).

1570–1.
fol. 288. [CCXXVII.]—An indenture betwixte the quiens majestie and Brien McCahir McArt Cavanagh:

This indenture made betwixte the righte honorable sir Henry Sidney, knighte of the noble order of the gartier, lorde president of the counsaile of Walles and lorde deputy generall of Ireland, for and in the behaulf of the quiens moste excellent majestie of thone parte and Brian McCahir McArt Cavanaghe of Ballyian, in the county of Wexford, gentleman, chiffe of his name and seipte called Slaght Dermod lawdarage, for and

in the behaulf of himself and all the rest of the gentlemen and free- 1570-1.
holders of the saide scipt in the baronies of Ballyian, St. Molinge and Clanhauricke and Fassaghesleabuy, in the county aforesaide, and in the county of Cathirloghe, as authorised by the saide gentlmen and freeholders under this deede and seale, of the other partie, wittnessethe :

That the saide Brian McCahir McArt Cavanaghe do for himself and all the rest of the saide gentlemen and freeholders of the baronies and places aforesaide for them, their heires and assignes, covenant, promes, graunt, agree and condiscend to and with the saide righte honorable the lorde deputy to surrender and give up in the quiens majesties moste honorable court of chauncery within this realme of Ireland, to the use of the quienes majestie, her heires and successors when he thearunto shalbe required, all suche mannors, castles, landes, tenementes, rentes, reversions and all other hereditamentes that they and every of them have within the saide borrowes and places aforesaide within the counties aforesaide, either in use or possession, and that the saide Briene McCahir and the fol. 288b.
rest aforesaide shall receave and take the same backe by letteres patentes from her majestie to have and to holde to them and their heirs for ever, yeldinge and painge unto her majesty, her heirs and successors suche yearelie rentes services and reservacions as shalbe expressed mentioned and conteined in the saide letteres patentes :

And the saide righte honorable the lorde deputy, for and in the behaulf of the quienes most excellent majesty, dothe promes and graunte to and with the saide Briane McCahir that the saide Brian and the saide gentlemen and freeholders, their heires and assignes shall not onelie have letteres patentes made unto them of the saide landes tenementes and hereditamentes accordinge as before is expressed but also shall from and after the date hearof be free and wholly dischardged, acquited and exonerated for ever of and from the bonoghte, accustomed to be paide oute of the saide baronies and places aforesaide and by the seipt aforeseide to the quienes galloglasses, and of all sesses, chardges, exactions and impositions of souldiors, horse, horsboy and all other maner cesses, chardges, dewties and exactions whatsoever they be other then the rentes, reversions and chardges hearafter specifiede :

In consideration of the discharge of which bonoght and other chardges aforesaide the saide Brian McCahir, for and in the behaulf of himself and all the rest aforesaide, have given and graunted like as fol. 289.
heareby he dothe give and graunte to the saide righte honorable the lord deputy to the use of the quiens majestie, her heirs and successors for ever one yearly rentchardge of fifty two marckes of good and lawfull money of Ireland, paiable at the feastes of St. Michaell and Easter by eevin portions :

The firste paiment to begyn at the feaste of Easter, which shalbe in the yeare of our lorde God a thousand fyve hunderid seavinty and two, and so yearly for ever at the severall feastes aforesaide, at her highnes exchequir within the saide realme of Irland, or to the handes of the vice theasauror or generall receivor of the same realm for the time beinge.

And if it fortune the saide rent of fifty two markes to be behind in parte or in the whole by the space of sex monethes next after eny of said feastes, that then it shalbe lawfull unto the saide righte honorable the lorde deputy or other governor or governors of this realme for the time beinge to enter and distreine in all and singuler the landes tenementes and hereditamentes within the saide countrye, baronies and places aforesaide, and the distresse so taken to deteine and kepe till the saide yearly rent be fully and wholly satisfied and paide.

1570–1. And further the saide Brian McCahir dothe for him self and the rest aforesaide, their heirs and assignes covenant, promes and graunt to
fol. 289b. and with the saide right honorable the lorde deputy for and in the behaulf of the quienes majesty, her heirs and successors, not onely to bear yearlie for ever to all and generall roddes, hostinges, journies and risinge out of three horsmen six kearne, as they have bene accustomed, but also to pay and yeld yearly to the quienes majesty her heirs and successors for ever suche auncient rent, custom and dewties as they have usually yelded heartofore, that is to saie: xiij markes lawfull mony of Ireland and thirtene busshels ottes, at suche tearmes, times, and places, as they have been accustomed.

And the saide right honorable the lorde deputy dothe promes and graunt for and in the behaulf of the quienes most excellent majesty, that the said Brian McCahir and the rest of the gentlemen and freeholders aforesaide ne none of their landes tenementes and hereditamentes aforesaide ne no parte parcell or member thearof shall from hence forthe be chardged, cessed, imposed or be contributory with the counties of Wexford or Cathirloghe in eny maner cesse, chardge, exaction, risinge oute or otherwise, by eny manner meane, but shalbe and remaine severid from them in the chardges aforesaide, eny custom or use heartofore to the contrary notwithstanding.

And the said right honorable the lord deputy, for and in the behaulf
fol. 290. of the quienes moste excellent majestie dothe promes and graunt to and with the saide Brian McCahir and the rest of the gentlemen and freeholders of the baronies and places aforesaide, that if it fortune at eny time heareafter eny parte and parcell the landes, tenementes and hereditamentes chardgeable with the said yearely rent of fifty two markes to be evicted, recoverid and taken out of the handes and possession of the said Brian or any of the rest of the gentlemen and freeholders of the places aforesaid by due order and ceremony of the quienes majesties lawes, that then and for so muche of the yearlie rent chardge of fifty two markes as the same landes tenementes and hereditamentes was chardged with to be defaulked and alowed in the saide yearlie rent chardge of fifty two markes, eny thinge heare in conteyned to the contrary notwithstandinge.

In wittnes wheareof to this parte of this endentur remaininge in the custody of the said Brian McCahir for him and the rest aforesaide, the saide righte honorable the lorde deputy, for and in the behaulf of the quienes moste excellent majesty have hearunto putt his seale, the xvth of Marche, in anno 1570[–71] and in the thirthenth year of the raigne of our soveraigne lady Elizabethe, by the grace of God quiene of England Fraunce and Ireland, defender of the faithe, etc.—H. Sydney.[1]

fol. 300. [CCXXVIII.]—At Drogheda, the third of June 1567, anno regni regine Elizabeth nono:

H. Sydney.

It is concluded by us, the lorde deputy, the lordes spirituall and temporall of this realme and the rest of her majesties counsell of the same, whose names are hereunto subscribed, the rest beeng uppon reasonable excuses and otherwise in the service of her majesty absent:

That for the service of her highness, and quyet and deffence of this realme, and of her majesties subjectes of the same, there shall be a

---

[1] Ff. 290b to 299b, inclusive, are blank.

generall hostyng proclaymed after the olde custome, by wrytt, for six weekes, at the rate of three plowland to a carte, the same to begynne the first of Julye next, to come, and to assemble the same day at Rose heeth, nighe to Dondalke, with also the rysinege owt of the contrey requysite to same. [1567.]

G. Kyldare.—H. Midensis.—R. Trimletiston.—Crystofer Howthe.—T. Louithe.—Jo. Plunket.—Robert Dyllon.—Warhame Sentleger.—W. Fytzwylliams.—Henry Draycott.—Thomas Cusake.—Francis Agarde.[1]

[CCXXIX.]—At Dublyn, the 9th of January, 1567[-8]. fol. 307*b*.

Robert Weston.—W. Fytzwylliams.—Wheare sir Christofer Nugent, knight, lorde baron of Delvyn, is by her majesties letteres patentes aucthorised to followe pursue and prosequute the proclaymed rebelles, the Omores, sonnes to Ferras MacRosse, and to have under his leading for that purpose from the xxith of October last past, one hondreth and fyftye kerne, tenne horsmen and fyftye boyes in holding, and to have the daylie allowance or entreteyment of twoo pence, Yrish, by the day for every kerne, and six pence, Yrish, for every of those horsemen: 1567-8.

It is nowe concluded by us, the lords justices, the lords spirituall and temporall of this realme, and the rest of her majesties counsell of the same, whose names are hereunto subscribed, the rest beeng uppon reasonable excuses, and otherwise in the service of her majesty absent:

That for the service of her highnes and the quyet, deffence of this realme, and of her majesties good subjectes in the same, that the saide holding shall have contynuance tyll the first day of Marche, next ensueng, and the said baron from the said xxith of October tyll the same first of Marche, for the aforesaid nomber of kerne and horsemen, to have the dailie allowance or interteynment as before is expressed, which, according the rates aforesaid, amounteth in the whole to ccxxvii*li*, tenne shillinges, Yrish, and do conclude the same shalbe contributed and cessed on the severall countyes of Dublyn, Meth, Westmeth, Kildare and Lowth, ratabely, according the extent of the plowlandes in the same, after the rate of six shillings, seven pence uppon every plowland, in maner folowing:

The countie of Dublyn - -	120 plowland	39 *li*. 10*s*.	
The countie of Meth - -	240 ,,	79 ,,	—
Westmethe - - - -	120 ,,	39 ,,	—
Kildare - - - -	120 ,,	39 ,,	—
Lowthe - - - - -	120 ,,	39 ,,	—

And this cesse or contribucion to be furthwith cessed and levyed, and the baron to be aunswered and satisfied thereof by the last of this present monthe:

(Provyded that suche baronyes in eche of the said counties whereon the said kerne or horsmen in the pursewte aforesaid have taken alredy or shall take any meate or drynke according the instruccions annexed to the said barons letteres patentes aforesaid shall be exonerated and exempted from such porcion of this cesse or contribucion as ratabely is due to be defalked according the said instruccions for eche moneth whilest so they have taken or shall take any meate or drynk uppon any the said baronyes during the tyme of this holding.)[2]

[1] Ff. 300*b* to 307*a*, inclusive, are blank.

[2] The portion within parenthesis is struck out in the MS.

[1567-8.] fol. 308. Postscripta: The said auctheritie and pursewte against the said rebelles was first concluded and agreed on by the lorde deputye and dyverse others the lordes and others of her majesties counsell, to be graunted to the said baron of Delvyn. And in respect the ending of that holding was not then concluded on, therefore the same is by us concluded on as aforesaid.

Adam Dublin.—Christofer Delvyn.—Francis Agarde.

fol. 308b. [CCXXX.]—At St. Sepulchres, the first of Marche, 1567[-8]:

Robert Weston.—W. Fytzwylliams.—It is concluded and agreed by us, the lords justices, the nobilitie and counsell, whose names are hereunto subscribed, the rest being uppon reasonable excuses and otherwise in her majesties service absent:

For that according her majesties expresse pleassure hither signified, especiall service is to be doune in the north partes of this realme, and that it were fitt some carriages were proporcioned for the better furnissing of the nomber of a cc. horsemen and a cc. fotemen, to be drawen downe thither herehence for service aforesaid, for their necessaries and victels during this rooade or journey; as well as for the better supplieng by lande the present wantes of victelles wanting to her majesties garrisons which there alredy be residing and remayning:

That therefore a cesse of twoo hondreth garrans, in the whole, shall be presently cessed, taken upp, and reyred ratabely on the plowlandes cessable and not beeng free or wast within the counties of Dublyn, Methe, Westmethe, Kildare, and Lowthe, and one leader to every twoo garrans, and one monethes vittell for every leader, to be in a redynes for service and to be brought at such day and place as we, the lordes justices, shall appoynct, which cesse is the rather nowe graunted of benevolent will to further the urgentnesse which her majesties service requirith at this tyme, and yet the contrey chardged with no greater proporcion by this cesse, in respect the same mought be the less burdenowse with suche a fewe nomber of garrans to exchewe the hinderance of their sowing, which mought otherwise, by a greater nomber to have been cessed, have arrysen and growen the more hinderfull in this tyme of the yere.

Postscripta: For that Westmeth hath wonted to pay their cariages in mony, it is agreed they shall be at choyse whether they will bye garrans or send garrans, this cesse notwithstanding, for this present necessytie.

Adam Dublin.—R. Trimletiston.—Christofer Delvyn.—H. Midensis. —H. Draycott.—Robert Dyllon.—Francis Agarde.—Thomas Cusake.

fol. 309. [CCXXXI.]—At St. Sepulchres, the xxth of May, 1568, anno regni regine Elizabeth decimo:

[1568.] Robert Weston.—It is concluded by us, the lordes justices, the lordes spirituall and temporall of this realme, and the rest of her majesties counsell of the same, whose names are hereunto subscribed, the rest beeng uppon reasonable excuses and otherwise in the service of her majesty, absent:

That for the service of her highness and the quyett and deffence of this realme, and of her majesties subjects of the same; and namely against such Skottes as are doubted to arryve to the disturbance of this realme, theare shalbe a generall hostyng proclaymed after the olde custome, by writt, for six weekes, at the rate of three plowland to a carte, the same to begynne within tenne dayes warning, at suche day and place after this hostyng proclaymed, as shall be lyking to the said lordes justices or other governor for tyme beeng to assigne, with also the rising owt of the countrey requisite to the same : [1568.]

Our meaning is, that if the warr in the north or the comming of the Skottes urge not this hosting, that then it shall not be converted into mony to eny other uses.

T. Armachanus.[1]—Adam Dublin.—H. Midensis.—Roland Baltynglas. —Thomas Cusake.—John Plunket.—Robert Dyllon.—H. Draycott.— Francis Agarde.—John Chaloner.

[CCXXXII.]—The copie of a lettere sent to the lordes of her majesties most honorable counsell for the erection of a scole at Galway: fol. 309*b*. [1569.]

It may please your lordeshippes: I have of late received a peticion from the whole inhabitantes of Galway, and chiefly in the name of one Dominicke Linche, a principall marchant of that towne, declaring an ernest desire in them for fondation of a free scole there to be builded at the charges altogether of the said Dominicke, who offerethe also to endow the master with certein perpetuities and enheritances for the better maintenance and continewance of this his godly purpose.

But forasmuche as he is not of suche grownded welthe as therby without his utter empoverishinge he is hable to performe of himself bothe the buildinge and the exhibicion to the scolemaister, his sute stretchethe thus farre that it might please the queenes most excellent majestie to endowe the schole for ever with the inheritance of her parte of the parsonage of Galway, beinge surveihed at viii*l*. xiii*s*. and viii*d*. per annum and with the scite of a ruined howse called Erlestone, surveed at iii*s*. per annum, which is alledged to be a place of most aptnes and comoditie for the buildinge of the same:

The greate honestie of the peticioner, together with the rarenes of his request, declaringe so vertuous a dispotition and zeale to his native soile as no man within this realme ever attempted, hathe made me looke into the demaundes and diligentlie to enquire the estate of that which he beseachethe of her highnes, and finde that the parsonage is devided into viii. partes, whereof fyve partes are impropried to a colledge of prestes in Galway, the other thre partes are percell of her highnes revenue, lett in lease for manie yeares yet to come, after the rate of vii*li*. xiii*s*. viii*d*., as aforesaid, and will not, as I am enformed, excede that value if the same lease for yeeres were presentlie determined:

The howse which he requirethe, is also of no greater rent then is before alledged beinge sometime parcell of the inheritance of the erle of Clanricarde. And like as the value of the thinge desired, without the which the worke intended cannot be performed, is so small as with respect to the common comoditie and utilitie that shall growe of it it is not to be greatlie estemed:

So consideringe that he and the inhabitants are contented that the schole shall take erection from her majestie, and her highnes and her successors to have the nominacion of the scholemaster, the honor of the godly foundacion, especially in this rude and fol. 310. barberowse countrie, may be a sufficient pourchase to her highnes to alienate from her self so small a revenew likely to conferre unto her hereafter an infinite nomber of lerned honest and dewtifull subjectes of all sortes.

[1] Thomas Lancaster, successor to Adam Loftus in the see of Armagh.

[1569.] Sure, my lordes, the greate wante of civilitie, especiallie in those partes where this towne is planted and in whose walles is conteined all the dew subjection of the province of Conaught, is a cawse that might move your lordeshippes to a comiseracion of this estate and to compell you to use mediation to the queenes majestie for her charitie to be extended to so good and Godlie a pourpose, wherby also religion shuld be greatly advanced, for throughe lacke thereof I see the discommoditie growinge by the careles education of the nobilitie and gentilmen of those partes where even thei of the best howses, the brothers of the erle of Clanricarde, yea, and one of his uncles and he a bysshop,[1] can neither speake nor understande in maner any thinge of ther princes language, which language by the old statutes of Galwey[2] everie man ought to lerne and must speake before he can be admitted to any office within ther corporacion.

What marvell is it then that where there is nether religion, lerninge, understandinge, nor civilitie, there want also dew obedience and conformitie to the lawes. All which by this meanes may take encrease, if it please her most excellent majestie to become, with this small charge, the founder and beginner of this well intended enterprise, the honor whereof shalbe as perpetuall as the worke, and the commoditie greate to her people but most to her excellencie that of barberous uncivill and undewtifull men shall reigne over a nomber of lerned dewtifull and reformed subjectes hereafter:

fol. 310*b*. And this I thoughte my parte to comunicate to your lordeshippes, desiringe that this private sute for a common benefite may receive your comendacions to the queenes most excellent majestie and that I may have answere of her highnes resolucion herein. And so I humble take my leave. At Dublin, the xx[th] of May 1569.

To my singuler good lordes and others of her majesties most honorable privey counsaill on hir highnes person attendant.[3]

fol. 311. [CCXXXIII.]—The copie of a lettere from the bishopp and chapter of Fernes touchinge theire collegiall residence at Fernes, dated at Dromcormocke, the vii[th] of Aprill, 1570:

1570. Our dutie remembered unto your honorable lordeshippe, advertisinge the same, that whereas wee received your lordeshippes letteres at Wexforde, willinge us the bishippe, deane and chapter of Fearnes, to conferr together, for an absolute answere in writinge subscribed with our handes, as concerninge our collegiall residence at Rosse, accordinge a concordatum in tyme paste taken in that behaulfe by consent of a fewe of the chapitre of Fearnes our predecessours:

Whereunto wee answere, that the said concordatum is insufficient and never tooke effect, inasmoche as Rosse is ferr distant from the more parte of our livinges and prebendes; further for that there were no edifices nor mansion places fit for any canonicall residence, and further that our said predecessours nor our selves, coulde not justlye forsake nor remove from the cathedrall churche of Fearnes, whereunto wee, whose names are hereunto subscrybed, will sticke whyle wee live, and have agreed, for buildinge and repairinge the same to our greate chardges,

---

[1] Roland de Burgh, bishop of Clonfert.

[2] In margin: "A lawe in Galway." *See* Tenth Report of Royal Commission on Historical Manuscripts, Appendix V., 1885.

[3] *See* Calendar of State Papers, Ireland, London: 1860, p. 302.

and meane to bring the same to suche plight to the uttermoste of our powers and habilitie, whereby wee may be there resident according our firste institicion and creacion for the behofe commoditie and greate comforte of all our countrey and diocese, albeit wee received sundrie letteres from divers governours for dwelling at Rosse and at Weixforde, which wee coulde not lawfully doe, contrarie to our foresaid institucion: 1570.

Besching your honour to accept this our answere and to further this our Godlie purpose accordinge your accustomed goodnes to whom wee wishe all increase of helth, welth and felicitie ffrom etc. fol. 311b.

Your lordeshippes humble suppliantes:

John[1] Fernis.—Walter Keting, chancellor of Fernes.—William Devrous, threasurer of Fearnes.—Robert Chevers, of Killange.—Sir James Laffane, prebendarie de Whitchyrche.—W. Devrous, prebendary of Tamonde.—Richard Sinot, prebendary of Edermen.—Stephen Hay, prebendary of Towme.—Nicholas Whittey, prebendarie of Clone.—Sir Morishe Odrehen, prebendarie of Crospatrike.

To the right honorable and our singuler good lorde the lorde deputie of Irelande.

[CCXXXIV.]—At Dublin, the first day of June, anno 1569: fol. 312.

H. Sydney.

It is condiscended, concluded and agreed by us, the lorde deputie, the lordes spirituall and temporall of this realme and the rest of the queenes majesties counsell of the same, whose names be here unto subscribed, assembled at Dublin, the daie and yeare above written, the rest beinge absent upon necessarie causes or emploied otherwaies: [1569.]

That for sonderie ernest respectes for the furtherance of her majesties service and more securitie of this realme, the terror and reducinge of rebells unto dew subjection and obedience, that there shalbe a generall hostinge proclaimed by writt, after the auncient custome, for sixe weekes, after the rate of three plowlandes to a carte:

The same to assemble att Ratheskeaghe, the xvth day of Julie next to come, or at suche day proroged after that day, as by further pclamacion set forthe by us the said lorde deputie and counsaill, shalbe assigned:

The same generall hostinge to be levied, divided, furnished, appointed and sorted as by scedules in that behalf directed to the sheriffes of the severall counties and cessors of the several baronies within everie shire shalbe prescribed:

Robert Weston, canc.—T. Armachanus.—G. Kyldare.—Roland Baltynglas.—H. Midensis.—R. Trimletiston.—T. Louithe.—Ed. Fyton.—W. Fytzwylliams.—H. Draycott.—Thomas Cusake.—James Bathe.—Francis Agarde.—John Chaloner.—N. White.

[CCXXXV.]—At Christes churche,[2] the vth of June, 1569, anno regni regine Elizabeth undecimo: fol. 312b.

Memorandum: That the vth of June, beinge Trinitie Sonday, Michaell Bee, then maior of the citie of Dublin, was committed to her majesties castell there, for his disobedience and arrogant contempt of a

[1] John Devereux, bishop of Ferns, 1566–1578.
[2] Dublin.

[1569.] commaundement[1] addressed unto him from the lorde deputie, and ordered and adjudged to pay so manie peckes of corne as by his meanes and wilfulnes in resistinge and disobeinge of the said lorde deputies commaundement shulde be sufficientlie and dewlie proved the garrison was appointed and unfurnished of :

And, moreover, a fine of one hundrethe pounde, currant money of this realme, to be levied of his goodes and cattels to the queenes majesties use was imposed upon him for that his contempt :

And upon the vii[th] day of the said monethe then next followinge, the counsell beinge assembled at the castell of Dublin, the maior submitted himself upon his knees to the said lorde deputie and the whoole boorde, humble acknowleginge and confessinge his fault and disobedience :

Where upon and likewise at the ernest sute and peticion of the recorder, aldermen, and the rest of the cobretherne of the saide citie, beinge likewise upon ther knees, and the rather to gratifie the whole corporacion in restoringe unto them againe ther hedde and chief officer it was thought good the said maior shulde be enlarged : and sett at libertie.

fol. 313. [CCXXXVI-1.]—At the castle of Dublin, the xvi[th] of June, 1569 :

It was condiscended concluded and agreed by us, the lorde deputy, the nobilitie and others of her majesties privie counsell, whose names be hereunto subscribed, the rest being absent upon necessary causes or imployed otherwise in her majesties service :

That sir Edmunde Butler, Edward Butler and Piers Butler, brethren unto the erle of Ormonde, should, for their disloyaltie and disobedience, contemptuously refusing to come in to the lorde deputie and counsell and to answere to justice, that for the cause abovesaid and for divers other haynous offences by them committed, shold therefore, except they doe come in and make their personall apparaunce before the lorde deputie or, in his absence, before the lorde chancelor, within xiiii dayes next after the publication of a proclamacion (bering date at Dublin the sixtene day of June, 1569, et anno regni regine Elizabeth, etc. undecimo, that they be from thencefourth)[2] denounced and published as rebelles and traitors unto the queens most excellent majestie :

And that all persons of what degree, nation or condicion soever he or they were that after the daye before lymitted shold be a follower, an aider an assister, abetter, a relever or mainetayner of the same rebelles or any of them or that shall give them meat, drincke, lodging or any succor, shalbe reputed and taken as outlawes, rebelles and traytors, and sufferr such penaltie, punishement and correction with such forfeitures of lives landes and goodes as by the lawes of this realme is dew to all rebelles felons and traitors.

Robert Weston, canc.—G. Kyldare.—H. Midensis.—T. Louithe.—W. Fytzwylliams.—P. Carew.—Ed. Fyton.—John Plunket.—Thomas Cusake.—N. Bagenall.—Robert Dyllon.—H. Draycott.—Francis Agarde.—N. White.—John Chaloner.[3]

---

[1] In margin : "Maior of Dublyn prisoner in the castle for disobeying the lord deputyes commandement."

[2] The passage within parenthesis is from transcript of the order on fol. 314 of the MS.

[3] Fol. 313*b*. is blank.

[CCCXXVI-2.]—At the castle of Dublin, the xvi[th] of June, 1569: [1569.]

[Transcript of preceding order, but without signatures.] fol. 314.

[CCXXXVII.]—Memorandum: That the xv[th] day of November, 1570, I, Edmunde Molyneux, clerke of the counsail of this state, delivered to the handes of John Thickepenny, her majesties surveiour of her victualls for the province of Mounster, two writtes and to every of the said writtes annexed two severall actes, to be delivered to the maiors of the cities of Cork and Waterforde, to be there proclaimed: fol. 314b.

The one entituled the acte for the attaindor of suche as be or shalbe endicted of highe treason or petie traison committed or to be committed from the first of Aprill, 1569, unto the first of Aprill, 1571, if thei shall not yelde ther bodies, etc.

The other, an acte authorisinge the governour for the time beinge, by advise of the most parte of the privey counsaill and upon her majesties plesure signified by instruction or lettere to graunte letteres patentes to the Irissherie and degenerated men of Englishe name of ther landes, etc., yeldinge to her majestie her heires and successors certaine reservacions, etc.

The which severall actes the said John Thickpenny confessethe himself to have received the day and yeare first above written:

By me, John Thickpenny.

Memorandum: That xx[th] day of November, 1570, I, the above named Edmunde Molyneux, delivered to the handes of Richard Arthure her majesties writte, addressed to the maior of Limericke for the proclaiminge of two actes, to the said writt annexed, videlicet, the acte intituled the acte for the attendor, etc. The other an acte authorisinge the governour to graunte letteres patentes to the Irissherie and degenerate men of Englisshe name of thor landes, etc., yeldinge to her majestie, her heires and successors certain reservacions, etc.

The which severall actes the said Richarde Arthure confessethe himselfe to have received the day and yeare first above written;

Rychard Arthur.

Memorandum: That the day last above written I, the above named Edmunde Molyneux, delivered to the handes of Edwarde White a like write, where unto the said two actes before mencioned were annexed, addressed to the maior of Galway:

The which severall actes the said Edwarde White confesseth himself to have received the day and yeare first above written.

Edwarde Whyte.

[CCXXXVIII-1.]—At the castell of Dublin, the xxv[th] of June, 1569. fol. 315.

H. Sydney.

It was condiscended, concluded and agreed by the lorde deputie, the nobilitie and others of her majesties counsell assembled, whose names be hereunto subscribed, the rest beinge absent in her majesties service or otherwise in necessarie affaires emploied:

That it shalbe lawfull to the lorde deputie, for the more spedie repressinge of suche rebellion as is presentlie in Mounster and in divers other places within this realme to encrease her majesties garrison, either of horsmen, footemen or kerne of suche nomber and as manie as to him shall seeme mete and convenient; the same to remaine as parcell of her majesties garrison, until her majesties plesure be knowen:

And to have suche wages, enterteignement and allowance as other of her majesties garrison have, videlicet, for everie harquebussier on horse-

[1569.] backe xiid. per diem; for everie lance, ixd. per diem, for everie foteman, harquebussier or archer, viid. per diem, and for every kerne, iiiid. per diem, provided alwaies that everie suche souldior so hired to be entered into the clerke of the checkes booke as well for his entrie as for his discharge:

And also it was further agreed that it shalbe lawfull for suche commissaries as the lorde deputie shall from time to time appoint to take upp and presse any suche person or persons as to them shall seme mete to be emploied in her majesties service, provided that the said commissaries shall not take up or presse any suche person or persons as be allredie in enterteignement with any nobleman, or gentilman nor suche as be their howshold servantes.

Robert Weston, canc.—G. Kyldare.—Christofer Delvyn.—R. Trimletiston.—W. Fytzwylliams.—Ed. Fyton.—Jo. Plunket.—Robert Dyllon.—H. Draycott.—N. Bagenall.—Francis Agarde.—N. White.

fol. 316. [CCXXXVIII-2.]—Copy of preceding.

fol. 316b. [CCXXXIX.]—After our hartie comendacions:

Where our verie good lorde, the lorde Mountjoye, had the last parliament here an acte passed in the same for confirmacion of the queenes majesties graunte made unto him by her highnes letteres patentes for the serchinge, magginge, findinge and makinge of allam and coppras, a matter never attempted here in this realme:

Forasmuche as her majestie is pleased to gratifie him also in respecte of his greate charge alredie herein susteined with the like acte of parliament to be passed therein her highnes realme of Irelande, we have thought good for that pourpose to sende you herewith not onlie the autentike copie of the saide acte but also a booke redie drawen by advice of lerned counsell here:

And shall therfore desire and pray you to conferre in that matter with her majesties counsaill and suche others as for this cawse shalbe requisite; and to use suche expedicion for the better accomplisshement hereof as the booke beinge perfected and the greate seale of that realme annexed thereunto, the same may be spedelie returned hither, to the ende her majestie may ratefie and allowe of it here as in other actes her highnes is accustomed.

And thus we bid you hartelie well to fare:

From Westmonester, the xxviiith of June, 1569.

fol. 317. [CCXL.]—At Dublin castell, the last of June, 1569.

H. Sydney.

It is concluded by us, the lorde deputie and counsell, whose names be hereunto subscribed, the rest beinge absent upon occasion of her majesties service or otherwaies necessarilie emploied:

That for the more spedie repressinge of suche rebellion as is presentlie in Mounster a contribution or cesse shulde be made of befes to be devided upon the shires as hereafter followethe, videlicet:

First: Of the countie of Dublin, xliiii. biefes.

Methe,	lxxx.	"
Westmethe,	xliiii.	"
Kildare,	xliiii.	"
Louid,[1]	xl.	"

W. Fytzwilliams.—Jo. Plunket.—H. Draycott.—Francis Agarde.—Thomas Cusake.—John Chaloner.

[1] Louth.

[CCXLI.]—By the lorde deputie and counsaill: 1570.

We greet you well: Where John Lie, the younger, of Ballinha, in the countie Kildare, gentilman, our interpretor, hathe bene a long sutor unto us for a fredome of one hunderethe acres of his lande belonginge to Ballinha, aforesaid, in consideracion of the greate wast of a parcell of his lande destroied by meane of a bridge late erected and builded upon his grownde for the commen benefite of all travelers passinge to and froo the river of Blackewater, or otherwise the said bridge to be put from thence:

Whereupon we, upon the viewe thereof, knowinge the greate discommodite that shulde come to all travelours by the removinge of the same:

And withall thinkinge the said Lies demaunde, as aforesaid, overmuche, in respect of that hinderance, have condiscended and agreed by tenor hereof that the said Jhon Lie shall have the fredome of fortie acres of his lande in the towne and fildes of Clonaghe, from henceforthe continewallie, with condicion that the said bridge beinge made but of timber, wattell and gravaell, nedinge daily reparacion, shalbe by the said Lie, yerely from henceforthe, in consideracion of the said fredome duely maintayned and keept upe upon his proper costes and charges:

Willinge and comaundinge the sheriffes, cessors and other her majesties officers from time to time beinge, even so, to permitt and suffer the said xl acres free to remaine from all cesses and imposicions, as for the contrarie doinge you and everie of you will answer at your perills.

Yeoven at Laighlin, the xviith of May, 1570.

To all sheriffes, cessors and other her majesties officers from time to time within the countie of Kildare and to everie of them to whom it shall or may apperteigne.

[CCXLII.]—At Dublin castell, the xi[th] of October, 1569: fol. 318.

H. Sydney. [1569.]

It is condiscended concluded and agreed by us, the lorde deputie, the lordes spirituall and temporall of this realme, and the rest of the queenes majesties counsaill of the same, whose names he here unto subscribed, assembled at the castell of Dublin, the day and yeare above written, the rest beinge absent upon necessarie cawses or employed otherwaies in her majesties service:

That for sunderie ernest respectes, the advancement of the presente service, and securitie of the realme, the terror and the reducinge of the rebells unto dew subjection and obedience, and for the more spedie repressinge and appeasinge of the presente troubles and sturres, that ther shalbe a generall hostinge proclaimed by writt, after the auncient custome, for one and twentie daies, after the rate of three plowlande to a carte. The same to assemble at the Newrie, the xxii[th] of this presente [monthe] or at suche daie proroged after that day as by further proclamacion sett forthe by us, the lorde deputie and counsaill, shalbe assigned:

The same generall hostinge to be levied, devided, furnished, appointed and sorted as by scedules in that behalf directed to the sheriffes of the severall counties and cessors of the severall barronies within every shire shalbe prescribed:

Robert Weston, canc.—James Cassellensis.—H. Midensis.—Adam Dublin.—G. Kyldare.—R. Darensis.—W. Fitzwylliams.—Jo. Plunket.

[1569.] —Thomas Cusake.—H. Draycott.—P. Carew.—Christopher Delvyn.—Francis Agard.—R. Trimletiston.—John Chaloner.

fol. 318*b*. This generall hostinge was afterwardes by the lorde deputie and counsell, for certeine ernest respectes proroged, and the assemblie and settinge forthe of the said hostinge defferred unto suche further tyme and place as shuld afterwardes be signified by letteres from the saide lorde deputie unto the sheriffes of the counties when and where the said assemble and settinge forthe to the hostinge shuld be: And then the countrie to be in arredines within ten daies warninge from tyme to tyme to advance and sett forwarde to the said generall hostinge as ther perills. This order and agrement was solemplie published by proclamacion, the xvi[th] of October, 1569.

fol. 319. [CCXLIII.]—At the castell of Dublin, the xi[th] of October, 1569:

Whereas Thomas Stucley, esquier, beinge the sixt day of June last past, accused before us the lorde deputie and counsaill, here assembled, aswell of fellonie as highe treason towchinge the queenes majesties most roiall person, was by order of this borde forthwith committed to close prison, within the castell of Dublin:

And now, havinge remained and continewed prisonner there for the space of xviii weekes to abide his triall, hathe not in the meane time either by his accuser or any other man bene detected of any matter arreignable or any other cawse, whereby he might have further triall, as by the judges and the rest of her majesties lerned counsaill of this realme we be enformed, to whom we referred the heringe, examininge discussinge and judginge of the matter.

Forasmuche as the said Thomas Stucley hathe made sundrie times humble sute and peticion unto us for that there is no matter fownde to charge him withall, whereby he ought to be deteined any longer in prison:

And also for that duringe the time of his imprisonment and by occasion thereof, as he alledgethe he hathe bene robbed and spoiled by the rebells and traitours, sir Edmunde Butler and Piers, his brother, with ther complices, and lost by them all his goodes and cattells, his tenantes are fledde and runne away, his growndes lie wast and unmanured:

It is therfore condissended, concluded and agreed by us, the lorde deputie and counsaill, whose names be here unto subscribed, that the said Thomas Stucley, shalbe enlarged and sett at libertie conditionallie, that is to say: that he the said Thomas Stucley, with sufficient suerties
fol. 319*b*. with him, shall first enter into good and sufficient bonde of recognisance of five hundereth pounde, currant money of England, before the lorde chauncellor, for his forthcominge and personall apparance at any time within xx[ti] daies after notice geven unto him or any one of his suerties, either by or from the lorde deputie or in his absence from the lorde chauncellor and counsaill, betwixt this and the last day of Hillarie terme next ensuinge, to answere any matter of accusation that may be apposed or laied against him:

And in the meane time if no further matter be objected and laid against him betwixt this and the said last day of Hillarie terme before specified, then presentinge him selfe before us, the lorde deputie, or in our absence, the lorde chauncellor and counsaill his bonde to be cancelled and he fullie discharged and sett at libertie.

[CCXLIV.]—An enterie made of a protection graunted to sir Edmunde Butler, knight, and his bretherne, Edwarde and Pieres Butler, by the erle of Ormonde, beringe date the ii[de] of September, 1569: [1569.] fol. 320.

Where it pleased the lorde deputie to geve me full power and aucthorite to parle[1] and enter into any speche or communication as well with any of my bretherne, as also with any other that have or dothe depende uppon them, or that have bene conversant with them, and to graunt to them or any of them protections to come to come to his lordeship, and to remaine with him and saulfelie to retorne from him which his lordeship promised to holde firme and to ratefie as if the same protections were under his owne graunt directelie passed to the severall parties:

I thought good for quietinge of the countrie, upon the humble submission and peticion of my bretherne sir Edmunde Butler, Edwarde Butler and Piers Butler, and all others ther companie and retinewe made to the quenes majestie upon theire cominge to me, to graunte unto them and everie of them the queenes majesties protection to goe to my lorde deputie, remaine with him, and saulfie to returne from him:

Willinge and commaundinge in the queenes majesties name all and singuler her majesties subjectes, officers and ministers, to suffer and permitt the said sir Edmunde, Edwarde and Piers and all and everie other that hathe or doithe depende upon them, or that hathe bene conversant with them, frelie to passe and repasse to and fro accordinglie, and in all respectes to deale with them as with lawfull subjectes, without doinge or procureinge any hurte to them or any of them in their bodies, goodes or otherwise in their journey towarde my lorde deputie, while thei shall remaine with him, and also till thei be salfelie returned from his lordeshippe:

In witness whereof I have here unto subscribed my name the seconde day of September, 1569.—Thomas Ormonde, Oss[ory].

The erle of Ormounde and Osserye, lorde highe thresurer of Irlande, hath undertaken for the furthecomyng of his two bretherne, sir Edmounde Buttler and Piers Buttler, for that nighte and to bring them present there afore the seid lorde deputie and counsell the nexte daye folowing. fol. 320b.

xx[mo] die Octobris, 1569, at Dublin castell, in the presence of the lorde deputy and the reste of the counsell.

[CCXLV.]—By the queene. fol. 321.

Right trustie and welbeloved, we greete you well: We have received letteres from our cosen, the erle of Ormonde, conteininge the maner of his procedinges from the time of his last arrivall in Irelande untill the time he tooke his journey to Limericke, with his two unworthie bretherne: And whatsoever may be conceived of our acceptacion we wolde have you assured that in suche matters of weight apperteininge to governement we doe not without good deliberacion either resolve with our selffes or notifie any thinge to others, but as may stande with our honor and service, and with the credit of suche as we employ in our service, whereof you are the principall for that our lande:

And therfore we have accordinglie written to our cosen the erle, as he may finde plainlie our good acceptacion of his faithfulness towardes us and our crowne, whereof indede we never fownde cawse to doubt:

---

[1] Parley.

[1569.] And, on the other parte, he may as plainlie see our mislikinge not onlie of his bretherne for ther rebellion, but also of the pretences and allegacions of ther disorders, which thei wold have us to thinke to have proceded upon some occasion of your harde dealinge towardes them and otherwise wherein as we meane never to belive the inferriors, beinge offendors, against ther governors, so yet for our satisfaction we require you to advertise us of the trew circumstances of suche matters as thei alledge for ther excuse:

And as for the erle himself we thinke it goode that by your frendlie usage of him, as may stande with our service, he may be encoraged to procede in the same. And if he shall for that pourpose open to you any overture wherein you may finde it probable that his credit may profet fol. 321*b*. our service in subduinge or stainge of the rebellious there or suche like, then you may doe well to committ trust to him so his doinges may allwaies take ther aucthoritie from you, for otherwise whilest you governe there we meane not that any person of any estate shall entermeddell with any matter of state, but that the same shalbe delivered and allowed by your self:

And consideringe this greete trust, you see we repose in you, we doubt not but you will more circumspectlie use it, and speciallie in the good usage of the said erle, wherby our service may take profett:

And so we have no other thinge at this tyme to writ, beinge fullie occupied in other matters, whereof we knowe you are and wilbe sorie to here; but by Goddes goodnes we doubt not but the successe of them wilbe to our honor and quietnes:

Yeoven under our signet at our castell of Winsore, the xv[th] of October, 1569, in the eleventhe yeare of our raigne.

To our right trustie and welbeloved sir Henry Sidney, knight of our order of our garter, and our deputie in our realme of Irelande.

fol. 322. [CCXLVI.]—At the castell of Dublin, the xxi[th] of October, 1569, and the xi[th] yeare of her majesties most prosperous raigne:

H. Sydney.

Where sir Edmunde Butler, knight, and Pierce Butler, appiered before us, the lorde deputie and counsaill, in her majesties castell of Dublin, the xviii[th] daie of October, and after some speches uttered concerninge the hainous treasons and horrible deedes by them committed, it was required of them whether thei wolde submitt themselves to the grace and mercie of our soveraigne ladie the queenes most excellent majestie: either of them answered for them self, and said that thei wolde stande to a protection to them graunted by the erle, theire brother, who was thereunto aucthorised by the right honorable the lorde deputie, which theire protection bare date the seconde daie of September last, and in effect was, that, in consideracion of ther submission to the queenes majestie, thei shuld come to the lorde deputie, remaine with him, and departe from him saffelie.

Against which theire protection was objected by her majesties lerned counsell, beinge commaunded so to doe:

First: Inasmuche as thei were received to protection in consideration of theire submission, and that thei now relied on their protection and refused to submitt themselves, that therfore the protection was dissolved and no longer of force:

Secondlie: It appearethe that ther protection was to them graunted the ii[de] day of September to come to the lorde deputie, to remaine with him, and to departe from him saffelie, and so thei protected in no parte but while thei were cominge to the lorde deputie, remaininge with him, and in the departure from him : [1569.]

Neverthelesse, upon theire protection to them graunted thei came to the erle, and after the erle came to the lorde deputie, to his campe niere Limericke; and the saide sir Edmunde and Pierce returned and staid from him, and continewed in the counties of Kilkenny, Waterforde and Tipperarie till this theire present repaire, by reason of severall letteres of commaundement sent by my lorde deputie to the said erle to the citie of Waterforde, to bringe them saffelie without sufferinge them to escape by lande or sea : fol. 322*b*.

By which theire staie from cominge imediatlie to the lorde deputie upon the graunte of their protection to them, theire said protection was likewise dissolved :

It was alledged further that in this intervall, betwixt the receipt of ther protection, and the cominge to the lorde deputie, bothe the said sir Edmunde Butler and Pierce had broken her majesties peace and comitted unlawfull actes which was offered to be proved. By which also their protection was clerelie avoided :

And forthelie there is not in the said protection any time limited when thei shuld departe, so as the lorde deputie and counsell were at libertie to staie them duringe ther pleasure, any speciall wordes in the protection to the contrarie thereof notwithstandinge :

Lastlie : Whereas upon ther first apparance, the xviiith of October, thei refused (as before is recited) to submitt themselves :

The lorde deputie then openlie pronounced that their said protection (suche as it was) shulde not be of force (if it had any) longer than that day, and after that night, at the request of the erle, the lorde deputie did graunte them protection for the next daie, being Wenesdaie, the xixth of October, to the ende the erle might use all waies and meanes he coulde to perswade them to submitte themselves.

And on Thursday, the xxth of October, thei, apperinge before the lorde deputie and counsell, refused to make any submission.

So as hereby it apperethe that not onlie the first protection was, by the lorde deputies sentence so published, dissolved but also the saffetie to them graunted duringe Wenesday was likewise determined. And, duringe the time theis objections remained unresolved, the said sir Edmunde and Pierce were committed to the custodie of the erle, ther brother, to be saffelie kepte till the next daie, beinge Friday the xxith of October : And on Friday for that the lorde deputie and counsell could not attende the same cause the archebisshop of Dublin, John Chaloner, her majesties secretarie, and Edmunde Molyneux, clerke of the counsell, were therefore sent to the said erle, chardginge him to see the said sir Edmunde and Pierce saffelie kept till Saturday, which the saide erle did undertake, but Pierce, that night, after the archbisshop and the rest had signified the lorde deputies and counsells pleasures to the erle, escaped ; and the next daie it was resolved, concluded and agreed by the lorde deputie, the nobilitie, counsell and justices, whose names are hereunto subscribed, that for the premised consideracions the said sir Edmunde Butler shulde be staied and committed to the castell of Dublin till the queenes majesties pleasure be knowen : fol. 323.

Provided if hereafter he shall showe any sufficient matter to maintaine the force of his said protection that he shall have allowance thereof, and if he shall finde sufficient suerties to be alwaies forthcominge, suche as

[1569.] the lorde deputie and counsell shall allowe of, that then he shall have the libertie of the citie of Dublin.

Robert Weston, canc.—H. Midensis.—W. Fytzwylliams.—Jo. Plunket. —N. Bagenall.—Thomas Cusake.—H. Draycott.—N. White.—Francis Agarde.—John Chaloner.

[CCXLVII.]—At Dublin, the xviii[th] of November, 1569, the xii[th] yeare of her majesties most prosperous reigne:

H. Sydney.—It was condiscended concluded and agreed by us, the lorde deputie, nobilitie and others of her majesties counsell, assembled, whose names be here unto subscribed, the rest beinge absent in her majesties service or otherwise in necessarie affaires emploied;

That the generall hostinge by her majesties writt, proclaimed the last monethe, for xxi. daies to have assembled at suche daie, proroged as we shuld within x. daies warninge appoint; shuld for divers greate and weightie consideracions, bothe the season of the yeare, and the condicion and sorte of the rebells and anoyers of the state and publike securitie of the realme be converted into money, with an accrece of x daies and a half, over and besides the xxi. daies, which likewise shuld be converted into money, to the hier and wages of greate nombers of chosen kerne, to be joyned with the horsemen and footemen of her majesties armie, to pursue and follow upon the rebells and ther mainteners, with suche diligence and continewance as may not onlie for the time propulce and disperce them, but so extirpe and banisshe them as thei be nomore hable to assemble and doe harme henceforthe.

This exploit is chieflie ment against the Cavenaughes and the rebells their adherentes and mainteners.

Robert Weston, canc.—G. Kyldare.—R. Trimletiston.—T. Louithe. —Jo. Plunket.—Robert. Dyllon.—H. Draycott.—Francis Agarde.— John Chaloner.

fol. 324. [CCXLVIII.]—At the castell of Dublin, the same daie and yere, videlicet the xxiii[th] of November, 1569, the xii[th] yeare of her majesties most prosperous reigne:

H. Sydney.

It was condiscended concluded and agreed by us, the lorde deputie, nobilitie and others of her majesties counsell, assembled, whose names be here unto subscribed, that for the necessarie provicion of her majesties garrison residinge in the northe partes that a proporcion and cesse of otes shuld be rered and levied upon these counties followinge: videlicet, upon

The countie of Dublin,	cccl.	peckes.
The countie of Kildare,	cccl.	„
The countie of Lowthe,	ccc.	„
Westmethe,	ccl.	„
The countie of Wexforde,	ccl.	„
The countie of Methe,	v[c].	„
The countie of Caterlaughe,	cl.	„
The countie of Kilkenny,	ccl.	„

And the same proporcion of otes, so rered, cessed and levied to be delivered to the handes of Thomas Might or his assigney, paienge redie money for the same after the rate of xvi[d] Irisshe the pecke.

Robert Weston, canc.—G. Kyldare.—T. Louithe.—Jo. Plunket.— Robert Dyllon.—H. Draycott.—Francis Agarde.—John Chaloner.

[CCXLIX.]—The copie of the quenes majesties lettere touching certaine sutes and peticions of the erle of Ormonde: [1569.]

Ryght trustie and welbeloved we grete you well: We have, upon certaine requestes made tous on the behalfe of the erle of Ormonde, now at his departure to that our realme, we thought mete to geve you knowledge of our plesure in the same as followethe, wherin we will you to shewe him suche reasonable favor as his causes shall require and as shall seme mete for the furtherance of our service to be done by him in that our realme:

First: We thinke it convenient that suche order as he shall shewe unto you in writinge, under our great seale of Englande, made and pronounced by the advice of our counsell, and the judges of our saide realme, for his title and right to the prise wines of Yochull, and Kinsale, be executed accordinge to the tenor of the said order, without delaie therin to be used; and the profites of the same to be aunswered unto him by the receivers, and suche as had charge by sequestration of the saide wines since the same order first geven.

We thinke it also convenient that upon the inquisition that was made by commission sent from us, and after past under our greate seale of that our realme, for the wronges and spoiles supposed to be made by the erle of Desmond and his tenantes, servantes, and followers, upon the saide erle of Ormond and his servantes and tenantes, there be suche order taken for the restitucion of the goodes spoiled, as dothe appere to be awarded and ordred in the boke, signed by the commissioners, and for default therof you cause to be delivered unto the saide erle of Ormond, or to his assignes so muche of the landes, castles, and manors, of the said erle of Desmond, and others the offenders, beinge of abilitie, and named in the said order, as you shall thinke mete to countervaile the summe contained in the saide decree: fol. 325.

And the saide erle of Ormonde and suche of his tenantes and others which have bene spoiled and damnified, the same to detaine untill satisfaction be made, according the effect of the said order, and as the usage and maner of that realme hath bene by lawe or order of counsell or commissiones, in the like cases upon suche inquisions had and made heretofore:

We thinke it also reasonable and our further pleasure is that the saide erle be exempted from all cesses and impositions for his owne landes and manors (the subsedies due to us onelie excepted), which he is willinge to paie accordinge to the old accustomed rate of plowelandes, heretofore used in the counties of Kylkenny and Tipperarie, in respect that he is [*sic*] and shall forbeare to levie and take suche profites of the inhabitantes of the saide two countreis for his expences, as we are enformed that heretofore he and his auncesters have used:

And for the same respect we also thinke it reasonable, that for some certaine time, as you shall thinke mete, the saide erle may have licence to provide necessarie victualls for his owne houshold onelie, at our prices in the said counties of Kilkenny and Tipperarie; and so muche the rather because he enformethe us that others have the like, and that his landes be so wasted, and his tenantes so sore impoverished, as he cannot by the helpe of them be provided as heretofore he hathe:

We also thinke it reasonable that upon the cessinge of the greate abuse of quinie and lyverie (whereunto the saide erle dothe as we perceive assent), it maie be provided the next parliament, that suche tenantes of his as have taken any estate of any his landes in farme, upon the abatement of the auncient rentes due therfore, in respect that they

[1569.] did also aunswere unto him and his a further charge under the title of quynie and lyverie, either by speciall reservacion or by prescription, maie either be compelled to compound with the said erle for bettering and encreasing of his rentes, in respect of the discharge of their burdens susteined by quynie and lyverie, or else that their leases and estates may ceasse upon reasonable recompence to be made for any fines by them paide for their saide leasses, or for any other charge by them susteined in bettering of their farmes, by building or any otherwise:

Where also the said erle affirmeth that our castle of Laghlin was builded upon his ground in the time of his minoritie, and that other his landes are occupied with the same castle, for the which he never had (as he saithe) any recompence, and in that respect hath often times made request to have restitucion or reasonable recompence: We thinke it reasonable that his allegacion be examined, and his demande considered, and suche recompence made to him as in reason shall seme mete, and therof to conferre with him and to advertise us therof, and also of your oppinion in this that he hathe for his recompence moved us to have a leasse in reversion for a number of yeres of the late possessions, as well spirituall as temporall, of the monastery of St. Marie,[1] by Dublin, of the late possession of Walter Peperd, excepting suche porcions therof as

fol. 326*b*. have ben graunted to others in fee farme, and as we shall understand your oppinion herein so will we geve you warrant to procede.

Geven under our signet, at our manor of Grenewiche, the last of June, in the eleventhe yere of our raygne.—Mdlxix.

To our ryght trustie and welbeloved sir Henry Sidney, knyght of our order of the garter, and our deputie in our realme of Irelande.

[1569–70.] fol. 327. [CCL.]—The submission of the Cavenaughes, made unto the lorde deputie in St. Peters churche, at Drogheda,[2] in the presence of the whole assemblie there, the viiith of Januarie, 1569[–70]:

Humbly submitte themselves unto your right honorable lordeship your most humble orators and peticioners, Brian McDonoughe, Cahir McMorought, Donell McGarralde, Brian McMorroughe, and Calaughe McOwen, Cavenaughes, for our selfes, our septes and followers, acknoleginge our offences to be suche against the queenes majestie as we yelde our selves, our lives, landes, and goodes wholy to her majesties mercie, desiringe your lordeship to extende your most gracious favour to pardon us: and we shalbe bownde to abide all orders that your honor shall thinke mete for us, to binde ourselves, our septes and all our followers never to faile of the duties and offices of trew and faithfull subjectes to her majestie and to her roiall crowne and dignitie:

And for your most gratious goodnes in this behalfe we shall pray for your prosperous successe duringe our lieves.

The examinacions of Brian McDonoughe, Cahir McMurroughe, Donell McGarralde and Caloughe McOwen, Cavenaughes, taken at Drogheda, the ninth of Januarie, 1569, by Edmunde Tremaine and Patricke Cusake, esquiers, and Edmunde Molineux, clerke of the counsaill of this state, commissioners appointed by the lorde deputie for the examinacions of the foresaid Cavenaughes towchinge the cawse of ther rebellion:

[1] *See* "Chartularies of St. Mary's Abbey, Dublin."—Rolls series.—London: 1884.
[2] *See* "Facsimiles of National Manuscripts of Ireland," Part IV. 1., p. xxi.—London: 1882.

Which examinacions, beinge the next day after redde in the presence [1569–70.]
of the saide lorde deputie and counsaill unto the said Cavenages, was there affirmed by them to be the trewe copie of ther examinacions, taken fol. 327b.
by the foresaid commissioners, humble acknoleginge the same upon ther knees:

1.—Brian McDonoughe Cavenaghe, chefe of his septe, beinge asked the cawse whie he rebelled and entered into conspiracie against the queenes majestie with sir Edmunde Butler and his associates, answered as followethe:

That he rebelled not with the said sir Edmunde, but kepte his castell warded only for his owne suertie: and that at the same time that sir Edmunde Butler returned from the spoile of Eniskorthie he sent a messenger unto him, called Callowe McOwen, to will him to come unto him, which if he shulde refuse to doe, he commanded the messenger to tell him that he wolde burne his castell:

And he saithe further becawse that neither the lorde deputie, nor yet sir Peter Carew were then in the conntrie, he was forced to yelde himself and his followers to be at the said sir Edmundes devocion:

And for any matter or other usage of sir Peter Carew towardes him or any of his septe he never fownde himself so agreved that for that cawse he wold have rebelled.

2.—Cahir McMoroughe, beinge demaunded as above, answered: that because he followed sir Peter Carew, sir Edmunde Butler spoiled him of all his goodes, and then he was forced to kepe his castell:

And that at the returne of sir Edmunde Butler from the spoile of Eniskorthie he passed that waie and threatened him that excepte he wolde yeld unto him he wolde burne his castell: and so he was forced to yeld himself and after that followed sir Edmunde from time to time as well against his owne neighboures, the Cavenaughes, that remained then good subjectes: as also to the Narrie[1] to praie sir Morice Fitzthomas. And at theis spoiles Piers Butler, sonne to the lord Mountgarret, was present and a follower of sir Edmunde Butlers; and also Walter fol. 328.
FitzEdmundes of Butlers woode: and for any usage of sir Peter Carew towardes him or any of his septe he never founde himself agreved in suche sorte to have rebelled.

3.—Donnell McGarrald, being demaunded as above, saiethe that he went with his uncles who wer tenantes to the erle of Ormonde and sir Edmunde Butler: And that he was perswaded by sir Edmunde that sir Peter Carew went aboute to take ther lande, and that was the cawse of his rebellion: and beinge servant to the saide sir Edmunde, he followed him contineawallie. He saithe further that ther was non within the Butlers countrie but wold have followed sir Edmunde before the cominge of the erle of Ormonde, if he had sent for any of them:

4.—Callow McOwen, beinge demaunded as above, saithe that he had nothinge ells to doe but to followe his master Morrough Oge of the Gargell[2] who gave him horse and harnesse.

[CCLI.]—At Drogheda, the xiii[th] of Januarie, in the twelfth fol. 328b.
yeare of her majesties most prosperous raigne, 1569[–70]:

H. Sydney.—It was condiscended, concluded and agreed by us, the lorde deputie, nobilitie and others of her majesties counsell assembled, whose names be hereunto subscribed:

[1] Narragh, co. Kildare. [2] Garrehill, co. Carlow.

[1569–70.] That at the humble peticion and sute of the nobilitie, gentilmen and freholders of the counties of Meethe, Dublin and Westmethe that the generall hostinge latelie proclaimed by writt for xxi. daies, with the accrew of x. daies and a half over and besides the xxi. daies, beinge, for greete and weightie consideracions, appointed to be converted into money for the waginge and hiringe of nombers of kerne and others to have served upon the Cavenaghes and the rebells their adherentes and maintenors, was remitted and forgeven, bothe in respect the Cavenaghes, against whom the service was chieflie intended, had humblie submitted themselffes: as also in consideracion of the greate povertie of the countrie who should have borne the bourden and charge of the said hostinge.

Robert Weston, canc.—Adam Dublin.—R. Trimletiston.—Cristofer Howthe.—T. Louithe.—N. Bagenall.—H. Draycott.—Thomas Cusake.—Francis Agarde.—John Chaloner.

fol. 329. [CCLII.]—The submission of the Cavenaghes, whose names ensue, to the lorde deputie and counsaill, at Laighlin the last of Januarie, 1569, and the order taken with them for ther better government and quiet of the countrie:

First: It was agreed by ther owne consentes that thei shulde deliver ther severall pledges into the handes of Henry Davells, esquier, within six daies after the date above written, saffelie to be kepte either within the castell of Caterlaughe or Dublin, ther to remaine, as well for the observacion of the peace as for the performance of all former orders taken with them: as also all other orders that hereafter shalbe prescribed unto them for ther better government and quiet of the countrie:

And for the better and more sure performans of the premises thei and everie of them have entered into bonde of recognisance of thre hunderethe pownde a pece, and besides have confirmed the same by a solempne othe taken upon the hollie Evangelist.

Moreover, we, the said lorde deputie and counsaill, have nominated and appointed the above named, Henrie Davells, to be capten of the said Cavenages for ther better staie and direction, till we take further order to the contrarie:

The names of suche of the Cavenaghes as submitted themselves :—	The names of the pledges that were offered to be delivered, and remaine for the performance of the order :—
1. Donell McDermond.	1. Brian McMorrishe McDermod.
2. Gerrall McCahir carre.	2. Caer McDonoughe and Edmudne Roe McTirrelaughe to remaine till he put in his pledge, Caer Doughe or Caer Rowe.
fol. 329b. 3. Moriertaghe Oge.	3. Caer Rowe.
4. Brian McDonoughe.	4. Art Doughe McArte.
5. Donnell Riogbe.	5. His sonne, Dermod.
6. Brian McCahir McArt.	6. Krean McCahir.
7. Brian Carraghe McMoriertaghe.	7. He did not appiere, but Henry Davells, with the rest, undertooke that he shuld put in his pledge, Morroughe McMoriertaughes sonne.

8. Cahir McMoriertaghe of Leeroghe.	8. He appiered not; neverthelesse Henry Davells, with the rest, undertooke for him that he shuld put in Arte Rowes sonne for his pledge.	[1569-70.]

Theis above written have not onlie undertaken for themselves to observe the peace to all the queenes majesties trew and faithfull subjectes: but also that all ther septes and followers shall so doe. And for performance thereof have put in ther pledges.

[CCLIII.]—Lisac McKeddow Omore, Rorie Oge Omore, Onne McLies Omore and Nell McLies Omore, beinge brought before the lorde deputie and counsell at Stradballie, the seconde of Februarie, 1569[-70], undertooke to put in ther pledges within six daies next after ensuinge to the handes of Frauncis Cosbie, esquier, senesshall of the queenes countie:

For performance whereof thei and euerie of them entered into bonde of recognisance of thre hunderethe pownde.

[CCLIV.]—At Laighlin, the xxx[th] day of Januarie, 1569[-70] in the xii[th] yeare of her majesties most prosperous raigne: fol. 330.

Whereas Nicholas Lumbarde, John Wise, James Walshe, and Patricke Doben, aldermen of the citie of Waterforde, stande bounden in recognisaunce of *ccli.* taken before Henry Draycot, esquier, master of the rooles, everie of them for ther severall apparance before the lorde deputie and counsaill or in his absence before the lorde chauncellor and counsaill at Dublin at or before the vi[th] day of Februarie next cominge and not to departe without licence: Thei have made ther apparance accordinglie and therfore are and remaine discharged of that bande:

Neverthelesse it was ordered that two of the aldermen of the said citie sufficientlie aucthorised from the whole corporacion should make ther personall apparance before the lorde deputie and counsaill at any time within ten daies warninge that thei shalbe demaunded and sent for, then to abide suche order as it shall please the said lorde deputie to direct and apoint.

[CCLV.]—The copie of the lettere and commission sent to the erle of Ormonde from Laig[h]lin, the last of Januarie, 1569[-70]:

Our verie good lorde, with our right hartie comendacions: Forasmuche as we have received letteres of advertisment from the lorde president and the rest of her majesties counsaill in Connaught (which we have imparted to your lordeship) of the erle of Thomondes grevous and notable misbehaviour not only in contempt of her majesties said president and counsaill and of the government by her highnes there fol. 330b.
ordeined and refusinge to come unto them beinge sent for by the sargeant at armes; but also in betrappinge and captivinge suche parte of the assistance sent for the gardinge of the said sargeant at armes as by his deceiptfull allurementes came within his castell of Clare, and also thereupon attemptinge the destruction of the rest of them that were within daunger of there throughe o[u]r shotte, and therby murtheringe one of them out of hande, and forthwith assemblinge greate nombers

[1569-70.] of galloglasses, horsemen and kerne in traiterous and rebellious maner to plasshe and entercepte the passage and waies of the said lorde president and counsaill assembeled; and in criminous and traiterous maner hurtinge of ther compagnie and killinge of ther horses, which his doinges tende to the apparance of an open defection and rebellion:

We have therfore thought fitt to require and by the tenor hereof to aucthorize your lordeship to assemble and use suche power of her majesties subjectes of this her majesties realme and also of her majesties garrisons by us written or to be written unto as to your discrecion shalbe thought fit to represse those and suche other the disloiall demeanors of the said erle of Thomonde, and of others whomsoever that are or shalbe therein assosiated, confederated or conspired with him or that shulbe or have bene counsaillors, aydors or furtherers thereof or of the doers thereof:

And suche and so manie of theis offenders or suspectes as shall refuse under your convoye to repaire unto us to answere for theis there demeinors to denownce and prosecute with fire and sworde, as open rebells against the queenes majestie and her estate roiall of this realme, unto the executinge of the premisses and of everie parte thereof theis our letteres shalbe your sufficient warrant.

And so we bid your lordeshippe right hartelie well to fare.

We likewise aucthorise your lordeshippe to parle with any of the said rebells or offendors and with any other rebells for the service aforesaid.

Your lordeshippes assured lovinge frendes.

To our verie good lorde the erle of Ormonde and Ossorie, lorde treasurer of Irelande.

fol. 331. [CCLVI.]—At Philipstowne, the vi^th^ of Februarie, 1569[-70:]

By the lorde deputie and counsaill:

i.—Trustie and welbeloved wee greete you well: Whereas it appierethe by an order taken at Dublin the xi^th^ of Marche, 1568, before us, the lorde deputie and counsell, for the matters in variance and contencion then dependinge betwixt sir Barnabie Fitzpatricke, knighte, partie plentif, and sir William Occarroll, knight, defendant, as well for and concerninge the murtheringe of Malaghlan McMourroughe; the stelthe of x. studde mares: A proclamacion [was] made by the said defendant prohibitinge that non of the pleintiffes countrie shuld come within the jurisdiction of the defendant or his countrie: As also for sunderie robberies and spoiles committed by certein of the servantes and followers of the plaintif against the said defendant:

For the appeasinge whereof and that either of the said parties the one to the other, ther servantes, followers and countries shuld from thenceforthe observe and kepe her majesties good peace, and shuld joyne and continew in unfained frendship, amitie and brotherlie love and serve togethers in any of her majesties affaires without quarelinge or grudginge one to the other and not revenge any disorder that shuld happen betwen them before complaint first made to the lorde deputie or other governor or governors for the time beinge, or to the senesshall of the countie, or to some other commissioners appointed to here and determine cawses in those partes:

It was condiscended and agreed for the better performance of that order that either of the said parties shuld bind themselves to forfaite five hunderethe kine; and besides for everie beast, cowe or other kinde of cattell that shulde thenceforthe be taken from any of the said parties, ther servantes and followers, either by stelthe or otherwaies, the partie greved to have of the trespasser thre kine or other beastes or cattell for [1569-70.] one so stolne and caried away; or ells the partie that shulde committ the facte and stelthe to be brought forthe and justified by the lawes, fol. 331*b*. accordinge to the trespas and offence.

Sithe which tyme the said sir Barnabie hathe exhibited his bill of complaint against the said sir William Occarroll, conteininge bothe stelthes, murders and other disorders committed by certein of his servantes and followers against the said sir Barnabe, his servantes and followers:

And the said sir William, beinge examined upon the said bill of complaint, in parte confessed, in parte denied, and in parte justified the factes committed, as may more at large appiere unto you by the said sir Barnabies bill and the said Occarrolls answere to the severall articles of the said bill, which herewith you shall receive.

Forasmuche as by the said Occarrolls owne confession, there manifestlie appiereth a breche of our said order, whereby the partie greved is to have the benefite, and for that some thinges conteined in the said sir Barnabies bill could not directlie be proved before us, which, neverthelesse, the said sir Barnabie hathe undertaken to prove before suche commissioners as we shulde appointe:

Know ye that, for the greate confidence we have of your fidelities, uprightnes and good judgementes, we have thought good by the parties consentes to nominate and appoint you Frauncis Cosbie, esquier, senesshall to the Queenes countie, and you, Owny McHughe, gentleman, and likewise, by tenor hereof, aucthorize you and either of you to be commissioners for the heringe, exameninge and discussinge of the matters yet remaininge unproved on the parte and behalf of the said sir Barnabie against sir William Occarroll, and, upon dew prove thereof, to ende and determine the same accordinge to our former order taken betwixt them: that is to say, that the partie greved shall have of the trespasser three kine or any other sorte of beastes or cattell for one stolne or caried awaie; or ells the partie offendinge against whom the prouf shalbe made, to be brought forthe to be justified by the lawes:

Neverthelesse our meaninge is that so manie kine, copells[1] or other cattell as be alredie delivered by the said Occarroll or his servantes and followers to sir Barnabie, his servantes and followers shalbe accounted by waie of defalkacion as parcell of those the said sir William ought to restore:

For the doinge whereof this shalbe your sufficient warrante:

Our order is that so muche as the said sir William Occarroll doithe fol. 332. confesse, as by the docquet here inclosed, you shall perceive that you cawse restitucion to be made to the said sir Barnabie at or before Easter next.

2.—The like order was taken on the behalf of sir William Occarroll as against sir Barnabie Fitzpatricke, mutatis mutandis, and referred by the parties mutuall consentes to the same commissioners to here and determine.

3. Memorandum: That the viiith day of Februarie, 1569[-70] sir William Occarrol, knight, came before us, the lorde deputie and counsaill, at Philipstone and there did acknowledge himself to owe to our soveraigne ladie the queenes majestie two hunderthe pounde currant money of Englande upon theis condicions followinge, videlicet:

That if the above bownden sir William Occarroll, knight, doe well and trulie observe fulfill and kepe her majesties peace, himself his

[1] Horses.

[1569–70.] servauntes tenantes and followers, against sir Barnabie Fitzpatricke, knight, his servantes, tenantes and followers and besides observe and kepe all orders heretofore taken by us the lorde deputie and counsaill or hereafter to be taken by us betwixt the said sir Barnabie and him, for the better government and quiet of ther countries: And moreover make triple restitucion for every stelthe comitted by himself, his servantes, tenantes and followers against or upon the said sir Barnabie Fitzpatricke, his servantes, tenantes and followers or ells apprehende the said partie or parties so offendinge or bringe them forthe to be justified by lawe:

And finallie pay or cawse to be paid two hunderethe kine to the use of our soveraigne ladie the queenes majestie: and likewise two hunderethe kine to the lorde deputie, dew by penaltie for the breche of the first order, taken at Dublin the xith of March, 1563, betwixt the said sir Barnabie
fol. 332b. and him at or before May day next ensuinge the date hereof, that then this present recognisanze to be voide and of non effect, otherwise to stande and remain in his full force streinght and vertu.

[CCLVII.]—By the lorde deputie and counsaill:

At Philipston, the vith of Februarie, 1569[–70]:

Whereas matter of contencion and striffe hathe bene moved and dependinge before us, betwixt Teige Odonne, chief of his name, on the one parte: and Tirrelaughe Odoine of Garihidert on the other partie, concerninge certein rentes dewties and other services which the said Teig claimethe of the said Tirrelaughe, as belonginge to him and his lordeship, which the said Teige affirmethe that he and his ancestors have from time to tyme received of the said Tirrelaughe and his auncesters:

It is therefore ordered concluded and agreed by the mutuall consent of bothe parties that the said Tirrelaughe shall yelde and pay from henceforthe all suche dewties, rentes and services to the said Teige, as he and his auncesters have paied or owght of dewtie to have paied: and on the other side the said Teig hathe undertaken and promised before us to defende the said Tirrelaughe in all his juste and honest quarrells against any that shall oppresse him or offer him wronge or injurie:

For the trew performance whereof bothe the parties have taken a solempne othe upon the hollie Evangelist before us, and in defaulte or breche of this order thei have entered into bonde to pay the forfeture of thre hunderethe kine, whereof two hunderethe to be paied to the use of our soveraigne ladie the queenes majestie, her heires and successors; and the other hunderethe to the lorde deputie or other governor or governors for the time beinge:

And for all other contencions that may hereafter chaunce to arrise
fol. 333. betwixt the said Teige and Tirrelauge thei have submitted them selves to the arbitrament and order of Dermod Oduggen and Rorie McDavie:

And if it shall chaunce that the said Dermod and Rorie cannot ende and determine the same; then thei have referred themselves to the sainge and orderinge of the freholders of the countrie of Oregan,[1] wherunto thei binde themselves to stande and obey.

It is further ordered that the said Teige shall pay to the queenes majesties use, by waie of fine for the burninge, murther and other disorders committed by him and his followers upon Tirrelaughe Odoine, one hunderethe kine at or before May daie next ensuinge:

[1] Now portion of the Queen's county.

And for the performance thereof [he] shall enter into good and sufficient bonde of recognizance before his departure, excepte it shall please the lorde deputie to discharge him thereof. [1569-70.]

[CCLVIII.]—Memorandum: that the xxith day of Februarie, 1569[70], Luke Dillon, esquier, her majesties atturney generall, Edwarde Fitzimons,[1] lerned in the lawes, and Edmunde Molyneux, clerke of the counsell of this state, were sent by the right honorable the lorde deputie to the lorde vicounte Mountgarret upon his repaire to the said lorde deputie, being sent for by a messenger at armes, to charge him upon the dewtie of his allegeance not to departe his lodginge within the citie of Dublin, where he lay, untill the saide lorde deputies pleasure were knowen:

Which comaundement beinge signified unto him by her majesties atturney, the said vicounte promised before the said atturney and the rest that he wold willinglie obey, and not to departe thence untill it shuld please the lorde deputie to licence him so to doe.

[CCLIX.]—The most humble submission of sir Edmond Butler, knight, and Piers Butler, esquier, brethren to the right honorable the erle of Ormonde and Ossory, made unto the right honorable and our very good lorde, sir Henry Sidney, knight of the most noble ordre of the garter, lorde president of her majesties councell in Wales, and lorde deputie generall of Irelande; and to the lords and others of her majesties councell in the saide realme of Ireland, the last of Februarie, 1569[-70], and in the xii[th] yere of her highnes raigne: fol. 333*b*.

We, Edmond Butler and Piers Butler, callinge to our mindes our most bounden and naturall duetie to our gracious soveraigne ladie the queenes most excellent majestie, doe most humblie acknowledge and confesse, before you, our verie good lorde and governour and this honorable table, that we have disloyallie swarved and declined from our allegiance to her highnes, by raising disorderly her majesties subjectes against her highnes peace and lawes; and have committed from the entrie into that our disobedience, sondrie offences and treasons, deserving extreme punishementes and sharpe corrections:

Which our heynous misdemeanour, as neither we meane nor indede can justifie or defend by any collour, so we doe for the same with most penitent and humble mindes prostrate before the estate of her most excellent majestie here to us represented by the presence of your lordeshippe, her most worthie governor humbly and with all reverence yeld and submitt freely and voluntarily our bodies, goodes, lives and livinges to the ordre and disposition of her highnes and of your lordeshipe our verie good lorde and governor under her majestie besechinge withall humilitie and due reverence your honour of your vertuous inclinacion and good nature, to remitt unto us all displeasures and indignacions, that we by any meane have moved your lordeshipe unto, as weil for your owne particular as otherwise: fol. 334.

And althoughe, you may judge our doinges to have bene suche as have not deserved favor nor favorable treatie, yet we doe make our most humble supplicacion, that your good lordeshippe our worthie governor and you, our verie good lordes, with the rest of her majesties honorable councell, will, in respect of this our most humble submission, and for the auncient service and trouthe of our house and also of the continuance of the same, be meane to the queenes majestie

[1] Appointed queen's sergeant in Ireland, 1573.

[1569-70.] that her highnes, who hath bene ever, to her majesties immortall fame, enclined to pitie and mercie, incomparablie beyonde the judgement of man, may be pleased to receave us to mercie, and extend upon us her most gracious pardon, upon trust of our assured loyaltie henceforthe:

And we shall according to our most humble dutie praye that God doe graunt her highnes a most happie and prosperous raigne:

And put into her majesties minde to graunt us our lives, that we may by our duetifull and most humble service acquite some deale of our most grevouse offences past.

[CCLX.]—The coppie of the lettere sent to the lordes and others of her majesties most honorable counsell in Englande for the erectinge of an universitie within this realme: Dated at Dublin the iiii[th] of Marche, 1569[-70]:

After our most humble dewties remembered unto your good lordeshippes: There hathe bene here upon knowledge of her majesties good likinge to have an universitie erected in this lande, a motion made in fol. 334*b*. parliament for the establishment of the same: the matter so well liked as hathe provoked manie good men to offer verie liberallie to helpe it forwarde:

And for our owne partes we thinke and judge the act to be so lawdable to the glorie of God, suche a worthie increase of estimacion to the roiall government of this lande, so necessarie for reformacion of the barbarisme of this rude people as no one thinge can be desired wherby to name good thinges shulde followe, beinge as it were a well of all vertu, from whence all goodnes shall flowe, in all states right commendable, where civilitie is most plenteous, but here most necessarie, where most vice and most rudenes is abundant:

Of suche magnificence and greatnes we accounte this enterprice, as we acknowledge no other foundacion fit for the same but the queenes majesties most gracious goodness, unto the which by the meanes of your lordeshipes we make most humble and ernest peticion, that it may please the same to devise, order, and direct it and to further it with her most bownteous liberalitie and good and gracious countenance, wherby all men, provoked by her highnes disposition towardes it so expressed, eche man in his degre will contribute to the best of his power:

And we for our selves like as we presume to this boldnes upon our good devocion towardes it and shall acknowledge your greate goodnes in followinge the same to obtaine her majesties most gracious favour and consent: So shall we not faile to use our uttermost endevours as well with our goodes and livinges as with our travells and encoraginge of others to bringe it to perfection.

Mr. Lucas Dillon,[1] beinge commended to your honors for parliament cawses, we have thought mete by him to exhibite to your lordeshipes this, our humble and ernest sute, that in consultacion of those matters it may please you to procure some direction to this: that havinge once a gracious beginninge the same may be followed with suche fortunate successe as to so godlie a cawse apperteinethe.

And so trustinge that even the goodnes of the matter shall worke more in your noble disposicions, enclined to vertu, then our weake perswasions to so worthie an acte, we commende it whollie to your handes, without trowbelinge of your lordeshippes with manie wordes, and pray

[1] Chief baron of exchequer in Ireland.

God bothe in this and all other your noble enterprises to send you good succes to his honor and glorie, and consequentlie to the benefite of her majesties service and the commoditie of all her good subjectes. [1569-70.]

[CCLXI]—At Wexforde, the xiii[th] of Marche 1569[-70], the xii[th] yeare of her majesties most prosperous raigne : fol. 335.

Where it pleased the queenes most excellent majestie to signifie unto us, the said lorde deputie, her princelie pleasure that our verie good lorde the erle of Ormonde shuld be exempted from all cesses and impositions for his owne landes and manors (the subsidies to her majestie only excepted) which the said erle is willinge to pay accordinge to the old accustomed rate of plowlandes, heretofore used in the counties of Kilkenny and Tipperarie : and in respect that he is, and shall forbeare to levie and take suche profet of the inhabitans of the said two countries for his expences as he and his auncesters have heretofore used, as by her majesties letteres signified as aforesaid, yeven under her signet at her majesties manor of Grenewich, beringe date the last of June in the eleventhe yeare of her highnes raigne more at large dothe and may appiere :

We the said lorde deputie and counsell, consideringe the queenes majesties pleasure advertised (as aforesaid) do by this our concordatum and agrement conclude, determine, agree and resolve that all the said erle of Ormondes manors, landes, tenementes and hereditamentes within the said counties of Kilkenny and Tipperarie shall from and after the date hereof be free and clerelie discharged of all and all maner of cesses, taxes, charges and imposicions whatsoever thei be wherewith the said countries are now charged by any maner of meane :

The subsidies aforesaid dew to her highnes out of the said manors, landes, tenementes and hereditamentes onlie excepted :

And for that some ambiguitie or dowt might happelie hereafter arrise of her majesties most gratious meaninge for the fredome of the rest of the said erles landes and manors not lienge and beinge within the two counties aforesaide althoughe the wordes of her majesties said lettere may in some apparance and favorable construction seme to be generall fol. 335b. and extende to the freedome of all his landes : and our meaninge is that the said erle shulde have and enjoy the full effect and benefite of her majesties said lettere, doe therfore further determine conclude and agree that the said erle shall have and enjoy all his landes and manors wheresoever within this realme free and manors of the cesses and imposicions aforesaid (the subsidies only excepted) till her majesties most gratious and princelie pleasure be knowen in that behalf : willinge and commaundinge all cessors and others her majesties ministers and officers, within the said counties of Kilkenny and Tipperarie and ellswhere within the realme to whom in this case it shall or may apperteigne as thei will answere the contrarie at ther perill from henceforthe not to cesse, taxe, charge or impose any the said landes and manors as heretofore hathe bene used and accustomed, but that thei and everie of them shall and may be free and discharged in as large and ample maner as eny fredome within the counties of Dublin, Methe or Kildare are or ought to be, eny custome usage or prescripcion to the contrarie in anywise notwithstandinge.

[1569–70.] [CCLXII.]—The copie of a lettere sent to the maior and corporacion of the citie of Waterforde by the lorde deputie and counsaill:

Whereas by supplication exhibited to us at Laighlin by certein of your citzens ther shewed an appearance of penitencie and submission of your faultes, and that for the assured testimonie thereof you were willed to confirme the same by the common seale of your corporacion as the consent of you all: forasmuche as the said testimonie hath bene hitherto delaied and in a maner denied, (whereby is to be gathered a firme perseverance of your accustomed stoutnes) an example unfitt to be suffered:

Theis be to require you, and her highnes name, straightlie to charge and commaunde you that you faile not to appiere before us, at her
fol. 336. majesties castell of Dublin, the first day of the next terme and to bringe with you the maior of the last yeare with foure more of your chiefest and most substanciall aldermen of the same citie:

And althoughe upon the towardenes of your humble inclination it was favourable graunted that two onlie of your compagnie shuld appiere upon convenient warninge, yet now forsomuche as your procedinges prove so contrarie to expectacion it is thought fit for the importance of the matter that you come no fewer then is afore required:

And therefore see you that you faile not as you will answere bothe the former recognisance and also the contempte of this our comaundement.

Dated at Weixforde, the twenty-first of Marche, 1569–[70].

Memorandum: That the maior and his bretherne of the citie of Waterforde appiered accordinglie before the lorde deputie, in the discharge of ther recognisance, and so were dismissed to appiere againe when thei shuld be sent for upon lawfull warninge which thei did afterwardes, and so were discharged by the lorde deputie.

1570. [CCLXIII.]—At Laighlin, the sixteenth of May, in the twelfth yeare of her majesties most prosperous raigne, 1570:

By the lorde deputie and counsell:

Wheare complaint was exhibited unto us in the behalffe of the three seiptes of Kinsellogh and the inhabitantes dwellinge under them, alledginge that Thomas Maysterson, fermer of her majesties castle of Fernes, over and above six score sparrs of bonought due to her majesties galliglasses upon the said three seiptes, dothe exact and impose upon them twelve sparrs, contrarie to right and equitie, and to theire greate hindraunce and impoverishinge:

We, therefore, for our better satisfaccion and knowledge of the truthe how the twelve sparrs ought to be answered, called unto us certeine of
fol. 336b. the aunciente and gravest men of the Odorans, Bolgirs and others in those parties, and for that purpose examined them upon there solemn othe: Thei confessed and declared that McMoroghowe, from tyme to tyme had allowed unto him twelve sparrs out of the said six score now appointed to the said galliglasse, which he bestowed and distributed at his owne will and pleasure, and that the said twelve sparrs so now demaunded above the said six score sparrs is onelie by extorcion and ought not of right nor dutie to be paide, to the which effect also Anthonie Colcloghe, esquier, deposed by lyke othe before us, declared that what tyme he was constable the said castle of Fernes and had

chardge in those countries, he receaved the said twelve sparrs of the galloglasse themselves, and out of the vearie six score sparrs due and graunted unto her majesties galliglasse, for there bonought, and never exacted ne levyed the same as anie surchardge: With which deposicion the Odorans agreed, and Hughe Obolgir, an auncient man, that some tyme in those countries was serjant to the said Coleloghe, and leavied and receaved the said twelve score sparres to the said Anthonie Colcloughs use of the galliglasse, confessed the vearie same : 1570.

Wherefore it is ordered and decreed by us, the lorde deputie and counsell, whose names are hereunto subscrybed, that the said twelve sparrs so used to be allowed to McMorghowe in like maner shalbe hereafter allowed, defalked and taken out of the said six score sparrs graunted or to be graunted for the bonought of the said galliglasse, and reserved and stayed from tyme to tyme to her majesties use, to be distributed and bestowed at the discrecion and pleasure of us, the said lorde deputie or enie the governor for the time beinge :

And that hensforthe it shall not be lawfull for anie fermor of the castle of Fearnes, or eni other officer to aske, levie or demaunde the said twelve sparrs or anie parte thereof upon the inhabitantes aforesaid untill better matter be shewed and allowed before us, the said lorde deputie, or other governor, for proffe of the same, but the said xii sparres to remeine and to be alwaies parcell of the said six score sparres and no surchardge to be used over and above the said six score sparres. fol. 337.

Thomas Cusake.—Francis Agard.

[CCLXIV.]—At the Newerie, the xvth of Julye, 1570, the xiith yeare of the queenes majesties most prosperous raigne : fol. 337*b*.

H. Sydney :

It was condiscended and agreed by the lorde deputie, nobilitie and counsaill, whose names be here unto subscribed, the rest beinge absent upon necessarie occasions and lawfull excuses of service and have neverthelesse particulerlie yelded ther consentes by ther severall letteres and promised to the entrie thereof made in this booke to subscribe ther names, whose letteres were likewise redde before the rest of the counsell here present, videlicet, the erle of Kildares lettere, the vicountes of Gormaston and Baltinglas, the barones of Hothe, Delven, Dunsanie, Trimleston and Lowthe :

That for divers greate weightie and urgent occasions, aswell for service to be done in the Northe against the rebell, Tirrelaughe Lenaughe, as ellswhere within this realme where it shalbe thought necessarie for the quiet and tranquillitie thereof and the better assurance of the good subjectes, that a generall hostinge shalbe proclaimed by writte, after the auncient custome, for vi weekes, after the rate of thre plowlandes to a carte, the same to assemble at the hill of Taraghe, the xvth of August next or ells at suche daie and place after that daie as the lorde deputie by his letteres or proclamacion, with the forwarninge of ten daies shall signifie and appointe.

Robert Weston, canc.—T. Armachanus.—G. Kyldare.—C. Gormanston.—H. Midensis.—Crystofer Howthe.—Christofer Delvyn.—Robert Dyllon.—R. Trimletiston.—Lucas Dillon.—H. Draycott.—Thomas Cusake.—Francis Agarde.—John Chaloner.

1570. [CCLXV.]—A certificat of suche rentes and customes as hathe
ol. 338. bene received by the capteins of the Birnes in Sylelo,[1] and now is dew unto her majestie, by the othe of those whose names insuethe, videlicet:

Robert Tallon of Downlovan, John Tallon of Kilmore, Edmonde Grace of Walterstone, James Ewstace of Fryertoune, Edmunde Tallon of Gylberstoune, Edmunde Ewstace of Curraneorne, Henry Curren of Knockedowne, Heughe Carraghe of Kylquyken, Gerald McKeon of Balleclan, Donogh Dowe of Ballekonill, Murgho McDonil of the Byrtace, Hughe McKgyllepatrike of Bynnore, Rory McKeyogho of Carnowe, and Elleaghe McCoulo:

1. The said jurors affirme that ther was yerely levied by the sergeant appointed in Sylelo by Obirne, as as chief captene of his name, five powndes, Irishe, indifferentlie, upon the freholders and ther tenantes, to the use of the said captein: And at the ende of everie vii yeares at least the said rent was dowbled, so that ten powndes was the seventh yeare paied by the name of galloglashe money.

2. Also thei affirme that the said Obyrne had every yeare twenty four shillings levied indifferentlie upon the freeholders ther for the expences of kerne, which money also thei finde to apperteigne to her majestie.

3. And that the said capten had of every freholder that died within the precincte of Sylelo, 6*s.* 8*d.* for heryot by custome, due nowe to her majestie.

4. And that the said capten had yerely one mutton in sommer, and one hogge or porke of a yeare old, at the least, everie winter, out of every towne within the said countrie and a custome plowday; and a
fol. 338*b*. custome rippe day of everie one that had a plowe within the countrey, dew now to her highnes.

5. Also thei affirme that sir John Travers, late of Munketon, knight, receved (as captein of Sylelo aforesaid) all the said rentes and customes. And that after the decease of the said sir John the erle of Kildare, by his conestables, received also the same.

By Mychall Fytzwyllyams, surveyor.

[CCLXVI.]—Omnibus Christi fidelibus, ad quos hoc presens scriptum pervenerit, Cornelius, alias Conor, comes Thomond, salutem in Domino sempiternam: Noveritis me, etc. (as at p. 213).

1570–71.
fol. 339*b*. [CCLXVII.]—At the castell of Dublin, the seventh of Februarie, 1570[–71], and in the thirteenth yeare of the queenes majesties most prosperous raigne:

H. Sydney:

It was condiscended, concluded and agreed by us, the lorde deputie and counsell, assembeled, whose names be hereunto subscribed, that forasmuche as by the composicion passed betwene the queenes majestie and Thomas Might, surveiour of her majesties victualls for this realme, beringe date at Grenwich, the xiiii[th] of May, 1568, the xi[th] yeare of her

[1] Shillelagh, co. Wicklow.

majesties raigne, that the said Might shuld have yearely for the provicion of her highnes garrison residing in the northe partes a proporcion and cesse of otes of two thousand four hundred peckes: 1570-71.

We have resolved and agreed that the said proporcion shall be reared and levied upon theis counties followinge, videlicet, upon

The countie of Dublin,	ccc.
The countie of Meathe,	cccccc.
The countie of Kildare,	ccc.
The countie of Lowthe,	ccc.
The countie of Westmethe,	ccc.
The countie of Wexforde,	ccc.
The countie of Kilkenny,	cc.
The countie of Caterlaughe,	cc.

We have further agreed and concluded that the same proporcion of otes so cessed, reared and levied shalbe delivered to the handes of Thomas Might or his assigney at the places specified in our warrantes; he painge redie money for the same, after the rate of sixteen pence Irishe the pecke, accordinge to the said composicion.

Robert Weston, canc.—W. Fytzwylliam.—N. Bagenall.—Jo. Plunket. Robt. Dyllon.—Thomas Cusake.—Francis Agard.

[CCLXVIII.]—The moste humble submission of the unworthie and moste unnaturall earle of Clancahir otherwise called McCarty More, made unto the right honorable sir Henry Sidney, knighte of the moste noble order of the gartier, lorde president of hir majesties counsaile in Walles, and lord deputy generall of Ireland, and to the lordes and others hir majesties counsaile of the said realme presented the xiiii[th] of Februarie [1570–1] in the the xiii yeare of hir highnes most prosperous reigne: fol. 340.

I, the moste unworthie and unnaturall earle of Clan Cahir, with inwarde sorrow of mynde and moste hertie repentance, callinge to mynd the greate benefittes and exeding bounty I have in sondry sortes receavid from the quienes most excellent majestie and the place of honor and preheminence I have bene moste unworthily called unto by hir highnes, far greater then I, accurssid creature, have or can desearve or that eny of myne auncestors heartofore have had, which with bitter teares and compunction of mynde, I moste humblie do confesse do so muche the more agravat the heiniousnes of my offences and heapith more haboundantly hir majesties most just indignation against me do most humbly acknowledge and confesse before you my dier lord and governor and this honorable table: That beinge seduced by that most pernicius rebell, James Fitzmorice, and other of the Geraldines, his asociates, uppon a faulse pretence to have a parle with me and to conclude a friendship betwixt the saide James and Mr. Richard Grenvile, then shirriffe of the county of Corcke, which when it toke no effect, I, forgettinge my ductie to Almightie God and obedience to hir majestie was by subtill intysementes and most wicked perswacions induced and brought to take an unadvised and rassh othe; which done, I consequently enterid into that fury and maddnes of unnaturall rebellion against my most gracious soveraigne, combyning myself bothe with sir Edmond Buttler and with all the rest of the principall rebels of Ireland, whearin in sondry degrees I have disloyally swearvid and declyned from

1570-71. fol. 340b. my alegience to hir highnes, by raising traiterously hir majesties subjectes against hir highnes peace and lawes, besieging hir tounes, shamefully mordering and distroinge hir subjectes, bourninge hir houses and castles: And besides have committed, sins my entery into that my disobedience, sondry grivïouse offences and heyniouse and detestable treasons, deservinge extreme punishment and sharpe correction, which my heynious misdemaynors, as I neither meane nor indeede can in eny sort justify or defend by eny coulor, so do I for the same, prostrate hear before your lordeshippes with most penitent and humble mynde, humblie with all reverence, voluntaryly and freely yeld and submitt my bodie, liffe, goodes and landes to the order and dispossission of hir highnes:

Beseeching with all humility and due reverence your good lordeshippe, my gracious lorde and governor, and you the rest lordes and others of hir majesties honorable counsaile to take compassion uppon me and to be meanes to the quiens majestie that hir highnes, who hathe bene ever to hir imortall fame, inclyned to mercy and petty, will now voutchsaulf to receave me, moste vile and unworthy wreache of hir creacion, to hir clemency and mercy and extend uppon me (above my desertes) hir moste graciouse pardon, uppon assuerid trust of my loyalty heareafter, for sithe I came first into sir Humfrey Gilbert and gave in myne onelie sonne into his handes, as a pleadg of my loialty, trouthe, and fidelity, I have sins contynued a good faithefull and true subject, and readie at all times to employ myself in hir majesties service so far forthe as my poore hability would extend unto, as bothe the earle of Ormond, when he had chardg, and likewise sir Humfrey Gilbert, in the time of his chardge, can well testify and declare, which if hir majesty shall do by your good meanes, and the rather for that I simply hear prostrate uppon my knees before your honors submitt myself,
fol. 341. liffe, landes and goodes and am come in to present myself voluntary before you, without eny pardon or protection which I had, either by word, letter or promes in eny sort, I utterly relinquish and forsake, reposeinge myself in your mercifull consideracions, and petifull regard of my poore and wretched estate and hoping that theise demonstracions and tokens of my loyalty hearafter may move your grave wisdoms to be meanes to the quenis majestie for me:

And I shall according to my moste bounden duety praie to Almightie God to grant her highnes a moste prosperous and happie raigne over all her dominions and subjectes and immortall triumphe over all her enemies, and likewise that it will please Him to unseele myne eyes and graunt me grace by my duetifull and humble service heareafter (which I do dedicat to her majesty to the last drop of my blud to be spent) to acquitt and recompence some part of my grivious offences past which I will endeavour myself to performe:

In testimony of all and singuler the premisses to be true, I, the said earll of Clancahir, have hearunto subscribed my name,—Donyll Clancare.

This peticion was exhibited the daie and yeare above written to the lord deputy and counsell assembled at the castle of Dublin, and, for testimony theareof, they have heareunto subscribed their names and have commanded the same to be enrolled.

Henry Sydney.—Robert Weston, canc.—T. Armachanus.—Adam Dublin.—Henry Draycott.—Thomas Cusake.—William Fitzwilliams.—John Plunket.—N. Bagnall.—Lucas Dillon.—Robert Dillon.—John Chaloner.

[CCLXIX.—An ordre passed for John Horne, of the cytty of Glocester, against the inhabitantes of the toune and county of Wexford, 1570[-1]: 1570–71. fol. 341b.

By the lord deputy and counsaile:
H. Sydney:
Right trustie and welbeloved, we greete you well: Wheareas uppon the longe, pettifull and just complainte of John Horne, of the cittie of Glocester, mariner, declaringe a robbery committed uppon a barcke of his factor, Henry Smithe, within Hampton poole, in the ryver of Wexforde, in the which William Warren, master of the said barcke, was morderid, and the saide Smithe, with diverse others grieviouselie wounded, and the somme of fourskore ten poundes, sterling, taken from the said barcke:

And notwithstandinge the truthe of the facte was certeinly knowne with undowbted presumptions that the doers thereof wear some of the inhabitantes theareabowte, yet, what throughe conseilement and corruption, and what throughe the negligence of them that should make searche, suche parsiality was used as the offenders could not be founde out:

Tendringe the case to be of suche weightie consideration as was neither, on the one part, to be so lett slipp unserched nor unpunnished, nor, on the other part, to lette so manifest a losse so duely folowed to be unrestored and unrecompensed, we directed to you and others our commission to call before you suche as you should thinke meete, bothe of the towne and countrey, and sending youe thearewith such examinations as moughte leade you to the better knowledge to finde oute the truthe, we required you to examine and try oute by all meanes possible, either by those examinacions or of eny thinge rysinge theareof, who wear the malefactors, with suche further instructions as we at that time thoughte convenient and was in the said commission further declared, which we thinck to be so well in your remembrance, as we accompte it not matteriall eftesones to repeate it:

But, even as then we directed our doinges accordinge to reason and good conscience, so, seeinge by your certificat how little that mylde kinde of procedinges hathe prevaled, and that you have taken their owne exposission of a pretence to take the money with lawe, as an excuse to purdge them from the suspition of takinge it as it was taken fol. 342.
in deede againste the lawe. And that in . . .[1] you rather retourned the mattir to us unperfected, then have done eny thinge to shew your diligence to do so muche as in this case is to be required:

Wee have thoughte mete uppon our first considerations to procede accordinge to our former determinacion to deale with more extremitty then we hoped that you should have had cause, sendinge againe theare-fore unto you the said examinacions to gather of the presumptions:

Thiese be to require you and, in hir majesties name, streightly to chardge and comaunde you and every of you to call unto you suche and so meny grave, honest and wise gentlemen, or other the inhabitantes of the towne and countrey as be of best credites by your judgment shalbe thoughte moste meet for your assistance:

And that you by their advise or so meny of them as shall joyne with you doe impose and sesse the saide somme of fourskore ten poundes, sterlinge, uppon the inhabitantes bothe of the towne and countrey, using thearein suche indifferency as it may appere that you be neither carried with favor nor malice, havinge neverthelesse good regard that

---

[1] MS. indistinct.

1570–71. you bear your hand in this case moste heaviest uppon suche as you finde cause moste vehemently to suspect to be culpable of the fact:

Gyvinge also unto you further authority, by vertue hearof, that when you have so imposed and sessed the said somme of fourskore ten poundes that within convenient time you do procede to the leavyinge theareof and every part theareof accordinge as you shall impose it:

fol. 342b. So as you or one of you by your agrement faile not to make payment of the same to the lorde justice that then shalbe, or to suche as he shall appoincte heare in Dublin, to receave the same, to the use of the complaynant before the xx[th] daie of Maie next cominge after the date heareof:

And if eny shall disobey you, or make default of payment contrary to your appoinctement, we give you hearby authority and power, to use your discretions, to leavy it, either by distresse or imprisonement, as you shall thincke most necessary, to recover the said payment:

And whear, peradventure, to thiese bad begyninges of their partes they shall so go onwarde as their malice shalbe suche as they shall maligne this order of our procedinge and theareuppon seeke to disobey it, wee doe earnestly pray you, and for the honor of this state, specially require you to publishe and make openly knowen unto them in our behaulf (that we hold the fact so horrible, the doinge of it so detestable, the poore mens losses so lamentable, the consielment so crafty and the searche so negligent and the bolsteringe of it so stowte,)[1] as we by oure discreacions do judge it more agreeable with reason, conscience and lawe and consequently more with the honor of this borde to make a president of it in this sort as we have appoincted, then by the sufferance of it unredressed or unpunisshed to minister occasion to breede so daungerous an exsample to give encoradgementes to others in like casses to use the like factes and practises:

fol. 343. And yet our meaninge is, and so we heareby signify bothe to you and them, that if by thiese meanes or any other waye that you or they can devise, that the verey offenders may be founde oute, and be brought to aunsweor accordinge to the lawe, that then this our order which we are dryven unto, for the extreme remedy, shall cease and be of non effect:

And otherwise we ernestly loke for, that you faile not in anywise to accomplishe the premisses in all the poinctes according this our order, as we shall thincke that you have good wills to assist or good porposes which we suerly determine to have to be performed:

And nothinge dowbtinge but you will deale thearein accordingly, we bid you righte hertily farewell. At Dublin the xvii[th] of February, 1570[–71].

Robert Weston, canc.—T. Armachanus.—N. Bagenall.—Lucas Dillon.—Thomas Cusake.—Francis Agarde.—H. Draycott.

[CCLXX.]—By the lord deputye and counsell:

H. Sydney:

Wheareas, for the better service of the queens majestie, as well in the sure and certaine delivery of the letteres directed from us, as also for the servinge of other proces from other the courtes of recorde within this realme, there he lately ordeyned certaine pursevantes or ordinarye messengers with ordinary allowances for their attendaunce in her

[1] The portion within parenthesis is underlined in the MS.

majesties causes, amongst whome we have admytted and allowed John Lynche alias Turcke, to be a pursevant or messenger for this bourd and all other her majesties courtes : 1570–71. fol. 343b.

Forasmuche as that many tymes chaunceth that the said pursevantes be sent for other mens causes either for disobedience of former letteres or to answere some other mysdemeanors by which the said pursevantes susteyne great cost and labor, as well of their horsses as themselves, we have thought it verye reasonable and doe hereby ordeyne that all persons upon whom the said pursevantes shall serve any proces from any court of recorde or to whome they shall bringe any lettere from us, the lord deputie, or from this bourd for any contempte, shall pay unto the pursevant that shall serve the proces or deliver the said lettere eche man according to his degree, videlicet,

Every archebishopp and earle, ten shillings ;

Every vicount, baron and bushoppe, six shillings, eightpence ;

Every knight degree twenty shillings; every esquier and gentleman two shillings, sixpence ;

And every other person of meane degree twenty pence currant money of this realme.

And for every day that any man shall remayne in the keepinge of the said pursevant after the proces served or his lettere delivered before his appearance the party so remayning shall gyve unto the said pursevant in degree above said :

Every archebushope and earle, four shillings ;

Every visconte, barone, bushoppe, three shillings ;

Every knight two shillings; every esquire and gentleman sixteen pence ;

And every other person of mean degree twelve pence of like money :

And the same some to be paied or agreed for before the partie be dischardged of his said appearance. Provided always that this order shall not extende to chardge any man that is sent for for the service of the queenes majestie without any former mysedemeanor or contempt made against hym :

And this our order to be observed as well of the partie of the pursevant, as of all others without any further demaund or refusall.

Yeoven the 22 of Marche, 1570-[71].

Robert Weston, canc.—T. Armachanus.—Adam Dublin.—John Plunket.—Lucas Dillon.—Francis Agard.

1570-71. fol. 1b. [CCLXXI.]—[1.]—The forme of the othe mynystred to suche as be admytted to be of the king and queenes majesties counsell :

Ye shall sweare to be true and faythefull to our soverayne lord and lady, the kings and queenes majesties, and their counsell, to conceale and kepe secrete from tyme to tyme. And for the better furtherance of their majesties servyce to geve your beste advyse and counsaill. And in all thinges concernyng their highnes honor and proffyte to use suche diligencye and cyrcomspectyon as to a true counsaillour shall appertayne. And that ye shall by no meanes consente to their disheryson or hynderances, but shall make declaracyon thereof to the lord deputie for the tyme beyng yf you have tyme therto, or otherwyse to such of their majesties counsaill as ar nexte to you, as well of that as all other mattiers that maye towche their majesties servyce or be prejudyciall in any condycion to their personnes, or to the person of their deputie for the tyme beyng. So helpe you God, in Christ Jesus, and all sainctes.

[2. Oath of supremacie :]

I, A. B., do utterlie testifie and declare in my consciens that the kings highnes is thounlie supprime governour of this realme, and of all other his highnes dominions and contries, as well in all spirituall or ecclesiasticall things or causes as temporall, and that no foren prince, person, prelate, state or potentate hath or ought to have eny jurisdiction, power, superioritie, preeminence or aucthoritie ecclesiasticall or spirituall within this realm; and therefore I do utterlie renownce and forsake all foren jurisdiccions, powers, superorities, and aucthorities, and do promise that from henceforth I shall beare faith and trewe alliegeaunce to the kings highnes his heires and successors, and to my power shall assist and defende all jurisdictions, pryveleges, preeminences and aucthorities graunted or belonginge to the kings highnes hys heires and successours or united and annexed to the imperiall crowne of this realme: So helpe me God, in Christ Jesus, and by the contents of this booke.

Bothe these oathes are written in the end of the Blacke Booke, begininge 1571.

fol. 2b. [3.]—The oath that shalbe ministred to Mr. William Ussher,[1] clarke of the councell, nowe to be sworne this day, beinge the 25th of Marche, 1594 :

Youe shall swere to the loyall and faithfull to our soveraigne lord the kings majestie, and to be secrett in all matters that shalbe handled in councell, and whereof you shalbe made privy, or shall come to your knowledge; and for the better furtherance of his majesties service you shall use your best endeavour to dischardge your place and office of clarke of the councell, whereunto by his majesties letteres patentes you are nowe preferred, and in all matters that maie touche his majesties service or be prejudiciall in any condicion to the state or common weale, and whereof you shall have eny intelligence, you shall not faile but to make presente declaracion in every suche case to the lord deputie, or other chiefe governour of this realme for the tyme beinge, yf you shall have tyme thereto, or otherwise to suche of his majesties councell as shalbe nerest unto you so helpe you God, etc.

---

[1] In margin, at head of fol. 1* : "I ended the table of all the particular matters contained in this book the 19th of September, 1609.—Wil : Uscher."

Sir William Ussher's Table to the Council Book, Ireland, 1556–1570–71 :

	Page	
[I.]—A proclamation for the payment of the kinges and queenes debtes, [Dublin, 27 May, 1556]	1	fol. 1.
[II.]—A letter to the maior and constable of Carrickfergus, concerninge some victuals pertaineinge to Hugh Mac Nele Oge, and concerninge Phelym Baccaghes sonnes	„	fol. 2.
[III.]—A generall hosteinge to begin at such time as the lord deputie should thinke fitt	2	fol. 3.
[IV.]—A commission to take up corne for the provision of the forts of Leix and Offalie	3	fol. 3.
[V.]—Instructions to John Baseinge and others, appointed to goe with the queenes shipps northward upon Scottland	„	fol. 4.
[VI.]—The baron of Upper Ossory committed to the castle for his arrogansie and disobedience in a matter betwixt him and the erle of Ormonde	4	fol. 5.
[VII.]—Order for the payment of sir Anthonie St. Legers debts, dureing the time he was deputie heere	5	fol. 5.
[VIII.]—Order that the erle of Kildare shall keepe the fort of Dyngan in Offalie	„	fol. 6*b*.
[IX.]—Letter to commanders of ships sent against the Scots	6	fol. 7.
[X.]—What rates horsemen and footemen shall pay weeklie for ther owne dietts, ther horseboys and horses, videlicet 2*s*. everie horseman and footeman for his owne diett weeklie; everie horse-boy, 7*d*. a weeke, and everie horse for day and night haveing six sheves double bande and hay and glay one penny, sterling	„	fol. 7*b*.
[XI.]—Orders, taken at Knockfergus, August 10 [1556], to sir George Stanley, made then Generall of Ulster, with certaine commissioners whose advise he was to use	„	
Note that the seconde of these orders was to maintaine the right of holy church, and to defend the ministers therof and to build churches	„	fol. 8.
[XII.]—Indentures betwixt the lord deputie and councell, and the erle of Tirone and McDonnelle for maintenance of four hundred galloglas, and one hundred shott for a quarter for the defence of Ulster against the Scotts.—[Latin.]	7	fol. 9*b*.
[XIII.]—A cesse of 3,100 beoves upon the lords, captens, and gentlemen in Ulster, for the expulsion of the Scotts	8	fol. 10*b*.
[XIV.]—A protection, in Latin, to John O Neile, sonne to the erle of Tirone	9	fol. 11.
[XV.]—Order, in Latin, betwixt Phelim Duffe and the sonnes of Phelim Bacaugh, for the division of the Clanndeboys, the one to have all on the one side the river, the other on the other side, except the castell of Belfast	„	fol. 12.

Page

fols. 8–13. [XVI.]—Instructions to Andrew Brereton, Generall of Ulster, and others joyned in comission with him - - - - 10

Note the first for the church, as before.

fol. 16. [XVII.]—Order that sir William FitzWilliams shall deliver to sir Henrie Sidney the remaine of 2,500*li.*, which he should have delivered to sir Edmond Rows, knight, then vice-threasurer 12

fol. 16*b*. [XVIII.]—A note of the entering and discharge of capten Williamsons company - - - - - - - ,,

[XIX.]—A note expressinge such persons as are to sett forth and owe riseinge out to a generall hostinge, with the number of their men and the number of carts in every barony - - 13

fols. 17–21*b*. Conferr this with the latter bookes, and the newe freedomes will appeare. Note that the totall to this hostinge was 612 horse and 662 kerne - - - - - - - - - ,,

fol. 22. [XX.]—Warrant to the erle of Kildare to deliver the fort of Dinghain to capten Henrie Cowley and William Derby, placed in the roome of gentleman porter in that fort, with one man in wages at eightpence sterling per diem - - - - - 18

fol. 22*b*. [XXI.]—Commission to appoint watch to be kept in everie towne dureing the winter, with the penaltie for default - - 18

fol. 23*b*. [XXII.]—Commission to hear a variance betwixt Henry Oneyle and Henry Dowdall - - - - - 19

fol. 24*b*. [XXIII.]—Proclamation that noe corne shalbe carried out of the English Pale into the Irish countries, and that if any forrener buy any in the marketts the same to bee forfayte - - 20

fol. 25. [XXIV.]—Articles then used to be annexed to the marshall law which seemed then to be granted to two or three - - ,,

fol. 27. [XXV.]—Order that the lord deputie may at all times cesse a holding upon the country, for reformation of Leix and other countries upon the borders - - - - - - 22

fol. 27*b*. [XXVI.]—Order for a cesse of wheat, malt, and beoves upon the country for furnishing the garrisons - - - - ,,

fol. 28. [XXVII.]—Commission to Robert Dillon and John Plunkett of Donsoughley, to enquire of the hurts done by the erle of Ormonde and the barron of Upper Ossorys people, one against the other, and to certifie - - - - - 23

fol. 30*b*. [XXVIII.]—A note of the submission of Connell Oge Omore and the rest of his sept; wherin they disclaimed all their right in Leix and tooke such parcell therof for rent as the lord deputie thought meete to give them - - - - - - ,,

fol. 32. [XXIX.]—Order that commission shall issue to take the fifth pecke of everie farmer of porte corne to the kinge, payeinge to the partie double the price he is to pay the kinge - - - - 24

fol. 33. [XXX.]—Order touchinge stolen goods and trackinge of them, with other things touchinge the apprehension of malefactors - 25

	Page	
[XXXI.]—Order to enlarge Saunders and Raubynson from prison at Dublin - - - - - - - -	27	fol. 35.
[XXXII.]—Order to proclaime Rory and Donough Oconner traytors, and that the earle of Kildare, the lord of Delvin, Omulloy, and Magohegan shall follow the slantie they gave for them to the uttermost - - - - - - -	„	fol. 35*b*.
[XXXIII.]—The proclamation proclaymeinge the Oconnors traytors and offeringe rewarde for the heade of the chiefe of them; wherunto, for that it concerned the life of man, the archbushop of Dublin, then lord chancellor, and the bushopp of Meath would not consent, least they should incurre the danger of irregularitie - - - - - - - -	29	fol. 38
[XXXIV.]—Proclamation chargeinge all such as had any of the proclaymed Oconnors goods or cattell upon [cummericke] or otherwise, should give notice therof to the lord deputie, or otherwise incurr the punishment provided for maintainors of rebels - - - - - - - -	30	fol. 39.
[XXXV.]—Order for generall musters for levieinge of labourers to be sent to Offaly to cutt passes and mend toughers -	„	fol. 40.
[XXXVI.]—Order betwixt the baron of Donganon and Shane Onele - - - - - - - - -	31	fol. 41.
[XXXVII.]—Order for takeinge of labourers to cutt passes and mend toughers in Leix, Offaly and other places, upon the charge of the country - - - - - -	32	fol. 42.
[XXXVIII.]—Coppie of the letter commandinge the said laborers to bee mustered - - - - - - -	„	fol. 43.
[XXXIX.]—A direction and commission for generall musters	33	fol. 43*b*.
[XL.]—A proclamation for the victualinge of the souldiers, in theire throughfare, for money, with the order how - -	„	fol. 44.
[XLI.]—Indentures, in Latin, betwixt the lord deputie and councell and William Ocarroll, made capten of Ely - -	34	fol. 45.
Note the first article for maintenance of the Church; note his rent 12*l*. yearlie, his riseinge out: twelve horsemen, and twenty-four kearne, bonaght for eighty galloglasses for a quarter, and 120 cowes to the lord deputie for makeinge him capten. - -	„	
[XLII.]—Order betwixt Brian Offerrall and Fiaughe McTege for the captainship of Offerrall Banes country - -	35	fol. 46*b*.
[XLIII.]—Generall hosteinge to begin the 2 of August [1557], 3 and 4 of Phillip and Marie - - - - - -	36	fol. 47*b*.
[XLIV.]—Act that the overcharge upon the country of the Englishe Pale to the two last generall hostinges shall be noe president - - - - - - - - - -	„	fol. 48.
[XLV.]—Indentures betwixt the lord deputie and John Brimingham and his sonne, Walter, for the castell of Kennafadda	„	fol. 48.

Page

[XLVI.]—Indentures, in Latin, betwixt the lord deputie and
fol. 49b. Barnabee Offarrall, capten of Offarrall Banes country - - 37
Note the first article for the Church; his riseing out: six horsemen, and thirty kearne; his rent fifty fatt beoves.

[XLVII.]—Order that neither the Tooles of the Fertry nor of Glancry shall have any spendinge upon the tenants of Glancap, but that they shall stand onelie to such impositions as the lord
fol. 51. deputie for the time shall lay upon them - - - - - 39

[XLVIII.]—Act to wage fifty kerne to goe to the generall
fol. 52. hostinge - - - - - - - - - ,,

[XLIX.]—A proclamation, in Latin, inhibitinge the reliefe of Denough Oconnor, and those that abandoned the castell of Mulighe, and for the good usage of those who weare laste to
fol. 53. keepe it - - - - - - - - - - ,,

[L.]—A proclamation that none shall keepe, upon paine of one hundred pounds, any horseman or kearne of Leix, Offaly, Slemarge, or Glanmoulyry, for that they releeved and joyned with the
fol. 56. rebells in the night although they appeared civill in the day - 41

[LI.]—Order that sir Henry Radclyf, leiutenant of Leix and Offaly, may by himselfe or his deputie procecute any the dwellers, upon the borders of those countryes, whom hee cann prove did
fol. 57. assist the rebells - - - - - - - - 42

[LII.]—A cesse of corne and beoves upon Meath, West Meath, and Kildare, for furniture of the fortes in Leix and
fol. 58. Offalye - - - - - - - - - - ,,

[LIII.]—Order that sharpe warr shalbe made upon Shane Onele, to bee from time to time ordered as the lord deputie
fol. 58b. should thinke fitt - - - - - - - 43

[LIV.]—Order on the spoyleing, burneinge, and takeinge of a great quantitie of victualls fownde at Armagh, the first jorney
fol. 59. made upon Shane Onele - - - - - ,,
Note what a superstitious care they had of the holy places, images, and other ornaments of the church.

[LV.]—Another cesse upon the counties of Meath, Westmeath,
fol. 59b. and Kildare, for the forts in Leix and Offaly - - - - ,,

[LVI.]—A proclamation that none shall carry corne out of the Pale into Irishmens countries, nor noe forreners to buy the same
fol. 60. in marketts upon paine of forfeture - - - - - 44

[LVII.]—Order that 200*li.* sterlinge shalbe taken up in Meath, which, with the default of the Polles kerne, is to be delivered to the thresurer to bee imployed for wageinge of kernes as the lords
fol. 61. justices, in the absence of the lord deputie, should thinke good - ,,

[LVIII.]—Order betwixt Francisco Dies, Spaniard, and
fol. 61. Henry Corneilson, defendant, for certaine merchandize - - 45

[LIX.]—Aug. 10, 1557.—Pledges taken of sundry the Irish
fol. 64. in Leinster - - - - - - - - - 47

1557-8, Feb 6.—Sir Henry Sidney, lord justice:

	Page	
[LX.]—An act wherby promise is made to Tibot Omolloye (upon the revoulte of his brother, Arte) to be cheife capten of Ferkeall - - - - - - - -	47	fol. 65.
[LXI.]—Indentures, in Latin, betwixt the lord deputie and Omolloye - - - - - - - -	,,	fol. 66.
Note the first concerninge religion. Note his riseinge out: four horsemen, twelve kerne, bonaught for halfe a quarter of a yeare to a battayle of galloglasses; one hundred beoves for his name of captaine.		
[LXII.]—A cesse upon the country for a proportion of corne to the forts in Leix and Offaly - - - - - -	49	fol. 68.
Note a marginall note why the countie of Dublin is cessed equally with Meath.		

1558.—Earle of Sussex, lord deputie:

[LXIII.]—Orders for watches and beacons upon the sea-coast, and for the bodderagges betwixt the Pale and Orayly -	50	fol. 69.
[LXIV.]—Order for the lord Power - - -	51	fol. 70.
[LXV.]—Order betwixt Anthony Colclough and Phillip Isam, for the mannor of Rosegarlande - - - - - -	,,	fol. 70b.
Note that Colclough, after the cancellinge of his lease, was restored to the possession upon a constat.		fol. 70b.
[LXVI.]—Order for removeinge Gerrald McOliver Fitzgerrald [from] forcible possession in the castell [of] Ardenegraghe in Dillons country - - - - - - - -	52	fol. 72.
[LXVII.—Order to mayor of Waterford, 1558, in relation to ship from Antwerp] - - - - - - - -	,,	fol. 72b.
[LXVIII.]—Orders, in Latin, betwixt Orayly and the State -	53	
Note, one article is that he shall cause the queenes money to passe in his country accordinge the value therof; belike it was copper.		fol. 73.
[LXIX.]—A generall hostinge, to sett forth within ten days after proclamation - - - - - - - -	54	fol. 75.

1558.—Sir Henry Sidney, lord justice:

[LXX.]—Order for one hundred kerne to lye upon the borders of Meath, next Offaly, at the charge of the country for six weekes - - - - - - - - -	55	fol. 75b.
[LXXI.]—Order that Thomas Fleminge shall have the leadinge of a hundred of the Polles kerne into the North at vid. sterling apeece per diem, where their pay to hostinges is but ivd. sterling	,,	fol. 76.
[LXXII.]—An oath taken by the erle of Thomond and the gentlemen of Thomond - - - - - - -	56	fol. 76b.
Note this one article—to be true and faythfull friends to the citie of Limericke. - - - - - -		

Page

fol. 77b. [LXXIII.]—Variance betwixt the earles of Ormonde and Desmonde, concerninge the prise wines of Youghall and Kinsale and the limits of the liberties of Tipperary - - - - 57

fol. 79. [LXXIV.]—Recognizance [in Latin] of 200li. acknowledged by the erles of Desmonde and Ormonde for the performance of a paire of indentures concerninge the variances before - - „

fol. 79b. [LXXV.]—Indentures betwixt the erle of Desmonde and the lord Roche; wherby the lord Roches country is freed from the erle - - - - - - - - - 58

fol. 81. [LXXVI.]—Indenture betwixt the erle of Desmonde and Teige McCormocke; wherin the erles clayme to Muskerry in right of his lady is mencioned - - - - - - 59

fol. 82b. [LXXVII.]—Indentures, in Latin, betwixt the State, the erle of Clanrycarde and the towne of Gallway, for good orders to be kept betwixt the saide towne and Clanrycarde - - - 60

fol. 86. [LXXVIII.]—Order deposing William Ower Okarwell from the captenship of Ely, and makeing Teige Okarwell capten; in which the breyhouns have libertie to end causes - - - 63

By this order the lord deputie and earle of Ormonde doe become slanty, to pursue the breakers therof to the uttermost.

fol. 87. [LXXIX.—Notes on sureties for Omore and Omolloy.] 64

fol. 87b. [LXXX.] Order that New haggarde in the baronie of Kenles, in the countie of Meath, shall beare with the country charge - „

fols. 88–91. [LXXXI.]—Kinge Henry VIII.: letteres for two goshawkes and four greyhoundes to the marquis of Saria and his sonne, yearlie out of this kingdome; with like letteres patents from king Edward VI., and kinge Philipp for the same - - - „

1558.—Sussex, lord deputie:

fol. 92. [LXXXII.]—Cesse of corne upon the Pale, and of beoves and swine upon the Irishe countries, for the provision of the garrisons - - - - - - - - - 66

fol. 94. [LXXXIII.]—An act for deliveringe a new great seale to Hugh [Curwen], lord archbushopp of Dublin, with cancellinge and defaceinge the old seale, and on deliveringe likewise of newe seales to the fowre courts - - - - - - 68

1558–9.—Sir Henry Sydney, lord justice, primo Elizabethæ:

fol 95. [LXXXIV.]—Indentures betwixt William Ower Ocarrwell and the State - - - - - - - - „

fol. 97. [LXXXV.]—Order betwixt the Offarrolls for halfe the tanisthippe which belonged to the captenshippe - - - 70

fol. 98. [LXXXVI.]—A generall hostinge, to begin the last of August, 1559, primo Elizabethæ - - - - - - - „

fol. 99. [LXXXVII.]—Commission to trie challenges betwixt the baron of Upper Ossorie, and Edmonde Butler, capten of the countie of Kilkeny - - - - - - - - - 71

[1] The figures XCI., XCI.A, on pages 74–5, should be XC, XCI., as above.

	Page	
Observe the meanes used to find out what monies were brought.		
[CXXI.]—A proclamation for punishinge of merchants and such as have anythinge to sell that doe indent and bargaine before they make price what coyne they will receive for payment	116	fol. 167*b*.
[CXXII.]—Order that noe monie but wares shalbe paid to any marchant stranger for such commodities as are brought thither, unlesse he enter into bonds to imploy the monie in commodities - - - - -	117	fol. 168*b*
[CXXIII.]—A proclamation inhibitinge the transportation of monie out of this realme - - - -	"	fol. 169*b*.
[CXXIV.]—Copie of the queenes letteres for sir William Fitzwilliams to be lord justice, in absence of the lord leiuetenant, directed to our right trustie, and right welbeloved and to our trustie and welbeloved our councellors and States of our realme of Irelande - - - - - - -	118	fol. 170*b*.
[CXXV.]—Order for sendinge garrans, laborers, and carres out of the counties of the Pale, to make certaine fortificacions, trenches and toughers in Leix and Offaly - - - -	"	fol. 171.
[CXXVI.]—Proclamation declareinge the value of the coynes how they should be taken heere - - - -	119	fol. 173.
[CXXVII.]—Proclamation inhibiting the transportation of coyne - - - - - - -	121	fol. 174*b*.
[CXXVIII.]—Order establishinge the rate of the redd Harpe and Rose halfpenny - - - - - -	122	fol. 175*b*.
[CXXIX.]—Generall hostinge, 1561 - - - - -	"	fol. 176.
[CXXX.]—Act abolisheinge the cheife captenry of the three seiptes of galloglasses, but that they should bee alike - -	123	fol. 176*b*.
Note castinge the dice for the indifferent levieinge theire bonnaght.		
[CXXXI.]—A cesse of wheate, mault, beofes, and other provisions for the forts of Leixe and Offaly - - - -	"	fol. 177.
[CXXXII.]—Another cesse for the forts and garrisons -	125	fol. 179.
[CXXXIII.]—An act for retaineinge in pay some souldiers which were discharged - - - -	127	fol. 181.
[CXXXIV.]—Instructions under the queens hand to sir Nicolas Arnold, knight, to take the musters of the companys in pay, grownded upon William Breminghams information -	"	fol. 181*b*.
[CXXXV.]—Generall hostinge, 1563 - - -	128	fol. 183.
Note the first conversion of cartes into garrons, after the rate of five garrons for each carte.		
[CXXXVI.]—Instructions to certaine commissioners to parle with the Moores - - - - - - - -	"	fol. 183*b*.
[CXXXVII.]—Resolutions for the prosecution of the Omoores - - - - - - -	130	fol. 184*b*.

Page

fol. 186. [CXXXVIII.]—Copie of the queens letter for sir Nicholas Arnolde to bee justice, 1564, the sixth yeare of her raigne - 132

fol. 186b. [CXXXIX.]—Letter from the lords, significinge the peace made with France - - - - - - „

fol. 187. [CXL.]—A remembrance of the deliverie of certaine instructions, toucheing the earle of Desmonde, to sir Thomas Cusake, with the queenes letter toucheinge Cormocke Oconor - - 133

fol. 187b. [CXLI.]—Letter to the earle of Kildare, toucheinge the bonaughte upon the Annalye - - - - „

fol. 188. [CXLII.]—Another letter toucheinge the same matter - 134

fol. 188b. [CXLIII.]—The election of sir Nicholas Arnold to be lord justice - - - - - - - - „

Observe that notwithstandinge her majesties letters, the lord chancellor issued writts to the lords and others who have to doe with the said election, according the ancient usage.

fol. 189b. [CXLIV.]—An opinion of the lord justice and councell that in respect of the general quiet except the Moores, the army might be reduced to 200 horse, comprehendinge therin 92 horse graunted to officers by letters patents, and to 500 foote - - 135

fol. 190b. [CXLV.]—Warrant for an intertainement of three shillings per diem to Arte Oneill, base sonne of the baron of Donganon, in respect of his service, for himselfe and his three horsemen - 136

fol. 191. [CXLVI.]—Answer to Odoneills peticion, 1564 - - „

fol. 192. [CXLVII.-VIII.]—Act for marshall law to be given to severall gentlemen in each countie - - - - 137

fol. 194. [CXLIX.—Order touching David Hay, of Wexford] - - 139

fol. 196. [CL.]—Act for prosecution of the Omores and Oconnors - 140

Note that the souldiers who weare removed out of the Pale to more fit places upon the borders where they weere to be victualled accordinge the markett those baronies where they weare before cessed, in the Pale, weare to beare the charge of soe much as those victuals cost, above that which the souldiers weare accustomed to pay.

fol. 196b. [CLI.]—Act authorizeinge the lord chancelor and others in the absence of the lord justice to order all such matters touchinge the State as the lord justice should write or send unto them in - „

fol. 197. [CLII.]—Consultations touchinge the service and defence of the country - - - - - - - 141

fol. 197b. [CLIIA.]—New commission to John Tirell - - - - „

fol. 198. [CLIII.]—Act for continuing the cesse of 150 holding kerne upon the county of Dublin for three weekes - - - „

fol. 198b. [CLIV.—Orders at Dublin, 26 October, 1564] - - - 142

fol. 199. [CLV.]—Order for holding kerne in several counties against the Occonnors - - - - - - „

	Page	
[CCXXXII.]—A letter to the lords of the council in England, for erectinge a free schoole in Galway - - - -	225	fol. 302*b*.
Observe the whole letter well written in a good cause: Note one of the lawes of Galway that none shall beare any office ther before he speak English.		
[CCXXXIII.]—A letter from the bishopp and chapter of Fearnes concerninge their residence at Fearnes - - -	226	fol. 311*b*.

Sir Henry Sidney, June, 1569:

[CCXXXIV.]—A generall hostinge - - - - -	227	fol. 312.
[CCXXXV.]—The maior of the cittie of Dublin, Michaell Bee, committed to the castle of Dublin, for disobeying the lord deputies commandment, fined in one hundred pounds, Irish, and after two days inlarged - - - - - - -	,,	fol. 312*b*.
[CCXXXVI. 1.]—An act for proclaimeinge sir Edmunde, Edward and Piers Butler, rebells, if they appeared not by a day	228	fols. 313, 314.
[CCXXXVI. 2.]—Transcript of preceding order - - - -	229	fol. 314.
[CCXXXVII.]—An entry of the delivery of certaine writts by Edmund Molyneux, clearke of the counsell - - -	,,	fol. 314*b*.
[CCXXXVIII.]—Act of counsell authorisheinge the lord deputy to increase the garrison - - - - -	,,	fols. 315–316.
[CCXXXIX.]—A letter from the lords toucheinge the lord Mountjoye for digginge for and making of allam, etc. - -	230	fol. 316*b*.
[CCXL.]—A cesse of beeves upon the five counties - -	,,	fol. 317.
[CCXLI.]—An entry of a freedome of forty acres to John Lie, the interpreter, in respecte of maintaineinge a bridge upon the Blacke water, in countie Kildare - - - -	231	fol. 317*b*.
[CCXLII.]—A generall hostinge for 21 days converted into money - - - - - - - - - -	,,	fol. 318.
[CCXLIII.]—Order for the release of Thomas Stucley, prisoner in Dublin castell - - - - - -	232	fol. 319.
[CCXLIV.]—Protection by the erle of Ormonde to his brethren, sir Edmund, Edward and Piers Butler - -	233	fol. 320.
[CCXLV.]—The queenes letter touching the earle of Ormonde and his brethren - - - - - -	,,	fol. 321.
[CCXLVI.]—Act for committinge sir Edmund Butler to the castle of Dublin upon his brother, Piers his escape - -	234	fol. 322.
[CCXLVII.]—A generall hosting converted into money to wage kerne - - - - - - - - -	236	fol. 323*b*.
[CCXLVIII.]—A cesse of oates after the rate of sixteen-pence, Irish, the pecke - - - - - -	,,	fol. 324.
[CCXLIX.]—The queenes letter touching certaine sutes and petitions of the erle of Ormonde - - - - -	237	fol. 324*b*.

	Page	
[CCLXX.]—Order for the pursevants fees from all degrees -	254	fol. 343.
[CCLXXI.]—(1.) The forme of the othe mynystred to suche as be admytted to be of the king and queenes majesties councell. (2.) Oath of supremacie. (3.) The oath that shall be ministred to Mr. William Ussher, clarke of the councell, the 25th of Marche, 1594 - - - - - - - -	256	fols. 1*b.*, 2*b.*

APPENDIX.

I.

A table to the redd counsell booke, beginning in king Henrie the eighths raigne, the thirty-fourth yeare [1542–3]:

Ordinances made in the castle of Baleingary by Thadus cecus . . [1] and others, January 9, 1543–4. fol. primo.

Indentures betwixt the lord deputie and sir Odo ODonnell, knight, wherein he acknowledgeth that he inhabiteth the kings lands without payeinge anythinge, and when the kinge shalbe pleased to reforme the kingdome hee would pay as much for those lands as any man.[2]—1531, May 6.

Sir Anthonie Sentleger, deputie.

The peticion of the lord FitzWilliam Bourke, wherein hee desireth to have the fee farme of the towne of Gallway, Roscomon, the townes of Loghregh, Clare, Cloncashell, Ballesorwer, and Leytrom, which the said Fitz William Bourke built, to have in fee farme the cocketts of Sligo, Porterarde and Leighbourne, with other kreekes; to have the nameinge to the lord deputie men for all the sperituuall liveinges within his rule, except bushopricks, to which he will nominate noe unlearned persons. The said McWilliam promiseth a rent of £10 sterling per annum. fol. 4.

Ordinances and provisions made in the great parliament held at Dublin the 33 yeare of Henry 8. for reformation of the inhabitants of Thomond and connaght; wherin note many good statutes for the Church and common-wealth. fol. 7.

1541. July 2.—Indentures of agreement betwixt the O Carrolls for the captenry of Ely O Carroll. fol. 11

See the division made betwixt them.

1542. May 13.—Indentures betwixt Rory O Moore for the captenry of Lex. fol. 14, 25.

Note in the ende a division of —[3] betwixt the capten and the constable of Catherlagh:

1541. August 14.—Indentures with Brian McMahon alias Bryan McMaghery. fol. 16.

Note in all these indentures a renounceinge of the Popes authoritie.

1542–3. Feb. 10.—The monasterie of the gray friers in Downe—unsuppressed: fol. 18*b.*

Quere, what is now become of it? Vide fol. 130*b.*, where it seemes it was a cathedral church.

---

[1] MS. indistinct.

[2] *See* State Papers, Ireland, 1834, ii. 151.

[3] Blank in MS.

1541-2. January 6.—The capteury of Fercall to Arthure O Mull-
fol. 19 moye, upon the decease of his father, Charles:—I take the same now to be O Molloye.

Articles whereby Conatius O Neale binds himselfe; in the last he
fol. 20 promiseth to build the churches in his commande.

A note of a concordat that the hospitall of the Maudlins, neere
fol. 22. Killkenie, should not be suppressed.

A note of a concordat that the towne of Galway should be freed from
fol. 22. appearance to the parliament.

An entry of an attornment betwixt lord FitzWilliam Bourke, capten
fol. 22. and ruler of Connaght and Rowland, bushopp of Clonfert:

There, likewise, a note of concordat for the not suppressinge of
fol. 22b. Killconell, in the diocese of Clonfert.

fol. 23. The like for the abbey of Cnochan, beside Gallway.

fol. 23b. The peticion of Gerrald Kavenagh, of Ballymoare in Idrone.

fol. 24. Parcell of lands claymed by some of the Kavanaghs.

fol. 27. Submission of Maquillen:

Note he desireth to be reputed an Englishman as his ancestors were and are: Three horses to the kinge yearlie and his riseinge out.

fol. 28b. Orders between O Neile and Phelim Rooe.

The submission of McDonnell, galloglasse: his risinge out: eighty
fol. 30. sparrs.

O Neiles answer touchinge his submission and such name and lands
fol. 31. as the kinge would give him.

1542. May 24.—The submission of Hugh O Kelly, abbot of Knock-
fol. 32. moy, in the diocess of Tuam:

Note that the parsonage of Gallway belongeth to this abbey. He promiseth to serve the kinge in Connaght with eighty horse accompanied of Scotts and sixty foote. He putteth in his sonne, Conner, pledge. A good abbot.

The submission of Owen McMorish Ochonor, captain of Irey:
fol. 33. riseinge out: eight horse; to cut passes.

The submission of James, earle of Desmonde:

fol. 34b. Note a priviledge claymed by the earle of Desmonde, not to come to parliament, graund counsell, or within any walled town (since the beheading of his grandfather at Drogheda).

John Gouldsmith and Dermitius Rian, batchelors of law and public
fols. 37, 38. notaries.

Order betwixt the lord of Upper Ossory and Rory O Moore, capten of
fol. 39. Lex, concerninge Killena:

Note: O Moore hanged two of the tenants there which was put to the erige of the parson of Athy and James FitzGerralde. Quere, what the nature of erige[1] is.

Order betwixt Brian O Connor, capten of Offalie, and his brother
fol. 40. Charles.

fol. 41. Order concerninge the killinge of O Toole by Tirlagh McShane.

fol. 43. Submission of Tady O Donn, capten of Oregan:

Note, his riseinge out: twenty-four kearne, and a rent of six kine yearlie. Quere, what Eastbrooke or Toghesuier[2] is?

Submission of Maguinnesse, witnessed by Robert Cooley, master of the rowles; Thomas Walsh, one of the barons of the exchequer in England;
fol. 45b. John Mynne and William Cavendishe, commissioners of he kinge.

fol. 47. Submission of O Donnell. His riseing out: sixty horse, 120 kerne.

fol. 49. Submission of Barnaby O Rourke:

[1] Ransom for murder or manslaughter. [2] Lordship in Queen's county.

Note his oath to the supremacie; his riseinge out of twenty-four horse, eight foot; the liveings of his country held by laymen to be presented unto by the kinge, 20*li.* rent yearlie, his pettie lords.

Indentures with the lord Barre, alias the great Barre, McCartie More, lord Roch, the O Suillivans, and many others in that part of Mounster: fol. 52.

Note ther confederacy to be revenged upon those that shall breake the articles.

Submission of Kedagh O Molaghlinn, of Cloncolman: His riseing out: four horse and twenty-four kearne, and xlvjs. viij.*d.* rent. fol. 62*b.*

Submission of McQuillyn and O Cahan. fol. 62*b.*

Note, the condicions for fishinge the Band.[1]

14 July, 1543.—Order betwixt Conn O Neile, earle of Tyrone and O Donnell: fols. 65, 68*b.*

Note: That neither of them is to have any authoritie out of Tyrone or Tirconnell; ther contention for Enishowen. They renounce the Popes authoritie; fine for contempt.

Order betwixt the O Carrolls and the erle of Ormonde: fol. 70.

Note, that the erle of Ormonde is adjudged to have nothing to doe in Ely. Quere, what an erick[2] is?

Controversie referred to brehownes. fol. 71*b.*

Two new seales sent out of England, the one for the great seale, the other for the exchequer, 28 March, 1543.

The two old seales defaced and sent into England. fol. 72.

Con, earle of Tyrone, sworne of the kings privie counsell. fol. 72*b.*

The riseing out of the countie of Tipperary (turned into money) and others, to wage kerne. fols. 73*b.*, 74.

The carriages of the gennerall hosting turned into money after the rate of four plowland to a cart, and for evrie cart, 2*s.* viij *d.* per diem: fol. 76.

Observe how this mony was disposed of:

Warrant for levieing this mony: fol. 76*b.*

Order betwixt Conn O Neale, earle of Tirone, and Neale Connelaugh. fol. 76*b.*

The castell of Coolerane to be delivered to the custodie of O Cahan for the kinge. fol. 79.

O Donells gifte to the kinge of halfe the coquet of Sligo, and halfe the heareings[3] or other fish taken at Arran, Inisheninycadrin, and one hundred beofes yearelie to the lord deputie. fol. 80.

Morice [Murrough] earle of Thomond, sworne of the privie councell, 35 Henry 8. fol. 81.

A portion of Leinster allotted to John Travers, master of the ordnance, to rule, wherin the castell of Fearns is. fol. 82.

The lord of Upper Ossory committed to the cittie of Waterforde till he make restitution of some preys made in Leix. fol. 82*b.*

Recognizances of the capten of Leix. fol. 83*b.*

Newcastle in the Birnes [country] leased to sir Edward Basnet, deane of St. Patricks, for 21 yeares at 26s. viii*d.*, yearelie. fol. 84*b.*

The Poules of the countie of Meathe. fol. 85.

The septs of the Cavenaghs. fol. 85*b.*

Poynings act touching the armeing of the country. fol. 86*b.*

An oath of allegeance ministred to all such Irishmen as did submitt themselves to the kings majestie. fol. 87.

A proclamacion that noe sale of cattell other then on the markett day shall alter the propertie from the true owner. fol. 88*b.*

---

[1] Bann, river in Ulster. [2] Ransom for murder or manslaughter. [3] Herrings.

fol. 89. 1543. Proclamacion against utteringe clipped money.

fol. 89*b*. The duties of the capten of the kings kearne.

fol. 90. Articles for the Cavenaughs country:

Note: Against cuddies; order to follow stelths; against cane, ericke, the capten of the country to hange theeves taken with and to have 10*s*.
fol. 90. of the lord deputie for everie one; against glibb, etc.

fol. 93. McMurroghs riseinge out: twelve horsemen, thirty kearne.

O Realy, capten of Clonkeyle, did pay 20*d*. out of everrie plowlande
fol. 94. of sixteen ploughland in the said cuntry.[1]

O Dwire did pay the like rent, and for his riseing out four horsemen
fol. 94*b*. and twelve kerne:

fol. 94*b*. Gillernow O Maghir the like.

Hugh Bourke for Burghs country paid yearlie to the kinge 40*li*.
fol. 94*b*. sterling, and for his riseing out: eighty galloglas and twenty horsemen.

O Mullryane for the country Oney payd 40*s*. sterling, and for his
fol. 95. riseinge out six horsemen and twelve kearne.

Mcyorris Breminchan, for everie carucate of land within Bremyn-
fol. 95. chams country, 12*d*. sterling, yearelie.

O Flarty for his country paid 5*li*. sterling yearlie; for his riseinge out:
fol. 95. forty kearne.

O Bryne, for the country of Arre, paid sixpence Irish out of every
fol. 95*b*. carucate; riseing out: six horsemen and twenty-four kearne.

Melaghlin O Maden paid yearlie for evrie plowland xij*d*., Irish;
fol. 95*b*. to the hostinge: four horsemen, twelve kerne.

Hugh O Maden paid 8*d*. sterling for everie plowlande; to the hosting:
fol. 95*b*. four horse, twelve kerne.

Tybbott Bourke besides Limerike paid 8*li*. sterling yearelie; to the
fol. 96. hosting: twelve horse, 24 kearne.

fol. 96. Art O Mollaghlen paid 4*li*. sterling per annum.

Magohegan, for Kinaleagh to the hosting: four horse and twelve foote,
fol. 96*b*. and four fat marts yearlie to the kinge.

O Carroll paid 120 fat marts yearlie; to the hosting: twelve horse,
fol. 96*b*. twenty-four kearne.

Barnard O Connor to send to the hosting a banner of horse and a
fol. 96*b*. banner of footemen well armed.

Tirlagh Roe O Connor, lord of Clonynyll, to pay yearly 8*li*. sterling;
fol. 96*b*. to the hostinge: six horse and twenty-four kearne.

fol. 97. O Kennedie: twelve horse, twenty-six kerne to the hostinges.

fol. 97. Hugh Roe McMahon: to hostinges twelve horse twenty-four kerne.

fol. 97. McMorrice: to hostinges, in person, with eight kerne.

Brian O Maghrie: to the hostinges into Ulster, sixteen horse and
fol. 97*b*. thirty-two foote, and to any other place, eight horse and sixteen foote.

Teige O Dwine: to the hostinge: twenty-four foote and six fat marts
fol. 97*b*. to the kinge yearelie.

Art O Molloy: to find such kearne and horse as the countie of
fol. 97*b*. Kildare and Kilkennie are bounde to finde.

Order betwixt therle of Desmond and Teige McCormocke for the
fol. 98. castell of Carricke Novar.

fol. 99. Subsidie of 30*li*. yearlie, out of the Pooren country.[2]

Sragha: an exaction of money taken by great lords to beare their
fol. 100*b*. charges in comeinge to parliaments, counsells or burgh townes.

fol. 101*b*. Penaltie for contempt.

fol. 103. Recognizances.

The waste lands to be inhabited within a yeare or forfeited; to such
fol. 106*b*. as weare not able the kinge lent money.

---

[1] MS. indistinct.

[2] *See* page 95.

The castells of Fearnes and Eniscorthy, the kinges : post, 306.
See this for the allottinge of lands to them. fol. 106.
Maurice [Morrough] O Brien, earle of Thomonde, Donagh O Brien, baron of Ibrecane : fol. 108.
Quere, how both are now in the erledome.
A concordatum of a chappell called Garribride or house for lepers in Balliloughreogh. fol. 113.
A concordatum for a remittal of the penaltie of the forfeiture for a recognizance to Gerrald Nugent, of Ballibrenogh. fol. 116.
A fortresse built neere Kinsale by Phillipp Roche, in consideracion of a licence granted him to transport a certaine proportion of graine. fol. 117.

1543-4, 4th Jan.—New seales to the kings bench and common pleas. fol. 117*b*.
Indentures with Redmond McRory of Fearney : He renounceth the Pope ; he sends to the hostinges tenn horse besides himselfe and sixteen foote ; he paid 10*li.* yearelie. fol. 118.
Orders for the rent of Low Leinster : fol. 120.
See the distribution thereof to severall governors whereof John Brearton, a grand capten, was one.

1543.—Articles agreed upon in counsell for the lord deputies goeing then into England to relate to the kinge concerninge the state of the whole kingdome : fol. 123.
Note the opinion held then of Low Leinster ; the union of Loughseudie to the bishoppric of Meath.

1544.—Instructions to the erle of Ormonde and others to goe into Clanrickarde, upon the death of the erle of Clanrikarde, to assure and settle the country. fol. 131.
A letter to Charles FitzArthur for sendinge a witche to the lord deputie, to be examined. fol. 133.
William Brabazon, esquire, lord justice, February, 35 [Henry VIII.]. fol. 134.

1543[-4], Feb. 23.—The kings letter for sendinge of three thousand kerne, one thousand to the north of England. fol. 134.
Instruction to William FitzHarris and Andrew Brerton upon their goeinge into O Donnells country to assist him to take the castell of the Lyffer. fol. 136.
The lord justice and counsells bill for 500*l.* sterling borrowed of the lady Agnes St. Leger, the lord deputies wife. fol. 139.
Two thousand sparres [1] in service for two dayes and two nights upon the baronies of ths English Pale. fol. 143.
An order that the citizens of Waterford shall for one yeare transport wooll to be died and returned. fol. 143*b*.
Instructions to Francis Harbert, etc. fol. 143*b*.
Thomas Ager going into Thomond to compound the variences [between] the erle of Thomond and the baron of Ybrecan, his sonne. fol. 144*b*.
Indenture with Tadie O Carroll : fol. 146*b*.
Note, 12*d.* out of everie carucate of land in Ely ; his riseing : twelve horse, twenty-four foote,—Scoticos, alias dictos galliglasses. Via arcta, a passe. fol. 146.
Recognizances. fol. 149.
Act for breaking the weares upon the Boyne betwixt Drogheda and Trim, and for the fishing of the river. fol. 150*b*.
Murther and all other offences put to arbitrament. fol. 152.

---

[1] Of galloglasses, *see* page 88.

fol. 158*b*. Recognizances taken before the lord deputie and other commissioners.
An entrie that the towne of Athenrie shall enjoy liberties of Galway,
fol. 159. and they of Galway the liberties of Athenrie, according a decree.

Order for the captenshipp of Clanrickard, upon the death of Ullicke
Bourke alias FitzWilliam de Burgo, the first earle of Clanrickard,
during the minoritie of his sonne, and untill it were determined who
was his lawfull heire male, for that he had three married wives at the
fol. 160. time of his death.

fol. 167*b*. Recognizance of David Sutton of Kildare.

Recognizance of the lord of Baltinglasse for the lord of Upper
fol. 168. Ossory.

The towne of Leytrim given to Thomas Bourke, one of the erle of
fol. 167*b*. Clanrickards sonnes, during the minoritie of his heire.

An act of Parliament, made [1459–60], 38 Henry VI., for finding an
archer for everie 20*l*. land which any nobleman or gentleman can
fol. 170. dispend.

The castle of Ballaughmore ordered to be delivered to Teige
fol. 171*b*. O Carroll, upon payment of the mortgage to the lord of Upper Ossory.

fol. 173. Recognizances.

Adward indented betwixt the lord of Upper Ossory and O Moore,
upon penaltie of one thousand kine, one halfe to the kinge, the other
fol. 173. halfe to the lorde deputie: the lord deputie and counsell, slantie.

fols. 176*b*., 177. Recognizances.

fol. 179. 1545, August 24.—Order betwixt the erle of Tirone and O Donnell.
Note the rent of sixty kine out of Inishowen, adjudged to Tirone for
observacion of the peace betwixt them. The archbushop of Armagh,
the archbushop of Dublin, and all others the spirituall prelates and
pastors are slantie who can thunder out the censures of the Church
against the offenders. A proper use of the Church censures.

fol. 181. Orders betwixt the erle of Ormonde and baron of Cahir.
Note, a Butler, baron of Chaire,[2] before him that was created in
queen Elizabeths time. Note the cantred of Clonmell, how it should
be charged, March last.

Recognizance for restitution, fastness, moneys, leachcrafte, cost of
fol. 183. those who pursue the goods.

fol. 183*b*. Recognizances.

Fredome to Blackney of Rikenhore, not to receive any of the kings
fol. 184*b*. armie unlesse he will, in respect he is bound to hostings.

The lord deputie would not licence the merchants of Limericke to
fol. 186. bargaine with certaine Frenchmen, being the kings enemies.

fol. 186*b*., 187. Noe pledges to be taken of noblemen.

[1545–6.] Sir William Brabazon, lord justice:

Agreement in counsell that the lord deputie, with the armie, should
fol. 189. goe into Leinster.

Order that Tirrell of Fertullagh shall take noe exactions upon the
fol. 192. country.

The erle of Tirone is licenced to intertaine as many of the kings subjects as will goe with him to assist John Brereton in regaining Oldcastell,
fol. 192*b*. which was taken from him by Neale Connolaghs sonne.

Act authorizeinge the prosecution of Shane McRemond and Hugh
fol. 194. McShane his sonne, in Cooleranill or Kilcoman, Ballynekenny, etc.

John Brereton, seneshall of the countie of Wexford, capten of
fol. 194*b*. fifteen archers on horsebacke and foote.

[2] Caher, Cahir.

Order, upon the death of the erle of Ormonde, that the lord justice with the armie should draw into those partes. fol. 195.

Sir Gerald McShane, prisoner in the castell, to attend the lord justice that journey, and to returne with him. fol. 196, *vide* 197.

Sir Anthonie St. Leger, lord justice:

1546.—Prise wines in controversie betwixt Waterford and Rosse. fol. 198*b*.

Hostages taken by the maior and his brethren of Gallway of the nobilitie and gentlemen of Clanrikard. fol. 199.

Riseing out according the statute[1] for everie 20*l*. a man to be kept armed within their houses readie at all arrayes. fol. 199*b*.

Proclamacion against releeving of rebels. fol. 203.

Sir Brian Johns, steward of Catherlagh. fol. 204.

Dame Elinor, the erle of Desmonds sister, divorced from sir Richard Butler, had in recompence of all her marriage goods but one hundred marks: fol. 204*b*.

The same ladie, married to Thomas Tobin, had but twenty marks yearlie for all her thirds. fol. 205.

Order wherby the rule of the counties of Kilkenie and Tipperary are committed to the government of the lady dowager of Ormonde, sir Richard Butler, and others. fol. 206.

Sir Edward Bellingham, lord deputie:

1548.—Order whereby the government of the counties of Tipperary and Kilkenie is given to sir Francis Brian. fol. 210*b*.

Order for the customer of Galway. fol. 211.

Carriages to the generall hosting turned into money. fol. 212*b*.

The number of the plowlands in each of the five counties, with the number of the carts after three plowland to a cart, and being turned into money what they amount to. fol. 213, post 217.

The Dorans challenge Cloghgrenan. fol. 220.

Sir Anthonie St. Leger, lord deputie:

Direction for the apprehension of the two sonnes of the lord of Killcullen and others. fol. 225.

Order that noe market shal be kept at Dromconragh, neere Ardie. fol. 232.

A generall hostinge and the carriages to be converted into money. fol. 233*b*.

[1548.] Sir Edward Bellingham, lord deputie:

John Parker, constable of the castle of Dublin, held Old Patricke.[2] fol. 234*b*.

Proclamation that noe distresse shall be taken for debt. fol. 236*b*.

Order for the rule of Leinster. fol. 238.

A subsidie of 50*l*. yearlie due to the king out of Kilkennie: Quere what is become of it now?

A subsidie of 50*l*. yearlie in the countie of Tipperary. fol. 243.

[1559.] Sir Francis Brian, lord marshall:

The countie of Dublin charged with carts to carry timber to the forte in Leix, after the manner of sending forth to an hostinge. fol. 246.

---

[1] *See* p. 278.

[2] Holmpatrick, near Skerries, co. Dublin.

fol. 246*b*. Order betwixt the captens of the galloglasse.
fol. 248. Order betwixt the erle of Tirone, Maguire, and others of Ulster.
fol. 249. Fernie noe parte of Tirone.
fol. 251, 253. 1549.—Maguire exempted from Tirone.
fol. 251*b*. Iniskene in Clancarroll adjudged to be the primates.
fol. 255. Clandeboy exempted from Tirone.
fol. 261. Dearby Rian, a worthie Irish learned man.

fol. 265. A gifte of certaine lands betwixt Catherlaugh, and Leighlene and in Idrone made to the kings majestie and his heires for ever.

fol. 268*b*. 1549, July 18.—Castell Finn built upon Twoe[1] Kinall Mohana, to which belonged the two Clanheyne, otherwise called the baronie of Clanheyne, which extendeth from the castell of Finn twelve miles westwarde towards the mountaynes.

fol. 269*b*. The Liffer had a parte of the two Kinelmoghana and the two Tooes[2] or baronies called Lagan and Tirebrassell extending from Derry to Liffer.

fol. 273 The fort in Leix called the protector:
Note tho proportion of vittall sent thither:
For a garrans travaile by the day 6*d*., and for a driver 4*d*.

fol. 274*b*. 1549.—Sir Francis Brian, lord marshall, chosen lord justice of this realme, 27th of December, third yeare of Edward VI. upon departure of sir Edward Bellingham.

Leix gotten by the sword, 3 Edward VI.:

fol. 276. O Moore banished, and after haveing of the kings mercy gotten an 100*l*. per annum, died, and a concordatum given his wife for twenty marks yearlie for her maintenance.

fol. 277. Instructions to the archbushopp of Cashell for government of Ormonde and all that parte of Leinster to the Shauen.

fol. 277*b*. Certaine abbies and manors evicted out of the kings hands by O Carroll, by the negligence and mis-government of Walter ap Howell.

Sir William Brabazon, 4 Edward VI., March [1549–50].

fol. 278*b*. Submission of O Carroll: his riseing out: twelve horse, twenty-four foote to find eighty sparrs of galliglas for one quarter yearlie, either to be taken in meate or sent in money; xij*d*. upon everie plowland in Ely O Carroll to the kinge for rent.

fol. 281*b*. Earl of Desmond, lord tresurer of Ireland.

fol. 282*b*. Order betwixt the erles of Desmond and Thomond: the prooffes of many things done betwixt them referred to the examination of both theyr ladies and some others, whereof the ladiics weare onlie of the quorum.

fol. 285*b*. Bunrattie in the possession of Tirlaugh O Brien.
fol. 288. General hosting for thirty dayes.

Sir Anthonie St. Leger, lord deputie, 4. Ed. VI.

fol. 289; post 303*b*. The parcells belongeing to the lordship of Catherlaugh:
Such as are exempt from the rule of Cahir McArte Cavenaugh:

fol. 290*b*. Inishcorthy, Fearnes, Cloughamon, and Clonnogan, which large territories exempt from the Cavenaughs, and taken for the kinge.

fol. 291*b*. fol. 292; post, 335*b*., 339*b*. Order for buildinge the parish churches in the Cavenaughs country, and for mayntenance of divine servise, and against such as bring provisions from Rome.

fol. 292*b*. Against orderinge of causes by Brehoun law, but by arbitrators.

[1], [2] In Irish Tuath.

Sir James Crofte, lord deputie, anno 1552. fol. 294.

The earle of Tirone stayed in the Pale from goeing into Tirone. fol. 295.

Order that noe letters, writings or orders of importance be signed before they bee read before the counsell. fol. 295*b*.

Order that the lord chancellor shall stay all such grants signed by the lord deputie and counsell, wherein any parsonages or tythe doe passe: fol. 295*b*.

Note it was not to bestowe them upon the Church.

Order concerninge Fearnes. fol. 298.

Kinsallaugh held of the kings mannor of Fearnes by paying yearlie at Fearnes twenty fat marts, twenty good sheep, and twenty peckes of oates, of the countie Wexford measure. fol. 298.

The clearke of the counsell to subscribe his name to all fiants of pardons, and shall keep register of evidence of such pardon. fol. 299.

Composition for concealment of fellonie inhibited. fol. 301.

The parcells belonging to the house of Leighlin. fol. 302.

The customes and duties paid to the house of Leighlin. fol. 302*b*.

The parcells which belonge to the castell of Fearnes. fol. 305.

The parcells thought meet to belonge to Cloughamon, with the services. fol. 305.

Order for inhabitinge the lands in O Morroues country. fol. 306.

Note that if they be not inhabited by a time, they are content the shalbe forfeited to the kinge; order for bringing ther stud to a competent number for that they are cause of much waste.

Indenture betwixt O Brien, earle of Thomonde, and sir Donnell O Brien, his brother, for a portion of land to the said sir Donnell. fol. 306*b*.

General hosteinge for thirty days. fol. 309.

The earle of Tirone and his counsell committed to John Money, of Dublin, marchant, to be safelie kept, which he undertooke. fol. 309*b*.

Sir John Allen, after he had beene lord chancellor, called before the lord deputies and counsell, touchinge some plate of the kinge of Portingales which came to his hands four yeares before. fol. 312.

The castle of Belferside,[1] in the country about Carickfergus. fol. 313*b*.

Mollogha holden of the baron of the Navan by knight service, who had Richard Teling, the heire, his warde. fol. 316*b*.

Sir Thomas Cusake, lord justice, 6 Edward VI., Thomas Lockewood, deane of Dublin. fol. 320.

A generall hostinge for twenty-one daye. fol. 320.

Four hoggshedds of salmon shipped for Englande seised on by the sheriffes of Dublin; valued at iiij*l*. each hoggshedd. fol. 321.

Sir Anthonie St. Leger, lord deputie, primo Marie: fol. 322.

Order for defence of Uriell. fol. 322.

Order for payment of 40*l*. sterling to the lord deputie, which he delivered to O Connors daughter goeing into England. fol. 325.

The armie and pentioners to be reduced to five hundred. fol. 325*b*.

Pentioners kept in pay upon secret intelligence that upon their discharge they would turn pirates. fol. 325*b*.

The armie, by instructions from the queene, to be reduced to five hundred, yet by advise in counsell, upon good grounds, the same was kept 1,000 stronge, four hundred and sixty horse and sixe hundred foote besides kearne. fol. 330.

Lord of Houth sent into Lecale with a hundred horse to banish the Scotts. fol. 331.

A generall hostinge for thirty dayes. Terens,[2] deane of Armagh, of the counsell. fol. 335.

---

[1] Belfast. [2] Terence Daniel.

fol. 337. Cesse for reliefe of the souldiers upon the borders.

fol. 339. Where the tract fayleth, there the goods stollen to be satisfied.

fol. 340. Generall hosting converted into money.

fol. 342. Henrie Cooley taken prisoner with the O Connors.

fol. 344. Recognizance for the peace.

fol. 345*b*. Order betwixt the earle of Thomond and Donalde O Bryane.

fol. 347*b*. Disposition of lands in Offaly to the O Connors.

fol. 350*b*. Direction to the erle of Kildare for prosecution of Phelim Ro.

Controversie betwixt Edward Galway of Corke and Andrew Leysagh,
fol. 353*b*. of Limericke, concerninge the bridge in Limericke.

fol. 354. General hostinge for thirty-one dayes after four plowland to a cart.

Prise wines of Rosse sequestred betwixt the erle of Ormonde and
fol. 354*b*. them.

Order, well drawne, after the manner of chancerie, betwixt certaine merchants of Chester and Gilliam Pippine of St. Malous for a shipp
fol. 355*b*. laden with secke taken by him.

Order for dissolving the sequestration of the prise wines of Rosse and if the erle of Ormonde cannot shew better matter, the towne to enjoy
fol. 359. the same.

Sir Thomas Cusake delivered the great seale to sir Anthonie St. Leger accordinge the kings and queens letters, who delivered the same
fol. 360. to William FitzWilliam.

fol. 360*b*. Articles of commission to Mr. Marshall concerning idle persons.

Order that it shalbe lawfull for the owner to take his goods though
fol. 362*b*. the same weare sold in open markett.

Orders betwixt the younge earle of Thomonde and sir Donnell
fol. 364. OBriane who claimed to be O Briane.

fol. 366*b*. Order for prosecution of them of Fearnie :

fol. 367. Instructions for the prosecution in Fearnie :

Note one that they should not burne houses nor townes and that they should spare and preserve all corne and haggards.

Order betwixt the erle of Ormond and barron of Upper Ossory,
fol. 368. with a forme of an oath which they both tooke.

The Scotts of the out Isles practise to get the castle of Karick-
fol. 370*b*. fergus.

Order that the clearke of the crowne and common pleas shall enjoy the clearkeshipp of the assise in all the English counties, as belongeing
fol. 372. to his office of clarke of the crowne and common pleas.

Finis of this councell booke, which I ended the 19th of October, 1609 :—[*Blank.*]

II.

Heare followeth a table of the principall matters contained in the counsell booke which begun the first of Aprile, 1571 :

1571.—William Fitzwilliams :

An act of counsell, wherin the earle of Clanrickard is fined in one thousand marks, for a contempt towards the lord president and counsell of
fols. 1–3. Connaught.

Beefe taken up in Connaught for the armie there at the rate of
fol. 3. vi*s*. viii*d*. sterling the peece.

fols. 5–8. A proclamation for raysinge the burden of cesse :

fol. 5. What freedomes weare allowed :

fols. 6, 7. Punishment for concealeinge of land chargeable with cesse :

The cessor shall have the quantitie of land allowed him free but in one place together. fols. 7, 8, after fol. 140.

An act for a generall hostinge, to begin the first of September, 1571. fol. 9.

A consultacion for tolleratinge with Rory Oge O More, and the reasons mouveinge therunto. fols. 10, 11.

An act for a generall hostinge, to begin the first of June, 1572. fol. 12.

A proclamacion of rebellion against Rory Oge. fols. 13–15.

An act for the first committinge of Richarde, earle of Clanrickarde, for not bringinge in his sonnes, Ullicke and John Burke. fol. 16.

Sir Edward Fitton, lord president of Connaught. fol. 16.

An act for the enlargement of the earle of Clanrickard upon 300*li.* bonds, to remaine in Marcus Barnewells house, in the Bridge street, [Dublin]. fols. 17–19.

Robert Dillon, second justice of Connaught. fol. 17.

The earle of Clanrickard the second time committed to close prison. fol. 20.

An act of counsell authorizinge the lorde deputie to levie such numbers of souldiers as he should thinke fitt and meet against Uliicke and John Burke. fol. 21.

An act for removeinge the earle of Clanrickard to the chamber over the green cloth with libertie to walke in the garden an houre in the forenoone and one houre in the afternoone of each day and to bee close prisoner. fol. 22.

An act for the enlargement of the earle of Clanrickard, by vertue of a clause in her majesties letters, which was well debated of. fols. 23–25.

Request made by the earle of Clanrickard the better to bringe in his sonnes. fols. 24, 25.

The earle of Clanrickardes undertakinge to pacifie his sonnes rebellion. fol. 27.

Her majesties gracious respect of her deputie and counsell and of the reputation of the place her president of Connoght held. fol. 23.

The earle of Clanrickards submission to the lord president. fols. 28, 29.

Intertaynement for one hundred archers given the master of the rolls against Brian McArte for killinge Browne. fol. 30.

Allowance of a beofe and a halfe and a pecke and halfe of wheat for a hundred foote a day. fol. 31.

Beofe at 12*s.* sterling the peece, and wheat iiii*s.* sterling the pecke. fol. 31.

The submission of Connor, earle of Thomonde; with articles annexed, whereof one is that from time he will further the contents of the booke of common-prayer and administration of the sacraments and the injunctions sett forth by the queene, wherto he has sworne. fols. 32–34.

An act for pacifiinge Magohegans sonns and Callagh McTirlaghs sonnes in rebellion. fols. 35–37.

An act concerninge the cesse of Odrone, in lieu of which cesse sir Peter Carew offred an hundred marks. fols. 38–41.

Warrant to Henrie Cooley, seneshall of the Kings countie, to intertaine thirty English souldiers. fol. 42.

An act that the lord deputie may retaine three hundred English for strengtheninge the armie. fols. 43, 44.

An act wherby is resolved that a writt of appeale against Brian McArte for the murther of Browne shall not be sealed: Note reasons against the course of justice. fols. 45, 46.

An act for retaineinge the erle of Desmonde and enlargeinge his brother, sir John of Desmonde. fols. 47–49.

The submission of sir John of Desmonde; with articles indented, wherof the first is that to his power hee shall procure that the lawes established for religion shalbe observed. fols. 49–51.

Against breons and breon law. fol. 54.

fol. 55. Against fines taken by great men for forsweareing their hands.

fol. 56. Against bardes, carroghs and rimors.

The objections of the erle of Claunrickarde and sir Edwerd Fitton,
each against other, and by an advised consultation the lappinge up of
fols. 58-67. their controversie.

The assignation of keepeinge the greate seale to Adam, lord archbushop
fol. 68. of Dublin:

Note he was sworne.

1573, June 4.—An act for the commitment of sir Edward Fitton, a
councellor and her majesties thresurer, for a contempt in keepinge the
fiant of a pardon in his hands and not deliveringe it when the lord
fols. 69, 70. deputie and counsell required the same.

1573, June 5.—Sir Edward Fittons refusall to sit in counsell after his
fols. 71, 72. inlardgment.

Letter to sir Edward Fitton to repaire into Connought, upon his
fol. 73. refuseinge to sit and assist in counsell heere.

fol. 74. A generall hostinge, to begin the twentieth of July, 1573.

An act for the lord deputies goeinge in person to prosecute the
O Mores and to take with him five hundred men out of the Pale, videlicet, three hundred out of the countie of Dublin, with ten dayes
fols. 75, 76. victualls, and two hundred out of Meath, with fifteen dayes victualls.

An act of counsell authorizeinge the lord deputie to encrease her
majesties armie, by puttinge in pay an hundred English souldiers and
fol. 77. an hundred kearnes.

An act of counsell that the lord deputie may intertayne two hundred
and fifty souldiers, besides two hundred warranted by her majesties
fols. 80-85. letters against the erle of Desmonde.

Copie of a letter to her majestie significing the proceedinge with the
fols. 86, 87. erle of Desmonde.

fols. 88-90. Copie of a letter to the lords, to the effect of the former.

An act that the erle of Desmond shalbe proclaymed traytor and
fol. 90. prosecuted.

A proclamacyon of rebellion, well penned, against Gerralde, earle of
Desmonde; with promise of one thousand pounds sterling, and 40
pounds pention to him that should by a time bringe him alive, and 500
fols. 91-99. pounds sterling and 20 pounds pention that should bringe his heade.

An act alloweinge the erle of Kildare one hundred horse in pay for
fols. 100, 101. defence of the English Pale.

An act that the earle of Kildare shall command the riseinge out of
fols. 102, 103. the Pale, beeinge five hundred horse and—[*Blank.*]

An act revokeinge Francis Agard, for the place of cheife commissioner
in Mounster, and appointinge James Dowdall second justice of the
bench in his roome (with allowance of xx*s.* per diem), with the assistance of Henrie Davells, with allowance of vi*s.* viii*d.* per diem for
fols. 104, 105. execucion of marshall affaires.

1575.—An act alloweinge capten Edward Moore twenty horsemen in
fol. 106. pay for the suppressinge of the O Connors.

Sir Henry Sidney:

fol. 107. A generall hostinge, to begin the 10 of Aprill, 1575.

1575, September 25.—A composicion of six thousand peckes of
wheate, 4338 pecks of beare malte, either at 40*d.*, Irish, the pecke; 8670
pecks of oate malte, at ii*s.*, Irish, the pecke; 13302 pecks of oates, at
xvi*d.*, Irish; 3252 fatt beoves at xii*s.*, Irish, le peece, given in lieu of
fols. 108, 109. cesse out of the five counties and the countie of Wexforde.

A warrant to the thresurer to pay money for the hire of cariages at xiiij*d.*, sterling, for one driver and two garrans. fol. 110.

Kings countie, Queenes countie, Catherlagh and Wexford charged with cariages. fol. 111.

Provision for the lord deputies house, for readie money, at these rates: a beofe, xijs., Irish; a pecke of wheate, iijs. iiij*d.* Irish; a mutton xvj*d.*, Irish; beare malte iijs. iiij*d.*, Irish, a pecke; oate malte, xxi*d.*, Irish; a porke, iiijs., Irish; for a gallon of butter, containeinge a 10 lb. weight, xijd., Irish. See the proportion of these things there. fols. 113, 114.

A warrant for a holdinge for the defence of the borders from the Windegates to Catherlagh, in the absence of the lord deputie, beinge to make some stay at Carrickfergus. fol. 115.

A lesseninge of the composicion granted in lieu of cesse. fols. 117, 118.

A generall hostinge, to begin the 10 of July, 1576, and to meet at the Newrie: fol. 119.

Note the baron of Lixnawe coulde not write, but made his marke to this act.

An order, in Latin, betwixt O Connor Sligo, and O Donell for three hundred and sixty markes rent, and other services of horse and foote demaunded by O Donell to be due to him upon O Connors country. fol. 121.

An act for giveinge William Gerrarde the oath of councellor and chancellor, in the absence of the lord deputie. fols. 124, 125.

A confirmacion of the composicion mentioned. fol. 117.

Rates allowed the constable to take for fine of irons and diett of prisoners of all sorts. fol. 126.

Articles wherunto Hugh McShane submitted himselfe. fol. 127.

Orders observed in the marches of Dublin against rimors, harpers, and against Irishmens sendinge ther horses a foyninge [1] into the barony of Radoune; with other good orders for followinge of stelthes. fols. 129, 130.

A tripartite indenture in Latine betwixt the lord deputie and counsell, Hugh O Donell, cheife of his name, of the other, and Conatius O Donell of therde, with the portion allowed to the said Conatius. fols. 131–133.

Indentures betwixt the lord deputie and counsell and Calvatus O Donell for Connatie, wherin note his riseinge out and his rent for that lande. fols. 135–137.

A proclamation explaineinge the statutes for freedomes made the 3d and 4th years of Philip and Mary, and in the 11th yeare of queen Elizabeth, explained, with allowances sett downe for the souldiers meat, ther boyes and horses. fols. 138–141.

Against compoundinge with the souldiers for money. fol. 142.

Against woemen and doggs. fol. 142.

How farr both horse and foote shall travaile by the day both summer and winter. fol. 142.

Covenants whereby the lord Barry yealdeth 150*li.* for one yeare in liew of cesse. fols. 145–147.

Fowre and twentie articles agreed upon betweene Walter, earle of Essex, and Tirlagh O Neale, contayninge many matters. fol. 149.

A warrant to man out the queenes shipp against pirats, upon the report of forrayne ayde to James FitzMorrishe. fol. 151.

A generall hostinge, to begin the 12 of August, 1577. fol. 157.

A recognizance of sir Donell O Connor Sligo, for the safe keepeinge of the castell of Bundroys. fol. 158.

The first composicion made with the cheife lords of Connoght by sir Nicolas Malby; note the riseing out of everie of them. fols. 159, 170–172.

---

[1] Free grazing.

An act whereby is discharged from cesse of souldiers and [of] the lord deputies house, everie plough lande that within a certaine time
fol. 174. would pay five marks, sterling.

A proportion of cesse for the lord deputies house, with a clause of discharge both of that and the victualing of the souldiers, upon payment
fol. 175. of five marks for everie plowlande.

An act for sendinge William Gerarde, lord chancelor into England, with 40*s*. per diem. The custodie of the seale committed to Adam, lord archbushop of Dublin, under two keyes, whereof Thomas Say kept
fol. 176. one.

An act for releaseing out of prison the noblemen and gentlemen
fol. 178. committed for the matter of cesse.

The submission of the lords and gentlemen committed for cesse;
fol. 179. wherupon ther enlargment was graunted.

A generall hosting converted into money after the rate of 2*s*. sterling, for everie cart; xij*d*. sterling per diem for everie horseman; xij*d*. sterling per diem for everie archer on horsbacke and 7*d*. sterling per
fol. 180. diem for every kerne.

Articles indented betwixt sir Nicholas Malby and Brian O Rourke;
fols. 181, 182. note his riseing out: sixty foote and twelve horse.

fol. 183. Warrant to enlarge Shane O Rely, who was nine years prisoner.

fol. 184. Coppie of her majesties letter concerninge the cesse.

An act wherbie many of the noblemen and gentlemen, for refusinge to signe a submission accordinge her majesties letters for cesse weare
fol. 185. againe committed.

An order for sequestringe the master of the rowles his office for
fol. 186. nonfezans.

The queens atturnes informacion against the master of the rowles, Nicholas White, esquire, for forfeiture of his office for not returninge
fol. 187. the estraites of the chancery into the exchequere.

fols. 188–190. The maister of the rowles answer to the informacion.

An order that the towne of Drogheda shall send to the hostinge but twenty-four besides their leaders; they have four carts allowed for ther
fol. 191. carriage, a cart to six men which is usuall to all the townes.

An order for Frances Shane against Robert Nugent for ninety-one
fols. 191, 192. cows; the titell of the Carne.

A warrant to sett forth the queenes shipp, 'the Handmaide,' upon
fol. 192. advertisement of foraine invasion.

A letter from the lords of the counsell for Kendall to have his office
fol. 192. of clarke of the starr chamber for his life.

A concordat to allowe Rosse Magohegan and Thomas FitzRedmond 90*li*. xiiij*s*. for a debt of a hundred twelve pounde due to them for
fol. 194. intertainement of kearnes.

A clause of a letter from the lords of the counsell, touchinge the release of those lords and gentlemen that weare committed for the
fol. 195. matter of cesse, with a resolution thereon.

fol. 196. The first submission of the foresaid gentlemen.

fol. 197. The second submission of the forsaid gentlemen.

The third submission of the said gentlemen, in all which they acknow-
fol. 198. ledge cesse to be due by the prerogative.

fols. 199, 200. An order against Feaugh McHue and Hue McShane his father, for restoringe goods taken from kearnes and for buildinge the cathedrall church burnt by them.

An order for compoundinge the great quarrells betwixt the lord of Mountgerrat and the lord of Upper Ossery, and restitution to be made to the poore of ther goods taken by either side, by which order both the lords weare committed to answer accordinge to justice. fols. 201-203.

The submission of the lord viscount of Moungerrat and Upper Ossory, whereby they promise noe other revenge to be done but by justice. fol. 203.

1578.—Sir William Drury:

An order to continue the erle of Clanricard in the possession of the castell of Clonmine, untill by order of law her majestie be duelie intiteled therunto. fol. 204.

A generall hostinge, to begin the 24 of December, 1578. fol. 205.

Order against Henrie Duke, for restitution to be made to Even Ro of such cowes as he tooke out of Fearnie. fols. 205-207.

Order whereby the maior and corporation of Corke are fined in xx*l.* for their negligence to appease a tumult in their citie. fols. 208, 209.

Order for the lady of Houth against her husband. fol. 212.

The first composition in leiwue of cesse for money which was the somme of 2000*li.* sterling which was borne by eleven counties besides Upper Ossory; see everie counties portion heere. fols. 212, 213.

The generall hostinge proroged to meet at Rosseke, the 18th of August, 1579.

Concerninge prise wines, where the case was, that the stranger sold and dispersed his wines before any agents for the earle of Ormonde demaunded the same, and how now he should be satisfied his prise wines was the question and sent into England for resolution. fol. 214.

Order whereby the lady of Houth hath eight poundes a month allowed her till the variance betwixt her and her husband the lord be ended. fol. 215.

1579-80.—Sir William Pelham:

A generall hostinge, to begin the 10 of January, 1579-[80]. fol. 220.

An act of reciprocation confirmed by the lord Grey. fol. 221.

The rates of the defaults of the risinge out of garrans: fols. 222, 223.

Note in the ende when there is noe forwarneinge given and yet the service of the hostinge remaininge dewe in such time by the country inhabitants the rate of viij*d.* sterling per diem for each garran, and the like for each driver is concluded and ordered, to be reared.

An act alloweinge an odd penny per diem to each souldier not victualed by the queene; three pence per diem given encrease to each horseman, from the 14 of October to the 18 of May, to provide oates for their horses. fols. 223, 224.

Letter from the lords in favore of doctor Forth that none should passe the reversion of any parcell he held in possession. fol. 224.

Letter from the lords that the erle of Kildare may execute the lord admirals deputation and that he bee not letted therin by the counsell borde. fol. 225.

Justices of oyer and terminer, Nicolas Walsh, cheife justice of Mounster, and others punished for ther contempt in executing one Morley, after they had received the lord justices letters to the contrary. fol. 224*b*.

Marmaduke,[1] bushop of Waterforde, committed to the castle for useing undecent speeches against the erles of Ormond and Kildare. fol. 226.

Petitions of O Neile sent the queene by capten Peirce. fol. 227.

An imposition of wheat, malt, beoves, etc. layd upon the cuntrie besides the composicion of 2000*li.* for that it was reserved at the makeinge of the composition that it should bee lawfull for her majestie in the time of foraine invasion or great inward rebellion soe to doe. fols. 228, 229.

---

[1] Marmaduke Middleton, bishop of Waterford, 1579-82.

Arthur, Lord Grey :

1580. October 3.—An act of councell, wherby is agreed that the
country shall beare six hundred men to advance the service, everie
fols. 231, 232. souldier to have 10*d*. sterling per diem and to victuall himselfe.

Acates[1] for the deputies house reserved, besides the composicion the
prises of the acates, and an order how to prevent the abuses of the
fols. 232, 233. accators.

fol. 234. An act of reciprocation.

A letter of the lords concerninge merchants of Waterforde who weare
fols. 234, 235. spoyled of 1300*li*. by some Frenchmen :

Note for their releife an imposition upon French commodities, rather
allowed then the arrest of French shippinge.

fol. 235. An act for committing the lord of Delvin close prisoner.

fol. 236. An act for committing the erle of Kildare close prisoner.

Contribution for labours and for oates for horsemen, with the places
fol. 237. thought fittest to place them in garrison.

1580–81. January 13.—An act for committinge to the castell [of
fol. 238. Dublin] the baron of Upper Ossery and his wife for matters of treason.

Allowances of cesse granted to the lord deputies houshoulde and
fols. 239–244. stable upon the endings of the cesse.

fol. 239. A generall hostinge, to begin the 25th August, 1581.

The queenes letter to displace Nicolas Nugent from the place of
cheife justice of the common pleas, and to give the same to sir Robert
fol. 240. Dillon.

The queenes letters for a pention of ii*s*. vj*d*. sterling to Mathias
fol. 241. O Cane.

Order on puttinge the horsemen in garrison for the ease of the
country, the proportion of horsemeat and mans meate allowed, and the
fols. 241, 242. prices paid the country.

Letter from the lords to give allowance to the cashered souldiers for
their transportation, soe much as the lord [deputie] should thinke
fol. 243. meete.

fol. 244. A generall hostinge, to begin the 19 of June, 1582.

A cesse of 1690 beoves for victualinge the armie, at 20*s*. Irish the
peece, to be delivered to Thomas Mollinex ; with that number plotted
fol. 244. upon the country.

The horsemen placed in garrison, with the allowance of horsemeat and
fol. 247. mans meat upon the contry.

Note the difference in the oates for horses, with hey and without, the
prices paid the country.

1582. November 12.—Archbishop of Dublin and sir Henry Wallop, justices :

The souldiers allowances changed into money, in liew wherof the
country was to pay everie souldier monthly 16*s*. sterling, paying one
fol. 248. month's cesse alwaies before hand.

fol. 248. A generall hostinge, to begin the 10th of June, 1583.

fol. 249. Order to muster the country according the statute.

Order to continue the horsemen in garrison at the rates of 15*s*. sterling
fol. 249. for 28 days.

A letter from the lords concerninge a composition to be made with the
fol. 250. country in liew of cess ; they mention 15 or 1600*li*.

A composition of 1500*li*. agreed upon in liew of cesse, and the same
fol. 251. proportion upon the five counties.

---

[1] Provisions purchased.

A commission to levie the composition of 1500*li.*, and to pay it to the vice-thresurer. fols. 252-254.

The division of the composition upon the baronies, and who weare made collectors, and the commission directed to them. fols. 254, 255.

Letters of the lords touching provision for the lord deputies, sir John Perrots house. fol. 256.

1584. June 21.—Sir John Perrot, lord deputy:

The bishop of Meath and sir Richard Bingham sworne counsellors, the first sittinge of sir John Perrot in counsell. fol. 258.

A generall hostinge, to begin the 10 of August, 1584. fol. 259.

Commission under the great seale, with instructions for general musters in everie countie. fol. 259.

John Norris, lord president of Mounster, sworn of the counsell, 25 of June, 1584. fol. 259.

Thomas Lestrange sworne of the counsell, the first of July, 1584. fol. 259.

Carriages hired upon the five counties, at 4*d.* sterling per diem, for everie driver; . . . drivers to five garrans. fol. 259.

Order that Ulicke, earle of Clanrickard, should bee pardoned. fol. 260.

A proportion for the victualinge of the souldiers in their travaile, the quantitie of ther meat, with the price. fol. 261.

Order for cariages upon the five counties for the lord deputies jorney into Conaught and Mounster, at the rate of 4*d.* sterling per diem for each garran, and as much for the driver, two drivers to five garrans. fol. 261.

An act of reciprocation. fol. 262.

A proportion of beoves plotted upon the Irishrie. fol. 262.

The riseinge out of the Pale turned into garrans, and a 150 Poll kernes turned into labourers. fol. 263.

Order to levie 500 foote upon the Pale, to be put into her majesties ordinary pay. fol. 263.

The proportion of cariage to a generall hostinge, how many carts everie countie doth containe, and how many garrans those carts make. fols. 265-268.

Order to take carriage garrans upon the countie at 4*d.* sterling per diem the garran, and as much the driver, to be payd by her majestie. fol. 269.

John [Long], Primate of Ardmagh, sworne of the counsell. fol. 269.

A note of such as did rise out on the generall hostinge into the north, 25 of August, 1584. fol. 269.

Letter from the lords to sir Henrie Wallop to allow the cittizens of Dublin a concordatum 2611*li.*, which they tooke in munition. fol. 271.

The queenes letter to make the Irish pay sterling to such horse and foote as served in the feilde and not the rest. fol. 272.

Letter of the lords for makeinge payment to the lord deputie of soe much as he had expended in househould more then he should have done yf he had cesse. fol. 273.

Composition ended, the lord deputie to use prerogative and cesse. fol. 274.

The proportion for sir John Perrot, the lord deputies, houshould to be borne by the country: fols. 275-283.

See heere the particulars:

Commissions for levieinge the proportion for the lord deputies househould. fol. 284.

Generall hostinge, the first of July, 1585. fol. 285.

Act to stay Edward Butler till he gave good assurance for his loyaltie; neverthelesse his pardon to be granted. fol. 286.

A proportion of beoves to the generall hostinge for the armie. fol. 287.

Allowance of 20*s.* given Jeffrey Fenton for his travayle and charges
fol. 287. in gooing to solicite busines at court.

An act respecting a yeares composition for victualing till order might
fols. 288–290. be taken by the next sessions of parliment.

An act to commit Richard Newtervill to the castle [of Dublin] upon
exhibitinge a bill against the country for money due unto him for beinge
fol. 288. their agent against the prerogative.

Act for the continuance of the foote-companies in Ulster, at the
fol. 289. charge of the Irishrie.

A letter from the lords, cheifetaines and knights of Conought, acknow-
fol. 290. ledging the benefit of the composicion.

A letter from the lords of the Pale to the queene, concerninge the
fol. 291. cesse for the lord deputies householde.

fols. 291, 292. An answer from the lord thresurer to that letter.

An act that the King and Queenes Counties shall beare composition
as the rest of the Pale doth, with consideracion of the fredome of ther
fol. 292. owne manuerance as the gentlemen of the Pale.

fol. 293. A generall hostinge, the first of May, 1586.

An act that such of the composition bands in Ulster as are forced to
leave ther places shall be victualed by her majestie, provided that the
fol. 294. same shalbe repayed upon the country.

An act renueinge the composicion 2100*li.*, in lieu of cesse and the
fol. 296. provisions for the deputies house.

fol. 298. Commission for levieinge the composicion.

The collectors charged with the receipt in the Pale, the sheriffes in the out counties and the lord of Upper Ossory for Upper Ossory.

An act to committ the sheriffe of the countie of Tipperary, and fine-
ing him in xx*li.*, for his contempts and delayes in levieinge the beoves
for the deputies household : Discharged of the fine by letters from
fols. 299, 303. England entred.

fol. 301. An act to proclaime Walter Reogh a traytor and to prosecute him.

Letter from the lords to free all the earle of Ormonds maunors from
cesse or other impositions, in regard he did foregoe the takeinge of coyne
fol. 302. and livery of his tenants.

Letter from the lords concerneing the manner of chargeing the counties
fol. 303. of Kilkeny and Tipperary with the composition.

fol. 304. The continuance of the composition for another yeare, endinge 1588.

An act ordering that the proportions for the lord deputies house layde
upon the out counties should be borne by the five counties of the Pale
fol. 304. (according to a former act entered in the booke, fol. 275).

fol. 308. Commission for levieinge the composition.

fol. 310. Generall hostinge, to begin the 20 of June, 1587.

fol. 311. A fiant, in Latin, to passe under the seale for general musters.

fols. 311–313. Instructions to be annexed to the commission for general musters.

Order for the commitment of Peirce Butler, shirife of Tipperary, for
his negligience in levieinge the composition, with a conditionall fine of
fol. 314. £100 layd on him.

Sir William FitzWilliams sworne lord deputie, in Christ church [Dublin], the last of June 1588.

fol. 316. A generall hostinge, to begin the 12 of August, 1588.

A letter to the lord thresurer concerninge O Ferrall Boy, with the
fols. 317, 318. case put downe and sent.

fol. 319. The composition continued the yeare, 1588.

Order that the countie of Kilkeny shall pay the porcion of the composicion layd at first upon them, and a tolleration to be had with the
fol. 319. counties of Catherlaugh and Wexford till certificates of their wasts.

Order for the lord deputie to goe against the Spaniards of the dispersed fleet landed in Ulster, with an act of reciprocation. fol. 320.

Order for the committinge of the pledges of Donell Spanagh, Dermot McMorrice and Dolin McBrene to the castle [of Dublin], being before in the custodie of sir Henrie Wallopp. fol. 321.

A generall hostinge, to begin the xxth of June, 1589. fol. 322.

Order betwixt sir Tir [lagh] O Neale and the earle of Tyrone. fol. 324.

Order against sir Rosse McMahowne for satisfying the subjects of the Pale. fol. 325.

Order for the viscount of Gormanstowne against the erle of Tyrone, Tirlagh McHenrie and McMahowne for spoyls done upon the Nobber. fol. 326.

Commission for leveing the remaines of carriages to a generall hostinge which are bestowed upon the country to helpe them to pay their composition. fols. 326, 327.

Order for deliverie of sir Edward Barkleys warrants to the lord deputie after the said sir Edwarde was dead, for that he was indebted to her majestie. fol. 328.

Order for George Cowley for the seneshallshipp of the baronie of Carbery. fol. 329.

Commission to appoint collectors in the absence of sir Geffrey Fenton, to levie the composition money. fol. 330.

Order that sir Murgh ne Doe shall have the benefit of a composition made with the country for him in liew of his cuttings and other services. fol. 321.

Order for sir Murgh ne Doe against Roger O Flartie for certaine quarters of land. fol. 332.

The examination of witnesses in the said case. fols. 333, 334.

A generall hostinge to begin the 18th of May, 1590. fol. 335.

Easter tearme adjoyrned untill mensis Pasche. fol. 335.

Division of the composition. fol. 336.

A generall hostinge to begin the 24 of July, 1591. fol. 339.

Arrearages of composition and order for levieinge of them: fols. 340–343.

Note in this the names of the five English baronies of the countie of Wexford and commission to examine wast in the out counties.

Recognizance of Nicholas Mason and others for payment of arrearages of composition due upon the countie of Wexford. fol. 344.

Commission to enquire in whom the fault was that the composition for two yeares together was not reared. fol. 345.

Recognizances of Peter Butler and others for payinge arrearages of the composition of the countie of Wexford. fol. 347.

Commission to the sheriffe of the countie of Louth for levieinge the arreares of the composition. fol. 349.

Commission to the sheriffe of Meath for the like: fol. 352.

Wherin note that the barons of the exchequer weare charged for a debt stalled by them upon a collector for that they had noe authoritie soe to doe.

Like commission for West Meath. fol. 356.

Like commission to the counties of Dublin and Kildare which follow one another. fols. 358, 359, etc.

Composition made for the yeare 1592 for 1500*li.* upon the Pale, the rest upon the out counties; with the names of the gentlemen of the Pale who consented. fol. 365.

Commission to the lord chancellor and others to appoint officers to levie the composition for the yeare 1592. fol. 368.

The apportioninge of the composition both upon the Pale and the out counties which the cheife baron hath undertaken to proceede in by course in the exchequer and not at the counsell boarde. fol. 370.

The queenes letters to sir Thomas Norris, sir Robert Gardener, and
fol. 370. other commissioners for makeinge a composition in Mounster.
Wherin note the barons of Donboine and Chaire [Caher] reproved.
Composition of 189*li.* made with the Crosse counties, and liberties of
fol. 372. Tipperary for five yeares, in which Eli O Carroll was not comprised.
Composition of 130*li.* made with the countie of Kilkenny for five
fol. 374. years, paying two years arrearages.
Recognizances on John Grace and others for payinge of the arrear-
fol. 374. ages of the composition in the countie of Kilkenny.
Commission to levie the arreare of 1200*li.* due upon the countie of
Tipperary, giveing allowance to the erle of Ormonde of such freedoms as
fol. 375. he hath in possession by vertue of the queenes letters.
fol. 376. Commission for levicinge the composition in the countie of Kilkenny.
fol. 377. The like for Tipperary.
Recognizance of Thomas Butler and others for payment of 400*li.*,
sterling, parcell of the arreareges of the composition in the countie of
fol. 378. Tipperary.
fol. 378. Like recognizance on James Laffan.
Composition with the countie of Wexford for 60*l.* sterling upon the
fol. 379. Irish countries.
Commission for levicinge the composition of the countie of Cather-
fol. 379. laugh, beinge 25*li.* sterling.
Like commission for levieinge the composition of the Kings countie,
beinge 50*li.* sterling:—consented to by Henry Warren, Anthony
fol. 380. Brabazon.
Commission to levie the composition of 35*li.* sterling, layd upon the
fol. 382. Queenes county.
fol. 384. Like commission for 140*li.* sterling on the countie of Wexford.
fol. 384. A generall hosting, to begin the 16 of July, 1593.
Recognizances of Michaell Keatinge and others for payment of 140*li.*,
fol. 385. sterling, of the arreare of the composition in the countie of Wexford.
Commission for levieinge the composition in the countie of Wexford
fol 385. for halfe a yeare.
Writts issued out of the exchequer for levieing the composition both
fol. 386. in the Pale and out counties for the yeare 1593.
Proportion of beoves for a generall hostinge both upon the Pale and
fol. 387. Irishrie.
fol. 388. A generall hostinge the 18 of April, 1593.
fol. 389. Proportion of beoves to this generall hostinge.

Sir William Russell entered the 3d of August, 1594:

1594.—An act that the lord deputie shall goe to releeve the castell of
fol. 390. Enniskillen, with reciprocall authoritie to the counsell divided.
An act wherby is ordered that a force of 1030 foote and 305 horse
shall be levied upon the country, and mayntaned at theire charge for 30
fol. 391. days for defence of the Pale:
Note that the counties of Mounster weare subject to this charge.
fol. 393. A generall hostinge, to begin 16th of August, 1596.

Lord Burgh.—May 23, 1597:

fol. 394. A generall hostinge, to begin the 16 of July, 1597:
fol. 395. A proportion of 2850 beoves for the armie, this hosting.
fol. 396. An act orderinge a reciprocall authoritie to the counsell divided.
Lord chancellor [and] sir Robert Gardener lords justices, 27 of
Aprill.

A general hosting, to begin the 6 of June, 1598. fol. 397.

Proportion of beoves to serve the armie this hosting, the number 3210. fol. 398.

A generall hostinge, to begin the first of May, 1598. fol. 399.

Earle of Essex.—May 8th, 1599:

An act authorizeing the counsell devided reciprocally. fol. 401.

Another act of the same nature. fol. 402.

The lord leiuetenants protestation that he would leave soe many of the forces he intended to carry into the north for the defence of the Pale as the councell should thinke meet, which forces the counsell thought too fewe to attend his lordship. fol. 404.

Lord Mountjoy:

1600. April 12.—A generall hostinge, to begin the 20th of May, 1600: fol. 405.

A proportion of beoves for that journey. fol. 405.

An act authorizeing the counsell devided reciprocally. fol. 406.

Another act of that nature. fol. 407.

Another act of the same nature. fol. 408.

An act that Mr. Tibbot Butler shall have the libertie of both of the courts of the castell [of Dublin] and the walkes upon the leades. fol. 410.

Another act of reciprocation. fol. 411.

A general hostinge, to begin the last of June, 1601. fol. 412.

A general hosting, to begin the first of June, 1602. fol. 413.

Another act of reciprocation. fol. 414.

Another act of that nature. fol. 415.

Another act of the same nature. fol. 416

A general hosting, to begin the first of August, 1603. fol. 417.

A proportion of beoves for that hostinge. fol. 418.

Sir George Cary:

1603. June 10.—An act authorizeing the counsell, divided by reason of the sicknes, parte with the lord deputie in the country and parte at Dublin. fol. 419.

An act for borroweing 1,100*li.* of the counties of the Pale for releife of the armie, being in want. fol. 420.

Sir Arthur Chichester.—11 of May, 1605:

A general hostinge, to begin the 3 of July, 1605. fol. 421.

The severall authorities of the agents of the five counties of the Pale for reviveing the composicion. fols. 422–424.

The agreement for reviveing the composition, subscribed by the lord deputie, counsell, and the foresaid agents. fol. 425.

Act of reciprocation. fol. 427.

A general hostinge adjourned. fols. 428, 429.

Act of reciprocation. fols. 430, 431.

General hostinge. fol. 433.

Act of reciprocation. fols. 434, 435.

Order betwixt sir William Steward and Daniell Mullinex, Ulster kinge at armes. fol. 436.

An act touchinge the fees, wages, intertainements and allowances to bee
granted to the lords justices, who were the lord chancelor and the lord
fol. 438. cheife justice.

fol. 438. The time when the said lords justices weare sworne.

fol. 438. Sir Oliver St. John sworne lord deputie [1616, August 30.]

fol. 439. Judges wages for holding assises made certaine.

fol. 439. Act touchinge the land of Trinity Colledge, neere Dublin.

fol. 440. Act for sowing hempe in the plantacion in Wexford.

Act of the vice provost of Trinitie College to observe the act of state,
fol. 440b. —entred the leafe before.

fol. 441b. Act for repaireinge the fort of Castellparke by sir Thomas Button.

fol. 442. Act touchinge the towne of Athlone.

Act upon the death[1] of Thomas [Jones] lord archbushop of Dublin
and lord chancellor, for delivery of the great seale to the lord cheife
fol. 445. justice, lord cheife baron, and master of the rowles.

III.

The table of the counsell booke which begun in the year 1589, and in
the time of Sir William Fitzwilliams government:

fol. 6b. Proclamation for restraint of corne and victuals upon payne of death.

fol. 7. Letter to publish the said proclamation:

Where note the names of all the maritime townes from Dublin to Elder-
fleete, and from Dublin to Rosse.

Proclamation inhibitinge the resort to the well neere Rathefernam
upon paine of death, which had beene better upon some other punishment,
fol. 25b. as the sequell declareth.

Letter from the lords, with articles inclosed for the reformacion of
fols. 31, 32. Tirone:

Wherin note one for rayseinge a composition in Ulster, and another that
he shall not wittinglie, keepe frier, munke, nun, or priest in his country
unlesse they conforme themselves.

Sir George Carew, knight, master of the ordnance, sworne of the
fol. 38. counsell, the 17 of October, 1590.

Sir Henrie Bagnall, knight, marshall of her majesties armie sworne
fol. 39. of the counsell, the 24 of October, 1590.

Order that the bishop of Waterford shall answer in cheife to captaine
Winckfeilde, though he tooke exception to the jurisdiction of the
fol. 45b. court.

fol. 49b. Order betwixt the bushop of Waterford and John Burnell.

fol. 56. Order betwixt Campion and Turnor for the deanery of Fearns.

Order betwixt Richard Winckfeild and the bushop of Waterford for the
fol. 56b. mannor of Ardmore.

A note that her majesties pleasure was signified to Charles Caltrop,
atturney generall, that he should be removed from his said office, and
fol. 60. discharged thereof, the 22 April, 1591.

fol. 61. Order betwixt John Money and sir John McCoughlan.

Letter from the queene, importinge a licence to the duke of Florence
fol. 67. to loade fifteen hundred quarters of wheate out of Mounster.

Order for the possession of the furrows in the countie of Dublin to be
given to Robert and James Hetherington, upon the attaindor of Michell
Fitzsimons, for which decree in the chancery past with them in Fitzsimons
fol. 68b. his lyfe time.

The devision of the countie of Monohan: the baronies it contayneth,
fol. 78. and how they are disposed.

---

[1] On tenth of April, 1619.

Warrant for the stay of two shipps of St. Malows at Galway by reason the towne revolted from the kinge of France and killed their governor; this stay was made upon letters out of England: fol. 78*b*.

Letters from the lords for stayinge those shipps. fol. 79.

Ambassador of the king of France his letter of authoritie, wherein note his stile, and that he useth the words we and our. fol. 79*b*.

Order for the release of the bushop of Clougher and his brother, indicted of treason. fol. 79*b*.

Order for passinge the lands of Monoghan to the chiefe lords and freehoulders: fol. 98.

Note the meanes devysed for the ease of the freehoulders in passinge their lands; note the last point in nature of an act of oblivion.

Order betwixt Colman and Phillips for the sheriffs patents, wherein is layd downe in the end what fees everie sheriffe shall pay. fol. 107*b*.

Letter from the lords touchinge sir Henrie Ughtredys signory, and the sygnory of Robert Strode, and touchinge Thomas Cams son, lord of Clenlishe. fol. 109.

Petition of Roger Wilbraham, her majesties solicitor, against Richard Colman, cheife remembrancer, for rasinge a fiant of a leasse to passe to Peirce Ovenden, and deminishing the rent. fol. 112.

Order for Edmonde Spencer against the lord Roche. fol. 146.

Proclamation restrayeneing hawkeinge. fol. 154.

The oath taken by Hugh Roe O'Donell: fol. 154*b*.

Note one that he shall not keepe any Romish bishops or preists comeinge from Rome, but shall expell and prosecute them.

Letter from the lords in behalf of sir Geffrey Fenton, reconcileinge him to the lord deputie, and that he shall have the fees of makeinge all warrants for pardons and other things which are to passe the great seale and to have the privie signet as belongeing to his office of secretarie. fol. 158.

Letter from the queene to admit sir Thomas Norreys of the counsell, who was sworne the 23 of November, 1592. fol. 166*b*.

Letters from the lords in favore of the archbushop of Cashell for redressinge the many wrongs offered him. fol. 171*b*.

Letter from the lords clearinge the sayd archbushop of some slanders and imputations booked against him, and cleareing him of an accusacion that he had made some informacions against the lord deputie. fol. 174.

Matter betwixt the lords of Delvin and Houth and sir Robert Dillon. fol. 197*b*.

Letters to the lords in the behalfe of doctor Hanmer, with his recognizance. fol. 200.

The petition of William Rian to the lords touching two frieries called Killala and Tipperary, desireinge pardon for his intrusion. fol. 201*b*.

Letter from the lords in his favour. fol. 202.

The risinge out of the five counties to the generall hostinge. fol. 211.

Letter from the lords in the behalfe of William Kearney for printinge the Irish testaments. fol. 227*b*.

Recognizance of Richard Boyle and Richard Lenan upon ther enlargement, wherein is mencioned the cause of ther commitment. fol. 229*b*.

Sir William Russell:

Letter from the lords to sir William Russell to hould the parsonage of Donboyne as sir William Fitzwilliams helde it. fol. 233*b*.

Letter from the lords for Gregory Cole against the lord chancellor. fol. 236.

Letters from the lords for new surveyinge of sir William Harbarts signorie of the island of Kery, and abating his rent. fol. 236*b*.

Letters to the lords, certificinge that Mr. Thomas Mollinex, chancelor of the exchequer, was borne under the dominion of the crowne of England in Callice. fol. 238.

A passe for Gillegrome Magragh, father to the archbushop of Cashell,
fol. 238. to repayre into Munster with his goods.
fol. 250*b*. Letter from the lords for Terbert to be past to Hugh Cuffe.
Letter from the queene, touchinge the devision of the towne of
Carrickfergus betwixt the burgesses, with propositions for wallinge the
fol. 253*b*. town.
The first submission of Hugh, earle of Tyrone, well penned, but with
fol. 259*b*. false meaneinge as the sequell shewed.
Concordatum for 20*li*., sterling, yearlie to William Daniell, preacher
fol. 273*b*. at Gallway.
fol. 273*b*. Letter from the lords, in the behalfe of Donnogh McCormocke,
fols. 273*b*., touchinge the remittall of arreares of rent upon the abbay of Mourne;
274*a*., 274*b*. with the referment and all the proceedings therupon.
fol. 283. An oath taken by Randall McSorleyboy McConnell.
Letter from the queene for the bushop of Limericke, touchinge a
castell, with a ploughlande and some cheife rents, to bee past to him
fol. 286. and his successors.
fol. 304. Sir Conniers Clifford sworne of the counsell.
Letter from the lords, for capten Audlies company to be bestowed
fol. 304. [on] sir Christopher St. Lawrence.

Lord Burgh.—3 June, 1597:

Commission to the lorde of Delvin to gather the force of the country,
to command the companies with authoritie to parle, and protect and use
fol. 323*b*. marshall law against any of the traytors.

Sir Thomas Norreys, lord justice, October, 1597:

fol. 330*b*. Commission for George Thorneton to be vice president of Mounster.

Lord chancellor and sir Robert Gardener:

Act that for all marshall causes, for payments of money for any such
cause the lords justices and lord lieutenant shall concurr, and such
warrants for those causes past by the justices or by the lord lieutenant
fol. 334*b*. shalbe ratified.
Petition of Sara Merideth, concerninge the profitts of the deanery of
fol. 335*b*. St. Patricks; with the referment, the returne, and the confirmation.
fol. 337*b*. Letters from the lords, toucheinge the lord Burghs goods.
The archbishop of Yorks letter to the lord chancelor of Ireland,
fol. 346*b*. toucheinge one Edward Potter, a recusant.
fol. 366*b*. Letter from the queene to sweare sir Henry Harington of the counsell.

Earle of Essex:

Commission from the counsell, in absence of the lord leiuetenant, to
fol. 370*b*. commande the forces at the Nasse and the counties adjoyninge.
Consultation upon the death of sir Richard Bingham for keepeinge the
ol. 372*b*. company of horse and foot under his charge from breakeinge.

INDEX.

A.

B.

C.

D.

E.

H.

I.

J.

K.

L.

M.

N.

O.

P.

Q.

R.

S.

T.

U.

V.

W.

Y.

Z.

CIRCULAR OF THE COMMISSION.

Public Record Office, Chancery Lane,
London, W.C.

HER MAJESTY has been pleased to appoint under Her Sign Manual certain Commissioners to ascertain what unpublished MSS. are extant in the collections of private persons and in institutions which are calculated to throw light upon subjects connected with the civil, ecclesiastical, literary, or scientific history of this country. The present Commissioners are :—

Lord Esher, Master of the Rolls, the Marquess of Salisbury, K.G., the Marquess of Lothian, K.T., the Earl of Rosebery, K.G., Lord Edmond Fitzmaurice, the Bishop of Oxford, the Bishop of Limerick, Lord Acton, Lord Carlingford, K.P., and Mr. H. C. Maxwell Lyte, C.B.

The Commissioners think it probable that you may feel an interest in this object and be willing to assist in the attainment of it; and with that view they desire to lay before you an outline of the course which they usually follow.

If any nobleman or gentleman express his willingness to submit any unprinted book, or collection of documents in his possession or custody to the examination of the Commissioners, they will cause an inspection to be made by some competent person, and should the MSS. appear to come within the scope of their enquiry, a report containing copies or abstracts of them will be drawn up, printed, and submitted to the owner, with a view to obtaining his consent to the publication of the whole, or of such part of it as he may think fit, among the proceedings of the Commission, which are presented to Parliament every Session.

To avoid any possible apprehension that the examination of papers by the Commissioners may extend to title-deeds or documents of present legal value, positive instructions are given to every person who inspects MSS. on their behalf that nothing relating to the titles of existing owners is to be divulged, and that if in the course of his work any modern title-deeds or papers of a private character chance to come before him, they are to be instantly put aside, and are not to be examined or calendared under any pretence whatever.

The object of the Commission is solely the discovery of unknown historical and literary materials, and in all their proceedings the Commissioners will direct their attention to that object exclusively.

In practice it has been found more satisfactory, when the collection of manuscripts is a large one, for the inspector to make a selection therefrom at the place of deposit and to obtain the owner's consent to remove the selected papers to the Public Record Office in London, where they can be more fully dealt with, and where they are preserved with the same care as if they formed part of the muniments of the realm, during the term of their examination. Among the numerous owners of MSS. who have allowed their family papers of historical interest to be temporarily removed from their muniment rooms and lent to the Commissioners to facilitate the preparation of a report may be named: The Duke of Rutland, the Duke of Portland, the Marquess of Salisbury, the Marquess Townshend, the Earl of Dartmouth, the Earl of Ancaster, Lord Braye, Lord Hothfield, Mrs. Stopford Sackville, Mr. le Fleming, of Rydal, and Mr. Fortescue, of Dropmore.

The costs of inspections, reports and calendars, and the conveyance of documents, will be defrayed at the public expense, without any charge to owners.

The Commissioners will also, if so requested, give their advice as to the best means of repairing and preserving any papers or MSS. which may be in a state of decay, and are of historical or literary value.

The Commissioners will feel much obliged if you will communicate to them the names of any gentlemen who may be able and willing to assist in obtaining the objects for which this Commission has been issued.

J. J. CARTWRIGHT,
Secretary.

HISTORICAL MANUSCRIPTS COMMISSION.

Date.	—	Size.	Sessional Paper.	Price.
				s. d.
1870 (Re-printed 1874.)	FIRST REPORT, WITH APPENDIX - - Contents :— ENGLAND. House of Lords; Cambridge Colleges ; Abingdon, and other Corporations, &c. SCOTLAND. Advocates' Library, Glasgow Corporation, &c. IRELAND. Dublin, Cork, and other Corporations, &c.	f'cap.	[C. 55]	1 6
1871	SECOND REPORT, WITH APPENDIX, AND INDEX TO THE FIRST AND SECOND REPORTS - - - - - - Contents :— ENGLAND. House of Lords; Cambridge Colleges; Oxford Colleges; Monastery of Dominican Friars at Woodchester, Duke of Bedford, Earl Spencer, &c. SCOTLAND. Aberdeen and St. Andrew's Universities, &c. IRELAND. Marquis of Ormonde; Dr. Lyons, &c.	"	[C. 441]	3 10
1872 (Re-printed 1895.)	THIRD REPORT, WITH APPENDIX AND INDEX - - - - - - Contents :— ENGLAND. House of Lords; Cambridge Colleges; Stonyhurst College; Bridgewater and other Corporations; Duke of Northumberland, Marquis of Lansdowne, Marquis of Bath, &c. SCOTLAND. University of Glasgow; Duke of Montrose, &c. IRELAND. Marquis of Ormonde; Black Book of Limerick, &c.	"	[C. 673]	6 0
1873	FOURTH REPORT, WITH APPENDIX. PART I. - - - - - - Contents :— ENGLAND. House of Lords; Westminster Abbey; Cambridge and Oxford Colleges; Cinque Ports, Hythe, and other Corporations, Marquis of Bath, Earl of Denbigh, &c. SCOTLAND. Duke of Argyll, &c. IRELAND. Trinity College, Dublin; Marquis of Ormonde.	"	[C. 857]	6 8
1873	DITTO. PART II. INDEX - - -	"	[C.857i.]	2 6

Date.	——	Size.	Sessional Paper.	Price.
				s. d.
1876	FIFTH REPORT, WITH APPENDIX. PART I. - Contents :— ENGLAND. House of Lords; Oxford and Cambridge Colleges; Dean and Chapter of Canterbury; Rye, Lydd, and other Corporations, Duke of Sutherland, Marquis of Lansdowne, Reginald Cholmondeley, Esq., &c. SCOTLAND. Earl of Aberdeen, &c.	Fcap.	[C.1432]	7 0
"	DITTO. PART II. INDEX - - -	"	[C.1432 i.]	3 6
1877	SIXTH REPORT, WITH APPENDIX. PART I. - Contents :— ENGLAND. House of Lords; Oxford and Cambridge Colleges; Lambeth Palace; Black Book of the Archdeacon of Canterbury; Bridport, Wallingford, and other Corporations; Lord Leconfield, Sir Reginald Graham, Sir Henry Ingilby, &c. SCOTLAND. Duke of Argyll, Earl of Moray, &c. IRELAND. Marquis of Ormonde.	"	[C.1745]	8 6
(Re-printed 1893.)	DITTO. PART II. INDEX - - -	"	[C.2102]	1 10
1879 (Re-printed 1895.)	SEVENTH REPORT, WITH APPENDIX. PART I. - - - - - - Contents :— House of Lords; County of Somerset; Earl of Egmont, Sir Frederick Graham, Sir Harry Verney, &c.	"	[C.2340]	7 6
(Re-printed 1895.)	DITTO. PART II. APPENDIX AND INDEX - Contents :— Duke of Athole, Marquis of Ormonde, S. F. Livingstone, Esq., &c.	"	[C. 2340 i.]	3 6
1881	EIGHTH REPORT, WITH APPENDIX AND INDEX. PART I. - - - Contents :— List of collections examined, 1869–1880. ENGLAND. House of Lords; Duke of Marlborough; Magdalen College, Oxford; Royal College of Physicians; Queen Anne's Bounty Office; Corporations of Chester, Leicester, &c. IRELAND. Marquis of Ormonde, Lord Emly, The O'Conor Don, Trinity College, Dublin, &c.	"	[C.3040]	8 6
1881	DITTO. PART II. APPENDIX AND INDEX - Contents :— Duke of Manchester.	"	[C. 3040 i.]	1 9

Date.	—	Size.	Sessional Paper.	Price.
				s. d.
1881	DITTO. PART III. APPENDIX AND INDEX Contents :— Earl of Ashburnham.	f'cap.	[C. 3040 ii.]	1 4
1883 (Re-printed 1895.)	NINTH REPORT, WITH APPENDIX AND INDEX. PART I. - - - - Contents :— St. Paul's and Canterbury Cathedrals; Eton College; Carlisle, Yarmouth, Canterbury, and Barnstaple Corporations, &c.	"	[C.3773]	5 2
1884 (Re-printed 1895.)	DITTO. PART II. APPENDIX AND INDEX - Contents :— ENGLAND. House of Lords, Earl of Leicester; C. Pole Gell, Alfred Morrison, Esqs., &c. SCOTLAND. Lord Elphinstone, H. C. Maxwell Stuart, Esq., &c. IRELAND. Duke of Leinster, Marquis of Drogheda, &c.	"	[C.3773 i.]	6 3
1884	NINTH REPORT. PART III. APPENDIX AND INDEX - - - - - - Contents :— Mrs. Stopford Sackville.	"	[C.3773 ii.]	1 7
1883 (Re-printed 1895.)	CALENDAR OF THE MANUSCRIPTS OF THE MARQUIS OF SALISBURY, K.G. (or CECIL MSS.). PART I. - - - -	8vo.	[C.3777]	3 5
1888	DITTO. PART II. - - -	"	[C.5463]	3 5
1889	DITTO. PART III. - - -	"	[C. 5889 v.]	2 1
1892	DITTO. PART IV. - - -	"	[C.6823]	2 11
1894	DITTO. PART V. - - -	"	[C.7574]	2 6
1895	DITTO. PART VI. - - -	"	[C.7884]	2 8
1885	TENTH REPORT - - - - - This is introductory to the following :—	"	[C.4548]	0 3½
1885 (Re-printed 1895.)	(1.) APPENDIX AND INDEX - - - Earl of Eglinton, Sir J. S. Maxwell, Bart., and C. S. H. Drummond Moray, C. F. Weston Underwood, G. W. Digby, Esqs.	"	[C.4575]	3 7
1885	(2.) APPENDIX AND INDEX - - The Family of Gawdy.	"	[C.4576 iii.]	1 4
1885	(3.) APPENDIX AND INDEX - - Wells Cathedral.	"	[C.4576 ii.]	2 0

Date.	—	Size.	Sessional Paper.	Price.
				s d.
1885	(4.) APPENDIX AND INDEX - - Earl of Westmorland; Capt. Stewart; Lord Stafford; Sir N. W. Throckmorton, Sir P. T. Mainwaring, Lord Muncaster, Capt. J. F. Bagot, Earl of Kilmorey, Earl of Powis, and others, the Corporations of Kendal, Wenlock, Bridgnorth, Eye, Plymouth, and the County of Essex; and Stonyhurst College.	8vo.	[C.4576]	3 6
1885 (Re-printed 1895.)	(5.) APPENDIX AND INDEX - - - The Marquis of Ormonde, Earl of Fingall, Corporations of Galway, Waterford, the Sees of Dublin and Ossory, the Jesuits in Ireland.	"	[C. 4576 i.]	2 10
1887	(6.) APPENDIX AND INDEX - - - Marquis of Abergavenny, Lord Braye, G. F. Luttrell, P. P. Bouverie, W. Bromley Davenport, R. T. Balfour, Esquires.	"	[C.5242]	1 7
1887	ELEVENTH REPORT - - - - - This is introductory to the following:—	"	[C. 5060 vi.]	0 3
1887	(1.) APPENDIX AND INDEX - - - H. D. Skrine, Esq., Salvetti Correspondence.	"	[C.5060]	1 1
1887	(2.) APPENDIX AND INDEX - - - House of Lords. 1678-1688.	"	[C. 5060 i.]	2 0
1887	(3.) APPENDIX AND INDEX - - - Corporations of Southampton and Lynn.	"	[C. 5060 ii.]	1 8
1887	(4.) APPENDIX AND INDEX - - - Marquis Townshend.	"	[C. 5060 iii.]	2 6
1887	(5.) APPENDIX AND INDEX - - - Earl of Dartmouth.	"	[C. 5060 iv.]	2 8
1887	(6.) APPENDIX AND INDEX - - - Duke of Hamilton.	"	[C. 5060 v.]	1 6
1888	(7.) APPENDIX AND INDEX - - - Duke of Leeds, Marchioness of Waterford, Lord Hothfield, &c.; Bridgwater Trust Office, Reading Corporation, Inner Temple Library.	"	[C.5612]	2 0
1890	TWELFTH REPORT - - - - - This is introductory to the following:—	"	[C.5889]	0 3
1888	(1.) APPENDIX - - - - - Earl Cowper, K.G. (Coke MSS., at Melbourne Hall, Derby). Vol. I.	"	[C.5472]	2 7
1888	(2.) APPENDIX - - - - - Ditto. Vol. II.	"	[C.5613]	2 5

Date.	—	Size.	Sessional Paper.	Price.
				s. d.
1889	(3.) APPENDIX AND INDEX - - - Ditto. Vol. III.	8vo.	[C. 5889 i.]	1 4
1888	(4.) APPENDIX - - - - - The Duke of Rutland, G.C.B. Vol. I.	"	[C.5614]	3 2
1891	(5.) APPENDIX AND INDEX - - - Ditto. Vol. II.	"	[C. 5889 ii.]	2 0
1889	(6.) APPENDIX AND INDEX - - - House of Lords, 1689–1690.	"	[C. 5889 iii.]	2 1
1890	(7.) APPENDIX AND INDEX - - - S. H. le Fleming, Esq., of Rydal.	"	[C. 5889 iv.]	1 11
1891	(8.) APPENDIX AND INDEX - - - The Duke of Athole, K.T., and the Earl of Home.	"	[C.6338]	1 0
1891	(9.) APPENDIX AND INDEX - - - The Duke of Beaufort, K.G., the Earl of Donoughmore, J. H. Gurney, W. W. B. Hulton, R. W. Ketton, G. A. Aitken, P. V. Smith, Esqs.; Bishop of Ely; Cathedrals of Ely, Gloucester, Lincoln, and Peterborough; Corporations of Gloucester, Higham Ferrers, and Newark; Southwell Minster; Lincoln District Registry.	"	[C. 6338 i.]	2 6
1891	(10.) APPENDIX - - - - The First Earl of Charlemont. Vol. I. 1745–1783.	"	[C. 6338 ii.]	1 11
1892	THIRTEENTH REPORT - - - - This is introductory to the following:—	"	[C.6827]	0 3
1891	(1.) APPENDIX - - - - - The Duke of Portland. Vol. I.	"	[C.6474]	3 0
	(2.) APPENDIX AND INDEX - - - Ditto. Vol. II.	"	[C. 6827 i.]	2 0
1892	(3.) APPENDIX - - - - - - - J. B. Fortescue, Esq., of Dropmore, Vol. I.	"	[C.6660]	2 7
1892	(4.) APPENDIX AND INDEX - - - Corporations of Rye, Hastings, and Hereford. Capt. F. C. Loder-Symonds, E. R. Wodehouse, M.P., J. Dovaston, Esqs., Sir T. B. Lennard, Bart., Rev. W. D. Macray, and Earl of Dartmouth (Supplementary Report).	"	[C.6810]	2 4
1892	(5.) APPENDIX AND INDEX - - - House of Lords, 1690–1691.	"	[C.6822]	2 4
1893	(6.) APPENDIX AND INDEX - - Sir W. FitzHerbert, Bart. The Delaval Family, of Seaton Delaval; The Earl of Ancaster and General Lyttelton-Annesley.	"	[C.7166]	1 4

Date.	—	Size.	Sessional Paper.	Price.
				s. d.
1893	(7.) APPENDIX AND INDEX - - - The Earl of Lonsdale.	8vo.	[C.7241]	1 3
1893	(8.) APPENDIX AND INDEX - - The First Earl of Charlemont. Vol. II. 1784–1799.	„	[C.7424]	1 11
1896	FOURTEENTH REPORT - - - - This is introductory to the following:—	„	[C.7983]	0 3
1894	(1.) APPENDIX AND INDEX - - The Duke of Rutland, G.C.B. Vol. III.	„	[C.7476]	1 11
1894	(2.) APPENDIX - - - - - The Duke of Portland. Vol. III.	„	[C.7569]	2 8
1894	(3.) APPENDIX AND INDEX - - The Duke of Roxburghe; Sir H. H. Campbell, Bart.; the Earl of Strathmore; and the Countess Dowager of Seafield.	„	[C.7570]	1 2
1894	(4.) APPENDIX AND INDEX - - Lord Kenyon.	„	[C.7571]	2 10
1896	(5.) APPENDIX - - - J. B. Fortescue, Esq., of Dropmore. Vol. II.	„	[C.7572]	2 8
1895	(6.) APPENDIX AND INDEX - - House of Lords, 1692–1693.	„	[C.7573]	1 11
1895	(7.) APPENDIX - - - - - The Marquess of Ormonde.	„	[C.7678]	1 10
1895	(8.) APPENDIX AND INDEX - - Lincoln, Bury St. Edmunds, Hertford, and Great Grimsby Corporations; The Dean and Chapter of Worcester, and of Lichfield; The Bishop's Registry of Worcester.	„	[C.7881]	1 5
1895	(9.) APPENDIX AND INDEX - - The Earl of Buckinghamshire, the Earl of Lindsey, the Earl of Onslow, Lord Emly, Theodore J. Hare, Esq., and James Round, Esq., M.P.	„	[C.7882]	2 6
1895	(10.) APPENDIX AND INDEX - - The Earl of Dartmouth. Vol. II. American Papers.	„	[C.7883]	2 9
	FIFTEENTH REPORT. This is introductory to the following:—			
1896	(1.) APPENDIX AND INDEX - - The Earl of Dartmouth. Vol. III.	„	[C.8156]	1 5

www.ingramcontent.com/pod-product-compliance
Lightning Source LLC
Chambersburg PA
CBHW021112270326
41929CB00009B/848

9783337323967